The Handbook of Political Change in Eastern
Europe, Second Edition

The Handbook of Political Change in Eastern Europe

Second Edition

Edited by

Sten Berglund

Professor of Political Science, University of Örebro, Sweden

Joakim Ekman

Doctor of Political Science, University of Örebro, Sweden

Frank H. Aarebrot

Professor of Comparative Politics, University of Bergen, Norway

Edward Elgar

Cheltenham, UK • Northampton, MA, USA

Published by
Edward Elgar Publishing Limited
Glensanda House
Montpellier Parade
Cheltenham
Glos GL50 1UA
UK

Edward Elgar Publishing, Inc.
136 West Street
Suite 202
Northampton
Massachusetts 01060
USA

A catalogue record for this book
is available from the British Library

Library of Congress Cataloguing in Publication Data

The handbook of political change in Eastern Europe / edited by Sten Berglund, Joakim Ekman, Frank H. Aarebrot.—2nd ed.
   p. cm.
   Includes indexes.
   1. Europe, Eastern—Social conditions—1989—Congresses. 2. Europe, Eastern—Politics and government—1989—Congresses. 3. Social change—Europe, Eastern—Congresses. 4. Post-communism—Europe, Eastern—Congresses. I. Berglund, Sten, 1947- II. Ekman, Joakim, 1970- III. Aarebrot, Frank H., 1947-

HN380.7.A8H36 2003
306'.0947—dc22
                                                            2003064235
ISBN 1 84064 854 6

Printed and bound in Great Britain by MPG Books Ltd, Bodmin, Cornwall

Contents

Tables and Figures

Tables

Figures

Notes on the Contributors

Frank H. Aarebrot (b. 1947) is professor of comparative politics at the University of Bergen, Norway. He is the author and co-author of numerous articles and chapters within the field of comparative politics, among others: 'Analysis and Explanation of Variation in Territorial Structure', in Stein Rokkan et al., *Centre–Periphery Structures in Europe* (Campus Verlag 1987). He has published *The Political History of Eastern Europe in the 20th Century* (with Sten Berglund, Edward Elgar 1997), *The Handbook of Political Change in Eastern Europe* (co-edited and co-authored with Sten Berglund and Tomas Hellén, Edward Elgar 1998), *Politics and Citizenship on the Eastern Baltic Seaboard* (co-edited and co-authored with Terje Knutsen, Nordic Academic Press 2000) and *Challenges to Democracy: Eastern Europe Ten Years after the Collapse of Communism* (co-authored with Sten Berglund, Henri Vogt and Georgi Karasimeonov, Edward Elgar 2001).

Sten Berglund (b. 1947) is professor of political science at the University of Örebro, Sweden. His previous publications include *The New Democracies in Eastern Europe: Party Systems and Political Cleavages* (co-edited and co-authored with Jan Åke Dellenbrant, Edward Elgar 1991 and 1994), *The Political History of Eastern Europe in the 20th Century* (with Frank Aarebrot, Edward Elgar 1997), *The Handbook of Political Change in Eastern Europe* (co-edited and co-authored with Tomas Hellén and Frank Aarebrot, Edward Elgar 1998), *Challenges to Democracy: Eastern Europe Ten Years after the Collapse of Communism* (co-authored with Frank Aarebrot, Henri Vogt and Georgi Karasimeonov, Edward Elgar 2001) and *Baltic Democracy at the Crossroads: An Elite Perspective* (co-edited with Kjetil Duvold, Norwegian Academic Press 2003).

Tomaž Boh (b. 1976) is a doctoral student at the Faculty of Social Sciences, University of Ljubljana, Slovenia, and a research assistant at the Centre for Political Research at the same faculty.

William Crowther (b. 1952) is professor of political science at the University of North Carolina at Greensboro, and co-director of the Parliamentary Documents Center, USA. He is the author of numerous scholarly works on various aspects of Romanian and Moldovan politics, and is currently engaged in a comparative study of post-communist legislatures.

Goran Čular (b. 1968) is a research assistant and a Ph.D. candidate at the Faculty of Political Science, University of Zagreb, Croatia. His research interests include political parties, party systems and democratic consolidation. His publications include 'Political Development in Croatia 1990–2000: Fast Transition – Postponed Consolidation', in *Croatian Political Science Review* (2000).

Kevin Deegan-Krause (b. 1968) is an assistant professor of political science at Wayne State University in Detroit, Michigan, USA. His teaching and research in comparative politics focuses on the relationship between attitudes and political behaviour in Central and Eastern Europe, especially the former Czechoslovakia and the former Yugoslavia. His works have appeared in journals including *Party Politics* and the *Journal of Democracy* and in a number of edited volumes. He is currently completing a book about the role of political parties and political cleavages in the democratic consolidation of Slovakia and the Czech Republic.

Kjetil Duvold (b. 1971) is a doctoral student at the University of Örebro, Sweden. He has been a visiting lecturer in Lithuania for the EuroFaculty and the University of Bergen for several years. He has published several articles on the Baltic countries, including 'From Homo Sovieticus to Balts: Colonisers, Migrant Workers or a New Diaspora?', in Frank Aarebrot and Terje Knutsen, eds, *Politics and Citizenship on the Eastern Baltic Seaboard* (Nordic Academic Press 2000), and he has published *Baltic Democracy at the Crossroads: An Elite Perspective* (co-edited with Sten Berglund, Norwegian Academic Press 2003).

Joakim Ekman (b. 1970) holds a Ph.D. in political science from the University of Örebro, Sweden. His current research interests comprise European politics, democratization and political socialization, and his most recent works include *National Identity in Divided and Unified Germany* (doctoral thesis, 2001) and 'Satisfaction with democracy: A note on a frequently used indicator in comparative politics', in *European Journal of Political Research*, Vol. 42, No. 3 (with Jonas Linde, 2003).

Marian Grzybowski (b. 1945), is full professor of constitutional comparative law, Head of Chair at the Jagiellonian University of Cracow, and Judge of the Constitutional Tribunal of the Republic of Poland. His research focuses on comparative constitutional studies of Scandinavia, Central Europe, the United States and Canada. He is the author of 14 books, including *Governments in Central-Eastern Europe* (1980), *The Modern Political Systems of Scandinavia* (1989), *The Federal Executive in the USA* (1992), *Electoral Systems of Central Europe* (1995) and *The Parliament of Canada* (1996).

Yuri Josanu (b. 1967) as an associate professor of political science at the International Institute of Management in Chishinau, Moldova. He received his doctorate in 1997 from Babes Bolyai University in Cluj-Napoca, Romania.

Mindaugas Jurkynas (b. 1972) is a lecturer and Ph.D. candidate at the Institute of International Relations and Political Science, Vilnius University, Lithuania. He is currently working in the project 'Baltic Sea Area Studies: The Northern Dimension of Europe', at the Humboldt University in Berlin, Germany. His research focuses on party politics and cleavages in Lithuania and region-building processes in the Baltic Sea region. He has written and published widely on Baltic politics.

Georgi Karasimeonov (b. 1949) is professor of political science at the University of Sofia, Bulgaria, managing director of the Institute for Political and Legal Studies in Sofia, and president of the Bulgarian Political Science Association. His main research interests and publications are in the fields of political parties, political institutions, post-communist transition and constitutional law.

Mikko Lagerspetz (b. 1963) is professor of sociology at the Estonian Institute of Humanities, Tallinn, Estonia. He was born and educated in Turku, Finland, but has been a resident of Estonia since 1989. His research has focused on social problems, cultural policies, and civil society. He has authored *Constructing Post-Communism: A Study on the Estonian Social Problems Discourse* (Turku University 1996) and *Estonian Cultural Policy and its Impact* (with Rein Raud, Council of Europe 1995). His recent publications include 'How Many Nordic Countries? Possibilities and Limits of Geopolitical Identity Construction', *Cooperation & Conflict*, Vol. 38, No. 1 (2003).

Zdenka Mansfeldová (b. 1950) is senior research fellow at the Institute of Sociology, Academy of Sciences of the Czech Republic. Her current research interests include political parties, institutionalization of interest representation and social partnership. Her publications include *Pluralistic*

System of Interest Representation in Czech Society (1996), *Zerfall der Tschechoslowakei: strukturelle Ursachen und Parteihandeln* (1995), *Social Partnership in the Czech Republic* (1997) and *Post-Communist Party Systems: Competition, Representation and Inter-Party Cooperation* (with Herbert Kitschelt, Radoslaw Markowski and Gábor Tóka, Cambridge University Press 1999).

Piotr Mikuli (b. 1977) is a constitutional lawyer and a doctoral fellow associated with the Chair of Comparative Constitutional Law, the Law and Administration Faculty of the Jagiellonian University in Cracow, Poland. He is interested in constitutional and administrative justice, political systems and constitutional rules in comparative perspective. His doctorate concerns the constitutional system of the United Kingdom. He is the author and the co-author of a number of publications dealing with Polish and European constitutional issues.

Hermann Smith-Sivertsen (b. 1962) is an assistant professor of political science at the Department of Business Administration and Political Science at Buskerud College in Kongsberg, Norway. His current research is focused on party systems, party organizations and mass politics in Latvia and Lithuania. His most recent English-language publication is 'Civil Society in the Baltic States: Participation and NGOs', in Frank Aarebrot and Terje Knutsen, eds, *Politics and Citizenship on the Eastern Baltic Seaboard* (Nordic Academic Press 2000).

Bojan Todosijević (b. 1966) is a doctoral candidate at the Department of Political Science of the Central European University, Budapest, Hungary. His research interests include political psychology, electoral behaviour, political tolerance, and political representation. His most recent publication is 'Structure versus culture again: Corporatism and the "new politics" in 16 Western European Countries', in *European Journal of Political Research* Vol. 42, No. 5 (with Zsolt Enyedi, 2003).

Gábor Tóka (b. 1962) is an assistant professor at the Department of Political Science of the Central European University, Budapest, Hungary. He is co-author of *Post-Communist Party Systems: Competition, Representation and Inter-Party Cooperation* (with Herbert Kitschelt, Zdenka Mansfeldová and Radoslaw Markowski, Cambridge University Press 1999), and author of the *Inventory of Political Attitude and Behaviour Surveys in East Central Europe and the former Soviet Union 1989–97* (Edwin Ferger Verlag 2000). He has published articles on electoral behaviour, political parties, and democratic consolidation, most recently in *Do Political Campaigns Matter?* (edited by David M. Farrell and Rüdiger Schmitt-Beck, Routledge 2002).

Henri Vogt (b. 1967) is senior research fellow at the Finnish Institute of International Affairs, Helsinki, Finland. He holds a D.Phil. in politics from the University of Oxford. His publications include *Between Utopia and Disillusionment: A Narrative of the Political Transformation in Eastern Europe* (Berghahn Books 2004) and *Challenges to Democracy: Eastern Europe Ten Years after the Collapse of Communism* (co-authored with Sten Berglund, Frank Aarebrot and Georgi Karasimeonov, Edward Elgar 2001). His current research concerns the dialogue between the European Union and Africa within the framework of globalization and democratization discourses.

Drago Zajc (b. 1938) is a professor at the University of Ljubljana, Slovenia, and president of the Slovene Political Science Association. His main fields of academic interest are human rights and parliamentary procedure. His publications include *The Role of the Slovene Parliament in the Process of Democratization* (1993) and *The Influence of the Electoral System on the Composition of Parliaments* (1996).

Nenad Zakošek (b. 1957) is professor of political science at the Faculty of Political Science, University of Zagreb, Croatia. His research focuses on voters' behaviour in Croatia, the development of political parties and party systems, and theories of social development. Since 2000, he has been editor-in-chief of *Politička misao*, the Croatian political science journal, the oldest such journal in Eastern Europe. His recent publications include 'Das politische System Kroatiens', in Wolfgang Ismayr, ed., *Die politischen Systeme Osteuropas* (Leske + Budrich 2002) and 'Wahlen in Kroatien 1990–2000', in Klaus Ziemer, ed., *Wahlen in postsozialistischen Staaten* (Leske + Budrich 2003).

Preface

The *Handbook of Political Change in Eastern Europe* provides the reader with standard handbook information on voting behaviour, cabinet formation, electoral and constitutional arrangements in 13 Central and East European countries from 1989–90 and onwards. But it is not just a handbook in the conventional sense of that term. The country-specific chapters have political cleavages as a common theme, and the handbook thus offers in-depth analyses of the changing cleavage structures in Central and Eastern Europe since the breakdown of communist rule. In the introductory and concluding chapters, the three editors make an attempt to apply a macro-level perspective to the process of democratic consolidation in the region.

The second edition of the *Handbook of Political Change in Eastern Europe* is based on the same concept as its predecessor, and many of the contributing authors are familiar from the 1998 version of the handbook. Their respective contributions have been updated, and in many cases rewritten completely on the basis of the current state of knowledge. Two separate authors – professors Zdenka Mansfeldová (Prague) and Kevin Deegan-Krause (Detroit) – now cover the Czech Republic and Slovakia in two separate chapters, and three new countries – Croatia, Serbia and Moldova – have been added to the long list of post-communist countries included already in the first edition of the handbook.

The successful completion of this book project must be attributed to the contributing authors. The editors want to avail themselves of this opportunity to thank all the contributing authors for their dedication and perseverance. The editors are also indebted to the Tercentenary Fund of the Swedish National Bank and to the universities of Bergen and Örebro for providing funding for an authors' meeting in Örebro in February 2003. The editors also remain indebted to the European Consortium for Political Research (ECPR) and Professor Hans-Dieter Klingemann at the Science Center in Berlin (WZB) who helped pave the way the first edition of the handbook.

Sten Berglund   *Joakim Ekman*   *Frank Aarebrot*

1. The Diversity of Post-Communist Europe

Sten Berglund, Joakim Ekman and Frank Aarebrot*

The topic of this book is political cleavages in 13 countries in Central and Eastern Europe. We are concerned mainly with the consolidation of democracy in a post-communist setting, and not so much with problems facing transitional societies. Indeed, to speak about 'transitional societies' or a 'transition from communism' in this part of the world would seem somewhat out of date. The democratic regimes that were installed in Central and Eastern Europe following the demise of communism have been able to cope with a number of significant challenges in the 1990s, and the relevant question today has not to do with the risk of democratic breakdown. Rather, it is a question of creating as favourable conditions as possible for the practical realization of democracy. This process, usually referred to in the literature as the consolidation of democracy, is not fundamentally different from the day-to-day process of coping with the challenges to democracy in Western Europe. The main concern regarding the future development of democracy – in Europe as a whole – has to do with the deepening of democracy in the face of European integration, globalization, the rise of xenophobia, and societal fragmentation, to mention just a few challenges to democracy in contemporary Europe (Berglund, Aarebrot, Vogt and Karasimeonov 2001). The theoretical link between consolidation and political cleavages is simple – the emergence of a stable party system and distinguishable and consistent voter preferences are indicators of democratic consolidation (cf. Whitefield 2002).

A Diverse Picture of Political Development

Since the publication of the first *Handbook of Political Change in Eastern Europe* in 1998, we have witnessed a gradual 'normalization' of political life in many places in Central and Eastern Europe. The original sample included ten countries: Estonia, Latvia, Lithuania, Poland, the Czech Republic, Slovakia, Hungary, Slovenia, Romania, and Bulgaria. Eight of these countries are foreseen for full membership of the European Union (EU) already in 2004, while Bulgaria and Romania are slated for membership in 2007. Furthermore, in March 1999, the Czech Republic, Hungary and Poland joined the North Atlantic Treaty (NATO). At a meeting in Prague on December 12, 2002, the remaining seven countries from our original sample were formally invited to join NATO as well. The Prague Summit may very well be remembered in the history books not only as the summit where the largest expansion in NATO's history was announced, but also as the definite end of the political division of Europe. Following a long history of artificial divisions in the 20th century, the countries of Central and Eastern Europe are finally free to choose for themselves which alliances they wish to join.

In this volume, we have added three countries to the original sample: Croatia, Serbia, and Moldova. We have thus settled for 13 countries. Several factors determine the inclusion of these states and the exclusion of others. There is the geographical argument: the former Soviet republics in the Caucasus and Central Asia are obviously beyond the scope of a book dealing with Central and Eastern Europe. A cultural and historical definition comes into play: we deal mainly with the 'interface' countries between the Baltic and the Aegean which are 'the East of the West and the West of the East' (Rupnik 1989, 4); the successor states of the German, Austrian, Russian and Ottoman empires which in the 1940s came under communist control, i.e. 'Eastern Europe' or 'the Soviet bloc'.

The term 'Eastern Europe' is ambiguous and in many ways outdated. It was the post-Yalta order which 'dictated a strict and single dichotomy [...] by subsuming under the label Eastern Europe all those parts of historic Central, East Central, and South-eastern Europe that after 1945 came under Soviet domination' (Garton Ash 1991, 161; Hellén 1996, 5–10). The term was not only an ideological precept pertaining to the East/West conflict but also denoted the perceived homogeneity of the bloc of European states oriented towards the Soviet Union. This is not say that there were no common denominators. There were, at least on the surface. The political systems of the socialist countries in Eastern Europe were initially copies of the Soviet model, and the rules of the political games were, in the final analysis, defined by Moscow until the very breakdown of Soviet-style communism. After the 1950s, the East European leaders were more free to embark upon what was commonly referred to as a national road towards socialism, but some things were simply not condoned by the Soviet leaders. The leading role of the Marxist-Leninist party must not be eroded, democratic centralism must not be questioned, and the 'eternal' friendship and alliance with the Soviet Union must not be violated. These principles lent themselves to different interpretations – as demonstrated during the Prague Spring of 1968 – but Moscow had the final say and its interpretation tended to give the East European leaders a short rather than a long leash (Schöpflin 1993; Berglund and Dellenbrant 1994).

The ambitious Soviet programme of industrialization, urbanization and modernization also served as a model and source of inspiration of long-lasting consequences for the East European countries. They went through a rapid, profound and occasionally dramatic process of socio-economic transformation under communism (Berglund and Aarebrot 1997).

Even so, national traits were not eradicated by the communist regimes, which frequently exploited communalism, nationalism and xenophobia. By 1989–90, history had begun to repeat itself. Without instructions from the centre, the 'Soviet bloc' almost immediately disintegrated into historic sub-regions. In some respects, disintegration went even further, as the collapse of the Soviet Union, Yugoslavia and Czechoslovakia led to the establishment of several independent republics with little recent or, in some cases, no historical experience of statehood. If the USSR itself is included, the pre-1989 socialist bloc in Europe encompassed nine states. In 1992, one could find no fewer than 27 independent states in the same area; 15 arising out of the defunct Soviet Union, five out of Yugoslavia, and two out of Czechoslovakia.

With the collapse of the communist regimes in Central and Eastern Europe in the late 1980s and early 1990s, and the dissolution of the Soviet Union, the artificial division of Europe into one democratic Western part and one communist Eastern part became obsolete. If the 'Soviet bloc' was a misnomer, falsely indicating a homogenous entity of states, contemporary 'Eastern Europe' is something of a misnomer as well, considering that developments in different parts of the region have been quite diverse. It thus makes little sense to lump all of the 'post-communist states' together, despite a common history of 40 years of communist rule (cf. Rose 2002).

In 1998, we argued that our ten-country sample largely reflected a wish only to include countries that had reached some level of political stability, in order for the analysis to be worthwhile (Berglund, Hellén and Aarebrot 1998, 4). This argument is still valid. Since we are primarily interested in analysing democratic stability with regards to party politics, we would be ill advised to include countries such as Russia, Georgia, Ukraine, Armenia, or Azerbaijan, not to mention Belarus. Instead, we have opted for a more distinct group of countries. In terms of democratic development, state of civil society and the rule of law, our sample could by and large be described as the more successful league of the post-communist countries (*Table 1.1*).

One of the most well-known indices of democratic development is the country rating provided by Freedom House. Since 1972, Freedom House has published an annual report on the state of freedom throughout the world – the *Freedom in the World* survey – by assigning each country and territory the status of 'free', 'partly free', or 'not free' according to their average political rights and civil liberties ratings. Political rights and civil liberties are measured on a one-to-seven scale, where 1 represents the highest degree of freedom and 7 the lowest. Countries with combined average ratings for political rights and civil liberties that fall between 1.0 and 2.5 are generally considered 'free'; between 3.0 and 5.5 'partly free'; and between 5.5 and 7.0 'not free'.[1]

Table 1.1: Freedom ratings of post-communist countries 2002–2003

Country	Political rights	Civil liberties	Freedom status
Slovenia	1	1	Free
Bulgaria	1	2	Free
Czech Republic	1	2	Free
Estonia	1	2	Free
Hungary	1	2	Free
Latvia	1	2	Free
Lithuania	1	2	Free
Poland	1	2	Free
Slovakia	1	2	Free
Croatia	2	2	Free
Romania	2	2	Free
Serbia and Montenegro	3	2	Free
Albania	3	3	Partly free
Macedonia	3	3	Partly free
Moldova	3	4	Partly free
Armenia	4	4	Partly free
Bosnia–Herzegovina	4	4	Partly free
Georgia	4	4	Partly free
Ukraine	4	4	Partly free
Russia	5	5	Partly free
Azerbaijan	6	5	Partly free
Kazakhstan	6	5	Not free
Kyrgyz Republic	6	5	Not free
Tajikistan	6	5	Not free
Belarus	6	6	Not free
Uzbekistan	7	6	Not free
Turkmenistan	7	7	Not free

Sources: Freedom in the World Country Ratings (www.freedomhouse.org); Karatnycky (2003).

In Table 1.1 we have outlined the 2002–03 freedom ratings for the post-communist countries, including the successor states of the Soviet Union. A rather clear-cut pattern is detectable. Among the highest-ranking countries ('free') we find the Central European countries Slovenia, the Czech Republic, Hungary, Poland, and Slovakia, as well as Bulgaria and the three Baltic countries Estonia, Latvia, and Lithuania. It should be noted that all these countries are ranked basically on a par with the 'old' democracies of Western Europe (e.g. United Kingdom, France, Belgium, and Spain). In some ways, this indicates the relevance of history: the 'Central' or 'East Central' European countries which went communist after the Second World War were once wholly or mainly subsumed in the great multi-national Prussian-German and Habsburg empires, and consequently, they are profoundly anchored in the Western tradition, which entails Western Christianity, at least a measure of experience of the rule of law, the separation of powers, constitutional government, and civil society (cf. Garton Ash 1991, 224). The three Baltic states, Estonia, Latvia and Lithuania, share a common history of Soviet occupation in the 20th century. In a longer historical perspective, however, these three countries have not been unaffected by Western thought, located as they are at the crossroads between Russia, Germany, and Scandinavia. Although the pattern is not perfect, these historical legacies nevertheless work to set the Central European and Baltic countries apart from the countries of South Eastern and Eastern Europe, with its traditions of Eastern Christianity or Islam, clientelism and Ottoman rule (*Table 1.1*).

Bulgaria stands out as an inspiring exception to this geographical pattern, which goes to prove that one should not overlook other explanations, no matter how important the historical legacy may be. Recent years' improved freedom scores in Bulgaria are ascribable to specific political actions, signifying increased tolerance towards ethnic minorities and non-traditional religious groups (Karatnycky 2003, 110).

Romania, Croatia, and Serbia and Montenegro are classified as 'free' in Table 1.1 as well, and according to the Freedom House ratings, basically on the same level as electoral democracies such as Mexico and India (cf. Karatnycky 2003, Diamond 2002). Among the countries designated as 'partly free', we find the post-Soviet states (Moldova, Armenia, Georgia, Ukraine, Russia, and Azerbaijan) as well as the Balkan countries Albania, Macedonia, and Bosnia–Herzegovina. Finally, the 'not free' category encompasses the post-Soviet states to the east of the Caspian Sea, i.e. Kazakhstan, the Kyrgyz Republic, Tajikistan, Uzbekistan, and Turkmenistan. Belarus ends up in the 'not free' category as well, with reference to the presidential dictatorship introduced by Alyaksandr Lukashenka in 1994.

Back in 1998, the successor states of the collapsed Yugoslav federation – with the exception of Slovenia – were still in a state of political flux. Developments in recent years, however, have justified a broader coverage of the Balkans. Thus, we are pleased to include in this revised and expanded version of the *Handbook of Political Change in Eastern Europe* chapters on post-Tuđman Croatia as well as on post-Milošević Serbia.

Bosnia–Herzegovina has been excluded on grounds of its status as a de facto international protectorate. The political system of what is commonly referred to as 'Bosnia' is in fact divided into two separate entities, the Serb Republic and the Croat-Bosniak Federation of Bosnia-Herzegovina. Furthermore, due to its multiethnic composition, the city of Brcko has since 1999 been placed under international administration, which in turn has divided the territory of the Serb Republic into two halves. The ethnic/territorial division is accompanied by a complex system of overlapping authorities. The central government is weak, and its power is basically limited to foreign affairs, trade, and monetary policy. All other areas of competence – including defence policy and taxation – are matters for the regional governments. In addition to the two basic political entities, there is the Office of the High Representative (HR), the main international body that oversees the civilian aspects of the implementation of the peace process. The HR is not accountable within the Bosnian political system, and answers only to the international Peace Implementation Council (PIC). Nevertheless, the HR holds considerable executive powers, and has among other things the right to impose laws and dismiss officials, in order to uphold the peace process (the Dayton Accords). These rights have been heavily used. For example, in 1999, the HR dismissed the president of the Serb Republic, and since the late 1990s, more than 100 laws and decisions have been passed (cf. Karatnycky, Motyl and Schnetzer 2002). In conclusion, the status as an international protectorate as well as its dysfunctional political system makes Bosnia–Herzegovina a less than ideal case for the present investigation, since we are interested in analyses of electoral politics and democratic consolidation.

The exclusion of Albania could arguably be justified on similar grounds. The civil unrest of 1997 left Albania in state of chaos, and although the situation has improved since, the subsequent elections have been characterised by violence, accusations of electoral fraud, open hostility between government and opposition, and low voter turnout. The most recent parliamentary elections in the summer of 2001 were indeed accompanied by irregularities, and no less than five rounds of voting had to be carried out before all the seats in the parliament had been filled. The pre-history of the 2002 presidential elections also testifies to the unstable political climate. The Foreign Affairs Committee of the European Parliament had to step in to mediate between the parties, in order to make the elections possible at all. The President of Albania is elected by the Parliament, but must have the support of at least 60 per cent of all MPs. Only days before the elections did Fatos Nano, leader of the Socialist Party, and opposition leader Sali Berisha finally agree on a joint candidate – Alfred Moisiu – thereby making the elections actually possible. Thus, the 2002 presidential elections were successfully carried out largely due to external pressure (Whyte 2002).

We have also chosen not to include Macedonia in this volume. The first ten years of independence saw reasonable levels of pluralism and respect for minority rights in this former Yugoslav republic. At the same time, however, Macedonia experienced repeated political and economic crises, and the Kosovo war in particular entailed a serious challenge to the stability of the country. In early 2001, Macedonia seemed to be on the verge of a fully fledged civil war. For the time being, however, it would seem that Macedonia managed to overcome this crisis as well. In the 2002–03 *Freedom House Country Ratings*, Macedonia's political-rights and civil-liberties ratings improved on grounds of its increased stability and the gradual implementation of the 2001 Ohrid Agreement that put an end to the hostilities between Macedonian security forces and armed Albanian rebels (Karatnycky 2003, 111).

Moldova, finally, is something of a deviant case in our investigation. The political development in Moldova is not really on a par with the rest of the countries in our sample (*Table 1.1*). Still, the country has some interesting characteristics, which justifies its inclusion in this volume. Moldova has strong cultural links to Romania, with which it shares a common history (see Chapters 11 and 15). Moreover, in some ways, the country resembles Estonia and Latvia. It is a former Soviet republic with significant minorities within its borders – 14 per cent Ukrainians and 13 per cent Russians (Karatnycky, Motyl and Schnetzer 2002). Like the Baltic countries, Moldova was occupied by the Soviet Union following the Molotov-Ribbentrop Pact. Unlike the Baltic countries, however, Moldova has no history of national independence. In the post-war era, it was a part of Romania (Bessarabia). The question of national identity is thus a central issue here, just like in contemporary Estonia and Latvia.

*

Just as in the original volume, the country-specific chapters in this book are arranged roughly in order of the geographical north–south axis, starting off with the Baltic Seaboard countries, proceeding down through Central Europe, then moving eastwards through the Balkans towards the Black Sea, and concluding with Moldova in the north-east, bordering on Ukraine.

This introductory chapter, the remainder of which will deal mainly with the concept of political cleavages, is followed by a framework chapter, which sets out to formulate some crucial questions without necessarily providing the final answers to them. What is the relevance of the historical legacy? Which are the prerequisites for the consolidation of democracy? What are the long-term prospects for democracy in Central and Eastern Europe? The 13 subsequent country-specific chapters address similar topics, albeit and obviously from slightly varying perspectives.

To sum up the first part of this chapter, this revised and expanded

Handbook of Political Change in Eastern Europe provides the reader with in-depth analyses of the political development in a broad range of countries in post-communist Europe. The country-specific chapters are written by scholars with well-documented area expertise on their respective cases. Each chapter includes appendices with detailed information about election results, government compositions, electoral laws, and constitutional frameworks. In addition to these in-depth and up-to-date analyses of the East European party systems and emerging cleavage structures, the concluding chapter of this volume makes an attempt at synthesizing the results of the country-specific analyses.

Analysing Political Cleavages

This volume is written within the tradition of comparative macro-sociology. As in the seminal book on cleavage structures edited by Seymour Martin Lipset and Stein Rokkan (1967), we focus primarily on the systems of contrasts and cleavages within national communities; on the factors important for development of a stable system of cleavages and opposition in national political life; and on the behaviour of rank-and-file citizens in the party-political systems. The historical dimension is important, as is the task of developmental comparison and the mapping of variations in the sequences of alternatives. As in the first version of the *Handbook of Political Change in Eastern Europe*, the fundamental assumption in this volume is that cleavages matter. They structure the behaviour of voters and parties alike and they determine the number of parties and the nature of partisan conflict; they are of obvious importance for the way democracy works. Indeed, the cleavage concept is crucial to the study of parties, party systems and regime change. And like many other key concepts, it is subject to many different interpretations. The country-specific chapters in this volume also testify to this.

Kevin Deegan-Krause (Chapter 8) contributes with a particularly interesting development of Seymour Martin Lipset and Stein Rokkan's classical account of 1967. Drawing on Bartolini and Mair (1990), Knutsen and Scarbrough (1995) and others, Deegan-Krause suggests that cleavages are operative on three levels of analysis – the demographic level, the attitudinal level, and the behavioural level. A 'full' cleavage thus requires an overlap on all three levels. For example, as a demographic category, 'workers' will have to display attitudinal and behavioural characteristics that set them apart from other social groups in order to qualify for cleavage politics along a left/right continuum. A partial overlap does not constitute a cleavage but a *divide*, and in Chapter 8 Deegan-Krause draws our attention to three such divides or partial cleavages – structural divides, issue divides, and caste divides:

1. A *structural divide* consists of overlap between demographic and attitudinal elements. A structural divide involves a relationship between particular material conditions or identities and specific sets of beliefs such as, for example, pro-redistribution sentiments of working-classes or attitudes favouring majority elections in a dominant ethnic group that may create a wide and enduring split in society. Yet without a behavioural component that produces, say, labour unions or labour parties, the split may yield little conflict and even less change. This corresponds quite closely to Mainwaring's description of 'salient social cleavages without clear party expressions' (Mainwaring 1999, 46).

2. An *issue divide* consists of overlapping attitudinal and behavioural elements. As such, it involves a relationship between particular beliefs and particular party choices. These divides may have an immediate political impact, but they may not endure from one election to the next because they lack roots in society. In fact, observers often refer to such cleavages as 'political cleavages' to distinguish them from 'social cleavages' that involve ties to particular social groups. These cleavages also correspond closely to the 'issue dimensions' of party competition discussed by Lijphart (1984).

3. A *caste divide*, finally, consists of a direct overlap between ascriptive or demographic elements, on the one hand, and behavioural elements, on the other. Lacking an attitudinal component, this is the least familiar of the three divides, but it may come into being when social groups have not consciously articulated the nature of an underlying group identity. If the members of a group can agree on questions of identity and formulate corresponding demands, this divide can develop into a full cleavage. If they cannot, caste divides are vulnerable to political entrepreneurs, who may try to seek support by emphasizing attitudinal factors that cut across group and party lines.

What about the relationship between full cleavages and parties, then? Lipset and Rokkan (1967) portray parties as the principal agents of transforming societal conflicts into political divisions. This is in contrast to the more traditional representation of parties as 'outgrowths' of social forces (cf. Knutsen and Scarbrough 1995). Chemists use the term 'cleavage' to depict the tendency of crystals to split in certain directions, and Lipset and Rokkan argue that political parties translate group interests to political oppositions by crystallizing and articulating conflicting interests, constructing alliances, setting up organizational networks, and devising electoral strategies. Thus, 'cleavages do not translate themselves into party oppositions as a matter of course' (Lipset and Rokkan 1967, 26).

Lipset and Rokkan identified four classical cleavages in Western Europe: those of state versus church and centre versus periphery, which arose during the era of nation-building, and those of land versus industry and employers versus workers, arising from the industrial revolution. These cleavage dimensions have since been reformulated and empirically operationalized with reference to late-20th-century society. The church/state cleavage is now commonly recast as secularized versus religious, and the employer/worker cleavage as middle-class versus working-class, while the centre/periphery cleavage captures resistance to the state – often based on ethno-religious conflicts – and the urban/rural cleavage is recast as sectoral conflicts.

Cleavages go beyond issues, conflicts and interests of a purely economic or social nature. They are in a sense more fundamental, as they are founded on culture, value orientations, and ideological insulation; they constitute deep-seated socio-structural conflicts with political significance. A cleavage is rooted in a persistent social division, which enables us to identify certain groups in society: members of an ethnic minority, believers of a particular denomination, and residents of a particular region. A cleavage also engages a certain set of values common to members of the group; group members share the same value orientation. And finally, cleavages are institutionalized in the form of political parties and other associational groups.

It follows from Lipset and Rokkan's well-known argument that the 'freezing' of a party structure needs a coupling to the cleavage structure. Electoral behaviour becomes more predictable when, and only when, parties find voters and voters find parties corresponding to their respective positions in the same cleavage structure. Indeed, the political quietude in Western Europe during the 1950s and 1960s indicated that the party systems had frozen along the lines of the cleavage structure. Conversely, the much higher degree of electoral mobility and emergence of new party-political forces thereafter – an 'unfreezing' of party systems – can be seen as the result of the erosion of old cleavage lines and the emergence of new ones. Some studies even argue that cleavage politics in the West is in the process of being replaced by 'new politics', anchored not in cleavages but in more fluid relationships between social groups, value orientations and party preferences (Inglehart 1984). In fact, an appropriate description of 'new politics' would be 'politics without cleavages' or 'post-cleavage conflicts' (Knutsen and Scarbrough 1995, 497).

Central and Eastern Europe emerged from socialism with what Wessels and Klingemann (1994) have described as 'flattened societies'. As a result of the communist regimes' levelling and modernizing policies they were much less socio-politically structured than the Western democracies or, for that matter, the pre-communist societies. The low level of socio-economic differentiation had the consequence that party preferences after 1989 were largely determined by 'cultural politics' rather than by interests related to the voters' individual positions in the social structure. It has indeed been argued that the political parties of the transitional era articulated only theoretical interests of social groups that did not exist at the time. Class certainly was a weak predictor of electoral behaviour, far behind the factors of age, education, union membership and, in particular, religion.

The volatility of electoral behaviour since the transition from communism seems to confirm the notion that the class cleavage remains weakly articulated. This does not, however, imply that the post-communist societies have moved directly from socialism to a 'new politics' mode. Indeed, the predominance of cultural politics over interest politics at the early stages of transition seems to testify to the existence of fairly strong cleavages particularly in the centre/periphery, ethnic, secular/religious and, in some cases, urban/rural dimensions. As indicated by the country-specific analyses, the Central and East European parties that have managed to garner stable support in the 1990s have often done so by articulating and exploiting these cleavages.

The country-specific chapters in this volume (Chapters 3–15) will provide an overview of how cleavages have made themselves felt after communism. Of particular interest is the extent to which there is a link between the cleavage structure and the emerging party systems. As mentioned above, Lipset and Rokkan have pointed out that the link between parties and cleavages is crucial for the development of stable party systems. The following chapters will demonstrate that most, if not all, Central and East European countries are still far from having established a cleavage–party linkage dominating the electoral arena. The party systems in the region are still in a state of flux, and electoral behaviour is characterized by a great deal of volatility. This makes the political systems vulnerable to various kinds of populist movements, including those of an anti-democratic hue. Even so, a historical perspective tells us that the prospects for consolidated democracy have never been better in Central and Eastern Europe than they are today.

NOTES

* This chapter is partly based on the introductionary chapter in the 1998 version of *The Handbook of Political Change in Eastern Europe*, written by Sten Berglund, Tomas Hellén and Frank Aarebrot.

1. It should be noted that these dividing lines are not unconditional. For example, a country that receives, say, a rating of 6 for political rights and 5 for civil liberties need not necessarily fall into the same category as a country that receives a rating of 5 for political rights and a 6 for civil liberties. Whether the country will be classified as 'partly free' or 'not free' has ultimately to do with the total number of raw points the country receive. Countries with combined raw scores of 0–30 points are 'not free', 31–59 points are 'partly free', and 60–88 points are 'free'. These raw points are decided by the Freedom House survey team, and are based on responses to a standardized checklist of political rights and civil liberties. The survey team also takes into account country specific factors, such as extreme violence or perceived future prospects. The specific circumstances in each country may or may not lead to a minor adjustment of the raw points. Somewhat simplified, the 'political rights' checklist encompasses the possibilities to participate freely in the political process – e.g. the right for all adults to vote in free and fair elections, the right to compete for public office, the right to organize political parties, the right for cultural, ethnic or religious minorities to have reasonable self-determination or autonomy. 'Civil liberties' include freedom of expression and belief, freedom of assembly, demonstration and open public discussion, the rule of law, personal autonomy, and economic rights. For a more detailed description of the survey and information about the criteria used to rate countries, see www.freedomhouse.org.

REFERENCES

Bartolini, Stefano and Peter Mair (1990), *Identity, Competition, and Electoral Availability: The Stabilisation of the European Electorates 1885–1985*, Cambridge, Cambridge University Press.

Berglund, Sten and Jan Åke Dellenbrant, eds (1994), *The New Democracies of Eastern Europe: Party Systems and Political Cleavages*, Aldershot, Edward Elgar.

—— and Frank H. Aarebrot (1997), *The Political History of Eastern Europe in the 20th Century: The Struggle Between Democracy and Dictatorship*, Aldershot, Edward Elgar.

——, Tomas Hellén and Frank H. Aarebrot, eds (1998), *The Handbook of Political Change in Eastern Europe*, Cheltenham, Edward Elgar.

——, Frank H. Aarebrot, Henri Vogt and Georgi Karasimeonov (2001), *Challenges to Democracy. Eastern Europe Ten Years after the Collapse of Communism*, Cheltenham, Edward Elgar.

Diamond, Larry (2002), 'Elections Without Democracy: Thinking About Hybrid Regimes', *Journal of Democracy*, Vol. 13, No. 2, April 2002, 21–35.

Freedom in the World Country Ratings, Freedom House website (www.freedomhouse.org).

Garton Ash, Timothy (1991), *The Uses of Adversity*, London, Granta and Penguin.

Hellén, Tomas (1996), *Shaking Hands with the Past: Origins of the Political Right in Central Europe*, Helsinki, The Finnish Society of Sciences and Letters and the Finnish Academy of Science and Letters.

Inglehart, Ronald (1984), 'The Changing Structure of Political Cleavages in Western Societies', in Russell J. Dalton, Scott C. Flanagan and Paul A. Beck, eds, *The Electoral Change in Advanced Industrial Democracies: Realignment or Dealignment?*, Princeton, Princeton University Press.

Karatnycky, Adrian, Alexander Motyl and Amanda Schnetzer, eds (2002), *Nations in Transit 2002. Civil Society: Democracy, and Markets in East Central Europe and the Newly Independent States*, Freedom House and Transaction Publishers, New Jersey.

—— (2003), 'Liberty's Advances in a Troubled World', *Journal of Democracy*, Vol. 14, No. 1, January 2003, 100–113.

Knutsen, Oddbjørn and Elinor Scarbrough (1995), 'Cleavage Politics', in Jan W. van Deth and Elinor Scarbrough, eds, *The Impact of Values*, Oxford, Oxford University Press.

Lijphart, Arend (1984), *Democracies*, New Haven, Connecticut, Yale University Press.

Lipset, Seymour Martin and Stein Rokkan (1967), 'Introduction', in Seymour Martin Lipset and Stein Rokkan, eds, *Party Systems and Voter Alignments*, New York, Free Press.

Mainwaring, Scott (1999), *Rethinking Party Systems in the Third Wave of Democratization: The case of Brazil*, Stanford, Stanford University Press.

Rose, Richard (2002), 'Advancing Into Europe? The Contrasting Goals of Post-Communist Countries', in Adrian Karatnycky, Alexander Motyl and Amanda Schnetzer, eds, *Nations in Transit 2002*, Freedom House and Transaction Publishers, New Jersey.

Rupnik, Jacques (1989), *The Other Europe*, London, Weidenfeld and Nicholson.

Schöpflin, George (1993), *Politics in Eastern Europe 1945–92*, Oxford, Blackwell.

Wessels, Bernhard and Hans-Dieter Klingemann (1994), 'Democratic transformation and the prerequisites of democratic opposition in East and Central Europe', Wissenschaftszentrum Berlin für Sozialforschung, FS III, 94–201.

Whitefield, Stephen (2002), 'Political cleavages and post-communist politics', *Annual Review of Political Science*, Vol. 5, 181–200.

Whyte, Nicholas (2002), 'The European Parliament flexes its muscles – in Albania', report published on-line by the International Crisis Group (ICG), June 27, 2002 (www.crisisweb.org).

2. The Challenge of History in Central and Eastern Europe

Sten Berglund, Joakim Ekman and Frank Aarebrot*

In the past century, Central and Eastern Europe has experienced three major political transformations: in 1917–19, after the First World War; in 1944–48; after the Second World War; and in 1989–91, after the demise of the Soviet Union and the end of the Cold War. External forces and sources have played a major role in all three of them, but the transformations were clearly also a product of domestic divisions and cleavages.

This chapter sets out to identify social divisions and political cleavages at work in Central and Eastern Europe throughout the 20th century. Some of these divisions and cleavages have their roots in the individual societies, others are linked to the broad international environment; the urban/rural cleavage would be an example of the former type; the divide between communists and their opponents highlights the latter family of cleavages. The roots of the cleavages are, however, of limited significance for our analysis. Our ambition is to describe the full set of cleavages at various critical junctures in the history of Central and Eastern Europe, for the additional purpose of evaluating the prospects for democratic consolidation in the most recent attempt at democracy in the region.

Much has changed in the eastern part of Europe over the past hundred years, but this should not make us oblivious to the importance of the historical heritage. Indeed, history sometimes rebounds with a vengeance when and where least expected. Social and political changes of a large magnitude often include an initial element of overshooting that tends to be corrected in the long run. The French Revolution is, of course, a classic case in point, but so too is the gradual adaptation of the Soviet puppet regimes in Central and Eastern Europe to their respective national constituencies. History clearly matters and must be taken into account by those who build political institutions and by those who analyse them.

The present chapter is structured first to provide the reader with a rough overview of the foremost social divisions and political cleavages in Central and Eastern Europe between, as well as after, the two World Wars. This predominantly historical section serves as a background for one more analytically cast sub-chapter on the prospects for consolidated democracy in Central and Eastern Europe today.

The Imperial Heritage

The First World War (1914–18) resulted in a cataclysmic shift in the power structure on the European continent. The German, Habsburg, Russian and Ottoman empires came out of the war fatally weakened, and as the victorious Western allies – the United States in particular – propagated the idea of national self-determination, the 'captive nations' of these empires were able to break free of their empires into independence, statehood and the first of three experiments in democracy thus far.

Already, in the mid-19th century, the quest for statehood and independence was attached to calls for social regeneration: in less-developed areas, by demands for land reform and an eradication of feudal and semi-feudal structures; in the more developed ones, by rising middle-classes and industrial working-classes. Thus, socio-economic conflicts and cleavages were often directly linked to ethnic and cultural ones; indeed, most mainstream theories see nationalism primarily as a function of different aspects of modernization (Deutsch 1953; Gellner 1983; Hobsbawm 1990). In any case, both nationalism as an ideology and the nation state as a mode of societal organization are incarnations of modernity.

The political culture in the newly independent states was strongly marked by the legacy of the past. The region, taken as a whole, had been an interface between East and West since at least the 10th century, when it became part of Christian European civilization. But with the onset of proto-industrialization in the 15th and 16th centuries, the distance to the European core again began to broaden. Since then, the bulk of the eastern part of Europe has remained relegated to the periphery or at least the semi-periphery of the European economic system; only some parts (in particular, Bohemia) have occasionally been within the core (Wallerstein 1974, 99). There is no doubt that all of Eastern Europe has been part of the broad pattern of European civilization and culture for at least a millennium, but 'slightly differently, less intensively, less fully' than the West, 'with the result that East European participation in the European experience was only partial' (Schöpflin 1993, 11). In political terms, the eastern part of Europe has been a transitional zone between the Western tradition of division of power and the Eastern tradition of concentration of power. This fault-line coincides with that between Western and Eastern Christianity; the Eastern tradition is at its strongest in territories once under Ottoman rule, and the Western tradition is strongest in areas marked by Lutheranism (*Figure 2.1*).

Figure 2.1: The main historical religious cleavage lines in Eastern Europe

The history of Central and Eastern Europe in the modern era is in many respects the history of the great empires. But these empires were different in character. By the late 19th century, the German and Habsburg empires had most of the trappings of a modern *Rechtsstaat,* and although they were far from being model democracies, civil society and representative democracy were developing fast. After 1871, Prussia developed into a great German power based on the mono-national principle, but within the Habsburg empire, nation-building accelerated during the decades prior to the First World War, just like state-building in the case of Hungary after the 1867

Ausgleich or Compromise with Austria. In contrast, the territories once subjected to the Russian and Ottoman empires reached independence almost totally void of state- and nation-building traditions.

This dichotomy between the German and Habsburg empires and their Russian and Ottoman counterparts, neatly coincides with the East/West fault-line between Central and Eastern Europe. The Western group shares traditions of Roman law, feudalism and relatively early national awakening; the Eastern group has a Byzantine heritage and a lack of strong feudal traditions, enabling ancient local authority relationships such as kinship and clientelism to survive longer. This tendency is stronger in the South than in the North. The North/South dichotomy is reinforced by the strength and autonomy of political authority versus religious leadership. The North/ South dimension separates the Protestant and substantially secularized states from the Counter-Reformation Catholic states, non-secularized Orthodox states, and the Muslim states (Berglund and Aarebrot 1997).

The Baltic states are characterized by their position at the crossroads of German, Russian, Polish and Scandinavian culture. Nevertheless, they are not a culturally homogenous group. In the late pre-modern and early modern era, the Lithuanian heartland was part of the Polish-Lithuanian commonwealth, at times ruling over vast tracts of land stretching down to the Black Sea; thus it has a tradition of itself being an imperial centre. Estonia and most of Latvia, on the other hand, have no pre-20th-century traditions of independence. They were ruled by the Teutonic Order, Denmark, Poland, Sweden and eventually by aristocratic Germanic agents of the Russian Tsar. This gave them a more Western cultural tradition, and a mainly German nobility and bourgeoisie, as opposed to Lithuania's mainly Polish and Russian landowners and Jewish artisan, merchant and professional classes. For these same historical reasons, Latvia and Estonia are predominantly Protestant while Catholicism is dominant in Lithuania. In linguistic terms, however, the cleavage runs otherwise: Estonian is a Fenno-Ugric language distinct from Latvian and Lithuanian, which both represent relatively distant branches of the Baltic family of languages.

The Structure of Conflicts in the Inter-War Era

The states formed in Eastern Europe as a result of the First World War did not settle once and for all the issue of state- and nation-building. In fact, in many cases they were as ethnically diverse as, or even more than, the empires from which they emerged. In the inter-war era (1919–39), all East European states had significant national minorities and/or substantial diasporas. Problems of state-building and nation-building were thus at the very top of the political agenda. Topics such as democracy, the rule of law and the distribution of wealth also played a prominent role in the Central and East European inter-war political debate, but the emphasis was more frequently than not on the survival of state and nation in what was felt to be a hostile environment. The odds were, in that sense, tilted against the survival of the new democracies, and by the end of the inter-war era Czechoslovakia was the only democratic survivor.

In Czechoslovakia, the Czech core nation constituted less than half of the total population; and the arguably artificial 'Czecho–Slovak' nationality added up to only two-thirds in the 1920 and 1930 official censuses. In Yugoslavia, similar figures applied to the core Serb and 'Serbo–Croat' nationalities, respectively; all in all, no less than 14 different languages were widely spoken in the State of the Southern Slavs. Moreover, of Poland's inter-war population, fewer than 70 per cent were ethnic Poles, and of Romania's, only about three-quarters could be defined as ethnic Romanians – what constitutes a 'Pole', 'Romanian', 'Macedonian' etc., has, of course, always been the subject of both controversy and manipulation (cf. Rothschild 1974, 1989; Crampton and Crampton 1996). Even in the most ethnically homogenous states in the region – the Baltic states, Bulgaria and Hungary – the proportion of the core populations were only in the 80–90 per cent range during the 1920s and 1930s (see *Table 2.5*, p. 48).

The ethnic mosaic also had a territorial dimension. In particular, the entire Hungarian polity was shell-shocked by the loss of no less than two-thirds of the territory and three-fifths of the population ruled from Budapest during the Habsburg era. While rump Hungary was by and large ethnically homogenous, one Magyar in three was left outside the country's borders – in Romania, Czechoslovakia and Yugoslavia – as territories were transferred to her neighbours by the Western allies of the First World War. This was done partly on strategic grounds, but also as a result of the Magyars' bad record on minority rights and because Hungary – like Austria proper, but as opposed to the Slavic nations of the Dual Monarchy – was considered a defeated aggressor nation. Not surprisingly, revanchist feelings became the determining force in Hungarian politics from the very outset of independence. Poland, which almost miraculously re-emerged as a sovereign state after a hundred and twenty years of partition, had territorial grievances with all her neighbours, some of which were settled by force during a confusing and violent process reminiscent of the conflicts that erupted after the break-up of Yugoslavia in 1991. All of Bulgaria's borders were disputed, and the post-1920 demarcation line between Lithuania and Poland cut right through an ethnically very mixed area; as did the borders between Poland and the USSR, between Lithuania and Germany, between Yugoslavia and Italy and between Albania and Yugoslavia. Czechoslovakia did, thanks to successful lobbying among the Western powers, hit a territorial jackpot and walked off with an extravagant settlement. In Eastern Europe, Czechoslovakia was alone in being solely on the defensive when it came to territorial conflicts.

All these new states in Central and Eastern Europe, save Bulgaria and Albania, retained substantial and/or influential German-speaking minorities – even when it came to the exclusively German-speaking areas in Austria and Bohemia directly bordering on Germany proper, the Western allies had refused to apply the nationality principle, since that would have left the *Reich* bigger and stronger than before the war. Jewish minorities were also present in great numbers throughout the region, Estonia, Bulgaria and Albania excepted. Polish Jewry counted about three million, equal to 9–10 per cent of the total population; of Carpatho-Ukraine's population, some 12 per cent were Jewish; of Lithuania's, 7 per cent; of Hungary's, 6.5 per cent; of Slovakia's, Romania's and Latvia's, 3–5 per cent. With no outside power to protect them, the Jews were particularly vulnerable to the rising tide of xenophobia. Most countries in the area introduced anti-Jewish legislation, such as quotas in higher education, during the 1930s.

Given the ethnic mix, the regimes were faced with two alternatives: either create multi-ethnic, consociational states (Lijphart 1968; 1980) or embark on a policy of national assimilation and/or exclusion. All eventually went for the latter alternative – even Czechoslovakia, where escalating German, Magyar and Slovak separatism and Czech hegemonic ambitions dashed Tomás Masaryk's hopes that the democratic process would eventually bring all ethnic components into a political nation. All over the eastern part of Europe, national and state consolidation were seen as prerequisites for each other.

The imposed policies of ethnic integration and ethnic exclusion had much to do with the absence of autonomous sub-system structures. During the Habsburg era, the cultural and linguistic integration of Jews, Slavs and Romanians into the politically dominant German and Magyar communities was welcomed and encouraged, while imperial Germany and Russia used much stiffer methods to impose their hegemony over Poland and in the Baltic states. Because this process encouraged both the integrators and those subjected to integration to perceive political structures and conflicts in national rather than in economic, social or class terms, genuinely autonomous structures had experienced great difficulties in forming. Here, the imperial centre of Hungary and the economically more advanced Bohemia and Moravia proved exceptions: already, by the late 19th century the Czechs had won the ethnic struggle for hegemony in Prague and Moravia. Long thereafter, the local German nobility remained in control in Estonia and Latvia, where national awakening was slow to commence; Germans, Magyars, Jews, Greeks, Italians and Armenians dominated urban life in the Balkans; Slovakia was ruled as any province of Hungary; and Poland was administered from the imperial centres of St Petersburg, Berlin and Vienna.

If the peace settlements and establishment of new states were intended to ease communal tension, defuse national conflicts and, in general, set the successor states on a path towards democracy and prosperity, this failed miserably. Even though national self-determination was a straightforward enough concept in theory, its practical application to the eastern part of Europe as things stood in 1919 created an abundance of new intra-state and inter-state conflict dimensions. The nation-states created were far from perfect, with borders designed to accommodate the victors and their protégés, and very little protection for the minorities, whose calls for cultural autonomy were considered seditious by the new ruling ethnic groups. Germans and Magyars in Czechoslovakia, Ukrainians, Germans and Jews in Poland, and Magyars, Jews and Ukrainians in Romania were among those who experienced harassment or even persecution (Tismaneanu 1993, 6).

In newly-independent Poland, Marshal Józef Piłsudski and the moderate left championed a multi-ethnic Polish state, but were, however, not prepared to grant any significant amount of autonomy to the minorities, particularly not to some five million ethnic Ukrainians and 1.5–2 million Belorusians who lived in the Eastern borderlands, which nationalist Poles perceived as the bastion of Western Christianity, the *przedmurze*. The failure to create a political state led to the eventual victory of Roman Dmowski's vision of a state founded on national kinship. President Beneš envisaged that Czechoslovakia would develop into an 'Eastern Switzerland', but others saw only a mini-replica of the Habsburg concoction – the difference being that Czechoslovakia, like the other successor states, lacked the Habsburg supra-national ideology which helped national minorities to feel included. And even for the ethnic groups that had not been content with that prospect, the imperial policy of ethnic favouritism had at least been more reversible than that of the successor states constructed around nation-building ethnic majorities.

The imperfect application of the nationality principle guaranteed that nationalism would remain the dominant issue in inter-war Central and Eastern Europe. The widespread irredentism encouraged states to intervene in their neighbours' affairs to protect minorities belonging to their own core nationality, and, as a counter-reaction, caused the host states to attempt forceful integration of their minorities, or even to deny their very existence. Social policies were strongly influenced by attempts at ethnic assimilation, economic policies drifted towards economic nationalism and competitive striving for autarky, and attempts at land reform were primarily motivated by the glory of expropriating 'alien' landlords. Moreover, resilient irredentist tension pre-empted the development of regional political and economic cooperation, and enabled Germany and the USSR, the revisionist great powers, to exploit the situation to their own advantage.

Ethnic cleavages often coincided with religious ones. Multi-ethnic and multi-denominational Poland was, despite its secular constitution, for all intents and purposes a state of and for Roman Catholics, just as Romania and Bulgaria were states of and for Orthodox believers. In Yugoslavia, an Eastern Orthodox dynasty ruled over not only Catholic Croatia and Slovenia but also over predominantly Muslim areas in Bosnia, Herzegovina and Southern Serbia. In Czechoslovakia, Slovak dissatisfaction was fuelled by the strong Catholic heritage, as opposed to the Protestant or secular outlook of the politically dominant Prague and Bohemian elites. Latvia was an amalgamation of three historical regions of which Livonia and Courland were mainly Protestant and Latgale mainly Catholic.

Apart from the ethno-religious cleavage, conflicts between the centres and the peripheries were also rife, due to the centralizing ambitions of the new elites. Czechoslovakia, where Prague was pitted against the rest of the country is a case in point. Hungary was divided between cosmopolitan Budapest and the countryside with feudal estates and subsistence farmers. In Romania, the anti-Magyar and anti-Jewish policies were complemented by Walachian chauvinism. Polish political life in the inter-war era was characterized by tensions between the formerly Russian areas, which provided most of the bureaucracy and military officers, and the previously German and Austrian territories, which dominated industry and commerce. In Yugoslavia, the relationship between politically dominant Serbia and the economically more advanced Northwest was of a similar nature.

The ethnic cleavage
Party formation in immediate post-independence Central and Eastern Europe was co-determined by ethnicity, class, ideology and religion, but as Table 2.1 indicates, ethnicity was the defining cleavage, to which other cleavages – including left/right – were subordinated. Typical in inter-war Central and Eastern Europe was the existence of parallel party systems for each ethnic group, a tendency which was reinforced by constitutional arrangements which had paved the way for extreme multi-partyism, particularly in the northern half of the region. The matrix depicts the party systems classified according to ethnicity and party families. The parties included in the matrix may have operated for only a short period in time or only as voting lists or parliamentary clubs. As Derek Urwin has noted: '[w]e find in these imperfectly integrated European states with substantial minorities that either the ethnic cleavage coincided with other cleavages, especially religion, or that the linguistic groups generated complete party systems of their own. This is generally the case in Eastern Europe, examples being the Germans and Magyars in Czechoslovakia, and the Jews and Ukrainians in Poland. These sub-cultural party systems often included an agrarian party' (Urwin 1980, 195).

Table 2.1: Relevant parties and their main ethnic bases

	Social Democratic	Agrarian	Liberal	Conservative	Nationalist/ Ethnic Defence
Estonia					
Estonian	x	x	x	x	x
Russian					x
German					x
Swedish		x		x	x
Latvia					
Latvian unitary	x	x	x	x	
Latgalian	x	x	x	x	x
Semgalian		x			x
Russian	x	x		x	x
German					x
Jewish	x				x
Polish	x				x
Lithuania					
Lithuanian	x	x	x	x	x
Polish	x	x			x
German	x				x
Jewish	x				x
Poland					
Polish	x	x	x	x	x
Ukrainian	x	x			x
Belorussian	x	x			x
German	x	x	x	x	x
Jewish	x	x	x		x
Czechoslovakia					
Czecho-Slovak	x				
Czech		x	x	x	
Slovak		x		x	x
German	x	x	x	x	x
Magyar	x	x	x	x	x
Ruthenian					x
Jewish					x
Polish					x
Hungary					
Magyar	x	x	x	x	x
Romania					
Romanian	x	x	x	x	x
Magyar	x	x	x	x	x
Jewish	x				x
German	x				x
Bulgaria					
Bulgarian	x	x	x	x	x

Indeed, agrarian parties were almost universally ethnically based (the Yugoslav Peasant Union was one exception), as were many of the liberal and conservative parties, and – for obvious reasons – the radical nationalist formations. But fragmentation according to ethnicity also applied to the left. The social democrats, faced by the bewildering ethnic array of the Austro-Hungarian empire, had already by the 1890s abandoned the territorial basis of nationality for a 'personal' principle. By the end of the First World War, the social democratic parties in the German, Habsburg and Russian empires had formally split into their national branches, and the disintegration continued within the newly independent states.

The main exception to the ethnic principle of party organization was the communist movement, which remained staunchly internationalist. This was only natural, since the one defining moment of the Marxist movement was the outbreak of the First World War, when the overwhelming majority of European social democrats rallied behind the respective governments and only a minority remained committed to supra-nationalism. In 1942–43, however, the communist strategy changed, and the communist parties founded or co-founded 'national' or 'patriotic' fronts which proved able to attract broad public support.

Table 2.1 strongly suggests an extremely high level of ethnic compartmentalization and political fragmentation, particularly in the Northern tier of the East European countries. In Czechoslovakia, there were moderate socialist, agrarian, liberal, Christian democratic and conservative parties catering for almost every single ethnic group. By way of example, Poland had a total of 92 registered parties by 1925, about half of which were ethnically Polish; in Latvia, ethnic fragmentation resulted in separate party systems for Latvians, Russians, Germans, Poles and Jews, while regional fragmentation prompted the emergence of parochial Latgalian and Semgalian parties (cf. Crampton and Crampton 1996). In Yugoslavia, the party system was also structured along ethnic lines, with the National Radical Party being dominant in Serbia proper and the Democratic Party among Serbs elsewhere, and the Croat People's Peasant Party, the Slovene People's Party and the Yugoslav Muslim Organization dominant within their respective ethnic constituencies; over 40 parties participated in the November 1920 election for the constituent assembly.

The new states invariably chose or were endowed with formally Western-style constitutions, albeit that Bulgaria and Romania had been monarchies since the 19th century and Yugoslavia and Hungary emerged as kingdoms in 1918–19. The constitutional formats were conducive to extreme multi-partyism. The problem was that these new, modern political systems largely had no base of autonomous spheres and power-centres. The nation-builders inevitably had to turn to the state, and paradoxically the state thus came to perform or organize many of the functions of civil society. These attempts to create a civil society from above were not entirely unsuccessful, but they also resulted in a high degree of state control of social and political interaction. The process of enforced social modernization formed the basis of the statism often mentioned as the main characteristic of inter-war Central and Eastern Europe. And even when the state did succeed in building structures of civil society, it often proved unwilling to relinquish control.

The Balkans were a special case. Bulgaria, Serbia and Romania had been ruled by local proxies of the Ottoman empire, and when independence arrived by instalments beginning in 1817, they simply cut their remaining ties with Constantinople. Contrary to their tight hold at the state level, the Turks allowed local governments considerable autonomy. After conquering an area, the Ottomans preferred to rule through intermediaries. Under the *millet* system, the Turks eliminated any residual local secular government and replaced it with a religious authority of local origin, or at least of local confession, with civic responsibilities. In the Balkans, the Orthodox Church came to serve as the Ottomans' agent for regional and local government, and the Church became strongly identified with the Ottoman state. When nationalism began to emerge within the region, non-Orthodox groups saw the Orthodox Church as an obstacle to their ethnic and nationalist goals. Religion thus tended to reinforce ethnic differences, exacerbating social divisions and complicating political development (cf. Jelavich and Jelavich 1965; Jelavich 1983a; 1983b).

As the Ottomans had eradicated the local aristocracies, the Balkan elites were not landed but rather military and clerical, and relative latecomers to political power, heavily reliant on the state and on clientelist relationships. Albania was even worse off than the other Balkan countries when it became autonomous in 1913, as it had only a rudimentary state administration; the country was in practice ruled by tribal structures dominated by the Muslim clans of the north and was reduced to an economic and political client of Italy.

As George Schöpflin (1993) has argued, the attempts by the weakly grounded semi-authoritarian or fully fledged dictatorships – in the Balkans as well as elsewhere in the eastern part of Europe – to build loyalty to the state through the promotion of nationalism raised two problems: it left open or exacerbated the national issue, and nationalism as a political doctrine provided answers to very few questions of political organization and the distribution of power.

> It created strong identities and a sense of belonging to the state for members of the dominant group, but said next to nothing about political structures, the resolution of conflicts of interests, the allocation of resources and values, participation and representation, i.e. the day-to-day problems of political, economic and social life.

[...] The comparative vagueness of the nationalist message, together with its emotional intensity, produced a somewhat contradictory result. East European nations in the inter-war era reached a fairly high state of national consciousness of their political identities as members of a nation and as those excluded as non-members. At one and the same time the implicit promise of equality and justice, encapsulated in the nationalist message, was left unfulfilled, with inevitable frustration and resentment at the social-political closures enforced against society by its rulers (Schöpflin 1993, 24–5).

From fragmentation to strongman rule

The institution of the government party operating in a pseudo-parliamentary system was common to all the post-independence polities of the successor states: the governing parties (or coalitions) were incarnations of the bureaucracies and the technocratic and military elites. Prime ministers tended to emerge from the administrative elite and then proceeded to 'elect' a parliament to serve them. This system was, however, hegemonic, not totalitarian, and parliamentary opposition both on the left and on the right – even radical opposition – was tolerated as long as it did not threaten the fundamental stability of the regime in power. Hungary was a case in point: the ruling Unity Party was an instrument for administration rather than an association of like-minded people, and as the electoral system – with suffrage restricted to less than 30 per cent and an open ballot in rural areas – virtually guaranteed it a permanent majority, most of the formal requirements of democratic rule could be observed. Likewise, Romania and Bulgaria had vocal parliaments, but their function was to legitimize the governments designated by the monarchs. In Poland and the Baltic countries, the representative systems also took on a façade character after the post-independence constitutions, modelled on Weimar and the French Third Republic, had shown the dangers of extreme multi-partyism.

Another effect of the marriage between the bureaucratic and administrative elite and the government was the personal, rather than ideological, nature of conflicts and of party loyalties. The influence of informal 'old-boy networks' – such as the Polish and Czech Legionnaires, the Estonian Freedom Fighters, the Lithuanian Light Infantry Association, the IMRO in Bulgaria and Macedonia – sometimes resembling secret societies, marked the clientelistic nature of political loyalties and encouraged opportunistic defections and sudden shifts in coalitions.

In Central and Eastern Europe of 1900–39, 'governments did not lose elections' (Schöpflin 1993, 12). The exceptions, Hungary in 1905 and Bulgaria in 1932, both resulted from divisions within the elite rather than being expressions of the popular will. Strong state control of the administrative machinery enabled the elites, when united, to produce the desired election outcomes. But while there was a strong element of façade politics, a large amount of outward and genuine respect for constitutional probity was observed; sensitivity to international opinion also put a lid on the most outrageous authoritarian ambitions.

The authoritarian systems which emerged after the experiment with Western-style parliamentarism were often based on a similar ideological cocktail as in Poland after 1935, when the 'Government of Colonels' united the rival forces of left and right into the Camp of National Unity: '40 per cent nationalism, 30 per cent social radicalism, 20 per cent agrarianism, and 10 per cent anti-Semitism' (Wandycz 1992, 226). In many cases one could add technocratism, as the modernization of industry and infrastructure was hailed as the programmatic solution to the problems of the states and the regimes, regardless of the social mobilization which rapid industrialization always entails (Rothschild 1974, 71–2). The rise of fascism in Italy and Nazism in Germany provided East European strongmen and nationalists with an outside blueprint for authoritarianism which they were increasingly eager to embrace – but only up to a point. In fact, the authoritarianism of the 1930s was as much directed against the radical, mass-based right as against the Marxist or utopian-agrarian left. The presidential coups in Poland and the Baltic states and the tightening of the Balkan royal dictatorships were prompted by – or at least said to be prompted by – the threat from anti-regime fascist or fascist-style movements: Estonia had its Freedom Fighters, Poland its *Falanga*; Czechoslovakia had the (Hlinka's) Slovak People's Party, the Czech National Party and the *Sudeten* subsidiary of the *Reich* NSDAP; Hungary the Arrow Cross; Romania the Iron Cross.

By the mid-1930s, the principle of parliamentary rule had been discarded and replaced by strongman rule almost throughout Central and Eastern Europe (*Table 2.2*). Czechoslovakia's experiment in democracy proved the most successful; despite strong centrifugal forces, it had a functioning parliamentary system, the rule of law and separation of powers until the 1938 Munich agreement – as a result of Masaryk's and Beneš's vision that social and economic development would pave the way for ethnic harmony. But even in Czechoslovakia, the political system was rigid, bureaucratic and non-participatory: in the inter-war era, the country was dominated by the *Petka* or 'Committee of Five', a loose cartel of five major Czech-dominated parties (Zeman 1976; Bankowicz 1994).

The argument that the ruling elites of inter-war Central and Eastern Europe were pursuing state-building rather than nation-building may seem surprising, given their exploitation of nationalism. But as Józef Piłsudski put it paraphrasing Massimo d'Azeglio, one of the founding fathers of the Italian state: 'It is the state which makes the nation and not the nation the state'; the first task of the rulers of the newly independent countries was to consolidate state structures, so as to be able to counter external and internal threats. Moreover, these ruling elites did not emerge from nowhere; there was indeed a marked continuity of the state-building elites, as witnessed by the strong military and aristocratic element.

Table 2.2: The breakdown of democracy

Country	Date	Strongman	Authoritarian orientation
Estonia	1934	Konstantin Päts	Centrist, corporatist
Latvia	1926	Kārlis Ulmanis	Centrist, corporatist
Lithuania	1926	Antanas Smetona	Corporatist, semi-fascist
Poland	1926	Józef Piłsudski	Initially left-oriented; then rightist and nationalist
Czechoslovakia			
Czech lands	1939		Corporatist, modelled on Italy
Slovakia	1938	Jozef Tiso	Clerico-Fascist, German puppet
Hungary	March 1919	Béla Kun	Soviet Republic
	August 1919	Miklós Horthy	Reactionary, semi-authoritarian
	November 1944	Ferenc Szálasi	Fascist, German puppet
Yugoslavia	1928	King Alexander	Royal coup
Romania	1920	King Ferdinand, Alexandru Averescu	Royal coup, fascist leaning military junta
Bulgaria	1934	King Boris	Royal coup

The elites were socially and economically conservative, and the truly revolutionary force in the predominantly rural eastern part of Europe before, during and after the First World War was the peasantry – not the working-class. There were only pockets of industrialization in inter-war Central and Eastern Europe – Bohemia, Silesia, Warsaw, Łódz, Riga, parts of Budapest, the Romanian oil district – and worker radicalism on issues other than wages and working conditions was ill-supported by the shallow roots of the working-class.

Modernization and the rural problem
The elites were aware of the dangers of rural backwardness, and the main concern of the state-builders became the issue of how to counter it through accelerated social modernization. There were land reforms and ambitious industrialization schemes in almost every East European country, and the depression of the 1930s prompted many of the regimes to further step up modernization. Poland built from scratch the gigantic Gdynia harbour complex, and in 1935 introduced a six-year plan which called for state intervention, capital regulation, nationalization of key industries and the creation of a Central Industrial Area to the east of Warsaw. The Hungarian government also experimented with Polish-style state planning and micro-management, spearheaded by the armament and investment programme centred on the city of Györ between Budapest and Vienna. Even so, the efforts at socio-economic modernization focused on rural life, which was characterized by insularity, rigid structures and a negative egalitarianism

which sought to equalize downwards (Schöpflin 1993, 26). Agriculture, the dominant livelihood in the eastern part of Europe, was backward and unproductive, and at subsistence level, almost everywhere.

The national independence project was initiated by the urban elites, and the majority of the East European peasantry remained deeply sceptical of the state-building efforts. Only a small portion of the peasantry was entrepreneurial, within the sphere of the money economy and aware of the possibilities and limitations of politics. The overwhelming majority, with very small or no land-holdings, either only occasionally or never entered into commodity production. It was deeply suspicious of the state, which was seen as a manipulator of the market or as an agent of the alien, parasitic 'city' that depleted the countryside of its resources. This was the world of the *Gemeinschaft*, resisting the emerging *Gesellschaft* (Schöpflin 1993, 26–8). In some of the cases, the urban/rural cleavage coincided with the ethno/religious one, as in Eastern Poland where the peasantry was mostly Orthodox or Uniate Catholic Ukrainian and Belorusian, but the landlords Roman Catholic Poles; also in Transylvania and the Banat, where the Orthodox Romanians were concentrated in rural areas and German and Magyar Catholics and Protestants dominated the towns and cities; or in Slovakia with its staunchly Catholic Slovak peasantry pitted against Jewish town-dwellers, largely Protestant Magyar landowners and the secular Czech political elite.

Peasant parties were strong already at the outset of independence. Some of the peasant movements were what Rokkan (1975) would have called 'parties of rural defence', while others had a more distinct class profile. The former had a reactionary touch as they tended to idealize the past and present it as a model for the future. The latter tended to be radical in the sense that they questioned and challenged the social order in the countryside as well as in the cities. Its targets were both the landed gentry and the urban bourgeoisie with Jewish, German or Magyar elements, thus creating a link between radical agrarianism and radical nationalism.

In post-First World War Bulgaria, the Agrarian Patriotic Union (BAPU) of Alexandr Stambolisky dominated the stage with its calls for land reform and social equality. Romania had a populist movement extolling traditional rural values. Poland had a strong, but divided, peasant movement with parliamentary offshoots. Hungary was confronted with agrarian socialism at an early stage and the Smallholders Party was to remain one of the dominant political forces throughout the inter-war era. Similar comments apply to the Agrarian Party in Czechoslovakia and the agrarian parties in the Baltic states (Berglund and Aarebrot 1997, 16). Most of the peasant movements, however, were unable to translate the numerical strength of their constituencies into political influence. The organizations were not strong enough and their leaders prone to cooptation by the ruling elites.

The elites could successfully play the game of divide and rule as the opposition was from opposite quarters: the national minorities, opposed mainly to the nation-building project, and the rural population opposed to the state-building project. For instance, the peasant movement in Yugoslavia was deeply divided between centralist and autonomist forces.

The radicalization of the peasantry is largely explained by the adverse economic circumstances, particularly the impoverishment brought on first by the agricultural crisis in the early- and mid-1920s, and later by the depression. The experience was particularly debilitating as the villages had only just initiated their integration into commodities production and the monetary economy; the adverse effects were thus largely interpreted as yet another example of urban society's efforts and ability to exploit the peasant. The experiences of the First World War had of course also whetted the appetites of millions of peasants to benefit from modernization, and demonstrated the dependence of urban societies on the fruits of rural labour. As their relative deprivation and exclusion from the general progress in Europe were ever more clearly exposed, large parts of the peasantry chose to identify groups outside 'the peasant way of life' as their enemies. This juxtaposition was both class-based – directed against the land-owners, the urban bureaucracies, industrialists and the socialist proletariat – and ethno-racial – directed at 'national outsiders' such as Jews, Gypsies and Magyars. In many instances these identifications coincided, such as the equation of Jews with both finance capitalism and internationalist, godless Bolshevism, or of Magyars in Slovakia with feudalism and cultural imperialism. At times the right proved their radical credentials to the peasants, as in Hungary where a second bill on land reform was pushed through on the eve of the Second World War.

The legacy of radicalism

Pressure arising from rapid and turbulent modernization has been identified as a source of popular radicalism in rural, backward and peripheral regions. This 'emerging radicalism' has often been left-oriented, not only in post-war Central and Eastern Europe but also in Scandinavia where support for communism has traditionally had two bases: in the established industrial regions and in the poorest rural areas. Support for the rural, emerging variety of left radicalism has been found to be consistent with the prevalence of economic and social instability (high unemployment or underemployment, large differences in living standards, wide fluctuations in income, and a high level of migration); rapid and widespread socio-economic change; weak socio-political traditions and norms; rootlessness and weak group identification; and expressive and momentary political activity (Allardt 1964; 1970).

In contrast to industrial communism, the rural variety of left-wing radicalism tends to emerge where individuals without strong class identification experience deprivation. But this deprivation is not relative and institutionalized, as is the case within the established urban working-class. It is 'diffuse', an effect of the modernization process which breaks down the traditional rural groups of reference and comparison. Rapid arrival at modernity opens up vistas to which isolated individuals cannot relate, while simultaneously obscuring their rural roots. In general terms, 'isolation and lack of opportunity to participate in social life tend to increase radicalism' (Allardt 1964, 55). This theory ties in neatly with the socio-economic dynamics in inter-war Central and Eastern Europe.

Even so, the communist opposition could not make itself felt in any significant way after the early 1920s. This may be attributed partly to the strategy and organization of the communist parties: they were cadre-driven, dogmatically proletarian and extremely suspicious of alliances with other social formations. The industrial working-class itself was small almost everywhere, and among the peasantry, communism was strongly identified not only with 'soulless', materialistic industrialism and an urban way of life, but also with 'alien' social and ethnic groups and with a foreign power – the Soviet Union – which was seen as threatening the hard-won national freedom. In Hungary, the rural *Lumpenproletariat* initially rallied behind the 1919 Soviet Republic, but support fizzled out once the revolutionaries had demonstrated their contempt for the peasantry. The other inter-war Bolshevik uprisings – in conjunction with the Soviet invasion of Poland in 1919–20, in Bulgaria in 1923 and in Estonia in 1924 (as well as the wave of communist-led strikes in Romania in 1921–3) – were based on severe overestimations of potential public support. Subsequently, the communists were marginalized throughout almost the entire region. The Czechoslovak Communist Party which consistently polled some 10 per cent of the vote was the main exception from this rule. This deviant case is generally seen as a by-product of a number of circumstances: Czechoslovakia had not experienced Soviet or Russian aggression; there was a substantial and class-conscious working-class in Bohemia and Moravia; and an anomic rural Slovak proletariat formally included in the national core but *de facto* excluded from influence. In Bulgaria, with its long-standing identification with Russia, the Communist Party also had a spell of success at the polls before it was banned in 1925, and it did quite well as it resurfaced under a new label in the early 1930s. Pockets of fairly stable communist support also existed in some blue-collar worker milieus (such as the Tallinn docks, the Romanian oilfields and some Budapest districts), and in backward areas in Yugoslavia, particularly in Montenegro.

Only occasionally did the communists manage to combine their internationalist critique of nation-building and socialist critique of state-building. 'Irredentist communism' had an appeal within minority Slavic communities in Central and Eastern Europe, notably in Eastern Poland, Eastern Estonia, Latvia, Slovakia, Ruthenia and Romania. This phenomenon linked rural discontent and ethnic separatism with the external challenge of the Russian Revolution. But this discontent rarely translated into real influence because of formal barriers – the Communist parties were eventually banned everywhere except in Czechoslovakia.

The link proposed by Allardt and others between *anomie* and relative deprivation to account for early left-wing radicalism can indeed be generalized. In the eastern part of Europe, communist parties were not the sole beneficiaries of such sentiments. In fact, the general radical mood in the immediate wake of the First World War is almost a dominant feature throughout Central and Eastern Europe, from Germany to Russia to Turkey. At this point in time, the entire region was marked by general fatigue, or even exasperation, with a war that everybody had lost. The imperial regimes, which had mobilized the masses for war but not succeeded in winning it, were felt to have lost their legitimacy. In a sense it may be argued that personalities with such different backgrounds or ideological outlooks as Hitler, Lenin and Piłsudski, all derived their initial political support from this anomic mode of exasperation. One country, Hungary, saw a pattern of revolution parallel to that in Russia, but in many other countries too, political actors had to consider these forces: the Legionnaires of Poland and Czechoslovakia, the agrarian radicals in Bulgaria, the semi-fascist or nationalist veterans' movements of the Baltic and Balkan states were all tributaries of the same river.

The possibilities for democratic survival were closely linked to the ability of civil society to integrate these forces. Hence, in Czechoslovakia – the socio-economically most advanced country in the region – discontent was channelled into social democratic and trade union movements, which, however, were ethnically divided. In Finland, democracy survived the onslaught first of left-wing and then of right-wing radicalism as a result of the Nordic traditions of civil society. But Finland and Czechoslovakia were the exceptions, not the rule. Most of the newly independent countries were marked by the failure to develop a modern civil society to replace the clientelistic structures of the imperial era. It may seem paradoxical that whereas populist radicalism – whether left-wing, right-wing, agrarian or royalist – in itself represented a rebellion against the old clientelistic networks, it offered no real alternative to them. Therefore, as the new states of Central and Eastern Europe moved from an era of democratic idealism towards a period when they were gradually reduced to buffer states squeezed between the new secular mass movements of communism and fascism, most of them did not succeed in developing participatory systems conducive to democratic consolidation. Instead they moved towards a new form of clientelism, where parties strongly associated with and linked to the state apparatus became the focal points of new clientelistic networks. When the Iron Curtain came down in 1946–47, the new Soviet-backed regimes simply took over the function as the nodal point in these new clientelistic networks.

So it should come as little surprise that the inter-war experiment in democracy failed, as did the following experiment in the immediate wake of the Second World War. Between 1919 and 1939, very little happened in terms of social and political regeneration. Nationalism and economic modernization served as instruments of political mobilization rather than as attempts at solving the problems of nation-building and economic reform. Ethnic diversity remained very high, rural economic development did not fulfil its promises and expectations, and industrialization remained largely confined to the industrial areas of the old empires. The democratic regimes of the early inter-war period, faced with populist challenges of almost every conceivable ideological shade, responded by ever grander promises of a swift entry into the modern world. But as they did not have the capacity to come through on most of these promises, they harvested dissatisfaction and disillusionment. This created a climate that played readily into the hands of non-democratic forces, which went on to develop a modern form of clientelism rather than a true civil society.

The Post-War Cleavage Structure

With the exception of the Baltic states which found themselves forcefully integrated into the Soviet Union, the arrival of the Red Army in Central and Eastern Europe at the end of the Second World War spelled the return of partial political pluralism and provided for a second experiment in democracy. But it was a pluralism that was closely monitored by Moscow and its allies in the eastern part of Europe. By 1949, the so-called popular democracies had been reduced to mere carbon copies of the supposedly superior Soviet model of democracy. The pluralism that remained was of a purely formal character, featuring domesticated non-socialist parties whose leaders had pledged allegiance to the Soviet model of government.

War and occupation was to leave a lasting imprint on the nation-states of Central and Eastern Europe. The map of Europe was drawn and redrawn several times, first by Nazi Germany and subsequently by the victorious anti-Hitler coalition (Berglund and Aarebrot 1997). In parallel with territorial revisions on a vast scale, the new rulers opted for policies of population transfers, inspired by Nazi and Soviet examples of ethnic cleansing, but with an additional antecedent in the 1923 Lausanne settlement after the Graeco-Turkish War of 1919–21.[1] Between 1936 and 1956, an estimated 22 million people were transferred from, to or within Poland, equalling no less than 70 per cent of the 1939 population (Davies

1986, 82). Throughout Central Europe, these drastic policies went a long way towards creating ethnically almost homogenous states (*Figure 2.2*). However, the Balkan states remained strongly multi-ethnic, and in the Baltic republics multi-ethnicity was reinforced by emigration, deportations and Slavic immigration. The USSR itself, of course, remained a multi-ethnic empire, albeit that Moscow pursued its own nation- and state-building agenda through Russification and attempts to create a *homo sovieticus*, with a Balkan parallel in the proclamation of a 'Yugoslav' nationality.

In 1947, when Europe had been divided by the allies into stable spheres of interest, millions of people – Poles, Russians, Latvians, Estonians, Lithuanians, Magyars and last but not least, Germans – had been driven away from their traditional settlement areas into truncated or redefined homelands by consecutive waves of ethnic cleansing. Estonia, Latvia and Lithuania were wiped out as independent states by the Soviet Union in 1940 and again – after an interlude under German domination – in 1944, when the German *Wehrmacht* had to give in to the advancing Soviet Red Army; and in the aftermath of the Soviet occupation, they were subjected to such an intensive process of Russification that the viability of a return to the pre-war formula was questionable, at least in Estonia and Latvia with the obvious majority potential of their large Russian-speaking minorities.

The other states of Central and Eastern Europe did return to the pre-war formula of national sovereignty, but under conditions dictated and closely supervised by the one remaining great power in the region. These conditions included acceptance of the border changes and the concomitant population transfer imposed and/or encouraged by the Soviet Union, and whatever else might be required to promote the 'friendly relations' between the Soviet Union and its Central and East European neighbours presupposed by the Yalta and Potsdam agreements among the allies of the Second World War; these constraints were imposed on friends and foes alike. Though technically an ally of the anti-Hitler coalition, Poland was not treated any more gently than Hungary which had fought the war as an ally of Nazi Germany. It was in fact the other way around, and probably for the simple reason that Hungary needed less monitoring by Russia than Poland (Hellén 1996). Hungary had been pushed back to the borders imposed on it by the Trianon Peace Treaty of 1919 and thus had to resign itself to the loss of the Magyar-dominated province of Transylvania on the border with Romania.

This was a serious blow to long-standing Hungarian national aspirations, but it was much less of a threat against the *Pax Sovietica* imposed on the region than the chaos that existed in Poland, in the wake of the massive border changes which had compensated Poland for the loss of its eastern provinces to the Soviet Union by extending Poland deeply into what had recently been Germany, east of the rivers Oder and Neisse. The border changes were accompanied by truly large-scale population transfers, involving tens of millions of refugees of German, Polish and Russian nationality (*Figure 2.2*).

Figure 2.2: Ethnic cleansing and resettlement, 1945–1949

Source: Crampton and Crampton 1996.

The task of implementing and supervising this social experiment – to say nothing about the actual integration of the new territories into Poland proper – made it imperative for the Polish provisional government not only to rebuild the war-torn state apparatus but also to improvize a state machinery, where there was none at all. The stage was clearly set for identity politics and state-building in early post-war Poland.

Poland was admittedly an extreme case of the turmoil that gripped all of post-war Central and Eastern Europe. Czechoslovakia was restored to its pre-war boundaries with the exception of Ruthenia (Carpatho-Ukraine) which was handed over to the Soviet Union upon the request of the war-time Soviet ally. This was in no way comparable to the Polish post-war trauma, but Czechoslovakia faced the dual task of overcoming the social, political and economic consequences of the expulsion of the some three million German-speaking residents in the Sudetenland along the German–Czechoslovak border, and of welding the Czech and Slovak parts of the republic together after war-time separation under German domination. The stage was set for a revival of the inter-war concept of a Czechoslovak nationality and, needless to say, for the resurgence of a strong Czechoslovak state.

The victory of the anti-Hitler coalition of the Second World War had put Hungary back to square one. The loss of predominantly ethnic Hungarian Transylvania to Romania, and the return of the Magyar-dominated southern rim of Slovakia to Czechoslovakia, reintroduced the well-known *diaspora* problem of the inter-war period into Hungarian politics and confronted Hungary with a refugee problem, albeit of limited magnitude. This was an open invitation to identity politics. With the economy in a shambles and the state apparatus partly dismantled by the retreating Germans, state-building was also of paramount importance to the post-war Hungarian authorities.

Romania regained Transylvania, which was hers by virtue of Trianon, but was deprived of Bessarabia, which had been occupied by the Soviet Union in accordance with the Molotov-Ribbentrop Pact and in defiance of the First World War peace treaties (Crampton and Crampton 1996). Moscow was – it turned out when it came to negotiations – no more willing to give up Bessarabia than any other territory seized within the framework of the ill-fated treaty with Nazi Germany. In the case of Romania, however, the transfer of territories was smooth without large-scale accompanying population transfers, but – as will be demonstrated later – this was to have a lasting impact on Romania's political agenda (cf. Chapter 11). The other countries of South Eastern Europe were only marginally affected by border changes and ethnic cleansing in the wake of the Second World War, but this should not be construed to imply that they were somehow safely beyond identity politics and state-building. The original ethnic mosaic had been preserved, with all which that entailed, by way of instability and the pre-war state apparatus often had to be rebuilt literally from scratch.

Yugoslavia is a case in point. The restoration of Yugoslavia to its pre-war borders spelled the revival of the inter-war concept of Yugoslav nationality as opposed to and as a substitute for Serb, Croat, Slovene and/or Macedonian nationalism, and the return to political centralization in a heterogeneous setting that might have called for far-reaching decentralization. But the bottom line was that the contradiction between nation-building elites and ethnically diverse populations had been markedly reduced, particularly in Central Europe. As the process of ethnic homogenization was largely instituted by the Soviet Union, the communist parties could claim credit for having, at least to an extent, solved the national problem.

The resilience of historical cleavages

The stage was set not only for a identity politics and ethnic cleavages, but also for a revival of the religious-secular dimension. But this dimension – it will be remembered – was not independent of identity politics. The Catholic Church, and the political parties close to it, had in fact been at the very centre of nation-building processes in Central and Eastern Europe ever since the Habsburg, Russian and German empires (Berglund and Aarebrot 1997; Hellén 1996). Similar comments apply to the highly salient urban/rural dimension in Central and Eastern Europe of the inter-war era. The social structure of the region had hardly changed since the First World War. With the exception of Czechoslovakia which belonged to the leading industrial nations of the inter-war era, Central and Eastern Europe remained basically rural and agrarian with pockets of industrialization in major cities and urban conglomerations. The countryside provided fertile ground for organized religion and for all kinds of agrarian movements, from the utopian to the pragmatic, which were likely to re-emerge with the backing of neat political majorities once democracy had been reintroduced.

The left/right dimension, however, did not seem to have particularly bright prospects in post-war Central and Eastern Europe. The parties of the left have traditionally been working-class parties and, with the exception of Czechoslovakia, there was not much of a working-class base in this basically rural region. The parties of the right have traditionally had a middle-class and/or entrepreneurial background which was yet another scarce commodity in the prevailing social structure of Central and Eastern Europe. The region had had its share of communist, social democratic, liberal and conservative parties in the 1920s and 1930s, but as a rule they had not performed particularly well. The liberal and conservative parties were successful only to the extent that they managed to link up to the strong and vocal nationalist and religious constituencies; the communists and the social democrats did not have an equivalent fall-back option.

The cleavage structure of the pre-war era had survived the Second World War intact, but with one important addition. War against and/or occupation by Nazi Germany had introduced a fascist/anti-fascist cleavage. By the end of the war, few, if any, Central and East Europeans were openly professing fascist sympathies; the overwhelming majority of them now pledged allegiance to anti-fascism. The day of reckoning had come for the fascists, the Nazi collaborators and other suspected war criminals. The methods ranged from lynchings, summary executions, and trials for war crimes, to political disenfranchisement of large segments of the population. There was only one drawback: how to define fascists and how to separate criminal fascists from mere Nazi fellow-travellers? These were questions with which the governments and courts of liberated Western Europe grappled for years after the war without producing any clear-cut answers. As a rule, the West European approach to the problem was cautious rather than rash and legal rather than political. In the Soviet-dominated part of Europe, however, justice and retribution was frequently meted out in a way that made sense only from the vantage point of political expediency. The initial Soviet concept for the so-called popular democracies in liberated Central and Eastern Europe called for these countries to be governed by broad 'anti-fascist' coalitions with their roots in the national fronts that had been part and parcel of the underground resistance against the German occupiers. The small and in many cases insignificant communist parties were cast for a major role within these anti-fascist coalitions. It was to the advantage of the communists and their allies, if part of the competition could be disqualified on real or trumped-up charges of harbouring pro-fascist sympathies; and the Soviet authorities actually did not agree to local or national elections until the old ruling elites and their potential followers had been barred from taking part in the electoral process.

The election results were in all likelihood a source of great concern to Moscow. Polling 38 per cent of the vote in the general elections in Czechoslovakia in May 1946, the local communists had done very well, particularly considering that this gave them, and their long-time social democratic coalition partner, a parliamentary majority (Broklová 1995). But this was all there was by way of reassuring electoral reports for Moscow.

In the Hungarian general elections of November 1945, almost two-thirds of the voters had come out in favour of the Smallholders' Party (Hellén 1996); in Poland, the Polish Peasant Party of Stanisław Mikołajczyk had apparently done considerably better than officially reported in the rigged plebiscite of November 1946 and the even more tightly controlled elections in February 1947 (Grzybowski 1994); in Bulgaria, the communist-dominated Patriotic Front had carried the general elections of November 1945 due to the boycott of several non-communist parties, including the majority faction of the Bulgarian Agrarian Union (BAU) of Nikola Petkov, which had unsuccessfully called upon the Allied Control Commission to supervise the election carefully so as to avoid fraudulent practices (Fowkes 1995); and in Romania, it took yet another openly fraudulent election to provide the communists and their allies with a majority in the 1946 parliament (Dellenbrant 1994).

These elections were followed by other elections which reduced the space for political pluralism until it had been eliminated altogether. The social democrats were forced to merge with the communists, and the non-socialist parties were either infiltrated by the communists or banned. Many of the popular democracies formally preserved the multi-party format, but the surviving non-communist parties were permanent allies of the ruling Marxist-Leninist parties, totally reconciled with operating within the framework of the fundamental principles of the world communist movement. These principles included unconditional acceptance of the leading rule of the Marxist-Leninist party, the consistent application of the principle of democratic centralism with its distinctly authoritarian components, and the unwavering support of the notion of eternal friendship and alliance with the Soviet Union (Berglund and Dellenbrant 1994).

Communism as a modernizing force

Within a few short years, the popular democracies of Central and Eastern Europe had been transformed into mere carbon copies of the Soviet political system. The party space was dominated by one single force, and the dominant Marxist-Leninist force was itself constrained by the Soviet mentor. The social and economic programme on which the new regimes embarked was one of radical modernization, inspired by the Soviet crash programme for industrialization of the 1920s and 1930s. The means of production were socialized; the agricultural sector was collectivized and a number of gigantic industrial projects – like the Nowa Huta steelworks in Poland – were initiated throughout the Soviet bloc. The long-term consequences were manifold. The traditional middle-class and rural constituencies of the liberal, conservative and agrarian parties were wiped out and the traditional working-class and urban constituencies of the left-wing parties were substantially strengthened; the countryside was impoverished and the role of traditional religious values was sharply reduced; illiteracy was wiped out or sharply reduced; the average level of education jumped upwards as dramatically as industrial output and the standard of living.

Several inferences may be drawn on the basis of the socio-economic indicators in Table 2.3. It is readily seen that communist Central and Eastern Europe trails behind the industrial nations of the West. The East European countries rarely come out at the very top of the list of socio-economic indicators and they seldom surpass West Germany, which entered the post-war era in a state of devastation and destruction, much like that of Central and Eastern Europe. Hence, when the East European countries actually rank at the top of the list, it is not necessarily an indicator that they are ahead of

Western Europe, the United States and the United Kingdom. The large share of industrial workers in the Hungarian labour force in 1978 (58 per cent) and the huge industrial output in the GDR, Bulgaria and Romania as of 1978 (62, 55 and 58 per cent of the GDP, respectively) testify to rapid social transformation and economic development, particularly compared to pre-war conditions (Hellén 1996) and also compared to the first decades of the post-war era. The data also serve as a reminder that Central and Eastern Europe did not provide fertile ground for what is sometimes referred to as the post-industrial society, with its emphasis on service production and small-scale enterprises.

The Soviet model of modernization, with its emphasis on industrialization, urbanization, collectivization and secularization, lost part of its attraction even for the local communists who had promoted it, when – after Stalin's death – the Soviet leaders openly admitted that there might be more roads than one leading to socialism, but the model was never entirely abandoned. Industry in general, and huge industrial conglomerates in particular, were promoted at the expense of the agricultural sector; collective farming was at the very least preferred to whatever there was left of private farming, and religion was at best tolerated. The net result was an unprecedented social transformation of the eastern part of Europe, with the exception of Albania which rejected one socialist partnership after the other – first with Yugoslavia (1948), then with the Soviet Union (1961) and subsequently with China (1977–78) – only in order to withdraw into splendid and self-imposed isolation as the only 'true exponent of socialism'.

By the end of the 1980s, Central and Eastern Europe was closer to Western Europe than ever before in terms of modernity, but with a class structure marked by the equalizing impact of almost fifty years of 'real socialism' (Wessels and Klingemann 1994). As indicated by Table 2.3, tremendous socio-economic changes took place under communism, mainly in favour of industry to the detriment of the agricultural sector. An almost equally important change, which is not shown in the table, is the change in life-style in rural areas due to collectivization. Briefly, collectivization entailed the introduction of an industrial life-style for agricultural workers. In sum, many of the advantages of a modern and urban organization of labour, such as fixed working hours, regulated holiday periods, pensions and fixed wages, were introduced without consideration for anything like cost-benefit analysis.

Thus, politics in the 1990s has inherited a new cleavage: the desirability of retaining a modern, urban-type life-style in agriculture and declining industries, as opposed to an understanding of the adaptation of life-styles to such uncomfortable facts of life as profit margins.

Table 2.3: Socio-economic indicators for Central and Eastern Europe

	Poland	CSSR	Hungary	GDR	Bulgaria	Romania	Albania	FRG	Highest
Urban pop. % in									
100,000+ cities									
1950	23	14	38	20	9	10	0	48	71 UK
1960	27	14	22	21	14	16	8	51	72 UK
1976	20	17	28	24	24	25	8	35	72 US
Labour force,									
% in industry									
1960	29	46	35	48	25	21	18	48	48 FRG
1977	38	49	58	51	38	31	24	48	58 Hun
GDP,									
% in industry									
1960	51	65	58	–	–	–	–	54	56 CSSR
1978	52	60	47	62	55	58	–	42	62 GDR
GDP,									
% in agriculture									
1960	23	13	20	–	–	–	–	6	n/m
1978	16	9	15	10	18	15	–	3	18 Bulg
Literacy rate, %									
1960	98	99	98	99	85	99	–	99	100
1970	98	n/a	99	99	91	98	–	99	100
Telephones									
per 1,000 pop.									
1966	41	105	56	75	–	–	–	108	481 US
1975	76	177	100	150	88	56	–	318	697 US
Newspaper circ.									
per 1,000 pop.									
1960	145	236	143	456	182	147	47	307	477 Swe
1975	248	300	233	463	232	129	46	312	572 Swe
TV receivers									
per 1,000 pop.									
1965	66	149	81	188	23	26	1	193	362 US
1975	180	249	223	302	173	121	2	307	571 US

Note: Dates may be approximate. The most recent Romanian data on urbanization were gathered in 1971 and not in 1976 and the East German data on newspaper circulation were collected in 1965 rather than 1960. The Bulgarian data on literacy were gathered in 1965 rather than 1960 and the Romanian and Albanian data on newspaper circulation are from 1974 and 1965 respectively.

Sources: Taylor and Hudson (1972); Taylor and Jodice (1983a; 1983b).

Another feature of communist policies was a marked increase in investment in education on all levels, particularly in technical fields. This produced large middle-classes, but not middle-classes structured in the same way as in Western Europe. Income distribution was weakly, or not at all, linked to education. Nor was political and social stratification only a matter of education. Who belonged to the ruling-class, the so-called *nomenklatura*, was defined by the ruling party and in terms of access to this party. But to the extent that education can be used as an indicator of modernity, the relative size of the population with a middle-class education has never been larger in Central and Eastern Europe than it is today. This is clearly a legacy of communist policies, and ought to be conducive to the establishment of a civil society and, in a similar vein, detrimental to the continuation of clientelistic relationships. The poor development of civil society in some East European countries today may be attributed to two interrelated factors: the harsh realities of daily life in transitional societies, and the lingering effects of professional specialization originally intended to fit the requirements of the communist system. We would, however, argue that the possibilities for developing a stable civil society to complement democratic institutions is better now than ever before.

The social transformation on which the communist regimes embarked called for a strong government presence; and there is indeed a case to be made for the notion that the communist regimes of Central and Eastern Europe had state-building as a top level priority (Berglund and Aarebrot 1997). The concept of a liberal state with the emphasis on individual rights and freedoms and the rule of law was obviously alien to the communist leaders, but they definitely needed a strong and efficient state machinery capable of levying taxes, mobilizing the masses and supervising the individuals. Nation-building or identity politics was also of obvious importance for the leaders of communist Central and Eastern Europe, particularly for the leaders of countries affected by large-scale border changes and population transfers. But identity politics in many ways represented a Pandora's box of horrors and had to be handled with great care. The territorial revisions and population transfers had, after all, been initiated by the Soviet Union; and, to the extent that the Soviet Union did not itself benefit from the changes, the beneficiary was a neighbouring socialist country also aligned with the Soviet Union.

The West German card could, however, be played with impunity. The refusal by West Germany to recognize the Oder-Neisse line *de jure* prior to a comprehensive peace settlement, was frequently used by the Polish United Workers' Party in its attempts to mobilize support for Poland's alliance with Russia (Hellén 1996); and Moscow was relentless in its references to German militarism and revanchism. The Jewish card could also be played with relative impunity, once Israel had been written off as a potential ally of Soviet Russia in an otherwise hostile Arab world. The history of the Soviet Union and communist Eastern Europe is in fact full of thinly veiled anti-Semitic campaigns, from Stalin's aborted crusade against Jewish doctors in the early 1950s to the recurrent verbal attacks on Zionism and cosmopolitan tendencies all over Central and Eastern Europe. The verbal abuse frequently carried over into outright punitive actions – purges of the party rank and file, imposed exile and stiff and summary sentences – which further reduced the importance of the survivors of Hitler's racial war against the European

Jewry. The notion of an overarching Czechoslovak national identity – which the leaders of post-war Czechoslovakia used to combat Czech and Slovak nationalism just as the pre-war leaders had done – was an acceptable form of nationalism in the new Central and East European setting. Similar comments apply to the idea of a Yugoslav nationality aggressively promoted by the post-war leaders of this multi-ethnic state and, for that matter, to the anti-Turkish undercurrents of Bulgarian nationalism. The Romanians had a licence to engage in anti-Magyar rhetoric ever since the Soviet Union had decided to hand over Transylvania to Romania. The communist regime in Bucharest was to use this option quite frequently in its attempts to come out as the true defender of the nation. The loss of Moldavia and Bessarabia was a more sensitive issue, but, by the end of the 1980s, this did not stop the beleaguered Ceauşescu regime from suggesting that this region be reincorporated into Romania.

The forty years of communism in Central and Eastern Europe included successive waves of political and economic liberalization, but – with Poland and Hungary as the two major exceptions – the fundamental features of the Marxist-Leninist system remained intact until the very end. The first (almost) free parliamentary elections in Poland in June 1989 and the gradual return to genuine political pluralism in Hungary in the late 1980s set a dangerous precedent for the hibernating Stalinist and neo-Stalinist regimes in Central and Eastern Europe and served as a source of inspiration for dissidents throughout the region. Marxist-Leninist tradition would have called for Soviet intervention sooner rather than later. Stalin would not have condoned free elections and the return to genuine political pluralism anywhere within the Soviet bloc, nor would Khrushchev, nor Brezhnev. But Gorbachev was willing to take a chance on reform communism in Central and Eastern Europe and thus paved the way for the breakdown of Soviet-style communism throughout the entire region. The countries of Central and Eastern Europe found themselves thrust into their third experiment in democracy in the 20th century.

A Third Try at Democracy

The focus of the present volume is on the current and most recent experiment in democracy. It has now been going on for almost a decade and a half, and we would perceive it as the most successful and most promising democratic experiment ever seen in Central and Eastern Europe. This is due to a number of factors:

• the existence of an international climate defined by the US, NATO and the European Union so as to promote the development of democracy in Central and Eastern Europe;

- the relatively high level of socio-economic development in contemporary Central and Eastern Europe with all which that entails by way of industrialization, urbanization and secularization;
- a historical legacy that favours inclusion and co-optation of the spiritual heirs to Marxism-Leninism;
- the development of the Central and East European countries towards the ethnic homogeneity presupposed by the nation-state model; and
- the skilful use of creative electoral engineering in order to put an end to political fragmentation and promote stable government as opposed to the political immobilism of the inter-war years.

There are factors pulling in the opposite direction, most notably the uncertain economic prospects in some East European countries; the strongly clientelistic heritage particularly in South Eastern Europe; the inclination towards populism of the nationalist variety and pronounced generational differences in the approach towards democracy, market economy and market reform as evidenced in the 1990s by the *Central and Eastern Eurobarometer* surveys; and, last but not least, more than a nagging suspicion by East Europeans that their respective governments have no interest in promoting human rights (Berglund and Aarebrot 1997).

Survey research is a post-Second World War phenomenon, but there is no reason whatsoever to assume that the Central and East Europeans of the inter-war era were less ambivalent in their approach towards democracy and more optimistic about the government's willingness and ability to respect human rights than the Central and East Europeans of today. Similar comments apply to the economic crisis, the clientelistic heritage and the inclination towards populism and strongman rule. If anything, the depression between the two world wars was probably stronger than the economic crisis that accompanied the transition from plan to market. A clientelistic heritage is probably more strongly felt in underdeveloped than in developed or developing societies. And populism is likely to be a more attractive option in underdeveloped countries with a long-standing imperial heritage, with its authoritarian appeal, than it is in developed or developing countries which have recently emerged from communist rule, with its formally egalitarian ideology. We would be inclined to conclude that the negative factors are of lesser – and definitely not greater – magnitude today than they were during the inter-war era. We therefore limit ourselves to a discussion of the five factors we believe favour the development of democracy in contemporary Central and Eastern Europe.

The international climate

The First World War (1914–18) was supposedly fought 'to make the world safe for democracy'. But with all due respect to President Wilson, it is probably fair to say that the architects of the Versailles world order, including the British and the French, struck a delicate balance between democracy on the one hand and national self-determination on the other. And with all due respect to the East European inter-war leaders, there is little doubt that they were under the sway of nation-state ideologies which tended to relegate the defence of democracy to a secondary position. Democracy was a beleaguered form of government throughout the inter-war era. It was questioned by the far left as well as by the far right; and the gradually increasing competition between the Soviet Union and Nazi Germany for political influence in Central and Eastern Europe certainly did not make things easier.

In the early 1990s there were no dictatorships left in the new European house, and the emphasis in Central and Eastern Europe was on democracy and on cooperation with the West, which was seen as the only safeguard against a possible revival of Soviet imperial ambitions. This West European and Atlantic orientation was not only the gut reaction of recently liberated states, marked by the anti-communist backlash of the early 1990s, but the considered opinion of nations most of which have since seen government by reform communists as well as by right-wing forces.

The East European commitment to the European Union and to NATO, and the favourable response by these international organizations, are in fact among the most important factors accounting for the rapid consolidation of democracy in most of the countries in the region. The Czech Republic, Hungary and Poland have been members of NATO since 1999; Estonia, Latvia, Lithuania, Slovakia, Slovenia, Bulgaria and Romania will follow suit in 2004. These ten countries have also been invited to join the European Union in two waves of accession – in 2004 (the Baltic and Central European countries) and in 2007 (Bulgaria and Romania), respectively.

Table 2.4: Results of the EU accession referenda (2003)

Country	Date of Referendum	Per cent yes	Per cent no	Voter turnout, per cent
Slovakia	16–17 May	92.5	6.2	52.15
Lithuania	10–11 May	91.0	8.9	63.3
Slovenia	23 March	89.6	10.4	60.3
Hungary	12 April	83.8	16.2	45.6
Poland	7–8 June	77.5	22.6	58.9
Czech Republic	13–14 June	77.3	22.7	55.2
Estonia	14 September	66.9	33.1	63.4
Latvia	20 September	66.8	32.5	72.5

Source: 'Enlargement referenda' (2003); 'Referendums on EU enlargement' (2003).

The EU accession referenda held in the first group of candidate countries in 2003 have paved the way for the biggest enlargement in the history of the European Union. Even if voter turnout has not always been that impressive, the post-communist citizens have clearly endorsed their respective countries' membership of the EU (*Table 2.4*). In a development that few would have predicted in 1990–92, Central and Eastern Europe is thus likely to be deeply embedded into Western political, military and economic power structures in just a few years.

Modernity makes for democracy

In their *Political History of Eastern Europe in the 20th Century*, Sten Berglund and Frank Aarebrot (1997) analyse the outcome of the inter-war struggle for democracy (read: breakdown versus survival of democracy) in Western as well as Eastern Europe in terms of two explanatory factors: state-building, and religious autonomy or secularization (*Figure 2.3*).

Figure 2.3: Democratic survival: a classification of European countries in inter-war Europe (short-lived and semi-independent state formations are parenthesized)

	State-building tradition	
Religious autonomy from state authority	*The City Belt, empire states and states devolved from these empire states: The Charlemagne Heritage*	*External Eastern historical empires and states devolved from these historical empires: The External Challengers*
Predominantly Protestant countries: State and Church integrated	Denmark Sweden Norway Finland Great Britain The Netherlands Switzerland	*Estonia* *Latvia*
&	*Germany*	
Secularized Catholic or Orthodox countries: Dominant state	France Belgium Czechoslovakia	*Russia (USSR)* *(Ukraine)*
Catholic counter-reformation countries, non-secularized Orthodox countries and Muslim countries: Continued dualism between Church and State	Eire *Spain* *Portugal* *Austria* *Hungary* *Italy* *(Croatia)* *(Slovakia)*	*Lithuania* *Poland* *Romania* *Bulgaria* *Yugoslavia (Serbia)* *Greece* *Albania* *Turkey*

The model is clearly inspired by Stein Rokkan's (1975) seminal conceptual map of Europe and the outcome could hardly have been neater. With only two exceptions, democracy survives in countries with a strong state-building tradition, which are either predominantly Protestant or secularized Catholic or Orthodox. The two deviant cases – Germany and Eire – can be accounted for in terms of another factor of general importance: structural or practical co-optation. The literature on inter-war Czechoslovakia – the sole democratic survivor in Central and Eastern Europe by the end of the inter-war era – emphasizes the dynamics of an intricate system of consociational devices (Lijphart 1968; 1980). The authors therefore conclude:

> Where the state-building tradition was weak and the legacy of empire strong, or where secular nation-building was still impaired by deeply rooted religious sentiments, or where significant segments representing major cleavages were not co-opted into a constitutional compromise, the chances for democratic survival in inter-war Europe were slim indeed (Berglund and Aarebrot 1997, 36).

Strictly speaking, this finding only pertains to the inter-war era, but the implications are nevertheless manifold. In the long run, even the most stable macro-sociological relationships are bound to change. The communists who were to take over Central and Eastern Europe after the brief semi-democratic interlude of 1945–49 had state-building and socio-economic change at the very top of their political agendas; and the primacy of politics, industrialization, urbanization and secularization became the catchwords of the day in the 1950s and 1960s.

Co-optation and democracy

Yet another difference between the inter-war era and the post-communist period, perhaps too obvious to be mentioned, has to do with the readiness of leaders and voters to integrate or co-opt parties and movements across the entire political spectrum. The fate of the former ruling parties is a case in point. With two notable exceptions – Czechoslovakia and the GDR – the initial call for de-communization and lustration did not make a lasting impression on the political system, and, in fact, the former communist parties were accepted as legitimate contenders for political power within the political system, once they had pledged themselves to parliamentary democracy. This policy of inclusion rather than exclusion was endorsed not only by the new political elites but also by the voters. The inter-war era was characterized by a tendency of exclusion rather than inclusion, as evidenced by the presidential coups in the Baltic states, which served to exclude the extreme left as well as the extreme right, or by the inverted power relationship between governments and parliaments in Poland, Hungary,

Bulgaria and Romania. The particularly harsh nature of this Czechoslovak and East German approach to the instruments of the former communist regime may be attributed to a number of factors: a strong civil society, the democratic legacy from the inter-war era, and the weak reform credentials of the defunct regimes. Nevertheless, the political systems of these two countries gradually adopted more integrative features.

It is a moot question whether it is good or bad for democracy that reform communism remains a viable political alternative in Central and Eastern Europe. We would be inclined to say it is good rather than bad. Exclusion of political elites is always conducive to instability of democratic regimes; and, other things being equal, circulation of power among competing political elites is preferable to the monopolization of power by one single political force, whether communist or not.

Stability and ethnic homogeneity

The ideals of what constitutes nation-states are often constant over time and across regimes, but they may also vary. It is indeed indicative of the fluid and adaptable nature of nationalism (Anderson 1991) that the very definition of nationality may be changed by political regimes in an effort to create new super-nationalities more suitable for the transformation of a multi-ethnic society into a 'national' society. The deliberate attempts to that end by Tsarist Russia in the 19th century, and by Soviet rulers in the 20th century, are good examples, as are the notions of Czechoslovak and Yugoslav nationalities advocated by the inter-war and the post-war leaders of these mini-empires.

In Poland, Bulgaria, Hungary, Romania and Albania, the nation-state ideals remained largely unchanged under communist rule. The anti-Semitic campaigns in the People's Republic of Poland and the systematic denial of the existence of a German community in post-war Poland testify to this (Hellén 1996). The Bulgarian communist regime also adopted the traditional nation-state concept. Todor Zhivkov's persecution of the Turkish-speaking minority and the pressures brought to bear on the Bulgarian-speaking Muslims – the Pomaks – are cases in point (Crampton and Crampton 1996). The communist regimes of Romania and Hungary maintained their respective nation-state ideals, which were reinforced by the constant conflicts between the two countries over the plight of the Magyar minority in Transylvania (Hellén 1996). Finally, in Albania, open enmity towards Yugoslavia over the Albanian majority in the Kosovo province of Serbia served as one of the pillars of the sultanistic and isolationistic Hoxha regime.

With the demise of the Czechoslovak and Yugoslav mini-empires, a new definition of nationhood was instated. This new definition is very similar to the ideals of the nation-state found in countries that have retained a constant concept of nationhood across regimes throughout the 20th century. This is brought out in the official Czech and Slovak statistics on the ethnic composition over time (*Table 2.5*). In the Czechoslovak censuses of 1921 and 1930, the core group was widely defined as people of 'Czechoslovak' nationality. No more than 65 per cent of the population could be subsumed as belonging to the artificial national core of this 'nation-state'. The minorities – that is, those who were not considered 'Czechoslovak' – included Germans, Poles, Ruthenes, Magyars and Jews. The nationalities excluded from the core thus consisted of Slavic as well as non-Slavic speakers, and one excluded group, the Jews, was not linguistically defined at all. Gypsies were not even listed. The Czechoslovak core population included Czechs, Moravians and Slovaks. The 1991 censuses list Czechs and Slovaks as the largest groups of the Czech and Slovak republics respectively. The definition of the core group is apparently much narrower today, but with more than 80 per cent of the national grand totals, these narrowly defined majority groups nevertheless account for considerably more than the 65 per cent reported for the Czechoslovak nationality in the censuses of 1921 and 1930. Similar observations can be made upon comparing the official statistics of Yugoslavia in the inter-war period with current censuses in the successor states. The old Serbo-Croat nationality has been discarded.

In this context, Estonia, Latvia, and maybe Macedonia, are deviant cases. Until the early 1990s, these have been countries with decreasing ethnic homogeneity, but with a linguistically defined, and thus limited, definition of nationhood that has remained stable across previous regimes. Moreover, the possibilities of increasing the core populations of these countries are hampered by the fact that the new large minorities mainly consist of a diaspora population of a former imperial ruler, or – in the case of Macedonia – of a potentially irredentist Albanian minority.

Table 2.5 classifies the Central and East European countries into four groups, using as a measure of ethnic homogeneity the percentage of the population reported as belonging to the core, or majority, population. It should be noted that the main purpose of the table is classification of countries. Estimates in terms of percentages have only been included where relatively reliable international sources are available.

The European house that emerged in the aftermath of the breakdown of communist totalitarianism had more rooms in it than the old and familiar Cold War European building of states. In this sense, the unification of Germany in October 1991 was unique. All the other recent border changes in Central and Eastern Europe have been by-products not of amalgamation but of secession and/or breakdown. Sometimes this process resulted in new, ethnically homogeneous entities – sometimes it did not. The Czech and Slovak republics are clearly more homogeneous than the federal

Czechoslovak republic from which they seceded, which in its turn had been more homogeneous than Masaryk's inter-war Czechoslovak republic. Due to a continuous and systematic influx of ethnic Russians into the Baltic region, Estonia and Latvia came out of the Soviet Union with much more by way of ethnic diversity than they had ever had before. On the whole, however, contemporary Central and Eastern Europe stands out as distinctly more homogeneous than its inter-war counterpart.

Table 2.5: Ratings of ethnic homogeneity in terms of the relative size of the regime-proclaimed majority nationality (percentages of total population)

			Censuses [*]		
	Country	*Majority Population*	*1920*	*1930*	*1993*
Stable approximate nation-states: stable definition of the majority nationality, large majorities	Lithuania	Lithuanians	81[1923]		80[1992]
	Hungary	Magyar		97[1992]	
	Bulgaria	Bulgarians	83	87[1934]	85-90[**]
Newer approximate nation-states: stable definition of the majority nationality, large majorities today but smaller majorities in the inter-war era	Poland	Poles	70[***]	70[***]	99
	Romania	Romanians		72	89
Recent approximate nation-states: devolved from dissolved 'Mini-Empires', large or medium-large majorities today, small majorities or minorities prior to the recent dissolution of the 'Mini-Empire' states	Czechoslovakia	'Czechoslovaks'	66[1921]	67	
	The Czech Rep.	Czechs			81
	Slovakia	Slovaks			86
	Yugoslavia	'Serbo-Croats'	74[1921]	77[1931]	
	Slovenia	Slovenes			99[1991]
	Croatia	Croats			78[1991]
Former approximate nation-states with a decreased majority population today	Estonia	Estonians		86[1934]	62[1992]
	Latvia	Latvians		77[1935]	53
	Macedonia	Macedonians			65[1991]

[*] The censuses of the inter-war period are generally unreliable in their estimates of the size of ethnic minorities. The figures are, nevertheless, interesting as expressions of perceived size of regime-proclaimed core populations. [**] For Bulgaria's current ethnic population our source only indicates that national minorities exceed 10 per cent. [***] The Polish inter-war estimates are highly questionable. Polish nationality was at last partly determined by the ability of the respondent to understand the census-taker when addressed in Polish.

Sources: Berglund and Aarebrot (1997, 161); data from Crampton and Crampton (1996).

Electoral engineering

It may also be argued that the current experiment in democracy in Central and Eastern Europe benefits from the laboratory provided by the inter-war era. Inspired as they were by the German Weimar constitution, the inter-war East European constitutions had encouraged multi-partyism to the point of creating a high degree of political fragmentation, which resulted in government instability and political immobilism. The post-communist democracies of Central and Eastern Europe have opted for a variety of oligopolistic devices designed to exclude minor political parties from parliamentary representation. Hungary did so prior to the founding elections in March/April of 1990. Poland held on to the Weimar notion of fair representation for a while, and then followed suit, just like Romania, another latecomer to oligopolistic devices such as strict thresholds of registration and parliamentary representation, as well as proportional representation tempered by distinctly majoritarian features, like French-style two-stage elections and the introduction of single-member constituencies. The net result is that political fragmentation has been all but wiped out in Central and Eastern Europe. There is nothing to prevent parties already in parliament from breaking up between elections, but there is a definite price tag, in the form of threshold requirements, attached to hasty and ill-considered political divorces to be met in the upcoming elections.

Not all Cats are the same Shade of Grey

The perspective, which we have applied in this historical overview, has been macro-sociological. We have taken a bird's-eye view on an entire region. This is a legitimate endeavour, but it should not be seen as a licence to neglect the between-country variations. As mentioned in the previous chapter, there are in fact at least three groups of countries in contemporary Central and Eastern Europe, all marked by distinctive historical heritages.

We have the five Central European countries of Hungary, Poland, the Czech and Slovak republics, and Slovenia, for all intents and purposes successor states of the German and Habsburg empires and firmly embedded in the Western tradition. They have all benefited from the improved international climate that has prevailed since the demise of communism. They all have some, if not all, of the attributes of modernity, including an emerging class cleavage that appears to have the potential of becoming a dominant factor in electoral behaviour and party structuring. With the exception of Hungary, ethnically homogeneous ever since 1919, they have all been on a conspicuous historical journey of nation-building. They have all but completed the transition from plan to market. As noted above, three of them – Hungary, Poland and the Czech Republic – already belong to NATO, and by the end of 2004 they will all be members of NATO as well as the European Union.

The three Baltic countries of Estonia, Latvia and Lithuania constitute yet another cluster. They benefited from the disintegration of the Soviet empire, which resulted in the re-establishment of sovereignty. They have oriented themselves towards the West, and embarked on a course of radical – and largely successful – transformation from plan to market economy. But with Russia as next-door neighbour and with minorities of hundreds of thousands of Russian-speakers who are not yet fully integrated into their societies, Estonia, Latvia and – to a lesser extent – Lithuania find themselves in a potentially explosive situation. It is explosive not only from a domestic point of view, but also by virtue of the foreign policy implications, since Russia sees itself as the guardian of the some 20 million diaspora Russians now living outside the borders of Russia proper. This goes a long way towards accounting for the preoccupation of Estonians and Latvians with identity politics (cf. Chapters 3 and 4). Identity politics is no less important in Lithuania, but has a somewhat different background: it does not only revolve around Russia and the Russians, but also around the historically problematic relationship to Poland. The Baltic countries are still in the process of nation-building and state-building, but they have nevertheless passed the litmus test of NATO as well as the European Union, of which they will become full members in 2004. This would not have been possible, if the political elites of Latvia and Estonia had not been willing to respond to the recommendations of the international community by modifying their initially harsh positions on ethnic minorities.

Finally, we have the countries of South Eastern Europe or the Balkans. This is by far the most heterogeneous region. It features countries like Bulgaria and Romania, that have passed the dual litmus tests of NATO and the European Union, as well as the former republics of the Yugoslav federation such as Croatia, Serbia and Montenegro, Bosnia–Herzegovina and Macedonia and the former Soviet republic of Moldova. Yet they all share some characteristics. The transformation from plan to market and from authoritarianism has been slow, to say nothing of democratic consolidation, that has failed to materialize in some parts of the region. It is tempting to attribute this pattern to yet another common denominator – a patrimonial, or clientelistic, past with its roots in the era of Ottoman rule. This tradition was actually skilfully manipulated, exploited and reinforced by the communist rulers. The countries in the region are also up against ethnic problems, which might possibly destabilize the democratic regimes introduced after 1989. The fate of the former Yugoslav federation gives ample evidence as to the severity of ethnic problems in a clientelistic setting. The cleavages likely to emerge in South Eastern Europe constitute a mixture of what Georgi Karasimeonov, in Chapter 12, refers to as 'residual' and 'transitional' cleavages. In the Balkans, the modern cleavages are likely to remain latent for quite a while yet.

The regionalization of the eastern part of Europe, which we have introduced, should not make us oblivious of the within-group variations. Hungary cannot be substituted for Poland, nor can Poland be substituted for the Czech Republic, or, for that matter, for Slovenia – not to mention

Slovakia, which throughout the 1990s has been somewhat of an outlier in the Central European group. The point, however, is that the five Central European countries have more in common with one another than with the Baltic or Balkan countries. Similar comments apply to the Baltic countries and the countries of South Eastern Europe. The country-specific data in Chapters 3–15 are therefore vital for the comparative analysis of the entire region in Chapter 16.

Politics Makes for Strange Bedfellows

In the following country-specific chapters, the reader will notice that two extreme positions are possible when evaluating the effect of historical cleavages on present-day politics in Central and Eastern Europe. Some authors choose to interpret the emerging party systems mainly as functions of stable historical cleavages. This approach is similar to that applied in Lipset and Rokkan's seminal article on Western Europe (1967); in this volume, the contributions by Zdenka Mansfeldová, Kevin Deegan-Krause, Marian Grzybowski and Piotr Mikuli, Gábor Tóka, and Nenad Zakošek and Goran Čular testify to the resilience of historical cleavages in the Czech Republic, Slovakia, Poland, Hungary as well as in Croatia. The opposite position would be to argue that historical cleavages are of little or no importance and that the structure of the current party systems must be explained by reference to new cleavages derived from new social structures. The argument would then be that the democratic development started in the 1920s and 1930s has been interrupted for a long period of time by authoritarian and totalitarian regimes, and that the societies have changed dramatically during the subsequent period. In this volume, this position is most strongly represented by Hermann Smith-Sivertsen, and by Kjetil Duvold and Mindaugas Jurkynas, in their eminent chapters on Latvia and Lithuania, respectively. Considering that the Estonian experience is similar, as evidenced by the fascinating analysis by Mikko Lagerspetz and Henri Vogt, it is tempting to infer that we have encountered an effect of more than forty years of forced integration with the Soviet empire. Nevertheless, in the broader East European perspective, the Baltic countries are outliers.

On the issue of historical continuity, the editors of the present volume would take an interim position. The basic dimensions of change in Central and Eastern Europe appear to follow three patterns, as illustrated by Figure 2.4:

1. *The pattern of ethnicity*: The old empires with their ethnic fragmentation have been replaced by states which today can legitimately refer to themselves as nation-states, with the notable exceptions of some countries in South Eastern Europe and on the Baltic rim. The pivotal role of the

national cleavage in a situation where nation-building has not run its full course is indeed one of the main themes in both William Crowther's enlightening contribution on Romania, as well as in William Crowther and Yuri Josanu's instructive chapter on Moldova;

2. *Modernity*: All countries covered by this book have undergone a fundamental process of modernization which entails industrialization at the expense of the previously predominant agrarian economy, as well as industrialization of the agrarian sector itself. The gap between urban and rural areas, both in terms of economic production and in terms of life-style, has narrowed;

3. *Clientelism and civil society*: The 20th century has entailed vast changes in the patterns of social authority from imperial clientelism via clientelistic one-party states towards patterns conducive to the establishment of civil society.

Figure 2.4: Three dimensions of continuity and their impact on the cleavage structure

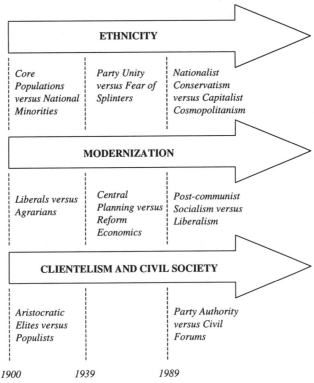

It is admittedly difficult to document a continuation of the manifest cleavages based on ethnicity, modernization and authority from the inter-war era to the present day. It is difficult to establish this linkage across time, it can even be difficult to document it contextually within the same time period – as evidenced by Drago Zajc's highly illustrative chapter on Slovenia. Bojan Todosijevic' very interesting contribution on Serbia also testifies to the difficulties involved in analysing cleavages in post-communist societies. Even so, we would argue that there is an indirect continuity in the salience of the patterns within each of three crucial areas of ethnicity, modernity and pattern of social authority, but that a juxtaposition of the political forces surrounding the three domains might indeed be dramatically different today than it might have been in the 1920s and 1930s.

Thus, in the case of ethnicity, after the First World War parties were formed in order to protect ethnic minorities or, conversely, to mobilize national core populations in defence of a real or imagined threat from such minorities. In some cases there is continuity, as shown, amongst others, by the post-1989 organization of Magyar parties in Slovakia and Romania. But in most cases, ethnicity has been transformed into an instrument for the political elites in a general nation-building project. Even though the Jewish minority in contemporary Poland is numerically insignificant, a Polish political leader may use anti-Semitic innuendo in order to position his party in relation to the cleavage between nationalism and cosmopolitanism.

In the inter-war period, most East European party systems included agrarian parties for rural defence (Urwin 1980). In Hungary and Romania, the old agrarian parties have re-emerged in the 1990s, sometimes even under their former labels, but they have a totally different function in post-communist society than they had in the inter-war era. Paradoxically, one may argue that many parties which label themselves 'agrarian' or 'green' actually work in favour of maintaining an industrial life-style among farmers and indeed, resist the dismantling of collective farming.

In the inter-war period, clientelism served to prevent the formation of strong, modern, mass-based organizations and to hinder the development of marked ideological conflicts between parties with different clienteles. Contemporary Central and Eastern Europe clearly is not a region where rivalling patrons can mobilize followers with any set of policies. Yet clientelism can account for a difference in mentality between a rent-seeking electorate, mainly concerned with extracting resources from the state, and a wage-earning electorate whose interest lies in minimizing taxes and expanding the space for individual initiative.

In short, ethnicity, modernization and clientelism have all played an important role in political life in Central and Eastern Europe throughout this century, but there is only a limited degree of direct continuity in the manifestation of cleavages if we compare the regimes of the 1920s and 1930s with the regimes of today.

NOTES

* This chapter is based on Chapter 2 in the 1998 version of *The Handbook of Political Change in Eastern Europe*, written by Tomas Hellén, Sten Berglund and Frank Aarebrot.

1. The peace settlement, which replaced the 1920 Peace Treaty of Sévres, gave Turkey all of Anatolia and Eastern Thrace. To prevent any future disputes, it also called for a compulsory population exchange; some 1.3 million Greeks and some 380,000 Turks were forced to emigrate (Jelavich 1983b, 172).

REFERENCES

Allardt, Erik (1964), *Social Sources of Finnish Communism: Traditional and Emerging Radicalism*, University of Helsinki, Publications of the Institute of Sociology, 22.
—— (1970), 'Types of Protest and Alienation', in Erik Allardt and Stein Rokkan, eds, *Mass Politics*, New York, The Free Press.
Anderson, Benedict (1991), *Imagined Communities: Reflections on the Origin and Spread of Nationalism*, Verso Books.
Bankowicz, Marek (1994), 'Czechoslovakia: From Masaryk to Havel', in Sten Berglund and Jan Åke Dellenbrant, eds, *The New Democracies in Eastern Europe: Party Systems and Political Cleavages*, Aldershot, Edward Elgar.
Berglund, Sten and Jan Åke Dellenbrant, eds (1994), *The New Democracies in Eastern Europe: Party Systems and Political Cleavages*, Aldershot, Edward Elgar.
—— and Frank Aarebrot (1997), *The Political History of Eastern Europe in the 20th Century: The Struggle Between Democracy and Dictatorship*, Aldershot, Edward Elgar.
Broklová, Eva (1995), 'Historical Roots for the Restoration of Democracy in Czechoslovakia', in Ivan Gabal, ed., *The Founding Election in Czechoslovakia: Analyses, Documents and Data*, Berlin, Edition Sigma.
Crampton, Richard and Ben Crampton (1996), *Atlas of Eastern Europe in the Twentieth Century*, London and New York, Routledge.
Davies, Norman (1986), *Heart of Europe: A Short History of Poland*, Oxford, Oxford University Press.
Dellenbrant, Jan Åke (1994), 'Romania: The Slow Revolution', in Sten Berglund and Jan Åke Dellenbrant, eds, *The New Democracies in Eastern Europe: Party Systems and Political Cleavages*, Aldershot, Edward Elgar.
Deutsch, Karl (1953), *Nationalism and Social Communication: An Enquiry into the Foundations of Nationality*, New York, MIT Press–Wiley.
'Enlargement referenda' (2003), www.euobserver.com, accessed on 30 October, 2003.
Fowkes, Ben (1995), *The Rise and Fall of Communism in Eastern Europe*, London, Macmillan, 2nd edn.
Gellner, Ernest (1983), *Nations and Nationalism*, Oxford, Blackwell.
Grzybowski, Marian (1994), 'Poland: Towards Overdeveloped Pluralism', in Sten Berglund and Jan Åke Dellenbrant, eds, *The New Democracies in Eastern Europe: Party Systems and Political Cleavages*, Aldershot, Edward Elgar.
Hellén, Tomas (1996), *Shaking Hands with the Past: Origins of the Political Right in Central Europe*, Helsinki, The Finnish Society of Sciences and Letters and the Finnish Academy of Science and Letters.
Hobsbawm, Eric (1990), *Nations and Nationalism since 1780: Programme, Myth, Reality*, Cambridge, Canto, 2nd edn.
Jelavich, Barbara (1983a), *History of the Balkans Volume 1: Eighteenth and Nineteenth Centuries*, Cambridge, Cambridge University Press.
—— (1983b), *History of the Balkans Volume 2: Twentieth Century*, Cambridge, Cambridge University Press.

Jelavich, Charles and Barbara Jelavich (1965), *The Balkans*, Englewood Cliffs, NJ, Prentice Hall.

Lijphart, Arend (1968), *The Politics of Accommodation: Pluralism and Democracy in the Netherlands*, Berkeley, University of California Press.

—— (1980), *Democracy in Plural Societies: A Comparative Exploration*, New Haven, Yale University Press.

Lipset, Seymour Martin and Stein Rokkan (1967), 'Introduction', in Seymour Martin Lipset and Stein Rokkan, eds, *Party Systems and Voter Alignments*, New York, Free Press.

'Referendums on EU enlargement' (2003), www.euractiv.com, 22 September, 2003.

Rokkan, Stein (1975), 'Dimensions of State Formation and Nation-Building: A Possible Paradigm for Research on Variations within Europe', in Charles Tilly, ed, *The Formation of National States in Europe*, Princeton, Princeton University Press, 562-600.

Rothschild, Joseph (1974), *East Central Europe between the Two World Wars*, Seattle and London, University of Washington Press.

—— (1989), *Return to Diversity: A Political History of Eastern Europe since World War Two*, New York, Oxford University Press.

Schöpflin, George (1993), *Politics in Eastern Europe 1945–92*, Oxford, Blackwell.

Taylor, Charles Lewis and Michael C. Hudson, eds (1972), *World Handbook of Political and Social Indicators*, 2nd edn, New Haven, Yale University Press.

—— and David A. Jodice, eds (1983a), *World Handbook of Political and Social Indicators: Cross-National Attributes and Rates of Change*, Vol. 1, 3rd edn, New Haven, Yale University Press.

—— (1983b), *World Handbook of Political and Social Indicators: Political Protest and Government Change*, Vol. 2, 3rd edn, New Haven, Yale University Press.

Tismaneanu, Vladimir (1993), *Reinventing Politics: Eastern Europe from Stalin to Havel,* New York, Macmillan.

Urwin, Derek (1980), *From Ploughshare to Ballotbox: The Politics of Agrarian Defence in Europe*, Lommedalen, Universitetsforlaget.

Wallerstein, Immanuel (1974), *The Modern World System: Capitalist Agriculture and the Origins of the European World-Economy in the Sixteenth Century*, London, The Academic Press.

Wandycz, Piotr S. (1992), *The Price of Freedom: A History of East Central Europe from the Middle Ages to the Present*, London, Routledge.

Wessels, Bernhard and Hans-Dieter Klingemann (1994), 'Democratic Transformation and the Prerequisites of Democratic Opposition in East and Central Europe', Wissenschaftszentrum Berlin für Sozialforschung, FS III, 94–201.

Zeman, Z.A.B (1976), *The Masaryks: The Making of Czechoslovakia*, London, Weidenfeld and Nicholson.

3. Estonia

Mikko Lagerspetz and Henri Vogt*

On 23 April 2001, a group of 26 Estonian social researchers published an open letter entitled 'Two Estonias' in the daily *Postimees,* in which they raised their concern about the course of development in the country. In their view, Estonia had drifted into a deep political, social and ethical crisis:

> The power elite has become alienated from ordinary people to the extent that it is appropriate to talk about two different Estonias. Two thirds of Estonian children grow up in poverty, people lack even elementary security, many young people would like to leave the country. Egotism and lack of ethics are nowadays accepted as self-evident in everyday political practice, and the very concept of responsibility has become blurred. Major economic and strategic decisions are made without any analysis of their social effects. The example of the [hurried and clandestine and eventually unsuccessful attempt to privatize the] Estonian Railways shows that people have become marginalized and been assigned the role of uninformed by-watchers, whose opinion is ignored even in issues which have direct relevance to them.

The letter also referred to the erosion of popular trust in such central political institutions as the parliament, government and prime minister, revealed by public opinion polls, and argued that '[t]he central institutions of the state are unable to carry out their tasks. The elitist and egotist behaviour of our political leaders has created a situation, in which people are unable to take their state seriously'. Finally, the writers wanted to emphasize that the question was not, after all, of individual politicians and their deeds or misdeeds:

> [...] We do not want the present political opposition to use this letter for its own advantage, interpreting it merely as a criticism of the government coalition. Most of our conclusions apply to Estonian politics in its entirety. It is not a question of names, but of the system and its principles.

The letter started a long and occasionally heated debate in the country, and many ordinary Estonians integrated the notion of 'two Estonias' into their daily vocabulary. Politicians, from the governing coalition in particular, became ardent critics of the idea. They claimed, for example, that the letter itself was an attempt to draw a deep division line into society and questioned the definition of poverty used by its authors. The reaction of the leader of the neo-liberal Reform Party and then Minister of Finance, Siim Kallas, was probably the most outraged of all. He turned the tables by accusing the less successful citizens of the 'second Estonia' for not having the will to meet the requirements of modern society:

> There are those who are well acquainted with the rules, possibilities and limits of the market economy and use these to gain success; there are others who have no wish to understand even the most elementary principles of the market economy and instead seek retreat from it by trying to re-introduce Soviet-time methods of economic and social policies. (*Postimees,* 19 October 2001.)

It is noteworthy that Kallas identified the then opposition leader Edgar Savisaar (Centre Party) as the main propagator of these dangerous and outdated ideas. But only three months later, Kallas became, against all odds, the head of a government coalition consisting his own and Savisaar's party.[1]

*

The notion of 'two Estonias' is the starting point of this chapter. More precisely, we will ask *how the present and also the future of Estonia's political order are related to this deep cleavage in society*, how the other cleavages – the ethnic one in particular – relate to it, and what possible ways there are to weaken its influence. We believe that the notion provides an apt description of the state of affairs in Estonian society: the distinction between the winners and the losers, between elites and ordinary people, between the powerful and the powerless, and between those active in politics and those with no faith in it is very clear indeed. Yet, as most notions introduced by social scientists, even the cleavage between the two Estonias contains a certain degree of ambiguity. It is composed of many different components, and it may also be difficult to decide to which category a person belongs – he or she may be economically well off but utterly disillusioned politically.

By macro-economic standards, Estonia's economic development has been in many respects positive since independence. It compares favourably with that of the two other Baltic states and even the countries of Central Europe. After the rapid decline of the early 1990s, the country's real GDP has steadily increased since 1994, and in 2001 it amounted to 89.8 per cent of the level of 1989; this was 20 per cent higher than the corresponding figures for Latvia and Lithuania. The average annual growth of the GDP was 4.9 per cent between 1995 and 2001, which raised Estonia, along with Latvia, Poland and Hungary, to the group of fastest growing economies in

East Central Europe (*Statistics in Focus* 2003, 2; *Economic Survey of Europe* 2002, 230).

The radical and decisive nature of Estonia's economic reforms, and especially its monetary policy, are often proposed as the main factors accounting for this relative success (Grennes 1997). The extremely rapid westward reorientation of Estonian foreign trade is particularly noteworthy. In 1991, the Soviet Union, including Latvia and Lithuania, took 95 per cent of Estonian exports, but already in 1995, 54 per cent of Estonian exports went to the EU, and a mere 25 per cent to the CIS countries, above all Russia. In 2002, the share of the European union was 68 per cent of the country's exports, whereas Russia accounted for only 3.3 per cent (*Statistical Yearbook of Estonia* 1994, 221–2; 1996, 235–6).

But despite these positive economic developments, the gap between material winners and losers has continued to grow. More and more people feel that they are permanently doomed to poverty.[2] The number of long-term unemployed has doubled since the mid-1990s, being over 6 per cent at the moment,[3] and the correlation between life expectancy, education and reported wealth has become stronger (Tiit 2002, 98–100). Moreover, the reorientation of Estonia's foreign trade towards the West, along with the government's refusal to subsidize exports or to support industries with public funding, have led to growing unemployment and poverty particularly in rural areas and in the industrial region of the Northeast mostly inhabited by Russian-speakers; the heavy industries of this area, as well as Estonia's agricultural sector, were closely integrated into the Soviet economy. The monetarist budget policies, along with the governments' reluctance to raise the level of taxation, has resulted in chronic under-funding of such public sector functions as education and health care. In all, poverty has not become more common, but it has become deeper and more visible. Even those who are well off – the young, urban, ethnic-Estonian, well-educated, male, private-sector employees – cannot avoid being influenced by its consequences.

People's widespread and open criticism of politics is another important indicator of the cleavage between the two Estonias; a significant part of the present chapter will deal with the reasons behind this criticism. Despite this, one should bear in mind that Estonia's political development has in many respects been successful. First of all, the restoration of the country's pre-Second World War independence in August 1991 took place without any political or ethnic violence. The constitutional and institutional framework was put in place very effectively after the Soviet era, and it has functioned well ever since. True, there have been as many as nine changes of the government during this time, but the changes have all been orderly and have not been preceded by prolonged crisis. According to the Corruption Perceptions Index 2002 of *Transparency International*,[4] the corruption of politicians and public officials was lower than in any other country of

Central and Eastern Europe, and even lower than in Italy and Greece. The Public Information Act of November 2000 states that everybody has access to the information produced by public institutions and enterprises fulfilling public service functions, provided that the information does not include state secrets or infringe on the personal privacy of individuals. All such information requests must be answered within five days. Finally, there are no serious signs of permanent polarization of political life – unexpected government coalitions have been built, and there is a relative consensus amongst parties in most key areas of policy.

The last point can also be interpreted negatively, however. After all, one elementary aspect of the notion of 'two Estonias' is the deep division line between the majority of the population and an internally consensual political elite, insensitive to the interests and preferences of ordinary people. This problem is also closely related to the starting point we had in our chapter on Estonia for the previous edition of this book. Then, more than five years ago, we started off from people's widespread indifference towards politics, an indifference that developed rapidly after the glorious days of the independence struggle of 1987-91. According to opinion polls 90 per cent of the population were interested in politics in January 1990, but by October 1993 this figure had already dropped to 43 per cent. By November 1996 the figure did not climb above 62 per cent at any stage (Vihalemm, Lauristin and Tallo 1997, 203). We also argued that this indifference formed the most crucial cleavage in Estonian society, a cleavage that undermined and underlay all other contradictions in society; and that it also reflected the cleavage between the winners and the losers of the economic transformation.

In the present chapter we actually take a step further: as we five years ago wrote a story about transformation, this time the story is essentially of consolidation. Indifference towards the world of politics seems to have become consolidated and to a certain extent even accepted by a great number of people. This in turn begs the question why has this actually happened? Why has it become almost self-evident that democratic politics fails to address the most relevant issues for a large part of the population? Why has it been accepted that ordinary people have no say in politics? On the other hand, is there any way of changing this prevailing situation? Or are there any signs of change visible already?

Before we turn into a more profound analysis of Estonia's political landscape, let us review the main patterns of development in Estonia's party system since the advent of the independence process. The review also creates an overall picture of political developments in the country. In the ensuing section, we will try to answer the questions we posed above through a simple conceptual scheme. In the final section, we will be more concerned with policies and actual cleavages in Estonian society.

The Development of the Party System

Estonia's return to full sovereignty started in 1987, when a popular movement with the aim of preventing the plans of Soviet central authorities to open new phosphorite mines in North-Eastern Estonia emerged, and lasted until 31 August 1994, when the last Soviet troops finally left the country.

This period can be subdivided into two parts: the first lasted until 20 August 1991, when the Supreme Council (the parliamentary body of the Soviet Estonia) and the Estonian Committee (the executive body of the Estonian Congress, see below) declared Estonia's independence. The Soviet Union recognized the independent Republic of Estonia less than three weeks later, on 6 September 1991.[5]

Before independence

It was the attitude towards the Soviet regime that paved the way for the development of a political spectrum in Estonia. In the late 1980s, the main strategic question of the Estonian popular movements was whether it was realistic to seek full independence or only extended autonomy within a renewed Soviet Union. Yet after the March 1990 Supreme Council elections at the very latest, it became clear that an overwhelming majority of Estonians and all major ethnic-Estonian-led movements were in favour of the former alternative. Even among ethnic Russians this was not an entirely illegitimate goal.

Eestimaa Rahvarinne, the Popular Front, was founded on 13 April 1988. This movement was, from the very beginning, meant to serve as an umbrella organization for various critical groups;[6] it never became a party. In practice, most of the groups that joined *Rahvarinne* supported relatively moderate strategies, avoiding dramatic confrontations with the Soviet Communist Party. The initial aim was to unite most of the population, to provide a platform for democracy, and to achieve more autonomy, especially economic autonomy, for Estonia within the Soviet Union.[7] *Rahvarinne* rapidly won a very large following among Estonians. It has even been claimed that 'a dual Communist Party-Popular Front power existed at that period' (Park 1995, 295). With respect to the Supreme Council, this state of affairs cannot be overstated: there, *Rahvarinne*-minded politicians, or at least its sympathizers, formed a majority from the very outset; even a great number of ethnic Estonian communists started to support the Front. This is why many dramatic decisions of this period made by the Supreme Council became possible.

Of these decisions, the Declaration of Sovereignty on 16 November 1988 is the most noteworthy. The Declaration effectively reserved the Estonian authorities the right to veto any legislation adopted by the Supreme Council of the Soviet Union, and paved the way for the adoption of similar documents by other Soviet Republics. This was also the first time the legal and political unity of the Soviet Union was questioned (Lagerspetz and Maier 2002, 96–7).

The unveiling of Estonia's true history was one of the first major tasks for the builders of independence, and the organizations founded by them. The Estonian Group for Making Public the Molotov–Ribbentrop Pact (*Molotovi–Ribbentropi Pakti Avalikustamise Eesti Grupp*, MRP–AEG) was brought to the public's attention in August 1987, when it organized a demonstration – the first of its kind – in a park in downtown Tallinn; on 10 August the next year the leading Estonian daily, *Rahva Hääl*, published the secret protocols to the Pact. In January 1988, the leaders of the MRP–AEG, founded the *Eesti Rahvusliku Sõltumatuse Partei* (ERSP), the Estonian National Independence Party; and a year later in February 1989, they formed the Estonian Citizens' Committees (*Eesti Kodanike Komiteed*) together with activists from the National Heritage Society (*Eesti Muinsuskaitse Selts*, EMS), a merger of several small heritage groups since December 1987.

Many of the founding fathers of the Citizens' Committees were well-known radical dissidents for whom the policy of *Rahvarinne* appeared far too cautious. The Committees presented the restoration of the pre-1940 Republic as the primary, indeed, as the only acceptable goal (Laar et al. 1996, 558). The major initial activity was the organization of a census of those who had been, or were descended from, citizens of pre-1940 Estonia, and to have them elect an Estonian Congress. Notably, this made the participation of émigré Estonians possible, both as candidates and electors. The Congress was designed to become the only true Estonian parliamentary institution, responsible to an ethnically defined Estonian constituency.

The attitudes among non-ethnic Estonians were different; they reacted with irritation to the nationalist elements of the Estonian movements. The most important counter-independence movement, the Inter-Movement (*Internatsional'noe dvizhenie*), was actually founded as a direct response to the emergence of *Rahvarinne*, only two months after the latter, in July 1988. The founders were mainly Russian-speakers who had moved to Estonia during the forty years of Soviet rule. It is hard to estimate the true level of support for the Inter-Movement, but many non-ethnic Estonians definitely did *not* support it. Inter-Movement itself claimed that it had 150,000 to 200,000 supporters in 1989 (Arter 1996, 140), but according to Taagepera (1993), who refers to a May 1989 survey, it had the support of some 50,000 people, or approximately 11 per cent of the non-ethnic Estonians. Hence, the only reliable figure for illuminating the mood among the non-ethnic Estonian population may be the one from the independence referendum of 1991, in which approximately two-thirds of non-Estonians voted in favour of staying within the Soviet Union.

Three important elections were held in 1989 and 1990: the elections to the Congress of the USSR People's Deputies (26 March 1989); the elections to the Estonian Congress (24 February–1 March 1990); and the elections to the Estonian Supreme Council (18 March 1990). The 1989 elections were the first almost free elections in Estonia since the inter-war era. Turnout was surprisingly high, 87.1 per cent, and the victory of *Rahvarinne* clear; it received 29 out of 36 seats. This was an open manifestation of the mood prevailing in the country against the Soviet system.

The Estonian Congress elections posed a serious problem to *Rahvarinne*. It initially considered the creation of the Congress too confrontational, and wanted instead to use the existing political institutions for proceeding towards independence. Only a week before the elections, *Rahvarinne* finally decided to participate. This was crucially important: it was the final confirmation of the radicalization of *Rahvarinne* in favour of full independence. From the point of view of electoral success, however, *Rahvarinne's* decision obviously came too late: 174 out of the 499 seats (464 in Estonia plus 35 abroad) went to candidates close to the Citizens' Committees (the EMS got 104 seats, the ERSP 70). *Rahvarinne* won 107 seats; independents 109; and the Estonian Communist Party 39 *(Helsingin Sanomat*, 6 March 1990; quoted in Arter 1996, 257).[8]

In the Supreme Council elections, *Rahvarinne* emerged as the victor, however, whereas the Citizens' Committees were critical about the very legitimacy of the elections. It is difficult to provide exact information about electoral behaviour in these elections due to the peculiarities in the electoral system. For example, a candidate could run for two different lists without even knowing it, and no party labels were used. In this sense, these elections were not yet really party-political, although nine registered parties or popular movements participated. In any case, 43 out of 105 seats went to candidates supported by *Rahvarinne*, and all in all the number of 'nationalist-inclined' representatives was between 70 and 80 (cf. Dellenbrant 1994, 99–100; Arter 1996, 257; Gerner and Hedlund 1993, 122; Raitviir 1996, 190). Two weeks later, on 3 April, the leader of *Rahvarinne*, Edgar Savisaar, became prime minister.

The Estonian Congress never acquired the decisive role that its founders had hoped for, although the radical example it showed was undoubtedly a major factor in making full independence a real alternative (Raitviir 1995, 186). From May 1990 onwards, the Congress became increasingly marginalized, apparently because its policy was too much dominated by the ERSP – many people simply chose to channel their political influence through the Supreme Council (over 40 individuals were members in both bodies). Yet, as a sign of national unity, the Council and the Congress nominated thirty members each to the Constitutional Assembly that started the preparation of a new constitution in September 1991.[9] Despite the occasionally dramatic controversies between these two parliamentary bodies, it should be kept in mind that many Estonians initially supported both of them, and also participated in both elections, as the high turnouts show – 71.0 per cent in the case of the Estonian Congress and 78.2 per cent in the Supreme Council elections (Raitviir 1995, 131). Indeed, the two bodies and the two popular movements behind them represented two different strategies of action, but their fundamental goals were not necessarily that different.

The referendum on independence of 3 March 1991 was the final major political event before the declaration of independence. As mentioned earlier, only 21.4 per cent of the permanent residents of Estonia voted against independence in a referendum with a turnout of 83 per cent (Raitviir 1996, 446). The majority of 'no' votes came from predominantly Russian-speaking areas. In Tallinn, however, at least one-third of Russians were in favour of independence.[10]

After independence
Once the leading role of the Communist Party in Soviet Estonia had been terminated by an amendment on 23 February 1990, the number of parties immediately mushroomed. Before the elections of September 1992, these numerous parties started to reorganize into electoral alliances, not least as a result of the 5 per cent electoral threshold that had been introduced. Later on, these alliances often became parties. Since 1999, electoral alliances are no longer permitted.

Rahvarinne had lost its function as an umbrella organization by the time of the elections of 1992, mainly due to the defection of three important political formations: the social democrats, the liberal democrats and the agrarians. An electoral alliance called *Rahvarinne* did participate in the first elections, though, but it obtained only 12.4 per cent of the votes and 15 seats out of 101 in the first *Riigikogu*. The most important component of this *Rahvarinne* alliance was the People's Centre Party (*Eesti Rahva Keskerakond*), led by the previous movement leader Edgar Savisaar; the prefix 'People's' was removed from the party label in 1993. In the elections of the 1990s, the party managed to create a relatively stable support basis for itself, and it has constantly had one of the biggest factions in the *Riigikogu*. In the elections of both 1999 and 2003 it gained 28 seats and was thus the biggest party.

The stable popular support of the Centre Party is in fact exceptional for Estonian conditions. It is partly a function of the party's image as a representative of the silent majority of ordinary people forgotten by the political establishment. But it is also to be attributed to the personality of its leader Edgar Savisaar, who keeps appealing to some people whilst being anathema to others. At the same time charismatic and authoritarian, Savisaar was probably also the main reason for the isolation of the party from other parties between November 1995 and January 2002, when it reassumed governmental power (until April 2003). The party has also received significant support among the Russian-speakers. This is clearly visible in Table 3.1, which gives an overall picture of the support basis of the main Estonian parties at present.

The Moderates *(Mõõdukad)* was the only *Rahvarinne*-derived party alliance to become part of the government, which was formed after the elections of September 1992. Originally a coalition of two parties, it became a party in 1996; it has later attracted politicians and political groups who have become disappointed with other parties. The Moderates' popularity has varied much more than that of the Centre Party; in this respect they represent Estonian standards well. In the elections of 1992, the alliance polled a respectable 10 per cent of the votes and gained 12 seats, but three years later its support dropped to 6 per cent. In the elections of 1999, the Moderates gained a clear victory with a respectable 15.2 per cent of the votes, but in 2003 they again hardly passed the electoral threshold, gaining only 7.0 per cent of the votes and 6 seats. The Moderates has proclaimed itself a social-democratic party, but to what extent it will develop into a representative of Scandinavian-style social democracy is still unclear; at the moment its policy seems to bear traits of new labour. It is also worth noting that the labour unions have usually turned to this party, when in search of political allies. The leader of the Central Organization of Estonian Labour Unions, Kadi Pärnits, was elected to the *Riigikogu* from its list in 2003.

Table 3.1: The support basis of the main Estonian parties (%)

	All respond-ents	Centre Party	People's Union	Mode-rates	Reform Party	Pro Patria Union	Res Publica
Estonians	85	71	93	89	90	98	93
Non-Estonians	15	29	7	11	10	2	7
Men	43	39	32	40	48	56	45
Women	57	61	68	60	52	44	55
Under 35	32	21	25	40	38	36	45
35–59	41	43	36	31	43	48	38
Over 59	27	36	40	29	19	16	17
Elementary education	17	24	28	14	5	9	12
Vocational education	62	64	63	50	65	59	65
Higher education	20	12	10	36	29	32	22
Tallinn	27	31	13	28	21	29	42
Other cities	37	41	21	29	61	38	25
Countryside	36	28	66	44	18	33	33
Under 1000 crowns/m	12	10	21	4	13	6	8
1001–2000 crowns	37	48	37	34	22	27	35
2001–3000 crowns	22	22	23	36	21	23	17
3001–4000 crowns	14	10	16	12	19	12	14
4001–6000 crowns	11	9	2	14	13	24	11
Over 6000 crowns	5	1	0	1	12	9	15

N = 808; a representative sample of Estonian citizens. The survey was conducted between 31 January and 10 February 2003 by Research Centre Faktum, Tallinn. The authors are grateful to Juhan Kivirähk, President of the Research Centre Faktum for providing them with these data.

The electoral alliance *Kindel Kodu*, Secure Home, which got 17 representatives elected to the first *Riigikogu* of 1992, was a joint platform for three party formations. The most important of them was the Coalition Party (*Eesti Koonderakond*), named after the Finnish conservative party but having as its key figures many reform communists along with a number of former managers of small and medium-size state companies (Arter 1996, 181). An electoral alliance of the Coalition Party and a group of four other, mainly rural, parties gained a landslide victory in the 1995 elections, with 41 out of 101 seats. The prime ministers of the three successive governments came from the Coalition Party. The party's heydays lasted until the elections of 1999, when its defeat (7 seats) was as convincing as its victory four years earlier. It no longer participated in the elections of 2003.

The Country People's Party (*Maarahva Erakond*), which changed its name to People's Union (*Rahvaliit*) in 1999, proved the most successful of the above-mentioned rural parties. The party was originally founded in 1994 by the former President of the Soviet Estonian Supreme Council, Arnold Rüütel, whose personal popularity was also the main factor that made it possible for the party to outplay its rural competitors.[11] After the abolition of electoral alliances in 1999, it campaigned without its previous allies and won 7 seats in the elections; its support increased to 13 seats in 2003. The party has been a proponent of protectionist policies – by Estonian standards – promoting state subsidies for agriculture, active regional politics, and conservative values. It was in the government between 1995 and 1999, and joined it again in April 2003.

Among the five main parties that formed the electoral alliance *Isamaa* (Pro Patria, literally 'Fatherland'), the clear winner of the 1992 elections, four originated from Citizens' Committees or groups close to them.[12] The core of *Isamaa* was the Estonian Christian Democratic Union (*Eesti Kristlik Demokraatlik Liit*), whose leaders, Mart Laar, Trivimi Velliste and Illar Hallaste had also been active in the National Heritage Society. In the *Isamaa*-led government that was formed after the 1992 elections, Laar became prime minister – aged 32 years, the youngest prime minister in Europe. All the parties in the *Isamaa* bloc merged in January 1993 under the name of the electoral alliance, but this new party soon began to disintegrate to the extent that it, together with the Estonian National Independence Party (ERSP), only got eight representatives in the elections of 1995. In December 1995, *Isamaa* merged with the ERSP to form *Isamaaliit*, the Pro Patria Union, and this new party succeeded well in the elections of 1999 (18 seats) – so well that Laar became Prime Minister again.[13] Pro Patria Union has established itself as a right-wing, strongly nation-oriented party, but it has suffered from fluctuations of popular support. Prior to the 2003 elections, many commentators doubted whether it would pass the 5 per cent threshold, but it gained 7 seats in the end.

Siim Kallas, then President of Estonia's Central Bank, founded the

Reform Party (*Reformierakond*) in November 1994. In a short period of time it gained substantial popularity within the electorate, and already in the elections of 1995 it came in second. The party has since been in government, and in 2002–3 Kallas headed the cabinet after the cooperation between Pro Patria Union and the Reform Party in Laar's government proved impossible. The party has consequently promoted neo-liberal policies, one of its major achievements being the abolishment of the corporate income tax in January 2000. Kallas's reaction in the context of the 'two Estonias' debate that we referred to above is a prime example of the underlying values of this party. The Reform Party was able to maintain its popular support in the 2003 elections, in fact gaining one seat more than it had in the previous parliament (18 seats in 1999, 19 seats in 2003).

Finally, the Russian-speaking population has been represented by a number of different parties or groupings since 1991. In 2002 all major Russian-speaking groups joined the United People's Party (*Eesti Ühendatud Rahvapartei*) that had parliamentary representation between 1999 and 2003 (6 seats). In the elections of 2003, the party failed to pass the national 5 per cent threshold, despite notable support in the North Eastern region. On the national level, none of the other parties has been willing to openly cooperate with the United People's Party, but on the local level it has been influential and also entered governing coalitions.

*

Hence, during the first decade after the Soviet era a more or less clear cleavage pattern seemed to emerge in the Estonian party system, and the system started to look reasonably stable. There were five effective parties, Pro Patria Union, the Reform Party, Moderates, the Centre Party and the People's Union (cf. Pettai and Kreuzer 1999, 170), of which the two latter clearly had more support among the potential representatives of the Second Estonia (see *Table 3.1*). Of these five parties, the Centre Party alone was held outside all government coalitions between November 1995 and January 2002, which made it look like the only real alternative to the prevailing policies of market liberalism (Lagerspetz and Maier 2002, 103). But after the Centre Party had formed a government coalition with the neo-liberal Reform Party in January 2002, the monotony of the party system appeared complete – taking the political programmes at face value, the Reform Party and the Centre Party are at opposite extremes. Hence, despite the individual identity of the main parties, basically any of them seemed to be able to cooperate with any other; pragmatic interests easily undermined programmatic controversies. Moreover, even the 'left' options have been clearly market-economy and nationally oriented – to the extent, in fact, that in many countries these parties might qualify as steadfast right-wingers. All in all, using the distinction left-wing versus right-wing is not very informative in the Estonian context.

This relative stability was challenged again in 2002–2003, however, and the elections of March 2003 were clearly influenced by protest voting. The number of empty and invalid ballots – 5,723 – was exceptional in Estonian circumstances, and surprisingly many new faces joined the ranks of parliamentary politics: only 44 of the 101 MPs were re-elected. The clearest sign of protest was that a new party, founded only 15 months earlier in December 2001, was able to gain 28 seats – a result equalling that of the Centre Party and making it one of the two biggest parliamentary factions. This party, *Ühendus Vabariigi eest* – *Res Publica* ('The Union in Defence of the Republic' – *Res Publica*), had staged an expensive and highly visible election campaign, based on the simple slogan 'Choose Order!' (*Vali kord!*), thus lashing out against the entire political establishment. The party had been founded by well-known émigré political scientist Rein Taagepera, and was subsequently to be led by Juhan Parts, who had resigned as State Auditor to enter politics. On 2 April 2003, the President assigned Parts to the task of forming the cabinet. He fulfilled the task successfully, and a new government consisting of Res Publica, the Reform Party and the People's Union was sworn in two weeks later. The Centre Party was right away excluded as a potential coalition partner.

Res Publica has defined itself as rightist and conservative, but its popular appeal is essentially based on its criticism of the corrupt tendencies of the other parties. It has thus gained significant support among the material winners of the transition, many of whom have also lost their confidence in the traditional political forces (see *Table 3.1*). Moreover, the party has utilized such common populist issues as fighting criminality and drug use. It is still premature to say what the role of Res Publica will be in the future, but one possible result of its emergence on the political scene may be renewed isolation of Savisaar's Centre Party and a further strengthening of the neo-liberalist inclination of Estonia's economic policy – essentially a continuation of the policies that have prevailed during the entire independence period.

Three Forms of Politics

In the previous edition of this book, we analysed people's indifference towards politics with the help of a simple conceptual scheme, composed of three different notions of politics, namely *institutional politics, identity politics* and *politics-as-such*. In the following, we will apply the same model as we explore the nature of the distinction between the 'Two Estonias' and its potential consequences for the development of the country's polity.

Up to a certain point, these three forms of politics are analogous to the processes of state-building, nation-building, and society-building, processes that have been highly relevant in Eastern Europe over the past ten to fifteen years. Institutional reforms have formed the basis of state-building under the new conditions. Nation-building is essentially a question of national identity, the redefinition of which has been one of the tasks of the new era. And the ways of understanding politics and political action in a society is indistinguishable from the nature of that society itself – during the communist times there was hardly any open political realm. The difference between these notions is that whereas 'building' denotes the whole process of creating a societal entity, 'politics' in its various forms is more of a *tool* in that process. In any case, just as the processes of 'building' are partly overlapping, so, too, are these three forms connected to each other in many ways. For example, many decisions made by the government have potential impact on the nation's understanding of itself, and once these become articulated in public debate, we are dealing with the world of politics-as-such.

Figure 3.1: Three concepts of Estonian politics: a conceptual scheme

Type of politics	'Building process'	People's present attitude	Main questions and factors
Institutional politics	State-building	Negative exclusion; very few partisans; has not improved in the past few years even though the system has become less turbulent.	Too high expectations after independence; political scandals; small and exclusive political elite.
Identity politics	Nation-building	Latent importance; independence and the new political system approved as such; the ideal of One Estonia at stake.	Relations with Russia; Future of non-Estonians; position in Europe and membership in the EU and NATO; *'longue durée'*.
Politics-as-such	Society-building	Scepticism towards political processes and ideologies; no true alternatives to be found in politics or to be achieved through politics; civic identity still underdeveloped.	The creation of civil society; individualism; business versus politics; successful economic transition.

*

By 'institutional politics' we simply refer to predominantly state-level politics, encompassing the parliament, government, presidency, political parties, corporate groups, and sometimes even the legal system; other possible names might be 'official' or 'high' politics. Political conflicts and their resolution, the actual politicking as well as policy-making, are included in our definition, and all the actions of the above-mentioned bodies, and people's interpretations of them, also need to be considered.

As has been indicated earlier, this 'traditional' form of politics has been highly unpopular in the country during the past ten or twelve years. The way the central institutions of the polity has worked has clearly disappointed many people. A clear reflection of people's scepticism regarding party politics are the election turnouts that seem to have stabilized on a very low level since the mid-1990s: only 57.4 per cent of the electorate voted in the parliamentary elections of 1999, and four years later the turnout was approximately the same, 58.2 per cent. A great part of those who have not been willing to cast their vote are prime representatives of the Second Estonia. Estonia is of course no exception in this sense: similar developments have taken place in both Eastern and Western Europe.

Trust in public institutions is another good indicator of people's relationship to their polity. In a poll conducted in May 2002, no more than about half of the respondents reported trust in the government, the prime minister and the *Riigikogu*. But trust in political parties has been much lower still, by far the lowest of all public institutions. In this poll, only 22 per cent of the respondents trusted the political parties, and 56 per cent did not.[14] From this perspective, one can even argue that the critical attitudes towards politics are essentially a by-product of the pessimism towards political parties. This is so clear that it allows David Arter – in his excellent and still relevant 1996 book on Estonian politics, *Parties and Democracy in the Post-Soviet Republics: The Case of Estonia* – to call Estonia an anti-party system.[15] Arter also argues that in the light of electoral behaviour in the first and second parliamentary elections of 1992 and 1995, the main characteristics of this anti-party system remained more or less constant. Our own evidence suggests that in this respect the situation has not changed markedly since then. Res Publica's success in the 2003 elections is a clear sign of prevailing anti-party sentiment in the country. All in all, it is noteworthy that the party system has consolidated under conditions where people's relationship to it has been highly suspicious.

In the chapter on Estonia in the previous edition of this book, we listed reasons for people's scepticism towards institutional politics, and especially political parties. We mentioned the initial shock of entering the new world. The material consequences of change were very different from what people had expected – the level of the GDP dived dramatically – and the lamentable turn from national unanimity to a day-to-day political tug-of-war took people by surprise. This 'surprise effect' is of course no longer there, but as for example the discussion around the 'Two Estonias' shows, politicians have not been able to create an impression of themselves as being there for the sake of the national community, but for their personal success. We also noted that the actual record of parties was not flattering, as numerous political scandals stained the escutcheon of politics in the 1990s. It seems that the situation has not become much better in this respect in the 2000s.

According to population surveys made in May and July 2002, scepticism towards politics is clearly correlated with socio-economic indicators (Rikmann et al. 2002). People with primary education only, those living in rural areas, and Russian-speakers without citizenship have less confidence in most institutions, feel less informed about the functions of these institutions, and are also more prone to deny any need for such information. Many of these people, generally 'losers' of the transformation, have become totally alienated from politics and lost their interest in the work of political institutions; this is the most common mode of expressing dissatisfaction with politics in today's Estonia.

It is also worth noting that the electoral system does not really promote sensitivity to new initiatives from the electorate or from local party organizations. On the contrary, it leaves much of the actual political outcomes dependent on the ranking of candidates by the leadership of the respective parties (see *Appendix 3.3*). Accordingly, an ambitious politician has more to win by being compliant to the leaders of his or her party than by seeking to represent a dissenting opinion originating from his or her local constituency. A change of the electoral system is currently under discussion in the country.

Finally, and as regards the distinction between the two Estonias, it is worth noting that even the representatives of the well-off business community are often considered to belong to the same bulk of the First Estonia as political elites. Indeed, after the political parties, trust in big business is also remarkably low: in the Candidate Countries Barometer 2001, only 28 per cent of Estonians said that they trusted big companies.

*

The second category in our tripartite division of politics, 'identity politics', represents all the questions that somehow refer to the nature of Estonia as a nation and country, and as a state among other states. The construction of a nation's identity is, of course, a never-ending story and one that pertains to all modern societies: a country's position in the world is a matter of continuous redefinitions. In Estonia in particular, institutional politics has been a self-regulating process exclusive to political elites, but identity politics, although it may often be expressed through these same elites, always needs to be connected in some way to the population at large.

It is obvious that the whole revolutionary process in Estonia started in the field of identity politics – that is, in the field that could not develop freely under the Soviet regime as long as Moscow's bear's paw was still strong. When the new era dawned in the mid-1980s, the nation had to be redefined in both time and space. As we mentioned above, one of the first things was to reveal and reformulate the 'true' history of the nation, the whole cultural heritage of Estonia, in a manner suitable to the new political conditions. Simultaneously, it was deemed imperative to preserve and defend the soil that Estonians had inhabited from time immemorial. The major movements during the independence struggle, *Rahvarinne* and the Citizens'

Committees, can also initially be seen as identity political movements, the nature of which they only lost after the declaration of independence in August 1991. But as the advent of independence became more and more apparent, the need for identity politics greatly diminished and institutional politics quite naturally started to dominate the public sphere.[16] More important still, as long as identity politics prevailed, with its emphasis on the future of the nation, people were politically very active. But as soon as politics became a matter of the state – that is, when institutional politics gained precedence – people turned away from politics in general; or, rather, they remained primarily identity-political, but this form of politics became latent or invisible.

This turn-away from institutional politics is not only a phenomenon of the present, however. One can contend that a historically determined sentiment glorifying the nation but condemning the state exists in Estonia. Not unlike other small nations in Central and Eastern Europe, national identity in Estonia contains a strong anti-statist element; there is a controversy between identity politics and institutional politics. This may also be the reason for the survival of this small nation, whose lands have been regularly conquered throughout history – 'Estonia' has had the ability to exist outside the realm of the state. Even the first experience of independence in the inter-war period can be seen as the ultimate confirmation of the inability of the state to protect the nation: democracy could not be preserved and many people thought that President Konstantin Päts, the embodiment of the state in the 1930s, simply handed over the country to the Soviet Union. Be that as it may, the documented criticism of, and indifference towards, institutional politics can also be seen as a mere return to the traditional historical path, to scepticism towards the state.

It is no easy task to give exact empirical evidence as to what the current significance of identity politics is. The discussion regarding 'two Estonias' offers once again a good point of departure, though. The notion truly touched a chord within the nation. One reason for this is apparently identity-political: the foundational myth of Estonia is based on unanimity, on 'One Estonia' against outside oppressors, a small community of people surrounded by great powers. From this perspective it is also highly interesting that in the *Candidate Countries Barometer* 2002, Estonians proved to be only moderately proud of their nationality. In Hungary as many as 94 per cent of the respondents were proud that they were Hungarians, whereas in Estonia the corresponding figure was only 59 per cent; only in Latvia, the figure was even lower, 55 per cent.[17] This may seem surprising at first sight, but it is obvious that the level of expectations has been so high in Estonia that current realities cannot but make people highly disappointed.

It is also important to note that regaining independence, gaining democracy, a parliament, president, political parties, was – and is – very important from the perspective of identity politics; acquiring all these was a confirmation of the Estonians' 'Europeanness' (Vogt 2003). The importance of all this has not vanished in the face of deepening cleavage between winners and losers. Although people may criticize the present parliament and laugh at the parties, only a very few Estonians are willing to return to anything reminiscent of communism; in the *New Europe Barometer* 2001 they amounted to only 7 per cent. In the same poll, however, a significant part of the respondents, almost 40 per cent, saw strongman rule as a desirable option for the country (cf. Ekman and Linde 2003). Again, we would be inclined to interpret this high figure, not as criticism of democracy *per se*, but as a disappointment with the prevailing distinction in society: a strongman could possibly rejoin the nation. Arnold Rüütel's rise to the country's presidency – he is, after all, a Soviet-time leader – can also be explained from this perspective; it was a result of the deep division between losers and winners. All in all, one can still say that a significant part of the Estonian population – the entire Second Estonia – is interested in politics only in so far as it deals with the question of identity.

*

The third major category of politics, 'politics-as-such', is undoubtedly even more difficult to analyse or even delineate than identity politics. Our definition bears traits of an Arendtian understanding of politics (Arendt 1958): it is how the role of politics is understood in society; the space that the business of politics is able to retain in society; the possibilities people perceive in political action. In this sense it is the precondition for any actual form of politics. In practice for example the development of civil society is essentially dependent on how people perceive their possibilities to influence in general.

A few points regarding politics as such are significant here. First of all, we have to ask how the era of communism and the widely spread disillusionment in relation to the new system have affected people's willingness to participate in any kind of political processes. This combination has obviously been a major hindrance to the development of civil society, but some clear signs of change have nevertheless been visible in this field recently. The number of non-governmental organizations has mushroomed during the past five years, and was in late 2002 already more than 17,500. Even if we take into account that half of the registered organizations have been founded for the maintenance of real estates and that many of the remaining are inactive or equipped with very poor resources, the development has been unprecedented (Trummal and Lagerspetz 2003). Moreover, new practices and structures of cooperation are rapidly emerging both within the non-profit sector and between it and the government. An example of the latter is the adoption of a Conception of the Development of Estonian Civil Society by the *Riigikogu* in December 2002. In the long run, these new practices may undoubtedly lead to new forms of political participation and empowerment of citizens through civic organizations, but many new initiatives still face inertia and suspicion among politicians and within the public administration (Rikmann 2003). These positive trends in the development of civic participation may in any case indicate a movement towards what Vihalemm, Lauristin and Tallo (1997, 200) called the critical-rational stage of political culture; it is the final stage of political transformation, hence the stage of consolidation.[18]

Second, we need to analyse the way politics is understood in relation to general societal trends, particularly in Estonia and in Europe generally. The most significant of such trends is probably the spread of individualist values and attitudes. According to Marju Lauristin (1997), increasing individualism is a fairly clear tendency in the country, both among ethnic Estonians and non-Estonians, and especially among the young and well educated. Along with some other Estonian commentators of this phenomenon (e.g. Realo and Allik 1999), she interprets it as a sign of the country's cultural 'Westernness'. This interpretation can be contested, however. Estonian individualism seems to be of the hedonistic kind, based on the idea that everyone should take care of oneself and not of the others (Vogt 2000). In consolidated Western democracies in contrast, individualism includes the ideas of pluralism and cooperation. What is important is that the egotist attitude, not uncommon elsewhere in Central and Eastern Europe either, can be understood as a carry-over from the atomizing practices of totalitarian mass society (cf. Arendt 1951/1994) and not necessarily as a sign of the adoption of 'Western' values. It has indeed become a moot question to what extent the *longue durée* of Estonian national sentiment, the traditionally strong national unity, can counterbalance this hedonistic individualism.

Finally, it seems that the range for political manœuvring has become extremely narrow in Estonia and the variation of political possibilities has been dramatically reduced. As we indicated earlier, in economic policy Estonia has followed a straight course despite the regular changes of government, and ideological differences between parties have become minimal. This absence of alternatives has probably made people believe that change may not be brought about through politics. Yet, politics as such is essentially a matter of producing alternative ways for political action, and arguing in favour of them while at the same time taking into consideration the views of the others. People should learn that being political, which includes a conflictual component – to be able to fight for, say, the future of a local school – makes a difference. This kind of understanding of politics is still far too often absent from Estonian politics, despite some signs of strengthening critical-rationalism.

*

In the first section of our analysis, we showed how the clear ideological cleavages of the early days of the independence process have been transformed into a party system that is essentially dominated by political pragmatism – if not opportunism – with the potential to undermine all ideological differences. We also concluded that this structure reflects the actual mood and opinions among the majority of the population – particularly those of the Second Estonia – to a very limited degree. In the preceding section, we noted that people's utter estrangement from the world of institutional politics is not the only factor that determines the nature of political life in the country, but we also have to take into consideration questions of identity and the fact that civil society has truly started to develop in recent years. In the ensuing sections we will try to deepen this picture by discussing two rather different issues: the ethnic cleavage and membership in the European Union.

Before turning to these themes, it is worth noting that in the previous edition of this book we wrote that 'the cleavage between the 'old guard' and the 'young professionals, is the only major cleavage that can be derived from the party structure'. We pointed at a distinction between those, whose personal interests were somehow related to Soviet times, and those young neo-liberals who demanded as clear a break with the past as possible. This observation has lost its significance during the past five years, and one can hardly see that the party structure would reflect it either. This is yet another sign of consolidation.

The Ethnic Cleavage

The relationship between native Estonians and the Russian-speaking minority has been high on the agenda throughout the years of independence, or actually long before that. This has also been a question of particular interest to outside observers, some of whom have criticized Estonia's democratic character by referring to the uncertain position of ethnic minorities. Of Estonia's 1.36 million inhabitants, approximately 68 per cent were native Estonians in 2002; the rest are mainly Russians (26 per cent). As a result of large emigration in the beginning of the 1990s, the number of Russians decreased quite significantly, so that as they were over 470,000 in 1989, they now number only 351,000. There are also close to 50,000 Ukrainians and Belorussians, who for all intents and purposes belong to the Russian-speaking community.

When the *Riigikogu* approved the Citizenship Resolution in February 1992, citizenship was automatically granted only to pre-1940 citizens and their descendants, irrespective of ethnicity. Those people who had arrived during the Soviet era were obliged to undergo a naturalization process, including a language test, two years of residency, and an oath of allegiance (Jurado 2003). This resolution, and the – in some respects – even stricter new Citizenship Law passed in 1995, effectively created a multi-layered society. Some 73,000 people living in the country still have Russian citizenship, and 170,000 people have no citizenship at all. There is also a completely marginalized group not even holding a residence permit and thus staying in the country illegally; their number is not known. Between 1992 and 2000, 115,000 people obtained citizenship through the naturalization process. Yet, one can also argue that having the idea of legal continuity of the pre-1940 Estonian state as its point of departure, the Law on Citizenship is strictly logical and not in conflict with international law. The principle of *jus sanguinis* applied here is no different from that of some other countries, notably Germany.

Since 1997 some positive steps regarding the assimilation of the Russian-speakers have been taken. Several successive governments have included a minister without portfolio with demographic and nationalities issues as the area of responsibility. The Citizenship Law has been amended several times, the most important of these amendments being the one of December 1998. According to it, children under the age of 15 whose parents are stateless and have lived in Estonia for at least five years are allowed to obtain citizenship without any examination. Moreover, a number of state-coordinated and state-funded integration programmes have been launched since 1997. The current main programme, Integration in Estonian Society 2000–2007 (*Integratsioon Eesti ühiskonnas*), is based on two principles. On the one hand, it seeks to create unity (*ühtlustamine*) in society by promoting Estonian language skills among the minorities, along with a sense of Estonianness. On the other hand, the idea is to make the preservation of cultural differences possible through improved cultural minority rights (*Integreeruv Eesti* 2000, 4). These policy measures are a sign of Estonia's willingness to cope with European standards in the sense they have been advanced by the European Union, the Council of Europe and the OSCE.

Nevertheless, one can argue that integration is still perceived one-sidedly. The implementation of the Integration Programme seems less preoccupied with the promotion of tolerance, cultural diversity and the preservation of ethnic differences than is declared by the text. Instead, authorities tend to see integration as equivalent to language learning by the minorities (Hallik 2002, 241). It is still taken for granted that Russians need to learn the Estonian language before they can be naturalized. Citizenship is thus understood as the main carrot that the Estonian state can offer to those Russians who are willing to learn the language. The existence of another kind of relationship between citizenship and language learning has thus been overlooked: obtaining the Estonian citizenship first might provide an impetus for learning the language as well, as the person's destiny would now be more firmly tied to the country (cf. the survey of Russians studying Estonian in Narva by Lindén, 2000).

Moreover, and as we noted earlier, the Russians have not had many opportunities to make themselves heard in party politics, although those residents who lack citizenship are allowed to vote in local elections (but not be elected themselves). In effect, the political dialogue about ethnic issues has taken place between Estonians deciding what to do with the 'non-Estonians' (*mitte-eestlased*), without much participation by the Russians and other minority groups. It is thus obvious that a significant part of the second Estonia consists of those predominantly Russophone residents who do not hold Estonian citizenship and who are not consulted when decisions concerning their future are made. Or perhaps we should refer to this as the 'third Estonia'?

All in all, 'The Russian Question' *(Vene küsimus)*, and all the interrelated problems, is still in many respects politically relevant; it creates the background against which the consensual nature of some key areas of Estonian policy-making can be explained. In Estonian political discourse, reference is made to what Estonians perceive as the continuing colonial ambitions of the Russian state as well as to the unresolved question of the integration of non-Estonian residents into Estonian society. Memberships in the EU and NATO have above all been presented as a means of distancing Estonia from Russia's sphere of influence. In this sense, the ethnic cleavage is essentially understood as a security issue, indeed as a matter of the nation's existence. We believe that the prospective membership in these two organizations will truly lessen the security concerns of the Estonians and in this respect also bring about positive changes as regards the position of Russians in the country.

Membership in the European Union

During Estonia's new independence, accession to the EU and NATO has been *the* foreign policy priority of all governments. The ambition to join the military alliance has motivated a steady rise in budget allowances for defence, but the impact of a prospective EU membership has been deeper and touched all spheres of politics and society. Discussions on all major policy issues have included the question of their compatibility with the norms and expectations of the EU.

NATO membership has not really given rise to dissenting voices, but the lack of popular support for accession to the EU has become a major concern for the country's governments. In fact, Estonia has become notoriously known as an applicant country with pronouncedly little popular support for EU membership. In June 2002, only 32 per cent of Estonians perceived EU membership as a good thing, while the average among the 13 applicant countries was 61 per cent; Romania came out at the very top, with 78 per cent of the respondents favouring EU membership (*Candidate Countries Eurobarometer* 2001). The development of Estonian public opinion is shown in Table 3.2. The overall picture is that the share of EU proponents has been relatively stable, whereas those who have been uncertain about their opinion have mostly joined the ranks of EU opponents.

Table 3.2: How would you vote in a referendum about EU membership? (%)

I would vote...	Nov 1995*	Nov 1996*	Nov 1997*	Nov 1998	Oct 1999	May 2000	Oct 2001*	Sept 2002*
In favour	44	29	35	27	38	34	38	39
Against	14	17	14	14	22	26	27	31
I would not vote	–	–	9	13	6	8	21	18
Undecided/ No answer	32	54	48	46	34	32	14	12

Sources: The question reads (with some minor variation over the years): 'If a referendum on the accession of Estonia into the European Union were held tomorrow, how would you vote?' All surveys conducted by Saar Poll. Surveys marked with an asterisk are from the *Central and Eastern Eurobarometer*; *Candidate Countries Barometer*; Kirch et al. (2002, 163); Raik (2003).

Interestingly enough, non-ethnic Estonians have been more favourably disposed towards joining the EU than ethnic Estonians. They apparently believe that membership in the EU would help solve Estonia's ethnic problems. It may also be noted that most non-ethnic Estonians are urban dwellers and thus belong to a segment of the population, which tends to be more pro-EU than the rural strata. Be that as it may, the relatively low overall support for membership in Estonia is truly astonishing, given the extent to which the country's economy is already integrated into the EU, the Estonians' general self-perception as 'European' and 'Western', and the consequentiality with which the goal of EU accession has been advocated by all governments since Estonia's independence was restored.

It seems to be precisely the last mentioned factor that explains the opposition. Estonia's EU accession has remained an elite project. Analyses of the results of various population surveys show that accession is opposed, above all, by pensioners, the unemployed, the rural population, the less educated, and those whose income is lower than average. The opponents are also likely to be pessimistic when assessing the overall development of democracy and economy in Estonia (Kirch et al. 2002, 166). Their trust towards politicians and domestic political institutions is lower than that of people in general. In short, the present opposition to Estonia's EU membership is essentially an expression of dissent against the policies of domestic decision-makers.

This can be seen as a paradox: the neo-liberal economic policies of Estonian governments have indeed spelled the rejection of regulatory devices that are likely to be reintroduced as the country joins the EU. The negotiation strategy of successive governments was therefore designed to protect Estonia's competitive advantage as a tax haven and reservoir of cheap labour, at least for a period of transition. In the long run, however,

Estonia's EU membership will almost certainly move the country's economic policies towards a more social and regulated direction. Membership will both force the political elite to adjust its policies with those of the other EU states, and offer civic organizations and labour unions opportunities for finding new partners and allies across the continent. These potential changes have been recognized by the political and economic elite, especially by those who oppose the accession and describe the EU as 'socialist in essence', but even many pro-EU politicians have been weary of them. For example Prime Minister Siim Kallas complained in an article published in the daily *Postimees* on 13 December 2002 that

> [I]t is disconcerting that the labour union leadership has heaped complaints about the Estonian government on Europe. After the actions by the inheritors of the *Interdvizhenie* in order to gain privileges for the Russians, this is indeed the first time that somebody seeks help from the European Union against the Republic of Estonia. [...] Their requirements are purely political, leftist and egalitarian, and have nothing to do with the interests of working people, but belong to the sphere of electoral campaigns. [...] The kind of Europe that the labour unions want is not the Europe that we have worked to join tremendously through all these years.

With all possible certainty, Estonia will join the EU in May 2004. A referendum will be held on the issue in September 2003, but given the relatively unanimous support of the political elite and the low organizational capacity of the Estonian EU opponents hitherto, it seems very unlikely that the result would be anything but positive. With this, one central aim of the Estonian political leadership will be reached. However, it may turn out that the entrance into a new economic and political environment renders it more difficult to reach another aim: the continuation of political stability in the terms that were defined by the country's political and economic elite during the formative years of the newly independent state.

Conclusion: The Consolidation of the Extraordinary?

When looked at by outside observers, the development of Estonia's economy, society and political life since independence is impressive, by virtue of its rapid pace in particular. The flow of investments, consultancy and aid from neighbouring Sweden and especially Finland have significantly contributed to this, but the domestic politicians themselves also saw the rapid reform of the country's economy and politics as imperative in the early 1990s. Until the withdrawal of the last Russian troops in 1994, there was still reason to be concerned about possible Russian revanchist ambitions. Approaching the 'West', primarily represented by the EU and NATO, was the obvious way of counterbalancing the Russian threat. The West, in turn, sought to safeguard the macro-economic growth and financial and political predictability of the region. For both the West and the domestic political leadership, maintaining the stability of the political system was a more important goal than heightening its sensitivity to initiatives from the grass-roots level. As a result, political parties were given a strong legal position, despite their weak organizational base and low popular legitimacy (Rosimannus 1995).

From the outside, then, it seems that Estonian democracy has become successfully consolidated. Through four parliamentary elections, the political system has proven its ability to function smoothly. The question is, however, to what extent this smoothness, the consensual and predictable nature of politics, has been reached at the cost of democratic participation. After all, one of the main arguments of the present chapter has been that a significant part of the population is not really represented on the level of institutional politics – a point also raised by the social researchers responsible for the letter about the 'two Estonias'. From this perspective, we could even say that 'democratic consolidation' itself is a paradox, or a contradiction in terms (Lagerspetz 2001, 416). Consolidation essentially means a narrowing of the range of possible alternatives, whereas democracy requires that the decision-making processes are kept open for new innovative initiatives. Focusing the study of Central and East European politics on the process of consolidation may mean that one overlooks the need for a continuation of the democratization processes that started in the 1980s.

Here, one could apply the concept of 'extraordinary politics' introduced by the Polish economist Leszek Balczerowicz (1993, 31) in the early 1990s. He argues that 'great changes' in a country's history create a reserve of 'political capital' at the disposal of the government in charge. This reserve enables the government to apply radical and drastic measures of economic reform, if concentrated in the period of 'extraordinary politics' shortly after the historical change.

We may be accused of extending the meaning of extraordinary politics too far, but we would nevertheless argue that its era has yet not quite ended in Estonia. In other words, the media and large parts of the population are still ready to accept such decisions by the government that they would otherwise basically resist, provided that these decisions seem to strengthen the country's independence. Although the Estonians were able to break away from the Soviet Empire, history has taught them not to take for granted their national independence, or indeed, their very existence as a people. This attitude serves as a strong incentive for overcoming internal social divisions – people are simply postponing their demands for better living standards because of the perceived Russian threat. This attitude has until recently given the governments a free hand to implement radical economic reform policies, without having to fear protests from the social groups most negatively affected. In short, the Estonians' emphasis on identity politics has made it possible to pursue consensual policies. This is what we consider the key factor explaining the radical nature of Estonia's post-socialist economic reforms.

There are also some signs of continuing efforts to reproduce and make use of the remaining reserve of political capital. A recent example is the discussion on the need of a new 'social' or 'national' contract (*rahvuslik kokkulepe; ühiskondlik kokkulepe*), which has been initiated by the President of the Republic Arnold Rüütel and actively promoted by the central organizations of employers. In practice, the national/social contract would be a document agreed upon and signed by all major political parties, employers' organizations, labour unions and other institutions and organizations of nation-wide significance. Such a document would define 'the long-term objectives of Estonia's development'. According to preliminary information from the Chancellery of the President (January 2003), these objectives would be concerned, at least, with the aging of the population; the financing of education and innovation; guaranteeing the continuation of present taxation policies and the 'enterprise-friendly economic environment'; and a gradual improvement of social services. A memorandum stating the need of such a document was signed before the March 2003 elections, the idea being that the document would provide the guidelines for politics pursued by the new parliament and government. The amount of realism underlying these ambitions remains to be seen.

To some extent, these preparations for a social contract constitute an answer by the political and economic establishments to the criticism voiced by the letter 'two Estonias': the document is supposed to show that the leaders of the country are able and willing to bridge the gaps between different political and economic interests. On the other hand, the country's prospective EU accession has certainly created a new need for cooperation amongst the domestic elites. Their ability to pursue neo-liberal economic policies without being challenged has hitherto been sustained by two factors (cf. Lagerspetz 2001, 414). First, people have believed that, in the long run, the continuation of present policies will lead to greater prosperity for all members of the nation; joining the EU has been presented as an important part of that strategy. Second, the losers of the economic reforms have been more or less unable to articulate any alternative visions of future development. This may be attributed to the low level of labour and civic organization as well as to the ideological reaction against socialist values that followed upon the struggle for independence. Until now, the neo-liberal policies have been supported both by their ideological hegemony and by the fragmentation of their adversaries. The national social contract could thus be interpreted as an effort to recreate the hegemony and curtail the possibilities of coordinated opposition.

Indeed, the above-quoted outburst by Prime Minister Kallas against contacts between Estonian labour unions and EU agencies shows that the political elite is aware of the possible consequences of the country's EU accession for domestic politics. With accession, the position of labour unions will certainly become stronger than hitherto, due to EU-level regulations and the new possibilities of concerted action with labour unions in other countries. Moreover, Estonia's taxation, environmental and social policies – to name just a few policy areas – will become objects of serious scrutiny and pressure by other member countries. Finally, the country's almost simultaneous accession to the EU and NATO signifies for many Estonians an end to the post-socialist transition period. The political reserve capital originating from the newly won independence thus requires new energy: the governments must simply present themselves as guardians of 'common Estonian interests', no longer that much against an alleged Russian threat, but within the enlarged EU.

The profound change of Estonia's international position is, thus, bound to thoroughly change the overall picture of Estonian domestic politics too. Even so, once initiated, the policy-making style described above as 'extraordinary politics' may well dominate, even after the situation has changed – the pattern of consensual policy-making could become a permanent feature of Estonian politics. Here, one is tempted to draw a parallel with Finnish political life during Urho Kekkonen's presidency (1956–81). He regarded the formation of broad-based coalition governments as crucial for a small state neighbouring a superpower. One may even see this pattern of domestic politics as something typical of small European states. Shmuel N. Eisenstadt (1985, 47–8) has argued that such states have historically developed two complementary patterns of political organization and activity. The 'real' decisions tend to crystallize in the course of negotiations between the executive, the bureaucracy, the parliamentary commissions and the relevant interest groups, while the 'open' parliamentary debate tends to be more of a symbolic and illusory nature. The function of the latter is to create legitimacy for the ground rules of the political system, while the first form of policy-making ensures smooth cooperation among different elites.

As it turns out, Eisenstadt's description of domestic politics in small European states is surprisingly well-suited for the actions of the seemingly fragmented and scandal-ridden, but, in fact, unequivocally 'centrist-rightist' Estonian political elite – despite the fact that the interests of different social groups are still clearly under-represented in the polity within the realm of institutional politics.

NOTES

* Acknowledgement: The authors are grateful to Kristi Raik for her learned comments on the manuscript.

1. Savisaar himself did not become a minister though, but he did become the chairman of the Coalition Board. The Board was formed of the leadership of the two parties and had the function of designing the general outlines of government policies.

2. It is worth noting, though, that the income ratio between the highest and the lowest 20 per cent of households has remained fairly stable since the mid-1990s (420/100 in 1996 and 377/100 in 2001; *Estonian Human Development Report* 2002, 120) while unemployment has increased only modestly (from 9.7 per cent in 1995 to 12.6 per cent in 2001; Vetik 2002, 119).

3. Unemployment for more than 12 months was 3.1 per cent of the total labour force in 1995; in 2001 it was already 6.1 per cent. *Estonian Human Development Report* 2002, 12.

4. See *www.transparency.org/cpi/2002/cpi2002.en.html.*

5. More thorough discussions of the revolutionary process can be found in Lagerspetz (1996) and Vogt (2000).

6. The political background of the delegates at *Rahvarinne's* founding congress, on 1 October 1988, were as follows: EKP members 28 per cent, National Heritage Society 19 per cent, *Rohelised* 10 per cent, religious organizations 2 per cent, Estonian National Independence Party 0.2 per cent and others 40 per cent (Arter 1996, 131).

7. This idea of economic autonomy became a force to be reckoned with in September 1987, when four members of the Estonian Communist Party (EKP) published the IME programme, which accepted the basic principles of capitalism and called for economic institutions to be put under Estonian control (IME is an abbreviation of *Isemajandav Eesti*, 'self-management of Estonia'; the term IME also means 'miracle'; Gerner and Hedlund 1993, 79).

8. The COE election was probably the only privately run general election ever staged (Arter 1996, 137).

9. The new constitution was accepted in a referendum on 18 June 1992. Voter turnout was 66.9 per cent.

10. In Narva, with its solid ethnic Russian majority of more than 90 per cent, 72.7 per cent voted 'no'. In Tallinn, the Pearson correlation between the number of Russians in a given area and the number of 'no' votes was no less than 0.96 (Data provided by Raitviir 1996, 448).

11. Rüütel became President of the Republic in 2002 as the parties of the government coalition failed to join forces behind a common candidate. Estonia's president is in the first instance elected by the Parliament, but if no candidate receives the majority of votes in the Parliament, representatives of local government councils together with the MPs form an electoral body (see *Appendix 3.3*). This undoubtedly favoured Rüütel as his support is mainly concentrated on rural areas.

12. Lennart Meri was originally *Isamaa's* candidate when he became President in 1992.

13. Interestingly enough, the name alludes to *Isamaaliit* (the Fatherland League), the ruling party subsequent to the coup of 1934.

14. www.riigikogu.ee/osakonnad/msi/sel_works/graph8.html. The figures presented by the *Candidate Countries Barometer* are even more alarming: in Estonia in 2001, only 12 per cent of the population said that they trusted parties; overall, this figure varied between 6 (Slovakia) and 18 (Hungary) per cent.

15. Arter defines his anti-party system in terms of three parameters: first, 'partisan allegiance provides the basis of candidate choice for only a minority of voters at general elections'; second, 'abstentionism should exceed one in three of those entitled to cast a ballot'; third, 'there exist numerically significant anti-parties' (Arter 1996, 252).

16. Yet, and as Lieven (1993, 215) noted, in the early stages of party structure development, the significant dividing lines between parties were their attitudes to history and national culture rather than, say, questions of economic policy.

17. A year earlier the same figure was 60 per cent. The *Candidate Countries Eurobarometer* surveys are available at http://europe.eu.int/comm/public_opinion.

18. Vihalemm, Lauristin and Tallo (1997, 202) refer to the first stage of the new political culture as 'the mythological stage' (1988–89/91). One of its most important characteristics was that '[l]arge mass demonstrations united the participants with an emotionally high voltage. Symbols, myths and rituals had a heyday, and the function of words during the mass rallies was magical. Speeches, songs and slogans represented a collective witchcraft, the symbolic fight of a small nation against the totalitarian machinery'. The next stage, when political differentiation started, was the ideological stage; the third would be the critical-rational stage. According to Vihalemm, Lauristin and Tallo, Estonian society had not yet entered that stage in 1997.

REFERENCES

Arendt, Hannah (1951/1994), *Totalitarianism,* San Diego, Harcourt Brace.
—— (1958), *The Human Condition,* Chicago and London, Cambridge University Press.
Arter, David (1996), *Parties and Democracy in the Post-Soviet Republics: the Case of Estonia,* Aldershot and Brookfield, Dartmouth.
Balczerowicz, Leszek (1993), 'Common Fallacies in the Debate on the Economic Transition in Central and Eastern Europe', *Working paper* No. 11, London, European Bank for Reconstruction and Development.
Candidate Countries Eurobarometer (2001), *http://europe.eu.int/comm/public_opinion.*
Dellenbrant, Jan Åke (1994), 'The Re-Emergence of Multi-Partyism in the Baltic States', in Sten Berglund and Jan Åke Dellenbrant, eds, *The New Democracies in Eastern Europe: Party Systems and Political Cleavages,* 2nd ed., Aldershot, Edward Elgar.
Economic Survey of Europe (2002), No.1, Economic Commission for Europe, United Nations, New York and Geneva.
Ekman, Joakim and Jonas Linde (2003), 'Demokrati och nostalgi i Central och Östeuropa', *Nordisk Østforum,* Vol 17, Nr 1, 65–84.
Eisenstadt, Shmuel N. (1985), 'Reflections on Centre-Periphery Relations and Small European States', in Risto Alapuro, Matti Alestalo, Elina Haavio-Mannila and Raimo Väyrynen, eds, *Small States in Comparative Perspective: Essays for Erik Allardt,* Oslo, Norwegian University Press.
Estonian Legislation in Translation: Legal Acts of Estonia, No. 1, January 1996, Estonian Translation and Legislative Support Centre.
—— No. 7, July 1996, Estonian Translation and Legislative Support Centre.
Estonian Human Development Report (1997), United Nations Development Programme.
—— (2002), United Nations Development Programme.
Gerner, Kristian and Stefan Hedlund (1993), *The Baltic States and the End of the Soviet Empire,* London and New York, Routledge.
Grennes, Thomas (1997), 'The Economic Transition in the Baltic Countries', *Journal of Baltic Studies,* Vol. xxviii, 1.
Hallik, Klara (2002), 'Minority Protection in Estonia: An Assessment of the Programme Integration in Estonian Society 2000–2007', in *Monitoring the EU Accession Process: Minority Protection, Volume I.* Budapest, OSI/EU Accession Program, 189–244.
Helsingin Sanomat 6 March 2000.
Integreeruv Eesti 1997–2000 (2000), Eesti Vabariigi Valitsuse raport, Tallinn.
Jurado, Elena (2003), *Complying with 'European' Standards of Minority Protection: Estonia's Relations with the European Union, OSCE and Council of Europe,* D.Phil. Thesis, Oriel College, Oxford University.
Kirch, Aksel, Toivo Palm and Koit Oole (2002), 'Changes in EU – Consciousness in Estonia in 1995–2002: Discussion and public opinion', in Aksel Kirch and Juhan Sillaste, eds, *Monitoring Preparations of Transition Countries for EU Accession,* Tallinn, The Institute for European Studies and The Office of European Integration of State Chancellery, 156–69.
Laar, Mart, Urmas Ott and Sirje Endre (1996), *Teine Eesti,* Tallinn, Meedia- ja Kirjastuskompanii SE & JS.
Lagerspetz, Mikko (1996), *Constructing Post-Communism: A Study in the Estonian Social Problems Discourse,* Turku, Annales Universitatis Turkuensis, Series B, 214.
—— (2001), 'Consolidation as Hegemonization: The case of Estonia', *Journal of Baltic Studies,* xxxii, 4, 402–20.
—— and Konrad Maier (2002), 'Das politische System Estlands', in Wolfgang Ismayr, ed, *Die politischen Systeme Osteuropas,* Opladen, Leske + Budrich, 69–107.
Lauristin, Marju (1997), 'Contexts of Transition', in Marju Lauristin and Peeter Vihalemm, eds, *Return to the Western World. Cultural and Political Perspectives on the Estonian Post-Communist Transition,* Tartu, Tartu University Press.
Lieven, Anatol (1993), *The Baltic Revolution: Estonia, Latvia, Lithuania and the Path to Independence,* New Haven and London, Yale University Press.

Lindén, Tove (2000), 'Subjektiva och strukturella faktorers inverkan på de ryskspråkigas val av språkstudier i Estland – vilka är det som studerar estniska i Narva, och varför?', *term paper presented at the Department of East Europan Studies of the University of Uppsala.*

Park, Andrus (1995), 'Ideological Dimension of the Post-Communist Domestic Conflicts', *Proceedings of the Estonian Academy of Sciences*, 44/3.

Pettai, Vello and Markus Kreuzer (1999), 'Party politics in the Baltic states: Social bases and institutional context', *East European Politics and Societies*, Vol. 13, No. 1.

Postimees, 23 April 2001; 19 October 2001; 13 December 2002.

Raik, Kristi (2003), 'Democratic Politics or Implementation of Inevitabilities? Democracy and Integration into the European Union of Estonia', manuscript of Ph.D. thesis, University of Turku.

Raitviir, Tiina (1996), *Eesti Üleminekuperioodi valimiste (1989–1993) võrdlev uurimine; Elections in Estonia During the Transition Period (1989–1993): A Comparative Study*, Tallinn, Teaduste Akadeemia Kirjastus.

Realo, Anu and Jüri Allik (1999), 'A Cross-Cultural Study of Collectivism: A Comparison of American, Estonian, and Russian students', *The Journal of Social Psychology*, 139, 2, 133–42.

Rikmann, Erle (2003), 'Kansalaisosallistumisen kulttuuri Virossa', *Idäntutkimus*, Vol. 10, No. 1.

——, Mikko Lagerspetz, Piret Pernik and Tarmo Tuisk (2002), 'Poliitilise osaluse dilemmad Eesti poliitilises kultuuris: kuuluvus ja kodanikuidentiteet. Uurimuse raport', *manuscript*, Chancellery of the Riigikogu, available at *http://www.riigikogu.ee/osakonnad/msi*.

Rosimannus, Rain (1995), 'Political Parties: Identity and Identification', *Nationalities Papers*, Vol. 23, No. 1, 29–41.

Statistical Yearbook of Estonia (1994), Tallinn, Statistical Office of Estonia (www.stat.ee, visited 23 March 2003).

—— (1996), Tallinn, Statistical Office of Estonia (www.stat.ee, visited 23 March 2003).

Statistics in Focus – Theme 2, 8/2003, Eurostat.

Taagepera, Rein (1993), *Estonia: Return to Independence*, Boulder, San Francisco and London, Westview Press.

Tiit, Ene-Margit (2002), 'Kihistumine ja sotsiaalpoliitika Eestis', in Raivo Vetik, ed., *Kaks Eestit: artiklite, ettekannete ja analüüside kogumik*, Tallinn, TPÜ kirjastus, 95–107.

Trummal, Aire and Mikko Lagerspetz (2003), 'Eesti kodanikeühendused täna', in Mikko Lagerspetz, Aire Trummal, Rein Ruutsoo, Erle Rikmann and Daimar Liiv, *Tuntud ja tundmatu kodanikeühiskond*, Tallinn, Avatud Eesti Fond.

Vetik, Raivo, ed., (2002), *Eesti inimarengu aruanne 2002: inimarengu trendid ja poliitika kujundamine*, Tallinn, Tallinna Pedagoogikaülikooli Rahvusvaheliste ja Sotsiaaluuringute Instituut.

Vihalemm, Peeter, Marju Lauristin and Ivar Tallo (1997), 'Development of Political Culture in Estonia', in Marju Lauristin and Peeter Vihalemm, eds, *Return to the Western World: Cultural and Political Perspectives on the Estonian Post-Communist Transition*, Tartu, Tartu University Press.

Vogt, Henri (2000), *The Utopia of Post-Communism: The Czech Republic, Eastern Germany and Estonia after 1989*, D. Phil. thesis, University of Oxford.

—— (2003), 'Res Publica among Youth in Finland and Estonia', in Valeszka Henze, Valeska Maier-Wörz and Henri Vogt, eds, *Youth around the Baltic Sea: Sharing Differences – Discovering Common Grounds*, Örebro, Örebro University.

APPENDIX 3.1: ELECTION RESULTS

PARLIAMENTARY ELECTIONS

1992 Elections
Date: 20 September
Turnout: 66.8%

Electoral Alliance/Party	%	Seats
Pro Patria (*Isamaa*)	22.2	29
Secure Home (*Kindel Kodu*)	12.4	15
Popular Front (*Rahvarinne*)	12.4	15
Moderates (*Mõõdukad*)	9.8	12
Estonian National Independence Party		
(*Eesti Rahvusliku Sõltumatuse Partei*, ERSP)	9.8	12
Independent Royalists (*Sõltumatud Kuningriiklased*)	7.2	8
Estonian Citizens (*Eesti Kodanik*)	7.0	8
Estonian Entrepreneurs' Party (*Eesti Ettevõtjate Erakond*)	2.2	1
The Greens (*Rohelised*)	2.5	1
Others	14.1	0
Total		101

Electoral Alliances:

Pro Patria (*Isamaa*): Christian Democratic Party, Christian Democratic Union, Liberal Democratic Union, Estonian Liberal Democratic Party, Conservative People's Party, Republican Coalition Party (*Eesti Kristlik-Demokraatlik Erakond, Eesti Kristlik-Demokraatlik Liit, Eesti Liberaaldemokraatlik Liit, Eesti Liberaaldemokraatlik Partei, Eesti Konservatiivne Rahvaerakond, Eesti Vabariiklaste Koonderakond*).

Secure Home (*Kindel Kodu*): Coalition Party, Rural Union, Democratic Justice Union (*Eesti Koonderakond, Eesti Maaliit, Eesti Demokraatlik Õigusliit*).

Popular Front (*Rahvarinne*): Popular Front of Estonia, People's Centre Party, Assembly of Nations in Estonia, Women's Union (*Eestimaa Rahvarinne, Eesti Rahva-Keskerakond, Eestimaa Rahvuste Ühendus, Eesti Naisliit*).

Moderates (*Mõõdukad*): Social Democratic Party, Rural Centre Party (*Eesti Sotsiaaldemokraatlik Partei, Eesti Maa-Keskerakond*).

Independent Royalists (*Sõltumatud Kuningriiklased*): Royalist Party, Royalist Association 'Free Toome' (*Eesti Rojalistik Partei, Rojalistik ühendus Vaba Toome*).

Estonian Citizens (*Eesti Kodanik*): Party of the Republic of Estonia, 'The Association of Legal Real Estate Owners in Tartu', 'Association of Healthy Life in Noarootsi' (*Eesti Vabariigi Partei, Tartu Õigusjärgsete Omanike Ühendus, Noarootsi Tervisliku Eluviisi Selts*).

Greens (*Rohelised*): Green Movement, Green Party, European Youth Forest Action in Estonia, Maardu Green League, Green Regiment (*Eesti Roheline Liikumine, Erakond Eesti Rohelised, Keskkonnakaitse- ja noorteühendus Euroopa Noorte Metsaktsioon Eestis, Ühedus Roheline Maardu, Roheline Rügement*).

1995 Elections
Date: 5 March
Turnout: 68.9%

Electoral Alliance/Party	%	Seats
Coalition Party and the Rural Union[*]		
(*Koonderakond ja Maarahva Ühendus*)	32.2	41
Reform Party (*Eesti Reformierakond*)	16.4	19
Centre Party (*Eesti Keskerakond*)	14.2	16
Pro Patria and Estonian National Independence Party		
(*Rahvuslik Koonderakond 'Isamaa'*		
ja Eesti Rahvusliku Sõltumatuse Partei)	7.9	8
Moderates (*Mõõdukad*)[**]	6.0	6
Our home is Estonia (*Meie Kodu on Eestimaa*)[***]	5.9	6
Right Wing (*Parempoolsed*)[****]	5.0	5
Others	12.4	0
Total	100.0	101

[*]   Coalition Party, Rural Union, Country People's Party, Pensioners' and Families' Union, Farmers' Assembly
[**] Social Democratic Party, Rural Centre Party
[***] United People's Party of Estonia, Russian Party in Estonia
[****] People's Party of Republicans and Conservatives

1999 Elections
Date: 7 March
Turnout: 57.4%

Party	%	Seats
Centre Party (*Keskerakond*)	23.4	28
Pro Patria Union (*Isamaaliit*)	16.1	18
Reform Party (*Reformierakond*)	15.9	18
Moderates (*Mõõdukad*)	15.2	17
Coalition Party (*Koonderakond*)	7.6	7
Country People's Party (*Maarahva Erakond*)	7.3	7
United People's Party (*Eesti Ühendatud Rahvapartei*)	6.1	6
Others	9.4	–
Total	100.0	101

2003 Elections
Date: 2 March
Turnout: 58.2%

Party	%	Seats
Centre Party (*Keskerakond*)	25.4	28
Res Publica	24.6	28
Reform Party (*Reformierakond*)	17.7	19
People's Union (*Rahvaliit*)	13.0	13
Pro Patria Union (*Isamaaliit*)	7.3	7
Moderates (*Mõõdukad*)	7.0	6
Others	5.0	–
Total	100.0	101

PRESIDENTIAL ELECTIONS

1992 Elections
First direct round
Date: 20 September
Turnout: 67.9%

Candidate	% Nation-wide	Tallinn	Tartu	Kohtla-Järve
Arnold Rüütel	41.8	37.8	27.8	50.4
Rein Taagepera	23.4	22.4	17.1	31.6
Lennart Meri	29.5	33.8	49.8	14.2
Lagle Parek	4.2	4.8	3.9	2.3
Invalid ballots	1.1			

Second Round
Votes in the Riigikogu
Date: 5 October

Candidate	Votes
Arnold Rüütel	31
Lennart Meri	59
Invalid ballots	11

1996 Elections
Votes in the Riigikogu

Candidate	1st Round 26 August	2nd Round 27 August	3rd Round 27 August
Lennart Meri	45	49	52
Arnold Rüütel	34	34	32

Votes in the Electoral Body

Candidate	1st Round 20 September	2nd Round 20 September
Lennart Meri	139	196
Arnold Rüütel	85	126
Tunne Kelam	76	
Enn Tõugu	47	
Siiri Oviir	25	

2001 Elections

Votes in the Riigikogu

Candidate	1st Round 27 August	2nd Round 28 August	3rd Round 28 August
Peeter Kreitzberg	40	36	33
Andres Tarand	38		
Peeter Tulviste		35	33

Votes in the Electoral Body

Candidate	1st Round 21 September	2nd Round 21 September
Peeter Kreitzberg	72	
Arnold Rüütel	114	186
Toomas Savi	90	155
Peeter Tulviste	89	

Note: Before the 1992 presidential elections, the Chairman of the Supreme Council was effectively 'president' and sometimes even called so. That office was held by Arnold Rüütel from 8 May 1990 until 5 October 1992.

APPENDIX 3.2: GOVERNMENT COMPOSITION

Time	*Prime Minister (party)*	*Parties; number of cabinet seats*	*Political orientation*	*Reason for change of government*
Apr 1990 – Jan 1992	Edgar Savisaar	Primarily non-party	Caretaker government with majority support in the Supreme Council.	Savisaar stepped down because of accusations he had not anticipated the cuts in fuel supply from Russia.
Jan 1992 – Oct 1992	Tiit Vähi	Primarily non-party	Caretaker government with majority support in the Supreme Council.	*Riigikogu* elections.
Oct 1992 – Nov 1994	Mart Laar (Pro Patria)	Pro Patria, 4 Nat. Ind. Party, 3 Moderates, 3 No affiliation, 4 (as of 21 Oct 1994)	'Right-centre' oriented majority government.	Vote of no confidence in Laar because of the roubles sale scandal.*
Nov 1994 – Apr 1995	Andres Tarand (No party affiliation; later to lead Moderates)	Caretaker government on same basis as above; premature elections not desired.	'Right-centre' oriented majority government.	*Riigikogu* elections.
Apr 1995 – Nov 1995	Tiit Vähi (Coalition Party)	Coalition Party, 5 Centre Party, 4 Country P. P., 1 No affiliation, 4	'Centre' oriented majority government.	Vähi stepped down because of the 'Tape scandal'. **
Nov 1995 – Mar 1997	Tiit Vähi (Coalition Party)	Coalition Party, 4 Reform Party, 4 Country P. P., 2 No affiliation, 4	'Right-centre' oriented majority government until 21 Nov 1995, when the Reform Party quit the coalition.	Vähi forced to step down because of 'Real estate scandal'. ***
Mar 1997 – Mar 1999	Mart Siimann (Coalition Party)	Coalition Party, 6 No affiliation, 6 Country P. P., 2 Progress Party, 1	Centre-right oriented minority government.	Parliamentary elections.
Mar 1999 – Jan 2002	Mart Laar (Pro Patria Union)	Pro Patria U., 5 Reform Party, 5 Moderates, 5	Right-wing oriented majority government.	Rivalry between the Pro Patria Union and the Reform Party.
Jan 2002	Siim Kallas (RP)	Reform Party, 6 Centre Party, 8	Centre-right oriented minority government.	Parliamentary elections.
April 2003	Juhan Parts (Res Publica)	Res Publica, 5 Reform Party, 5 People's Union, 4	Right-centre oriented majority government.	

* 2.3 billion roubles that had been obtained when Estonia introduced its national currency, the kroon, had been sold clandestinely for 1.9 million US dollars.

** Edgar Savisaar had allegedly organized the taping of conversations with other political leaders during the government negotiations in April.

*** Vähi was accused of having arranged a cheap flat for his daughter in the centre of Tallinn.

APPENDIX 3.3: THE ELECTORAL SYSTEM

According to the *Riigikogu* Election Act of 11 July 1994, an Estonian citizen who has reached the age of eighteen by election day has the right to vote, and an Estonian citizen who has attained twenty-one years of age by the election day may run as a candidate.

Regular *Riigikogu* elections are held every fourth year – the first *Riigikogu*, however, was elected for only three years. Regular and extraordinary *Riigikogu* elections are called by the President of the Republic. The President may call extraordinary elections upon the request of the Government, or upon expression of no confidence either in the government or in the Prime Minister, pursuant to the Constitution.

Estonia is divided into eleven multi-member electoral districts. The 101 seats are distributed among electoral districts in proportion to the number of citizens with the right to vote.

An independent candidate or candidate list may be nominated by a political party. An independent candidate may be nominated by any Estonian citizen with the right to vote, including the prospective candidate himself or herself. If a political party nominates candidates in more than one electoral district, a national list of candidates specifying the rank order of candidates must be presented to the National Election Committee.

The distribution of mandates in the electoral districts is determined by three rounds of counting:

1. *First round of counting.* A simple quota is calculated for each electoral district by dividing the number of valid votes cast in the electoral district by the number of mandates. A candidate is elected in favour of whom the number of votes exceeds or equals the simple quota.

2. *Second round of counting.* In the lists competing for the national pool of equalizing mandates, the candidates are ranked according to the number of votes received. The votes cast in favour of all candidates running on the same list are added up. A list receives as many mandates as the number of times the votes it receives exceeds the simple quota, but an individual candidate on the list must receive at least 10 per cent of the simple quota in order to be elected.

3. *Third round of counting.* Mandates, which are not distributed in the electoral districts, are distributed as compensation mandates among the national lists of political parties, the candidates of which receive at least 5 per cent of the votes nationally, but not between fewer than two lists. A modified d'Hondt distribution method with the distribution series of $1, 2^{0.9}, 3^{0.9}$, etc., is used.

Political parties and independent candidates shall, within one month after the announcement of the election results, submit a report to the National Election Committee concerning expenses incurred and sources of funds used for the election campaign.

The electoral system has been the same since the 1992 elections, the major amendment being that electoral alliances were forbidden before the elections of 1999.

According to the President of the Republic Election Act of 18 May 1996, the President of the Republic is elected by the *Riigikogu*. If the *Riigikogu* fails to elect the President, an electoral body shall convene to elect the President. Anyone born an Estonian citizen and at least forty years of age, may be nominated as candidate for the presidency. The right to nominate a candidate for the presidency rests with no less than one-fifth of the 101 members of the *Riigikogu*. A member of the *Riigikogu* may nominate only one candidate. A person can be elected President only for two consecutive five-year terms. In 1992-96, however, a four-year term was applied.

In all three rounds in the *Riigikogu*, a candidate who receives a two-thirds majority of the full caucus of the Riigikogu (i.e. at least 68 votes) is elected President. If no candidate receives the required majority in the first round, a second round of voting is held on the following day, preceded by a new round of nomination of candidates. In the case of a third round of voting, the members of the *Riigikogu* have a choice between the two most successful candidates in the second round of voting.

If no candidate receives the required majority in the third round, the Chairman of the *Riigikogu* convenes an electoral body for the election of the President of the Republic. The electoral body consists of the members of the *Riigikogu* and of representatives of the local government councils (in 1996, there were 273 representatives; thus the total number in the electoral body was 374). A minimum of 21 members of the electoral college has the right to nominate a candidate for election. No member of the electoral body may nominate more than one candidate. A candidate obtaining a majority vote in the electoral body is considered elected. If no candidate receives a majority, a second round of voting shall be held on the same day between the two candidates who received the greatest number of votes in the first round.

Source: Estonian Legislation in Translation: Legal Acts of Estonia, No. 7, July 1996, Estonian Translation and Legislative Support Centre.

APPENDIX 3.4: THE CONSTITUTIONAL FRAMEWORK

Adopted in a referendum on 28 June 1992, the Constitution of the Republic of Estonia vests legislative power in the *Riigikogu*. The *Riigikogu* shall: pass laws and resolutions; decide on the holding of a referendum; elect the President of the Republic; ratify or reject international treaties; authorize the candidate for Prime Minister to form the Government of the Republic; pass the state budget and approve the report on its implementation. Upon the initiative of the President, it appoints the Chief Justice of the Supreme Court, the Chairman of the Board of the Bank of Estonia, the Auditor General, the Legal Chancellor and the Commander or the Commander-in-Chief of the Defence Forces; upon the proposal of the Chief Justice of the Supreme Court, it appoints Justices of the Supreme Court. The *Riigikogu* decides upon the expression of no confidence in the Government, the Prime Minister or individual Ministers. Upon the proposal of the President, it is entitled to declare a state of war, and order mobilization and demobilization.

The President of the Republic shall: represent the Republic of Estonia internationally; initiate amendments to the Constitution; designate the candidate for Prime Minister; appoint to and release from office members of the Government; serve as the Supreme Commander of the Defence Forces; and appoint the President of the Bank of Estonia on the proposal of the Board of the Bank.

The President shall, within fourteen days after the resignation of the Government of the Republic, designate a candidate for Prime Minister. The candidate for Prime Minister shall, within seven days, present his/her government to the President, who shall appoint the government within three days. If a candidate for Prime Minister does not receive a majority of votes in the *Riigikogu*, or is unable to or declines to form a government, the President has the right to present another candidate for Prime Minister within seven days. If the President does not present a second candidate or if the second candidate is rejected by the *Riigikogu*, the right to nominate a candidate for Prime Minister is transferred to the *Riigikogu*. The *Riigikogu* shall then nominate a candidate for Prime Minister who shall present his/her government to the President. If the membership of a government is not presented to the President within fourteen days after the transfer to the *Riigikogu* of the right to nominate a candidate for Prime Minister, the President of the Republic shall declare extraordinary elections to the *Riigikogu*.

The Government shall resign upon: the convention of a newly elected *Riigikogu*; the resignation or death of the Prime Minister; the expression of no confidence in the government or the Prime Minister by the *Riigikogu*. The *Riigikogu* may express no confidence in the Government of the Republic, the Prime Minister, or an individual Minister. If no confidence is expressed in the Government or in the Prime Minister, the President may, upon the proposal by the Government and within three days, call extraordinary elections to the *Riigikogu*. The Government may tie the approval of a bill it introduces to the issue of confidence. If the *Riigikogu* does not approve the bill, the government shall resign. An individual member, faction, or committee of the *Riigikogu*, and the Government of the Republic have the right to initiate laws. The President of the Republic may only initiate amendments to the Constitution. The majority of the *Riigikogu* has the right to call upon the Government to initiate legislation desired by the *Riigikogu*.

The *Riigikogu* has the right to refer a bill or any issue to a referendum. A law, which is passed by referendum, shall promptly be proclaimed by the President. If the referendum does not produce a majority for the bill, the President shall declare extraordinary elections to the *Riigikogu*.

Laws shall be proclaimed by the President of the Republic. The President may refuse to proclaim a law passed by the *Riigikogu;* within fourteen days, he must return the law to the *Riigikogu* for a new debate and decision, along with his/her reasoned resolution. If the *Riigikogu* again passes the law unamended, the President shall proclaim the law or propose to the Supreme Court to declare the law unconstitutional. If the Supreme Court declares the law constitutional, the President shall proclaim the law.

Source: Estonian Legislation in Transition: Legal Acts of Estonia, No. 1, January 1996, Estonian Translation and Legislative Support Centre.

4. Latvia

Hermann Smith-Sivertsen

In this chapter we will sketch a proposal on the emerging cleavage structure of Latvian mass politics of the late 1990s and the first decade of the 21st century. It was argued as a tentative proposition that Latvia around 1997 had developed four basic cleavages of political relevance. The first was the independence cleavage. The second was the ethnic inclusion/exclusion cleavage. The third was the rural/urban cleavage. The fourth emerging cleavage was claimed to be that between the disadvantaged strata versus the managing, occupational elites (Smith-Sivertsen 1998).

The proposal that current Latvian mass politics – to a large extent expressed as popular participation through elections and parties – could be analysed in terms of these four cleavages will require a few notes on the concept of cleavages. After only five national elections, each of which significantly changed the party system, it can be argued that the short time span and the instability of the party system make possible only the observation of political divisions of a temporary nature, not cleavages. When such divisions continue to stay relevant (even if there are changes in terms of older or newer parties representing the divisions) and when these divisions also can be linked to social structure, then what we observe are probably emerging cleavages. Issue voting and voting according to social cleavages do not necessarily exclude each other; the two forms of voting can exist side by side.

The four divisions or cleavages treated here are likely to remain important – those who opposed independence and those who struggled for it at the critical historical junctures will be remembered for a long time to come. Besides, the incorporation process of the non-citizens will probably be a lasting feature. The linguistic interests of the Russophones in Latvia are also fundamentally different from those of the Latvian-speakers, and this too is a lasting feature. Also, many rural dwellers have economic needs different from those in the metropolitan areas. The introduction of market economy in a society in which most people were (and still are) living on a modest income and egalitarian by outlook, created a setting in which some groups turned out more adaptable and other groups came out as losers. When trying to make sense of political participation in Latvia from the transition and onwards, political contradictions embedded in socio-economic interests or related to specific social groups, are increasingly identifiable.

The cleavage approach applied on Latvia in this chapter is primarily a model based on data about the parties' electorates assessed within the particular context of this country. The model is based on the assumption that a certain degree of correlation exists between the main policy messages of the parties and the social and ethnic characteristics of the parties' electorates. Even so, the cleavage model of Latvian mass politics that we propose is a tentative one: the cleavages are weakly institutionalized as the parties' memberships are small and the interest organizations are not powerful. We also lack data about the level and quality of the diffusion of mass consciousness about cleavages in Latvia. Furthermore, our cleavage model may later be corroborated or challenged by new electoral data as well as new interpretations of the context.

The Relevance of History

From the point of view of the perspective applied by Lipset and Rokkan (1967), cleavages become significant at different stages in history; they are developed over time; and the historical roots of current manifest and latent cleavages are often regarded as important in explaining the nature of the current cleavages. Thus, a cleavage model should be related to history. Yet in fact, the social and political similarities between Latvia by the turn of the millennium and Latvia of the inter-war era are few. During the previous period of independence, Latvia was predominantly agrarian: in 1935, farming accounted for more than two-thirds of the labour force (Spekke 1951). In Latvia as of 2000, the total share of agriculture, hunting, forestry and fishing was 13.5 per cent only, while more than two-thirds of the population live in towns and urban areas. In inter-war Latvia, the social democrats were always the largest and the Farmers' Union the second largest party. Party fragmentation was extreme, with 22 to 27 parties gaining representation in the 100-seat *Saeima* in the four elections from 1922 to 1931. Regional parties proliferated, and the German, Jewish and Russian ethnic minorities had their own parallel party systems. Grand coalitions were a rare occurrence too. All these political features have been absent since Latvia regained independence. The introduction of an electoral threshold of 4 per cent in 1993 – stepped up to 5 per cent in 1995 – probably accounts for some features of the new party system.

So what is left of inter-war Latvia? The constitutional framework and the political-institutional model were resurrected after independence was regained in 1991, and the legitimacy of the republic has its foundation in the inter-war republic. The core body of citizens was defined by their or their families' relationship to the republic before 1940. Two other current traits can be traced back to the inter-war era. One is the absence of large parties: even the two largest parties cannot form an absolute parliamentary majority in the *Saeima*. This was the case during the inter-war era, and again from 1994. The second quality is the apparent weakness of Russian ethno-political mobilization. In 1925, 12.6 per cent of Latvia's citizens were ethnic Russians, yet in the inter-war years the Russians never had more than 6 per cent of the seats in the *Saeima* despite the highly proportional electoral system. The small German minority in 1925 of 3.8 per cent normally won 6 per cent of the seats, and there were always at least as many German as Russian *Saeima* deputies (Garleff 1976).

Other historical periods than the inter-war era are arguably more important for the current cleavage formation. The crucial phase of Latvian nation-building took place in the 19th century when Latvia was an integral part of the Russian empire. The nation-building effort was a two-front struggle against linguistic Russification and Baltic German economic dominance. Current disagreements regarding the capacity of the Latvian nation and state to integrate ethnic non-Latvians can probably be traced back to this period, but even so, developments during the Soviet era are probably more important for recent cleavage formation. The post-communist economic problems in Latvia are rooted in the industrialization and urbanization processes that took place during the Soviet era. The fundamental change in the ethnic balance in Latvia also took place in these years, mainly due to immigration and deportation.

The influx of Russian-speakers was reinforced by the extensive purge of the Latvian national communists from the party in 1959–60 (Misiūnas and Taagepera 1993); in Soviet Latvia, Russians and Russian-born Latvians dominated the Communist Party. As Kjetil Duvold and Mindaugas Jurkynas point out in the following chapter, there were no such purges in Lithuania; the Lithuanians were allowed to take full control of the republic Communist Party there. The destiny of the national communists in Latvia was probably also important for the later transition to democracy. In the late 1980s, the national communists found themselves too weak to sustain a significant political party, and chose to join or endorse the main independence movement. As opposed to Poland, Hungary and Lithuania, Latvia has not experienced a return to power of the communist successor parties. This is partly due to the fact that the prominent national communists of Latvia have aligned themselves with many different parties and groups. The diverse political career patterns of the former members of the Latvian *nomenklatura* paved the way for a party system dominated by dimensions other than the pro- versus anti-communist division, prevalent in many other post-communist East European countries (cf. Chapters 6 and 12).

A Tentative Model of Cleavages and Parties

In this chapter, four cleavages – pertaining to independence, ethnic inclusion/exclusion, rural versus urban, and the disadvantaged strata against the occupational elites – are presented according to the sequence in which the conflict became manifest in the party system. We claimed in early 1998 (Smith-Sivertsen 1998) that the most salient cleavages in Latvia in the late 1990s were those of ethnic inclusion/exclusion and the socio-economically disadvantaged versus the occupational elites. The citizenship referendum in the autumn of 1998, the pensions referendum in November 1999 and the successful popular referendum drive to stop the privatization of the Latvenergo company in 2000 proved our predictions right. With these two cleavages as our point of departure, we may suggest a tentative model of cleavages and parties of current Latvia:

Figure 4.1: Party positions on the national and socio-economic cleavages

	Parties with over-representation of the adaptable and the emerging middle-classes	*Parties with over-representation of the disadvantaged strata*
Latvian nationalist parties	For Fatherland and Freedom (LNNK) 1995 and 1998	
		Latvian Farmers' Union and Latvian Christian Democratic Union 1995[*]
	Peoples Party (TP) 1998	
Socio-economic parties	Latvia's Way 1995	People's Movement for Latvia (Siegerist Party) 1995
	Democratic Party–*Saimnieks* 1995	The 'New Party' 1998
		Social Democratic Alliance LSDP/LSDSP [**] 1995 and 1998
		'Latvian Unity Party' 1995
Russophone-friendly parties		National Harmony Party 1995 and 1998
		Latvian Socialist Party 1995

[*] The 1995 electoral alliance between the Farmers' Union and the Christian Democrats took an intermediate position between the nationalist parties and the socio-economic parties.
[**] Survey data from the 1995 elections show that those voting for the social democratic alliance 'Labour and Justice' were in a socio-economically intermediate position. In Figure 4.1, this coalition is listed as belonging to the 'disadvantaged strata' category due to the type of voters it seems to have attracted when it had its electoral breakthrough, in the local elections of 1997. However, survey data to corroborate this assumption is not available.

Everyone who has read political science studies of post-Soviet Latvia must have noticed that ethnic Latvians now only constitute a rather modest majority of the residents there, with 36.1 per cent of the current inhabitants having Russian as their mother tongue, including ethnic Russians, Belorussians and Ukrainians. In January 2003, only 42.9 per cent of the resident Russophones possessed Latvian citizenship, 54.2 per cent of the Russian-speakers living in Latvia were non-citizens, and the remaining were citizens of other countries.

So to ask if 'class' matters to current and future Latvian politics can indeed seem bold and/or irrelevant. Party names tell a story too. In Latvia, not a single party claiming to be socialist, social democratic, workers' or representing the underprivileged or defrauded, won significant support in the 1993 and 1995 elections. None of these parties entered parliament in 1993, and in 1995 only one of them, the Latvian Socialist Party (LSP), won parliamentary representation after having polled 5.6 per cent of the vote.[1] In these two elections, not a single party in Latvia marketed itself as 'leftist' or 'communist'. When looking at the election result of 2002, we are faced with the same absence of explicit references to the left in the party labels. Some leftist hardliners (of the LSP) did manage to get elected, though.

This quick glance at party labels corroborates Anton Steen's suggestion (1997a, 8; 1997b, 207) that the emergence of class-based parties seems unlikely in Latvia. Steen asserts that this is due to the dominance of the issue of ethnic cohesion. He argues that socio-economic cleavages are unlikely to de-politicize ethnic tensions by cutting across ethnic groups, and that a party system along ethnic divisions is gradually emerging. In this case, Russian-speaking citizens will vote for Russophone parties to the extent that they vote at all. Steen builds this claim on the argument put forth by Graham Smith (1996), that the Russian-speakers in Latvia opted for ethnically distinct political parties in 1995. However, Smith did not corroborate his argument with survey data. As opposed to Smith, other observers (Kolstø and Tsilevich 1997, 376) claim that Latvia is a special case in Central and Eastern Europe due to the absence of ethnic-minority political parties of significance. A voter survey of the 1995 general election suggested that the picture of ethnic voting is too simplistic. Ethnicity does matter, but so do other factors. By way of example, the NORBALT living conditions project concluded that, as far as mass attitudes go, 'ethnic affiliation does not play the dividing role we may have anticipated' (Jacobsen 1996).

In a 1996 research report, Steen (1996, 196) concludes that the 'deep ethnic cleavages' between the Russians and the Latvians have been the 'overriding basis of conflict' in Latvia (and also in Estonia). When state-building and nation-building processes dominate the agenda, such a statement may be true. Empirical research on the elite level may also convey another picture than research on the mass level. We would argue that severe socio-economic hardship strongly affects the everyday lives of most of the residents regardless of ethnicity. When the socio-economic conflicts of interest become clarified, these questions can also cause increased tensions inside the core nation and sooner or later demonstrate a significant mobilizing power. Nørgaard et al. (1996) suggest that the parties in Latvia should be placed within a two-dimensional matrix, with a radical/moderate dimension on the ethno-political issue and a 'political/economic left/right cleavage'. The Nørgaard model is indeed helpful, but it was constructed without corroboration by voter survey data. The model seems to be founded solely on the author's evaluation of the policy positions of the parties prior to the 1995 election campaign.

This chapter will offer another perspective than that of Steen and Smith. Our position is closer to that of Nørgaard: we will argue that the dominant conflict issues in Latvian politics have changed in recent years. From 1988 until 1991, the relationship to the Soviet Union was the dominant issue. Between 1991 and 1994, economic hardship was a significant issue, but the political-cultural inclusion/exclusion issue regarding the Soviet-era Russophone immigrants and the Citizenship Law created the most heated debate. Since 1995, however, the socio-economic predicaments have constituted the most important issues in Latvian politics. The issue of cultural and political inclusion/exclusion remains at the centre of an important but less heated political conflict, which flared up as the most salient issue during the autumn of 1998 (due to the referendum that the Latvian nationalists initiated and lost). The inclusion/exclusion or 'ethnic' issue is not only a Latvian/Russophone conflict but also a Latvian/Latvian conflict. During the early 1990s, it basically boiled down to a disagreement over citizenship laws. After 1998, however, the focus is mainly on issues of language and education policies.

The Independence Cleavage

The dominant conflict from 1988 to 1991 was the question of independence. In the single-seat constituency elections to the Latvian Supreme Council in March–April 1990, the pro-independence side needed to win a minimum of 134 seats. Under Soviet statutes, a two-thirds majority was required to enact constitutional changes. At a time when the Latvian share of the electorate was only about 52 per cent, with an 81.3 per cent turnout, 68.2 per cent of the votes cast were for the candidates of the pro-independence Latvian People's Front. It elected 144 deputies, of whom 138 voted for the resolution of independence in May 1990. Without Russophone support or indifference, this outcome would not have been possible (Lieven 1993; Dreifelds 1996). But ethnicity did matter. Opinion polls conducted in March 1991 showed that 38 per cent of the non-Latvians and 94 per cent of the ethnic Latvians supported independence. The independence referendum that month resulted in 73.7 per cent of the participants voting in favour, with an impressive 87.6 per cent turnout. The result would have been much more ambiguous if significant Russophone support for independence had not been forthcoming. According to Dreifelds (1996, 69), the pro-Soviet Communist Party and the Interfront attracted 20–30 per cent of non-ethnic Latvians in 1990, while an equal share of that group supported the Latvian People's Front (*Latvijas tautas fronte,* LTF).

The struggle for independence created the strongest political mass movements Latvia had seen in decades. The Latvian People's Front mustered a membership of 110,000 in October 1988 (Dreifelds 1996), and Karklins claims that the Front's membership had grown to 230,000 registered members by the spring of 1989 – i.e. one member for every ninth inhabitant (Aasland 1996). The more radical independence activists organized themselves within the framework of the National Independence Movement (LNNK), which had joined forces with the Front. Outside the LTF stood the weaker and more radical Citizens committees (Congress Movement). The independence issue mainly mobilized and unified the Latvians and divided the Russophones; thus it both was and was not a contradiction defined by ethnicity. Yet the over-representation of Russian-speakers on the losing side may have fostered suspicions about loyalty to the state among the Russophones, thereby legitimizing their non-inclusion.

Was the independence cleavage a transitional cleavage that determined political divisions only at an early stage? Soon after independence, the LTF started to disintegrate into factions and nascent political parties. In the pro-independence camp, this cleavage was indeed transitional, but it divided the Russophone group more permanently. Russia recognized Latvia's independence in late August 1991. Some years later, those parties in Latvia which were most dependent on the Russophone vote and which advocated citizenship rights to non-citizens, were split by the independence cleavage. The Equal Rights Movement and the Socialist Party (LSP) were the political heirs to the groups that resisted full independence. The pro-independence National Harmony Party (TSP) in the 1993 and 1995 elections attracted support from Russophone groups and from some anti-nationalist Latvians. The independence cleavage contributed much to prevent the creation of one significant, unified party, which would advocate citizenship for stateless residents and be sympathetic to Russophone interests. With a potential constituency of nearly 20 per cent of the post-1991 electorate, a successful Russophone party could have had an impressive parliamentary impact, I claimed in early 1998 (Smith-Sivertsen 1998). And in the elections of late 1998 and 2002 we witnessed the electoral success of a united Russophone-friendly bloc of TSP, LSP and Equal Rights. First the coalition ran under the label of TSP and in 2002 the bloc was called 'For Human Rights in a United Latvia' (PCTVL). The three parties in it never merged but for four and a half years the partners had a common caucus in the *Saeima* and joint lists in elections. However, in February 2003, the historical independence cleavage seemed to resurface within the Russophone-friendly camp. The 12 TSP-deputies left the PCTVL faction and were joined by four deputies who are members of Equal Rights. The rump PCTVL only has five strongly leftist LSP members and three Equal Rights deputies.

However, even if the independence cleavage in the course of time loses its significance, the Russian-speaking electorate may still split along at least two dimensions: rejection of or compliance with Latvian nation-building policies, as well as along a socio-economic axis.

The independence cleavage also seems to have been branding the Equal Rights Movement and the Socialist Party as pariahs in Latvian politics. This has reduced the likelihood of mutual cooperation between the Russophone-friendly parties and the ethnic-Latvian leftist and centre-left parties. Still, such cooperation turned out to be possible in the Riga local government from 2001, in the national referendum drives over pensions, and in the Latvenergo-privatization scheme.

A Single Dominant Ethnic Cleavage?

The citizenship issue became crucial in Latvian politics when the bulk of the resident Russophones – the Soviet-era settlers – were legally defined as non-citizens in October 1991. The Latvian Supreme Council ruled that citizenship should be granted to pre-1940 citizens and their descendants; other residents could be naturalized contingent upon a set measure of knowledge of spoken Latvian, sixteen years of residency and the renouncement of non-Latvian citizenship. These guidelines for naturalization were not passed into law because of opposition from Latvian nationalists who thought this policy was too inclusive. From 1991, a conflict between moderate Latvians and radical nationalist Latvians started to develop. Legislation regulating the mode and pace of naturalization was not enacted until 1994, and actual naturalization began only early in 1995. Latvian moderates advocated limited, slow and strict naturalization with a quota to be decided annually. This had been the policy of the 1993–94 ruling elitist-liberal Latvia's Way and the Farmers' Union. The Latvian nationalist position was to oppose any naturalization of Slavic non-citizens or to create a quota regime, which would make naturalization virtually impossible. It was proposed that the annual quota should not exceed 10 per cent of the natural growth rate of the Latvian population, a proposal that left virtually no room for naturalization given the low birth rate in Latvia. The 'For Fatherland and Freedom' movement and the Latvian Independence Movement (LNNK) proposed such policies in 1993 (Røeggen 1997). Being a part of the ruling grand coalition from December 1995, these two parties gradually learned to live with the policy of Latvia's Way, as well as with the liberalizing international pressures in this regard. Due to pressure from the latter, quotas were rejected and instead, annual application windows were introduced from 1996 for different age groups. In 1998, these windows were abolished and all non-citizens permanently living in Latvia could apply for naturalization. Until 1 January 1998, a modest 6,993 individuals had been naturalized. There were many reasons why so few of the eligible residents applied for naturalization: the language proficiency requirement; the military draft; the visa regime between Latvia and Russia; and the high naturalization fee (Hendra 1997). These fees were significantly reduced in 2001. By December 2002, a total of 59,239 persons had been naturalized. The referendum in 1998 also gave children of non-citizens, born in Latvia after August 1991, the right to become citizens without screening procedures. By late 2002, as many as 995 children had become Latvian citizens this way (data from the Naturalization Board).

Since the naturalization process started, the political conflict over the citizenship question has gradually become less heated (Dreifelds 1996, 98). In January–February 1996, during the early months of the Šķēle grand coalition, the leading nationalist 'For Fatherland and Freedom' party initiated a petition for a more strict citizenship law. But the party failed, although only just, to mobilize 10 per cent of the electorate to sign the proposal, which would have set annual quotas equivalent to a maximum of 0.1 per cent of the citizenry to be naturalized. If the parliament had rejected a petition for stricter citizenship legislation with the required number of signatures attached to it, the proposal could have become the object of a popular referendum already in 1996. The nationalists succeeded in the 1998 referendum drive, but lost the popular vote.

In 1997, 28 per cent of the registered residents of Latvia were non-citizens. By early 2003, this share had been reduced to 22 per cent. The non-citizens are mainly Russian-speaking. The gradual integration of these Russian-speakers may make for political tensions for a number of years to come. However, tensions can also be managed. In the cooperation agreement of the 1995–98 ruling grand coalition, consensus among the ruling parties was required for any amendments to the legislation on citizenship and naturalization. This agreement seemingly provided the nationalist parties with a veto against legislation that would speed up naturalization. At the end of the day, the nationalists did not manage to halt the softening of the citizenship policies that was passed from 1998 and onwards. Still the climate of the grand coalition partly stabilized and partly postponed the citizenship issue, and this paved the way for the socio-economic issues to attract more of political attention.

This inclusion/exclusion question could be understood in terms of the conflict about the nature of the Latvian nation and its relationship to the outside world. The liberal nationalists in Latvia's Way, other moderate Latvian parties, and the patriotic nationalists who in 1997 united in the 'For Fatherland and Freedom' (LNNK) all agree that Latvia should be a 'one-community nation-state giving the traditional minorities the right of cultural autonomy'. The disagreement is more a question of optimism or pessimism regarding the prospects of integration of the Russophones in the one-community state. This sentiment is probably influenced by the view of the Latvian nation as the victim or the prospective victor. In the Soviet epoch, Latvians had to be bilingual while resident Russian-speakers were mainly monolingual. For Latvian school children, English has now become the first and compulsory foreign language while the study of the Russian language is no longer compulsory. Russophone school children face a different emerging situation. The educational system for the minority is still in the making, but it seems that Russian-speaking school children will be taught both in Russian and Latvian. In the future, resident Russophones will have to be bilingual while the Latvians may act as monolinguals in domestic public life. Other trends also favour this vision of one community. Differences in birth rates between ethnic Latvians and Russian-speakers will probably increase the ethnic Latvian share of the population from 56.7 per cent in 1997 to about 60 per cent in 2007.

Moreover, more residents regard themselves as Latvians than indicated by official statistics (Aasland et al. 1996, 34). The 1995 *Central and Eastern Eurobarometer* survey also found that 60.1 per cent of the population of Latvia thought of themselves as Latvians, which gives an ethnic Latvian share more than three percentage points higher than the officially reported share at that time (Berglund and Aarebrot 1997). This is probably due to the fact that some people speak Latvian at home, but may be registered as ethnic Russians or ethnic Poles in their passports. The census of 2000 reported that the share of Latvian residents was 57.6 per cent and that 62 per cent of the population claim that Latvian is their native language. The fact that Latvian passports state the holders' ethnicity contributes to the complications for those Latvian-speaking citizens who are officially ethnic non-Latvians so they hardly feel co-opted into the nation. Latvian national identity is basically ethnic (Kruks 1997). However, back in 1991, citizenship was granted on the 'First Republic' option, which was more inclusive to non-Latvians than an ethnic definition of citizens would have been.

The Russophones

The human rights situation for non-citizens in Latvia was rather serious in 1992–94. When the status of non-citizens was legally defined in 1995, the human rights situation improved. By the mid-1990s, the number of restrictions on non-citizens had decreased; by way of example, they no longer receive 90, but 100 per cent of the basic pension to which all Latvians are entitled. Opinion polls also suggest that there has been a significant decline in ethnic tensions after 1993 (Hendra 1997).

Citizenship was not all that mattered. Did the Russophones react strongly when their language lost status due to the strict language laws? A thorough Latvification of the ministries and government agencies was carried out in 1992–93 through mandatory language tests for those with a non-Latvian education (Kolstø and Tsilevich 1997), and as a result, almost all jobs in the state apparatus have been occupied by Latvians. Language tests were also carried out in the private sector. Despite this, the Russophones responded with political inactivity. Indeed, in the parliamentary elections of 1993 and 1995, the proportion of non-Latvians elected was less than half the non-Latvians' share of the electorate. Kolstø and Tsilevich (1997) argue that ethnic mobilization of Russians and other Russian-speakers has been largely absent in Latvia. However, the electoral success of the Russophone-friendly coalition 'For Human Rights in a United Latvia' (PCTVL) – which polled 19.04 per cent of the votes in the 2002 election – is an important exception. The salient issues of language rights in secondary schools and local governments probably have a stronger mobilizing impact on the Russophones, than the issues of citizenship and language requirements for ministry jobs. But, it is also worth noting that no less than 30 per cent of the PCTVL-*Saeima*-candidates in 2002 were ethnic Latvians. This testifies to the reluctance of the elites of Latvia to accept ethnic electoral lists.

The Salience of the Ethnic Inclusion/Exclusion Dimension

So far, Latvian post-communist politics has mainly been a product of two sets of conflicts. The first to become manifest pertained to the processes of state-building and nation-building, i.e. issues regarding independence, ethnicity and power, citizenship and language. The second set of conflicts, which has a distinct socio-economic flavour to it, has gained in importance since naturalization proceedings opened up and, particularly, since the approach to ethnicity by the nationalist parties became tempered by their need to maintain working parliamentary coalitions. Anti-elitist sentiments and the emerging social stratification are increasingly making themselves felt; and the socio-economic conflicts between ethnic Latvians are mainly independent of their attitudes towards naturalization and citizenship.[2]

Indeed, it is very hard to explain Latvian elections only in terms of state-building and nation-building conflicts, such as independence and inclusion/exclusion. The victors in the 1993, 1995 and 1998 *Saeima* elections and in the 1997 and 2001 local elections were neither the Latvian nationalist parties nor the Russophone-friendly parties. Instead, parties stressing socio-economic issues and downplaying inter-ethnic issues came out on top. The popularity of the individual candidates, campaign funding and success in attracting the media obviously played a role in facilitating the electoral success or failure of the parties, but it would be too cynical to disregard the main policy messages of the parties at the time when they made their electoral breakthroughs.

Socio-economic issues were already important in the 1993 elections. In fact, the failure of the ruling Latvian People's Front to win any seats at all may be attributed to two factors related to this dimension: the deteriorating living standards and the increasing gaps between social strata (Cerps 1994, 89). Income differentiation is not popular in Latvia. In the mid-1990s, more than 80 per cent of the population had the opinion that the income differences 'should be less' (Jacobsen 1996, 180). The victor of the 1993 election, Latvia's Way, was heterogeneous, composed of both radicals and moderates from the Latvian People's Front, and held together by basic agreement on economic reform (Lieven 1993, 301). Latvia's Way included some former members of the *nomenklatura* as well as Latvian *émigré* organizations in the West. The most successful electoral lists in 1993 were those that were most seriously preoccupied with the socio-economic area (Freimanis and Semanis 1994, 66). Surveys conducted in 1993 indicated that the issues with the highest priorities among the voters were economic problems, unemployment and agriculture; citizenship was only the seventh important issue.

The 1993 electoral programme of Latvia's Way was basically concerned with economic questions. It was also helpful that this electoral list had the most popular politicians and the biggest campaign budget (Dreifelds 1996). Centre-right Latvia's Way won 36 per cent of the seats in 1993. The nationalist-oriented Latvia's National Independence Movement (LNNK), which won 15 per cent of the seats, was one of the medium-sized parties to make an electoral breakthrough. LNNK changed its name to Latvia's National Conservative Party (LNNK), and in 1997 it merged with the other main nationalist party. The Russophone-friendly, centre-left 'Harmony for Latvia–Revival for the Economy' was yet another successful, newcomer, winning 13 per cent of the seats. In 1994, this party split into the National Harmony Party and the Political Union of Economists, of which the latter participated in the Gailis cabinet but did not survive the 1995 elections. The Farmers' Union was the fourth largest party in 1993. Four more parties each obtained 5–7 per cent of the seats in 1993. Of the eight parties represented in parliament, the Equal Rights Movement was alone in not endorsing independence; the bulk of the remaining seven were offshoots from the People's Front.

The ethnicity of the respondents, categorized as ethnic majority or ethnic minority, was recorded in a 1993 opinion poll on electoral preferences. The results indicate that 44 per cent of the ethnic Latvians would vote for moderate parties, such as Latvia's Way, the Democratic Centre and the Harmonists, while 39 per cent expressed preference for the parties, which were to form the 'National Bloc' (the LNNK, Fatherland and Freedom, the Christian Democrats and the Farmers' Union) in 1994. Among the ethnic minorities, 25 per cent expressed a preference for the Equal Rights

Movement and 19 per cent for the Harmony party – i.e. the two main Russophone-friendly parties had a total share of 44 per cent among the non-ethnic Latvians. But 36 per cent of the non-ethnic Latvians responded that they would vote for Latvian parties, mainly Latvia's Way and the Farmers' Union (Klingemann et al. 1994). The data corroborate the theory that ethnic mobilization among the minorities was quite weak in 1993, and that a very sizeable proportion of the ethnic Latvians did not endorse the least inclusive parties even in 1993, when the citizenship law was undecided.

Survey data on ethnic voting are not available for the 1993 *Saeima* elections, but for the 1995 and 1998 elections, the voting behaviour of ethnic Latvians can be compared with that of non-Latvians. The 1995 election was a serious blow both for the ruling Latvia's Way and for the main opposition parties, the LNNK and the Farmers' Union. The elections spelled breakthrough for the Democratic Party–*Saimnieks*. It advocated support for Latvian industry, emphasized professionalism, and at the time seemed centre-left. The populist parties (the Siegerist Party and the Unity Party) and the nationalist-oriented 'For Fatherland and Freedom' party also fared well. After the election, Maris Grinblats of 'For Fatherland and Freedom' was nominated as Prime Minister, but failed to win the vote of confidence. He was supported by the nationalist parties, the Farmers' Union and the Christian Democrats as well as by Latvia's Way. President Guntis Ulmanis then proposed Ziedonis Cevers of the DP–*Saimnieks* for Prime Minister, but the coalition of the DP–*Saimnieks* and the Unity, Siegerist and Harmony parties fell one vote short of obtaining the confidence of the *Saeima*. Eventually, a grand coalition was formed including the former governing party, Latvia's Way, as well as the nationalist parties, DP–*Saimnieks*, the Unity Party and the Farmers' Union. The Russophone-friendly parties and the largest populist party were left out in the cold.

This raises the question to which degree the Russian-speakers in the electorate mainly supported Russophone-friendly and non-citizen inclusive parties in the 1995 and 1998 elections.

Table 4.1 indicates that in 1995, some 52 per cent of the Russophones voted for the three parties that rank at the very top as regards inclusion of non-citizens and integration of Russian-speakers: the Socialist, the Harmony and the Russian parties. The communist successor Socialist Party offers the voters the option of a symbolic 'exit', while the centre-left Harmonists provides a 'voice' option (cf. Hirschman 1972). It will be remembered that the Russophone-friendly parties of Latvia do not express support for the current state-building and nation-building efforts; thus, Russian-speaking voters concerned about socio-economic issues while at the same time accepting the ongoing process of state- and nation-building, have to turn to other parties. Indeed, both in 1995 and 1998 no less than 46 per cent of the Russian-speakers opted for predominantly Latvian parties, most of them campaigning on a socio-economic platform, including issues such as the mode and pace of the transition from plan to market and of privatization, the plight of workers and the poor, anti-elitism, local industry and rural economic interests, and, last but not least, the importance of international trade and EU membership. The data would seem to suggest that the proportion of Russian-speakers supporting Latvian parties increased by 10 percentage units between 1993 and 1995. A collective wish among Russian-speakers to strengthen moderate ethnic Latvians against radical ethnic Latvians may partly explain this voting pattern.

Table 4.1: The ethnic Latvian and Russophone vote in the 1995 and 1998 elections (%)*

Party	Ethnic Latvian vote 1995	Ethnic Latvian vote 1998	Russophone vote 1995	Russophone vote 1998
Alliance Latvia's Way	16.2	17.2	8.0	14.7
Democr. Party–*Saimnieks*	15.8	0.7	12.6	2.6
The New Party	–	7.7	–	6.4
Peoples Movement for Latvia (Siegerist Party)	15.4	0.7	12.4	0.0
Union 'For Fatherland and Freedom' (TB/LNNK)	15.0	19.9	0.0	1.3
L. National Conservative Party** and L. Green Party	8.0	–	0.0	–
Peoples Party	–	29.2	–	10.2
Farmers' Union (LZS) and Christian Democrats	7.5	2.8 (only LZS)	2.2	0.0
L. Unity Party	6.8	0.4	7.8	1.3
L. Social-Democratic Union***	4.9	14.9	3.4	9.6
National Harmony party	1.8	2.7	21.7	50.3
Latvia's Socialist party (LSP)****	1.6	–	23.4	–
Party of Russian Citizens of Latvia	0.0	–	6.8	–
Other lists	7.0	3.7	1.7	3.8

* The Russophones consist of ethnic Russians and other non-Latvians. About two-thirds of the latter are Russophone. The data draw on surveys by the *Baltic Data House* as well as official statistics.[3] In 1995, the Russophones counted 175,656 voters as opposed to an estimated number of 758,469 ethnic Latvian voters.
** Merged with TB/LNNK in 1997.
*** In 1995, this list was labelled 'Coalition Labour and Justice' and consisted of the same parties as in 1998.
**** Ran on the Harmony list in 1998.

In the 1995 elections, 23 per cent of ethnic Latvians voted for the main Latvian nationalist parties: 'For Fatherland and Freedom' and the LNNK. Thus, ethnic Latvian support for the parties of the 'National Bloc' fell from 39 per cent in 1993 (Klingemann et al. 1994), to 30.5 per cent in 1995. This phenomenon was paralleled by an increased Russophone tendency to vote for ethnic Latvian parties, which would seem to suggest that ethnicity had lost salience between 1993 and 1995. Table 4.1 shows that 3.4 per cent of ethnic Latvians opted for one of the Russophone parties. This was of crucial importance: neither Socialists nor Harmonists would have overcome the 5 per cent electoral threshold in 1995 without some ethnic Latvian support. It should also be noted that more than half of ethnic Latvians voted for those predominantly Latvian parties that also enjoyed significant support among the Russian-speakers.

Some parties had an equally strong base of support among Russian-speakers and ethnic Latvians: the agrarian-oriented, rural-populist Unity Party; the anti-elite populist People's Movement for Latvia led by Joachim Siegerist; and the Democratic Party–*Saimnieks* for the support of local industry. These three parties made an electoral breakthrough in 1995, together polling no less than 37.4 per cent of the total vote. The electorally less successful social democratic coalition for 'Labour and Justice' also enjoyed similar levels of support among Latvians and Russian-speakers. Moreover, about 10 per cent of those who voted for liberal/elitist, centre-right Latvia's Way in 1995 were Russian-speakers, and Latvia's Way can be added to the list of the other four socio-economic parties. In 1995, these parties accounted for 56.7 per cent of the total vote, scoring 44.2 per cent among the Russian-speakers and 59.1 per cent among the ethnic Latvians. Also, in 1998, there were several parties well over the electoral threshold that all enjoyed support among Latvians as well as non-Latvians: the New Party (centrist), the social democratic alliance and pro-market Latvia's Way.

We may thus conclude that Latvia has an inclusion/exclusion cleavage that defines three groups: Russophone-friendly and Russophile parties, Latvian nationalist parties, and socio-economic parties, which enjoy support among ethnic Latvian as well as among Russian-speakers.

The Urban/Rural Cleavage

In the inter-war era, Latvia had several significant rurally based parties. The leading rural party was reborn when Latvia regained her independence and today several parties vie for the rural vote. In 1993, the Farmers' Union with its rural appeal (Freimanis and Semanis 1994, 67) became the fourth largest party, which does indeed raise the topic of the importance of the rural/urban cleavage in modern Latvia.

Economic reforms took off in the countryside. The Supreme Council passed legislation on land reform as early as June and November 1990. In 1991, collective and state farms held 92 per cent of all agricultural land in Latvia; four years later, this proportion had fallen to a mere 17 per cent. In 1996, private farmers controlled 80 per cent of the agricultural land. There are two kinds of individual farms: 64,000 family farms accounting for 47 per cent of the farmland in 1995, and part-time farms and private subsidiary plots accounting for 32 per cent (Zecchini 1996). By 1997, privatization was almost complete. Agriculture, forestry and fishing were significant job providers, accounting for 18.5 per cent of employment in 1995 (European

Commission 1997).

When represented in the *Saeima* (1993–98 and again from 2002), the Farmers' Union has been included in all governments save one. The exception was the 1994–95 Gailis cabinet dominated by Latvia's Way; the Farmers' Union left the government in the summer of 1994 after a controversy over import tariffs and farming subsidies (Dreifelds 1996). Following independence, Latvia adopted a liberal trade regime, but the agricultural sector remained sheltered from international competition, even though Latvia's free trade agreements with Estonia and Lithuania were extended to agricultural products in January 1997 (European Commission 1997). Latvia's limited financial resources restrict the scope for agricultural subsidies and credits for farming. Due to lack of investment, agriculture is backward and in decline (Hendra 1997). It remains to be seen what impact the EU membership will have from the spring of 2004 and onwards.

Farmers have their own interest organization, the Farmers' *Saeima*. *Lauku Avize* (Rural Newspaper), a biweekly with the highest circulation of any newspaper in Latvia, is close to the Farmers' *Saeima* (Prikulis 1997), but until 1998, it was sceptical of all parliamentary parties, including the Farmers' Union.

An urban/rural cleavage normally manifests itself in the form of parties with distinct rural constituencies and an equally distinct rural platform catering to farmers' interests. In Latvia, it still remains to be seen which political parties will permanently occupy the rural end of the urban/rural spectrum. In 1995, the electoral coalition of the Farmers' Union and the Christian Democrats stood out as strongly rurally oriented by polling 71.5 per cent of its votes in rural constituencies. The more populist Unity Party had 70 per cent of its voters in the countryside (Ikstens 1997). The People's Movement for Latvia (also known as the Siegerist Party) had a high share of rural votes – 60.5 per cent – but it also had strongholds in the urban environment of small towns, although not in metropolitan Riga. It is worth noting that only 31 per cent of the total population lived in rural areas as of 1995 (European Commission 1997); the rural areas, however, accounted for a slightly higher proportion of the electorate.

The main Russophone-friendly parties and the ethnic Latvian nationalist parties are clustered towards the urban end of the urban–rural continuum. The leading nationalist party, 'For Fatherland and Freedom', received in 1995 only 22.5 per cent of its votes from rural constituencies as opposed to 40.5 per cent from Riga, which accounted for 26 per cent of Latvia's electorate. The Democratic Party–*Saimnieks* and Latvia's Way both had mixed urban/rural support (Ikstens 1997). In 1995, the parties of socio-economic protest came out strongest in the countryside, while Latvian nationalist and Russian-speaking protest voters were mainly found in urban areas.

Data from the 1995 election testify to the emergence of an urban/rural cleavage. This can be interpreted as an actual cleavage or, for that matter, as a historical cleavage (cf. Chapters 2 and 16).

The *Lauku Avize* served as mouthpiece for the important new centre-right party that emerged in 1998, Andris Šķēle's People's Party (TP). The founders of the party (among them many farmers and persons with jobs connected to rural businesses) printed their manifest in that newspaper in the spring of 1998. The TP was founded and funded by Prime Minister Andris Šķēle (1995–97) who also was the owner of a huge food- processing conglomerate. Elected on the TP list to the *Saeima* in 1998 were three former prominent politicians from the Farmers' Union, two former *Saeima* deputies from the Christian Democrats, two former deputies from the Latvian Way, and one ex-minister and deputy of the former LNNK party. The TP had a catch-all profile in 1998, but it got particularly strong support from voters living in the villages, countryside and small towns, from voters in high income families and from ethnic Latvians. Despite receiving 80 per cent of its 1998 votes from rural areas, the Farmers' Union (LZS) dropped out of the *Saeima* in the 1998 election. However, it got 9.44 per cent of the votes in 2002, in an alliance with the small Green Party. Considering that the LZS lost its more rightist politicians to Šķēle in 1998, and compensated for this loss by recruiting some centre-left politicians as well, the author of this chapter would be inclined to see the LZS as a centrist party from 2002 and onwards. After 2002, TP is clearly to the right of LZS.

The Disadvantaged Versus Occupational Elites

Latvia has a historical labour/capitalist cleavage. Between 1922 and the 1934 *coup d'état,* the Latvian Social Democratic Party consistently came out as the strongest party, controlling 20–31 per cent of the parliamentary seats. In the 1990s, however, it was an open question whether, how or when this cleavage would reappear. In 1993, the historical Latvian Social Democratic Workers' Party (LSDSP) won only 0.7 per cent of the vote, while the former Latvian nationalist Communists – now campaigning on a social democratic platform as the Democratic Labour Party (LDDP, later renamed LSDP) – obtained an equally disappointing 0.9 per cent of the vote. Andris Siliņš, the chairman of the most important trade union, LBAS, ran together with the Pensioners' Association and received only 0.4 per cent (Cerps 1994). Two years after the 1993 electoral debacle, the two social democratic parties LSDSP and LDDP joined the tiny Justice Party and Siliņš (who by then had resigned as LBAS leader) in an electoral coalition. This coalition fell short of the five per cent threshold. To the extent that the disadvantaged strata voted differently than other strata in 1995, these voters must have preferred parties other than those of a social democratic flavour. Several opinion polls from late 1997 suggested that support for the social democrats was on the increase.

Employment and Trade Unionism

Already in early 1993, the majority of the total work force was privately employed. At the beginning of 1997, the private sector accounted for 64 per cent of employment and for 55 per cent of the GDP (Hendra 1995; 1997). In the late 1990s, privatization of large-scale industrial enterprises was remarkably slow as compared to the swift privatization of the agricultural sector and small-scale businesses (European Commission 1997). In 2000, the private sector accounted for 71 per cent of total employment and 67 per cent of the GDP (European Commission 2001). The position of labour is not strong in Latvia. However, the new paragraphs in the Constitution from 1998 may help to strengthen the position of employees. It is stated in paragraph 107 that '[e]very employed person has the right to receive, for work done, commensurate remuneration which shall not be less than the minimum wage established by the State, and has the right to weekly holidays and a paid annual vacation'. Paragraph 108 offers trade unions a significant legally protected position: 'Employed persons have the right to a collective labour agreement, and the right to strike. The State shall protect the freedom of trade unions.'

According to official statistics, 7.2 per cent of the economically active were unemployed in 1996 (Hendra 1997). However, using ILO methodology, the real unemployment rate at the end of that year was estimated at 18.3 per cent (European Commission 1997). LBAS, the most important trade union, has 300,000 members, including pensioners and unemployed, but no central strike fund. Only a few of the LBAS member organizations had started to collect such funds in 1997. Some LBAS officials cooperate with political parties, but LBAS leaders are expected to be non-partisan. As LBAS sees it, strikes are very rare in Latvia due to the fact that striking workers have been at risk of losing their jobs, and the union itself tends to prefer demonstrations or negotiations with the government to strikes.

The labour/capital cleavage may be reinforced if the LBAS becomes wealthy enough to finance significant political parties. Before the 1998 election, the People's Movement For Latvia (the Siegerist Party) did stand out as closer to LBAS than to any other of the parties represented in the 1995–98 *Saeima*, when it came to willingness to act in support of union interests.[4] Even so, there were no formal connections between the Siegerist party and LBAS. A labour/capital cleavage is unlikely to become manifest until trade unions are strong enough to carry out effective strikes, and several unsuccessful strikes in the late 1990s bear witness to the weakness of organized labour.

In 1997, no less than 26.3 per cent of Latvia's population were pensioners, who had experienced a dramatic drop in living standards in the wake of the economic transition. The real income of pensioners declined between 1994 and 1996; and according to a 1997 report from the United

Nations Development Programme (UNDP), the average income of pensioners covers only 74.3 per cent of the 'crisis subsistence level'. The average monthly pension in November 1997 was 46 lats, the equivalent of 78 US dollars. The Socialists, the Siegerist Party and the social democrats (LSDSP/LSDP) are among the parties strongly advocating the cause of pensioners and other people with fixed incomes (Ikstens 1997; Prikulis 1997).

According to the 1997 UNDP report on Latvia, households with children or with unemployed members account for the bulk of the disadvantaged strata. Poverty is more widespread in the countryside than in urban areas, and particularly common in the eastern Latgale province. Between 44 and 67.9 per cent of Latvia's population was estimated to live in poverty. In 1995, per capita GDP adjusted for purchasing power was among the lowest in Central and Eastern Europe and the lowest among the three Baltic states (Hendra 1997). In this light, it would be unrealistic to expect poor people to vote mainly according to conflicts related to state-building and nation-building in one election after the other, to the detriment of their own economic interests.

Social Strata and Voting

The *Baltic Data House* voter survey of 1995 contained data about income, education, occupation and age of the surveyed voters. An analysis of the data indicated that voters in households with a monthly per capita income of less than 20 lats were over-represented among the supporters of the Harmony Party, the People's Movement for Latvia (Siegerist Party), the Unity Party, and the Farmers' Union-Christian Democratic alliance. More than 40 per cent of Siegerist Party voters belong to this low-income group, compared with only 21 per cent of those voting for 'Fatherland and Freedom'. The Russophone-friendly parties, the rural parties, and the populist Siegerist Party were the most successful among voters with 30 lats or less monthly income per household member. On the other end of the income axis, the better-off voters preferred Latvia's Way and 'Fatherland and Freedom'.

Latvia's Way and the DP–*Saimnieks* had the highest shares of entrepreneurs among their voters: 15 and 9 per cent, respectively. On the other hand, the two Russophone-friendly parties – the Harmonists and the Socialists – and the two populist protest parties (the Siegerist and Unity parties) obtained 14–29 per cent of their votes from among the unemployed – a category which did not include the retired, students and housewives.

Not surprisingly, voters with gloomy prospects in the transition from plan to market were over-represented among the voters of the Unity, Harmony and Siegerist parties. These parties were particularly successful among the 50 to 64-year-olds. Pro-market Latvia's Way was strongest among voters aged 18–24 years. In a similar vein, it may be noted that the Siegerist and Unity parties had strong bases of electoral support among voters with little education. The two nationalist parties, 'Fatherland and Freedom' and LNNK, were popular among university graduates, while the Siegerist and Unity parties found very little support within this group (Ikstens 1997).

The bottom line is that stratification probably mattered in the polling booth, but in a way that benefited not only more or less leftist parties but also protest-populist parties such as the Siegerist Party and the Unity Party. Latvia's Way and the DP–*Saimnieks* both emphasized economic issues and were capable of attracting ethnic Latvians as well as Russian-speakers. Both these parties provided some prominent former communists with a new political platform, which made them vulnerable to populist, anti-elitist attacks. The support for protest-populist parties indicates an inclination of disadvantaged groups – Latvians and Russophones alike – to join together in protest against social and economic hardship.

Indeed, a division between the emerging middle-class and the disadvantaged strata may be developing. In 1995, however, the tensions between the disadvantaged and the occupational elites were more dependent on age, education and place of residence than on position along the capital/labour dimension. The younger, the well-educated, the well-off and the urban dwellers tended to vote differently from the old, the unemployed, those with the lowest levels of education, the low-income groups and the rural population. The emerging middle-classes could accept the hardships of the transition to market with relative ease, due to their professional positions, their education, or their youth, and the time horizon deriving from youthfulness. The disadvantaged strata, on the other hand, have pronounced difficulties in coping with the transition, and the bleakest prospects in the market economy.

In their chapter, Mikko Lagerspetz and Henri Vogt point to a similar socio-economic cleavage in Estonia: the young, the city-dwellers, the well-educated and private-sector employees are those best off in the new system. However, this socio-economic cleavage has not yet had a fundamental impact on the Estonian party system. What makes Latvia a special case is the widespread anti-elitism in the country. This sentiment may reinforce the pattern of protest voting among the disadvantaged. It must not be forgotten that voter turnout in Latvia has surpassed that of Estonia and Lithuania for several consecutive parliamentary elections.

With 12.88 per cent of the votes and 14 seats, the social democratic alliance (LSDP and LSDSP) entered the *Saeima* in 1998. Despite the demand for centre-left alternatives, the merged social democrats – under the name of the historic party – got only 4.01 per cent and no seats in 2002. What was the reason? After 1999, there were serious conflicts within the merged party. Also, the party leader was easy to attack in the media because of his background in the KGB. The social democratic *Saeima* faction split and by

2002, three electoral lists used the label social democratic. The electoral defeat in 2002 prompted the leader of the merged party to resign. So during the 8th *Saeima*, the PCTVL, the National Harmony party and the Farmers' Union will have to carry the torch of a leftist, anti-market position without the benefit of social democratic support. The parties most in favour of market economy will be the new party of former president of the Bank of Latvia, Einars Repše, known as 'New Era' and the People's Party. In 1998, the latter party got strong support both from members of high-income households and from the unemployed. This shows the catch-all potential of pro market parties: some voters believe such parties can provide jobs.

Can quantitative research of electoral behaviour in Latvia confirm that disadvantaged strata vote in a similar way regardless of ethnicity? Yes, this is what regression analysis of a 1998 voter survey tells us (N = 860 party voters who used the franchise and were willing to reply to the questions). Left-wing and centre-left voting behaviour were in 1998 determined by three variables: being non-Latvian, being male, and having a low income. Of those in the lower-income brackets, 43.8 per cent voted centre-left as opposed to 28.6 per cent of those in the higher-income brackets. When controlling for ethnicity, we found that 35.2 per cent of low income ethnic Latvians vote centre-left – the preferred choice of just 23.3 per cent of those ethnic Latvians who are financially better off. In a similar vein, it may be noted that ethnic Latvians with higher education are more inclined to vote centre-right than those with only primary or secondary education; the difference is nine percentage points. Place of residence is also significant. Urban dwellers – ethnic Latvians and non-Latvians alike – are more inclined to vote left or centre-left than the inhabitants of small towns and rural areas. In 1998, the Farmers' Union and the People's Party were both regarded as centre-right parties. So this outcome may seem to reflect an urban–rural dimension.[5]

Emerging Socio-economic Cleavages in Riga

Of Latvia's five multi-seat *Saeima* electoral constituencies, Riga has shown the clearest signs of Latvian/Russophone political polarization. Of Riga's inhabitants, the majority of whom are Russian-speakers, the ethnic Latvians dominate the electorate with a share of 70 per cent (Kolstø and Tsilevich 1997); of all Latvian regions, Riga has the highest proportion of non-citizens among the local non-Latvian population (Aasland et al. 1996, 37). The stage is, in a sense, set for ethnic confrontation. In the 1995 parliamentary elections, Riga stood out as the stronghold of the two main Latvian nationalist parties ('For Fatherland and Freedom' and LNNK); together they polled 27.7 per cent of the Riga vote, as compared to 18.3 per cent of the total national vote. The pattern repeated itself in 1998, but the difference in TB/LNNK support in Riga and in the whole of Latvia was a little bit smaller in 1998. Surpassed only by Eastern Latgale, Riga was also a stronghold for the Russophone-friendly parties, which in 1995 won 18.8 per cent of the Riga vote as against 12.4 per cent nation-wide.

Riga municipal politics provides additional cues about the developing polarization between Latvian nationalists and Russian-speakers. In the 1994 city council elections, 14 parties gained representation on the council; three years later, 17 parties entered. These parties may be divided into three groups with respect to their main policy objectives at the time of their electoral breakthrough. One group consists of Latvian nationalist parties with a manifest non-inclusive policy as regards non-citizens. The parties in this group could get elected, even when their socio-economic policies were not well defined. The second group of parties includes those that are favourably inclined towards the Russian-speakers and in some cases have a socio-economic orientation too. The third group counts parties with vague inter-ethnic political profiles but with strong views on a variety of socio-economic issues, such as market reforms, privatization, and the promotion of businesses, the plight of the disadvantaged, poverty, crime, pensions and taxes. Some of these 'socio-economic' parties are pro-market and pro-business; others are populist and/or centre-left. What they have in common is that they leave it to others to campaign on inter-ethnic issues.

In the 1994 city council elections, the Latvian nationalist parties conquered 52 per cent of the Riga votes, the Russophone-friendly parties 9.1 per cent, and the socio-economic parties 31.5 per cent with the centre-left *Saimnieks* as the largest in this group. Three years later, however, the picture had changed. In the March 1997 local elections, the nationalist parties obtained 28.5 per cent of the Riga votes, the Russophone-friendly parties 14.3 per cent, and the socio-economic parties 49.8 per cent. Within the latter group, tensions increased as the centre-left social democrats took the lead with an 18.7 per cent share of the vote – up from a modest 4.7 per cent in 1994 – while centre-right pro-market Latvia's Way also improved strongly, from 3.5 per cent in 1994 to 14.1 per cent in 1997. The main issues in the 1997 campaign were social and economic. The social democrats attempted to appeal to low-income groups on issues such as rent control, heating and housing subsidies (*The Baltic Times,* Vol. 2, No. 49). The social democrats also set out to 'rid Riga of corruption and mafia influence', another pressing social problem. The social democrats were not alone in raising these socio-economic issues, but their pay-off was the best.

This changing centre of political gravity from nationalist to socio-economic parties in ethnically divided Riga is an important demonstration of how political cleavages in Latvia have developed. The most successful populist parties as of 1995 – the Siegerist and Unity parties – together polled a meagre 3.7 per cent of the Riga vote in 1997, down from 13.5 per cent in 1995. The populist failure and the social democratic success story were probably connected; it is not unlikely that many economically hard-pressed voters moved from the populists to the social democrats. In the 2001 local elections, the social democrats in Riga increased their support to 23.4 per cent of the votes, and the leftist PCTVL obtained 21.4 per cent. Supported by three small parties, the centre-left parties had the city council majority and the social democrats got to appoint the mayor. On the other side of the political spectrum, Latvia's Way and TP had jointly 19 per cent of the votes while the nationalists in TB/LNNK got 17.3 per cent. So on both sides, the socio-economic parties got more votes and seats than the ethno-linguistic parties.

A Model With Limitations

Many things still happen in Latvian politics that cannot be explained in terms of the four cleavages discussed at some length in this chapter. Every *Saeima* gets to greet parties not represented in the outgoing *Saeima*. And every election seems to produce a winner that is a new electoral option. Some times a political party takes over the general ideological position of one of its competitors. The 'For Fatherland and Freedom' party did this to LNNK in 1995, and Einars Repše's 'New Era' played the same trick on Latvia's Way in 2002.

A quick glance at the changing electoral coalitions, the changing party labels and the results of the four parliamentary elections between 1993 and 2002 conveys the impression of a party system in a state of flux. Though true, this interpretation does not provide the whole truth. There is in fact much more structure and stability to the Latvian party system than meets the eye in a simple inspection of party labels and electoral alliances. The candidates of the Latvian Socialist Party and those of the Equal Rights party have, for example, always stood together in every election during the last decade, but this is not readily apparent from the ballot labels. First these candidates used the label of the Equal Rights movement, then that of the LSP; in 1998 they were on the Harmony ballot lists, and in 2002, the entire coalition behind the Harmony lists of 1998 now labelled itself PCTVL. In 2002 a new party – 'Latvia's First Party' – emerged with several religious leaders among its candidates. For all intents and purposes, however, this party is the electoral vehicle for the remnants of the Christian Democratic Union; the rump of the People's Front (that ran for office in 1993 and 1995), as well as a third of the 1998-deputies of the 'New Party'. Known party actors often re-emerge under new labels and in new electoral coalitions. What seems novel is not really new.

Conclusions

The author of this chapter emphasized the importance of the socio-economic dimension in Latvian politics, also when writing his contribution to the first edition of the *Handbook of Political Change in Eastern Europe*. The following year, another scholar published an in-depth analysis of the programmatic and economic profiles of contemporary Latvian parties (Nissinen 1999). It is an excellent piece of work; gratifying to this author are the many parallels between her approach and his own. She criticizes the overemphasis on ethnic problems in most studies of Latvian politics. She documents the significant differences between Latvian parties with respect to economic policies. She sorts out parties that mobilize on socio-economic matters from those that do so on ethno-linguistic issues. And just like this author, she finds more socio-economic parties than strictly ethno-linguistic parties.

Latvian parties do not have stable bases of electoral support, but Latvian mass politics is not completely unstructured. In 1995, more than 40 per cent of the voters postponed their voting decision until the very last week prior to the elections (Zepa 1996). The independence cleavage and the ethnic inclusion/exclusion cleavage currently seem to be clearly linked to the party system. The rural/urban cleavage seems significant, but the relationship between rural parties and rural voters is less permanent. The emerging cleavage between the disadvantaged strata versus the occupational elites is also unstable. This fourth cleavage might be interpreted as protest voting, but it has a strong socio-economic component attached to it that might be reinforced in the future.

Acronyms of Parties and Movements

DP–*Saimnieks*	*Demokratiska partija–Saimnieks* (Democratic Party–Saimnieks)
LBAS	*Latvijas Brīvo arodbiedrību savienībā* (Free Trade Union Confederation of Latvia)
LC	*Latvijas ceļš* (Latvia's Way)
LDDP	*Latvijas Demokratiskas darba partijas* (Latvian Democratic Labour Party)
LNNK	*Latvijas Nacionālās neatkarības kustības* (Latvian National Independence Movement)
LSDP	*Latvijas Socialdemokratiska partija* (Latvian Social Democratic Party)
LSDSP	*Latvijas Socialdemokratiska stradnieku partija* (Latvian Social Democratic Workers' Party)
LSP	*Latvijas Socialistiska partija* (Latvia's Socialist Party)
LTF	*Latvijas Tautas fronte* (Latvia's People's Front)
LZS	*Latvijas Zemnieku Savienība* (Latvian Farmers' Union)
PCTVL	*Par cilveka tiesibam vienota Latvija* (For Human Rights in a United Latvia)
TB	*Apvienība Tevzemei un Brīvībai* (Alliance For Fatherland and Freedom)
TB/LNNK	*Apvienība 'Tevzemei un Brivībai'/LNNK* (For Fatherland and Freedom/LNNK)
TP	*Tautas partija* (People's Party)
TSP	*Tautas saskanas partija* (People's Harmony Party)

NOTES

1. The post-communist ballot not endorsing independence was labelled 'Equal Rights Movement' in 1993 and 'Latvia's Socialist Party' in 1995. The former is a movement and was allowed to run in 1993; in 1995 only registered parties could submit lists. All in all, the same political groups stood behind these two ballots in 1993 and 1995.

2. A correlation between ethno-political cleavages and socio-economic stratification may be present or may emerge, as the economic conditions of various ethnic groups are influenced by the ethnic distribution of political power. The NORBALT living conditions project found that the rate of unemployment among citizens of Latvia was 16 per cent, as opposed to 20 per cent among the non-citizens in the labour force as of September 1994. However, the NORBALT report on Latvia claimed that the differences between the two groups were too small to be considered systematic (Priede 1996, 135). The NORBALT project maintained that non-citizens were not much worse off than citizens, and that gender, age and geography were stronger variables in influencing living conditions (Aasland et al. 1996, 212).

3. The percentages were calculated by the author from the *Baltic Data House* (BDH) exit poll at the 1995 *Saeima* elections published by Brigita Zepa (1996), and from a 1998 BDH data set. The BDH data report the share of ethnic Latvians, Russians and 'other nationalities' for parties with more than 4 per cent of the votes. Of the electorate, 78.7 per cent were Latvians and 16.3 per cent Russian. 'Other nationalities' include Poles (2.2 per cent), Belorussians (1.2 per cent), Lithuanians (0.4 per cent), Jews (0.4 per cent), Roma (0.4 per cent) and Ukrainians (0.2 per cent). The majority of the Lithuanians speak Latvian at home, the Roma speak their own language, while the other minorities usually use Russian. In this case, the estimate is that two-thirds of the respondents counted as 'other nationalities' are Russian-speaking, as are all Russians. The tiny 'Party of Russian Citizens of Latvia' was not included in the BDH data, but is estimated to have a 100 per cent Russophone electorate, as suggested by Kolstø and Tsilevich (1997, 376). The Russophone share of the electorate of the category 'Other lists' is not provided by BDH; here other minor parties (gaining less than 1.5 per cent of the vote) are estimated to have some 5 per cent Russian-speaking voters.

4. Interview with Lilija Babre, International Secretary of the Free Trade Union Federation of Latvia (LBAS), 25 March 1997.

5. Political scientist Frode Berglund performed the logistic regression, and the author is very grateful to him for his kind assistance. The author helped him put the parties in the proper categories, and was present while he did the quantitative analysis. The *Baltic Data House* provided the data set.

REFERENCES

Aasland, Aadne et al., eds, (1996), 'Latvia: the impact of the transformation', *The NORBALT Living Conditions Project, Fafo report* 188, Oslo.

Baltic Data House (1998), data set, BDH, Riga.

Berglund, Sten and Frank Aarebrot (1997), *The Political History of Eastern Europe in the 20th Century: The Struggle Between Democracy and Dictatorship*, Aldershot, Edward Elgar.

Cerps, Uldis (1994), 'The Leftist Parties in Latvia and Their Performance in the 1993 Parliamentary Elections', in Jan Åke Dellenbrant and Ole Nørgaard, eds, *The Politics of Transition in the Baltic States*, Umeå, Umeå University.

Dellenbrant, Jan Åke (1994), 'The Re-Emergence of Multipartyism in the Baltic States', in Sten Berglund and Jan Åke Dellenbrant, eds, *The New Democracies in Eastern Europe: Party Systems and Political Cleavages,* 2nd edn, Aldershot, Edward Elgar.

Dreifelds, Juris (1996), *Latvia in Transition,* Brock University, Cambridge University Press.

European Commission (1997), *Agenda 2000: Commission Opinion on Latvia's Application for Membership of the European Union,* Brussels, European Commission.

Freimanis, Aigars and Einars Semanis (1994), 'The Transition of the Political Regime in Latvia', in Jan Åke Dellenbrant and Ole Nørgaard, eds, *The Politics of Transition in the Baltic States*, Umeå, Umeå University.

Garleff, Michael (1976), *Deutschbaltische Politik zwischen den Weltkriegen: Die parlamentarische Tätigkeit der deutschbaltischen Parteien in Lettland und Estland*, Bad Godesberg.

Hendra, John (1995), *Latvia Human Development Report 1995*, Riga, UNDP.

—— (1997), *Latvia Human Development Report 1997*, Riga, UNDP.

Hirschman, Albert O. (1972), *Exit, Voice and Loyalty: Responses to Decline in Firms, Organizations, and States*, Cambridge, Harvard University Press.

Ikstens, Janis (1997), *Cleavage-related information about Latvia*, Mimeo.

Jacobsen, Birgit (1996), 'Political Attitudes', in Aadne Aasland et al., eds, 'Latvia: the impact of the transformation', *The NORBALT Living Conditions Project, Fafo report* 188, Oslo.

Klingemann, Hans-Dieter, Jürgen Lass and Katrin Mattusch (1994), *Nationalitätenkonflikt und Mechanismen politischer Integration im Baltikum*, FS III 94-205, Wissenschaftzentrum Berlin für Sozialforschung, Berlin.

Kolstø, Pål and Boris Tsilevich (1997), 'Patterns of nation building and political integration in a bifurcated postcommunist state: ethnic aspects of parliamentary elections in Latvia', *East European Politics and Societies*, Vol. 11, No. 2.

Kruks, Sergei (1997), *Identity Discourse in Contemporary Latvia*, Department of Media and Communication, University of Oslo.

Lieven, Anatol (1993), *The Baltic Revolution: Estonia, Latvia and Lithuania and the Path to Independence*, Yale University Press.

Lipset, Seymour Martin and Stein Rokkan (1967), 'Cleavage Structures, Party Systems and Voter Alignments: An Introduction', in Seymour Martin Lipset and Stein Rokkan, eds, *Party Systems and Voter Alignments: Cross-National Perspectives*, New York, The Free Press.

Misiūnas, Romuald and Rein Taagepera (1993), *The Baltic States: Years of Dependence 1940–1990*, London, University of California Press, expanded and updated edition.

Nissinen, Marja (1999), *Latvia's Transition to a Market Economy: Political Determinants of Economic Reform Policy*, Basingstoke, Macmillan Press Ltd.

Nørgaard, Ole with Dan Hindsgaul, Lars Johannsen and Helle Willumsen (1996), *The Baltic States after Independence*, Cheltenham, Edward Elgar.

Priede, Zaiga (1996), 'Employment and Working Conditions', in Aadne Aasland et al., eds, 'Latvia: the impact of the transformation', *The NORBALT living conditions project, Fafo report* 188, Oslo.

Prikulis, Juris (1997), *Latvian Political Parties and Their Electorate 1995–1997*, Mimeo.

Røeggen, Vidar (1997), *Statsborgerskapspolitikk i Latvia: et spørsmål om suverenitet*, Hovedoppgave, Inst. for Administrasjon og Organisasjonsvitenskap, Bergen, University of Bergen.

Smith, Graham (1996), 'The ethnic democracy thesis and the citizenship question in Estonia and Latvia', *Nationalities Papers*, Vol. 24, No. 2.

Smith-Sivertsen, Hermann (1998), 'Latvia', in Sten Berglund, Tomas Hellén and Frank H. Aarebrot, eds, *The Handbook of Political Change in Eastern Europe*, Edward Elgar, Cheltenham.

Spekke, Arnolds (1951), *History of Latvia: An Outline*, Stockholm.

Steen, Anton (1996), 'Elites, democracy and policy development in post communist states: A comparative study of Estonia, Latvia and Lithuania', *Research Report* 02/96, Department of Political Science, University of Oslo.

—— (1997a), 'Cleavage Structures, Elites and Democracy in Post Communist Societies: The Case of the Baltic States', in Anton Steen, ed., *Ethnicity and Politics in Estonia, Latvia and Lithuania*, Forskningsrapport 02/97, Departement of Political Science, University of Oslo.

—— (1997b), *Between Past and Future: Elites, Democracy and the State in Post-Communist Countries: A Comparison of Estonia, Latvia and Lithuania*, Ashgate, Aldershot.

Zecchini, Salvatore (1996): *Review of Agricultural policies: Latvia*, Paris, OECD.

Zepa, Brigita (1996) 'Veletaju uzvedība Saeimas un pasvaldību velesanas 1990–1995', *Sociologijas un Politologijas Žurnals*, No 7 maijs.

APPENDIX 4.1: ELECTION RESULTS

PARLIAMENTARY ELECTIONS

1990 Elections to the Supreme Council of the Republic of Latvia
Date: 18 March (first round; 170 deputies elected);
   25 March, 1 April and 29 April (run-off elections)
Turnout: 81.3%

Party/list/caucus	%	*Mandates May 1990* [*]	*Mandates Aug. 1990* [**]
Latvian People's Front (*Latvijas Tautas fronte*)	68.2		131
Independents	10.3		8
Communist Party members and sympathizers[***]	21.5		59
Deputies not belonging to any faction			3
'Latvian People's Front and associated deputies'[*]		144	
'Equal Rights faction and associated deputies'[*]		53	
Total	100.0	197	201

Sources: [*] Lieven 1993; [**] Dellenbrant 1994; Misiūnas and Taagepera 1993; Dreifelds 1996.
Note: [***]'Members of the Communist party and its sympathizers' is a category proposed by Dellenbrant (1994); this group was mainly defined by its opposition to the Latvian People's Front (LTF). It should be noted that the LTF contained many former members of the Communist Party of the Soviet Union. Lieven (1993) labels the category of candidates which received 21.5 per cent of the vote as 'opponents of independence'.

1993 Elections to the 5th Saeima
Date: 5 and 6 June
Turnout: 89.9%

Party/list	%	*Seats*
Latvia's Way (*Latvijas Ceļš*)	32.4	36
Latvian National Independence Movement–LNNK (*Latvijas Nacionalas Neatkarības Kustība*–LNNK)	13.4	15
Harmony for Latvia–Revival for the Economy (*Saskana Latvijai–Atdzimšana Tautsaimniecībai*)	12.0	13
Latvian Farmers' Union (*Latvijas Zemnieku Savienība*)	10.6	12
Equal Rights Movement (*Lidztiesība*)	5.8	7
For Fatherland and Freedom (*Tevzemei un Brīvībai*)	5.4	6
Latvian Christian Democratic Party (*Latvijas Kristīgo Demokratu Savienība*)	5.0	6
Democratic Centre Party (*Demokratiska Centra Partija*)	4.8	5
Latvian People's Front (*Latvijas Tautas fronte*)	2.6	–
Others	9.5	–
Total	100.0	100

1995 Elections to the 6th Saeima
Date: 30 September–1 October
Turnout: 71.9%

Party/coalition	%	Seats
Democratic Party–*Saimnieks*		
(*Demokratiska partija–Saimnieks*)	15.2	18
People's Movement for Latvia (Siegerist Party)		
(*Tautas kustība Latvijai [Zigerista partija]*)	15.0	16
Alliance 'Latvia's Way' (*Savienība 'Latvijas ceļs'*)	14.7	17
Union 'For Fatherland and Freedom'		
(*Apvienība 'Tevzemei un Brivībai'*)	12.0	14
Latvian Unity Party (*Latvijas Vienības partija*)	7.2	8
United list of Latvian Farmers' Union, Latvian Christian		
Democrat Union and Latgale Democratic Party		
(*Latvijas Zemnieku savienibas, Latvijas Kristīgo*		
Demokratu Savienība un Latgales Demokratiskas		
partijas apvienotais saraksts)	6.4	8
Latvian National Conservative Party–LNNK and Latvian		
Green Party (*Latvijas Nacionali konservativa partij–*		
LNNK un Latvijas Zala partija)	6.4	8
Latvian Socialist Party (*Latvijas Socialistiska partija*)	5.6	5
National Harmony Party (*Tautas saskanas partija*)	5.6	6
Coalition 'Labour and Justice': Latvian Democratic		
Labour Party, Latvian Social Democratic Workers		
Party, Party for the Defence of Latvia's Defrauded		
People 'Justice' (*Latvijas Demokratiskas darba*		
partijas [LDDP], Latvija Socialdemokratiskas		
stradnieku partijas [LSDSP] un Latvijas Apkrāpto		
cilvēku aizstavības partijas 'Taisnība' [Taisnīiba]		
koalicija 'Darbs un taisnīgums')	4.6	–
Latvian People's Front (*Latvijas Tautas fronte*)	1.2	–
Others	6.3	–
Total	100.0	100

Comparison of parliamentary election results (1990–1995)

Party/electoral coalition	1990	1993	1995
Latvian People's Front	68.2	1.2	1.2
Communists and Interfront	21.5	–	–
Alliance Latvia's Way	–	32.4	14.7
Latvian National Independence Movement (LNNK) *	–	13.4	–
Latvian National Conservative Party (LNNK) and Latvian Green Party**	–	–	6.4
Harmony for Latvia–Revival for the Economy *	–	12.0	–
National Harmony Party **	–	–	5.6
Latvian Farmers' Union *	–	10.6	–
Latvian Farmers' Union, Latvian Christian Democrat Union and Latgale Democratic Party **	–	–	6.4
Equal Rights Movement *	–	5.8	–
Latvian Socialist Party **	–	–	5.6
Union For Fatherland and Freedom	–	5.4	12.0
Christian Democratic Union***	–	5.0	–
Democratic Centre Party*	–	4.8	–
Democratic Party–*Saimnieks***	–	–	15.2
People's Movement for Latvia (Siegerist Party)	–	–	15.0
Latvian Unity Party	–	–	7.2
Coalition 'Labour and Justice' (LSDSP/LDDP)	–	–	4.6
Others	10.3	9.4	6.2

Note: Each electoral list from 1993 marked with one asterisk [*] has its main successor in the 1995 election marked with two asterisks.[**] The Democratic Centre Party relabelled itself the Democratic Party and in 1995 merged with *Saimnieks*, which had won 17.8 per cent of votes in the 1994 Riga local elections. The word 'Saimnieks' can be translated as 'host', 'master', or 'in charge'.

[***] The Christian Democratic Union ran jointly with the Latvian Farmers' Union in 1995.

Percentage of seats in the 1993 and 1995 Saeima *elections
and* Saeima *party caucuses in the autumn of 1997*

Party/electoral coalition	1993	1995	1997
Latvian People's Front	0	0	–
Alliance Latvia's Way	36	17	16
Latvian National Independence Movement (LNNK)	15	–	–
Latvian National Conservative Party (LNNK) and Latvian Green Party*	–	8	–
National Reform Party and the Greens*	–	–	6
Harmony for Latvia–Revival for the Economy	13	–	–
National Harmony Party	–	6	5
Latvian Farmers' Union	12	–	–
Latvian Farmers' Union and Latvian Christian Democrat Union and Latgale Democratic Party	–	8	13
Equal Rights Movement	7	–	–
Latvian Socialist Party	–	5	4
Union For Fatherland and Freedom*	6	14	–
Fatherland and Freedom/LNNK*	–	–	17
Christian Democratic Union	6	–	–
Democratic Centre Party	5	–	–
Democratic Party–*Saimnieks*	–	18	20
People's Movement for Latvia (Siegerist Party)**	–	16	9
Latvian Unity Party**	–	8	1
Coalition 'Labour and Justice' (LSDSP/LDDP)***	–	0	1
Freedom faction**	–	–	5
Independents	0	0	3

* The LNNK merged with 'Fatherland and Freedom' in 1997. The National Reform Party is primarily a platform for those of the old LNNK (Andrejs Krastins, Alexander Kirsteins and others) who did not want to merge with the 'Fatherland and Freedom'.

** The Unity Party lost most of its *Saeima* members in March 1997; the bulk of them went over to the Farmers' Union–Christian Democratic caucus. The Freedom faction is composed of three former Siegerist party deputies, one ex-Fatherland and Freedom deputy plus one ex-Unity Party deputy. Ex-Siegerist party deputies are also to be found in the DP–*Saimnieks*, Fatherland and Freedom/LNNK, and National Reform party caucuses (Ikstens 1997).

*** The historic social democratic party LSDSP got one deputy in 1996 when *Saeima* deputy Janis Adamsons defected from Latvia's Way. In the autumn of 1997, Adamsons became chairman of the LSDSP. Adamsons was one of the most popular candidates of Latvia's Way in the 1995 elections; among the party's candidates, only Anatolijs Gorbunovs obtained a higher number of personal votes.

1998 Elections to the 7th Saeima
Date: 3 October 1998
Turnout: 71.89%

Party/coalition	%	Seats
Peoples Party		
(*Tautas partija*)	21.3	24
Alliance 'Latvia's Way' (*Savienība 'Latvijas ceļs'*)	18.2	21
Union 'For Fatherland and Freedom'/LNNK		
(*Apvienība 'Tevzemei un Brivībai'/LNNK*)	14.7	17
National Harmony Party (*Tautas saskanas partija*)	14.2	16
Latvia's Social Democratic Alliance (*Latvijas Socialdemokratu apvieniba*)	12.9	14
The New Party (*Jauna partija*)	7.4	8
Latvian Farmers' Union (*Latvijas Zemnieku savienibas*)	2.5	–
Labour Party, Latvian Christian Democrat Union, and Latvian Green Party (*Apvieniba: Darba partijas, Latvijas Kristigi demokratiskas savienibas, Latvijas Zalas partijas*)	2.3	–
People's Movement for Latvia (Siegerist Party) (*Tautas kustība Latvijai [Zigerista partija]*)	1.7	–
Democratic Party–*Saimnieks* (*Demokratiska partija–Saimnieks*)	1.6	–
Others	3.3	–
Total	100.0	100

2002 Elections to the 8th Saeima
Date: 5 October 2002
Turnout: 71.51%

Party/coalition	%	Seats
'New Era' (*Jaunais laiks*)	23.9	26
'For Human Rights in a United Latvia' (*Par cilveka tiesibam vienota Latvija*)	19.0	25
Peoples Party (*Tautas partija*)	16.6	20
Latvia's First Party (*Latvijas Pirma Partija*)	9.5	10
Greens and Farmers' Union (*Zalo un Zemnieku savieniba*)	9.4	12
Union 'For Fatherland and Freedom'/LNNK		
(*Apvienība 'Tevzemei un Brivībai'/LNNK*)	5.4	7
Alliance 'Latvia's Way' (*Savienība 'Latvijas ceļs'*)	4.9	–
Latvia's Social Democratic Workers Party (*Latvijas Socialdemokratiska stradnieku partija*)	4.0	–
Others	6.9	–
Total	99.6	100

PRESIDENTIAL ELECTIONS

1993 Elections
In the Saeima

		1st Ballot	2nd Ballot	3rd Ballot
Candidate	Party	6 July	7 July	7 July
Gunars Meierovičs	Latvia's Way	35	did not run	did not run
Aivars Jerumanis	Christian Democratic Union	14	10	–
Guntis Ulmanis	Latvian Farmers' Union	12	46	53
Against all		no option	no option	26

Guntis Ulmanis won an absolute majority among the 100 *Saeima* deputies in the 3rd ballot and was duly elected. Gunars Meierovics recalled his candidature after the first ballot and endorsed the candidacy of Guntis Ulmanis. 'Harmony for Latvia' boycotted the *Saeima* vote; the party wanted direct elections to the presidency.

Sources: Dreifelds (1996) and the *Saeima* Interparliamentary Relations Bureau.

1996 Elections
In the Saeima

		1st Ballot
Candidate	Party	18 June
Guntis Ulmanis	Incumbent	53
Ilga Kreituse	DP–*Saimnieks*	25
Imants Liepa	People's Movement for Latvia (Siegerist Party)	14
Alfreds Rubiks	Latvian Socialist Party	5
Did not vote		3

Incumbent State President Guntis Ulmanis won an absolute majority among the *Saeima* deputies in the first ballot, and was duly elected for a second three-year term.

Source: OMRI Newsletter No. 118, 1996.

1999 Elections
In the Saeima

Candidate	Party	1st Ballot (17 June)
Anatolijs Gorbunovs	Latvia's Way	21
Arnis Kalniņš	Latvian Social Democratic Workers's Party	14
Vaira Paegle	People's Party	24
Jānis Priedkalns	Fatherland and Freedom/LNNK	17
Raimonds Pauls	New Party	24

	2nd Ballot (17 June)	3rd Ballot (17 June)	4th Ballot (17June)
A. Gorbunovs	21	23	22
A. Kalniņš	14	–	–
V. Paegle	24	25	24
J. Priedkalns	17	17	–
R. Pauls	24	32	23

	5th Ballot (17 June)
A. Gorbunovs	–
A. Kalniņš	–
V. Paegle	24
J. Priedkalns	–
R. Pauls	33

Having received the least votes in the 5th round, Mrs Vaira Paegle was excluded from further ballots. Mr Raimonds Pauls recalled his candidacy after the 5th ballot. The political parties were then asked to nominate new candidates. The Latvian Social Democratic Workers's Party and the Fatherland and Freedom/LNNK nominated Mrs Vaira Vīķe-Freiberga.

Candidate	Party	6th Ballot (17 June)
Vaira Vīķe-Freiberga	No political affiliation	50
Valdis Birkavs	Latvia's Way	21
Ingrīda Ūdre	New Party	12

Due to unclarity regarding one vote (it was not clear wheather one MP voted against all three candidates or just against Mr Birkavs and Mrs Ūdre), the decision was taken to repeat the 6th ballot.

Final Ballot (17 June)

Vaira Vīķe-Freiberga	53 votes
Valdis Birkavs	20 votes
Ingrīda Ūdre	9 votes

Thus Vaira Vīķe-Freiberga was elected President for a four-year term.

APPENDIX 4.2: GOVERNMENT COMPOSITION

Date of inauguration	Prime Minister	Party of PM	Parties in Cabinet	Left–Right position
May 1990	Ivars Godmanis	Latvian People's Front	Latvian People's Front	Centre
July 1993	Valdis Birkavs	Latvia's Way	Latvia's Way, 10 Farmers' Union, 3	Centre
Sept. 1994	Māris Gailis	Latvia's Way	Latvia's Way, 10 Pol. U. of Economists, 2 Independent, 1	Centre
Dec. 1995	Andris Šķēle	No affiliation	DP–*Saimnieks*, 4 Fatherland & Freedom, 4 Latvia's Way, 3 LNNK, 2 Unity Party, 1 Farmers' Union, 1	Centre
Feb. 1997	Andris Šķēle	No affiliation	DP–*Saimnieks*, 3 Fatherland & Freedom, 4 Latvia's Way, 3 LNNK, 2 Farmers' Union, 2	Centre
Aug. 1997	Guntars Krasts	F. Fatherland and Freedom/LNNK	Fatherland & Freedom/LNNK, 4 DP–*Saimnieks*, 4 Latvia's Way, 3 Farmers' Union, 2 Christian Democrat, 1	Centre
Nov. 1998	Vilis Krištopans	Latvia's Way	Latvia's Way, 6 Fatherland & Freedom/LNNK, 6 New Party, 2	Centre-right
Jul. 1999	Andris Šķēle	People's Party	People's Party, 5 Fatherland & Freedom/LNNK, 5 Latvia's Way, 5	Centre-right
May 2000	Andris Bērziņš	Latvia's Way	People's Party, 5 Latvia's Way, 4 Fatherland & Freedom/LNNK, 4 New Party, 2	Centre-right
Nov. 2002	Einars Repše	The New Era	The New Era, 8 Latvian First party, 3 Farmer's Union, 2 Fatherland & Freedom/LNNK, 2 Green Party, 1 Without party, 2	Centre-right

APPENDIX 4.3: THE ELECTORAL SYSTEM

The Supreme Council of the Republic of Latvia elected in March–April 1990 established a transitional period for restitution of independent state power, and this period terminated with the convening of the first post-Soviet *Saeima* (parliament), which since the election of the Fifth *Saeima* on 5 and 6 June 1993 is the highest legislative body in Latvia. The one-chamber *Saeima* counts 100 deputies and is elected in direct, proportional and secret elections by citizens 18 years of age and over. Until the term of the 6th *Saeima* expired in 1998, the *Saeima* deputies served for three years; a constitutional amendment, valid from the election of the 7th *Saeima* in 1998, extended the term of the *Saeima* to four years.

The 100 members of *Saeima* are elected proportionally on party candidate lists or electoral coalition candidate lists in five multi-seat constituencies: in the 1995 elections, Riga had 27 seats, Vidzeme province 25, Latgale province 19, Zemgale province 15, and Kurzeme province 14 seats. The allocation of mandates to the constituencies is made 100 days before each election; the number of mandates is proportional with respect to the constituency's relative share of the total electorate. In 1993, there was a 4 per cent national electoral threshold; the threshold was raised to 5 per cent in 1995.

The *Satversme* (constitution) of Latvia proscribes the *Saeima* to be elected in 'general, equal, direct and secret elections, on the basis of proportional representation', but it does not mention the method for achieving proportional representation nor any electoral threshold. The 1995 Election Law prescribes the St. Lagüe method of distributing mandates among parties, with the divisors being 1, 3, 5, 7, 9, etc. The individual voter can give a plus sign to candidates on the ballot list, or delete the names of candidates. Parties can enhance the possibilities of candidates to be elected by putting them on the ballot in several constituencies.

Citizens over 21 years of age are eligible for election to the *Saeima*. The 1995 election law ruled that several groups were not eligible to run as candidates, among them prison inmates, former KGB employees, those who had been active in certain communist, pro-Soviet organizations after 13 January 1991, and those who do not master the national language of Latvia to the highest (third) level of competence. In May 2002, the language proficiency requirements for candidates for public office were abolished. Still, an elected deputy can – by a decision of the *Saeima* – lose his/her seat if he/she is unable to use the state language while performing his/her duties in the *Saeima*.

The *Saeima* elects the President by secret ballot. For a candidate to be elected, he or she must receive a minimum of 51 votes. The President serves a maximum of two consecutive terms. Persons aged 40 or over are eligible for the office of President. When Guntis Ulmanis' second term expired in 1999, the presidential term of office was extended from three years to four years.

APPENDIX 4.4: THE CONSTITUTIONAL FRAMEWORK

Latvia is a parliamentary republic first established on 18 November 1918. Its *de jure* independence was recognized on 26 January 1921. The *Satversme* (Constitution) was adopted on 15 February 1922, and it was reintroduced in full, with amendments, on 6 July 1993, when the 5th *Saeima* (Parliament) was elected.

The main function of the *Saeima* is law-making and adopting the state budget, but it also elects the President of the State, the State Auditor, and the Central Election Commission, and ratifies international agreements. The *Saeima* may give a vote of confidence or no confidence in the government. Draft laws may be presented to the *Saeima* by the President of State, the Cabinet, the Committees of the *Saeima*, no less than five individual members of the *Saeima* or, in cases and in a manner provided for in the Constitution, by one-tenth of the electorate.

The members of the *Saeima* shall be exempt from judicial, administrative and disciplinary prosecution, in connection with in the fulfilment of their duties, although not for the dissemination of defamatory information with the knowledge that it is false, or the dissemination of defamatory information about private or family life. Members of the *Saeima* may not be arrested or searched, nor may their personal liberty be restricted in any way, without the sanction of the *Saeima*. According to the Rules of Procedure of the *Saeima*, a deputy may be expelled from the *Saeima* by a *Saeima* decision if he or she during the period of a current session has been absent from more than half of all the *Saeima* sittings without a valid excuse. A deputy may be expelled from the *Saeima* by a decision of the *Saeima* if, upon approval of his/her mandate, it is established that he/she lacks command of the official language at the level necessary for the performance of his/her professional duties.

According to the *Satversme*, executive power is held by the Cabinet of Ministers. The Cabinet consists of the Prime Minister, full Ministers and State Ministers, the latter resembling junior ministers in other countries. State Ministers cannot be regarded as fully-fledged Cabinet members, but have voting rights in the issues concerning their field. An incoming Prime Minister must be nominated by the President. A nominated Prime Minister must then receive a vote of confidence in the *Saeima*, in which an absolute majority among those deputies present is required. The Prime Minister nominates the members of Cabinet, who also must receive a vote of confidence in the *Saeima*. All presidential decrees shall be countersigned by the Prime Minister, or by the Minister concerned, who thereby assumes full responsibility for the decrees.

If the *Saeima* expresses a vote of no confidence in the Prime Minister, the whole Cabinet shall resign. If the *Saeima* expresses a vote of no confidence in a particular minister, the Minister shall resign and the Prime Minister shall nominate another person to take his or her place. According to the *Saeima* Rules of Procedure, draft resolutions about a vote of no confidence in the Cabinet, the Prime Minister, Ministers or in Ministers of State, may be submitted by at least ten deputies or by a *Saeima* Committee. A question to any member of Cabinet in the regular *Saeima* 'questions and answers' sittings must be submitted in writing by no fewer than five deputies. Five deputies is also the minimum size of a *Saeima* faction.

The President promulgates laws passed by the *Saeima*. He may suspend the promulgation of a law for a period of two months at the request of not less than one-third of the members of the *Saeima*. A law thus suspended shall be submitted to a referendum if a minimum of 10 per cent of the electorate so requests. A referendum shall not be taken if three-quarters of the *Saeima* members pass the law once again, or, generally, on budget matters and foreign policy. The President (1) represents the State in an international capacity; (2) carries out the decisions of the *Saeima* concerning the ratification of international treaties; (3) is Commander-in-Chief of the Armed Forces and in time of war appoints a Commander-in-Chief; (4) declares war on the basis of a decision of the *Saeima*; (5) pardons criminals; (6) has the right to convene extraordinary meetings of the Cabinet and presides over such meetings; (7) has the right of legislative initiative; (8) has the right to propose the dissolution of the *Saeima*. A proposal to dissolve the *Saeima* shall be followed by a referendum. If, in the referendum, more than one-half of the votes are cast in favour of dissolution, the *Saeima* shall be considered as dissolved and new elections shall held within two months. If, in the referendum, the dissolution of the *Saeima* is opposed by a majority, the President shall be regarded as dismissed and the *Saeima* shall elect a new President of State for the remaining period of office of the President.

On the motion of not less than one-half of the members of the *Saeima*, the *Saeima* may at a secret sitting decide by a two-thirds majority to dismiss the President and immediately appoint a successor. Should the President resign, die or be dismissed, the duties shall be carried out by the Chairman of the *Saeima* pending the election of a new President of State.

In 1998, the *Satversme* was amended. A Constitutional Court was established and 27 paragraphs on civil and human rights were added to the *Satversme*. Language policies are also dealt with in the *Satversme* after the amendments of 1998 and 2002. The constitution now says that '[t]he working language of local governments is the Latvian language' (§101) and that '[e]veryone has the right to address submissions to State or local government institutions and to receive a materially responsive reply. Everyone has the right to receive a reply in the Latvian language' (§104).

5. Lithuania

Kjetil Duvold and Mindaugas Jurkynas

Lithuanian politics came to be regarded as comparatively stable throughout the politically, socially and economically turbulent 1990s. In the first edition of *The Handbook of Political Change in Eastern Europe*, Darius Žeruolis notes, 'Lithuanian party and electoral politics have entered a "dull" stage' (Žeruolis 1998, 121). Five years later, the picture looks somewhat different. New actors have emerged on the political stage and a more fluid centre-ground has replaced earlier bipolar tendencies of the moderately fragmented party system. In this chapter we will attempt to explain these changes by looking at electoral and party system dynamics, before we sketch out some underlying conditions for the overall political development of Lithuania, such as socio-economic differentiation and general political attitudes.

Fifty years of Soviet domination disrupted independent state- and nation-building in Lithuania and put an end to all possibilities to revive the path to democracy. Soviet-style modernization, combined with repression, deportations, emigration and, obviously, passing generations, changed society beyond recognition. Consequently, the beginning of the 1990s represented a *tabula rasa* for Lithuanian politics.[1] Ties with inter-war Lithuania were at best weak, based on memories rather than individuals or institutions, but rather frequently they were merely invented. Like all post-communist countries, Lithuania emerged from communist dictatorship as a 'flattened' society (Wessels and Klingemann 1994). The Soviet regime did a thorough job in wiping out relevant socio-political divisions by monopolizing all organized and collective activities and, accordingly, deprived society of the type of structural divisions that characterize established democracies. Most ironical was the absence of division between capital and labour. The single most important cleavage in virtually every West European polity and the basis for 'Left' and 'Right' lacks roots in Lithuania and other Central and East European countries because the property-owning classes were absent. Nevertheless, political parties emerged as an integral part of democratization in most post-Communist regimes, and acted as entrepreneurs for emerging political dimensions. Party

133

competition in new democracies is essentially shaped and driven by parties and party actors (Sitter 2001, 87). Such competition, in turn, presumes the presence of an axis where voters and political actors can identify different parties. Left and Right provide the most usual basis for party placement – at least on the semantic level (Kitschelt, Mansfeldová, Markowski and Tóka 1999). What 'Left' and 'Right' actually mean, can either be historically derived or appear as basically speculative terms. In the former case, they have evolved out of specific conflicts between social movements and political parties (Bobbio 1996, 1). In the latter case, they appear merely as 'empty boxes', in which country-specific *problematique* fills up the boxes (Sartori 1976, 337). Dominant divides are politicized by party actors and tend to become configured along the Left/Right axis.[2] Political discourses inform us about the relevant political, societal and economic *problematique* at a specific point in time. The emergence of parties prior to significant stratification of society enables us to study such discourses as independent expressions from political actors, which, in turn, affect the development of political conflict. In the following, we will discuss how, in Lithuania, these boxes became filled with value-laden – or regime-oriented – conflict, and how these have gradually been transformed into a more classic dimension based on socio-economic issues.[3] The process also reflects a shift from a bipolar party system with centrifugal tendencies to a moderate pluralist system with a much higher degree of coalition-potential. Patterns of political conflict and numbers of party splits and mergers might reveal to what extent there is a sound potential for coalescent practices. However, the emergence of new parties, actors and issue dimensions might obviously break existing patterns. Such changes have to some extent taken place in Lithuania over the last few years.

The Emergence of Bipolarity

The embryo of a multiparty system in Lithuania emerged in the late 1980s, during the national revival (*Atgimimas*) and collapse of Soviet one-party rule.[4] The very first party-groups appeared under the Popular Front – or *Sajūdis* – umbrella. While the actual number of organizations mushroomed, they failed to develop coherent networks across the country. Only between 1990 and 1992, a period of fragmentation and increasing tensions within the *Sajūdis*, did parties begin to develop coherent organizations and seek more stable electoral footholds. Cultural or value-laden politics, related to independence and Soviet domination, stood above interest politics, and the inter-war period provided scant material for emerging cleavage structures. The political parties did not yet serve as representatives of different economic and social interests.

The initial core parties emerged over two brief periods. The first stage, between 1989–90, took place when informal affinity groups developed into political parties. Established in June 1988, *Sajūdis* was the first political movement to emerge outside the framework of the Lithuanian Communist Party (LKP). *Sajūdis* was registered as a social movement in support of *perestroika,* as the Soviet constitution banned any political organizations other than the Soviet Communist Party.[5] Nonetheless, there were clearly *political* objectives involved in the movement, although they ranged from modest claims for autonomy to full independence. Other proto-parties included the Social Democrats, Christian Democrats, Nationalists' Union, Greens, Humanitarians and Union of Political Prisoners and Exiles. Some of them claimed to have roots in inter-war politics or even earlier. They were all characterized by lack of organizational stability and ideological cohesion, and apart from their names there were no actual links to any pre-Soviet parties in terms of organizational or human resources.

The second wave of political parties surfaced with the dissolution of the *Sajūdis* and the fragmentation of the Supreme Council/Constitutive Assembly between 1990 and 1992. The *Law on Political Parties and Political Organizations* in 1990 provided legal setting for party development. The Liberal Union (LLS) and the Centre Movement (the Centre Union [LCS] from 1993) entered the political arena at that time, although the *Sajūdis* as a broad political movement remained the key platform for opposition to the Soviet regime. The overall goal of national independence and the prevalence of fairly moderate forces within the *Sajūdis* put a lid on political polarization in the period up to the declaration of independence in March 1990. *Sajūdis* and most other political groupings, including large sections of the reformed Communist Party (the Lithuanian Labour Democratic Party [LDDP] from December 1990) endorsed the idea of national independence. So did the overwhelming majority of the population, which was confirmed in a national plebiscite in February 1991.[6] The first free and constitutive elections vested political powers in the *Sajūdis* umbrella, which shows that the independence question was the common denominator for electoral support at the outset.

The Constitutive Assembly of 1990–92 saw rapid escalation of political animosity. *Sajūdis* became increasingly radicalized, leading to political fragmentation. The value-laden political climate in the *Seimas* added to the polarizing and centrifugal tendencies in the nascent party system. A certain polarization might perhaps occur in any settings marked by severe conflicts, but the emotional assessments of the Soviet regime penetrated nearly all political issues in Lithuania, thus making compromises between the Labour Democrats on the Left and *Sajūdis* on the Right virtually impossible. Even ideologically kindred parties like the Labour Democrats and the Social Democrats kept dodging each other. *Sajūdis*-leader Vytautas Landsbergis bore a clear imprint on the radicalization of politics, as he and his closest political entourage ascribed 'communist' or 'Moscow' labels to a wide range of opponents on the 'Left' of *Sajūdis*. The emotionally charged atmosphere also affected society profoundly. Although socio-economic interests began to crystallize, value-laden issues hindered them from affecting voting preferences and party competition. Few other parties had sufficient organizational capacity or coherent party programmes, which made it difficult for them to break the patterns of conflict, set by *Sąjūdis* and Labour Democrats. Nevertheless, polarization actually gave birth to smaller parties like the Liberal Union, Centre Union and others, squeezed in between the Left/Right poles as they were. But it would take several years before credible alternatives were in place. Each side of the Left/Right divide agreed on essential macro-economic choices, although they may have parted somewhat in terms of pace and priorities. To a much larger extent than in Estonia and Latvia, the economic priorities of the main parties mirrored a leftover from Soviet times, with an emphasis on egalitarian values and an active role of the state in the economy (Lieven 1994, 269).

The political climate mellowed somewhat by the time, as agreements over constitutional and electoral questions were reached. New parliamentary elections, using newly adopted electoral rules, were launched. The 1992 elections represented a substantial change in the sense that political parties for the first time became the main vehicles of electoral choice. In 1990, all parties (save a few hard-line communists) advocated similar macro-strategic objectives – independence, democracy and market economy. In any event, coalition practices during the election campaign were meagre. Major parties failed to cooperate and only two right-wing parties (or party coalitions), led by the *Sąjūdis* and the Christian Democrats, overcame the 4 per cent electoral threshold for representation.[7] The electoral outcome was, on the other hand, highly favourable for the Brazauskas-led Lithuanian Democratic Labour Party, which astonished observers and pollsters by winning an absolute majority of parliamentary seats and, thus, needed no coalition partner to form a government.[8] *Sąjūdis* lost its leading position largely due to internal fragmentation, but also due to its focus on value-laden issues and its confrontational approach to political opponents. It gradually alienated several actors who stood in opposition to Landsbergis. It also experienced difficulties in transforming itself from a mass movement into a political party. The core nationalist elements within the *Sąjūdis*, led by Landsbergis, turned the party into the Homeland Union – Lithuanian Conservatives (TS[LK]) in May 1993.[9] Nevertheless, the ensuing battlefields in the *Seimas* continued to focus on the same old issues. The opposition focused their ammunition on the alleged 'Soviet-mentality' of the new government, '*nomenklatura* privatization', murky business deals and related topics. Public trust in the political class dropped accordingly. Despite their common 'anti-communist' position, collaboration practices were poorly developed within the opposition. No political forces outside the quadruplet of the Labour Democrats, the Social Democrats, the Christian Democrats and the Homeland Union entered the political playground. There was simply no space for new parties in the black-and-white world of Lithuanian politics in the early 1990s. Besides, the organizational strength of the Labour Democrats and the Homeland Union – inherited from respectively the Lithuanian Communist Party and the *Sajūdis* – played an important role in preventing the emergence of new parties. Although fragmentation remained moderate, the Lithuanian party system must be classified as highly polarized in the early 1990s (*Figure 5.1*).

Although the Lithuanian president is supposed to refrain from party politics when in office, the political parties try to promote their preferred choices all the way up to the second round of voting – a practice which tends to reinforce the bipolar patterns of Lithuanian politics. In 1993 only two candidates, Labour Democrat leader Algirdas Brazauskas and diplomat Stasys Lozoraitis, patronized by the Right, ran for the office.[10] The election campaign confirmed the same old division-line between 'communists' and 'anti-communists'. The centre/right threw its support in favour of Lozoraitis in order to prevent the 'communists' from winning. Ironically, even the leftist Social Democrats supported Mr Lozoraitis due to their perennial rivalry with the Labour Democrats. As it turned out, Mr Brazauskas won rather convincingly, with 60 per cent of the votes, thus entrenching the Labour Democrats' grip on power.

Figure 5.1: Seats and votes of LDDP* and Sajūdis/TS[LK] combined, 1992–2000 (%)

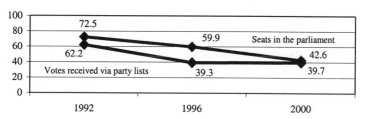

* LDDP and LSDP formed an electoral alliance for the 2000 elections and formally merged into the Social Democrats (LSDP) in January 2001.

The parliamentary elections of 1996 also bore out bipolar tendencies, although the electoral pendulum – in terms of electoral outcome – had swung back to the Right.[11] The Homeland Union, still led by Vytautas Landsbergis, won an absolute majority of seats and formed a new government.[12] Although they did not actually need coalition-partners, the Christian Democrats and the Centre Union were invited to join the government.[13] The election results showed the prevalence of the old value-laden conflict, but perhaps a more important conclusion is that the electorate tended to vote against the existing government.[14] Turnout plummeted drastically, and it appeared that many likely Labour Democrat voters simply abstained. Compared with the municipal election just one year before, the combined votes received by the Labour Democrats, Social Democrats, Christian Democrats and the Homeland Union shrank from 67.1 to 55.8 per cent, which indicates that the old conflict patterns were slowly ebbing out. Significant support for the Centre Union may also be interpreted as a sign of a new opening of the electoral market.

With the benefit of hindsight, it appears that the main bearers of bipolarity and value-laden conflict – the Labour Democrats and the *Sajūdis*/Homeland Union – have lost support after each consecutive parliamentary election.

The presidential election in December 1997 turned out to be a symptom of changes to come. The perpetual opponents from the Left and Right, Algirdas Brazauskas and Vytautas Landsbergis respectively, either did not participate at all or lost in the first round.[15] Instead, two independent candidates attracted 72.3 per cent of the votes already in the first round.[16] The atmosphere of the campaign was less tense than the rather heated campaigns of previous elections. The winner, American-Lithuanian Valdas Adamkus, managed to stay aloof from the old regime division. But that did not change the fact that party configuration in the *Seimas* stayed intact all the way up to the parliamentary elections of 2000. Overall, the period between 1990 and 1997 disclosed meagre coalescent behaviour among all major actors, both in terms of electoral campaigning and cooperation in parliament. The Homeland Union and the Christian Democrats were inclined to collaborate, but – as before – essentially on the basis of 'anti-communism'. Moreover, party mergers were absent and, with the small exception of the Centre Union, no new parties emerged. The four main parties – the Labour Democrats, Social Democrats, Christian Democrats and the Homeland Union – received on the average 69 per cent of the votes between 1992 and 1997. Although party system fragmentation remained fairly moderate, the nature of party competition was decidedly centripetal.[17]

Figure 5.2: Distribution of relevant political parties along the value-laden/ideological dimension, 1990–1998 [18]

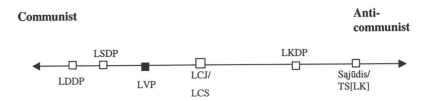

To sum up thus far, the bipolar structure of the Lithuanian party competition throughout the 1990s was borne out of a division that manifested itself already towards the end of the 1980s (*Figure 5.2*). Always more national-oriented and native-dominated than its Estonian and Latvian counterparts during Soviet times, the Lithuanian Communist Party managed to translate its considerable organizational network and professionalized leadership into a credible political alternative to the frontrunners of independence in the *Sajūdis* movement. In Estonia and Latvia, the communist parties collapsed into pitiful, small groupings without political muscle to return to the race. The hot issue of ethnic minorities seems to have played a significant role in eliminating the communist parties from the political scene. The Soviet legacy and the role of the Communist Party came to overlap with the question of 'illegitimate' immigrants from the Soviet Union. It was trickier to 'externalize' the communist past for Lithuania. A significantly lower rate of immigration from other Soviet republics, coupled with a more indigenous communist party leadership, brought all these issues closer to home. For all intents and purposes, it was harder to discredit communist elites that by and large were of Lithuanian background. Surely that did not prevent several *Sajūdis* leaders from highlighting the issue. Nonetheless, the legacy of communism could hardly be sustained as an enduring social cleavage. The role of the past is by its very nature a transitional phenomenon (Hellén, Berglund and Aarebrot 1998, 370). What seemed to be a rather relentless conflict dimension between the Left and Right in Lithuanian politics in the 1990s, eventually ebbed out. Although Landsbergis and his followers launched a 'Nuremberg-style' trial against communism as late as in 2000, the charges made were directed against Russia as the legal heir of the Soviet Union, not 'collaboration' among ordinary Lithuanians. Overall, there has been no Lithuanian equivalent to the Czech and German lustration laws against former communist 'collaborators'. Such a large-scale process could have had dramatic impact on society, potentially whipping up much resentment among the general population. The fierce attacks on former communists, launched by Mr Landsbergis and some of his allies, may indeed have backfired. To the astonishment of many outside observers, the great independence leader became highly unpopular among many ordinary voters.

From Value-laden Politics to a New Political Ground

Municipal elections are difficult to apply in an evaluation of party system development. Local issues seem to prevail and, due to the proportional electoral system, the number of relevant parties is higher. Moreover, turnout is generally lower, since local politics is considered to be of relatively low importance, controlled and politically dependent upon the centre as they are. It is in any case hard to trace similar bipolar and centripetal tendencies in local politics, since the majority of municipalities are run by coalitions that are dissonant with coalitions at the national level. Moreover, pre-electoral coalitions differ from one constituency to another. However, it is noteworthy that local elections to some extent have disclosed tendencies of upcoming parliamentary elections. New parties first appear in local elections, priór to the hunt for votes on a grander scale.[19]

The municipal elections of 2000 represented the breakthrough for party system change, producing no less than eight parties with at least 5 per cent of the votes. The New Union (NS) and the Liberal Union (LLS), led by youthful and charismatic Artūras Paulauskas and Rolandas Paksas respectively, smashed into the political arena. These parties, in addition to the Centre Union and the Peasants' Party (LVP) represented altogether new dimensions than the old value-laden conflict and gained 52.4 per cent of the votes cast. Parliamentary elections followed suit the same year, which essentially confirmed the electoral change, although only four parties and electoral alliances overcame the 5 per cent threshold. The Liberal Union and the New Union formed Lithuania's first minority government after the election, but the *New Politics* bloc, which enjoyed the blessings of President Adamkus,[20] ultimately failed to form a stable coalition – partly due to the surprising defeat of the Centre Union. A second noticeable change was the electoral alliance between the Labour Democrats and the Social Democrats, which gave a substantial regain for the Left, assisted by the political comeback of Algirdas Brazauskas. When the Paksas-led coalition collapsed the following year, the Social Democrats were waiting in the wings to form a broader and more stable government together with the New Union. The Conservatives, for their part, lost severely, plummeting to a meagre 8.6 per cent – quite a drop from the 30 per cent they received in 1996. Vytautas Landsbergis' unsuccessful presidential campaign in 1997, combined with increasing discontent with the Conservative-led government, reduced the party's leeway to exploit the value-laden conflict, which eventually appealed to only a very narrow constituency of voters.[21]

Figure 5.3: Percentage of votes received by the 4 'old' main parties (the LDDP, LSDP, LKDP and TS[LK]), 1992–2002

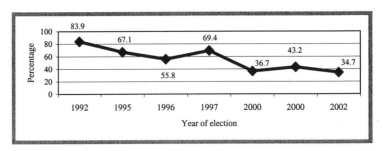

Overall, the election resulted in greater voter volatility, but also in the rise of new political actors with other sets of political goals. It should also be pointed out that the coalition potential increased significantly. More than 70 per cent of the votes went for cooperation minded parties, be it the four-party *New Politics* bloc or the Social Democratic alliance. The number of relevant parties remained identical, since two newcomers (the New Union and the Liberal Union) pushed out two 'old' parties (the Christian Democrats and the Centre Union). Nevertheless, the two newcomers, together equipped with 61 new members of the *Seimas*, introduced a political style and approach that differed from the old regime-dimension, which changed the nature of party competition. The Lithuanian party system is still in a certain flux since the 2000 elections. New parties have emerged, old parties dropped out and significant mergers have either taken place or are in the pipeline (*Figures 5.3 and 5.4*) Electoral volatility reached comparatively high levels as the voters drastically shifted their preferences. The variability of the Lithuanian party system since 2000 represents rather a qualitative than quantitative oscillation – which will be either confirmed or refuted by the general election of 2004.[22]

Figure 5.4: Effective number of legislative parties

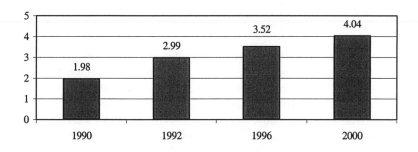

Source: Herron 2002, 14; Krupavičius and Žvaliauskas (2003).

Finally, municipal and presidential elections in 2002 corroborate that the value-laden regime dimension has vanished. Socio-economic issues prevailed in the electoral campaign and no parties made charges related to the Soviet past. Moreover, virtually all parties and political actors approve of major foreign policy choices. Crucially, coalition-potential seems to have increased drastically, as three major party mergers took place and others seem to follow this pattern. The Social Democrats and the Labour Democrats merged under the name of the Social Democratic Party. The Christian Democratic Union and the Christian Democratic Party became the Christian Democrats and the Peasants' Party and New Democracy (the Peasants' Party and New Democracy Union) followed the same path shortly afterwards, although they were slower than the Social Democrats at moving towards unification (Krupavičius and Žvaliauskas 2003). Perhaps more significantly, a merger among the Liberal Union, the Centre Union and the relatively marginal Modern Christian Democrats took place in 2003. A splinter from the Liberal Union, the Liberal Democrats (LDP), did not create any major upset, since the split essentially represented personal animosities among the Liberals, rather than ideological rifts. On the other hand, the Liberal Democrats performed rather well in the 2002 local elections and may well continue upwards, since the party is intimately linked with Paksas, Lithuania's current president. Overall, the elections revealed a more fragmented 'local level party system' of eight parties, and only the upcoming general election will give a full answer as to who will stay in the political game after 2004.

Cleavages and Political Representation in Lithuania

What we have outlined thus far is essentially restricted to the political arena. Political actors in rapidly changing societies have to a very large extent been able to engineer the configuration of political 'cleavages'. But they are by no means unrestricted by the very context they operate within. We will therefore shift our focus somewhat by offering an examination of underlying socio-structural 'traits', on the one hand, and general political attitudes, on the other. Rae and Taylor's (1970) seminal definition of social cleavages containing *ascriptive*, *attitudinal* and *behavioural* aspects may serve as a theoretical backdrop for our distinction between the political arena and contextual factors. Ascriptive divisions such as ethnicity and, to some extent, religion and socio-structural position, obviously exist even in societies that have undergone intensive Soviet homogenization. How and to what extent these elements can provide a sound basis for cleavages after communism is another matter. The second aspect, popular attitudes and values, have kept changing very rapidly in all new democracies. Consequently, they inevitably appear rather fluid compared with those found in more established societies. Just as socio-structural differentiation takes shape, the scope for political 'engineering' of opinions, attitudes and values is considerable. Political actors and institutions play a pivotal role in engineering issue dimensions that may eventually turn into salient issue dimensions (Mainwaring 1999). Whereas ascriptive and attitudinal aspects of cleavages are essentially sociological, behavioural aspects are linked to the organizational level of politics. However, democratic consolidation requires political institutions that roughly correspond with the values and interests of the citizenry (Klingemann and Fuchs 1995, 3). To what extent do 'sociological' and 'political' aspects of cleavages actually coincide? In other words, to what extent do political parties mirror and channel popular preferences and interests? Parties may proclaim themselves as 'conservative', 'liberal' or 'social democratic', yet appear far removed from the values and goals of the voters. At the outset it seems reasonable to assume that Lithuanian parties are poorly linked with the electorate. Membership is low by West European standards, although a few parties have throughout the 1990s had membership pools that make them at least reminiscent of traditional mass parties.[23] Moreover, most Lithuanian parties are elite creations – initiated and operated by ambitious political leaders with weak loyalty to party organizations. A large number of party splits and factionalism in the parliament testify to this pattern. We may indeed reasonably question the role of political parties in Lithuania.

Studying *perceptions* of cleavages among citizens represents one way of scrutinizing the link between political parties and voters and to establish the extent to which parties actually represent voters. If cleavage crystallization is relevant for the development of party systems, we must assume that voters have their own perceptions of cleavages and, moreover, are in a position to locate parties according to at least some of these cleavages. Although we do not have data that support voters' perceptions of individual parties, the *New Europe Barometer* (NEB) from 2001 enable us to tap general perceptions of cleavages – in other words, which issue dimensions that are relevant for distinguishing between parties (*Table 5.1*).

Table 5.1: Relevance of cleavages in the Baltic countries (%)

	Estonia	Latvia	Lithuania
Legacy of the communist regime	24	13	29
State intervention versus market	29	27	50
Urban versus rural	35	12	24
Ethnic representation or not	17	12	10
Nation versus European integration	35	31	33
Personality versus political ideals	33	33	40
No opinion on cleavages	12	31	6

Note: The exact introductory question is: 'Here are some reasons that people give about the difference between political parties. Which of the following best explains these differences?'. The respondents made two choices. The figures above show primary and secondary choices of cleavages.

Source: New Europe Barometer (2001).

A quick glance at Table 5.1 reveals that cleavages simply seem to matter more in Lithuania than in Estonia and, in particular, Latvia. Only 6 per cent have no opinion at all of cleavages in Lithuania, as opposed to a staggering 31 per cent in Latvia. Similarly striking, the role of state intervention versus market solutions seems to be of far greater importance to Lithuanian citizens than to Estonians and Latvians. Clearly, citizens appear to acknowledge a solid division between personalities in politics and political ideologies. Strong personalities, not necessarily conducive for cleavage-based politics, still seem to be among the strongest factors behind party choice among all Baltic constituencies. However, *Left* and *Right* – the most salient of all cleavages in Western Europe, but a dimension that is often assumed to be of fairly marginal importance in Central and Eastern Europe – is actually perceived as the single most important issue dimension of Lithuanian politics.

Redefining 'Left' and 'Right'

The bipolar nature of Lithuanian politics in the 1990s was to a large extent driven by a zealous anti-Communist Right on the one side, and a reformed communist party on the other. There are clear indications that this dimension has been replaced by a socio-economic divide. Although Jakub Zielinski (2002, 185) notes that conflict between labour and capital in new democracies is likely to emerge only after party system consolidation, the Lithuanian case actually indicates that the socio-economic divide has surfaced prior to party system consolidation. The last decade has entailed enormous societal changes, not least brought about by market reforms. Income differences have increased rapidly. The Gini coefficient, a standard measure of income distribution, shows that Lithuania, at 0.327, has higher income inequality levels than the EU average: quite a change for a country where income differences were comparatively small some 15 years ago. Rapid marketization has clearly produced new 'winners' and 'losers'. For instance, failing industrial enterprises created soaring unemployment, concentrated in industrial 'pockets' once designed by Soviet planners. Many people are too old to readjust to this entirely reshaped labour market. Recent labour market surveys reveal that unemployment remains relatively high.[24] Lithuania – like other post-communist countries – has developed a far more diverse social stratification than during communism. Something reminiscent of a middle-class has emerged, at the same time as the number of 'have-nots' has increased.

For a long time considered 'sluggish' compared with its Baltic neighbours in terms of market reforms and economic development, Lithuania started to catch up towards the end of the 1990s.[25] Currently, the private sector accounts for 75 per cent of the GDP, and more than 70 per cent of the workforce. Sectors like banking, energy, transport and communication have been up for large-scale, ambitious privatization schemes, or are in the pipeline. However, the privatization process has had repercussive effects for the general political climate of Lithuania. Sell-offs of state properties have given birth to several political scandals, cronyism and alleged corruption affairs. It has also helped sustaining the old regime dimension, where former *nomenklatura* appointees have been accused of exploiting their channels, networks and influence for their own personal benefit. This issue has had yet another side: fear of excessive Russian influence in Lithuania. Several political actors are alarmed by the prospect of Lithuania making herself vulnerable to Moscow by being dependent on Russian raw materials and investments into the energy sector. The sale of the Mažeikių Nafta oil refinery in 1999 illustrates this dimension rather well: the Conservative-led government wanted, almost at any price, to strike a deal with American energy giant Williams International instead of Russian Lukoil. The deal came at a high price, though: as part of the parcel, Lithuania was forced to take up substantial foreign loans and full responsibility for business risks. The deal upset the public and ultimately led to the collapse of the government. In an ironic twist, Williams subsequently sold its shares to Russian Yukos. Nevertheless, the story gives a picture of how emotive the privatization question at times has been, and how it has been tangled up in a 'West versus East' discourse, in which the Homeland Union has been playing first violin.[26] There has been an almost unanimous desire to loosen the ties with Russia and be anchored to the 'West', where most Lithuanians feel they rightly belong.[27]

Marketization is, on the whole, likely to be controversial among the general public. 'Winners' are likely to be in favour and 'losers' against it. By way of illustrating, NEB data from 2001 clearly show that attitudes towards the present economic system are contingent on income: those who are comparatively well off are evidently more in favour of market economy (*Table 5.2*). Age matters as well, but perhaps less than we could expect. Individuals in the lower age brackets are slightly more pro-market than are individuals who started their career within the Soviet system, but it could nevertheless be maintained that surprisingly many young people seem negative about market economy and positive about the Soviet economic system (*New Europe Barometer* 2001).

Table 5.2: Evaluation of former and current economic systems by income quartiles (%)

Income quartiles	1 (low)	2	3	4 (high)	Total
Positive about the socialist economy	86	78	75	56	73
Positive about current economic system	25	32	46	54	40

Source: New Europe Barometer (2001).

If there is a socio-economic dimension in Lithuanian politics, it seems plausible to assume that leftist parties appeal more to the less well-off strata of voters. 'Socialism' may have been turned into a rather discredited ideology all over post-communist Europe. Nonetheless, the Social Democrats (and previously the Labour Democrats) describe themselves as 'social democratic' and 'labour', thus trying to appeal to the average worker and public official. Similarly, the party attempts to align itself with the large

European family of social democratic parties. Whatever the case might be, social democracy in the context of post-communism does make a difference, if only because the communist regimes for decades 'monopolized' socialism and deprived citizens of choosing between reformist and 'revolutionary' socialism. Whereas socialism and social democracy in long-standing democracies are associated with social change and demand for greater economic equality, it will almost inevitably remain identified with *status quo* in post-communist societies. Another point is that ex-communist parties are more strongly associated with members of the old *nomenklatura*, who happened to be among the main beneficiaries of the privatization process. We may initially ask to what extent the Social Democrats actually represent the unprivileged and worse-off segments in Lithuania. Recent data from the NEB reveal that only some 35 per cent of Left and centre/left supporters[28] are satisfied with their personal economic situation, as opposed to 50 per cent of centre/right sympathizers.[29] Almost identical patterns emerge when centre/left and centre/right respondents are asked about future prospects: approximately 50 per cent of the former group and 30 of the latter group believe that their situation will stay the same or deteriorate in the future. Along a broader dimension, only one-third of the left-wing sympathizers appear to be content with the current economic system, whereas more than half of those who support the centre/right parties are satisfied with it. A positive rating of the previous socialist economy among 85 per cent of centre/left-wingers and 'only' 54 per cent among centrists/rightists fits into this picture (*Table 5.3*).

Table 5.3: Evaluation of former and current economic systems by party preference (%)

	Centre/ Left	Centre/ Right	Other party	Not vote or don't know	Total
Positive about the socialist economy	85	54	82	74	73
Positive about current economic system	38	56	36	32	40

Source: *New Europe Barometer* (2001).

A further inspection reveals that rural voters and those with low income are most likely to vote for parties of the Left. In a similar fashion, young people are most likely to prefer centre/right parties. These figures will hardly surprise anyone who follows politics in Central and Eastern Europe: likely winners of marketization support it and likely losers of it oppose the speed and pace of economic reforms. In any case, it does strengthen our suggestion that Left-Right identification in Lithuania follows certain socio-economic patterns that are reminiscent of the socio-economic space in more established democracies. Although we can tentatively conclude that there is a link between socio-economic groups and voting patterns, the tricky issue of *policy-making* remains. Indeed, there is little to suggest that Left/Right matters very much in policy terms. A few critical issues may appear as salient political divisions in the eyes of the electorate, but they are nevertheless likely to be of comparatively low importance. Profound conflicts over macro-economic priorities, Trans-Atlantic alignment and European integration are unlikely to reach prominence on the political arena. A large informal sector and inefficient tax collection contribute to a relatively low capacity for public spending.[30] For Lithuania, like other Central and Eastern European countries, most essential political decisions almost appear to be a *sine qua non*: to prosper or to stagnate.

Although suspicion towards authorities and public institutions runs deep among many Lithuanians, some are likely to feel strongly attached to the idea of a strong state. The communist regime provided security, stability and welfare for citizens. Yet, it was a highly patronizing system, which essentially turned individuals into subjects. The result was that most people got used to turning to the state for help or ways of improving their lives. A strong emphasis on individual responsibility has certainly taken root after communism, but it seems apt that a certain 'dependency culture' lingers on among certain segments of the population – in spite of the 'rolling back of the state'. This discrepancy between expectations and delivery could, in turn, give us some clues as for why approval of the Soviet economy outweighs support for the current economic system (*Tables 5.2 and 5.3*). On the other hand, no significant parties in Lithuania actually try to exploit this discontent.

Although many people in Lithuania remain worse off economically even after well over a decade of marketization, there are also many 'winners' of the transformation. Young, educated city-dwellers have accessed high-ranking positions in business, politics and the media. They are likely to reside in the capital and other major cities and their income is likely to outstrip that of their parents. Moreover, they are unlikely to have much affinity for the Soviet past, but also little understanding for the emotionally charged anti-Soviet claims made by former *Sajūdis* leaders or members of the émigré community. Several former members of the Soviet *nomenklatura* make up another 'winning' group. They had social and political capital at their disposal, and were able to profit personally from many privatization arrangements (Matonytė and Mink 2003, 52). '*Nomenklatura* privatization', prevalent in virtually every post-communist country, infuriated many anti-Communists and produced a rather curious situation in which it was the old communists who went ahead with ambitious privatization plans, whereas the anti-Communists appeared to drag their feet because they opposed the way privatization was handled. Again, it shows that the regime – or value-laden – cleavage played a significant role in shaping the socio-economic axis from the very beginning. And it may have come as some surprise to some observers that many old *nomenklatura* members turned out to be the most cunning capitalists, and that the old communist party proved to be more pragmatic and flexible as market-reformers.

Mapping Ethnic Divisions

In terms of party system development, the ethnic question stands out as perhaps *the* chief difference between Lithuania on one side, and Latvia and Estonia on the other. As pointed out by Mikko Lagerspetz, Henri Vogt and Herman Smith-Sivertsen in Chapters 3 and 4 of this volume, the relationship between the indigenous core populations and the predominantly Russian minorities has played a decisive role in defining party competition and issue dimensions in the two other Baltic countries. The issue has continued to dodge Estonian and – in particular – Latvian politics for years, possibly blocking other cleavage dimensions from surfacing. Identity politics has clearly been of immense importance in all three Baltic countries, being essentially new state creations as they were. But the absence of large-scale influx of Russians during Soviet times paved the way for so-called 'zero-option' citizenship laws in Lithuania, which removed the issue from the political agenda by offering citizenship to all inhabitants. Besides, compared with the larger share of ethnic minorities in Estonia and Latvia, Lithuania's less than 20 per cent ethnic minorities gives a different balance and makes overall integration more feasible.

Lithuania has two sizeable ethnic minorities: Russians and Poles. The Russian-speaking population, some 8 per cent of the total, is essentially a legacy of Soviet domination. The majority of the Soviet immigrants came as labour migrants, attracted by vacancies within rapidly expanding industrial plants, or were simply sent there. Most of them reside in the capital, the port city of Klaipėda, or near the Ignalina nuclear plant in Eastern Lithuania. The Polish minority, at 7 per cent of the total population, has quite different and more complex origins, being a long-term interface minority in the borderlands between Lithuania, Poland and Belarus. They are largely concentrated in the outskirts of the Vilnius region and the South Eastern corner of Lithuania.

The Polish minority clearly represents a more intricate issue for Lithuania than the Russians. To some extent, they symbolize a quite traumatic relationship between Lithuania and Poland, particularly concerning the historical status of Vilnius. Fractions of the Poles expressed secessionist views during the Lithuanian independence struggle and some Lithuanian nationalists expressed open hostility towards the Poles. It would not be far-fetched to make comparisons to, for example, the Hungarian minority of Slovakia. The ultimate difference, however, is that no mainstream Lithuanian political leaders has tried to exploit the issue, like Mečiar played out the 'minority card' in Slovakia to tremendous effects.

There are two distinct ethnic parties in Lithuania, the Electoral Action of

Lithuanian Poles (LLRA) and the Union of Lithuanian Russians (LRS). Neither of them is sizeable enough to pass the 5 per cent electoral threshold, but they have both captured some seats each in the *Seimas* either as part of electoral alliances, as in the case of the Russian party, or due to geographical concentration in single-member constituencies, as in the Polish case. Moreover, the Polish party is visibly represented in several local councils and has even gained political prominence in Vilnius.[31] Despite the fact that many Russians and Poles vote for specific ethnic parties (curiously, ethnic parties are actually better represented in the *Seimas* than Russian parties are in the Estonian *Riigikogu*) most of the minority votes go to mainstream leftist parties. The presence of specific ethnic – and, in the Polish case *regional* – parties does not affect the overall party competition or issue spectrum of Lithuanian politics. A more disturbing pattern is that Russians and, particularly, Poles are much less than average likely to participate in elections.[32] Moreover, ethnic minorities appear to be less satisfied with the way democracy works and less in favour of the current regime, according to data from the *New Europe Barometers*. On the other hand, they are not less trustful of parties, politicians or key state institutions than ethnic Lithuanians.

Urban-Rural Discrepancies

Lithuania has significant – and increasing – divisions between urban and rural areas. Nearly all foreign investments go to the capital or other major urban areas. The countryside lags further and further behind. Currently, the primary sector accounts for the bulk of income for some 17 per cent of the Lithuanian workforce, significantly above the average level in the European Union. On the other hand, the share of agricultural production of the GDP is less than 6 per cent, a mere quarter of its 1994 share.

Table 5.4: GDP share of the agricultural sector in Lithuania, 1994–2001 (%)

1994	1995	1996	1997	1998	1999	2000	2001	2002 (Janauary–June)
21.1	23.1	20.1	16.6	14.3	11.9	10.0	9.4	5.9

Source: Department of Statistics, Vilnius.

Farms are typically small, rather unproductive and probably unsustainable in the long run. Attempts to modernize and restructure the countryside have proved slow and difficult. Large sections of farmers are old and unable to readjust, and sceptical towards selling their land.[33] Suspicion about commercialization of land is deep, and attachment to own 'ways of life' seems to be genuine. At the same time, their disposable income is significantly lower than the national average and rural unemployment is in some cases several times higher than in the main urban areas.

Presumably, the urban-rural disparity is a source of salient political divisions in Lithuania. The question is what kind of rural representation we can expect to find. Most visibly, the Peasants' Party has managed to build up a substantial body of electoral support, doing particularly well in certain rural districts. At the same time, the party seems to attract considerably more votes in municipal elections than in parliamentary elections, which may indicate that voters indeed make different calculations when they participate in local and national contests. Peasant Party supporters are more than twice as likely as the average Lithuanian to belong to the lowest income group.[34] But, although the sheer scale of the urban-rural division makes it easy to explain the presence of at least one significant party for rural protection, the electoral strength of the Peasants' Party should not be overstated. They do not attract anything like a plurality of votes among farmers, and their organizational ties with other rural interest groups seem limited. There were two agrarian parties in the first republic of Lithuania – the right-wing Farmers' Union and the left-wing Peasant People's Party. The latter was actually the single largest party throughout the period up to the suspension of parliament in 1926 (Žeruolis 1998, 125). Specific agrarian parties have been particularly successful in Lutheran countries of Western Europe, particularly in the Nordic countries. In predominantly Catholic countries of Europe, agrarian interests have tended to ally with Christian Democratic and conservative forces across the urban-rural divide (Lipset and Rokkan 1967, 46). There are few signs of similar alliances in contemporary Lithuania. Conservative parties like the Homeland Union are distinctively urban in outlook. They are overwhelmingly anti-protectionist, big-business oriented, and in favour of membership of the European Union. The Christian Democrats have been more eager to stress issues like rural protection, and enjoy a certain degree of rural support.[35] Overall, most agrarian voters belong to the 'losers' of economic liberalization and are clearly suspicious about further marketization. Besides, the speedy de-collectivization conducted by the Conservatives in the very early period of independence was painful and deeply unpopular among farmers, a factor that accounts for much of the loss of support by the Conservatives in the 1992 elections.

Who do rural dwellers and farmers tend to support? Many in the primary sector were collective farmers during Soviet times and are likely to consider themselves as 'workers' even today. Many of them are negative about market economy altogether. By way of illustration, according to the *New Europe Barometer* (2001), some 10 per cent more rural dwellers than urban dwellers are positive about the communist regime and socialist economy of the past. In a similar vein, considerably more rural dwellers admit that they would prefer to abolish parliament and install a strong leader instead. To answer the question 'Who do rural dwellers support?' is moot, but it seems clear that a majority of them have voted for left-of-centre parties. It may be that many of them believe the leftist parties will give them better protection from harsh market reforms. Alternatively, they may vote for them for entirely sentimental reasons. 'Conservatism' and 'anti-change' clearly have different meanings in a post-communist setting. In any event, certain successful agriculture pressure via road blockades and lobbying through the Chamber of Agriculture on decision-making has taken place, for instance in determining minimum-price for certain agricultural products. But the truth is that rural interests are poorly represented in Lithuanian party politics. The rural dimension is obviously unlikely to disappear, but it is difficult to make any predictions as far as future representation of rural interests is concerned. More radical market reforms, continuing depopulation of the countryside and integration into the European Union are factors that in all likelihood will have profound consequences for this issue and for the countryside as a whole.

The chief division line between 'urban' and 'rural' interests would supposedly lie between protectionists and advocates of a free market. If that is the case, urban interests are perhaps best taken care of by the liberal and strongly pro-market Liberal Union, but to some extent also by the Conservatives and the Centre Union. Lifestyle and moral issues might comprise another set of urban-rural divisions. We will return to the latter issue below. As for lifestyle values, it seems apt that Vilnius and a few other urban spots are changing at a dramatically faster pace than rural areas, appearing increasingly cosmopolitan and pluralistic. Although alternative lifestyles and post-materialist values have yet to be expressed through party preferences, it is noteworthy that the New Democracy Party, led by former Prime Minister Kazimiera Prunskienė, forged an alliance with the Peasants' Party in 2002. Whether the alliance will attempt to combine a rural and environmental profile, in a way reminiscent of the Nordic centre parties, remains an open question. Interestingly enough, the first organizations to challenge the Soviet regime had post-material flavours, especially after the Chernobyl catastrophe in the mid-1980s. On the other hand, the environmental question was closely linked with the emerging independence movement. In any case, post-communist transformation posed rather pressing material issues for most people and only rising living standards could pave the way for a post-material agenda.[36]

The Relevance of European Integration

Together with NATO membership, the most profiled political issue in Lithuania over the last few years has undoubtedly been the membership application to the European Union. This process will itself have immense impact on domestic politics.[37] EU membership does not really represent a division between political parties and elites in Lithuania. There are no strong and well-organized anti-EU movements. The issue has hardly stirred any political rifts or given birth to novel alignments among the political elites. Virtually all major actors on the Lithuanian political stage are unanimously in favour of membership. Across almost the entire political spectrum, the question of membership of the European Union, together with that of NATO membership, represent the very core of political anchoring and national identification: to align itself with the 'West', or to remain under the sway of Russia. Arguably, democratic consolidation has been even more complex for Lithuania and the Baltic countries than for many other Central and Eastern European countries. As former Soviet republics, they did not only face a radical shift from authoritarian rule and centrally planned economy to democracy and market economy, but also to national independence. They have, in brief, faced a 'triple transition' (Offe 1992). This is why identity formation has been at the very heart of post-Soviet politics in Estonia, Latvia and Lithuania. Membership of the European Union has been a highly important component in this process. Baltic elites have faced the intricate tasks of juggling de-communization, nation-building and 'Europeanization' (Duvold and Berglund 2003). However, it leaves few options for the political elites but to adapt to an already existing framework of politico-legal practises. The scope for 'home-made' solutions is severely limited.

Even if the European question has yet to produce new political divisions in Lithuania, it seems apt to assume that it will do so at some point. A solid majority of Lithuanians support membership, which was confirmed in a referendum on the question, held in May 2003. Over 90 per cent voted in favour. Prior to the two-day referendum, there were serious concerns about the turnout, which must reach 50 per cent to be valid. Many feared that political apathy, lack of an organized anti-movement, over-confident supporters, and several hundred thousand 'absent' voters could trigger a very low turnout.[38] As it turned out, more than 60 per cent cast their vote. Nevertheless, a significant minority remains oblivious of or even negative about EU membership. According to the *Candidate Countries Eurobarometer* (2002), there is a slim majority of Lithuanians who think that membership would be 'a good thing', who think that Lithuania will benefit from membership, and who tend to trust the European Union. Approximately one-fifth holds the opposite view. There seems to be an obvious potential for exploiting weary public sentiments as soon as EU membership become part of domestic politics. The European Union might to some extent become a scapegoat for anything 'bad' – just like it has in several current member states. Furthermore, EU membership may actually reinforce some of the existing inequalities between 'winners' and 'losers', including urban-rural divisions. Although certain sections will be able to enjoy regional funds provided by the EU, the farming sector will inevitably go through a painful restructuring that will cost many livelihoods. Membership may also give birth to a certain nationalist backlash. Lithuania, like Latvia and Estonia, has emerged from Soviet domination and many people are truly sensitive about national self-determination. It should come as no great surprise that many Lithuanians, Latvians and Estonians appear to be rather uncommitted 'Europeans'. According to the *New Europe Barometer* from 2001, 44 per cent of the Lithuanians identify primarily with the nation-state.[39] That is more than twice as many as the average Central and East European country, and more than any country in the region. At the same time, 9 per cent identify primarily with Europe, slightly lower than the regional average, but up more than double since the mid-1990s. At the same time, according to the *Candidate Countries Eurobarometer* only 55 per cent of Lithuanians are 'proud of their country' – 30 per cent less than average in the region. In some other countries where dissatisfaction with own political system is high, like Romania, Bulgaria and Slovakia, support for the European Union is high. In Lithuania, dissatisfaction with domestic institutions is not matched by great trust in the EU. Just over 50 per cent trust the EU – considerably less than in the aforementioned countries. Only 41 per cent claim to be 'positive about the EU', more than 10 per cent less than average in the region (*Candidate Countries Eurobarometer* 2002).[40]

Traditionalists and Modernists

The 'Europe versus nation' dimension is about more than simply membership of the European Union. As we pointed out above, it goes to the very core of nation-building. It is quite plausible to draw a distinction between 'modernists' and 'traditionalists' in Lithuanian politics. In somewhat simplified terms, 'modernists' are young, educated urbanites with fairly cosmopolitan values and perceptions. They are likely to identify with a liberal agenda in terms of economics and politics, and support Lithuania's further integration into NATO and the EU. 'Traditionalists' are harder to identify, for the simple reason that being 'traditional' is a rather perplexing phenomenon in a society that underwent revolutionary changes just over a decade ago. For a start, there are those who might be called 'Soviet-style traditionalists', who struggle to accept that the Soviet economic system was unsustainable and, accordingly, mourn the disintegration of the predictable and humdrum Soviet society. A significant number of Lithuanians actually believe that Soviet communism was a superior political and economic system, although few of them actually want to turn back the clock to the Soviet times. Many Soviet-style traditionalists take a moralist approach to personal lifestyle and family values. They are likely to share that approach with many 'anti-Communist traditionalists', represented by the Catholic Church and parties like the Homeland Union and the Christian Democrats, let alone fringe parties like the Nationalist Union and the Freedom League. Some of them seem almost hostile to modernity and liberal values. Anti-Communist traditionalists are undoubtedly very national-minded, and a few of them seem to prefer to rebuild a 'pure' Lithuania as of two or three generations ago, rather than facing a cosmopolitan and technologically advancing democracy for the 21st century. However, most mainstream conservatives take a more pragmatic position towards the contemporary world, and consequently support market reforms and membership of the European Union and (particularly) NATO.

The religious dimension does to some extent have roots in inter-war times. The Christian Democratic Party was a dominant force in Lithuanian politics up to the 1926 *coup d'état*, drawing support particularly from rural and clerical sections of the electorate (Žeruolis 1998, 124). The Christian Democratic Party and the smaller Christian Democratic Union[41] have represented the religious dimension in post-communist Lithuania. The anti-Soviet resistance from the Catholic Church made the party a fairly important player during the independence struggle. However, the political 'space' the party tried to occupy, particularly on moral issues, simply submerged with the value-laden anti-Communist conflict, which meant that the Christian Democrats had to compete with, and being largely overshadowed by, the Conservatives. The party has also been a victim of the decline of the old regime conflict. However, it is worth noting that the Christian Democrats are closer to the Social Democrats than the Conservatives in terms of social spending (Žeruolis 1998, 132).

Finally, farmers, a potential stronghold for the Christian Democrats in the future, also represent the 'traditionalist' flank of this modernist-traditional dichotomy. But with the agriculture sector likely to undergo radical modernization in the years to come, they face an uphill battle to keep their way of life. The change might well be met by vocal protests.

Strong personalities

The preferences for some form of authoritarian rule are disturbingly prevalent in Lithuania (*Tables 5.5–5.7*). Forty per cent of the Lithuanian respondents in the NEB survey as of 2001 agree or strongly agree with the statement 'Best to get rid of Parliament and elections and have a strong leader who can quickly decide everything'. Authoritarian preferences have been consistently high in Lithuania throughout the 1990s and are considerably higher than in most other Central and Eastern European democracies. Who are those who want to abolish democracy? Authoritarian sympathies do follow certain sociological patterns: rural dwellers, old people and – notably – those with low education harbour more authoritarian preferences.[42] On the other hand, some of these differences, particularly the age factor, are perhaps smaller than expected. Age, education and territoriality all appear to be poor predictors of variations in attitudes to communist rule. Party preference accounts for larger variations. Some 19 per cent among centre/left supporters would actually prefer to return to communist rule. Only 4 per cent of those who support centre/right parties hold the same opinion. Similarly, 69 per cent of the centre/left supporters rate the former communist regime in positive terms, compared with a mere 31 per cent among the centre/right supporters. The large discrepancy between the number of people who want to return to communist rule and those who evaluate the communist system of the past in positive terms is rather unique for the Baltic countries. Having been annexed and incorporated into the Soviet Union, the notion of actually returning to communist rule seems to be closely associated with the return of Soviet occupation, thence undesirable. However, that does not seem to prevent many people from giving positive ratings of the former political and economic system, embodied by the Soviet Union.

Table 5.5: Alternatives to democracy by age (%)

	18–29	30s	40s	50s	60+	Total
Return to communist rule	12	13	15	16	15	14
Military rule	4	3	4	7	9	6
'Strong-man' rule	35	34	39	50	45	40
Rejection of all authoritarian alternatives	59	60	58	44	48	53

Source: New Europe Barometer (2001).

Table 5.6: Alternatives to democracy by education (%)

	Elementary	Secondary Vocational	Secondary Academic	University	Total
Return to communist rule	18	16	14	6	14
Military rule	12	5	5	1	6
'Strong-man' rule	58	46	40	18	40
Rejection of all authoritarian alternatives	39	48	53	79	53

Source: New Europe Barometer (2001).

Table 5.7: Alternatives to democracy by party preference (%)

	Centre/Left	Centre/ Right	Other party	Not vote or don't know	Total
Return to communist rule	19	4	25	14	14
Military rule	4	5	10	6	6
'Strong-man' rule	42	30	62	39	40
Rejection of all authoritarian alternatives	48	68	32	54	53

Source: New Europe Barometer (2001).

The idea of military rule does not appeal to many Lithuanians. Overall, lack of enthusiasm for army rule sets post-communist Europe apart from several countries in Latin America, Africa and the Middle East: the army does not provide a realistic regime alternative. This is in all likelihood a legacy of the communist era, when the military was under heavy political control and dominated by Moscow. Looking back to inter-war times, however, there were surely elements of 'army rule' and military leaders – like Poland's Marshal Piłsudski. Lithuania's very own Antanas Smetona was not actually a military leader, but his dictatorship was preceded by a military coup in 1926, also supported by the Catholic Church. Although a comparatively mild dictatorship, Smetona's regime had militaristic and even some fascist properties.[43] Soviet occupation pre-empted any possibilities for Lithuania to have an open and liberal re-evaluation of the Smetona period. The issue became buried under official Soviet rhetoric and re-emerged only after independence. Some Lithuanians, particularly among the elderly, are likely to consider Smetona as a significant statesman – even a national hero. In their opinion, he gave Lithuania a sense of order and direction, and his reign does indeed mark a period of relative prosperity. For fringe nationalists, the Smetona regime continues to symbolize a more 'pure' Lithuanian path – undiluted by either Russian or Western influences. On the other hand, the chances of a latter-day Smetona appearing on the Lithuanian political stage today are slim. The decline of the vehemently anti-Communist 'old' Right, and the recent success of more pragmatic centre/right parties make a new Smetona even less probable. Extremist parties like the Freedom League and the Nationalist Union – the latter being the heir of Smetona's party – are hardly in a position to exercise influence on the national level, although some are present in a few local councils. Most people probably do not want a full-fledged dictator, but many – perhaps a majority – would in all likelihood prefer to see a Gaullist-style president: a strong, decisive leader with whom they can identify.

The second and decisive round of the presidential elections in 2003 probably testifies to a certain yearning for a strong leader.[44] The winner, Rolandas Paksas, fought an aggressive campaign, containing more than a touch of populism, whereas outgoing president Valdas Adamkus campaigned on a ticket of handsome foreign policy achievements – the chief domain of the president. Paksas, on the other hand, stressed rather domestic issues like law and order, which happen to be responsibilities of the government. In all possibility, he may have succeeded in convincing many voters that his powers *would* extend to domestic issues. A lot of Lithuanians appear to be in favour of a stronger presidency – to the detriment of a parliamentary model of government. MPs and political parties, cornerstones of parliamentary democracy, enjoy the support of less than 10 per cent of the population. The Prime Minister and President, on the other hand, can expect support from more than half the population, although this support is obviously rather erratic, depending on current performance as it is. What seems clear is that institutions in general enjoy very low legitimacy in Lithuania. As in most former communist countries of Central and Eastern Europe, voters put their trust in certain political leaders. To be sure, political parties are at the very heart of elections, parliamentary legislation and government formations. Parties are designed to be prime vehicles for representation – in Lithuania as in most European democracies. At the same time, post-communist parties tend to be instruments for personal ambitions, thence the large number of splinter groups and factions. To illustrate this point, even the support for a relatively well-organized and broad 'church' like the Social Democrats seems very much contingent on the popularity of its current leader, Algirdas Brazauskas. During the 2000 parliamentary election, the temporary alliance (prior to the official party merger) between the Labour Democrats and the Social Democrats focused heavily on Mr Brazauskas' personal appeal. In fact, the alliance was simply named the 'Social Democratic Coalition of Algirdas Brazauskas', and its stunning victory was clearly due to the popularity of Mr Brazauskas himself (who had semi-retired from politics only a couple of years before). Another case in point is the Homeland Union, which also has a fairly solid party organization, including a relatively large membership pool. Yet, the increasing unpopularity of its longstanding leader, Vytautas Landsbergis, contributed to the party's near-collapse in the 2000 general election. The simultaneous rise of Artūras Paulauskas' New Union represents a contrasting example. Following the rising popularity of former presidential candidate Paulauskas, the party went from nowhere to become the second largest party in the 2000 general election.[45] Yet, the sudden decline of the New Union after just two years points to a decline in support for Mr Paulauskas himself. The party has failed to build up a stable party organization, and the image of the party is indistinguishable from that of its leader. Besides, the ideological inconsistency of the party together with the dominant position of its government-partner, the Social Democrats, has drained the support for the party.[46] Finally, the rise of the Liberal Union in 2000 was almost equally linked to the popularity of its then new leader, Rolandas Paksas. The sudden rise of Mr Paksas' new party – the Liberal Democratic Party – in the 2002 local elections is evidently linked to his high profile during the presidential elections, which were held simultaneously. It seems reasonable to infer that his strategy includes a strong showing for the Liberal Democrats in the next general elections, giving Paksas more political clout.

Besides political parties, there are two other institutional factors that reinforce the role of personalities in Lithuanian politics: the electoral system and the presidency. The electoral system is a hybrid of single-members constituencies and proportional party lists, similar to the German system (see *Appendix 5.3*). It was born out of a compromise between the Right, which preferred a majoritarian system, and the Left, which promoted a proportional system. When the party system is strong, as in the German case, the proportional elements of the system will largely determine the outcome. In Lithuania, however, the proportional lists somewhat paradoxically account for less party fragmentation than the single-member lists – an outcome that must be attributed to the weak and fluid party system.[47] The 'presidential factor' is another feature that reinforces the role of personalities in Lithuanian politics. Lithuania is by and large a parliamentary democracy, with semi-presidential features (see *Appendix 5.4*). But the fact that the president is elected by popular mandate certainly enhances the prestige of the position. Arguably, the presidency is the 'big prize' for many ambitious political leaders, and this does little to diminish the role of personalities in Lithuanian politics. However, a bolder and more optimistic scenario is that the role of the presidency will diminish somewhat as the political game turns increasingly routinized and institutionalized.

Citizen involvement

As pointed out earlier in this chapter, recent elections indicate that the Lithuanian party system is less stable than some commentators were led to believe in the late 1990s. Darius Žeruolis, for instance, noted that launching a 'third force' of parties (or a coalition of parties), linked to neither of the main parties, had been attempted but been 'refuted' by the bipolar patterns of the party system (Žeruolis 1998, 123). As it turned out, a 'third force' of parties *did* emerge and brought about a redefinition of the Left/Right dimension. But Žeruolis' second suggestion for a possible party system change, the arrival of anti-system parties, has not materialized. A quick glance at various attitudinal data that have been compiled in Lithuania would make many commentators wonder why. Trust in institutions is often exceptionally low and many citizens seem to favour less-than-democratic alternatives. Although more than 40 per cent claim to be 'satisfied with the way democracy works' (above average in Central and Eastern Europe), very few people actually participate in politics. According to one major survey, 70 per cent believe that politics is too complex for them to understand.[48] Some 55 per cent admit that they are not interested in politics. Moreover, hardly any citizens have signed a petition, donated money, or participated in a rally or strike etc. (*Norbalt Living Conditions Survey* 1999). According to the same survey, only some 16 per cent are members of some kind of organizations.[49] Party and trade union membership is rather low by West European standards.[50]

Voluntary organizations supposedly 'instil in their members habits of cooperation and public-spiritedness, as well as the practical skills necessary to partake in public life' (Putnam 2000, 338). In other words, associationalism may act as leverage on politics, protecting citizens from arbitrary and unjust legislation. There are several possible ways of explaining the low level of participation in Lithuania, including mistrust in organizations in general, after decades of communist-imposed institutions (in which participation often was mandatory) and disappointment with the democratic performance after the early enthusiasm about independence and democracy. Other factors include reliance on friendship and other informal networks, which might be characterized as substitutes for associations. Lack of personal resources, scant public resources and possibly also lack of government determination to build frameworks for participation are also important factors. According to the 2001 *NGO Sustainability Index* for Lithuania, the number of Lithuanian NGOs flourished towards the end of the 1990s and afterwards. Broadly speaking, there are more than 3000 such organizations today, and the number is growing. Nevertheless, most of them have insufficient funding, are poorly linked with other organizations or public institutions, and, crucially, mass participation remains rather limited.

Corruption and the black economy have accounted for some serious problems in the marketization process. The black market reportedly accounts for one-fifth of the entire economy,[51] although the real size and nature of it is difficult to measure. But it has obviously been a necessary survival strategy for many individuals through difficult times. The other side of the coin, however, is infallible: widespread tax evasion, weakened state capacity and legitimacy, and simply elimination of whole sub-sections of the population from the social protection radar (Rosenberg 2001). Several proposals to curtail corruption and bribery, perceived to be particularly widespread in public procurements, have been made but are often not implemented, and some of those that have been implemented have been widely ignored.[52] The general public has rarely voiced its opposition to these phenomena, but it has certainly built up disdain for politicians, public officials and business people. Accordingly, about half the population distrust private enterprises, and some 70 per cent distrust political parties and MPs. According to the *New Europe Barometer* from 2001, more than 90 per cent believe that all or most public officials accept bribes. Moreover, in a recent report on corruption, two-thirds of those who were polled admitted that they were prepared to offer a bribe if necessary.[53] There have, moreover, been numerous reports of unethical links between business and politics.[54] Transparency International ranks Lithuania 36 in their 2002 *Corruption Perception Index* – below Estonia (ranked 29), but well above Latvia (at 52). Curiously, only some 10–15 per cent Lithuanians distrust newspapers and TV – considerably less than the Central and Eastern European average. This is particularly striking since, according to the *Candidate Countries Eurobarometer* 2002, less than 30 per cent of Lithuanians claim that they actually read newspapers every day. Whatever the case, trust in the mass media and distrust in the political class seem to be intimately linked: for many people the media appears as a 'white knight' who informs the public about the 'corrupt political class'. But there is, according to data from the *New Europe Barometer* 2001, little evidence to suggest that political distrust is linked with party preferences. Except that centre/right-wing supporters are twice as likely to trust the army, contempt for politicians, public institutions and business leaders is evenly spread among the public.

Lack of interest in politics may to some extent account for low electoral turnout. Elections – perhaps the most basic form of political involvement – fail to attract more than approximately 6 out of 10 voters. Gorbachev's *perestroika* and the national revival in the late 1980s and early 1990s spurred a broad movement against the Soviet regime. Two million Balts joined hands in an extraordinary 370-mile human chain in 1989. More than 70 per cent of the electorate cast their vote in Lithuania's founding election in 1990, and the turnout was even higher in the first multi-party elections two years later. Subsequent elections, however, saw a plummeting of the turnout, which currently hovers around 55–60 per cent of the electorate. It would seem reasonable to assume that many 'non-voters' are less-than-average satisfied with Lithuanian democracy. However, data from the *New Europe Barometer* reveal a fairly weak relationship between non-participation and satisfaction with democracy. We cannot conclude that there is a distinct segment of the Lithuanian population who never takes part in elections. But in any case, the low turnout makes it necessary to raise some questions about electoral volatility and political stability in Lithuania.

Conclusions

Due to the predominance of solid government majorities, a fairly small number of relevant parties, and a party system that encountered only moderate fragmentation, Lithuanian politics preserved a significant degree of stability and continuity throughout the 1990s. However, developments since the last edition of the *Handbook of Political Change in Eastern Europe* point to a certain reorganization of Lithuanian politics. The breakthrough of change came with the 'earthquake' elections of 2000, which saw the rise of several new trends. Centre/right parties with new agendas surfaced and marginalized the old regime discourse. Increasing coalescent behaviour among political actors (and, as it currently looks, even merger-oriented practices between parties) has turned the old value-laden conflict into a more 'classic' socio-economic divide, which also has put an end to the bipolar tendencies and opened up for a more centripetal party competition. The reorganization of 'Left' and 'Right' in Lithuanian politics clearly brings with it a political climate that is more conducive to cooperation. It also stands a better chance of forging links between socio-economic interests and voting preferences – to facilitate the location of individual parties along policy dimensions *vis-à-vis* rivals, rather than relying on the emotional outbursts that characterized Lithuanian politics of the 1990s.

Notwithstanding these positive trends, electoral volatility has increased significantly during the last elections, which obviously explains much of the party system change. High volatility may indicate that there is a fair amount of voter dissatisfaction and that societal interests continue to lack a clear expression on the elite level. Such discrepancy also makes it easier for charismatic personalities to surface. The 2002/03 presidential elections, which saw the surprise defeat of much-lauded Valdas Adamkus, testify to the existence of a potentially unpredictable political landscape. The victory of Rolandas Paksas could be interpreted as a turn towards greater populism, which might cast shadows on the Left/Right dimension in the future. Paksas scored particularly well among rural and deprived segments of the population, leaving Adamkus with a majority of the votes in only a handful of constituencies,[55] prompting one Lithuanian commentator to assert that 'we are living in two Lithuanias'. Losers, pessimists and nostalgic people have flocked to Paksas.[56] It is too early to assess the impact of the presidential elections, but it seems apt that many voters simply gave their vote of no confidence to the Lithuanian political establishment.

Although the main parties still can be identified along a Left/Right axis, there is also scope for breakthroughs of other issue dimensions that may cut across it. We have already hinted at several unpredictable factors of Lithuanian politics, ranging from low levels of trust in politicians, via lack of satisfaction with the economic and political performance and urban-rural disparities, to the rather loose party organizations that form the basis of elections. Naturally, we are unable to make strong predictions about potential 'upsets' and 'shock results' in the future. There are, in truth, few signs of an imminent radical turn in Lithuanian politics. Moreover, rising prosperity will in all likelihood produce higher regime support and more sophisticated means of articulating interests in the coming years. On the other hand, it goes without saying that non-involvement of almost half the electorate, coupled with lack of political trust and low regime rating, creates a degree of uncertainty. Against this backdrop, it should not come as a major surprise that Lithuanian politics is still marked by fluidity. And for all intents and purposes, very many opinions are simply not heard or represented in Lithuanian politics. To what extent these voices – whatever they might express – will eventually join forces and become more strongly heard is a moot question. Upcoming general elections may provide answers as to whether the current post-2000 period is marked merely by a temporary oscillation, signalling further reshuffles, or if it amounts to more invariable patterns of party interaction and even the emergence of cleavage-based politics.

Acronyms

LCJ/LCD – Lithuanian Centre Movement/Union (*Lietuvos centro judėjimas/sąjunga*)
LDDP – Lithuanian Labour Democratic Party (*Lietuvos demokratinė darbo partija*)
LDP – Lithuanian Democratic Party (*Lietuvos dekokratų partija*)
LDP – Liberal Democratic Party (*Liberalų demokratų partija*) [since 2001]
LKD – Lithuanian Christian Democrats (*Lietuvos krikdčionys demokratai*)
LKDP – Lithuanian Christian Democratic Party (*Lietuvos krikščionių demokratų partija*)
LKDS – Lithuanian Christian Democratic Union (*Lietuvos Krikščionių demokratų sąjunga*)
LKP – Lithuanian Communist Party (*Lietuvos komunistų partija*)
LLENS – Union of Lithuanian Poles (*Lietuvos lenkų sajunga*) [relabelled LLRA]
LLRA – Electoral Action of Lithuanian Poles (*Lietuvos lenkų rinkimų akcija*)
LLS – Lithuanian Liberal Union (*Lietuvos liberalų sajunga*)
LMP – Lithuanian Womens' Party (*Lietuvos moterų partija*)
LNPJL – Lithuanian National Party 'Young Lithuania'
(*Lietuvių nacionalinė partija 'Jaunoji Lietuva'*)
LPKTS – Union of Lithuanian Political Prisoners and Deportees
(*Lietuvos politinių kalinių ir tremtinių sajunga*)
LRS – Union of Lithuanian Russians (*Lietuvos rusų sajunga*)
LSDP – Lithuanian Social Democratic Party (*Lietuvos socialdemokratų partija*)
LTMA – Alliance of Lithuanian National Minorities (*Lietuvos tautinių mažumų aliansas*)
LTJS – Lithuanian National Youth Union 'Young Lithuania'
(*Lietuvos tautinio jaunimo susivienijimas 'Jaunoji Lietuva'*) [relabelled LNPJL]
LTS – Lithuanian Nationalist Union (*Lietuvos tautininų sajunga*)
LVP – Lithuanian Peasants' Union (*Lietuvos valstiečių partija*)
LŽP – Lithuanian Green Party (*Lietuvos Žalioji Partija*)
ND – New Democracy (*Naujoji demokratija*)
NP – Independence Party (*Nepriklausomybės partija*)
NS – New Union (*Naujoji sśjunga/Social liberalai*)
TS[LK] – Homeland Union-Lithuanian Conservatives
(*Tėvynės Sajunga [Lietuvos konservatoriai]*)

NOTES

1. On 'tabula rasa' theories in new democracies, see for instance Shabad and Slomczynski (1999).
2. Although some political divisions merely separate one party from another independently of the Left/Right axis (Lijphart 1984, 127–29).
3. Also, see Jurkynas 2001 and Jurkynas 2003.
4. Mikhail Gorbachev's liberalization of the Soviet regime under the slogans *glasnost* and *perestroika* in the mid-1980s provided the basis for popular fronts across Central and Eastern Europe. Due to the conservative nature of the Lithuanian Communist Party, *perestroika* started to make an impact in Lithuania only in 1988 (Žeruolis 1998, 20).
5. The 1989 amendments of the Soviet Lithuanian Constitution scrapped the ban on political organizations.
6. The anti-independence and pro-Moscow organization *Edinstvto*, mainly backed by reactionary Russian and Polish politicians, did not exert as extensive political campaigns as similar anti-independence organizations in Latvia and Estonia.
7. In 1992, coalitions won 17.5 per cent of the votes and only 2.1 per cent in 1996 (Žeruolis 1998, 124). In 2000, however, coalitions won 72 per cent of the votes cast.
8. The Labour Democrats attracted over 800,000 votes and won 73 parliamentary seats out of 141.
9. The remains of the old *Sajūdis* turned into a social movement in December 1993 (Nørgaard et al. 1999, 88).
10. Vytautas Landsbergis did not run for office after his party lost heavily in the general elections the previous year. Therefore, the *Sajūdis* decided to support another right-wing candidate.
11. The pendulum effect was only visible in terms of the distribution of seats, since the majority of voters seem to have abstained rather than actually changed party preferences.

12. The Homeland Union received 70 mandates out of 141. However, four constituencies did not elect any candidate at all, since the turnout was lower than the 40 per cent required for valid result. Elections in the relevant constituencies were organized between 1997 and 1999, but three parliamentary seats remained vacant.

13. The choice indicates that the Homeland Union preferred a broad centre-right coalition as a bulwark against the Left.

14. Polls of political elites in 1994–1996 revealed that the ideological cleavage was tenacious (Žeruolis 1998, 96–9).

15. Brazauskas declined to run for office for a second time, urging voters to choose new and young politicians. He himself threw his support in favour of Artūras Paulauskas. Landsbergis failed to qualify for the second round.

16. In the first round, Adamkus was supported primarily by the Centre Union, whereas Paulauskas had the support of the Labour Democrats, the Peasants' Party, the Party of Electoral Alliance of Lithuanian Poles and the Women's Party. Paulauskas and his followers established the New Union/Social Liberal Party (NS) after the elections.

17. Based on a survey of political parties, Žeruolis (1998, 130) concludes: 'it is obvious that issues outside socio-economic conflict dominate the Left/Right divide in Lithuanian politics'.

18. The dimensional placement of parties is based on their ideological self-understanding and identification among the voters (*Research on political culture* 1996; Žeruolis 1998, 129–31). Black boxes portray parties with low parliamentary representation.

19. According to the head of the Central Electoral Commission, Zenonas Vaigauskas, data from the very first local elections (1990) were unavailable, since the archives had remained in the municipalities and parts of the documents had either been lost or not retrieved (E-letter to Mindaugas Jurkynas, 11 December 2002).

20. In his annual address to the *Seimas* in 2000, President Valdas Adamkus criticized the style and performance of the Conservative-dominated parliament and raised the idea of a 'new politics' that could break the old patterns of conflict. The appeal found response among several centre-oriented parties. The resulting 'New Politics' bloc consisted of the Liberal Union, the New Union, the Centre Union and the Modern Christian Democrats.

21. As demonstrated by Darius Žeruolis, the Homeland Union and the Christian Democrats benefited from strong level of socio-psychological attachments among their respective core constituencies (Žeruolis 1998, 134).

22. Gordon Smith (1989) suggests a three-election time span in order to evaluate the relevance of party system change.

23. The Social Democrats had 15,000 members in 2001, the Homeland Union had 13,000, and the Christian Democrats 10,000 (Krupavičius and Žvaliauskas 2003, 112).

24. Labour surveys conducted by the Lithuanian Department of Statistics reveal that the unemployment rate reached, on average, 13.8 per cent in 2002.

25. Lithuania's GDP growth in 2000 was 3.8 per cent; in 2001 it was 5.9 per cent; and 6.7 per cent in 2002 (Lithuanian Department of Statistics).

26. The Homeland Union was most active in paying attention to a strong Russian influence in the Lithuanian economy, especially in connection with recent privatization deals of the energy sector, such as Russian Gazprom's purchase of the Kaunas electric power station and shares in Lithuanian Gas.

27. A curious feature is that the Lithuanian Constitution explicitly prohibits Lithuania from joining any post-Soviet Alliances, such as the Commonwealth of Independent States (CIS).

28. We have included the Social Democratic Party and the New Union (Social Liberals) as 'centre/left'.

29. We have included the Modern Christian Democratic Union, Liberal Union, Centre Union, Homeland Union (Lithuanian Conservatives) and the Christian Democrats as 'centre/right'. Fringe parties on the Right, like the Freedom Union and 'Young Lithuania', are not included. Similarly, rural or ethnic parties – Action of Lithuanian Poles, Union of Lithuanian Russians, the New Democracy Party and the Peasants' Party – are excluded.

30. The level of general government expenditures in relation to GDP is reduced to a level well below the EU average (TransMONEE Database 2000, quoted in Rosenberg, 2001).

31. In April 2003, the Electoral Action of Lithuanian Poles switched side on the eve of the election of mayor for Vilnius, thus toppling their former coalition partners, the Liberal Union, and mayor Artūras Zuokas. The 'coup' got several thousands on to the Vilnius streets in protest.

32. Turnout in Polish-dominated Šalčininkai, Trakai and Vilnius districts hovers around 40 per cent.

33. Restrictions on sale of land to foreign purchasers were lifted in 2002 as part of the membership negotiations with the European Union.

34. Calculations are based on questions of voting intentions in the *New Europe Barometer* (2001).

35. As of May 2003, the Christian Democrats and the New Democracy and Peasants' Party (which merged in 2002) are reportedly considering some type of merger.

36. None of the two parties with post-material profile – the Greens and the Women's Party – were successful in playing out the 'life quality' card (Jurkynas 2003).

37. Membership requires the daunting task of transferring some 80,000 pages of legal text that comprise the *acquis communautaire* on to different branches and levels of administration.

38. According to the 2001 census, some 200,000 Lithuanians have emigrated since 1989. Many of them work illegally and were unlikely to use their vote.

39. The Latvian and Estonian figures are also rather high, and if we exclude Russians – who tend to identify with Russia or local regions primarily – the figures would be quite similar in all three countries.

40. Perhaps the EU appears as some kind of 'Groucho Club' for many Lithuanians: they do not particularly want to join a club that accepts them as members!

41. The two parties merged and became the Lithuanian Christian Democrats (LKD) in May 2001. A splinter of LKDP – the marginal Modern Christian Democratic Union (MKDS) – was set up in April 2000.

42. The greater importance of education for the support of democracy, compared with other social structural factors, has been highlighted in other studies of post-communist Europe (see Rose, Mishler and Haerpfer 1998, 139).

43. Smetona's party, the Nationalists (*Tautininkai*), was organized along fascist principles – with strong discipline and loyalty to the Leader. Similarly, the Veterans' Association, linked with the party, was organized as a state-run paramilitary force (Lieven 1994).

44. According to a survey that was compiled just after the elections, 46 per cent of those who voted for Paksas stressed 'youth' as important for their choice (clearly related to Adamkus being considered too old). Twenty per cent focused on his 'energy', 'boldness' and 'firmness' and 16 per cent mentioned 'promise of change' (*Prezidento rinkimai*, Vilmorus/Open Society Fund Survey, Vilnius 2003).

45. But the party became only the third largest in the *Seimas*, since the Liberal Union was more successful than the New Union in terms of gaining single-member seats.

46. As of May 2003, the Social Democrats and the New Union/Social Liberals are considering to forge closer ties, if not an outright merger.

47. See for instance Krupavičius and Žvaliauskas 2003 for further discussions on how the electoral system affects the party system in Lithuania. See also Shugart and Carey (1992).

48. The corresponding figures for Estonia and Latvia are 51 and 56 per cent respectively (*Norbalt Living Conditions Survey 1999*).

49. The corresponding figure for Estonia was 26 per cent and 23 per cent in Latvia. In terms of average number of organizational membership per person, Lithuania ranks at the very bottom in Central and East Europe (*World Values Survey* 1995–97, quoted in Howard, 2002).

50. According to party declarations of membership pool, approximately 3–5 per cent of the population are members of a political party. However, according to the 1999 *Norbalt Living Conditions Survey* of some 3000 Lithuanians, only 1 per cent holds membership in a political party. According to the same survey, some 5 per cent are members of a trade union.

51. See report on Lithuania in *Nations in Transit*, 2002.

52. See report on Lithuania in *Nations in Transit*, 2002.

53. On the other hand, some 50–60 per cent of business people and ordinary citizens claimed that they had not actually given any bribe over the last 5 years (Dobryninas, Zilinskiene and Alisauskiene, 2003).

54. See *Corruption and Anti-corruption Policy in Lithuania*, Open Society Institute, 2002.

55. Adamkus received a majority in Vilnius city, Kaunas city, Kaunas district, Palanga and Birštonas.

56. Raimundas Lopata, Director of the Institute of International Affairs and Political Science, Vilnius University, quoted on CNN.com on 5 January, 2003.

REFERENCES

Bobbio, Norberto (1996), *Left and Right: the Significance of a Political Distinction*, United Kingdom, Polity Press.

Candidate Countries Eurobarometer, Report 2002.2, Brussels 2002.

Corruption and Anti-corruption Policy in Lithuania (2002) EU Accession Monitoring Program/Open Society Institute, Vilnius.

Dobryninas, Zilinskiene and Alisauskiene (2003), *Map of Corruption in Lithuania, 2002*, Transparency International, Lithuanian chapter, Vilnius.

Duvold, Kjetil and Sten Berglund (2003), 'Democracy, Citizens and Elites', in Sten Berglund and Kjetil Duvold, eds, *Baltic Democracy at the Crossroads: An Elite Perspective*, Kristiansand, Nordic Academic Press.

Hellén, Thomas, Sten Berglund and Frank H. Aarebrot (1998), 'From Transition to Consolidation', in Sten Berglund, Tomas Hellén and Frank H. Aarebrot, eds, *The Handbook of Political Change in Eastern Europe*, Cheltenham, Edward Elgar.

Herron, S. Erik (2002), 'Failed Promises: Mixed Electoral Rules, Party Systems and Representation in Unconsolidated Democracies', Paper prepared for the *Consolidation of New Democracies* Conference, Uppsala, June 2002.

Howard, Marc Morjé (2002), 'The Weakness of Post-Communist Civil Society', *Journal of Democracy*, Volume 13, Number 1, January 2002.

Jurkynas, Mindaugas (2001), 'Politinio konflikto kaita ir takoskyros', in Algimantas Jankauskas, ed., *Lietuva po Seimo rinkimų*, Kaunas, Naujasis lankas.

—— (2003), 'Decline or Loss of Old Ideological Conflict? The Case of Lithuania', paper presented at the International workshop *Loss, Decline and Doom in the Baltic Sea Area*, Greifswald, Germany, February 2003.

Kitschelt, Herbert, Zdenka Mansfeldová, Radosław Markowski and Gábor Tóka (1999), *Post-communist Party System: Competition, Representation, and Inter-party Cooperation*, New York, Cambridge University Press.

Klingemann, Hans-Dieter and Dieter Fuchs, eds (1995), *Citizens and the State*, Oxford University Press.

Krupavičius, Algis and Giedrius Žvaliauskas (2003), 'Political Parties and Elite Recruitment in Lithuania', in Sten Berglund and Kjetil Duvold, eds, *Baltic Democracy at the Crossroads: An Elite Perspective*, Kristiansand, Nordic Academic Press.

Lieven, Anatol (1994), *The Baltic Revolution: Estonia, Latvia, Lithuania and the Path to Independence*, New Haven, Yale University Press.

Lijphart, Arend (1984), *Democracies: Patterns of Majoritarian and Consensus Government in Twenty-one Countries*, New Haven, Connecticut, Yale University Press.

Lipset, Martin Seymour and Stein Rokkan (1967), *Party Systems and Voter Alignments: Cross-National Perspective*, New York, Free Press.

Mainwaring, Scott P. (1999), *Rethinking Party Systems in the Third Wave of Democratization: the Case of Brazil*, Stanford, California, Stanford University Press.

Matonytė, Georges and Irmina Mink (2003), 'From *Nomenklatura* to Competitive Elites: Communist and Post-communist Elites', in Sten Berglund and Kjetil Duvold, eds, *Baltic Democracy at the Crossroads: An Elite Perspective*, Kristiansand, Nordic Academic Press.

New Europe Barometer (2001), data file, the research project *Conditions of European Democracy*, Örebro University/Centre for the Study of Public Policy (CSPP), University of Strathclyde.

Norbalt Living Conditions Survey (1999), data file, Fafo Institute for Applied International Studies, Oslo.

Nørgaard, Ole et al. (1999), *The Baltic States After Independence*, Cheltenham, Edward Elgar.

Offe, Claus (1992), 'Capitalism by Democratic Design? Democratic Theory Facing the Triple Transition in East Central Europe', *Social Research*, Vol. 58, No. 4, 865–92.

Partijų programos: sutrumpintas variantas (2000), *Vyriausioji rinkimų komisija*, Vilnius.

Prezidento rinkimai, Vilmorus/Open Society Fund Survey, Vilnius 2003.

Putnam, Robert D. (2000), *Bowling Alone: The Collapse and Revival of American Community*,

New York, Simon and Schuster.

Rae, Douglas W. and Michael Taylor (1970), *The Analysis of Political Cleavages*, New Haven, Yale University Press.

Report on Lithuania in *Nations in Transit* 2002, Freedom House.

Research on political culture (1996), UAB SIC *Rinkos tyrimai and TSPMI*, Vilnius University, Vilnius.

Research on political culture (1999), UAB SIC *Rinkos tyrimai and TSPMI*, Vilnius University, Vilnius.

Rose, Richard, William Mishler and Christian Haerpfer (1998), *Democracy and its Alternatives: Understanding Post-communist Societies*, Baltimore, The John Hopkins University Press.

Rosenberg, Dorothy J. (2001), 'Eastern Enlargement of the European Union: Problems of Convergence', unpublished paper.

Sartori, Giovanni (1976), *Parties and Party Systems. A Framework for Analysis*, Vol. 1, Cambridge, Cambridge University Press.

Shabad, Goldie and Kazimierz M. Slomczynshi (1999), 'Political Identities in The Initial Phase of Systemic Transformation in Poland: A Test of the Tabula Rasa Hypothesis', *Comparative Political Studies*, 32, 6.

Shugart, Matthew S. and John M. Carey (1992), *Presidents and Assemblies: Constitutional Design and Electoral Dynamics*, Cambridge, Cambridge University Press.

Sitter, Nick (2001), 'Beyond Class vs. Nation? Cleavage Structures and Party Competition in Central Europe', *Central European Political Science Review*, 2, 3.

Smith, Gordon (1989), *Politics in Western Europe: A Comparative Analysis*, Aldershot, Dartmouth.

Wessels, Bernhard and Hans-Dieter Klingemann (1994), *Democratic Transformation and the Prerequisites of Democratic Opposition in East and Central Europe*, Wissenschaftszentrum Berlin für Sozialforschung, Berlin.

Žeruolis, Darius (1998), 'Lithuania', in Sten Berglund, Tomas Hellén and Frank H. Aarebrot, eds, *The Handbook of Political Change in Eastern Europe*, Cheltenham, Edward Elgar.

Zielinski, Jakub (2002), 'Translating Social Cleavages into Party Systems: The Significance of New Democracies', *World Politics*, 54 (January 2002).

APPENDIX 5.1: ELECTION RESULTS

PARLIAMENTARY ELECTIONS

1990 elections to the Aukščiausioji Taryba/Atkuriamasis Seimas
First round
Date: 24 February
Turnout: 71.7%

	MPs elected	of which Sajūdis MPs
No party affiliation	48	46
LKP	22	13
LKP–TSKP	7	0
LSDP	9	9
LŽP	2	2
LKDP	2	2
Total	90	72

Second round
Date: 4, 7, 8 and 10 March;
new elections to vacant seats after two rounds on 7 and 21 April
Turnout: 66.4%

	MPs elected	of which Sajūdis MPs
No party affiliation	25	21
LKP	19	6
LKP–TSKP	2	0
LDP	3	2
Total	49	29

1992 elections to the 2nd Seimas
Date: 25 October and 15 November
Turnout: 75.3% (average of two rounds)

	%	Seats in MMD	Seats in SMD
LDDP	42.6	36	37
Sąjūdžio santara	20.5	17	11
LKDP, LPKTS *ir* LDP *jungtinis sąrašas*	12.2		
LKDP		3	6
LPKTS		3	2
LDP		4	–
LSDP	5.5	5	3
LKDS *ir Lietuvių tautinio jaunimo 'Jaunoji Lietuva' susivienijimas už vieningą Lietuvą*	3.4		
LKDS		–	1
LTJS *'Jaunoji Lietuva'*		–	–
LCJ	2.4	–	2
LLENS	2.1	2	2
LTS *ir* NP *sąrašas*	1.9		
LTS		–	3
NP		–	1
Independent candidates	–	–	1
Total		70	71

1996 elections to the 3rd Seimas
Date: 20 October (first round) and 10 November (second round)
Turnout: 52.9% (first round), 38.2% (second round)

Party/coalition	%	**Mandates** Total	in MMD	in SMD
TS(LK)	29.8	70	33	37
LKDP	9.9	16	11	5
LDDP	9.5	12	10	2
LCS	8.2	13	9	4
LSDP	6.6	12	7	5
LNPJL	3.8	1	–	1
LMP	3.7	1	–	1
LKDS	3.1	1	–	1
LLRA	3.0	1	–	1
LTMA	2.4	–	–	–
LTS and LDP coalition	2.1		–	
LTS		1	–	1
LDP		2	–	2
LLS	1.8	1	–	1
LVP	1.7	1	–	1
LPKTS	1.5	1	–	1
Independent candidates	–	4	–	4
Total		137	70	67
Total number of seats		141		

2000 elections to the 4th Seimas
Date: 8 October
Turnout: 55.9%

		Mandates		
Party/coalition	*%*	*Total*	*in MMD*	*in SMD*
Social-Democratic Coalition of Algirdas Brazauskas	31.1	51	28[*]	23[**]
NS	19.6	28	18	11
LLS	17.3	33	16	18
TS-LK	8.6	9	8	1
KDS	4.2	1		1
LVP	4.1	4		4
LKDP	3.1	2		2
LCS	2.9	2		2
NKS	2.0	1		1
LLRA	1.9	2		2
LLS	1.3	1		1
JL/PKS	1.2	1		1
MKDS		1		1
Non-partisan		3		3
Total		141	70	71

[*] LDDP 13; LSDP 11; LRS 3; NDP 1
[**] LDDP 14; LSDP 7; NDP 2

PRESIDENTIAL ELECTIONS

1993 Elections
Date: 14 February
Turnout: 78.6%

Candidate	Votes	%	Party affiliation
Algirdas Mykolas Brazauskas	1,212,075	60.0	LDDP
Stasys Lozoraitis	772,922	38.3	Non-affiliated, supported by *Sąjūdis*, LKDP, LCJ, LSDP and small non-left-wing parties
Invalid ballots	34,016	1.7	

Source: *Prezidento rinkimų komisijos protokolas* (Protocol of the Presidential Election Commission), 17 February 1993.

1997–98 Elections
First round
Date: 21 December 1997
Turnout: 71.4%

Candidate	Votes	%	Party affiliation
Artūras Paulauskas	838,819	44.7	Non-party, supported by LLS, LDDP, LMP, LLRA, LVP, LŪP
Valdas Adamkus	516,798	27.6	Non-party, supported by LCS, LTS, LDP
Vytautas Landsbergis	294,881	15.7	TS(LK), endorsed by LKDP
Vytenis Povilas Andriukaitis	105,916	5.6	LSDP
Kazys Bobelis	73,287	3.9	LKDS
Rolandas Pavilionis	16,070	0.9	Independent
Rimantas Smetona	6,697	0.4	*Nacionaldemokratis judėjimas 'Už nepriklausomą Lietuvą'*
Invalid ballots	22,680	1.2	

Second round
Date: 4 January
Turnout: 73.6%

Candidate	Votes	%
Valdas Adamkus	968,031	50.0
Artūras Paulauskas	953,775	49.2
Invalid ballots	15,980	0.8

Source: *Vyriausioji rinkimų komisija* (Central Electoral Committee of Lithuania).

2002–03 Elections
First round
Date: 22 December 2002
Turnout: 49.2%

Candidate	Votes	%
Valdas Adamkus	475,850	35.53
Rolandas Paksas	267,971	19.66
Artūras Paulauskas	109,630	8.31
Vytautas Šerėnas	106,829	7.75
Vytenis Povilas Andriukaitis	98,167	7.30
Kazimira Danutė Prunskienė	68,739	5.04
Juozas Edvardas Petraitis	51,322	3.74
Eugenijus Gentvilas	42,750	3.08
Julius Veselka	30,350	2.23
Algimantas Matulevičius	29,803	2.22
Kazys Bobelis	25,148	1.91
Vytautas Antanas Matulevičius	25,030	1.86
Kęstutis Glaveckas	7041	0.52
Vytautas Šustauskas	4863	0.37
Vytautas Bernatonis	3121	0.25
Algirdas Pilvelis	1844	0.14
Rimantas Jonas Dagys	1115	0.09
Total	1,349,573	100

Second round
Date: 5 January 2003
Turnout: 48.4%

Candidate	Votes	%
Rolandas Paksas	777,769	54.2
Valdas Adamkus	643,870	44.8
Invalid ballots	14,683	1.0

Source: *Vyriausioji rinkimų komisija* (Central Electoral Committee of Lithuania).

APPENDIX 5.2: GOVERNMENT COMPOSITION

Partisan composition of governments and the cause of their termination since 1990

March 1990 – 10 January 1991
Premier: Kazimiera Danutė Prunskienė
Government parties: Sajūdis, LKP and non-party ministers
Political orientation: Oversized rainbow coalition government
Cause of termination: No confidence in the Supreme Council/Constitutive Assembly

10 January 1991 – 13 January 1991
Premier: Albertas Šimėnas
Government parties: Sajūdis, LKP and non-party ministers
Political orientation: Oversized rainbow coalition government
Cause of termination: Soviet intervention in Vilnius and 'disappearance' of the premier

January 1991 – July 1992
Premier: Gediminas Vagnorius
Government parties: Sajūdis
Political orientation: Right-wing, majority government
Cause of termination: Lack of confidence in parliament

July 1992 – December 1992
Premier: Aleksandras Algirdas Abišala
Government parties: Sajūdis
Political orientation: Right-wing, caretaker government
Cause of termination: Pre-term parliamentary elections

December 1992 – March 1993
Premier: Bronislovas Lubys
Government parties: LDDP
Political orientation: Left-wing majority government
Cause of termination: Lubys refused to continue after the presidential elections

March 1993 – February 1996
Premier: Adolfas Šleževičius
Government parties: LDDP
Political orientation: Left-wing majority government
Cause of termination: Lack of confidence in parliament

February 1996 – December 1996
Premier: Laurynas Mindaugas Stankevičius
Government parties: LDDP
Political orientation: Left-wing majority government
Cause of termination: Parliamentary elections

December 1996 – June 1999
Premier: Gediminas Vagnorius
Government parties: TS[LK]; LKDP; LCS (*de facto*)
Political orientation: Right-wing majority government
Cause of termination: Vagnorius criticised by President Adamkus and steps down

June 1999 – November 1999
Premier: Rolandas Paksas
Government parties: TS[LK]; LKDP
Political orientation: Right-wing majority government
Cause of termination: Dispute over privatization of oil company and Paksas steps down

November 1999 – October 2000
Premier: Andrius Kubilius
Government parties: TS[LK]; LKDP
Political orientation: Right-wing majority government
Cause of termination: Parliamentary election

October 2000 – June 2001
Premier: Rolandas Paksas
Government parties: LLS, NS
Political orientation: Centre-right minority government with support from smaller parties
Cause of termination: Internal strife; NS quits after failure to change prime minister

June 2001 –
Premier: Algirdas Mykolas Brazauskas
Government parties: LSDP, NU(SL)
Political orientation: Centre-left majority government

APPENDIX 5.3: THE ELECTORAL SYSTEM

The Lithuanian electoral system consists of elections to the parliament, the office of the president, the councils of local governments and referenda.

The parliament (*Lietuvos Respublikos Seimas* or *Seimas*) consists of 141 parliamentarians elected for a four-year term. The parliament is considered to be elected when three-fifths of parliamentarians have been elected. Regular elections to the *Seimas* are held no earlier than two, and no later than one month prior to the expiry of the term. Pre-term elections to the *Seimas* may be held (1) upon the decision of a three-fifths majority of all parliamentarians; (2) upon the decision of the President if the *Seimas* fails to adopt a decision on a new programme of the Government within 30 days of its presentation; (3) if the *Seimas* twice in succession disapproves of the Government programme within 60 days of its initial presentation; (4) or, upon proposal of the Government, if the *Seimas* expresses direct no confidence in the Government. The President may not, however, announce early elections to the *Seimas* if his own term expires within less than six months, or if six months have not passed since early elections to the *Seimas*. The election to the new *Seimas* must be held within three months from the adoption of the decision on pre-term elections.

The first name of the Lithuanian parliament was the Supreme Council of Lithuania (*Lietuvos Aukčiausioji Taryba* or *Aukščiausioji Taryba*), renamed the Constitutive Assembly (*Atkuriamasis Seimas*) in 1996. It contained 141 representatives, whose selection took place in single-mandate constituencies in the election of 1990. For the elections to be valid, a turnout of 50 per cent was required. If the turnout in individual constituencies was lower, new elections had to be called. For a straight win, candidates had to receive an absolute majority of the votes. If a winner emerged in the first round, the two top candidates advanced to a second round, in which the winner was declared by a simple majority.

The electoral system was changed prior to the 1992 *Seimas* elections. Seventy-one of the 141 mandates were to be contested in single-member constituencies, while the remaining 70 were to be elected under proportional representation in a single, countrywide district. The deputies were to be elected for a four-year term. Any citizen of the Republic of Lithuania who, on the day of election, has reached the age of 25 and is a permanent resident in Lithuania, can run for parliament.

A turnout of more than 40 per cent is required for the elections to be valid in the single-mandate constituencies. Up until 2000, a candidate who obtained more than 50 per cent of the votes in the first round was declared as the winner. When no winner emerged, the two front-runners had to contest a second round. When only two candidates participated in the first round and both failed to obtain 50 per cent plus one vote, new elections had to be held. In the second round, a simple majority was sufficient. In the multi-member constituencies, more than 25 per cent turnout is required for the elections to be valid. In order to qualify for seat distribution, parties and political movements must overcome a nation-wide threshold, originally set at 4 per cent, but raised to 5 per cent for individual parties and 7 per cent for joint lists in 1996. There was no threshold for national minority parties in the general election of 1992. This exemption was abolished before the 1996 general elections. Seats are distributed according to the Hare quota, where all votes for parties above the electoral threshold are pooled. The pool is divided by 70, equivalent to the total number of seats allocated in multiple-member constituencies. The votes of the individual parties are divided by the divisor. Remaining unallocated mandates are allocated to parties whose remainder is closest to the divisor.

The electoral system was again modified prior to the 2000 *Seimas* election. According to the amendments, the two-round format in single member constituencies was abandoned in favour of a simple form of plurality system – the First Past the Post system. If candidates receive an equal amount of votes, the older candidate becomes parliamentarian.

The President is elected in direct elections. A candidate who obtains more than 50 per cent of the votes in the first round cast is considered elected, provided that at least 50 per cent of all eligible voters participate in the election. If the turnout is below 50 per cent, the candidate who receives the majority of votes and at least one-third of all registered voters is declared as the winner. If no candidate obtains more than 50 per cent of the votes, a second round between the top two frontrunners is to be held within two weeks. The candidate who obtains the majority of all votes cast in the second round is considered elected, regardless of the turnout. If only two candidates run in the first round and neither obtains an absolute majority, or at least one-third of votes of all eligible voters, new elections are called. The President is elected for a five-year fixed term and may be elected for a maximum of two terms. The president-elect must immediately suspend his or her party membership.

In 1992–96, members to local representative bodies (*Savivaldybių tarybos*) were to be elected for a two-year term, which was extended to a three-year term in December 1996, and to a four-year term in June 2002. Mandates for lists of candidates are distributed according to the number of votes received by each list in each constituency. The number of local governments increased from 56 in 1997 to 60 in 2000. The threshold for entering local assemblies is 4 per cent for parties and 6 per cent for coalitions.

All issues that are considered to be of uttermost importance for the state and its citizens are to be decided by referendum. Referenda are either mandatory or consultative (deliberative). Petitions of at least 300,000 eligible citizens can also call for a referendum. A group of at least one-fourth of all MPs may also submit a proposal to the *Seimas* to call a referendum.

Mandatory referenda are called for the following issues: amendments to the provision of Article 1 of the Constitution of the Republic of Lithuania that 'the State of Lithuania shall be an independent and democratic republic'; amendments to the provisions of Chapter I of the Constitution ('the State of Lithuania'); amendments to the provisions of Chapter 14 of the Constitution ('Amending the Constitution'); amendments to the Constitutional Act, dated June 8, 1992 ('On Non-Alignment of the Republic of Lithuania to Post-Soviet Eastern Alliances'); regarding participation by the Republic of Lithuania in international organizations, should this participation be linked with partial transfer of the scope of competence of Government bodies to the institutions of international organizations or the jurisdiction thereof. Mandatory referendums may be held also with regard to other laws or provisions in which 300,000 citizens have signed a petition for, or the *Seimas* can submit a proposal to be decided in a referendum. Consultative (deliberative) referendums may be held with respect to other issues of great importance, but when a mandatory referendum is not deemed necessary. They are either proposed by at least 300,000 eligible voters or by the *Seimas*.

A mandatory referendum is considered valid if the turnout is above 50 per cent of all registered voters. Resolutions regarding the provision of Article 1 of the Constitution of the Republic of Lithuania ('The State of Lithuania shall be an independent, democratic Republic') and concerning the Constitutional Act of June 8, 1992 ('On Non-Alignment of the Republic of Lithuania To Post-Soviet Eastern Alliances') are considered adopted if at least 75 per cent of all eligible voters have approved them. Resolutions regarding amendments of the provisions of Article 1 of the Constitution ('The State of Lithuania') and Chapter 14 ('Amending the Constitution') are considered adopted if more than 50 per cent of all eligible voters have given their approval. Resolutions regarding other issues, laws or provisions that have been deliberated in a mandatory referendum are considered passed if more than 50 per cent of votes cast and at least one-third of all eligible voters approve them (for instance in the case of the referendum on the European Union membership, held on 10–11 May, 2003). Decision on issues regarding participation by the Republic of Lithuania in international organizations, should this participation be linked with partial transfer of the scope of competence of Government bodies to institutions of international organizations or the jurisdiction thereof, are deemed adopted if it has been approved by more than 50 per cent of votes cast. A consultative (deliberative) referendum is considered valid if the turnout is more than 50 per cent of all eligible voters. Resolution is adopted if at least 50 per cent of votes cast are in favour.

Sources:

Constitution of the Republic of Lithuania [*Lietuvos Respublikos Konstitucija*], Valstybės žinios, 1992, Nr. 33-1014, amendments included.

Law on the Amendment of the Law on Elections to the Seimas [*Lietuvos Respublikos Seimo rinkimų įstatymo pakeitimo įstatymas*], Valstybės žinios, 2000, Nr. 59-1760.

Law on Presidential Elections, [*Lietuvos Respublikos Prezidento rinkimų įstatymas*], Valstybės žinios, 1993, Nr. 2-29, amendments included

Law on the Amendment of Article 119 of the Constitution [*Lietuvos Respublikos Konstitucijos 119 straipsnio pakeitimo įstatymas*], Valstybės žinios, 1996, Nr. 122-2863.

Republic of Lithuania Law on the Amendment of Article 119 of the Constitution [*Lietuvos Respublikos Konstitucijos 119 straipsnio pakeitimo įstatymas*], Valstybės žinios, 2002, Nr. 65-2629.

Law on Elections to Municipal Councils [*Lietuvos Respublikos savivaldybių tarybų rinkimų įstatymas*], Valstybės žinios, 1994, Nr. 53-996, amendments included.

Law on Referendum [*Lietuvos Respublikos referendumo įstatymas*], Valstybės žinios, 2002, Nr. 64-2570.

APPENDIX 5.4: THE CONSTITUTIONAL FRAMEWORK

The Lithuanian Constitution was passed by a referendum on 25 October 1992. The Basic Provisional Law (*Laikinasis Pagrindinis Įstatymas*), passed by the Supreme Council-Constitutive Assembly on 11 March 1990, had regulated the political system between 1990 and 1992. The Provisional Law was in fact a revised version of the Constitution of the Lithuanian Socialist Soviet Republic, but without references to the Soviet Union. Up until the adoption of the constitution, Lithuania was formally a parliamentary republic, but due to the extraordinary political circumstances of this period, the central figure in Lithuanian political life was not the Prime Minister, but the Chairman of the Supreme Council-Constitutive Assembly (who was Speaker of Parliament *de jure*, but Head of State *de facto*). Lithuania introduced a system of partial separation of powers as a consequence of political compromises in the summer and autumn of 1992. The Constitution foresees a directly elected president partly due to personal ambitions and partly as a safeguard against hung parliaments. Lithuania is regarded as a semi-presidential republic due to power balance between the President and the Parliament (*Seimas*).

The Parliament

The Parliament (*Seimas*) (1) debates and enacts amendments to the Constitution; (2) legislates; (3) decides on holding referenda; (4) announces presidential elections; (5) establishes state institutions as provided by law, and appoints and dismisses their chief officers; (6) approves or rejects a candidacy for Prime Minister proposed by the President of the Republic; (7) considers the programme of the Government submitted by the Prime Minister, and decides on its approval; (8) upon the recommendation of the Government, establishes or abolishes ministries of the Republic of Lithuania; (9) supervises the activities of the Government, and may express no confidence in the Prime Minister or in individual Ministers; (10) appoints judges and Chairs to the Constitutional Court and the Supreme Court; (11) appoints (and dismisses) members of the Office of State Controllers and the Chair of the Board of the Bank of Lithuania; (12) announces elections to the councils of local government; (13) forms the Central Electoral Committee and changes its composition; (14) approves the State budget and supervises the implementation thereof; (15) introduces taxes and other obligatory payments; (16) ratifies or rejects international treaties to which the Republic of Lithuania is a party, and considers other issues of foreign policy; (17) establishes administrative divisions of the Republic; (18) establishes state awards; (19) grants amnesty; and (20) imposes direct administration and martial law, declares state of emergency, announces mobilization, and decides on the use of the Armed Forces.

The *Seimas*, the Government, the President and the signatures of at least 50,000 citizens have the rights to take legislative initiative, which can either be adopted or rejected by the *Seimas*. A law is adopted when a majority of parliamentarians who participate in the sitting vote in favour. Constitutional laws are adopted when more than 50 per cent of all parliamentarians vote in favour. Amendments of Constitutional laws must be approved by at least three-fifths of all members of the *Seimas*. The President must sign laws that are passed. Unless the President either signs or returns the law to the *Seimas* for reconsideration, the Chairperson of the Parliament signs the law. In order for the *Seimas* to enact a law that has been vetoed by the President, an absolute majority of parliamentarians must vote in favour (three-fifths in the case of a constitutional law). Provisions of the laws may also be adopted in a referendum.

In case of gross violations of the Constitution, breach of oath, or upon the disclosure of a felony crime, the *Seimas* may remove from office the President, the Chair and judges of the Constitutional Court, the Supreme Court and the Court of Appeals, as well as *Seimas* members, by a three-fifths majority vote of all parliamentarians. The *Seimas* may also dismiss other appointed or elected officers by a simple majority vote of all MPs. The parliament may dissolve itself if three-fifths of all *Seimas* members vote in favour.

The President

The President officially promulgates laws passed by the *Seimas*, but has also the right to veto. He or she can return laws to the *Seimas*, which in turn may override the presidential veto (see above). The President names the Prime Minister who, upon investiture by the *Seimas*, forms the

Government. The Ministers are either appointed or dismissed by a presidential decree, upon the request of the Prime Minister. Only the *Seimas* can effectively censure or dismiss Ministers and the Government. The President may dissolve the *Seimas* if the Government is defeated in a vote of no confidence in the *Seimas*, but only if the Government asks the President to call early elections. The President may also call early parliamentary elections if the *Seimas* fails to make a decision on the Government's programme within 30 days, or if it rejects the Government's programme twice within 60 days from the day the programme was first submitted to the *Seimas*.

The President nominates the Chairman and judges of the Supreme Court and the Appeals Court; lower-level judges, three (out of nine) judges and the Chairman of the Constitutional Court, the Chairman of the State Control Office; and the Chairman of the Board of the National Bank. All these appointments have to be confirmed by the *Seimas*. The President also appoints (and dismisses) the Commander of the Armed Forces, Prosecutor General and the Head of the Security Services – all upon the approval of *Seimas*. The President can issue decrees, but in order to be valid some of them must be signed by the Premier or an appropriate Minister.

Under normal circumstances, early presidential elections can be called when the President dissolves the *Seimas* and at least three-fifths of the newly elected parliament call for early presidential elections. The powers of the President are terminated either upon the expiry of his/her term; upon holding pre-term presidential elections; upon the President's resignation or death; in the case of the Parliament removing the President from office via impeachment procedures; or when the *Seimas*, taking into account conclusions of the Constitutional Court and a three-fifths majority parliamentarian vote, conclude that the President cannot fulfil his or her duties for health reasons.

The constitutional set-up and political practice suggest that Lithuania is what Shugart and Carey (1992) would classify as a premier–presidential state, leaning towards parliamentarism. All presidential powers are matched by countervailing powers vested in the *Seimas*. In the areas where separation of powers is not very clearly stated, presidential supremacy is assumed (e.g. in foreign policy domains), but according to the constitution, both the President and the parliament can take the initiative and, hence, the personality of the President becomes a decisive factor. For instance, President Brazauskas chose to keep a low profile, staying out conflicts even when his former party held the majority in the *Seimas*. The Chairperson of the *Seimas,* Vytautas Landsbergis, heavily influenced foreign and defence policies in this period. However, Mr Brazauskas profile was more visible towards the end of his presidential term. By contrast, Valdas Adamkus, Brazauskas' successor, was far more active, enjoying considerable respect among the public. His moral authority allowed him to unseat Conservative Prime Minister Gediminas Vagnorius in 1999 in spite of the Conservative-dominated *Seimas*. The period after the presidential election of 2003 confirms that, without great legitimacy in the face of the public, the authority of the President is limited. Adamkus' successor, Rolandas Paksas, has held the office since February 2003. At the time of writing, it is too early to assess his abilities to exercise influence, but during the first months in office, he was largely overshadowed by a strong Premier with wide support in the *Seimas*.

The Government

The Government consists of the Prime Minister and Ministers. The President appoints and dismisses the Prime Minister with the approval of the *Seimas*. The President also appoints Ministers upon the nomination of the Premier, who presents the members of the Government and the programme to the *Seimas* within 15 days of his or her appointment. A new Government is installed when the *Seimas* approves its programme by a majority vote of participating MPs. The Government returns its mandate after parliamentary and presidential elections. When more than half of the Ministers are being replaced, the Government must be reinvested with authority from the *Seimas*, or resign. The Government must also resign if the majority of all MPs express no confidence in the Government or in the Prime Minister in a secret ballot, or if the Prime Minister resigns or dies. A Minister must resign if more than half of all MPs express no confidence in him or her in a secret ballot. Resignations are to be accepted by the President. Upon the request of the *Seimas*, the Government or individual Ministers must account for their activities.

The Government of the Republic of Lithuania: (1) runs the affairs of the country; (2) protects the inviolability of its territory, and safeguards national security and public order; (3) implements laws and *Seimas* resolutions (concerning Government implementation of laws) and presidential decrees; (4) coordinates the activities of the ministries and other governmental institutions; (5)

prepares drafts of state budgets and submits them to the *Seimas*; implements state budgets and reports to the *Seimas* on the implementation; (6) drafts bills and submits them to the *Seimas* for consideration; (7) establishes diplomatic relations and maintains relations with foreign countries and international organizations; and (8) discharges other duties prescribed by the Constitution and other laws.

The Government resolves affairs of the state administration. Government decisions must be passed by a majority vote of all members of the Government. Government directives are signed by the Prime Minister and the responsible Minister, but the Government is collectively responsible to the *Seimas*. Ministers are responsible to the *Seimas* and the President and are directly subordinated to the Prime Minister within their sphere of competence.

A member of the *Seimas* may be appointed Prime Minister or Minister but may not take up other posts, whether private or public. Members of the *Seimas* have the right to submit inquiries to the Prime Minister, individual Ministers, and the heads of other state institutions formed or elected by the *Seimas*. These persons or bodies must respond orally or in writing at a *Seimas* session. A group of no less than one-fifth of the *Seimas* deputies may ask for a vote of no confidence in the Prime Minister or in a Minister. After having considered the response of the Prime Minister or the Minister to such a motion, the *Seimas* may, by an absolute majority vote of all MPs, express no confidence in the Prime Minister or a Minister.

The Constitutional Court

The Constitutional Court consists of nine judges appointed for a non-renewable nine-year term. The Parliament appoints three candidates. Every three years, one third of the Constitutional Court is reconstituted. The *Seimas* appoints all candidates. The President, Chairperson of the Parliament, and the Chairperson of the Supreme Court each nominates three candidates. The Parliament also appoints the Chairperson of the Constitutional Court, who is nominated from among the judges by the President.

The Constitutional Court decides whether laws and other legal acts passed by the *Seimas* conform with the Constitution, and whether legal acts adopted by the President and the Government violate the Constitution or laws. The Constitutional Court also decides: (1) on the legality of presidential elections or elections to the *Seimas*; (2) whether the health of the President of the Republic is limiting his or her capacity to continue in office; (3) whether international agreements conform with the Constitution; and (4) on the compliance with the Constitution of specific actions of MPs or other state officers against whom impeachment proceedings have been instituted. The Government, one-fifth of all parliamentarians and the courts (the Supreme Court, the Court of Appeal, district courts, and local courts) can address the Constitutional Court concerning the conformity of parliamentary laws with the Constitution. At least one-fifth of MPs and the courts can address the Constitutional Court concerning the conformity of presidential acts with the Constitution and laws. At least one-fifth of MPs, the President and the courts can address the Constitutional Court concerning the conformity with an act of the Government with the Constitution and laws. If the *Seimas* and the President turn to the Constitutional Court to investigate the conformity of an act with the Constitution, the applicability of the act is suspended. The *Seimas* can request a conclusion from the Constitutional Court. The President can also request a conclusion in cases regarding parliamentary elections and international agreements. Laws and acts adopted by the *Seimas*, the President and the Government are not valid from the day of official promulgation of the Constitutional Court if the act in question, or parts of it, is inconsistent with the Constitution. Decisions of the Constitutional Court on issues assigned to its jurisdiction are final and cannot be appealed.

Source: Constitution of the Republic of Lithuania [*Lietuvos Respublikos Konstitucija*], Valstybės žinios, 1992, Nr. 33-1014; Amendments included.

Acknowledgement: The authors are grateful to Darius Žeruolis for his permission to include sections of his description of the constitutional framework and electoral system of Lithuania, published in the first edition of the *Handbook of Political Change in Eastern Europe*, in this edition.

6. Poland

Marian Grzybowski and Piotr Mikuli

Stein Rokkan's notion of six phases of transmission of social cleavages into party systems (Rokkan 1970, 90–97) does not quite do justice to the divisions and the party relations in the new democracies of Central and Eastern Europe, nor does Lipset and Rokkan's general theory on the interplay between cleavages and the party systems (Lipset and Rokkan 1967). With the benefit of hindsight, it is obvious that the typology of cleavages ought to be modified (Rae and Taylor 1970, 23–5; Flanagan 1971, 47–76). In two more recent articles (1995, 154–79; 1996, 43–5, 47–51), Georgi Karasimeonov identifies at least four types of socio-political divisions: (1) historical or residual cleavages, (2) transitional cleavages, (3) current ('actual') political divisions, and (4) prospective (or potential) divisions.

The general acceptance of Karasimeonov's typology should not be construed as an acceptance without reservations. The first group of cleavages – the historical or residual cleavages – seems to play a particularly important role in Poland. The social divisions, whether ideological or strictly political, inherited from the pre-communist society, are still of obvious significance in post-communist life. A religious cleavage with deep and strong roots in Polish history still makes itself felt in the views of numerous social groups in post-1989 Poland (Taras 1993, 23–4; Olson 1993, 416–41).

Intensive social divisions accompanied the dual transition from authoritarianism to democracy and from plan to market. As a rule, these cleavages have survived the transition of the early 1990s, albeit in modified form. But their long-term prospects are nevertheless bleak by virtue of their almost exclusive focus on substantive as well as procedural matters of transition.

The divisions determined by current politics are more elusive. It is quite difficult to judge which of the present social divisions and differentiations are of crucial importance for the shaping of party lines and party formations. The current debates and political infighting may easily give way to new issues and rivalry. In this sense the structure of conflict in Poland does indeed remain fluid.

Similar comments apply to the potential or expected divisions. Ongoing economic and political reform processes do contribute towards shaping the emerging new cleavage structure. But it is anybody's guess which of the potential cleavages, including the increasingly modern left/right cleavage, will have a lasting impact on the conflict structure in Poland.

The political parties are the crucial actors in all four cleavage categories. They exploit the existing cleavages for the purpose of mobilization and consolidation of their respective rank and file. In the process, they may contribute significantly towards the institutionalization of the existing cleavages and towards the emergence of new ones.

With one major exception, there is no evidence that new cleavages have gained ground to the detriment of historical change in Poland after 1989. The tension between those bringing down the pre-1989 communist regime and those committed to more or less limited reform within the framework of the communist regime, has had a special impact on and importance for the entire period, particularly the first three or four years of system transformation. At least three of the historical cleavages have preserved their importance in the current stage of social and political development.

First of all it may be noted that the paternalistic and traditional, and frequently religiously-inspired way of life of village and countryside (small-town) strata and, to some extent, the life-style of first-generation urban dwellers, remain at a distance from and in contradiction with the more open, modern way of life of the lion's share of the intelligentsia, the students, and the young and well-educated urban strata.[1]

Second, the gap between those earning their livelihood as proprietors and salaried employees and workers seems to retain its significance, even to grow in importance. This social division, which was quite visible – even overestimated – in the formative years of the Solidarity movement, lost ground in the early 1990s, only to reappear with a vengeance in the advanced stage of transition of the late 1990s.

Third, the legacy of the communist past has carried over into the present in the form of a division between those who are opposed to secular socialism and highly critical of the practices of the old regime and of Soviet political domination, and those more favourably disposed to 'real socialism'. The careful 'thick line' policy adopted by the first non-communist government of Tadeusz Mazowiecki – with all its omissions and inconsistencies – did not contribute towards eliminating or reducing the tension (Jasiewicz 1993a; 1993b). The division remains in place, interfering with other conflict dimensions structuring the interplay between the post-Solidarity camp and its rivals.

1989–91: Years of Political Fragmentation

After the parliamentary elections of 4 and 18 June 1989 (first and second rounds, respectively), the Polish United Workers' Party (PUWP) lost political power (Małkiewicz 1994, 20–21). With the benefit of hindsight, well-known journalist and former secretary of the PUWP, Mieczysław Rakowski, has identified the most important causes of the breakdown of communism in Poland (Rakowski 1991, 227–30). The PUWP had exhausted all its political possibilities and, under a barrage of criticism, found itself forced to change its organizational and programmatic formula. The party members and even the party apparatus embarked on a search for a new party line (Jaruzelski and Orzechowski 1991). The Eleventh Party Congress of the Polish United Workers Party on 27–29 January 1989 transformed the PUWP into a social democratic party – Social Democracy of the Republic of Poland – under the leadership of Aleksander Kwaśniewski. But the decision was not unanimous. A minority faction under the leadership of Tadeusz Fiszbach founded the Polish Social Democratic Union (PUS). PUS had little electoral success and was dissolved in 1991. A group of its members subsequently defected to the Union of Labour and the Social Democratic Movement, the last a co-founder of the Democratic Union (and next, the Union of Freedom).

The political transformation also affected the remaining party segments of the pre-1989 political order. At its Eleventh Extraordinary Congress on 26–27 November 1989, the United Peasant Party replaced most of its leaders, revised the party programme and then renamed itself the Polish Peasant Party 'Revival' (Dehnel-Szyc and Stachura 1991, 101–3; Paluch 1995, 29–33). Almost simultaneously, two other peasant parties were established: one based on the pre-war independent peasant movement, the other on Rural Solidarity. In May 1990, the PPP 'Revival' merged with the majority of the moderates of the pre-war peasant party, while the rest of that party and the Polish Peasant Party 'Solidarity' decided to continue their independent activities (Sokół and Żmigrodzki 1994, 41–3).

The efforts by the urban middle-strata of the Democratic Party (DP) – a former ally of the PUWP in the pre-1989 hegemonic multi-party system – to adapt to the new political situation were less successful. The party changed its leadership and programme and joined Mazowiecki's Solidarity-based cabinet (together with the UPP), but to no avail. The DP's reputation as a loyal and quiet ally of the PUWP before 1989 did not serve as the very best letter of recommendation for the non-communist future and it was hard for the DP to carve out a niche for itself within the space recently captured by the newly formed post-Solidarity centre and other liberal political formations and parties (Dudek 1995a, 80–115; 1995b, 35–8).

At the same time, the newly re-established massive Solidarity movement, and in addition a large number of new non-communist groups with a history of organized underground activities, started to function openly as political parties. Among them were the anti-communist and sometimes populist Confederation for an Independent Poland (*Konfederacja Polski Niepodległej*, KPN) of Leszek Moczulski, the conservative liberal Union of Real Politics (*Unia Polityki Realnej*, UPR) of Janusz Korwin-Mikke, the Polish Socialist Party (*Polska Partia Socjalistyczna*, PPS) of Jan Józef Lipski, the ephemeral Polish Socialist Party-Democratic Revolution (PPS-RD of Piotr Ikonowicz) and the radical Fighting Solidarity of Kornel Morawiecki. Most of these parties were small and played but a marginal (or temporary) role in Polish party politics. Two of them, however, constituted exceptions to this rule.

The secular (even laic) and pro-European Liberal-Democratic Congress (*Kongres Liberalno-Demokratyczny*, KLD), initially formed in Gdańsk in November-December 1989 and then officially established in Warsaw on 29–30 June 1990, was to have a major impact on Polish political life. Among the founders of this party were the young political activists Janusz Lewandowski, Donald Tusk and Jan Krzysztof Bielecki, of whom the latter went on to serve as Prime Minister in 1990–91. The KLD articulates the interests of secular and liberally-oriented groups of young, well educated, urban and entrepreneurial strata, open to modernization and committed to European integration, economically as well as culturally.

Another newly formed party, namely the Christian National Alliance (*Zjednoczenie Chrześcijańsko-Narodowe*, ZCHN), was also to be of major significance. With its close links to Polish Catholicism, the Alliance lands squarely on the opposite pole of the religious/secular cleavage. It was strongly sceptical of European integration and any kind of liberalization, especially within the fields of religion, education, culture and morality. Officially established on 28 October 1989, the Alliance has become a rallying-point for numerous Catholic, Christian Democratic and national-democratic organizations, such as 'Order and Freedom', 'Freedom and Solidarity', as well as various Catholic academic clubs and associations. The organization known as 'National Revival of Poland' joined the Christian National Alliance for a while, but left it in February 1990 (Dudek 1997, 110).

The appearance of new political parties resulted in parliamentary realignments. The so-called 'Contract' Polish *Sejm* of 1989–91, partly freely elected, went through a series of splits and secessions (*Table 6.1*).

Immediately after Solidarity's landslide victory in the June 1989 elections, the trade union wing of the Solidarity movement found itself engaged in a power struggle with the so-called citizens' committees, which had fulfilled a remarkable role in mobilizing voters during the election campaign. On 17 June 1989, the trade-unionist core of the National Committee of Solidarity had decided to dissolve the regional citizens' committees, as they were felt to be superfluous after the elections and even potentially disruptive. As a result, the political role of Solidarity's numerous advisors was curtailed, a development that met with protests from intellectuals like Adam Michnik and Bronisław Geremek. The efforts of converting the citizens' committees into a social movement, linking the open-minded and pro-European bid for democracy with modernized national traditions, did not meet with success. Instead of institutional integration, the personal factor became dominant. Lech Wałęsa started to play the role of integrator for most of the movement (Grzybowski 1996, 54; Wojtaszczyk 1995, 243–4).

Table 6.1: Composition of the Sejm *in 1989–1991*

	July 1989		Dec 1990		Feb 1991		Oct 1991	
Party	seats	%	seats	%	seats	%	seats	%
United Workers' Party (PZPR)	173	37.6	–	–	–	–	–	–
Democratic Left (PKLD)	–	–	104	22.7	104	22.7	102	22.3
Pol. Soc. Dem. Union (PUS)	–	–	41	8.9	40	8.7	–	–
Confed. for Indep. Pol. (KPN)	–	–	10	2.2	9	2.8	7	1.5
KPW	–	–	7	1.5	7	1.5	7	1.5
PKP	–	–	–	–	–	–	39	8.5
Citizens' Parliamentary Club (OKP)	161	35.0	155	33.7	111	24.1	105	23.0
Democratic Union (UD)	–	–	–	–	46	10.0	49	10.7
Solidarity of Labour (SP)	–	–	–	–	–	–	5	1.1
Solidarity camp total	161	35.0	155	33.7	157	34.1	159	34.8
UPP (ZSL)	76	16.5	–	–	–	–	–	–
Polish Peasant Party (PSL)	–	–	73	15.9	73	15.9	65	14.2
Mikołajczyk's PPP	–	–	4	0.9	4	0.9	4	0.9
Peasant parties total	76	16.5	77	16.8	77	16.8	69	15.1
Democratic Party (SD)	27	5.9	22	4.8	22	4.8	21	4.6
Others (Pax, UChS, PZKS)	23	5.0	22	4.8	22	4.8	22	5.0
Independents, new groups	–	–	21	4.6	21	4.6	30	6.8
Total	*460*	*100*	*459*	*100*	*459*	*100*	*456*	*100*

Source: Wasilewski and Wesołowski (1992), 82.

The autumn of 1989 and the first months of 1990 were marked by elite-level infighting and the gradual disintegration of the Solidarity camp. The personal rivalry between Lech Wałęsa and Tadeusz Mazowiecki, who both ran for the office of president, added fuel to the controversy within Solidarity. But the internal conflicts were not confined to the very top (Paszkiewicz 1996).

The competition between the evolutionist concepts of transition, supported by Mazowiecki, Geremek, Kuroń, Michnik and their followers, and the radical demand for 'acceleration' represented by Wałęsa himself and his sympathizers, began to overlap with the 1990 presidential race. A group of small centrist parties and political groupings formed the Alliance Centrum coalition – led by Jarosław Kaczyński, at that time one of Wałęsa's closest associates – which officially announced its support for Wałęsa's candidacy. Together with Solidarity itself, the Alliance became one of the two major engines of Wałęsa's presidential campaign. The political polarization instigated by the Alliance and by Solidarity leaders met with suspicion among left-oriented Solidarity activists; a left-wing group of former Solidarity activists decided to form the Citizens' Movement-Democratic Action (*Ruch Obywatelski – Akcja Demokratyczna*, ROAD). The growing gap between those who advocated an evolutionary and open concept of transition, and those in the nationalist- and religious-flavoured integrationist movement was to be significant for the cleavage structure. By the end of June 1990, the association of citizens' committees had broken up, with the majority of them rallying behind Wałęsa as presidential candidate.

The Solidarity movement was split along the lines of one of the most distinct cleavages in transitional Poland. The split separated those clusters of Polish society which tend to support the concept of a modernized, open, primarily laic state and society, with pro-European sympathies, from those keen on national traditions and values. The latter have remained favourably disposed to the values and norms of traditional Catholicism and harbour some suspicion of European integration and rapid modernization. De-communization was an issue of importance for the advocates of modernization, mainly up to the liquidation of the PUWP and the abolition of its former political hegemony. The traditionalists, on the other hand, only regarded the dissolution of the communist party as a small step in a long-term fight against communism and against all the remnants of the old regime.

At this juncture, the efforts towards preserving the unity of the Solidarity movement were bound to fail. But the split, once it had had occurred, did not separate the chaff from the wheat with anything even approaching accuracy. Within the Wałęsa camp, fervent Catholics allied with liberals, just as nationalists coexisted with moderate supporters of European integration, and determined sympathizers of 'acceleration' cooperated with cool pragmatists.

On the other hand, the supporters of Mazowiecki's candidacy included moderate Catholics with liberal socialists as their next-door neighbours; social-democrats (like Zbigniew Bujak) in coalition with progressive conservatives (like Alexander Hall), and former PUWP members in some cooperation with communist-era political prisoners (Wiatr 1993, 2–16). This kind of realignment did not promote the stabilization of the party system, but it was instrumental in paving the way for a further restructuring of the political preferences.

The results of the 1990 presidential elections (*Appendix 6.1*), confirmed the existence of deep cleavages cutting across the main Polish strata. The rivalry between Mazowiecki and Wałęsa testifies to the resilience of the liberal-secular versus traditional-Catholic division among the voters. Wałęsa drew his electoral support mainly from among the elderly, the less well educated, whether villagers or industrial workers in urban environments. He had his electoral strongholds mainly in Eastern and South Eastern Poland as well as in the Gdańsk area.

Mazowiecki, on the other hand, did particularly well among better-educated city dwellers of Western and Southern Poland, particularly in Cracow, Warsaw and Poznań, while he performed poorly especially in the villages (with only 7.4 per cent of the vote there), and generally in Central and Eastern Poland.

The same electoral results brought out the politically and personally weak position of the Peasant Party candidate Roman Bartoszcze. He won only 7.2 per cent of the vote in a country with roughly 38 per cent of its inhabitants somehow linked to farming. Similarly, the electoral results highlighted the limited chances of the militant anti-communist and populist option, represented by the Confederation for an Independent Poland and its leader Leszek Moczulski. The fact that the candidate supported by the Alliance of the Democratic Left came in fourth was a tribute not only to the personal skills of Włodzimierz Cimoszewicz, but also led to the renaissance of the post-communist-socialist option. The unexpected success of self-styled populist leader Stanisław (Stan) Tymiński was interpreted as a by-product of the nagging suspicion by many voters that the political establishment was neither willing to alleviate the widespread social misery in the immediate aftermath of the rapid transition from planned to market economy of the early 1990s, nor capable of achieving this goal.

The 1990 presidential elections had an additional impact on the Polish party system. In December 1990, just after the second round, Mazowiecki called upon his sympathizers to form a new party, the Democratic Union (*Unia Demokratyczna*, UD), based on the election committees supporting his candidacy. In May 1991, after some hesitation, two other organizations supporting Mazowiecki's candidacy joined the Democratic Union: the Citizens' Movement-Democratic Action (ROAD) and the Forum of Democratic Right with Alexander Hall (Żukowski 1992, 45–7). ROAD subsequently disintegrated, with some of the ROAD activists joining forces with Zbigniew Bujak to establish the Social Democratic Movement (*Ruch Demokratyczno-Społeczny*, RDS), which next merged with Solidarity of Labour and launched itself as the Union of Labour (*Unia Pracy*, UP) in June 1992. The UP obtained additional support from a faction within the disbanded Polish Social Union (PUS) and became, under the leadership of Ryszard Bugaj, the second leading non-communist party of the Polish left (Michta 1993, 49–52, 145–8).

*

Inspired by Cimoszewicz's promising results in the presidential race, the Social Democracy of the Republic of Poland set out to broaden its social and political base before the upcoming parliamentary elections. In February 1991, Kwaśniewski and Cimoszewicz called upon left-wing organizations and groups all over the country to form a broad electoral alliance. Some twenty organizations, including the trade union federation OPZZ, the post-communist youth organization and the Democratic Union of Women, responded favourably to the appeal and by July 1991 they had joined Kwaśniewski and Cimoszewicz in forming the Alliance of the Democratic Left (Gebethner and Raciborski 1992). The newly formed Alliance concentrated its efforts on the short-term goal of maximizing the socialist vote in the forthcoming parliamentary elections. Fierce criticism of governmental policies – most notably its 'dogmatic' monetarism, the impact of traditional Catholicism on public life and the marginalization of the political left – served as a unifying platform in the struggle against the post-Solidarity parties (Antoszewski, Herbut and Jednaka 1993, 49–53; Markowski and Tóka 1995, 199–205).

At this juncture, the Polish Peasant Party elected a new leader. Thirty-one-year-old Waldemar Pawlak replaced Roman Bartoszcze. The new party leader broke the electoral cooperation pact with the Polish Peasant Party 'Solidarity' and the rural Solidarity trade union. This was not acceptable to Bartoszcze, who responded by forming a new peasant party, the Polish Peasant Party 'Homeland' (*Ojcowizna*).

Lech Wałęsa, sworn in as President of the Republic in December 1990, had embarked on a course which led to political isolation. Instead of forming a strong presidential party, he lashed out against the Alliance Centrum of the Kaczyński twins, who were running a well-organized political machine with some 30,000 dues-paying members and had a recent record as staunch Wałęsa supporters (Żukowski 1992, 177–84).

The parliamentary elections of 27 October 1991 were notable for the low turnout. Out of 27.5 million eligible voters, only 11.9 million (43.2 per cent) showed up at the polling stations (*Appendix 6.1*). The young, the poor, the less well educated and those living in rural areas tended to be over-represented among those who opted out of the political process. Abstention was far more common in backward Eastern Poland than in more prosperous Western parts of the country; and there is, in fact, a case to be made for the notion that the losers of the transition process were more likely to express their discontent by opting out of the political process altogether than by voting for the opposition.

The results of the 1991 parliamentary elections testify to the complex underlying conflict structure. The level of fragmentation in the *Sejm*, elected in 1991, actually exceeds the levels scored in the inter-war era, when one-third of the population belonged to various ethnic minorities and electoral thresholds were unheard of.

Formally, victory belonged to the Democratic Union, but with no more than 12.3 per cent of the votes cast, it was a limited triumph. The Union failed dismally in its attempts to mobilize the 1990 Mazowiecki presidential vote (*Appendix 6.1*). No less than 20 per cent of Mazowiecki's voters opted for the Liberal Democratic Congress, while some 15 per cent of them chose the Alliance of the Democratic Left. The Democratic Union remained the party of the intelligentsia; as many as 28 per cent of the votes for this party came from people with academic education, as opposed to a meagre 9 per cent from those with primary education. The party had its strongholds in the bigger cities, and it remained particularly weak in the Eastern parts of the country (Jasiewicz 195, 62–3).

The Alliance of the Democratic Left came in second, defending its post-communist constituency. In addition, it benefited from substantial influx – almost 20 per cent – from the Tymiński camp and a trickle of votes from the Mazowiecki camp. The Alliance stood particularly strong among the elderly and among middle-aged voters with secondary education and professional degrees, in small and medium-sized urban agglomerations. It performed well in Northern Poland excluding the Gdańsk and Szczecin *voievodships*, in Western Poland, in Łódź, Kielce and in Sosnowiec.

Somewhat surprisingly, the Confederation for an Independent Poland came out as one of the five strongest party formations in the *Sejm*. The party did well among workers (who constituted 11.6 per cent of its electorate), among the retired and among young men without the benefit of secondary education. Voters with higher education, farmers and women rarely counted among the party's supporters. The party did rather well in Southern and South Eastern Poland and less well in the Western and Northern *voievodships* (Januszewski et al. 1993, 91–3).

The Polish Peasant Party (PPP) consolidated its position as the main party of the rural electorate. The party could count on the loyalty of the majority of those who had supported Roman Bartoszcze's bid for the presidency, and in addition it gained a remarkable portion of Wałęsa's presidential electorate.

The Polish Peasant Party (PPP) and its main competitor for the rural vote, the Peasant Alliance, remained distinctly rural organizations; 75 per cent of their voters lived in the countryside. The peasant parties dominated in Central and Eastern Poland. With its ties to the inter-war agrarian movement and to the United Peasant Party (of the communist-dominated multi-party system), the PPP received more votes than the pro-Solidarity Peasant Alliance in the Central and South Eastern *voievodships*.

The Catholic Election Action alliance could also claim victory. With its national, Christian (read: Catholic) appeal, the alliance enjoyed the support of the clergy. It was strongest among the older generations, particularly among elderly women. Among voters above the age of 60, the Catholic Election Action polled 15.6 per cent, as opposed to a meagre 5.4 per cent among those less than 25 years old. It had its strongholds in rural areas and its weak spots in industrial Upper Silesia and in the *voievodships* of Northern Poland.

The Citizens' Alliance Centrum came out of the elections seriously weakened. The coalition gained its votes mostly in small towns, among pensioners, and less-educated white- and blue-collar workers. The results were more encouraging in Warsaw and, for that matter, in South Eastern and Eastern Poland.

The Liberal Democratic Congress did well among the young, the well educated and the entrepreneurial strata, in some of the bigger cities (in those with over a hundred thousand inhabitants, the Liberals collected an average of 13.2 per cent of the votes), in its heartland of Gdańsk, in Warsaw and in some other towns. The party had almost no support in the rural East.

The defection of most Solidarity leaders to other political formations reduced the electoral prospects of Solidarity. In the elections, Solidarity was only the third most popular list among blue-collar workers, overtaken by the Democratic Union as well as by the Confederation for an Independent Poland. As of 1991, the typical Solidarity voters were recruited from among the less educated, among pensioners of working-class backgrounds and among the lower middle-class. The Gdańsk and Bydgoszcz regions provided Solidarity with a solid base, which compensated for the uphill battle in the rural and Western *voievodships*.

Only one-third of voters below 25 participated in the elections, and the young evidently felt sceptical towards most of the major parties (*Gazeta Wyborcza*, 6-13 July 1992). With the exception of the Democratic Union and the Liberal Democratic Congress, the major parties did not mobilize the young; close to 10 per cent of the young vote went to the cabaret-style Polish Party of Friends of Beer.

In general terms, the 1991 parliamentary elections marked the end of the transition from People's Poland to democratic Poland. The election results highlighted the disintegration of the former Solidarity movement. Most of the Solidarity sympathizers continued to support parties of the centre or the centre-right, a rather remarkable fact considering that Solidarity had started out as a trade-union movement. In a similar vein, it may be noted that Solidarity veterans, white- and blue-collar alike, divided their sympathies across a wide range of political parties – from the Democratic Union with its intellectual appeal, to the Confederation for an Independent Poland with its distinctly populist image. Most of the parties of the right and of the left remained city-based. The rural electorate became dominated by the two peasant ('class-type' or 'sectoral') political formations: the dominant Polish Peasant Party (centre-left-oriented) and its competitor, the Peasant Alliance (PL).

The Democratic Union and the Liberal Democratic Congress had become visible exponents of young, successful and educated city-dwellers. They campaigned on similar platforms, and the rational choice for them was amalgamation rather than mutual competition. Indeed, the two parties soon decided to merge into the Union of Freedom (*Unia Wolności*, UW).

The political centre and Christian Democratic cluster remained fragmented. The Citizens' Alliance Centrum came out greatly weakened by the bitter and fierce quarrel between party leader Jarosław Kaczyński and the President of the Republic, Lech Wałęsa. The Catholic Election Action was the only openly Christian party to have risen to a position of relative influence, no doubt due to its commitment to the Catholic Church hierarchy and the religious devotion of its supporters (mostly women in the upper age-brackets).

The 1991 elections to the *Sejm* spelled a modest revival for the political left. The post-communist Alliance of the Democratic Left moved from the level of 9.2 per cent of the voters (Cimoszewicz's result in the presidential first round in 1990) up to slightly less than 12 (11.99) per cent.

With the possible exception of the two major peasant formations, no party was able to dominate any social group or cluster. Party programmes and policies did not coincide neatly with well-defined socio-economic cleavages. Yet, there were indeed linkages between the changing cleavage structure and the emerging party system. The peasant parties, the populist and radical Confederation for an Independent Poland, and, to some extent, the Alliance Centrum and the Catholic Election Action, did represent the small-town, less well educated, traditionally minded groups of society.

The Democratic Union and the Liberal-Democratic Congress represented the young, urban, entrepreneurial strata, which tend to be liberal-minded and favourably disposed towards market reform and European integration.

The increasingly stable political geography of Poland also strongly suggests that there is a pattern to the political fluctuations. The parties of the right and of the centre, including the Catholic parties, seem to have found a particularly hospitable environment in Eastern and South Eastern Poland, while Northern Poland (excluding the cities of Gdańsk and Gdynia) and the Western territories appear to provide fertile ground for the parties of the left and of the centre-left. The relative alienation of numerous young Poles from party politics does, however, serve as a reminder that the process of consolidation is far from complete.

The Consolidation of 1991–93

Cabinet formation after the 1991 elections was not an easy venture, since the fragmented *Sejm* did not contain any self-evident basis for a majority. President Wałęsa tried to exploit this situation in order to strengthen the influence of the presidency. He saw himself as the main political player, as the maker of prime ministers and the architect of government coalitions. The first presidential initiatives, concerning the candidacies of Jacek Kuroń (Democratic Union), Jan Krzysztof Bielecki (Liberal Democratic Congress) and Bronisław Geremek (Democratic Union), remained politically ineffective.

The creation of the new cabinet was preceded by long, drawn-out negotiations. Almost two months after the elections, on 21 December 1991, the coalition government of Jan Olszewski was formed and confirmed by a vote of confidence in the *Sejm*. The parliamentary base of the new government was rather narrow: only 235 of the 460 representatives voted for confidence; 60 votes were cast against, mainly by the Alliance of the Democratic Left and by the conservative-liberal Union of Real Politics, while no fewer than 139 deputies abstained, predominantly representatives of the Democratic Union, the Liberal Democratic Congress and the Confederation for an Independent Poland (Dudek 1997, 265-9).

The newly formed government was openly anti-communist and, at the same time, quite sceptical towards a strict monetary approach to the economy. Many of the ministers tended to favour limited state interventionist policies with respect to internal as well as external economic activities. Within the field of foreign policy, the government seemed to prefer broad European cooperation, inspired by the Organization of Security and Cooperation in Europe, to the institutional kind of integration represented by full membership of the European Union. The majority of the ministers, including Prime Minister Olszewski himself, remained fiercely critical of the round-table agreement and of any form of participation by former communists in public life.

The Olszewski cabinet always kept a certain distance from the presidential office and from Wałęsa himself. The efforts undertaken to widen the parliamentary basis of the cabinet, towards the Democratic Union and the Confederation for an Independent Poland as well as towards the Polish Peasant Party, were to no avail. The demise of the Olszewski cabinet was brought about by the unexpected resolution of the *Sejm* – upon the initiative of Janusz Korwin-Mikke, leader of the Union of Real Politics – to institute lustration of leading state and government officials and to publish, under the auspices of the Ministry of Interior, a list of 'collaborators' of the communist security services, featuring, among others, President Wałęsa.

The cabinet faced a vote of no confidence on 4 June 1992. The motion obtained the backing of 273 deputies from the Democratic Union, the Liberal Democratic Congress, the Alliance of the Democratic Left, the Confederation for an Independent Poland and the Polish Peasant Party. Only 119 deputies of the *Sejm* voted against the motion and for the government; these were mainly representatives of the Catholic Action, the Alliance Centrum and the Peasant Alliance and Solidarity (Grzybowski 1996, 49–54). Once again, the political right had appeared divided and politically inconsistent.

Waldemar Pawlak, the 32-year-old leader of the Polish Peasant Party designated by President Wałęsa to take over as Prime Minister, was unable to form a centre-based government. His potential coalition partners, the liberal Democratic Union and the populist right-oriented Confederation for an Independent Poland, were not ready to agree on a compromise programme. After 33 days as caretaker Prime Minister, Pawlak was forced to resign.

The fact that Pawlak, and nobody else, was called upon to form a new government was nevertheless a remarkable phenomenon. For the first time since the transition, a non-Solidarity politician – and a leader of a party 'connected' with the old regime – was promoted to such an office. According to Aleksander Kwaśniewski, it was a 'historical step' towards 'normalization' of Polish political life (cf. *Polityka*, 18 July 1992).

Pawlak's failure paved the way for a coalition of the Democratic Union, the Liberal Democratic Congress, the Peasant Alliance (PL), the Christian-National Alliance and the small Polish Christian Democratic Party. The new cabinet, formed by centrist Democratic Union politician Hanna Suchocka, obtained the support of 226 deputies. The number of deputies who voted against was 124, mainly representatives of Olszewski's Movement for the Republic, the Polish Peasant Party, and the Union of Real Politics. Twenty-eight parliamentarians, mainly from within the Alliance Centrum and the Democratic Left, abstained from voting (Gebethner 1995a; 1995b).

Seven (subsequently eight) parties formed the parliamentary base of the Suchocka cabinet, of which three – the Democratic Union, the Liberal Democratic Congress and the National Christian Alliance – served as the main pillars. In fact, the Suchocka government often found it extremely difficult to mobilize even a fragile majority for its proposals. A wave of strikes spread through the industrial centres of Upper Silesia, the Głogów copper mining district and the aviation industry centre of Mielec. The unrest increased in magnitude. In 1990, 116,000 workers struck; in 1991 the number had risen to 222,000; and in late 1992 no less than 753,000 workers had been taken out on strike. Unemployment was also on an upward trend: from 2.5 million in 1992 (14.3 per cent of the labour force) to 2.9 million (16.6 per cent) at the end of 1993.

The good news was that the recession was coming to an end and the inflation rate was assuming more manageable proportions, down from 43 per cent annually in 1992 to 35 per cent in 1993. Even so, the man in the street remained adversely affected. In 1993, the average income fell by 1.8 per cent and the average pension by 2.7 per cent. The economic and social inequalities kept growing, as did the gap between the winners and losers of the economic reforms. The government was able to accelerate the pace of privatization, but the ambitious – and controversial – programme of self-government reform never left the drawing board.

The issues of constitutional reform, abortion and European integration dominated a political agenda played out against the background of economic difficulties. The austerity budget of 1993 did not satisfy the regional organizations of the Solidarity unions. The four-day general strike in Łódź, the protests of public sector employees and the teachers' strike paralyzed important parts of society. The Minister of Agriculture, Gabriel Janowski, a member of the Peasant Alliance, handed in his resignation when he could no longer guarantee minimum prices for agricultural products. The Peasant Alliance's withdrawal of support thrust Suchocka's government into a minority position.

The negotiations between the government and Solidarity about public sector salaries broke down twice, on 10 and 18 May 1993. A vote of no confidence was clearly in the making, and in late May, Alojzy Pietrzyk of Solidarity introduced a motion to this effect. On 26 May 1993, Hanna Suchocka found herself defeated by the narrowest of margins (223 out of 445). Three days later President Wałęsa decided to dissolve the *Sejm* as well as the Senate and call new elections. The Suchocka cabinet served as a caretaker government until the new elections on 19 September 1993. On 28 July 1993 – i.e. well after the vote of no confidence – the government signed a concordat with the Holy See, which brought an end to negotiations that had been going on since late 1992. The concordat contained stipulations concerning marriage, religious cemeteries, and subsidies for Catholic schools, which made for controversies and delayed its ratification.

The parliamentary situation was paradoxical in the sense that a post-Solidarity government had been ousted upon the initiative of a representative of the Solidarity trade union; but such was the position of strength then enjoyed by Solidarity and its numerous offspring parties. President Wałęsa, who called the pre-term elections, also failed to predict the 1993 victory of the post-communist Alliance of the Democratic Left.

The 1993 elections were held according to the new electoral law of 15 April 1993, approved by the President on 1 July 1993 (with some modifications introduced by the Senate). It was designed to curtail political fragmentation and introduced a 5 per cent threshold for political parties and an 8 per cent threshold for political cartels (coalitions). This spelled serious difficulties for more than half of the parties in the outgoing (1991–93) parliament. Some minor changes – including a switch from St Lagüe's to d'Hondt's method of distributing the parliamentary seats among parties (party lists) under proportional representation, and a reduction of the size of the voting districts – also played into the hands of the Alliance of the Democratic Left and the Polish Peasant Party (Gebethner 1995a; 1995b).

1993–97: The Era of Centre-Left Domination

In 1992–93, there was a pervasive swing to the left, as the centre-right government grew more and more unpopular. In late 1991, 52 per cent of those polled had expressed dissatisfaction with the government and most of its policies. By early 1993, the rate of dissatisfaction had reached 64 per cent (Janicki 1993). In the opinion polls, the Alliance of the Democratic Left took over the leading position with a support of some 20 per cent of the electorate. It was well ahead of the Democratic Union (with 16 per cent), and the Confederation for an Independent Poland and the Polish Peasant Party, both hovering around the 10 per cent mark (*Rzeczpospolita*, 2 October 1993).

For the 1993 race as many as 34 election committees registered lists of candidates, but only 23 of them in more than one electoral district. Only three committees declared themselves electoral cartels, subjected to the requirement of having to poll at least 8 per cent of the votes to gain parliamentary representation.

The primary beneficiaries of the swing to the left were the Alliance of the Democratic Left and the Union of Labour. When the Alliance tried to broaden its appeal, the Union of Labour countered by emphasizing its non-communist roots, while articulating serious doubts about privatization and the impact of Catholicism. The Union of Labour also jockeyed for the position as main defender of the interests of ordinary working people. This differentiation continued after the elections, marking a kind of institutionalization of the division of the Polish left.

The political appearance of the Non-Partisan Bloc for Supporting Reforms (*Bezpartyjny Blok Wspierania Reform*, BBWR), initiated by President Wałęsa in June 1993, was yet another feature that made the 1993 parliamentary elections unique. The President quite optimistically counted on an overwhelming electoral victory of some 400 out of a total of 460 seats. But not a single one of the parties participating in Suchocka's coalition joined the newly formed organization. The Bloc launched former Minister of Foreign Affairs, Andrzej Olechowski for Prime Minister and introduced a group of hopeful post-Solidarity activists as advisors and support team. The rather populist economic proposals initially earned the Bloc popularity ratings of around 18 per cent – a quite remarkable level it could not defend for long (Wiatr 1993, 80–89).

The arrival of the new post-Solidarity formation threatened the existence of the established post-Solidarity parties. The pre-election campaign thus became marked by a fierce propaganda battle between the Bloc, on the one hand, and the Democratic Union and – but only to some extent – the Liberal Democratic Congress, the Alliance Centrum and Jan Olszewski's Movement for the Republic (*Ruch dla Rzeczypospolitej*, RdR), on the other.

At the same time, the Movement (RDR) and the Alliance Centrum continued their campaign against the post-communists and the Democratic Union. Janusz Korwin-Mikke of the Union of Real Politics put forward an ultra-liberal programme designed to minimize the role of the state in order to attract the young and frustrated. Andrzej Lepper of the populist and anti-European rural organization 'Self-Defence' (*Samoobrona*) tried to rally support by exploiting the increasing dissatisfaction of the peasantry.

Voter turnout in the 1993 elections to the *Sejm* and the Senate was 52.1 per cent, some 10 percentage points higher than in 1991. The seats in the *Senate* were distributed in the following way: the Alliance of the Democratic Left, 37; the Polish Peasant Party, 36; Solidarity (trade union), 9; Democratic Union, 4; the Non-Partisan Bloc, 2; Union of Labour, 2; the Liberal-Democratic Congress, 1; Alliance Centrum, 1; independents, 4; small parties/election committees, 4.

The new electoral system contributed towards increasing the representation of the Alliance of the Democratic Left and the Polish Peasant Party. The Alliance obtained one-fifth of the votes but one-third of the seats in the *Sejm* and the Senate. The Polish Peasant Party obtained twice as many seats as it would have obtained under the old electoral law. The Confederation for an Independent Poland (KPN) and the Non-Partisan Bloc (BBWR) did not reach the 7 per cent threshold required to benefit from the distribution of seats from the national list. No less than 4.8 million votes (34.6 per cent of all cast) were wasted in the sense that they did not go towards representation in the *Sejm* (*Polityka*, 24 October 1994).

The elections spelled defeat for the Solidarity camp and victory for the parties of the left. Together, the parties supporting Suchocka's outgoing cabinet gained 23.3 per cent of the votes, only a few percentage points more than the Alliance of the Democratic Left scored in its own right. The latter almost doubled its share of the Polish electorate compared with the 1991 elections. The Alliance remained a party supported by small-town dwellers, but it had also made inroads into new constituencies including some business and academic communities. Seventeen per cent of the entrepreneurs voted for the Alliance lists, as opposed to 13 per cent for the lists of the Democratic Union and 9 per cent for those of the Liberal Democratic Congress. The Alliance won 134,000 voters from the Democratic Union and 72,000 from the Confederation of an Independent Poland (Dudek 1997, 332–3).

Farmers and their families as in 1991, formed the core of the Polish Peasant Party's electorate, but the party was also gaining ground in small towns. The PPP victory was accompanied by the political marginalization of the remaining peasant political formation, particularly the Peasant Alliance. But this party had not yet resolved its existential dilemma: whether to be an exponent of rural interests or a centre party in general.

The Democratic Union remained the party of urban, well-educated people. Academic centres, like Poznań and Cracow, provided the party with a badly needed electoral base, in the face of losses it incurred in the small towns of Lower Silesia and throughout all of Eastern Poland. Almost a quarter of the voters with academic education supported the Union. The electoral support was strongest among those aged over 60 or under 25.

The left-oriented Union of Labour tripled the share of votes obtained by its predecessors, the Social Democratic Movement, 'Solidarity of Labour' and the Greater Poland Social Democratic Union. It stood out as the party of salaried workers and minor civil servants, mostly in Greater Poland and Mazovia (Paszkiewicz 1996, 86-7, 202–3).

The victory of the non-Solidarity parties was brought about by a number of factors. In Poland, like most of the countries of Central and Eastern Europe, the difficulties of the economic transition produced a swing to the left. The post-Solidarity formations were busy running the country and vying for political influence and either overlooked the swing or underestimated it real impact. As a result, the heirs to the parties of People's Poland came back with a vengeance, as they represented the only alternative to a government suffering increasing popularity losses. Sociological surveys at hand suggest that well over 50 per cent of those who voted for the Alliance of the Democratic Left did so out of dissatisfaction with the post-Solidarity government. It may also be worth noting that only 43 per cent of the voters for the Alliance said that they considered the ex-communists better prepared to run the country (Planeta and Chrabąszcz 1996, 11–15).

After the 1993 election, a ten-point coalition agreement was signed between the victorious Alliance of Democratic Left and the Polish Peasant Party. The Union of Labour did participate in political negotiations preceding the cabinet formation but eventually declined to join the government. Waldemar Pawlak, the ambitious PPP leader, shouldered the role as Prime Minister, while the Alliance took over the crucial economy-related ministries and had one of its leaders, Józef Oleksy, elected Chairman of the *Sejm*. The Alliance was also prepared to go to great lengths to rid itself of the stigma attached to its communist past.

The Alliance and the Polish Peasant Party held an absolute majority in the *Sejm* and enjoyed the informal support of the Union of Labour until June 1994. The President had a decisive impact on the nomination of three ministers, those of the Interior, Defence and Foreign Affairs. The government was in fact loosely integrated from the very beginning. It remained marked by the efforts of the two coalition partners to widen their respective spheres of influence, and the three ministries indirectly controlled by President Wałęsa became something of a focal point in the tug-of-war between the Alliance and the PPP. In terms of issues, the government was, from the very outset, divided on decentralization and insurance reform.

The forthcoming 1995 presidential elections served as a constant reminder that unity was crucial for the success of the right and centre-right in Poland. Even the Catholic Church made an unofficial and in fact unsuccessful attempt to bring the parties of the right and centre-right together under the auspices of the Convent of St Catherine. Nevertheless, between 1994–95, there were several initiatives designed to bring the right-wing parties together. The national and the Catholic image, as well as the sceptical approach towards the idea of European integration cultivated by the Alliance Centrum and in particular by the National Christian Alliance, made these two parties obvious partners, but only in an unstable political alliance. The smallish parties of the right and the centre-right also made efforts to set up loose alliances.

Some parties split however. Two formations broke out of the Non-Partisan Bloc for Supporting Reforms (BBWR); a new political party, known as the Republicans; and a group of liberal activists who eventually co-founded the Committee of the One Hundred (*Komitet Stu*). Within the Union of Freedom, the establishment of the leftist faction Democratic Forum (*Forum Demokratyczne*), made the party less cohesive. In April 1995, Leszek Balcerowicz, the architect of the economic austerity programme of the early 1990s, replaced former Prime Minister Tadeusz Mazowiecki as leader of the Union of Freedom.

The ruling coalition tightened its grip on political and economic life, including the major state-owned companies, the banking system and, in addition, local government administration. However, the Foreign Ministry, the security services and the military, and to some extent public television, remained immune to the attempts at political domination by the coalition of the Alliance of the Democratic left and the Polish Peasant Party.

In the presidential elections of 5 and 19 November 1995, the candidates were evidently miles apart. In the first round, the candidate of the left, Aleksander Kwaśniewski, polled 35.1 per cent of the valid votes as opposed to 33.1 per cent for the incumbent (Lech Wałęsa). In the second round, Kwaśniewski defeated Wałęsa by a slim margin (*Appendix 6.1*). Kwaśniewski's victory was particularly evident in North-Western and North-Eastern Poland as well as in the centre of the country, while Wałęsa took Gdańsk, Warsaw, Cracow, Tarnów, Bielsko-Biała and South-Eastern Poland. In bigger cities (over 200,000 inhabitants) Wałęsa won by 58 per cent of the votes cast, whereas Kwaśniewski prevailed in medium-size (by 55 per cent) and small cities (by 56 per cent) and in rural areas (by 53 per cent). Those less than 60 voted predominantly for Kwaśniewski, while the upper age brackets tended to prefer Wałęsa.

Shortly after the presidential race Wałęsa's followers set out to destabilize the left by accusing Prime Minister Oleksy (the Alliance of the Left) of having acted in collusion with Soviet intelligence. This affair marked the beginning of a drawn-out crisis of confidence that lingered on long after the accusations had been refuted.

In late 1995, the leaders of Solidarity had embarked on a programme designed to bring the post-Solidarity parties together on a common platform, prior to the parliamentary elections of September 1997. The initiative by Solidarity trade union national chairman, Marian Krzaklewski, met with the slightly reluctant approval of the parties concerned. A broad coalition was formed in the summer of 1997, including almost all post-Solidarity right-wing formations. This move was to pave the way for a subsequent return to power.

Solidarity Comeback

The 1993 success of the Alliance of the Democratic Left and the post-communist-peasant coalition was, to a large extent, caused by the fragmentation of the post-Solidarity political forces. Neither the post-Solidarity parties nor President Wałęsa were in a position to act as effective links. Though marginalized on the national level, the post-Solidarity parties and political formations remained influential in the local arena, including local self-government, as well as on the factory floor. In its capacity as a politically active trade union federation, Solidarity preserved its mobilizing potential in most of the large- and medium-sized enterprises. In a number of localities – particularly in South Eastern and Southern Poland, as well as in cities like Gdańsk, Poznań, Warsaw and Cracow – the Alliance of the Democratic Left remained overshadowed by post-Solidarity parties. The ideological cleavage between the pro-Solidarity forces and those of the left-wing coalition, with its roots People's Poland, kept shaping consciousness and political behaviour among large segments of the electorate.

Casting itself as an exponent of modern, pro-European social democracy in favour of a mixed economy and political pluralism, the Alliance of the Democratic Left (SLD), lost credibility and appeal among the losers of the transition from plan to market. This loss of support was difficult to compensate for, since the new middle-class, and most of the intelligentsia, were solidly sceptic about formations with roots in the communist past.

The 1993–97 leftist government coalition was programmatically and politically inconsistent. The Alliance (and its main constituent party, the Social Democracy of the Republic of Poland, SDRP) remained openly secular, liberal, pro-European and open to many aspects of economic, cultural and behavioural modernization. In contrast, the Polish Peasant Party underlined the necessity of cultivating national and Catholic traditions and norms of social life, in line with the outlook of its predominantly rural constituency. The Alliance had the bulk of its electorate among city dwellers and salaried employees, i.e. among net consumers of agricultural products. The Polish Peasant Party, on the other hand, remained an interest party for food producers. Tensions were in a sense built into the leftist-peasant coalition from the very beginning.

The Solidarity opposition, now chiefly consolidated within the framework of the Election Action 'Solidarity' (AWS), lashed out at the governing leftist coalition which was portrayed as a government by the heirs to the very parties, which had been removed from power in 1989–90. The AWS campaign called on all former Solidarity members and sympathizers to recuperate the spirit of 1989–90. The AWS also, quite skilfully, exploited the differences between the two government parties on sensitive topics like privatization, abortion, the role of Catholicism, the Concordat with the Holy

See (firmly supported by the PPP, but not well received by the SLD), local self-governance and decentralization.

A number of factors contributed to the declining popularity of the governing parties, particularly the Polish Peasant Party: the poor performance of the authorities during the catastrophic floods in July 1997; the allegations that Prime Minister Oleksy had links with Soviet intelligence; the postponement of health care reform; and the feeble agricultural policy. The PPP faced a classical paradox: the bulk of the urban voters perceived it as a party of narrow and particular interests, and rural voters increasingly saw it as an inefficient exponent of rural interests, due to its weak position in the coalition. At the same time, Catholic-oriented media stepped up their pressure on the predominantly Catholic voters, portraying the Alliance-dominated government as anti-Catholic and libertarian. The entrepreneurial and business sectors shifted allegiance to the Union of Freedom, which was seen as liberal, pro-European and reform-oriented without having the stigma of a linkage to the defunct communist type regime. The Union of Freedom has so far rejected the option of a coalition with the post-communist Alliance of the Democratic Left, with which it does indeed share many issue positions. Instead, it has repeatedly emphasized its Solidarity roots.

The 1997 campaign revived the division between the Solidarity camp and the heirs of the old regime, which largely coincided with the division between traditionalists and modernists. But there were also traces of a re-emerging socio-economically defined left/right cleavage. The Union of Freedom campaigned on an explicitly pro-European and pro-market platform, while the PPP, the Union of Labour and some union-affiliated groups within the Alliance of the Democratic left emphasized the social costs of the transition to market, the high unemployment rate, social inequalities, the bleak prospects of Polish agriculture, and growing economic dependence on the outside world. The trade union wing of the Solidarity Election Action (AWS), the National Christian Alliance, and elements of the Confederation for an Independent Poland and the Movement for Rebuilding Poland (ROP) also voiced scepticism towards the liberal vision of the market economy. In fact, only the Union of Freedom was unconditionally in favour of full liberalization.

The Alliance and the PPP chose to run on different agendas in 1997. The campaign of the Alliance of the Democratic Left was based on the party's track record in macro-economic management – inflation and unemployment were falling and GDP growth for 1997 was estimated at 7 per cent. The Alliance steered clear of criticizing the liberal programme of the Union of Freedom, thereby attempting to set the stage for post-election political cooperation between the two reform-oriented, secular and pro-European parties. Even so, the leaders of the Alliance considered it more likely that any post-election government in which they would participate would include the Polish Peasant Party and possibly also the Union of Labour and the left-oriented Pensioners' Party (KPEIR).

*

In 1999, the Buzek government initiated comprehensive reforms of local and regional government, health care, social security and education. The reforms were generally seen as poorly planned and inefficiently executed. Jerzy Buzek was well aware of the widespread dissatisfaction with the government and set out to reshuffle his cabinet. The unpopular ministers of health and agriculture were dismissed. And so was the President of the Social Security Office (ZUS), who was responsible for a particularly problem-stricken government agency.

In May 2000, the crisis within the ruling coalition deepened. The crisis was in fact triggered by an open conflict between two of the coalition partners – AWS and the Freedom Union (UW) – within the Warsaw city council. The open tensions between the two partners finally made the Freedom Union withdraw from the government coalition altogether. This reduced the Buzek government to a minority government.

Presidential elections were held in October 2000. Aleksander Kwaśniewski polled 53.9 per cent of votes and was elected in the first round. With 17.3 per cent of the vote, Andrzej Olechowski, former Minister of Foreign Affairs and Finance, came in second. Solidarity trade union leader, Marian Krzaklewski, generally perceived as Kwaśniewski's main rival, polled only 15.6 per cent of votes. Lech Wałęsa finally only obtained about one per cent of the valid votes cast – an indication as good as any that the historical divisions in Polish society no longer played the same role as they did at the beginning of the transition process.

The presidential elections spelled serious problems for the Union of Freedom (UW). The party had not nominated a candidate of its own, even though a significant part of its voters favoured Andrzej Olechowski. The latter was subsequently to launch a new political movement known as the Civic Platform (PO) along with Donald Tusk, who had lost the struggle for the UW party chairmanship to Bronisław Geremek and Maciej Płażyński, Speaker of the *Sejm* and one of the leaders of AWS. As a result, support for the UW dropped sharply, and tensions mounted within the AWS. The Conservative People's Party under the leadership of Jan Rokita left the AWS and joined the Civic Platform. Lech Kaczyński, the increasingly popular Minister of Justice, decided to establish a new party – Law and Justice (*Prawo i Sprawiedliwość*, PIS) – with a distinct law and order profile. As if this were not enough, the AWS somehow had to cope with the negative fall-out of the screening process candidates had to go through in order to prove that they were not tainted by collaboration with the secrete service of the communist regime. This screening process provided fertile ground for a variety of accusations, some of them true and some of them false; and the various factions of the AWS never hesitated to capitalize on whatever accusations suited them best in the internal struggle for power and influence. The fate of deputy Prime Minister Janusz Tomaszewski is a case in point. The accusations against him were rejected by a court of law, but he was never reinstated in the state and party functions he had been forced to give up as a result of the unfounded allegations against him. By the spring of 2001 even the Solidarity trade union movement decided to opt out of the AWS.

In the autumn, it turned out that the budget deficit risked reaching 88 billion złoty. As a consequence, Buzek dismissed the Finance Minister, Jarosław Bauc, who was brought into the government, following the breakdown of the coalition with the UW. Leszek Balcerowicz, President of Poland's National Bank and Bauc's predecessor as minister of finance, confirmed the prognosis of his colleague.

Buzek, however, said he was taken by surprise and dismissed his minister on the ground that he had drawn attention to the deficit far too late. The difficult financial situation was not really due to any spectacular mistakes by the Buzek government. It was primarily a product of well-established budgetary practices. Debts incurred by the government were simply transferred from one year to another with the implicit understanding that they would have to be repaid somehow and some time, but preferably not right now.

All these changes of the political landscape discouraged the voters, who were sick and tired of what they perceived as political infighting. The AWS and the UW both lost popularity in the process, even though the UW was no longer part of the government. The Buzek government was also thoroughly discredited, first of all due to the drastic cuts in social welfare, for which the AWS was largely held responsible. Many people felt they had been deceived and lied to. Populist parties and movements became more and more attractive options, especially the Self Defence (*Samoobrona*) movements of Andrzej Lepper and the League of Polish Families (*Liga Polskich Rodzin*, LPR). Self Defence was particularly successful in the rural parts of the country. The party resorted to unconventional methods like blocking roads, pouring corn out of trains and the occupation of public buildings. LPR was promoted by Father Tadeusz Rydzyk, the director of the Catholic Radio station 'Maryja'. His radio station reaches an audience of about four million and is perceived as a bastion of old-fashioned and fundamentalist views. Its vision of religion and society draws constant criticism from the Polish Catholic Church. The LPR has successfully absorbed the most radical factions of the AWS. The associations of Catholic families with ties with Radio 'Maryja' also proved to be fertile recruitment ground for the LPR.

Opinion polls are not always reliable, but by the end of the period covered in this section there was little doubt that the stage was set for a change of guards in Warsaw. Support for the Solidarity Electoral Action (to be exact, this movement changed its name into 'the Solidarity Electoral Action of the Right' – AWS Prawicy, AWSP) and for the Union of Freedom (UW) was still decreasing. The most likely candidate to form the next government was the coalition of the Alliance of the Democratic Left (SLD) and the Union of Labour.

The Comeback of the Left

Parliamentary elections were held on 23 September 2001. With 41 per cent of the valid votes cast, the Alliance of the Democratic Left (SLD) and the Union of Labour (UP) were the undisputable winners. Civic Platform (PO), which gained the support of 12.7 per cent of the voters, came in second, followed by Self-Defence (*Samoobrona*) and Law and Justice (PIS) with an electoral backing of some 10 per cent each (10.2 and 9.5 per cent respectively). With an electoral support of 9 and 7.9 per cent respectively, the Polish Peasant Party (PSL) and the League of Polish Families (LPR) also did rather well. The Alliance of the Democratic Left (SLD) and the Union of Labour (UP) conquered 75 out of the 100 seats in the Senate. The Solidarity-based *Blok Senat 2001* (supported by AWSP, PO, UW, PIS) got 15 senators; the Peasant Party four; Self-Defence and the League of Polish Families two senators each; two senators were elected on a non-party ticket. The turnout was 46.3 per cent.

Table 6.2: Trust in political parties by education (%)

Party	Education			
	Elementary	*Technical*	*Secondary*	*Higher*
Alliance of Dem.Left (SLD), Union of Labour (UP)	40	42	47	42
Civic Platform (PO)	7	9	14	19
Law and Justice (PIS)	7	8	10	12
Self Defence (*Samoobrona*)	15	16	8	3
Polish Peasant Party (PSL)	14	11	7	5
League of Polish Families (LPR)	10	7	6	6

Table 6.3: Trust in political parties by place of living (%)

Party	Domicile			
	Towns, more than 200,000 inhabitants	*Towns, 51,000 – 200,000 inhabitants*	*Towns, fewer than 50,000 inhabitants*	*Countryside*
SLD, UP	45	50	49	35
Civic Platform (PO)	18	14	13	9
Law and Justice (PIS)	14	11	8	7
Self Defence (*Samoobrona*)	4	6	8	15
Polish Peasant Party (PSL)	2	3	6	19
League of Polish Families (LPR)	6	5	7	8

Table 6.4: Trust in political parties by age groups (%)

Party	Age			
	18–24	*25–39*	*40–59*	*60+*
SLD, UP	42	38	46	46
Civic Platform (PO)	20	17	11	11
Law and Justice (PiS)	9	10	10	10
Self Defence (*Samoobrona*)	8	10	10	10
Polish Peasant Party (PSL)	7	10	9	9
League of Polish Families (LPR)	5	6	6	6

Source: Tables 6.2–6.4 all draw on a pre-election opinion poll carried out by *Sopocka Pracownia Badań Społecznych* and published immediately after the elections (24.09.2001) by the on-line journal *Rzeczpospolita*: (www.rp.pl/dodatki/wybory01_010924/wybory_a_15.html).

The preference for a left-wing alternative was apperent even before the elections. Drawing on pre-election opinion polls, tables 6.2–6.4 provide an overview of trust in political parties by education, place of living and age.

The political circles behind the ill-fated Buzek government suffered serious setbacks in 2001. With an electoral backing of 5.6 and 3.1 per cent respectively, the AWSP and the UW did not even pass the threshold for parliamentary representation. This was a spectacular outcome and strong indication of the deep and widespread distrust in the Buzek government. The strength of the radical and populist vote also came as somewhat of a surprise, even though the writing had been on the wall for some time in the form of strong anti-European sentiments in recent opinion polls. The Polish Peasant Party (PSL) lost half of its parliamentary seats, mainly to *Samoobroona*. But Andrzej Lepper's influence was not confined only to the countryside; his party was quite successful also in small urban communities. Its catchy slogans and its call for the introduction of a guaranteed minimum wage paid off well. The structure of support for Self-Defence (*Samoobrona*) and the League of Polish Families (LPR) may be gauged from Table 6.5.

Table 6.5: Structure of support for Self-Defence and LPR (%)

	Self Defence	*LPR*
Total votes	10.2	7.9
Towns	7.1	7.5
Rural areas	17.8	8.7
Farmers	29.9	6.9
Unemployed	14.4	8.2

Source: Fedyszak-Radziejewska 2002, 61.

The 2001 parliamentary elections strengthened the impression, conveyed already by the presidential elections, that the historical past had lost its significance as a cleavage in Polish politics. This interpretation is partly at odds with the views presented by a number of sociologists in the wake of the elections of 1997. They had predicted that the historical cleavage would become a permanent fixture. It could also be argued that the cleavage has not disappeared but merely changed its form. If so, it manifests itself along the dividing between friends and foes of the 'open society' (Rychard 2002, 52). This split could cut right through parties, governments and parliamentary coalitions. Whatever the long-term implications might be, the changing cleavage structure must be attributed to ideological incoherence within the Solidarity camp (Kolarska-Bobińska 2002, 9). A significant part of the centre-oriented voters supported the SLD-UP coalition, which they perceived as an integrated team, capable of pushing important matters forward. The strong parliamentary presence by the Alliance of the Democratic Left and the Union of Labour and some other mainstream parties was generally seen as an indication that most Poles still support liberal democracy (Dudek 2002, 507).

With 41 per cent of the votes, the left-wing coalition did not win enough parliamentary seats to form a majority government in its own right. The number of potential coalition partners was rather limited, but a collation agreement was eventually worked out with the PSL. An attempt was made to integrate Andrzej Lepper and his followers into mainstream politics. Lepper was elected Deputy Speaker of the *Sejm*, but his parliamentary career came to a rapid halt in the face of the extra-parliamentary activities in which he engaged. He achieved certain notoriety for instigating a riot; he made a number of defamatory statements, and was eventually charged with slander by the public prosecutor.

On 4 October 2001, President Kwaśniewski appointed Leszek Miller as Prime Minister. Jarosław Kalinowski, the PSL leader, was appointed as his deputy, along with Marek Belka who also took over the Ministry of Finance. The *Sejm* approved the new government two weeks later.

Miller's cabinet focused on the urgent need to improve public finances and introduced austerity measures. But the struggle against the high level of unemployment was also given high priority. During the first few months in office, Miller came out strongly against the reforms that had been introduced by the Buzek government. The three-partite coalition (SLD-UP-PSL) went to great lengths to induce the Monetary Policy Council to lower interest rates.

Miller opted for a pro-European foreign policy. He set out to accelerate the negotiation process with the European Union and to close the gap that had opened up between Poland and the other candidate countries. Jan Truszczyński replaced Jan Kułakowki as the main negotiator. Some of the negotiating positions of the previous government were modified, including the controversial issues of agricultural subsidies and the purchase of land by foreigners (the previous cabinet had called for a ban of 18 years on land purchases by foreigners, but Miller opted for a 12-year transition period). The most important phase of the negotiations occurred in the autumn of 2002. The EU suggested that for the first three years subsidies for Polish farmers should amount to 25, 30 and 35 per cent respectively of the subsidies then enjoyed by farmers within the European Union.

These proposals added fuel to the anti-European sentiments in Poland. Many politicians, including some who had never questioned the Polish decision to 'go west', expressed their concern. In a public statement, Lech Kaczyński thus dissociated himself from Polish EU policy in general and from the negotiation process in particular. This change of heart was partly inspired by the results of the local elections that were held on 27 October 2002. Radical and populist parties, including *Samobroona* and the League of Polish Families, had once again done much better than expected which was a natural source of concern for the leaders of the mainstream political parties. The local elections also sent a clear message from rural Poland to Poland's EU negotiators in Copenhagen.

The Danish Prime Minister, who represented the EU in the negotiations with the candidate countries in 2002, subsequently suggested that resources from EU structural funds be used to increase subsidies to Polish farmers to 40 per cent of the then current EU level. The Polish government initially accepted this, but Poland later called for the system to be modified. And, when the negotiations were over, on 13 December 2002, Poland had gained acceptance for most of its demands by the EU summit in Copenhagen. The EU agreed to direct subsidies *to* Polish farmers for the years 2004–2006, amounting to 55, 60 and 65 per cent respectively of the level then enjoyed by EU farmers.

Most of the Polish political parties (SLD-UP, PSL, PO) are satisfied with the results of the EU summit. But the successful negotiations in Copenhagen were not sufficient to make *Samobroona* and the League of Polish Families (LPR) more favourably disposed towards Poland's EU membership. Law and Justice (PIS) – the party of the Kaczyński twins – also remained rather sceptical.

In March 2003, after two years in government, the ruling coalition (SLD-UP-PSL) broke up. By then, the Polish Peasant Party had already dissociated itself from its coalition partners on a number of social and economic issues for quite some time, and the Prime Minister finally decided to remove the party from the government when faced with its refusal to support an important bill which was to be submitted in the name of the entire cabinet. Shortly thereafter, the government was confronted by a series of difficult decisions (including military support for Anglo-American intervention in Iraq and the need for public finances reform). Its popularity dropped.

Conclusions

The division between the post-Solidarity parties and those linked to People's Poland has remained of major significance for Polish political life. It was crucial in 1989–90 and revived in the run-up to the 1997 elections. It served as the glue holding together the AWS electoral cartel and the AWS-UW parliamentary and cabinet coalition.

Even so, this division is likely to be of transitional nature. For a growing number of voters, particularly those in their twenties and early thirties, the organizational history of parties and election coalitions are of little consequence. One interpretation of the electoral results of 1997 is that the post-Solidarity parties played the role as 'guarantors' of the systemic transition, while the Union of Freedom was given the role of 'guardian' of modernization. The AWS-UW coalition somehow had to play both roles at the same time, which made for tensions between the two coalition partners. The coalition collapsed in May 2000; and the AWS minority did not survive the parliamentary elections in 2001.

The most recent presidential and parliamentary elections (2000 and 2001 respectively) would seem to suggest that the historical cleavages have lost their significance. But, it is yet too early to count them out. The controversy between those advocating a stronger role for Catholicism in public life and education, and those preferring public institutions to be neutral *vis-à-vis* religion and Christian values, is a case in point. This particular dimension cuts right through the post-Solidarity post-communist divide, as evidenced by the strongly Catholic flavour of the Polish Peasant Party and a number of the AWS parties. So far we have not seen any unified 'socialist' cluster of parties. The two parties claiming to be Social Democratic – the SDRP and the Union of Labour – joined forces in an electoral alliance prior to parliamentary elections in September 2001. The government coalition formed after the Solidarity comeback in late 1997 could hardly be considered right-wing. Trade-unionist elements cultivate many typically leftist social arguments and visions, far removed from liberal concepts of market, state and society. But there are nevertheless strong intimations of a re-emerging left/right cleavage in the form of the divide between the winners and the losers in the social and economic transformation processes.

As time goes by, the impact of the transition from communism to democracy is likely to lose salience. The 'de-communization' of SLD youth sympathizers, the gradual decrease of public sector employment, the fading out of basic, historically rooted, ideological controversies between parties linked to People's Poland, and those once in opposition to the communist regime, all lend support to this thesis. For the time being, the emerging cleavage structure is not clearly defined: post-communist Poland has not yet left the cleavage-forming stage of development. The parties and electoral coalitions cannot rely on stable constituencies defined in terms of stable social divides. The AWS (post-Solidarity) electoral alliance withered away after the defeat in the parliamentary elections of September 2001, and is yet to be replaced by a dominant party of the political right. The Polish party system clearly has not 'frozen' yet.

On the other end of political spectrum, the SLD has consolidated its role as the dominant factor within the new Left-Centre ruling coalition (including the Polish Peasant Party and the Union of Labour). But this three-party coalition is not likely to remain a permanent fixture in Polish politics. The SLD is in a process of transforming itself from a rigid leftist party representing blue-collar workers and left-oriented white-collars into a centre-left social-democratic formation with broad electoral support (including the business community). The Polish Peasant Party shares the uncertain prospects of its basically rural constituency. And the Union of Freedom tries to carve out a niche for itself as a spokesman for the economically and socially most deprived, but tends to be squeezed out by its senior socialist coalition partner.

The parties of the right and the centre-right form an even more heterogeneous group. Civic Platform (PO) and the remnants of the Union of Freedom represent a strongly pro-European stance and promote the ongoing process of political and economic modernization. The League of Polish Families and, to some extent, also Law and Justice cultivate euro-scepticism and advocate traditional, national and Catholic values.

Self-Defence finally remains quite successful at exploiting social unrest and mobilizing the populist vote. It has its constituency among the losers of the dual transition process in Poland, and its electoral performance may serve as an indicator of the extent of political dissatisfaction in contemporary Poland.

NOTE

1. Flanagan (1971) refers to these cleavages as segmental cleavages. Eckstein's approach to this concept is somewhat broader. By segmental cleavages he understands the 'lines of objective social differentiation' (Eckstein 1966).

REFERENCES

Antoszewski, Andrzej, Ryszard Herbut and Wiesława Jednaka (1993), *Partie i system partyjny w Polsce: Pierwsza faza przejścia ku demokracji*, Wrocław, Wrocław University Press.
Dehnel-Szyc, Małgorzata and Jadwiga Stachura (1991), *Gry polityczne: Orientacje na dziś*, Warsaw, Volumen.
Dudek, Antoni (1997), *Pierwsze lata III Rzeczypospolitej*, Cracow, GEO.
—— (2002), *Pierwsze lata III Rzeczypospolitej 1989–2001*, Cracow, 'Arcana' Publ.
Dudek, Beata (1995a), *Geneza i działalność postsolidarnościowych partii politycznych w latach 1989–1991*, Cracow, un-published doctoral dissertation, Jagiellonian Library of Cracow.
—— (1995b), 'Dekompozycja "Solidarności"', *Ad Meritum* 1995, No. 1, 35–7.
Eckstein, Harry (1966), *Division and Cohesion of Democracy: A Study of Norway*, Princeton, Princeton University Press.
Fedyszak-Radziejewska, Barbara (2002), 'Wieś polska w wyborach: radykalizacja nastrojów', in *Przyszłość polskiej sceny politycznej po wyborach*, Warsaw, Instytut Spraw Publicznych.

Flanagan, Scott, C. (1971), 'Models and Methods of Analysis', in Gabriel Almond, ed., *Choice and Change: Historical Studies on Development*, Boston, Little, Brown and Company.

Gebethner, Stanisław, ed. (1995a), *Wybory parlamentarne 1991 i 1993*, Warsaw, Wydawnictwo Sejmowe.

—— (1995b), '*System wyborczy: deformacja czy reprezentacja*', in Stanisław Gebethner, ed., *Parliamentary Elections 1991 and 1993*, Warsaw, Wydawnictwo Sejmowe.

—— and Jacek Raciborski, eds, (1992), *Wybory '91 a polska scena polityczna*, Warsaw, Fundacja Inicjatyw Społecznych.

Grzybowski, Marian (1996), *Electoral Systems of Central Europe*, Kielce and Cracow, A. Wiśniewski Publ.

Janicki, Mariusz (1993), *Polityka*, No. 22, September, 1993.

Januszewski, Stanisław et al. (1993), *Leksykon opozycji politycznej 1976–1989*, Warsaw, BIS.

Jaruzelski, Wojciech and Marian Orzechowski (1991), *Koniec epoki*, Warsaw, BGW.

Jasiewicz, Krzysztof (1993a), '*Polski wyborca w dziesięć lat po Sierpniu*', in St. Gebethner and Krzysztof Jasiewicz, eds, *Dlaczego tak głosowano? Wybory prezydenckie '90*, Warsaw, ISP PAN & IPN UW.

—— (1993b), '*Polish Politics on Eve of the 1993 Elections: Toward Fragmentation or Pluralism*', in *Communist and Post-Communist Studia*, No 4, Vol. XXVI.

—— (1995), '*Anarchia czy pluralizm? Podziały polityczne i zachowania wyborcze w roku 1991 i 1993*, in *Wybory parlamentarne 1991 i 1993*, Warsaw, Wydawnictwo Sejmowe.

Karasimeonov, Georgi (1995), '*Differentiation Postponed: Party Pluralism in Bulgaria*', in Gordon Whightman, ed., *Party Formation in East Central Europe*, Aldershot-Brookfield, Edward Elgar.

—— (1996), '*The Legislatures in Post-Communist Bulgaria*', in David M. Olson and Philip Norton, eds, *The New Parliaments of Central and Eastern Europe*, London, Frank Cass & Company.

Kolarska-Bobińska, Lena (2002), '*Polska Scena Polityczna po wyborach 2001*', in *Przyszłość polskiej sceny politycznej po wyborach 2001*, Warsaw, Instytut Spraw Publicznych.

Lipset, Seymour Martin and Stein Rokkan (1967), 'Cleavage Structures, Party Systems and Voter Alignments', in Seymour Martin Lipset and Stein Rokkan, eds, *Party Systems and Voter Alignments*, New York, The Free Press.

Małkiewicz, Andrzej (1994), *Wybory czerwcowe 1989*, Warsaw, ISP PAN.

Markowski, Radosław and Gábor Tóka (1995), *Zwrot na lewo w Polsce i na Węgrzech pięć lat po upadku komunizmu. Wybory parlamentarne 1991 i 1993*, Warsaw, Wydawnictwo Sejmowe.

Michta, Andrew A. (1993), 'The Presidential–Parliamentary Systems', in Richard F. Staar, ed., *Transition to Democracy in Poland*, New York, St. Martin's Press.

Olson, David M. (1993), '*Compartmentalized Competition: The Managed Transitional Elections Systems of Politics*', *Journal of Politics*, May.

Paluch, Piotr (1995), *PSL w systemie partyjnym Rzeczypospolitej*, Toruń, Adam Marszałek Publ.

Paszkiewicz, Krystyna A., ed. (1996), *Polskie partie polityczne: Charakterystyki, dokumenty*, Wrocław, Wrocław University Press.

Planeta, Piotr and Ryszard Chrabąszcz (1996), '*I tura wyborów prezydenckich w prasie polskiej*', in *Zeszyty Prasoznawcze/Press Studies*, 1996, No. 1–2.

Rae, Douglas W. and Michael Taylor (1970), *The Analysis of Political Cleavages*, New Haven, Yale University Press.

Rakowski, Mieczysław (1991), *Jak się stało*, Warsaw, BGW.

Ramet, Pedro (1992), '*The New Poland: Democratic and Authoritarian Tendencies*', *Global Affairs*, VII (Spring).

Rokkan, Stein (1970), 'Nation Building, Cleavage Formation and the Structuring of Mass Politics', in Stein Rokkan, ed., *Citizens, Elections, Parties: Approaches to the Comparative Study on the Process of Development*, Oslo, Scandinavian University Press.

Rychard, Andrzej (2002), '*Scena polityczna a scena społeczna*', in *Przyszłość polskiej sceny politycznej po wyborach 2001*, Warsaw, Instytut Spraw Publicznych.

Sokół, Wojciech and Marek Żmigrodzki (1994), '*Functions of Political Parties in Poland at the Time of Systemic Transformation*', *Polish Political Science*.

Staar, Richard F., ed., (1993), *Transition to Democracy in Poland*, New York, St. Martin's Press.

Taras, Raymond C. (1993), '*Voters, Parties and Leaders*', in Richard F. Staar, ed., *Transition to Democracy in Poland*, New York, St. Martin's Press.

Wasilewski, Jacek and Włodzimierz Wesołowski (1992), *Początki parlamentarnej elity. Posłowie kontraktowego Sejmu*, Warsaw.

Wiatr, Jerzy J. (1993), *Wybory parlamentarne 19 września 1993: Przyczyny i następstwa*, Warsaw, Agencja SCHOLAR.

Wojtaszczyk, Konstanty Adam (1995), '*Prawica i lewica na polskiej scenie politycznej*', in *Wybory parlamentarne 1991 i 1993*, Warsaw, Wydawnictwo Sejmowe.

Żukowski, Tomasz (1992), 'Wybory parlamentarne '91', in *Studia Polityczne*, 1992:1.

APPENDIX 6.1: ELECTION RESULTS

PARLIAMENTARY ELECTIONS

1991 Elections
Date: 27 October
Turnout: 43.2%

Party/coalition	*Sejm*		*Senate*	
	%	*Mandates*	%	*Mandates*
Democratic Union	12.2	62	20.0	21
Alliance of the Democratic Left	12.0	60	12.3	4
Polish Peasants' Party	9.2	50	11.5	9
Catholic Action	9.0	50	12.2	9
Confederation for an Independent Poland	8.9	51	7.7	4
Alliance Centrum	8.7	44	13.2	9
Liberal Democratic Congress	7.5	37	10.4	6
Peasant's Alliance (PL)	5.5	28	13.2	7
Solidarity	5.0	27	14.2	11
Party of Friends of Beer	3.0	16	–	–
German Minority	1.2	7	1.1	1
Christian Democracy	2.2	5	2.1	1
'Solidarity of Labour'	2.1	4	–	–
Polish Christian Democracy	1.1	4	3.9	3
Union of Real Politics	2.2	3	2.6	–
Party X (Tymiński)	0.5	3	3.2	–
Movement for Silesian Autonomy	0.4	2	–	–
Democratic Party	1.4	1	–	–
Social Democratic Movement (RDS)	0.5	1	–	–
Mountaineers' League	0.2	1	–	–
Great-Poland Social Union	0.02	1	–	–
Social Christian Union	0.1	1	–	–
Solidarity '80'	0.1	1	–	–
Union of Great Poland	0.1	1	–	–
Other parties/coalitions	6.2	–	5.7	8
Independent Senators	–	–	3.4	7

Note: The simple majority system and the varying density of population of the *voievodships*, or Senate elections voting districts, makes the electoral swing more visible in the Senate than in the *Sejm* elections. Each *voievodship*, regardless of population, was granted two seats in the Senate, with the exception of the Warsaw and Silesian (Katowice) *voievodships*, which were granted three mandates.

1993 Sejm *Elections*
Date: 19 September
Turnout: 52.1%

Party/coalition	Votes	%	Mandates	(%)
Alliance of the Democratic Left	2,815,169	20.4	171	37.2
Polish Peasant Party	2,124,367	15.4	132	28.7
Democratic Union	1,460,957	10.6	74	16.1
Union of Labour	1,005,004	7.3	41	8.9
Confederation for an Independent Poland	795,487	5.8	22	4.8
Non-Partisan Bloc (BBWR)	746,653	5.4	16	3.5
German Minority	78,689	0.6	4	0.9
Homeland (*Ojczyzna*) coalition	878,445	6.4	–	–
Solidarity	676,334	4.9	–	–
Alliance Centrum (PC-ZP)	609,973	4.4	–	–
Liberal-Democratic Congress (KLD)	550,578	4.0	–	–
Union of Real Politics (UPR)	438,559	3.2	–	–
Self Defence (Samoobrona)	383,967	2.8	–	–
Party X	377,480	2.7	–	–
Coalition for Republic (KDR)	371,923	2.7	–	–
Peasant Alliance	327,085	2.4	–	–
Others	155,557	1.1	–	–

Source: 'Proclamation of the State Electoral Commission, 23 September 1993', *Rzeczpospolita*, 27 September 1993.

1993 Senate Elections
Date: 19 September
Turnout: 52.1%

Party/Coalition	%	Mandates
Alliance of Democratic Left	21.4	37
Polish Peasants' Party	18.7	36
Democratic Union	15.7	4
Union of Labour	7.5	2
Confederation for an Independent Poland	11.4	–
Non-Partisan Bloc (BBWR)	10.7	2
German Minority	1.2	1
Catholic Election Committee *Ojczyzna*	5.9	–
Solidarity	15.4	9
Alliance Centrum	3.8	1
Liberal Democratic Congress (KLD)	6.5	1
Union of Real Politics (UPR)	2.6	–
Self Defence (*Samoobrona*)	3.0	–
Party X	0.2	–
Coalition for Republic (KDR)	1.8	–
Peasants' Alliance	1.6	–
Polish League	3.8	1
Polish Christian Democracy (PCHD)	0.6	–
Other parties	0.3	3
Independent senators	2.3	4

1997 Sejm *and Senate Elections*
Date: 21 September
Turnout: 47.9%

Party/coalition	%	Sejm Mandates	Senate Mandates[*]
Election Action 'Solidarity'	33.8	201	51
Alliance of Democratic Left (SLD)	27.1	164	28
Union of Freedom (UW)	13.4	60	8
Polish Peasant Party (PSL)	7.3	27	3
Movement for Rebuilding Poland (ROP)	5.6	6	5
German Minority	0.4	2	–
Union of Labour	4.7	–	–
Bloc for Poland	1.4	–	–
National Alliance of Pensioners (KPEIR RP)	1.6	–	–
Union of Republic's Right	2.0	–	–
National Party of Pensioners (KPEIR)	2.2	–	–
Polish National Community (PSN)	0.07	–	–
Self Defence (*Samoobrona*)	0.08	–	–
German Social-Cultural Association of Częstochova	0.04	–	–
Orthodox Slavonic Minority of the Polish Republic	0.1	–	–
German Social-Cultural Association of Katowice	0.1	–	–
German Social Cultural Association of Elbląg	0.005	–	–
Non-partisans	0.007	–	–
German Committee 'Reconciliation'	0.03	–	–
Olsztyn German Minority	0.01	–	–
People's Alliance 'Poland-Labour'	0.005	–	–
Independents			5

[*] Candidates to the Senate tended to run as individual candidates, though supported by political parties or coalitions. After the election most of the elected Senators joined the parliamentary caucuses of the parties or coalitions with which they had been affiliated.

2001 Sejm *and Senate elections*
Date: 23 September
Turnout: 46.28%

Party/coalition	%	Sejm Mandates	Senate Mandates
Alliance of Dem. Left (SLD)–Union of Labour (UP)	41.04	216	75
Bloc Senate 2001	–	–	15
Civic Platform (PO)	12.68	65	
Self-Defence of The Republic of Poland	10.20	53	2
Law and Justice (PiS)	9.50	44	
Polish Peasant Party (PSL)	8.98	42	4
League of Polish Families (LPR)	7.87	38	2
Electoral Action 'Solidarity of the Right' (AWSP)	5.60	–	
Union of Freedom (UW)	3.10	–	
Social Movement Alternative	0.42	–	
German Minority	0.36	2	
Polish Socialistic Party (PPS)	0.10	–	
Economic Polish Union	0.06	–	
Polish National Community (PSN)	0.02	–	
Independents	–	–	2

PRESIDENTIAL ELECTIONS

1990 elections
First round
Date: 25 November
Turnout: 60.6%

Candidate	Number of votes	%
Lech Wałęsa	3,569,889	40.0
Stanisław Tymiński	3,397,605	23.1
Tadeusz Mazowiecki	2,973,264	18.0
Włodzimierz Cimoszewicz	1,514,025	9.2
Roman Bartoszcze	1,176,175	7.2
Leszek Moczulski	411,516	2.5

Second round
Date: 9 December
Turnout: 53.4%

Candidate	Number of votes	%
Lech Wałęsa	10,622,969	74.3
Stanisław Tymiński	3,683,098	25.7

Source: Dudek 1997, 126.

1995 elections
First round
Date: 5 November
Turnout: 64.8%

Candidate	%
Aleksander Kwaśniewski	35.1
Lech Wałęsa	33.1
Jacek Kuroń	9.2
Jan Olszewski	6.9
Waldemar Pawlak	4.3
Tadeusz Zielinski	3.5
Hanna Gronkiewicz-Waltz	2.8
Janusz Korwin-Mikke	2.4
Andrzej Lepper	1.3
Jan Pietrzak	1.1
Tadeusz Koźluk	0.15
Kazimierz Piotrowicz	0.07
Leszek Bubel	0.04

Second Round
Date: 19 November
Turnout: 68%

Candidate	%
Aleksander Kwaśniewski	51.7
Lech Wałęsa	48.3

2000 elections
Date: 8 October
Turnout: 61.1%

Candidate	Number of votes	%
Aleksander Kwaśniewski	9,485,224	53.9
Andrzej Olechowski	3,044,141	17.3
Marian Krzaklewski	2,739,621	15.6
Jarosław Kalinowski	1,047,949	6.0
Andrzej Lepper	537,570	3.1
Janusz Korwin-Mikke	252,499	1.4
Lech Wałęsa	178,590	1.0
Jan Łopuszański	139,682	0.8
Dariusz Grabowski	89,002	0.5
Piotr Ikonowicz	38,672	0.2
Tadeusz Wólecki	28,805	0.2
Bogdan Pawłowski	17,164	0.1

APPENDIX 6.2: GOVERNMENT COMPOSITION

Mazowiecki's Cabinet
Date of investiture: 24 August 1989

Party/Coalition	Parliamentary seats		Cabinet posts	
	Number	%	Number	%
Solidarity	160	34.8	12	50.0
Polish United Workers' Party	171	37.2	4	16.7
United Peasant Party	76	16.5	4	16.7
Democratic Party	27	5.9	3	12.5
Association Pax	10	2.2	–	–
Christian-Social Union	8	1.7	–	–
Polish Catholic Social League	5	1.1	–	–
Independents	–	–	1	4.2

Bielecki's Cabinet
Date of investiture: 4 January 1991

Party/Coalition	Parliamentary seats		Cabinet posts	
	Number	%	Number	%
Solidarity-OKP	130	28.3		
Liberal Democratic Congress			4	20.0
Alliance Centrum			3	15.0
National Christian Alliance			1	5.0
Democratic Party	27	5.9	1	5.0
Democratic Union	30	6.5	1	5.0
Non-partisan	n/m	n/m	10	50.0

Olszewski's Cabinet
Date of investiture: 23 December 1991

Party/Coalition	Parliamentary seats		Cabinet posts	
	Number	%	Number	%
Alliance Centrum (POC)	44	9.6	4	20.0
National Christian All. (ZCHN)	48[*]+2	10.9	3	15.0
Peasants' Alliance (PL)	28	6.1	2	10.0
Party of Chr. Dem. (PCHD)	4	0.9	1	5.0
Non-partisan	n/m	n/m	10	50.0

[*] In the 1991 elections, the National Christian Alliance ran in the 'Catholic Election Action' electoral alliance, which won a total of 48 seats.

Suchocka's Cabinet
Date of investiture: 11 July 1992

Party/Coalition	Parliamentary seats		Cabinet posts	
	Number	%	Number	%
Democratic Union (UD)	62	13.5	5	20.8
National Christian All. (ZCHN)	48+2	10.9	6	25.0
Liberal Democr. Congress (KLD)	37	8.0	4	16.7
Peasant's Alliance	28	6.1	4	16.7
Party of Chr. Dem. (PCHD)	4	0.9	1	4.1
Peasant Christian Association	–	–	1	4.1
Polish Economic Programme[*]	12	2.6	1	4.1

[*] A splinter party from the Party of Friends of Beer.

Pawlak's Cabinet
Date of investiture: 26 October 1993

Party/Coalition	Parliamentary seats		Cabinet posts	
	Number	%	Number	%
All. of Dem. Left (SLD)	171	37.2	6	28.6
Polish Peasant's Party (PSL)	132	28.7	5	23.8
Non-partisans	–	–	10	47.6
Of which endorsed by PSL			1	
former members of Union of Labour	41	8.9	1	

Oleksy's Cabinet
Date of investiture: 4 March 1995

Party/Coalition	Parliamentary seats		Cabinet posts	
	Number	%	Number	%
All. of Dem. Left (SLD)	171	37.2	8	
Non-partisans, SLD endorsed			3	52.4
Polish Peasant's Party (PSL)	132	28.7	6	
Non-partisan, psl endorsed			1	33.3
Non-partisans	n/m	n/m	3	14.3

Cimoszewicz's Cabinet
Date of investiture: 7 February 1996

Party/Coalition	Parliamentary seats		Cabinet posts	
	Number	%	Number	%
All. of Dem. Left (SLD)	171	37.2	8	
Non-partisans, SLD endorsed			1	45.0
Polish Peasant's Party (PSL)	132	28.7	7	35.0
Non-partisans	n/m	n/m	4	20.0

Buzek's Cabinet
Date of investiture: 17 October 1997

Party/Coalition	Parliamentary seats		Cabinet posts	
	Number	*%*	*Number*	*%*
Electoral Action 'Solidarity' (AWS)	201	43.7	15+1	69.6
Union of Freedom (UW)	60	13.0	5+1	26.1
Alliance Centrum/indep. member	–	–	1	5.3

Miller's Cabinet
Date of investiture: 10 October 2001

Party/Coalition	Parliamentary seats		Cabinet posts	
	Number	*%*	*Number*	*%*
All. of Dem. Left (SLD)–Union of Labour (UP)	216	47.0	11	73.3
Polish Peasant's Party (PSL)	42	9.1	2	13.3
Independents[*]	–	–	2	13.3

[*] In March 2003, the two representatives of the PSL were dismissed from the Miller cabinet and replaced by two independents. As a result the Miller cabinet became a minority cabinet.

APPENDIX 6.3: THE ELECTORAL SYSTEM

Up until 2001, the elections to the *Sejm* were regulated by the Election Act to the *Sejm* of 28 May 1993 (slightly amended in 1995), which replaced the Election Act of 28 June 1991. The elections to the Senate were regulated by the Election Act to the *Senate* of 10 May 1991, amended in 1994. (For the full text of the laws and the amendments, cf. *Dziennik Ustaw*, No. 45, 1993, 205; No. 132, 1993, 640; and No. 54, 1994, 224.). Since 2001, a unified Election Act was established dealing with elections to the *Sejm* and the *Senate (Senat)*. The elections are now regulated by the Election Act of April 12, 2001 (cf. *Dziennik Ustaw* 2001, No. 46, 499; No.74, 786; No.154, 1802; 2002 No. 14, 128; No. 113, 984; No. 127, 1089).

Every citizen who has reached the age of 18 on the day of the election is eligible to vote. Every citizen of the Republic of Poland over 21 years of age is eligible to stand as a candidate. Citizens banned from public life are deprived of the right to vote and to run as a candidate.

The 460 seats of the *Sejm* are distributed in multi-member constituencies. Parties must surpass a 5 per cent threshold nationally in order to qualify for the allocation of seats; electoral cartels or coalitions must obtain 8 per cent of the valid votes cast nationwide. In 1991, the Hare–Niemeyer formula of seat allocation was applied on the constituency level and the St Lagüe formula on the national level. As of 1993, these formulas were replaced by the d'Hondt method.

Candidates may be nominated by political parties, coalitions of parties or by electoral committees, upon the request of at least 3,000 eligible voters in the given constituency. Electoral committees participate in distribution of mandates when their lists are supported by 3 per cent of voters (party committees) or by 5 per cent of voters (coalition-type committees).

The 100 Senators were elected according to the simple majority system, within the *voievodships*. Each *voievodship* was previously entitled to two mandates, with the exception of the densely populated *voievodships* of Katowice and Warsaw, which were entitled to three mandates each. The administrative reform of 1998 divided the 16 *voievodships* into electoral constituencies. Candidates for the Senate (*Senat*) may run on a party ticket or independently. The election committees may nominate as many candidates as there are seats in a given constituency. Each candidate may run in one constituency only, and not simultaneously for the *Sejm*.

The elections are supervised by the State Electoral Commission, chaired by the Judge of the Constitutional Tribunal. The Supreme Court has the final word on the validity of the elections to the *Sejm* as well as to the Senate.

The President is elected for a five-year term in general and direct elections, in one or two rounds. During the first round, a candidate must obtain an absolute majority of the valid votes to be considered elected. If no candidate obtains that level of support, a second round is held between the two front-runners from the first run. In the second run, the candidate who wins a majority is elected. The President may be elected for only two consecutive terms.

APPENDIX 6.4: THE CONSTITUTIONAL FRAMEWORK

The constitutional framework of Poland has undergone several changes since 1989. The Constitution of the People's Republic of Poland, enacted on 22 July 1952, was amended more than thirty times, most extensively on 7 April and 29 December 1989, and again on 8 March and 27 September 1990. As a result of these amendments, the official name of the state was changed from 'People's Republic of Poland' to 'Republic of Poland', the principle of the rule of law was codified, as was the formula for the division of power.

A bi-cameral system of representation, with a lower house (the *Sejm*) and an upper house (*the Senate*), was introduced. A President, first elected by the National Assembly (a joint session of the *Sejm* and the Senate) and, since 1990, by popular vote, replaced the State Council as a Head of State. Directly elected municipal councils with broad autonomy vis-à-vis the state administration replaced the local 'people's councils', which had been integrated into the state apparatus.

A so-called Short Constitution was enacted on 17 October 1992, pending agreement on a new and comprehensive constitution. In the form of a Constitutional Act, the Short Constitution summarized the constitutional changes of 1989–90 in a comprehensive form. It specified the powers of the President and the legal framework for government formation and government responsibilities. The role of the Prime Minister was strengthened and the autonomy of local self-government was enhanced.

On 2 April 1997, the National Assembly approved the new comprehensive constitution for the Republic of Poland. It was endorsed by the voters in a national referendum of 25 May 1997 with 53.4 per cent of the votes in favour. The Constitution defines Poland as a unitary democratic state, abiding by the rule of law and applying a parliamentary formula for the division of power. The *Sejm* and the Senate share legislative power. Executive power is divided between the President and the Council of Ministers.

The Council of Ministers, consisting of the Prime Minister, the Deputy Prime Ministers (optional), the Ministers and the Chairmen of Committees defined by law, is nominated by the President and subject to the approval of the *Sejm*. The Council of Ministers and its members remain responsible to the *Sejm*, but can be removed by the *Sejm* only through a constructive vote of no confidence. The President may dissolve the *Sejm* and the Senate only in the event that the Budget Bill submitted by the Government is not acted upon within the three months after its submission, or in case the *Sejm* and the Senate cannot agree on the formation of a new Government.

The President has a suspensive veto. He represents the state abroad; he ratifies international treaties (some of them subject to approval by the *Sejm* and the Senate in the form of a law); he nominates representatives of Poland to foreign countries and to international organizations. The President serves as Head of State and as Commander-in-Chief of the Armed Forces.

The constitutionality of statutes and legal acts is controlled by the Constitutional Tribunal upon the initiative of the President of the Republic, the Marshals of the *Sejm* or the Senate, the Prime Minister, the Presidents of the Supreme Court and of the Highest Administrative Court, the President of the Supreme Chamber of Control, the General Prosecutor and the Defender of Citizens' Rights, or at least 50 deputies of the *Sejm* or 30 Senators. The Constitutional Tribunal, composed of a President, a Vice President and 13 justices, is elected by the *Sejm* for a 9-year term.

The *Sejm* passes ordinary laws and budget laws. It elects the President of the National Bank of Poland (for six years, upon the initiative of the President of the Republic), the President of the Supreme Chamber of Control (for six years), and the Defender of Citizens' Rights (with the consent of the Senate, for five years). The Senate has the right to amend or oppose laws passed by the *Sejm*. The *Sejm* can reject the amendments or corrections made by the Senate, by an absolute majority. Laws can be passed upon the initiative of the President, the Senate, the Council of Ministers and at least 15 deputies of the *Sejm*. In addition, legal acts (statutes) can be proposed through a popular-initiative signed by at least 100,000 citizens. The *Sejm*, as well as the President (with the consent of the Senate), may call national referenda. A referendum may also be initiated by no fewer than 500,000 citizens.

A broad catalogue of civil rights and freedoms are protected by the Constitution and by statute. The list of freedoms includes: personal freedom, human dignity, the secrecy of communication as well as the freedom of thought and religion, of speech and of assembly. A number of political and social rights are also guaranteed by the Constitution: the right to vote and to be elected, the right to choose one's own profession and place of work, the right to safe working conditions, the right to rest, the right for social care and health care, the right to attend public schools free of charge, and the protection of maternity and childhood. Different kinds of ownership are equally protected by law. Public power shall be decentralized and the competencies of local self-governmental bodies protected by constitutional or by statutory regulations.

7. The Czech Republic

Zdenka Mansfeldová

When we try to analyse and judge more than one decade of post-communist transformation and democratic development, cleavages can provide us with a suitable framework for interpretation and a useful category of analysis. We can hardly recapitulate and evaluate various theories and concepts of cleavages in this introduction; suffice it to refer to Andrea Römmele who says that 'cleavage is a difficult concept, one on which agreement is limited and debate is enthusiastic' (Römmele 1999, 3).

We search for the cleavages that seemed to exist at the beginning of the 1990s, and try to determine to what extent they structured – and keep structuring – voting and party behaviour. The questions formulated by Kay Lawson for post-communist countries also apply to the Czech Republic:

> Do true cleavages presently exist in these nations? Are they revivals of old cleavages? Whether old or new, or a combination, are the parties capitalizing on them, presenting themselves as a representative of those on one side of such a cleavage? (Lawson 1999, 19)

The focus here will be on *political cleavages* representing 'relatively stable patterns of political polarization, in which certain groups support certain policies or parties, while other groups support opposing policies or parties. The groups in question may or may not be *social* groups; what counts is that there are divisions that are given *political* form' (Römmele 1999, 6–7). The analysis will also be inspired by Kay Lawson's definition of cleavages as 'long-term structural conflicts that give rise to opposing political positions, which may or may not be represented by parties' (Lawson 1999, 22), which fits the Czech situation very well.

*

After November 1989 and in the course of the democratic transformation, a variety of social problems emerged along different axes of conflict. In some cases, the issues and the tensions never went beyond the latent position of non-articulated, known and evident co-existing value differences; in other cases they developed or were mobilized, articulated, manifested and interlinked by various actors, to the extent that they began to work as cleavages of a different intensity and duration. Certain issues, which dominated the political scene in some elections, were not carried over into the following elections, because they were not anchored in society. They simply did not have the *social and structural* roots required for long-term survival.

When analysing cleavages in the Czech Republic, we must remember that current problems spring from past events and the cleavages therefore do not lend themselves to ready-made generalizations (Brokl 1999). Many of the contemporary tensions, conflicts and cleavages in transitional and consolidating democracies may in fact be triggered by events of little lasting impact, and they are therefore likely to fade out with the passage of time. The four-fold cleavage typology, suggested by Bulgarian political scientist Georgi Karasimeonov, is particularly well suited for the sometimes-fluid state of affairs in the new democracies of Central and Eastern Europe. The cleavages that he identifies are either of the residual (read: historical), transitional, actual or, for that matter, of the potential variety (Karasimeonov 1999, 2; see also Chapter 12).

The five elections that have so far been held in the Czech Republic since 1990 – in 1990, 1992, 1996, 1998, and 2002 respectively – represent landmarks, which may be used to demonstrate the political, economic and social development and its reflection in citizens' behaviour and attitudes. This chapter will focus on the process of cleavage crystallization along the way from one election to another – a process that has seen the arrival of new cleavages but also the extinction of temporary and partial cleavages.

In their study, Oddbjørn Knutsen and Elinor Scarbrough make an important distinction between cleavage politics and 'new politics'.

> Whereas the cleavage model suggests a relatively robust structuring of mass politics, the 'new politics' perspective points to the more fluid, volatile relationship between social groups, value orientations and party preferences which might be expected of a politics unanchored in cleavages. A more appropriate description for this kind of politics would seem to be 'politics without cleavages' – or 'post-cleavage conflicts' (Knutsen and Scarbrough 1995, 497).

For the purposes of the present study – and possibly also in analyses of other post-communist countries – it is probably advisable to refer to 'pre-cleavage conflicts' or potential cleavages rather than to search for cleavages at any cost.

The 12 years of transformation and the five elections already behind us provide us with cues about the underlying structure of Czech politics, about the pattern of conflict and cooperation among the political parties, and about the determinants of voting behaviour. The data frequently lends itself to interpretations in terms of cleavages, but chances are that the cleavages we find will be of the transitional variety. Actual cleavages, i.e. structurally rooted conflicts, as presented more or less distinctly by actors on the Czech political arena, are likely to emerge only during the processes of democratization and consolidation of democracy.

The Initial Phase of Transformation

The first post-transition elections in Czechoslovakia were held on 8–9 June 1990, following the so-called Velvet Revolution of November 1989. They were the first free elections since 1935, as the first post-war elections in May 1946 cannot be considered fully free (Broklová 1996). Three bodies were elected: two chambers of the Federal Parliament, and Czech National Council.

The transition in Czechoslovakia was not of the negotiated variety. The hard-line communist regime was in full control almost until the very end and collapsed within a period of only ten days. Kitschelt et al. describe the Czech Republic as an example of the bureaucratic-authoritarian model of communism, characterized by an all-powerful, rule-guided bureaucratic machine governed by a planning technocracy and disciplined, dogmatic communist party (Kitschelt, Mansfeldová, Markowski and Tóka 1999). The new political parties thus could emerge only after the transformation, albeit that some parties were grounded in certain embryonic structures existing beforehand. The 'historic parties' such as the Social Democrats, also experienced a renaissance after 50 years of suppression and they gradually tried to carve out electoral niches for themselves. The space of time between the collapse of the communist regime and the first elections was too short for voters to gain a clear understanding of the differences between the parties. Equally, the parties did not have enough time to present the electorate with distinct profiles and they were busy with the process of their own formation.

The electoral law provided for a single-round system with proportional representation within the constituencies. Voters cast their ballots for parties or lists, but had the possibility of naming preferred candidates. A 5 per cent threshold for individual parties was introduced. This electoral system has remained in place during all five elections held in the Czech Republic, though subject to modifications, and its possible change became a significant political issue after the elections of 1998. The electoral period was set at four years, but the first period was exceptionally shortened to two years. One reason for that was the expectation that party formation would proceed and a new constitution would be enacted within the two-year period after the elections.

Many of the new or 'reborn' parties were elite driven and anticipated the existence of cleavages or – for instance, in the case of the Agrarian Party –

the continuation of historical cleavages. But some of the historical cleavages, which were mobilized, failed to find political representation. The civic versus nationalist cleavage, which manifested itself in the problematic relationship between the Czech lands and Slovakia, is a case in point. It mainly manifested itself on the Slovak side, where it also found its political representation (see Chapter 8).

The elections of 1990 served as plebiscite on the future of the country rather than as an arena for partisan conflicts. Four Czech parties gained parliamentary representation, but they were far from representing well-defined constituencies. The overwhelming rejection of communism testifies to the value-driven character of electoral behaviour at this point in time. Anti-communism was an expression of a value judgement rather than of a real cleavage, and it was definitely not an issue of contention. Within this framework, the historical civic versus national cleavage began to develop and manifest itself, but it was not yet crystallized and institutionalized. In Slovakia, national sentiments were strongly articulated, while civic attitudes prevailed in the Czech lands. Other classical cleavages were also visible within this climate of general anti-communism, i.e. the centre versus periphery cleavage in the intricate relationships between the Czech lands and Slovakia, between Bohemia and Moravia, and between Prague and the rest of the Czech lands.

The 1990 elections were characterized by an extremely high voter turnout – 98.8 per cent of the electorate took part in the polls. Apart from the absolute victors – the Civic Forum (OF)[1] – three other formations gained seats in Parliament. The second largest political force in both the federal and the national parliament, far behind the OF, was the Communist Party, isolated but with a stable electorate. In addition, two parties managed to gain representation in the Czech parliament. One was the Movement for Autonomous Democracy–Society for Moravia and Silesia (HSD–SMS), a movement that presented itself as an advocate of Moravian and regional interests, but which later proved to be more regional than national and an agent in the struggle between centre and periphery. The main focus of its electoral programme was the introduction of regional autonomy and the reinvigoration of the Moravian–Silesian lands with the Moravian metropolis Brno as capital. In some constituencies the HSD–SMS won more votes than the OF. The other party to gain representation was the Christian Democratic Union–The Czech People's Party (KDU–ČSL), a bloc party gathering some historical parties from the Czech political scene. It had a traditional electorate among Czech and, mainly, Moravian Catholics.

From 1991 onwards, after the first phase of party formation, a process of differentiation commenced. The internal differentiation within the Civic Forum was the most important event in this process. Particularly in the Czech lands, this differentiation reflected diverging opinions about how the common goal of political and economic transformation should be reached.

The interest was, at the time, focused on the sphere of the economy: economic democracy, privatization and anti-statism. The emerging plurality of subjects and their activities were yet not organically fully attached to the social stratification and the structure of economic interests; the differentiation was rather based on identification with values. Early in 1991, the variegated orientation of representatives and members and the conceptions of political and economic transformation led to the disintegration of the Civic Forum into several new parties. The most notable of these were the liberal-oriented Civic Movement (OH) – which claimed the political middle ground – and the liberal, market economy-oriented Civic Democratic Party (ODS), which captured the right-hand side of the left-right spectrum. A third party with its roots within the Civic Forum was the Civic Democratic Alliance (ODA).[2]

After the 1992 elections, the number of parties represented in parliament more than doubled from four to nine. This raises the question of whether new cleavages have emerged or cleavages had started crystallising and found political representation. Apart from the ODS, another civic, right-oriented party gained representation in parliament: the Civic Democratic Alliance (*Občanská demokratická strana*, ODA). New in parliament were also the Social Democrats (ČSSD), which thereafter have gained increasing strength; and the Liberal Social Union (*Liberální sociální unie*, LSU), which represents agrarian and ecological interests and was formed as a coalition between the Greens, the Agrarian Party and the Czechoslovak Socialist Party. The LSU had its widest base of support in the agrarian regions of the country. Also represented in parliament after the 1992 elections was the Republican Party (SPR–RSČ), a vehicle for xenophobic and nationalist tendencies. The party had its largest base of support in the mining districts of Northern Bohemia, in regions with distinct economic problems and a higher than average proportion of Roma, and it was at its weakest in Prague (Kostelecký 1996; 2003). The Movement for Autonomous Democracy–Society for Moravia and Silesia (HSD–SMS) remained in parliament, but its distinct regional profile did not pay off on the federal level; it gained representation only in the Czech National Council.

Table 7.1: Satisfaction with development: In general, do you feel things in the Czech Republic are going in the right or in the wrong direction? (%)

	1991	*1992*	*1993*	*1994*	*1995*	*1996*	*1997*
Right	51.7	58.1	66.8	58.9	56.7	50.9	28.3
Wrong	30.5	33.8	33.2	30.0	30.0	36.6	58.2
Don't know	17.9	7.8	–	11.1	13.3	17.3	13.4

Source: Central and Eastern Eurobarometer (CEEB), 2–8.

In the 1992 elections, the ODS was the indisputable winner (see *Appendix 7.1*). The most important differentiating factor between the elections of

1990 and 1992 was the impact of economic reform. Satisfaction with the way reforms progressed showed a high correlation with support for the ODS, a party which identified itself with liberal democratic values and individualism (*Tables 7.1, 7.2* and *7.3*). The Civic Movement appealed to similar values, but did, however, not manage to gain representation in the 1992 parliament.

Table 7.2: Evaluation of the economic transformation in 1993–2001 (%)[*]

Year	93	94	95	96			97			98	99	00	01
Month	3	3	2	3	10	2	3	5	7	2	2	2	2
Succesful	26	28	31	28	23	18	20	10	8	5	7	8	11
Partly succesful	42	47	44	43	42	44	34	40	32	31	28	27	36
Not succesful	26	17	18	19	26	27	36	44	53	61	53	52	41

[*] Percentages calculated excluding those who say they 'don't know'.

Source: SOÚ AV ČR – CVVM (Centre for Public Opinion Research), Prague, 1 February 2000.

Critical attitudes towards economic reforms were associated with support for left-oriented parties, particularly for the Communist Party, and partly also with support for the right-wing Republican Party, which appealed to citizens with oppositional, radical or even extremist preferences. Support for economic reform and long-term support for the new political order prevailed within the parties of the right and the middle.

*

The coexistence of Czechs and Slovaks in a common state became more and more of a problem for the Federal Republic. In Slovakia it developed into the dominant cleavage. In the Czech Republic the parties did have somewhat different opinions on the future of the federation, but none of them called for independence; and the survival of the federation had no major impact on party preferences in the Czech Lands.

The common Czech-Slovak state, joining two nations with diverse historical experiences, forms a historical cleavage, which may be seen as civic rather than national. The cleavage gained particular importance after the early 1930s, when the Slovaks emerged as a modern nation. In 1968, however, it again came to the forefront, resulting in the federative re-organization of the Czechoslovak state. In 1990, the cleavage again appeared in its full strength in conjunction with the so-called hyphen war – the issue was whether the state should be called Czechoslovakia or Czecho-Slovakia. During 1990 and 1991, this resulted in a heated debate on federalism and the division of power between the two republics, as illustrated by the Competence Law of December 1990.

Contradictions between the two nations, Czechs and Slovaks, previously suppresed, were articulated again in the period between the elections of 1990 and 1992 and manifested themselves as a national cleavage in Slovakia. The political landscape developed in different directions in the two parts of the Federal Republic; even terms such as left and right carried different connotations in the two republics. Unlike the Czech lands, the right-wing segment of the left/right continuum remained unoccupied in Slovakia. Public against Violence (*Verejnost' proti násiliu*, VPN), the Slovak equivalent to Civic Forum (OF), which was a political formation of the middle with the potential of a civic movement, had no competition whatsoever on its right-wing flank. Czechs and Slovaks were therefore inclined to advocate different strategies for economic development as well (*Table 7.3*).

Table 7.3: Preferred economic system (%)

	January 1991			November 1991		
	Fed.	*CR*	*SR*	*Fed.*	*CR*	*SR*
Market economy	48	52	39	45	52	33
Mixed economy	36	33	43	44	39	53
Socialist plan economy	4	3	6	6	5	8
Don't know	12	12	12	5	5	6

Source: AISA, Research Report, November 1991.

From the very beginning, two separate and parallel party systems emerged, with their roots in the socialist federation. Nevertheless, in the elections of 1990 and 1992, several parties ran throughout the federation, and part of the new political elite was indeed concerned with mobilizing a federation-wide electorate. But in contrast to inter-war Czechoslovakia, such an electorate was no longer to be found (Brokl and Mansfeldová 2003; Broklová 1996).[3] The federation-wide parties were subsequently to be dissolved through the emergence of a dual structure with two sets of independent, national parties – one for each of the republics. This development was reinforced by electoral legislation, which provided representation in the federal parliament for parties that made it past the 5 per cent threshold in either of the constituent republics. The emergence of two autonomous party systems was an important precursor for the later break-up of the Czechoslovak Federation.

Apart from the legal prerequisites, the two somewhat differentiated party systems were the result of the divergent conditions in the two halves of the federation. In particular, this went for economic conditions and for the progress of economic reforms. During 1990–92, Czechoslovakia was marked by a serious fall in economic performance and increasing economic divergences between the two republics, with the Slovak economy hit particularly hard. In both parts of the federation, this led to the politicization of the transformation process and to conflicts pertaining to economic policy. The national cleavage nevertheless remained at the very top of the agenda in Slovakia; and it was readily apparent that the two parts of the federation were drifting apart.

The new democracies of Slovakia and Czech Republic in the first decade after their transition exhibit similarities and differences that help to illuminate the process of cleavage formation and dissolution. Despite broad similarities, these two countries emerged at the end of the 1990s with quite different relationships between opinion and political representation (Krause 2002, 2).

The collapse of the federation was one possible outcome of the 1992 elections, as the successful parties had widely diverging views on economic reform and on the federation, and manifested differences pertaining to democratic traditions and liberal values. For the Czech Republic, the national cleavage appears to have been solved through the dissolution of the federation. It may be considered a cleavage on the assumption that there are such things as one-sided cleavages. It was a Slovak issue only, without equivalent in the Czech lands. Contrary to Slovakia, the Czech Republic did not feature parties calling for the dissolution of the federation and the formation of an independent state (Brokl and Mansfeldová 2003).

The more left-oriented stance of the Slovak citizens, as compared to the Czechs, is often explained by a more positive attitude towards the previous regime. Krivý, Feglová and Balko (1996, 41) argue that traditional Slovak society did not turn to socialism immediately after the Second World War, but was attracted to it later due to its paternalism, collectivism, closed character, egalitarianism and anti-intellectual attitude. Indeed, it probably makes more sense to compare the two countries in terms of liberalism versus paternalism than in terms of left and right (Tymowski and Petrusek 1992). But the more positive attitude of Slovak citizens towards the past should be construed not as an expression of particularly socialist sentiments, but rather as a preference for the paternalistic mission of the state, as a manifestation of economic thought, and as an evaluation of the economic reforms and their anticipated costs. Of importance were also attitudinal differences between Czechs and Slovaks with respect to style of political leadership, methods of conflict resolution, and the implications of democratic governance (Krivý 1993).

The different orientations of Czech and Slovak citizens, as represented by the political parties, are best described with the help of two reference axes – paternalism versus liberalism and civic versus national, or state paternalism versus liberal market economy and libertarian-authoritarian – both of which illustrate why the Czech and Slovak party systems took on different forms (Kitschelt 1992; Brokl et al. 1994).

The two countries also differed with respect to religion. In Slovakia, the proportion of devout believers is considerably higher than in the Czech Republic. This difference did not, however, lead to a conflict between the countries, as it was sublimated into the civic-national cleavage. The nationally oriented Slovak parties appealed to the Catholic community rather than to secular, Greek Catholic and Orthodox voters (Krivý, Feglová and Balko 1996).

The developments covered thus far lead up to the resolution in 1992 of the historic Czechoslovak civic-national cleavage. At the polls, Slovak voters preferred actors who supported the national principle, while the Czech electorate embraced actors who represented the civic principle.

From Independence to the Third Elections

The years of 1992 and 1993 were marked by the dissolution of the federal state. The economy took off in 1994 and remained in an up-beat mode with a low inflation rate, a low rate of unemployment and a stable foreign exchange rate until approximately 1996.

Voter attitudes towards economic reform formed such distinct clusters that the Czech political system was sometimes characterized as 'one-dimensional' (Kitschelt 1994, 36). This dimension was consistent with the left-right axis. Opinion polls made between the second and third elections show that the positions on the left-right axis on which the parties placed themselves corresponded with their positions as perceived by the voters (Markowski 1995; Večerník 1996; Vlachová 1997). The conformity of the self-perception of the parties with that of the electorate was also reflected in inter-party interaction during the electoral campaign of 1996 and thereafter (Krause 1996, 428).

Opinion polls carried out in the first part of 1994 testify to a fragile social equilibrium, and growing public dissatisfaction with the way the country was run. The Velvet Revolution was by no means challenged. Czech voters remained committed to the principles and values of democratic governance, the market economy and even the general thrust of economic reform, but they were getting increasingly critical of the government's performance record as the social impact of economic reform made itself felt (Šimoník 1996, 457–8).

Several circumstances made the parliamentary elections of 1996 particularly important. They completed the formation of the Czech political system. They were the first elections held in the Czech Republic after the dissolution of the federation. They were also the first elections to the Senate, which commenced its work only three years after the constitution had provided for the establishment of the body and after long discussions about the wisdom of having a second chamber. In 1996, no new party managed to enter the lower chamber of the parliament of the Czech Republic, while three of the nine parties represented earlier lost out.[4] Of the six remaining, two were civic, right-oriented parties; one was Christian in character; one was social democratic; and one each on the extreme left and the extreme right of the political spectrum, the Communist Party and the Republican party, respectively – the term 'extreme' carrying the same connotations as in Sartori's *Parties and Party Systems* (1976).

The 1996 elections resulted in the emergence of a party of equal strength as, and a weighty rival to, the previously dominant Democratic Citizens' Party: the Social Democrats (ČSSD). The ČSSD is different from other post-communist leftist parties in the sense that it is not a renamed or transformed Communist Party. Instead, it harks back to a historical social democracy, defining itself against both the political right and the existing Communist Party. Brokl has pointed to the interesting effect created by the electoral formula: the first chamber was elected by proportional representation, while the second was elected through a majority system (Brokl 1996, 392–3). The larger parties were the beneficiaries of the majority effect, which resulted in a rather large portion of votes cast – some 10 per cent – being squandered. The 5 per cent hurdle also had a psychological effect, as voters were reluctant to cast their ballot for parties with little chance of gaining parliamentary representation (Novák 1996, 411).

What can be inferred from the election results? Brokl sums up three main explanations for the electoral success of the Social Democrats (Brokl 1996):

1. Domestic observers tended to interpret it as a result of the renewal of the social class structure, which provided also for the renewal of the classical role of the social democratic party, creating a marked linkage between a political party and a social class.

2. Foreign observers, in many cases, saw the success of the Czech Social Democrats as a parallel to the successes of leftist political parties in other post-communist countries, and feared that it would lead to a setback for the transformation process. Due to the existence of the more left-wing Communist party (KSČM), Czech Social Democracy was able to present itself as a social democratic party rather than as a crypto-communist successor party. The survey data show that the evaluation of the current situation and the pre-1989 regime did not change rapidly (*Tables 7.4 and 7.5*).

3. The third interpretation sees the electoral success of the Social Democrats as a manifestation of the emergence of a standard political spectrum, and as a result of the electoral formula with its 5 per cent hurdle for parliamentary representation. An analysis of the election results indicates that the ČSSD won voters who had previously supported smaller parties, likely not to clear the 5 per cent threshold, and who were prepared to vote neither for the parties in government, nor for the Communists and the extremists. A comparison of electoral preferences over time shows that a large portion of the electoral support for the Social Democrats did not

emanate from its core constituency, but from voters who made up their minds very late in the campaign. Sympathies also played a role. According to the Centre for Empirical Social Studies (STEM) 14.7 per cent of 'non-decided' voters mentioned the ČSSD as the most sympathetic party.

Table 7.4: Evaluation of the current situation and the pre-1989 regime (%)

The current regime is...	9/91	3/96	6/97	10/97	3/98	3/99	10/99	3/00
Better	39	34	26	29	25	27	29	28
About the same	44	41	40	37	37	43	36	36
The regime before 1989 was better	14	18	25	24	28	21	23	23
Don't know	3	7	9	10	10	9	12	13

Source: SOÚ AV ČR – CVVM (Centre for Public Opinion Research), Prague, March 2000.

Table 7.5:Left–right self-placement of Czech voters, 1990–1996 (%)

	6/90	6/91	6/92	6/93	6/94	5/95	12/95	7/96
Left-wing	19	20	16	20	21	23	22	22
Centre	51	43	33	40	41	41	41	41
Right-wing	30	37	51	40	38	36	37	37

Sources: STEM, *Trendy 1993–1996* and *Vývoj společensko-politické situace v letech 1990–1992.*

Opinion polls show that the right-oriented ODS and the left-oriented ČSSD were seen as alternative political parties. Yet in the 1996 elections voting behaviour did not follow social stratification; in fact, it cut right through the political spectrum, which leads to centripetal rather than centrifugal tendencies. One may talk about crosscutting cleavages. Of the 'poor', i.e. groups with lowest levels of income, 39 per cent voted for the right. Fifty-six per cent of the 'poor' voted for the left, not the 100 per cent a class interpretation would predict. Conversely, 25 per cent of the 'rich' – citizens in the highest income brackets – and 30 per cent of entrepreneurs voted for the left. The Czech electorate at the time was characterized as being in a state of flux. Voting behaviour nevertheless lends itself to some generalizations. Of the two main parties, the ODS represents the upper part of the social hierarchy, while the ČSSD may be seen as a representative of dependent persons. Even so, at the same time both parties present themselves as broad all-national parties attractive to the members of most social groups. A positive development in parliamentary politics has been the emergence of a new political elite with a degree of political experience. Of 200 members in the 1996 lower chamber, 74 had had seats in the previous parliament.

The 1996 elections, and developments thereafter, also demonstrate that the once strong socio-economic dimension, which overlapped with the right-left dimension, is receding in importance. As privatization is almost completed, the role of the state and the juxtaposition of economic populism and market principles constitute the main political issues. This is closely connected to the question of social security, where the idea of redistribution through a paternalistic state is contrasted with a social policy guided by market-oriented principles.

The cosmopolitan–nationalist antagonism is brought out by attitudes towards the European Union and NATO, attitudes towards neighbouring countries – particularly Germany – and towards foreign influences and foreign capital. Associated with this conflict dimension are attitudes towards ethnic minorities, in particular the Roma, and to asylum policy. The political parties have well articulated opinions on this dimension, as has the public. This conflict dimension is above all exploited by the populist Republican Party, and cannot be accounted for by socio-political variables. The Republican Party opposes all supranational institutions, and advocates that contention with an extreme nationalist posture.

The government formed after the 1996 elections with prime minister Václav Klaus included the same three parties as the one which took office after the 1992 elections: the right-wing ODS and ODA and the right of centre KDU-ČSL. The other three main parties – the ČSSD, the KSČM and the SPR-RSČ – remained opposition parties, but the Communists and the Republicans lacked 'coalition potential'. The Communists do represent the extreme left, but the Republicans are actually incorrectly thought of as a party of the extreme right.[5] The new government was a minority coalition government formed by three parties – ODS, ODA and KDU-ČSL – with only 99 MPs out of 200. The predictions that the government would be weak and unstable were fulfilled in December 1997, when the Klaus cabinet resigned. Growing economic problems and the decreasing confidence in constitutional institutions made for growing tensions among the coalition partners and within the ODS.

Electoral Change Without Regime Change

After the overthrow of Klaus' government in November 1997 and the subsequent split within the ODS, the general expectation was for an easy social democratic victory, the rise of the KDU-ČSL, a strong performance by the new Freedom Union (US), significant increases for extremist parties such as the SPR-RSČ and the KSČM, and populist parties like Pensioners for Life Security (DŽJ). The widespread dissatisfaction with the performance of democratic institutions, and an array of other social and political indicators, paved the way for such predictions (*Table 7.6*).

Table 7.6: Satisfaction with democracy in the Czech Republic (%)[*]

Month/year	1/97	3/97	1/98	1/99	1/00	4/00	1/01	7/02
Satisfied	55	39	36	33	40	36	37	42
Not satisfied	37	56	56	59	50	60	54	46

*Percentages calculated excluding those who say they 'don't know'.

Source: SOÚ AV ČR – CVVM (Centre for Public Opinion Research), Prague, 2002.

The electoral victory of the Social Democrats (ČSSD) in 1998 was therefore hardly surprising. The relative success of the ODS – it came in second – and the failure by the SPR-RSČ and DŽJ to gain parliamentary representation provided more food for thought.

The verdict of the voters was for the left – which gained in prominence – and against populism and extremism. It may even be seen as a tribute to the strength of a democratic political culture with little tolerance for political radicalism. But the failure of the SPR-RSČ was also partly of its own making, the logical consequence of internal strife and waning party cohesion. The bulk of its original sympathizers probably opted for the ČSSD; the rest of them either abstained from voting or went KSČM (Kreidl and Vlachová 2000, 80).

Five parties gained representation in the Chamber of Deputies: two left-oriented parties (ČSSD and KSČM) with a combined electoral support of 43.3 per cent, and three centre-right parties (ODS, KDU-ČSL and the new US) with a joint electoral backing of 45.3 per cent. The elections marked a shift to the left, but only in the upper age cohorts, that is among those 45-years old or older (Řeháková 1999, 322). Personal animosities and internal strife made it impossible for the parties of the centre-right to form a coalition cabinet, which paved the way for a social democratic minority government. With 32.3 per cent of the votes, the ČSSD only had 74 mandates in the Chamber of Deputies, but with the backing of the ODS – the strongest opposition party with an electoral support of 27.7 per cent and 64 of the deputies – Prime Minister Miloš Zeman could count on a comfortable parliamentary majority of 138 out of 200. The parliamentary coalition between the two parties was based on a formal agreement known as the 'Contract regarding the formation of a stable political environment in the Czech Republic between the two strongest parties, the ČSSD and ODS'. The contract defined the relations between the two parties and laid down the terms and conditions of the parliamentary coalition between the ČSSD and the ODS.

In a study inspired by Kitschelt's distinction between left/right (read: economic populism versus market liberalism) and libertarian versus authoritarian, Czech sociologist Plecitá-Vlachová tries to determine the relative importance of these two dimensions of conflict:

> [T]he left/right dimension declined slightly in importance between 1996 and 1998, to the advantage of libertarianism–authoritarianism. This was particularly obvious after the formation of the Freedom Union (US), which introduced politically liberal (read: libertarian) values into Czech politics (Plecitá-Vlachová 2003).

But – as noted by the same author – the groping by this party in political space in its efforts to strengthen the libertarian-authoritarian dimension did not pay off. Instead left/right came out strengthened as evidenced by the elections of 2002. The Opposition Agreement of 1998, modified in 2000 by the so-called Toleration Patent, included a pledge to embark on electoral engineering with the explicit objective of 'finding an electoral system that would significantly simplify the creation of a functional majority government consisting of a maximum of two political parties' (Lebeda 2003, 141). An amendment to the Constitution was ruled out as politically impossible, and a new electoral formula was therefore sought within the framework given by the proportional electoral system. This resulted in a proportional electoral system that favoured strong parties to the detriment of the weak, less successful parties (see *Appendix 7.3*). In 2001 the Constitutional Court invalidated key portions of the electoral reform as incompatible with the principle of proportional representation. The rules that applied in 2002 introduced 14 precincts; and the high threshold for coalitions was preserved (see *Appendix 7.3*).

The electoral campaign of 2002 revolved around the leading personalities of the major political parties, to an extent not formerly known. The electoral results were surprising on at least two counts. First of all, there was a dramatic decline in the electoral turnout – 58 per cent as compared to 73.9 per cent of eligible voters in 1998. Moreover, the Communist Party of Bohemia and Moravia (KSČM) made considerable gains. With 18.5 per cent of the popular vote and 41 seats in the Chamber of Deputies (as compared to 11 per cent of the votes and 24 seats in 1998), the Communist Party now ranks as the third strongest party in the Czech Republic. This shift in voter party preferences may also be gauged from their self-placement on the left/right scale (*Table 7.7*).

Table 7.7: Left–right self-placement of Czech voters, 1994–2002 (%)[*]

	1994[**]	1995	1996	1997	1998	1999	2000	2001	2002[***]
Left-wing	18.5	19.2	19.4	19.4	22.1	22.5	22.4	21.8	22.8
Centre	31.4	31.8	29.2	34.4	32.4	31.5	31.4	31.0	31.8
Right-wing	40.9	37.8	39.5	34.8	35.4	34.8	36.0	37.3	33.8

[*]   Percentages calculated excluding those who say they 'don't know'.
[**] Including the first survey of November 1993.
[***] Averages for the period from January to June.

Source: SOÚ AV ČR – CVVM (Centre for Public Opinion Research), Prague, 2002.

The apathy of a portion of the population, disgust among voters with politics (in German: *Politikverdrossenheit*), and the gradual normalization of politics that no longer dominates the social agenda are among the explanations most frequently given for the low electoral turnout. Analyses have shown that most non-voters and most KSČM voters are among the least satisfied with the political situation in the Czech Republic; but in contradistinction to the KSČM voters, the non-voters are socially and politically among the least active (Seidlová, Červenka and Kunštát 2003, 101). Despite the drop in the electoral turnout, 75 per cent of ODS voters, 66 per cent of KSČM voters, and 53 per cent of ČSSD voters remained loyal to their parties.

The current cabinet of Prime Minister Vladimír Špidla includes parties of the left as well as of the right – the ČSSD, KDU-ČSL and US-DEU. It has only a narrow majority in the Chamber of Deputies (50.5 per cent). Due to the differences in the political programmes of the coalition parties, the cabinet literally has to fight for the decisive vote whenever there is an important role-call. The formation of parliamentary coalitions and cabinets in the Czech Republic is governed by the personal preferences and animosities of the party leaders. This became obvious during the formation of the cabinet in 1998, and was confirmed again in 2002.

Contemporary Divisions of Opinion: Continuity and Change in the Czech Republic

Cleavage crystallization can be defined as a process through which the cleavage of interests and identity are crystallized and articulated in a political formation, which is able to influence decision-making. One can observe distinct phases of cleavage crystallization in the five elections in the Czech Republic. We have seen that the Czech Republic has a small number of parties with stable parliamentary representation. These parties possibly represent underlying structural conflicts, but all structural conflicts and social contradictions may not find their expression within the party system. In all likelihood, the Czech cleavage structure has not settled yet, but the longitudinal perspective offered by the five elections may help us define the contours of the cleavage space as of now. This has been the basic thrust of our inquiry, and a short summary of our findings is now in order.

In the first part of the 1990s, the Czech party system came close to being one-dimensional. It was dominated by one divide but with minor crosscutting axes (Kitschelt, Mansfeldová, Markowski and Tóka 1999, 230). In the Czech Republic, the divide between the advocates of social protectionism and the exponents of market liberalism has socio-cultural and political features that link liberal economic policy preferences to anti-communism, religion and Christian morality (Kitschelt, Mansfeldová, Markowski and Tóka 1999, 226). The 1992 elections revolved around questions of economic reform to the extent of giving the impression of an almost one-dimensional voter and party space.

The following elections resulted in further differentiation, and eventually the break-up, of this one-dimensional party space. As privatisation was drawing to a close, the role of the state and the combination of economic populism and market principles became the major political issues. This is closely related to the question of social security, where the notion of redistribution through a paternalistic state stands in contrast to social policy guided by market principles.

The *socio-economic cleavage* survived the 1996 elections, in collusion with a number of issues and contradictions of a short-term variety. When privatization had been removed from the agenda, the political debate focused on the role of the state. The struggle between social protectionism and market principles is part and parcel of this conflict. Similar comments apply to the controversy between advocates and opponents of redistributive measures to promote social security and equality. Redistribution played a prominent role in the campaigns leading up to the two most recent elections, 1998 and 2002 respectively. The impact on voting behaviour by socio-economically related issues such as old-age benefits, social security, and the responsibility of the state for law enforcement in economic matters also testifies to the resilience of the underlying socio-economic cleavage (Krause 2002; Plecitá-Vlachová 2002).

The presence of a *cosmopolitan versus national* orientation may be gauged from attitudes towards European integration in general and the European Union in particular, towards NATO and even towards cooperation within the Visegrad Four. The Czech parties are yet to find stable positions on this issue divide, and change positions as they see fit. The ODS is a case in point. Originally an outspoken advocate of EU membership, this party contested the 2002 elections on a platform of outright Euro-scepticism. European integration nowadays has all the trappings of a crosscutting cleavage in the Czech Republic.

The relationship to Germany in general and to *Sudeten* Germans in particular, sometimes simply referred to as the *German question*, has been a hot issue in Czechoslovakia and the Czech Republic since the beginning of the 1990s. The debate has focused on the decrees issued by President Beneš in the immediate aftermath of the Second World War. These decrees addressed themselves to regulation of Nazi crimes, crimes against humanity and Nazi occupation, and served as the basis for the transfer of ethnic Germans from the Czech lands to Germany and Austria.[6] In the first part of the 1990s, the Czech parties were split on this issue. Most of them approached it in terms of human rights, within the framework of a feeling of collective guilt and in the spirit of Europeanism; others, most notably the KSČM and SPR-RSČ, used it for nationalistic leverage. By the end of the 1990s, when Germany and Austria called for the abrogation of the Beneš decrees by the Czech Republic as part of the terms and conditions for EU membership, the political parties rallied in defence of what they perceived as the national interest and the issue ceased to be divisive within the Czech context.

Green politics or *ecology* has not made much of a breakthrough in the Czech Republic. In the elections of 2002, the Green Party campaigned on a platform of anti-globalization and sustainable development, but with limited electoral success. It did not get past the threshold for parliamentary representation, but it did obtain enough votes to qualify for reimbursement of its campaign expenditures and may thus turn out to be a force to be reckoned with in the future.[7]

Traditional conflict structures, such as *State versus Church*, are not articulated in Czech politics, or at least not in electoral behaviour. Secularization has long deprived organized religion of its importance, and the Czech Republic stands out as a solidly secular entity. Recent census data suggest that the process of secularization has not yet culminated. The Roman Catholic Church counts the largest number of believers, but it is not particularly strong in terms of absolute numbers, even though it benefited from a post-communist religious revival after 1989. One of the political parties – the Czech People's Party-Christian Democratic Party (KDU-ČSL) – has a steady support in traditionally Catholic regions. Nevertheless, its electoral gains did not surpass 15 per cent during the phase of transition. But it cannot be seen as an exponent of a State-Church cleavage (Rakušanová 2003). The issues advocated by the party relate to conservative values and morals, in other words to the libertarian-authoritarian dimension.

Nowadays the *urban/rural* cleavage does not seem to exist in the Czech Republic. The restitution of agricultural land and property did not promote the emergence of a significant layer of private farmers, and large parts of the agricultural land are cultivated by collective farms transformed into co-operatives of owners. Negative attitudes towards economic reform in general and government agricultural policy in particular, and apprehensions about the future within the EU, sometimes carry over into demonstrations and protests; and they definitely have an impact on party preferences, but they have not led to a revitalization of the old urban/rural cleavage. Several parties have in fact laid claim to the rural heritage of the Agrarian Party, one of the most influential parties of inter-war Czechoslovakia, but so far with limited success. An agrarian party gained representation in the wake of the 1992 parliamentary elections, but only as part of an electoral cartel *Liberální sociální unie* (Liberal Social Union), and it subsequently failed to carve out a stable electoral niche for itself. For the time being at least, left-wing parties, the KDU-ČSL and professional associations cater for the interests of the potential agrarian voters.

Parties, Movements and Coalitions

ČMUS	Bohemian and Moravian Union of the Centre (*Českomoravská unie středu*)
ČSSD	Czech Social Democratic Party (*Česká strana sociálně demokratická*)
CZ	Road of Change (*Cesta změny*)
DEU	Democratic Union (*Demokratická unie*)
DŽJ	Pensioners for Life Securities (*Důchodci za životní jistoty*)
HSD-SMS	Self-governing Democracy Movement–Association for Moravia and Silesia (*Hnutí za samosprávnou demokracii–sdružení pro Moravu a Slezsko*)
KDS	Christian Democratic Party (*Křesťansko demokratická strana*)
KDU-ČSL	Christian Democratic Union/Czechoslovak Peoples' Party (*Křesťansko demokratická unie/Československá strana lidová*)
KSČM	Communist Party of Bohemia and Moravia (*Komunistická strana Čech a Moravy*)

LB	Left Block (*Levý blok*), a coalition consisting of Left Bloc and the Communist Party of Bohemia and Moravia
LIRA	Liberal Reform Party (*Liberální reformní strana*)
LSNS	National Socialist Liberal Party (*Liberální strana národně sociální*)
LSU	Liberal Social Union (*Liberálně sociální unie*), a grouping consisting of three collective members: Czechoslovak Socialist Party, Green Party and the Agrarian Party
ODA	Civic Democratic Alliance (*Občanská demokratická aliance*)
ODS	Civic Democratic Party (*Občanská demokratická strana*)
OF	Civic Forum (*Občanské hnutí*)
OH/SD	Free Democrats/Civic Movement (*Občanské hnutí/Svobodní demokraté*)
SPR-RSČ	Association for the Republic–Republican Party of Czechoslovakia (*Sdružení pro republiku–Republikánská strana Československa*)
SZ	Green Party (*Strana zelených*)
US	Freedom Union (*Unie svobody*)
US-DEU	Freedom Union–Democratic Union (*Unie Svobody–Demokratická unie*)
ZS	Agrarian Party (*Zemědělská strana*)
4K	Four Coalition (*Čtyřkoalice*) formed by KDU-ČSL, US, DEU and ODA

NOTES

1. The Civic Forum, formed in November 1989, was the largest newly formed political subject. It was a movement in character; it provided a platform and served as an umbrella for a broad range of independent initiatives and anti-communist opposition forces. The Civic Forum party manifesto advocated in broad terms the transition to a free society and a market economy. The Civic Forum had a substantially broader base of support in Bohemia than in Moravia.

2. As early as the beginning of 1990, two competing notions of economic reform were articulated in Czechoslovakia. The first (liberal) one appeared on the federal government level and was prepared by right-oriented economists around Minister of Finance Václav Klaus. It included features such as market prices, foreign trade liberalization, settlement of exchange rate, and privatisation of state property. In particular it emphasized a fast pace of reform, a so-called shock therapy. The second (gradualist) approach appeared on the Czech government level and was prepared by rather left-oriented (or social democratic) economists (V. Komárek, M. Zeman and M. Matějka). While the first concept gained the citizens' support in the 1992 elections, won by the parties that represented it (above all the ODS and the ODA), the second approach remained in opposition up to the victory of Social Democrats in the 1998 elections.

3. The 1918–38 Czechoslovak Republic was a multi-national state, incorporating some of the most backward regions of the Austro–Hungarian monarchy, with their particular contradictions and newly crystallising cleavages. For 20 years (1918–38), the Czechs and Slovaks attempted to build a common political system; Czechoslovak politicians strove to solve the cleavage on a civic basis. During the communist era, the split was in fact checked through the asymmetrical constitutional arrangement.

4. One of them, the Christian Democratic Party, merged with the Civic Democratic Party in the spring of 1996.

5. A number of analyses (Vlachová 1997; Kitschelt, Mansfeldová, Markowski and Tóka 1999) show that the Republican Party is the only relevant party in the Czech Republic not to have a party manifesto dominated by right-wing rhetoric. Voter perceptions of the party's position in a space determined by dimensions tapping socio-economic values (left/right) and libertarianism versus authoritarianism put the party somewhere in the middle. The Republican Party thus at best qualifies as a party of the 'centrist extreme' (Kreidl and Vlachová 2000).

6. During the provisional situation after the Second World War and through the elections of 1946, presidential decrees had the force of law. More than three million *Sudeten* Germans were expelled from Czechoslovakia after the Second World War in accordance with the Beneš decrees. The *Sudeten* Germans were subsequently excluded from restitution because the law called for the return of property nationalized after, and not prior to, the Communist takeover on 25 February 1948.

7. Apart from the Green Party (2.4 per cent), another successful group – the Association of the Independent (2.8 per cent) – had its election costs reimbursed. It represents city mayors and

prominent local representatives. They are charismatic personalities with a record in local government but with limited prospects for election on the lists of the major political parties, even though the odds nowadays are tilted in favour of personality.

REFERENCES

AISA, Research Report, Prague, November 1991.

Brokl, Lubomír et al. (1994), 'Politický prostor České republiky', *Lidové noviny*, 11 November, 8.

—— (1996), 'Parlamentní volby 1996', *Sociologický časopis*, Vol. 32, No.4, 389–406.

—— (1999), 'Cleavages and Parties prior to 1989 in the Czech Republic', in Kay Lawson, Andrea Römmele and Georgi Karasimeonov, eds, *Cleavages, Parties and Voters: Studies from Bulgaria, the Czech Republic, Hungary, Poland, and Romania*, London, Praeger.

—— and Zdenka Mansfeldová (2003), 'The 1992 Election and the End of Common Co-existence', in Zdenka Mansfeldová, ed., *Czech Republic – 1992 and 1996 Elections: Analyses, Documents and Data*, Berlin, Edition Sigma.

Broklová, Eva (1996), 'Historical Roots for the Restoration of Democracy in Czechoslovakia', in Ivan Gabal, ed., *The 1990 Election to the Czechoslovakian Federal Assembly: Analyses, Documents and Data*, Berlin, Edition Sigma.

Central and Eastern Eurobarometer (CEEB), No. 2–8, Cologne, Zentralarchiv für Empirische Sozialforschung.

Centre for Empirical Social Studies (STEM), *Trendy 1993–1996* and *Vývoj společensko-politické situace v letech 1990–1992*.

Karasimeonov, Georgi (1999), 'Past and New Cleavages in Post-Communist Bulgaria', in Kay Lawson, Andrea Römmele and Georgi Karasimeonov, eds, *Cleavages, Parties and Voters: Studies from Bulgaria, the Czech Republic, Hungary, Poland, and Romania*, London, Praeger.

Kitschelt, Herbert (1992), 'The Formation of Party Systems in East Central Europe', *Politics & Society*, Vol. 20, Nr. 1.

—— (1994), 'Party Systems in East Central Europe: Consolidation or Fluidity', Paper presented at the Annual Meeting of the American Political Science Association, New York, September 1–4.

——, Zdenka Mansfeldová, Radosław Markowski and Gábor Tóka (1999), *Post-Communist Party Systems. Competition, Representation, and Inter-Party Co-operation*, Cambridge: University Press.

Knutsen, Oddbjørn and Elinor Scarbrough (1995), 'Cleavage Politics', in Jan van Deth, ed., *The Impact of Values*, Oxford University Press.

Kostelecký, Tomáš (1996), 'Results of the 1990 Election in a Regional Perspective', in Ivan Gabal, ed., *The 1990 Election to the Czechoslovak Federal Assembly: Analyses, Documents and Data*, Berlin, Edition Sigma.

—— (2003), 'Results of the 1992 and 1996 Parliamentary Elections in the Czech Republic from a Regional Perspective', in Zdenka Mansfeldová, ed., *Czech Republic – 1992 and 1996 Elections: Analyses, Documents and Data*, Berlin, Edition Sigma.

Krause, Kevin Deegan (1996), 'Systém politických stran v České republice, demokracie a volby roku 1996', *Sociologický časopis*, Vol. 32, No. 4, 423–38.

—— (2000), *Accountability and Party Competition in Slovakia and the Czech Republic*, Doctoral Dissertation, University of Notre Dame.

—— (2002), 'Once More unto the Breach: The Politics of Cleavage in Slovakia and the Czech Republic', Paper presented at the *APSA* convention, Boston, Massachusetts, 31 August 2002.

Kreidl, Martin and Klára Vlachová (2000), 'Rise and Decline of Right-Wing Extremism in the Czech Republic', *Czech Sociological Review*, Vol. 8, 69–92.

Krivý, Vladimír (1993), 'Slovenská a česká definícia situácie. Čas: 1992, január', *Sociologický çasopis*, Vol. 29, No. 1, 73–87.

——, Viera Feglová, and Daniel Balko (1996), *Slovensko a jeho regióny. Sociokultúrne dúvislosti volebného správania*, Bratislava, Nadácia Médiá.

Lawson, Kay (1999), 'Cleavages, Parties, and Voters', in Kay Lawson, Andrea Römmele and Georgi Karasimeonov, eds, *Cleavages, Parties, and Voters: Studies from Bulgaria, the Czech Republic, Hungary, Poland, and Romania*, London, Praeger.

Lebeda, Tomáš (2003), 'Vybrané dopady volební reformy', in Lukáš Linek, Lidislav Mrklas, Adéla Seidlová and Petr Sokol, eds, *Volby do Poslaneckéo sněmovny 2002*, Praha, Sociologický ústav AV ČR, 141–51.

Markowski, Radosław (1995), *Political Competition and Ideological Dimensions in Central Eastern Europe*, Studies in Public Policy No. 257, Glasgow, University of Strathclyde.

Novák, Miroslav (1996), 'Volby do poslanecké sněmovny, vládní nestabilita a perspektivy demokracie v ČR', *Sociologický časopis*, Vol. 32, No. 4, 407–22.

Plecitá-Vlachová, Klára (2002), 'Volby do Poslanecké sněmovny 2002 – voličské profily stran podle názorových štěpení', in Lukáš Linek, Ladislav Mrklas, Adéla Seidlová and Petr Sokol, eds, *Volby do Poslanecké sněmovny 2002*, Prague,: Sociologický ústav AV ČR.

Rakušanová, Petra (2003), *Cleavage Theory in Comparative Perspective: the Case of the Czech Republic and Poland*, Mimeo.

Řeháková, Blanka (1999), 'Předčasné volby 1998: Volební chování různých skupin voličů', *Sociologický časopis*, Vol. 35, No. 3, 311–34.

Römmele, Andrea (1999), 'Cleavage Structures and Party Systems in East and Central Europe', in Kay Lawson, Andreas Römmele and Georgi Karasimeonov, eds, *Cleavages, Parties, and Voters: Studies from Bulgaria, the Czech Republic, Hungary, Poland, and Romania*, London, Praeger.

Sartori, Giovanni (1976), *Parties and Party Systems*, Cambridge, Cambridge University Press.

Seidlová, Adéla, Jan Červenka and Daniel Kunštát (2003), 'Voliči a nevoliči – The Comparative Study of Electoral Systems', in Lukáš Linek, Ladislav Mrklas, Adéla Seidlová and Petr Sokol, eds, *Volby do Poslaneckéo sněmovny 2002*, Prague, Sociologický ústav AV ČR, 98–111.

Šimoník, Pavel (1996), 'Politické spektrum v České republice: Český volič mezi pravicí a levicí', *Sociologický časopis*, Vol. 32, No. 4, 457–70.

SOÚ AV ČR – CVVM (Centre for Public Opinion Research), Prague, 2000–2002.

Tymowski, Alexander and Miloslav Petrusek (1992), 'Grafika politické scény: Československo a Polsko', *S-Obzor* No. 1, 31–5.

Večerník, Jiří (1996), 'Levice a pravice jisté, střed nejistý', *Lidové noviny*, 16 September, 8.

Vlachová, Klára (1997), 'Czech Political parties and their Voters', *Czech Sociological Review*, No. 5, 39–56.

APPENDIX 7.1: ELECTION RESULTS

1990 Elections
Date: 8–9 June 1990
Turnout: 96.8%

Party	Federal Assembly Chamber of People		Czech Republic Chamber of Nations	
	% of votes	Mandates	% of votes	Mandates
OF	49.9	50	53.1	68
KSČ	13.8	12	13.1	15
HSD–SMS	9.1	7	7.9	9
KDU	8.8	6	8.7	9
Others	18.4	–	16.8	–
Total	100.0	75	100.0	101

Czech National Assembly

Party	% of votes	Mandates
OF	49.55	127
KSČ	13.24	32
HSD–SMS	10.03	22
KDU-ČSL	8.42	19
Others	18.81	–
Total	100.0	200

1992 Elections
Date: 5–6 June 1990
Turnout: 85.1%

Party	Federal Assembly Chamber of People		Czech Republic Chamber of Nations	
	% of votes	Mandates	% of votes	Mandates
ODS-KDS	33.43	37	33.90	48
LB	14.48	15	14.27	19
ČSSD	6.80	6	7.67	10
SPR-RSČ	6.37	6	6.48	8
KDU-ČSL	6.08	6	5.98	7
LSU	6.06	5	5.84	7
Others	26.8	–	25.8	–
Total	100.0	75	100.0	99

Czech National Assembly

Party	% of votes	Mandates
ODS-KDS	29.73	76
LB	14.05	35
ČSSD	6.53	16
LSU	6.52	16
KDU–ČSL	6.28	15
SPR–RSČ	5.98	14
ODA	5.93	14
HSD-SMS	5.87	14
Others	19.1	–
Total	100.00	200

1996 Elections to the Lower House of Parliament (Chamber Of Deputies)
Date: 31 May–1 June
Turnout: 76.41%

Party	% of votes	Mandates
ODS	29.6	68
KDU-ČSL	8.1	18
ODA	6.4	13
ČSSD	26.4	61
KSČM	10.3	22
SPR-RSČ	8.0	18
Other parties	11.1	–
Total	100.0	200

1996 Elections to the Upper House of Parliament (Senát)
Date: First round 15–16 November, second round 22–23 November
Turnout: First round 35.03%, second round 30.63%

Party	Total	Members elected for 2 years	for 4 years	for 6 years	% of votes
ODS	32	13	13	6	39.51
ČSSD	25	5	9	11	30.86
KDU-ČSL	13	4	3	6	16.06
ODA	7	4	–	3	8.65
KSČM	2	–	1	1	2.46
DEU	1	–	1	–	1.23
Independent	1	1	–	–	1.23
Total	81	27	27	27	100.00

1990 and 1992 parliamentary elections for the Czech National Council and 1996 elections for the Upper House of Parliament of the Czech Republic (parties winning with more than 5 per cent of the votes)

Party	1990 %	1990 Mandates	1992 %	1992 Mandates	1996 %	1996 Mandates
OF	49.55	127	–	–	–	–
ODS/KDS*	–	–	29.73	76	29.62	68
KDU-ČSL	8.42	19	6.28	15	8.08	18
ODA	–	–	5.93	14	6.36	13
HSD-SMS	10.03	22	5.87	14	–	–
LSU	–	–	6.52	16	–	–
ČSSD	–	–	6.53	16	26.44	61
KSČM	13.24	32	–	–	10.33	22
LB	–	–	14.05	35	–	–
SPR-RSČ	–	–	5.98	14	8.01	18
Others	18.81	200	19.11	200	11.1	150

* The Christian Democratic Party merged with the Democratic Party in 1996.

1998 Elections to the Lower House of Parliament
Date: 19–20 June
Turnout: 73.86%

Party	% of votes	Mandates
ODS	27.74	63
KDU-ČSL	9.00	20
ČSSD	32.31	74
KSČM	11.03	24
US	8.60	19
Other parties	11.32	–
Total	100.0	200

1998 Elections to the Upper House of Parliament (Senát)
Date: First round 13–14 November, second round 20–21 November
Turnout: First round 37.29%, second round 20.2%

Party	New Seats	Members elected % of votes
ODS	9	33.4
ČSSD	3	11.1
KSČM	2	7.4
Four coalition	13	48.1
Total	27	100.0

2000 Elections to the Upper House of Parliament (Senát)
Date: First round 12 November, second round 19 November
Turnout: First round 31.8%, second round 21.41%

Party	New Seats	Members elected % of votes
ODS	8	29.6
ČSSD	1	3.7
KDU-ČSL	8	29.6
ODA	1	3.7
US-DEU	8	29.6
Independents	1	3.7
Total	27	100.0

2002 Elections to the Lower House of Parliament
Date: 14–15 June
Turnout: 58%

Party	% of votes	Mandates
ODS	24.47	58
Coalition*	14.27	31
ČSSD	30.20	70
KSČM	18.51	41
Other parties	12.55	–
Total	100.0	200

* *Coalition formed by KDU-ČSL and US-DEU*

2002 Elections to the Upper House of Parliament (Senát)
Date: First round 25–26 October, second round 1–2 November
Turnout: First round 24.1%, second round 32.55%

Party	New Seats	Members elected % of votes
ODS	9	33.3
ČSSD	7	25.9
KDU-ČSL	1	3.7
KSČM	1	3.7
US-DEU	1	3.7
CZ	1	3.7
LIRA	1	3.7
Independents*	6	22.2
Total	27	100.0

* Included in this category are the Electoral Movement of Independents, the Association of Independents, Independent Candidates, and the Movement of Independents for the Harmonious Development of Communities and Cities.

APPENDIX 7.2: GOVERNMENT COMPOSITION

Federal Government

The Federal Government after the 1990 Elections
Date of investiture: 27 June 1990
Prime Minister: Marián Čalfa (VPN)

Party	Number	Cabinet posts (percentage)
OF	9	(56.25)
VPN	4	(25.0)
KDH	2	(12.25)
Independent	1	(6.25)

The Federal Government after the 1992 Elections
Date of investiture: 3 July 1992
Prime Minister: Jan Stráský (ODS)

Party	Parliamentary seats number	(percentage)	Cabinet posts number	(percentage)
ODS	48	(32)	4	(40)
HZDS	24	(16)	4	(40)
KDU-ČSL	7	(5)	1	(10)
Independent	–	–	1	(10)

Czech Governments

Pithart Cabinet
Date of investiture: 30 June 1990
Prime Minister: Petr Pithart (OF)

Party	Parliamentary seats		Cabinet posts	
	Number	Per cent	Number	Per cent
				17
OF	127	49.5	10	48.0
KDU-ČSL	19	8.4	2	9.0
HSD-SMS	22	10.0	1	5.0
Independent	–	–	8	38.0
Total	168	67.9	21	100.0

Klaus I Cabinet
Date of investiture: 3 July 1992
Prime Minister: Václav Klaus (ODS)

Party	Parliamentary seats		Cabinet posts	
	Number	Per cent	Number	Per cent
OF	66	33.0	11	58.0
KDU-ČSL	15	7.0	4	21.0
ODA	14	7.0	2	10.5
KDS	10	5.0	2	10.5
Total	105	52.0	19	100.0

Note: The table depicts the situation as of 4 January 1993. After the break-up of the federation the Czech Republic added two ministries, those of defence and transportation, which had previously existed only at the federal level.

Klaus II Cabinet
Date of investiture: 1 July 1996
Prime Minister: Václav Klaus (ODS)

Party	Parliamentary seats		Cabinet posts	
	Number	Per cent	Number	Per cent
ODS	68	34.0	8	50.0
KDU-ČSL	18	9.0	4	22.5
ODA	13	6.5	4	22.5
Total	99	49.5	16	100.0

Tošovský Cabinet
Date of Investiture: 28 January 1998
Prime Minister: Josef Tošovský (non-partisan)

Party	Parliamentary seats		Cabinet posts	
	Number	Per cent	Number	Per cent
KDU-ČSL[*]	18	9.0	3	17.6
US[**]	31	15.5	4	23.6
ODA	13	6.5	3	17.6
Without party affiliation	2	1.0	7	41.2
Total	64	32.0	16	100.0

[*] Two ministers were non-affiliated but nominated by KDU-ČSL.
[**] Former ODS members, the so-called rebel faction or opinion platform, later formed the Freedom Union (registered 22 January 1998).

Zeman Cabinet
Date of Investiture: 19 August 1998
Prime Minister: Miloš Zeman (ČSSD)

Party	Parliamentary seats		Cabinet posts	
	Number	Per cent	Number	Per cent
ČSSD	74	37.0	18	94.7
Independent	–	–	1	5.3
Total	74	37.0	19	100.0

Špidla Cabinet
Date of Investiture: 9 July 2002
Prime Minister: Vladimír Špidla (ČSSD)

Party	Parliamentary seats		Cabinet posts	
	Number	Per cent	Number	Per cent
ČSSD	70	35.0	11	64.70
KDU-ČSL	21	10.5	3	17.65
US-DEU	10	5.0	3	17.65
Total	101	50.5	17	100.0

APPENDIX 7.3: THE ELECTORAL SYSTEM

An electoral system based on proportional representation was adopted prior to the first elections in June 1990. It was almost identical for all three parliaments in the Federation (the Federal Assembly, the Czech National Council, the Slovak National Council).

The original Election Act was slightly amended before the elections in 1992. In 1995 a new Act on the Elections to the Parliament of the Czech Republic (No. 247/1995) was adopted, which included amendments of the elections to the Chamber of Deputies as well as new elections to the Senate, which was elected for the first time in 1996. The members of the Chamber of Deputies are elected in proportional elections. The Senators, on the other hand, are elected according to the principles of majority elections.

The proportional system that applies to the Chamber of Deputies has the following features:

• multi-mandate constituencies, the number of deputies (mandates) for one constituency is calculated proportionately according to the number of valid votes in the constituency;

• competition among party lists;

• possibility of preference voting for the selection of candidates within the list;

• a 5 per cent threshold for individual parties and a higher one for coalitions (from 7 to 11 per cent);

• allocation of mandates within the constituency with the help of a quotient defined by the total number of valid votes divided by the number of mandates for the election district plus one (the Haggenbach-Bischoff formula).

The Senate is permanently active, the term of election is six years and every two years one third of 81 senators is elected. The elections take place in one-mandate constituencies. In the first round candidates who win an absolute majority are elected. If no one gets an absolute majority, the two candidates with the greatest number of votes proceed to a second round.

An amendment to the Electoral Act, initiated by the ČSSD and the ODS and approved in 2000 (Act No. 204/2000 Sb) paved the way for the following changes. Non-resident citizens were allowed to vote. The number of constituencies was increased from the original 8 to 35. In individual constituencies no less than four and a maximum of eight mandates were distributed. The proportional system was preserved but there was a motion to strengthen the majority elements in it. A modified version of d'Hondt's electoral formula was proposed, based on the divisors 1.42, 2, 3, etc. The 5 per cent threshold was retained for parties contesting the elections alone, but the effective threshold was nevertheless increased by the requirements imposed on cartels. A cartel of two had to poll at least 10 per cent as opposed to the original 7; a cartel of three had to obtain a total of 15 per cent instead of the original 9, and cartels of four or more parties had to get the backing of no less than 20 per cent of the votes compared to the 11 per cent originally required. The 10 per cent requirement for preferential mandates remained intact, as did the rule giving each voter a maximum of two preferential votes.

In a decision by the Constitutional Court the amendment to Act No. 247/1995 was proclaimed unconstitutional, and the 2002 elections were held based on another amendment (Act No. 37/2002 Sb). The most important changes include a decrease of the number of constituencies from 35 to 14, and an increase of the maximum number of candidates on a party list to 36. The advantage of strong parties was reduced by the return to the original version of d'Hondt's formula with the divisors 1, 2, 3, etc. The 10 per cent requirement for preferential mandates was reduced to 7, but the thresholds for electoral cartels were preserved.

APPENDIX 7.4: THE CONSTITUTIONAL FRAMEWORK

The Government is the supreme body of executive power. It consists of the Prime Minister, Deputy Prime Ministers and Ministers. The Government coordinates the activities of ministries and central bodies of State administration. It holds the right of legislative initiative and the right to express its opinion on each and every bill. The Government makes decisions collectively. The adoption of a Government resolution calls for the consent of more than one half of all its members. The Government is authorized to issue Government decrees, signed by the Prime Minister and the appropriate member of the Government, and to implement acts. The Government is accountable to the Chamber of Deputies for the fulfilment of the State budget and it disposes of the Government budget reserve and controls the management of the funds of the State budget and the State Funds of the Republic.

The Prime Minister is appointed by the President of the Republic, who appoints other members of the Government upon his proposal and entrusts them with the control of ministries or other authorities. Within 30 days after its appointment, the Government is bound to appear before the Chamber of Deputies and request its vote of confidence. Should the newly appointed Government not receive the confidence of the Chamber of Deputies, a new Government is appointed. Should thus appointed Government not receive the confidence of the Chamber of Deputies, the President appoints the Prime Minister upon the proposal of the Chairman of the Chamber of Deputies.

The Government may request the vote of confidence of the Chamber of Deputies at any time. It may combine the question of confidence with the request that the Chamber of Deputies should resolve on a Government Bill within three months. The Chamber of Deputies may express its lack of confidence in the Government at any time. However, a motion for a vote of no confidence will be discussed by the Chamber of Deputies only if submitted in writing by at least fifty deputies. The Government must resign after the constituent meeting of the newly elected Chamber of Deputies. Otherwise the Government resigns if the Chamber of Deputies has refused it a requested vote of confidence, or if it has expressed its vote of no confidence.

The President of the Republic is elected for a term of five years at a joint session of both houses of Parliament. He/she may not be elected for more than two terms in a row. Any citizen qualified to stand for elections to the Senate is qualified to stand for election to the office of President. The President of the Republic cannot be held accountable as a result of the performance of his office. The President has the following powers: (1) He/she names and recalls the Prime Minister and members of the government, as well as accepts their resignations; (2) convenes sessions of the Assembly of Deputies; (3) dissolves the Assembly of Deputies; (4) empowers the government whose resignation he has accepted or which he has recalled with the temporary execution of its office until the naming of a new government; (5) appoints judges to the Constitutional Court and its chairman and vice-chairman with the approval of the Senate; (6) appoints the Chairman and Vice-Chairman of the Supreme Court; declares amnesties and grants pardons; (7) has the right to send laws, except for constitutional laws, back to Parliament; (8) signs laws; (9) appoints a president and vice-president of the Auditor General's Office; and (10) appoints members of the board of governors of the Czech National Bank.

APPENDIX 7.5: CZECH POLITICAL PARTY FACT SHEET

Czech acronym	Czech name	English name	Party leader	Date founded	Party history	Current status
ČSSD	*Česká strana sociálně demokratická*	Czech Party of Social Democrats	Vladimír Špidla (since 2001)	1990	Social democratic party formed shortly after revolution with some ties to pre-Communist predecessor. Led government from 1998 to present.	Government party
KDU-ČSL	*Křesťanská a demokratická unie–Česká strana lidová*	Christ. Dem. Union–Czech People's Party	Cyril Svoboda (since 2001)	1919	Catholic party co-opted as satellite party between 1948 and 1989, subsequently reconstructed as Christian democratic party.	Government party
KSČM	*Komunistické strany Čech a Moravy*	Comm. Party of Bohemia and Moravia	Miroslav Grebeníček (since 1993)	1921	Ruled from 1948 until 1989 revolution; retained considerable continuity with pre-1989 ideology and organizational structures.	Parliamentary opp. party
ODS	*Občanská Demokratická Strana*	Civic Dem. Party	Mirek Topolánek (since 2002)	1991	Party formed by members of the anti-Communist Civic Forum (OF) movement who sought an ideologically coherent party instead of a broad movement.	Parliamentary opp. party
Unie (US-DEU)	*Unie (Unie Svobody-Demokratická Unie)*	Freedom Union	Ivan Pilip (since 2002)	1998	Party formed by discontented members of ODS and ODA (Civic Democratic Alliance) after losing leadership struggles over party finance scandals.	Government party
ANO	*Aliancia noveho obcana*	Alliance of New Citizens	Pavel Rusko (since 2000)	2000	Pro-reform party.	Opp. party

Note: Table reprinted with permission and updates by Kevin Deegan-Krause. Original version appeared first in Krause (2000).

APPENDIX 7.6: CHARACTERISTICS OF PARLIAMENTARY POLITICAL PARTIES

English translation (Original name)	Characteristics
Communist Party of Bohemia and Moravia (Komunistická strana Čech a Moravy, KSČM)	Not reformed Communists
Czech Social Democratic Party (Česká strana sociálně demokratická, ČSSD)	Social democrats
Civic Forum (Občanské hnutí, OF)	Broad anti-communist umbrella movement
Liberal and Social Union (Liberálně sociální unie, LSU)	Three left-wing mini parties (Agrarians, Socialists and Greens) created the so-called LSU (Liberal and Social Union), which was a classic electoral coalition. They were clever enough to register themselves as a 'movement'. Under the then law, movements could include political parties. If they had taken part in the election as a 'coalition' they would not have entered the Parliament in 1992 with their 6.5 per cent of the votes.
Self-governing Democracy Movement–Association for Moravia and Silesia (Hnutí za samosprávnou demokracii–Sdružení pro Moravu a Slezsko, HSD-SMS)	Regionalist centrist party
Civic Democratic Party (Občanská demokratická strana, ODS)	Right liberals
Civic Democratic Alliance (Občanská demokratická alliance, ODA)	Right liberals, but more conservative than ODS
Freedom Union (Unie svobody, US)	Liberals
Freedom Union–Democratic Union (Unie svobody–Demokratická unie, US-DEU)	Liberals
Christian Democratic Party (Křesťansko demokratická strana, KDS)	Christian democrats
Christian and Democratic Union–Czechoslovak People's Party (Křesťansko demokratická unie–Československá strana lidová, KDU-ČSL)	Christian democrats, more Catholic, but not solely
Association for the Republic–Republican Party of Czechoslovakia (Sdružení pro republiku–Republikánská strana Československa, SPR-RSČ)	Extreme right

8. Slovakia

Kevin Deegan-Krause

In its 'us or them' politics of the mid-1990s, Slovakia emerged with one of the most polarized political systems in the post-communist sphere. The chasm between coalition and opposition parties went so deep that voters simply did not cross it, no matter how dissatisfied they became with their own side. Yet even when the gap was at its deepest, a well-trained student of Slovak public opinion could not have boarded a random tram and predicted which passers – young or old, expensively-dressed or shabby, well educated or not – supported which side. In fact, the deep divide among parties cut across many underlying social and cultural differences.

The tram-watcher's observations would not be useless, however. The same characteristics that offered little insight into preference between opposition and coalition at the same time offered enough information for very good guesses about the riders' attitudes on a whole variety of questions, particularly the desirability of economic reform. Divisions between these groups were also strong and not easily crossed, but they had little to do with political choice.

Slovakia during the 1990s thus possessed a sharp political divide without strong social roots and a strong social divide without much political relevance. In such cases, many of the standard tools for dealing with societal and political divisions break down. By rigid standards of definition, Slovakia lacked much in the way of cleavages. Its political divisions were softer, less rooted, and its more deeply rooted divisions remained largely non-political. And yet Slovakia's political divisions still played a peculiarly strong role in shaping political outcomes, particularly the outcome of its democratic consolidation. An unusual configuration of attitudinal differences among successive coalitions and oppositions caused violent oscillation between near-authoritarianism and a reverence for democratic principles and began to weaken only with the most recent parliamentary election.

The peculiarities of Slovakia's case provide strong motivation to study the phenomena associated with cleavages, but the absence of many 'true' cleavages in this environment suggests that the concept requires some reconsideration. This chapter revisits the question of cleavage, finding important subsets – partial cleavages – that may be used to draw important distinctions even when society and politics are not driven in the same way at the same time. Applying the concepts of partial cleavage to Slovakia helps to explain the country's political change since 1989 and to show the interaction between social roots and political party choice through the mediation of attitudes on questions of economy, national identity and authority. Further investigation uncovers the relative importance of social forces, institutions and even powerful individuals in shaping political outcomes in new – and established – democracies.

Cleavages and Partial Cleavages

Although Lipset and Rokkan began the serious study of cleavages as a political question in 1967, their work avoided both explicit definitions and offered a relatively cursory treatment of European political development after the 1920s (Lipset and Rokkan 1967). Application of the cleavage concept to more contemporary developments requires a more explicit definition, as does any effort to apply quantitative data from surveys or elections. In 1970, Rae and Taylor obliged by identifying three fundamental types of cleavages: (1) ascriptive or 'trait' cleavages such as race or caste; (2) attitudinal or 'opinion' cleavages such as ideology or, less grandly, preference; and (3) behavioural or 'act' cleavages such as those elicited through voting and organizational membership (Rae and Taylor 1970, 1). In 1990, Bartolini and Mair employed a similar set of relationships but suggested a high degree of interconnection:

> [T]he concept of cleavage can be seen to incorporate three levels: an *empirical* element, which identifies the empirical referent of the concept, and which we can define in social-structural terms; a *normative* element, that is the set of values and beliefs which provides a sense of identity and role to the empirical element, and which reflect the self-consciousness of the social group(s) involved; and an *organizational/behavioural* element, that is the set of individual interactions, institutions, and organizations, such as political parties, which develop as part of the cleavage (Bartolini and Mair 1990, 215).

In contrast to their predecessors, Bartolini and Mair explicitly define cleavages as consisting of all three aspects *together*, and this connection entails a new understanding of how cleavages function: 'cleavages cannot be reduced simply to the outgrowths of social stratification; rather, social distinctions become cleavages when they are organized as such [...] A cleavage has therefore to be considered primarily as *a form of closure of social relationships*' (Bartolini and Mair 1990, 216). This definition possesses certain intuitive advantage. 'Cleavage' as defined by Rae and Taylor exists everywhere and always; 'cleavage' as defined by Bartolini and

Mair is far less common and depends on the overlapping of a variety of particular differences. The more completely these difference overlap, the more complete is the closure of social relationships and the more significant are the political consequences.

Between ubiquitous but shallow 'difference' and deep but uncommon 'cleavage' lies an intermediate realm. Partial overlap between particular differences may play an important role in politics even if the resulting relationships do not approach the levels of closure found in full cleavages. Figure 8.1 offers a schematic explanation of the relationships between the concepts of difference and cleavage and the intermediate level defined in this chapter. Whereas differences can emerge in any of the three categories – hence demographic (ascriptive) difference, attitudinal difference or behavioural difference – a full cleavage requires all three differences to overlap. Cases, where only two differences overlap, represent a third and often under-studied category of partial cleavages; they take three distinct forms, based on the three possible parings of two differences; looked at in the negative, these can also be understood as a full cleavage *minus* each particular kind of difference. Each of these partial cleavages – this chapter will use the label 'divides' – displays distinct characteristics and has its own distinct effects on the social and political fabric:

1. A *structural divide* consists of overlap between demographic and attitudinal elements. A structural divide involves a relationship between particular material conditions or identities and specific sets of beliefs such as, for example, pro-redistribution sentiments of working-classes or attitudes favouring majority elections in a dominant ethnic group that may create a wide and enduring split in society. Yet without a behavioural component that produces, say, labour unions or labour parties, the split may yield little conflict and even less change. This corresponds quite closely to Mainwaring's description of 'salient social cleavages without clear party expressions' (Mainwaring 1999, 46).
2. An *issue divide* consists of overlapping attitudinal and behavioural elements. As such, it involves a relationship between particular beliefs and particular party choices. These divides may have an immediate political impact, but they may not endure from one election to the next because they lack roots in society. In fact, observers often refer to such cleavages as 'political cleavages' to distinguish them from 'social cleavages' that involve ties to particular social groups. These cleavages also correspond closely to the 'issue dimensions' of party competition discussed by Lijphart (1984).
3. A *caste divide*, finally, consists of a direct overlap between ascriptive or demographic elements, on the one hand, and behavioural elements, on the other. Lacking an attitudinal component, this is the least familiar of the three divides, but it may come into being when social groups have not

consciously articulated the nature of an underlying group identity. If the members of a group can agree on questions of identity and formulate corresponding demands, this divide can develop into a full cleavage. If they cannot, caste divides are vulnerable to political entrepreneurs, who may try to seek support by emphasizing attitudinal factors that cut across group and party lines.

In Central and Eastern Europe, where few full cleavages have emerged, these divides provide useful tools of analysis. Furthermore, because cleavages do not always spring into existence fully formed, study of partial cleavages may offer insights into where cleavages come from and how they decline. The remainder of this chapter analyses the types of partial cleavages that have emerged in Slovakia and how they have interacted with one another.

Figure 8.1: Three-level model of cleavages and partial cleavages

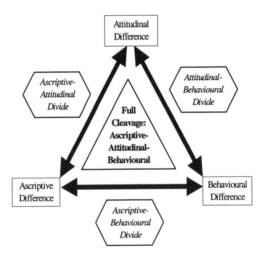

Issue Divides in Slovakia

The notion of partial cleavages offers a useful framework for studying Slovakia. In particular, it is helpful to begin with the strongest of the partial cleavages, the attitudinal-behavioural or issue divide. Such divides emerged almost immediately, are easy to trace and played a demonstrably important role in Slovakia's political outcomes over time. The most convenient means of tracing Slovakia's issue divides is to look briefly at the country's recent political history, with particular emphasis on the attitudinal basis of party appeals and coalition agreements. During the 1990s, Slovakia experienced four cycles of parliamentary elections. Two successful no confidence votes meant mid-cycle changes in government, bringing the total to six governments between 1990 and early 2003 when this chapter was completed.

The first government of Vladimír Mečiar, June 1990 to April 1991

Public Against Violence (VPN), the broad anti-communist movement that led the 1989 revolution in Slovakia, took the largest single bloc of seats in Slovakia's first popularly elected parliament, but the movement fell far short of a majority and found it necessary to form a governing coalition that also included the second-place Christian Democratic Movement (KDH) and representatives of smaller parties. Although far from unified on the role of the Church and national identity, the parties shared a common commitment to dismantling the institutional legacies of communism and creating a market economy. Opposition to the coalition, furthermore, remained divided into two groups with few common preferences: former communists with an interest in a common state, on the one hand, and the proponents of an independent Slovakia who tended to prefer open markets, on the other. The few methodologically sound public opinion surveys from this period show clear divisions only in a few areas: a sharp difference in attitudes on economic policy between the former communist Party of the Democratic Left (SDĽ) and all other parties, and a similarly sharp difference in attitudes about Slovakia's place in Czechoslovakia between the pro-independence Slovak National Party (SNS) and all other parties.

As might be expected in a broad anti-communist movement without a coherent opposition, conflict emerged more from within than from without. Coalition conflicts followed no clear ideological course either, and the major internal division centred around personality and leadership style, ultimately leading to a sharp division within the top-echelon of VPN and ultimately the creation of two separate parties. A splinter party led by Premier Vladimír Mečiar, lured away the vast majority of VPN's voters, but the VPN leadership and other Mečiar opponents retained a majority of seats in the parliament's presidium and removed Mečiar from the premiership in the spring of 1991.

The government of Jan Čarnogúrsky, April 1991 to June 1992

After Mečiar's removal 1991, remnants of Public Against Violence (VPN) remained in government in a coalition led by the chair of the Christian Democratic Movement (KDH), Jan Čarnogúrsky. In the reshuffle the government did not much alter its pro-market and pro-Czechoslovakia orientations, but the emergence of an effective opposition party in the hands of a popular leader changed the political landscape.

Figure 8.2: Positions of party supporters on key issues during the
Čarnogúrsky government (1991–1992). Coalition parties highlighted,
linked by line

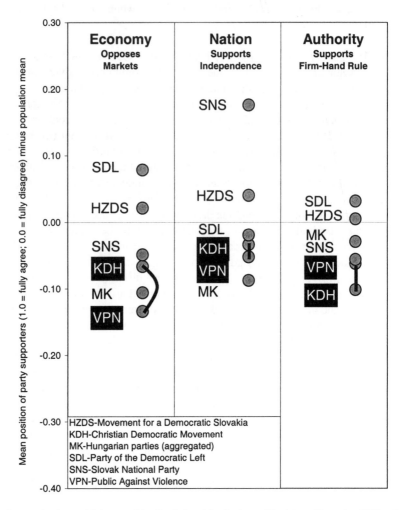

Source: Academy of Sciences of the Czech Republic, Institute of Sociology (December 1991 and June 1992).

Mečiar in opposition exhibited a stronger scepticism toward economic reform than had the VPN, but his big innovation came on the question of Slovakia's international position, on which he succeeded in formulating a position that called for greater autonomy for Slovakia without necessarily committing himself to Slovakia's independence. VPN voters overwhelmingly shifted to Mečiar's Movement for a Democratic Slovakia (HZDS) and he succeeded in attracting supporters of other parties as well.

Figure 8.2 provides the positions of party supporters on three key issue areas: the economy, the nation, and the exercise of political authority.

In staking out popular middle-ground positions on both national and economic issues, Mečiar radically transformed the relationship between attitude and party support in Slovakia, adding a second, larger party to those who sought renegotiation of the Slovak–Czech relationship and at the same time undercutting left-right differences on economic questions, pulling voters away from parties at both extremes. The magnitude of these differences intensified as the issue of Slovakia's place within Czechoslovakia became increasingly important in the 1992 election campaign. On authority issues both the parties and their voters remained extremely diffuse. The former communist party, in becoming the Party of the Democratic Left (SDL'), abandoned hard line politics, though voters were slow to follow; Mečiar, while showing some hints of a ruthless political style did not yet begin to attract more hard-line voters.

During this period, the institutional basis of Slovakia's party system also remained in flux and party organization remained fragile. In fact, the break-up of the VPN signalled the beginning of a wave of reshuffling that over the course of two years affected all major Slovak parties.

The second government of Vladimír Mečiar, June 1992 to March 1994

Mečiar returned to power in June 1992 in a major electoral victory, with the parliamentary deputies of his Movement for a Democratic Slovakia (HZDS) outnumbering those of the next largest party by more than two-to-one and falling just two seats short of a majority. The combined force of Mečiar's victory in Slovakia coupled with the victory of an equal and opposite force in the Czech Republic – Vacláv Klaus – led quickly to negotiations about the status of Czechoslovakia between the two premiers and from there to separation. The respective goals of Mečiar and Klaus remain in dispute, though evidence strongly suggests that responsibility for separation lies as much with Klaus as with Mečiar (Innes 2001). Whatever his initial goals, Mečiar proclaimed the outcome as a victory and soon began to take credit for it. Unlike the Czech Republic, which could rely on a higher degree of institutional continuity and *de facto*, if not *de jure* status as Czechoslovakia's successor state, most Slovaks found the split to be traumatic, and many retained a strong preference for continued union with the Czechs. Once independence had become reality, few of the leaders who had opposed the split dared to revisit the question, but the hostility between the two sides found its way into other issues and became increasingly sharp. Mečiar's aggressive political style created further rifts, some along the same opposition-coalition lines and others within his own party and within the closely associated Slovak National Party (SNS). The defeat and expulsion of more centrist factions within HZDS and SNS pushed the governing parties even further toward extremes.

Figure 8.3: Positions of party supporters on key issues during the second Mečiar government (1992–1994). Coalition partners highlighted, linked by line

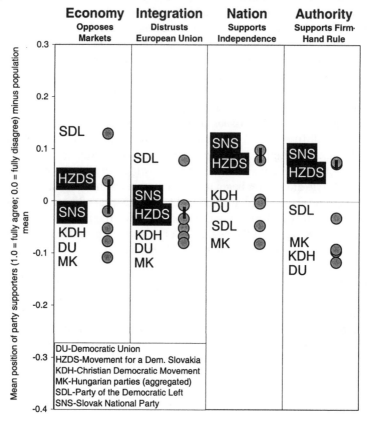

Source: FOCUS survey (October 1993).

Mečiar's embrace of independence and his increasingly aggressive political tactics cost him some votes but attracted others. The reshuffling of voters that began after independence deepened the differences among the support bases of various parties on questions of authority and independence, and in the process it erased many differences on economic questions. As Figure 8.3 indicates, HZDS and its closest ally, SNS, remained close to the centre on questions of economic policy, flanked on either side by opposition parties, though it maintained closer relationships with the left-leaning Party of the Democratic Left (SDL) than with the more market-oriented Christian Democratic Movement (KDH) and the Hungarian coalition parties.

Figure 8.4: Positions of party supporters on key issues during the Moravčík government (1994). Coalition partners highlighted, linked by line

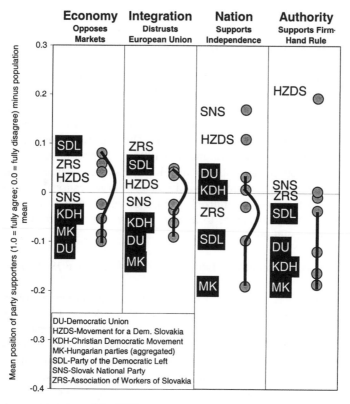

Source: FOCUS survey (May 1994).

The government of Jozef Moravčík, March 1994 to December 1994

The brief Moravčík government is notable for the formal emergence of a coalition against Mečiar, in effect splitting the party system into roughly equal halves. Formed specifically in opposition to Mečiar's increasingly combative tactics toward his political opponents, the coalition brought defectors from the Slovak National Party (SNS) and Meciar's Movement for a Democratic Slovakia (HZDS) together with both the Christian Democratic Movement (KDH) *and* the former communist Party of the Democratic Left (SDĽ) with the tacit support of Slovakia's Hungarian parties. Since the coalition had little in common except a distrust of Mečiar, its members almost immediately agreed to call new elections for later in the same year. In their few efforts at policy-making, the coalition found it extremely difficult to negotiate the conditions for an additional round of voucher privatization.

Surveys show that the voters of the coalition parties, like their party leaders, differed significantly. As Figure 8.4 indicates, coalition supporters occupied both poles of the socio-economic spectrum and differed widely on questions of authority (with SDĽ standing closer to opposition parties than to its own partners). A similarly wide spread emerged on the question of independence, where most coalition party voters took mean positions closer to those of HZDS and SNS voters than those of the Hungarian minority parties upon whom the coalition depended for its majority.

The party system during this period experienced continued moderate levels of fragmentation; both HZDS and SNS lost a large share of their parliamentary deputies while SDĽ lost significant numbers of voters to a splinter group from its own delegation. The process of reshuffling that occurred between early 1992 and mid-1994 did, however, contribute to a subsequent stabilizing of the political party system. Parties during this period show a slow progress toward increased organizational capacity, but still remained highly centralized, such that when serious disagreements emerged, party leaders opted to leave or to push others out rather than find compromise solutions.

The third government of Vladimír Mečiar, December 1994 to October 1998

In retrospect, it is clear that Mečiar's third government marks not only the most serious post-communist threat to Slovakia's democratic development, but also the high point in the emergence of authority- and nation-related questions as the dominant issue divide within Slovakia's politics. The coalition created by Mečiar in late 1994 shared a strong common focus on Slovak national identity and the dangers posed by non-Slovaks. Coalition parties shared a willingness to accept leadership by strong hand with little regard for the checks and balances necessary for the endurance of democracy. The parties opposing Mečiar held the opposite views on these questions. They defended the prerogatives of rival institutions and over time became more vocal in opposing the government's xenophobic rhetoric and in emphasizing the positive aspects of Western integration.

Even economic issues became subsumed within this framework. The Mečiar government did not abandon economic reform but re-oriented it to align with the needs of authority and nation: in public discussion, the government justified a switch from voucher privatization to direct sales as 'creating a layer of *Slovak* capital'; in its actual distribution, the government heavily favoured those who were already tied to the regime or who were willing to remit some of their significant financial gains.

As Figure 8.5 shows, public support for political parties mirrored these developments. The parties of the Mečiar coalition formed an increasingly coherent bloc on questions of authority and national questions. Furthermore, not only did the coalition parties become closer together on national issues, but attitudes on those very issues also became more coherent. Over time it became increasingly possible to predict Slovaks' attitudes towards the European Union, for example, on the basis of their attitudes towards Czechoslovakia or the Hungarian minority. By 1997, hostility towards Czechs, Hungarians, the West and 'non-national Slovaks' closely overlapped. On economic questions, HZDS and SNS supporters remained solidly in the middle, surrounded by opposition parties. Not until the mid-point of this government did this profile show any signs of change on economic questions. Although survey results offer an ambiguous picture, a number of polls conducted in 1997 and 1998 show the emergence of a left-wing orientation among HZDS and SNS voters.

Figure 8.5: Positions of party supporters on key issues during the third Mečiar government (1994–1998). Coalition partners highlighted, linked by line

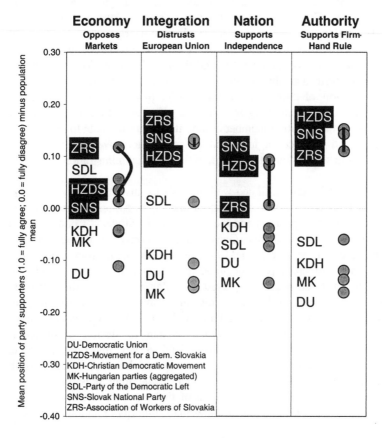

The first government of Mikuláš Dzurinda, October 1998 to October 2002

The polarization of Slovak voters around national and authority issues appears to have helped Mečiar maintain political control during the mid-1990s and to sustain the impression that the party did not need to adjust its increasingly xenophobic and authoritarian policies. The polarization worked against Mečiar in the long run, however. As Mečiar's violations of democratic norms became increasingly severe, opposition parties began to fear for their survival and began to engage in an otherwise unlikely degree of cooperation, even though they had little in common except an antipathy to Mečiar and a fear of authoritarianism and international isolation if he remained in power. Already by 1997, a coalition of parties ranging from Christian democratic to social democratic and green had begun to discuss an electoral coalition to defeat Mečiar. Changes in the electoral law aimed at disrupting this coalition only produced further integration, forcing the opposition coalition to reinvent itself as a single party: the Slovak Democratic Coalition (SDK). This party proved a strong rival to Mečiar's HZDS, and in the 1998 parliamentary election nearly matched its vote totals. In a repetition and amplification of the brief Moravčík coalition, SDK joined with the former communist SDĽ and the new Party of Civic Understanding (SOP) to form a coalition that also included (for the first time) the open participation of Slovakia's Hungarian parties. But having achieved its primary goals of removing Mečiar from office and reopening dialogue with the West, the coalition members found it difficult to come to terms on other issues and engaged in long and bitter conflicts over economic reform, religion in schools, and the reform of territorial administration, among other issues.

Mečiar's legacy continued well after his exclusion from government, but without his control over state media and privatization resources, his party lost its dominant position and the issue basis of Slovakia's politics began to show slow signs of change. Questions of authority and nation continued to unite the anti-Mečiar parties and distinguish them from others, but as support for Mečiar's party declined (particularly in the final months of the campaign), these questions played a smaller role in the shaping of party choice. Almost all of the major new parties that emerged during this period stood on the pro-integration and anti-authority side of the population mean. As national and authority attitudes began to decline in importance, economic questions re-emerged. In a 2002 survey, questions of economic reform continued to show weaker ties to party choice than questions about authority or the nation, but at higher levels than previously recorded. Furthermore, support for the largest of the new parties, *Direction* (SMER) depended more on economic attitudes than authority or national questions.

Figure 8.6: Positions of party supporters on key issues during the first Dzurinda government (1998–2002). Coalition partners highlighted, linked by line

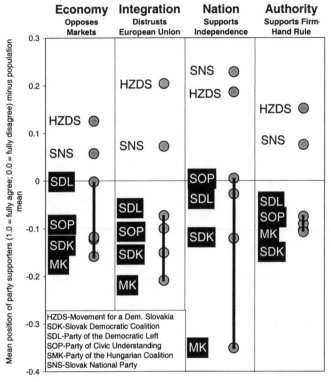

Source: FOCUS survey (January 1999).

Despite European and American fears about the possible return of Mečiar, the 2002 parliamentary elections confirmed the party's 1998 defeat. Isolated, plagued by internal strife and haemorrhaging voters, the Slovak National Party (SNS) found itself pushed into a marginal position and was unable to overcome the 5 per cent threshold for parliamentary representation. Splintering also sundered the former communist SDĽ, as voters opted instead either for the more radical (largely unreconstructed) Communist Party of Slovakia (KSS) or the idiosyncratic SMER. As a result of weakness among both of these families of parties, Mikuláš Dzurinda managed not only to retain the premiership but to do so on the basis of a smaller but more ideologically coherent coalition of parties with moderate pro-market and pro-integration positions and a categorical rejection of Mečiar's authoritarian political tactics. After nearly a decade in which economic questions remained secondary or tertiary, Slovakia thus found itself again moving toward an economic issue dimension (*Figure 8.6*).

Issue Divides in Comparative Perspective

Close attention to the configuration of Slovakia's coalitions and its coalition voters suggests the emergence of strong issue divides involving national questions that began to emerge during 1992 and became the central focus of party competition and voter party choice during the 1990s. In parallel, Slovakia also experienced the emergence of a dimension based on questions of authority and its proper exercise within democracy. Although hampered by irregular sequences and changes in questions, survey evidence allows for a more systematic test of this pattern.

Kitschelt and his co-authors measure the breadth of party positions, the coherence of positions within each party, the association of multiple issues, and the relationship to left and right (Kitschelt, Mansfeldová, Markowski and Tóka 1999). Slovakia challenges the presumption that 'left' and 'right' offer a universally meaningful scale for judging issue divides (Krause 2000). Other methods compare the attitudes of respondents on particular issues to their party preference. In a two-party system, the relationship is not problematic but in multi-party systems the task becomes more difficult. Torcal and Mainwaring look at each possible pairing of major parties in an attempt to determine the attitudes most closely related to voter choice (Torcal and Mainwaring 2000). Knutsen and Scarbrough use multinomial discriminant analysis and logistic analysis to explore the distinctiveness of voting within the system as a whole (Knutsen and Scarbrough 1995). The author, in previous works, uses thermometer scores of sympathy for or trusts in major parties to conduct a one-dimensional array of party preferences that can be compared to arrays of supporters on other issues (Krause 2000). Using the available data, all of these methods point to a similar set of developments.

Unfortunately, the data does not lend itself to a systematic analysis of issue divides. Ideal circumstances would involve long-term and frequent repetition of a stable questionnaire that included questions on economic policy, authority and democracy, religion and various aspects of national identity and sovereignty as well as detailed questions about political party preference. Most regular surveys fall far short in one or more of these categories, with too limited or unstable a set of questions or insufficient party information. The most comprehensive set of surveys – those conducted by the Central European University (CEU) – includes a wide set of questions consistently repeated. The time span of the CEU surveys covers only a four-year period, however, and omits regular questions on authority or Western integration. Surveys conducted by FOCUS are less systematic and consistent in the phrasing of questions over time, but they cover a large number of important issues and span the entire decade of the 1990s.[1]

Figure 8.7: Correlations between party preference and attitudes over time

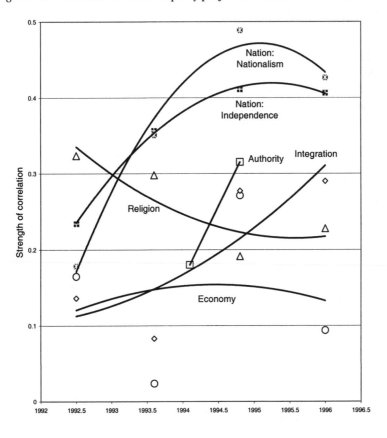

△ Religion: Trust in church

□ Authority: Preference for firm-hand rule

✳ Nation: Minority vs majority rights

○ Economy: State ownership vs free markets

✚ Nation: Preference for Slovak independence

◇ Integration: Trust in the European Union

Source: CEU surveys 1992, 1993, 1994, 1996.

The large number and broad range of attitudinal measures in the CEU surveys allow not only for measures of the relationship between attitudes and party support but also for measures of how attitudes cluster together. Factor analysis allows for the creation of broad summary measures corresponding to particular themes. Analysis of data for Slovakia produces the same factors on all four annual surveys: economic reform, the costs of transition, the role of religion, nationalism and the split of Czechoslovakia.[2] Simple correlation between the mean positions of party supporters on this one-dimensional scale and the attitudinal factors shows high initial levels of correlation for economy, religion and national questions, but the former two decline steeply between 1992 and 1994 leaving the national dimension as the primary dimension (along with questions of authority on the two occasions that those appeared in the CEU surveys). Analysis checking for the positions of individual voters on the same spectrums yields similar results. As Figure 8.7 demonstrates, religion played a more important role in party choice than economic or national questions. A dramatic rise in the role of national questions coupled with a gentle decline in the role of other attitudes demonstrates the clear supremacy of national issues by late 1994. A multiple regression using all five factors reproduces these same patterns.[3]

Figure 8.8: Correlations between party preference and attitudes over time

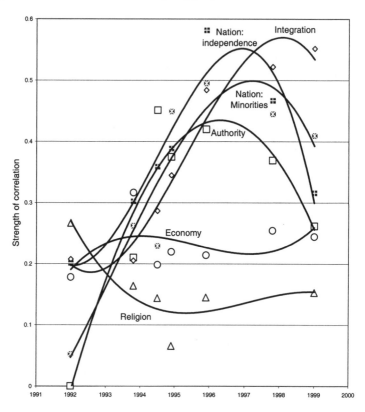

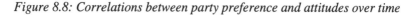

Δ Religion: Trust in church   O Economy: State ownership vs free markets
□ Authority: Preference for firm-hand rule   ✚ Nation: Preference for Slovak independence
✱ Nation: Minority vs majority rights   ◇ Integration: Trust in the European Union

Source: CEU surveys 1992, 1993, 1994, 1996; FOCUS (1992–1999).

Results from FOCUS surveys displayed in Figure 8.8 confirm these same basic patterns and adds some additional information. Like the CEU surveys, the FOCUS surveys show a variety of attitudes related to overall party choice in 1992 and 1993, but by mid-1994 questions about authority and national related attitudes (towards firm-hand rule, the European Union, Slovakia's independence, minority rights, and Hungarians as potential neighbours) far surpass questions about economy or religion. The role of attitudes toward independence and firm-hand rule had declined by 1999 and economy showed a slight rise, but minority rights remained important and the role of the European Union continued to climb in importance from its already high position (*Figures 8.7 and 8.8*).

Application of party coherence and party-spread methods to CEU and FOCUS data also suggest that nation-related attitudes played a more important role in Slovakia than any other, though religion produced wider spreads and tighter coherence within parties in the early years of the 1990s and authority produced some of the same effects in the middle years of the decade. Discriminant analysis, which determines the ability of particular variables to distinguish groups of respondents, also suggests a marked distinctiveness in the relationship between religious attitudes and support for particular parties, but not for overall coalitions. Only national issues and occasionally authority issues distinguish party supporters from one another and at the same time distinguish coalition from opposition voters. In accord with previous tests, the role of national and authority issues shows a significant increase over time.[4]

Since none of the relevant series of surveys are available through 2002, it is difficult to offer comprehensive evidence of the emergence of a new, post-authority and even post-national issue divide. It is apparent from FOCUS surveys conducted through 1999 that while national issues overall had not declined in importance, the emphasis shifted from national questions with cultural overtones involving minority groups to national questions with stronger economic overtones, such as European integration.

Issue Divides in Structure and Culture

The interaction among issue divides in Slovakia in the 1990s offers a useful set of circumstances that can help explain not only Slovakia's own political development, but also the relationship among issue divides. In particular, it is important to understand why national questions trumped economic ones in the early 1990s, whereas national and authority questions developed in parallel and even appeared to reinforce one another. To answer these questions, it is necessary to look more deeply at the social and cultural roots of particular issue divides, to understand their relationship to structural divides based on the relationship between ascription and attitude.

The economic divide

The relationship between the economic issue divide and the underlying socio-economic structural divide is so pervasive in twentieth-century democracies that it receives little scrutiny. Lipset and Rokkan noted the pervasive nature of the worker/owner cleavage that linked occupational ascription with redistributive attitudes and support for social democratic, socialist and communist parties (Lipset and Rokkan 1967). Rokkan noted the relatively homogeneous character of this cleavage across industrialized countries (Rokkan, Flora, Kuhnle and Urwin 1996), and Lijphart found socio-economic issues to be the only ones that proved at least moderately divisive in every one of the 36 countries in his survey (Lijphart 1999).[5]

Slovakia's political developments could in theory be explained by basic underlying weaknesses in the social conditions that might cause voters to take economic questions into account when making their choices. Investigations of social structure, however, show that measures of structural difference for Slovakia – class and occupational structure, income level and income distribution – did not differ markedly from those of the Czech Republic, Hungary or Poland (Matějů 2000; Tuček 1996). Furthermore, a wide range of opinion surveys indicates a relatively robust structural divide among Slovaks on socio-economic questions. Poorer, older and less educated Slovaks were considerably more likely than others to prefer socio-economic redistribution and the slowing of market-oriented reforms. Not only were the differences statistically significant, but rivalling those of the neighbouring Czech Republic which developed one of the most robust economic issue dimensions in the region (Mansfeldová 1998; Matějů and Vlachová 2000). Furthermore, the above evidence suggests that Slovakia had already begun to develop an economic issue divide during the early 1990s. The virtual disappearance of the economic issue divide, furthermore, does not correspond to any weakening of the socio-economic differences in Slovakia or in its structural divide; these actually increased in strength over time.

Slovakia's experience does not directly contradict the notion that social inequality produces certain attitudes about its redress and institutions to enforce redistribution, but it does call into question the strength of this imperative. As elsewhere in the post-communist sphere, the emergence of social inequality in Slovakia did produce the expected attitudinal results and the structural divide does appear to have shaped the development of Slovakia's political party system at least to some extent. Yet so weak was this second link that it could not prevail over a rival basis for political choice.

The national divide

The ubiquity of socio-economic structural divides in industrial societies has a near parallel in the prevalence of national structural divides in societies with ethnic minorities. Slovakia, on the surface, appears to be no exception. Tensions between Czechs and Slovaks within Czechoslovakia and between Slovaks and Hungarians in independent Slovakia provide strong motives for the emergence of differences in attitudes and political institutions, and indeed such differences did appear. But in fact such differences play a relatively small role in the account of Slovakia's politics discussed above. Czechs and Hungarians together represented considerably less than one-fifth of Slovakia's electorate and findings regarding the national issue divides discussed in the previous section actually change little even when all non-Slovaks are excluded from the sample. A 'full' cleavage did emerge between Slovaks and Hungarians in Slovakia – ascriptive, attitudinal as well as behavioural – but it played only a marginal role. Slovakia's issue divide on national questions was not primarily a conflict between Slovaks and other ethnic groups but a conflict *among* Slovaks *about* other ethnic groups.

The structural and cultural roots of Slovakia's national divide are harder to identify than are the roots of its economic issue divide. In the first place, the attitudes forming the basis of Slovakia's national issue divide – the independence of Slovakia and the role of the Hungarian minority – show virtually no connection to any underlying socio-economic structures. The vast majority of surveys conducted between 1991 and 1994 show no sustained and statistically significant connections to age, education level, urban residence, occupation, or income. Spatial patterns of residence show a stronger connection, but the relationships are still fairly weak. Residents of eastern Slovakia typically expressed a slightly lower preference for independence, and those Slovaks who lived in mixed Hungarian–Slovak districts were somewhat less likely to express hostility toward Hungarians. Even these patterns, however, explain only a small portion of the propensity to vote according to national attitudes.

A stronger but less tangible structural basis for Slovakia's national issue dimension can be found in the legacies of Czechoslovakia. Slovaks face a relatively recent history of intra-ethnic competition on national issues most notably expressed in the competition between pro-Slovak and pro-Czechoslovak parties during the inter-war Czechoslovak Republic, and open military conflict between factions during the wartime Slovak state. In addition, during the communist era the common Czechoslovak state provided a series of cultural and material tradeoffs for Slovakia (far more than for the Czech Republic), and sustained attitudinal differences about the merits of independence.

Yet despite these cultural and structural underpinnings, a national issue divide among Slovaks remained slow to develop and remained closely intertwined with the tactics of particular political parties. In the 1990 election, only the Slovak National Party (SNS) pursued the question actively, and it gained in the process less than one-sixth of the ethnic Slovak electorate.

Figure 8.9: Mean position of party supporters on questions of separation and free market over time (arrows indicate direction of change)

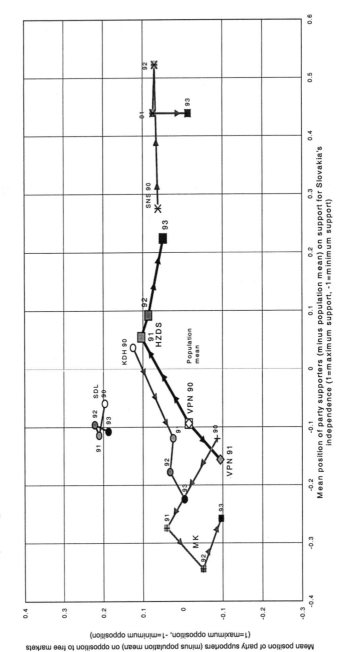

Source: Academy of Sciences of the Czech Republic, Institute of Sociology (1990, 1991, 1992, 1993).

Nation-related questions emerged in both the Czechoslovak and Slovak parliaments, but not until the splintering of VPN and the creation of HZDS did they take centre stage. As Figure 8.9 indicates, the emergence of HZDS in the spring of 1991 produced a change in the array of Slovak parties. Mečiar's new party proved extremely successful at attracting voters from all sides of the political space. In fact, a late 1991 survey suggests that he managed not only to hold on to nearly half of the former VPN voters, but also to pull away between 20 and 30 per cent of the supporters of the other three major Slovak parties, communist, Christian democratic and nationalist alike. In doing so, he shifted the political centre of gravity from the moderately pro-market and pro-Czechoslovakia position occupied by VPN to the very heart of both conflicts, simultaneously narrowing the range of competition on the more dominant economic divide and expanding competition on the then-weaker national divide. Further shifts occurred over time as Mečiar's party – by far the largest party in the country – shifted increasingly to the independence end of the national spectrum while remaining near the centre of the economic spectrum.[6]

The role of political choice here is difficult to assess. Mečiar's political acumen allowed him to occupy a large and largely empty political space, just as it was being abandoned by KDH. Such political insights are usually not limited to just one individual, and it is possible that another party might have found it advantageous to fill the same space. But even though it is likely that another contender would have done so as quickly or as well, the leaders of SNS and KDH certainly did not take full advantage of the moderate non-separatist national position while it was still available to them in 1990 and early 1991.[7] Individual parties played a role in shaping timing, if nothing else, but with the fast pace of changes in the post-communist era, timing had an important effect on outcomes.

Economy against nation
The relative dominance of economic and national issue dimensions illustrates the same interplay between underlying socio-economic and cultural factors as the more chaotic scramble of political parties for electoral advantage. At least one reason for the ultimate weakness in Slovakia's economic issue dimension can be found in the presence of its powerful rival: the obvious culprit is the national dimension that emerged at the same time that the role of economics in party choice began to decline. The link is not merely coincidental. Rather than reinforce an existing economic divide – as it did in the Czech Republic – the question of Slovakia's independence remained almost completely unrelated. Surveys conducted in 1991 and 1992 only rarely show any statistically significant relationship between attitudes towards the split and attitudes towards underlying economic questions.[8] As long as the two issues remained unrelated, the relationship between the two issue divides followed a zero-sum pattern: any shifts towards voting on the

basis of independence would draw similarly from both sides of the economic spectrum and weaken the strength of the economic dimension.

Since the first years after the fall of communism, political scientists have attempted to discern which of the possible issue divides would shape party competition in the post-communist period. Offe's work on the 'triple transition' suggested an implicit hierarchy of cleavages in which questions of economic distribution required the prior resolution of conflict over political institutions, and questions of institutions depended upon a broadly acceptable definition of the national community and its role within the state (Offe 1991). Kitschelt's work, beginning in 1992 and continuing through a series of books and articles, upends this hierarchy, placing more emphasis on historical socio-economic development and its consequences for the structure of political systems and party competition. Kitschelt in his later works suggests that national issue divides would be more likely to emerge where communist regimes had been less ideological in their economic policy (thus minimizing the post-revolution difference between communist and anti-communist forces on economic questions) and where repressive communist parties managed to keep a hold on power in the post-communist period, using national appeals to justify authority and economic isolation (Kitschelt 2001). Both models suggest that post-communist democracies face little real choice in determining their issue divides: Offe's conception implies choice only to the extent that conflicts at more fundamental levels can be resolved and other conflicts then attended to; Kitschelt's model sees national issue divides as dependent upon the weakness of economic divides or contingent on the needs of ruling parties for alternative bases of legitimacy.

Since both models predict a national issue divide for Slovakia, it is not possible to test them simply by looking at the success of the prediction. Rather, it is necessary to look at the means by which they reached their conclusions. As Kitschelt and his co-authors note, Slovakia is a difficult case and does not fall readily within any of the model's categories (Kitschelt 1999). Even accepting that Slovakia can be categorized as 'national accommodative' or 'patrimonial communism', Slovakia's national issue divides can only loosely be understood according to the patrimonial model in which 'unreconstructed communist-successor parties' make ethnic appeals or the 'national accommodative' model in which communist and anti-communist parties do not offer clear alternatives on economic issues. Other factors appear to play at least some role in the development of Slovakia's issue dimensions, and while Slovakia's example does not invalidate Kitschelt's otherwise sophisticated and well-grounded model, it does point to weaknesses in the evidence upon which it is based. In particular, the four countries studied most closely by Kitschelt and his co-authors are among the least ethnically diverse in the region (of the four, only Bulgaria has a significant ethnic minority) and among the most established (of Europe's 13 new post-communist states, the study included only the Czech Republic, the member of the group with the fewest traumas related to new statehood). The study, therefore, does not provide adequate grounds for testing Offe's notion that the identity questions of new and ethnically heterogeneous states might overwhelm all other divides.

Offe's insights about the power of national questions to shape issue divides conform quite closely to Slovakia's experience, but require some elaboration from an institutional perspective. Although Slovaks expressed dissatisfaction about their relationships with Czechs and Hungarians from the first post-communist opinion surveys, the national dimension did not overwhelm its economic rival until a particular party found a way to use the issue in obtaining political support. Furthermore, if other Slovak parties had quickly followed Mečiar's lead in adopting a moderate nationalist position, his national advantage might have faded and allowed questions of economic reform to remain foremost. In the mid-1990s, the overt role of political institutions became even more pronounced as Mečiar sought to build upon his early success with national issues through a deliberate effort to cast his government as the only viable defender of Slovaks against a range of enemies that included Hungarians, Westerners and unpatriotic Slovaks, as well as the leadership of virtually all opposition parties (Šipošová 1998). Without this state-supported encouragement, the national issue divide might have begun to fade shortly after independence and the question of European integration might have followed the pattern that then prevailed in the Czech Republic and emerged first as an economic divide.

The authority divide
Questions of authority and democracy rarely appear in discussions of issue divides. Support for the democratic exercise of authority does not appear explicitly in the framework of cleavages laid out by Lipset and Rokkan (1967), and plays only a tangential role in either the materialist/post-materialist cleavage proposed by Inglehart (Inglehart 1977) or a global-parochial cleavage alluded to by Kreisi and others (Kriesi 2000). In a framework of 'full' cleavages based on distinct ascriptive bases of support, authority does not provide a compelling case. A focus on partial cleavages, by contrast, suggests such questions as an important area for further research. This is particularly true in Slovakia.

Slovakia's authority divide holds the key to understanding that country's wide swings between the authoritarian tactics of Mečiar and the more moderate governments that came before and after. The emergence of an issue divide on questions of authority between 1992 and 1994 meant in practice that one side of the political spectrum had ever fewer qualms about the abuse of political power (at least by its own officials). By drawing authoritarians to Mečiar's side and causing democrats to defect, this self-reinforcing divide removed most effective restraints on Mečiar's use of power. Ultimately the process worked to Meičar's detriment, repelling more voters than it attracted, but in the parliamentary election of late 1994 he achieved perhaps the best possible balance between the goals of 'more voters' and 'more-authoritarian voters'. For four years, Slovakia paid a steep price in political corruption, violations of the rule of law and international isolation. The victory of Mečiar's opponents in 1998 offered at least some compensation, bringing to power a coalition of those who explicitly opposed their predecessor's abuses of power and promised to restore the accountability of political leaders to voters and other institutions.

The presence of an authority dimension played a fundamental role in Slovakia's development and helps to explain how the country could perform so much worse than its neighbours and yet so quickly catch up. Its origins, however, remain poorly understood. Survey evidence shows a moderate structural divide in which authority attitudes related closely to a variety of socio-economic variables including education level, age, urban residence and class, but this divide was no stronger than in the neighbouring Czech Republic, Hungary or Poland and cannot explain Slovakia's unique position. Other authors suggest a unique regional basis for authority attitudes (Buerkle 2002; Krivý, Feglová and Balko 1996) but statistical tests show only a moderate relationship to the authority issue divide.

More significant, perhaps, is the role of the political leader. Although Slovaks show no more propensity than Czechs or others in the region to prefer charismatic leaders, the devotion to Mečiar within his party and his central role within his party are unique in the region, resembling more the efforts of Tudjman in Croatia or Milošević in Yugoslavia than those of any Central European leader. Mečiar managed the difficult task of building a party that was both organizationally dense and yet wholly centralized around himself; he also demonstrated a remarkable ability to connect with Slovak voters. Since personal charisma has difficulty coexisting with institutional restraints and limits on power, it is not surprising that the emergence of a figure like Mečiar could create an authority dimension (Madsen and Snow 1991).

Yet scholars of charisma frequently suggest that the origins of charismatic leadership lie not only in the talents of an individual but in the ability of that individual to tap directly into deep societal needs (Geertz 1983). Since Mečiar was also the champion of Slovakia's national interests against the world, it is useful to ask whether his demand for unrestricted authority and his nationalism were not intrinsically related. The twentieth-century ideologies of Fascism and Nazism certainly offer ample precedent for the unity of nationalism and authoritarianism, and Greenfeld suggests an inherent connection between authoritarianism and collectivistic ideologies (Greenfeld 1992). But survey evidence for Slovakia suggests certain complications. Most important of these is the almost complete absence of a connection between various expressions of nationalism and authoritarianism in Slovakia in the early 1990s. Not until 1992 do surveys show the beginnings of statistically significant relationships between preference for 'firm-hand rule' and distrust of Czechs or Hungarians and even then the relationships remain uneven (FOCUS 1992–99; Academy of Science of the Czech Republic Institute of Sociology 1990–96). Only in 1993 do all survey questions begin to point the same way and do so with statistical significance. Furthermore, the connection between the two remained inextricably bound up with the figure of Mečiar himself. When controlling for respondents' trust in Mečiar, we find that the rate of growth in the correlations between 'firm-hand rule' and a variety of national questions drops by more than half between 1992 and 1997. Many of the statistical relationships are in fact insignificant until the second half of the decade. The statistical hard evidence corresponds closely to observable developments in Mečiar's own political orientation as he moved from a no-nonsense, straight talking spokesman for Slovak grievances to the 'father of the Slovak nation' and the 'steamroller' of HZDS. Slovakia's independence allowed Mečiar to claim the first title; an increasing fear of political betrayals conferred the second upon him. Although only weakly connected at the outset, the two qualities became increasingly intertwined in Meciar's persona and in the outlook of both his supporters and his detractors. Mečiar not only played a central role in creating Slovakia's authority divide but in linking it to an increasingly important national divide that in 1992 and 1994 provided enough votes to form a government. As Mečiar's political importance declined, so did the role played by the authority divide.

Conclusion

The issue divides that shaped Slovakia's politics in the 1990s exhibited little stability. An authority divide built on Mečiar's charisma rose and sank with his own political fortunes. A national divide endured for longer but only by transforming from a debate over Czechoslovakia to a debate over Hungarians to a debate over the European Union. An economic divide emerged quickly, but found itself pushed aside by other issues and did not threaten to emerge again until early in the next decade. This volatility reflects both conditions that were specific to Slovakia and others that affect nearly all contemporary democracies.

Slovakia's voters during the 1990s did not reach any long-term consensus answer to the question 'what issue should shape my vote?' The structural and cultural factors that determined attitudes did not determine which attitudes were most important in shaping political choice. In part, this reflects the nature of the underlying factors: historical and contemporary experiences of national conflict provided Slovak politicians with an alternative that did not exist in countries with less diverse populations and conflictual histories. But circumstances alone do not explain the lack of a stable issue dimension. The historical antecedents of an authority divide in Slovakia were no deeper than in Hungary, Poland or most other countries in the region and yet Slovakia alone found itself with a pervasive conflict on authority questions.

In Slovakia, as in many other countries in the post-communist world, issue divides emerge not only from historical patterns but also from the configuration of post-communist political competition. Issues compete for space in minds just as parties do, and parties encourage competition over issues that will maximize their own voters, members, and funding. Parties use the structural divides that are available to them, but they do not leave them as they found them. Rather, they deliberately seek to elevate some and diminish others, to link issues together or to disentangle them.

Even when political choice in Slovakia did rest on social or cultural roots, these often remained shallow and showed little explicit connection to Slovakia's history. Each of the contending issue divides resembles a divide that once shaped political competition in Slovakia, but often the resemblance was only superficial. The economic divide of the 1990s and the worker/owner cleavage of the 1930s both concerned inequality, but the intervening 70 years – 40 under a state socialist regime – radically altered both the class structure and the means of production. Likewise the national and authority divides of the two periods shared common rhetoric, but few in the 1990s would be willing to accept that the 'leader' should have 'supreme right to speak for and make decisions on behalf of the Party and thereby also on behalf of the nation' (Nedelsky 2001) as many did in the 1930s. Many of the broad themes remained – inequality, national recognition, and the need for order – but the specific circumstances had changed dramatically.

In Slovakia these changes are fairly obvious because of the 40-year hiatus during which issue divides were not acknowledged, but the change is not unique to Slovakia or even to the post-communist world. Changes in party systems and social structures have reshaped the connection between structural divides and issue divides in many democracies. Whether this marks the gradual erosion of full cleavages or merely a transition period in the emergence of new cleavages remains an open question. In either case, however, the exploration of partial cleavages can help to understand the process.

Acronyms of Parties, Movements and Other Significant Electoral Actors

ANO	*Aliančia nového občana*	New Citizen's Alliance
DS	*Demokratická strana*	Democratic Party
DSA	*Sočiálnodemokratická alternatíva*	Social Democratic Alternative
DU	*Demokratická únia*	Democratic Union
ESWS	*Együttélés–Spolužitie-Wspólnota-Soužití*	Coexistence
HZD	*Hnutie za demokračiu*	Movement for Democracy
HZDS	*Hnutie za demokratické Slovensko*	Movement for a Democratic Slovakia
KDH	*Kresťansko-demokratické hnutie*	Christian Democratic Movement
KSS	*Komunistická strana Slovenska*	Communist Party of Slovakia
MK/MKP	*Magyar Koalíció/Magyar Koalíció Pártja*	Hungarian Coalition
MKDM	*Magyar Kereszténydemokrata Mozgalom*	Hungarian Christian Democratic Movement
MPP	*Magyar Polgári Párt*	Hungarian Civic Party
ODÚ	*Občianská demokratická únia*	Civic Democratic Union
PSNS	*Pravá Slovenská národná strana*	Real Slovak National Party
SDK	*Slovenská demokratická koalícia*	Slovak Democratic Coalition
SDKÚ	*Slovenská demokratická a kresťanská únia*	Slovak Democratic and Christian Union
SDL'	*Strana demokratickej ľaviče*	Party of the Democratic Left
SDSS	*Sočiálnodemokratická strana Slovenska*	Social Democratic Party of Slovakia
SKDH/KSÚ	*Slovenské kresťansko-demokratické hnutie/ Kresťansko-sočiálna únia*	Slovak Christian Democratic Movement/ Christian Social Union
SMER	*Smer*	Direction
SNS	*Slovenská národná strana*	Slovak National Party
SOP	*Strana občianského porozumenia*	Party of Civic Understanding
SV	*Spoločná volba*	Common Choice
SZ	*Strana zelených*	Party of the Greens
SZS	*Strana zelených na Slovensku*	Party of the Greens in Slovakia
VPN	*Verejnosť proti násiliu*	Public Against Violence
ZRS	*Združenie robotnikov Slovenska*	Association of Workers of Slovakia

NOTES

1. Other long-term surveys – *Central and Eastern Eurobarometer*, *New Democracies Barometer*, and *Department of State* – include relatively meagre information about party choice and relatively few relevant questions in key areas, but in general these confirm the results of other surveys.

2. The CEU questions on nationalism factor closely together with the question on Czechoslovakia's dissolution, but for clarity the two are here detailed separately.

3. This form of measurement suggests a smaller role for attitudes about authority, but still larger than for any other non-national attitudes. Regression analysis for the late 1994 survey shows no relationship for questions about 'firm-hand' leadership, but if the closely associated questions on the nation are excluded, firm-hand leadership immediately becomes the strongest factor.

4. In Slovakia, questions of religion tend to fall in what Kitschelt refers to as a 'niche market' and usually serve only to distinguish supporters of Christian democratic parties (Slovak and Hungarian) from the rest of the population (Kitschelt, Mansfeldová, Markowski and Tóka 1999). In some surveys, supporters of the former communist SDL' occupy a reverse niche, at the anti-religious end of the spectrum.

5. The worldwide pervasiveness of the descriptors 'left' and 'right' with at least some common attributes also contributes to impressions of the inevitability of socio-economic cleavage (Inglehart and Klingemann 1976).

6. This configuration foreshadows the later and even more extreme developments highlighted

above. The pattern also corresponds extremely closely to Kitschelt's notion that national parties will choose to occupy economically centrist positions so as to maximize their appeal. Unless the notion of 'non-nationalism' or 'anti-nationalism' develops strong resonance with the population (as it did in Slovakia near the end of Mečiar's third government), parties occupying this position cannot afford to rely on this issue alone and will be more likely to occupy more distinct positions on economic questions (cf. Kitschelt 1999; 2001). Thus, even when national questions become the dominant issue divide, a second economic divide may continue to exist, but will have disproportionate effects on the non-national forces, a fact that nationalists may use to their advantage.

7. Cohen's account of the 'lack of historical consciousness' in Slovakia's political elite supports the notion that unlike leaders of the Christian Democratic Movement (KDH), some of whom retained consciousness of Slovakia's recent history that compelled them ultimately to move towards a more Western and Czechoslovak orientation, the ahistoric worldview of Mečiar and other 'mass-elites' allowed more flexibility in the combination of issue configurations and therefore a tactical advantage (Cohen 1999).

8. Surveys do show a relationship between attitudes about the split and those concerned with economic reform, but largely because such 'reform' remained tied in the minds of many Slovaks to Czech initiatives that did not consider Slovak needs. Questions that avoid this implication show no meaningful relationship between economy and independence.

REFERENCES

Academy of Sciences of the Czech Republic, Institute of Sociology (1990–1996), 'Economic Expectations and Attitudes Survey I–IX' [Computer file]: Czechoslovak Academy of Sciences/Academy of Sciences of the Czech Republic.

Bartolini, Stefano and Peter Mair (1990), *Identity, Competition, and Electoral Availability: The Stability of European Electorates, 1885–1985*, Cambridge, Cambridge University Press.

Buerkle, Karen (2002), 'Problems of Democracy Before Civil Society: Fathers of the Nation in Pre- and Post-Communist Slovakia', *Slovak Foreign Policy Affairs*, Vol. III, No. 1.

Central European University (1992–1996), 'Party Systems and Electoral Alignments in East Central Europe'. [Computer file]

Cohen, Shari J. (1999), *Politics without a Past: The Absence of History in Post-Communist Nationalism*, Durham, N.C., Duke University Press.

FOCUS (1992–1999), 'Public opinion survey'. [Computer file]

Geertz, Clifford (1983), 'Centers, Kings and Charisma', in Clifford Geertz, ed., *Local Knowledge*, New York, Basic Books.

Greenfeld, Liah (1992), *Nationalism: Five Roads to Modernity*, Cambridge, Mass., Harvard University Press.

Inglehart, Ronald (1977), *The Silent Revolution: Changing Values and Political Styles among Western Publics*, Princeton, N.J., Princeton University Press.

—— and Hans Dieter Klingemann (1976), 'Party Identification, Ideological Preference and the Left-Right Dimension among Western Mass Publics', in Ian Budge, Iwor Crewe and D. Farlie, eds, *Party Identification and Beyond: Representations of Voting and Party Competition*, New York, Wiley.

Innes, Abby (2001), *Czechoslovakia: The Short Goodbye*, New Haven, Yale University Press.

Kitschelt, Herbert, Zdenka Mansfeldová, Radosław Markowski and Gabor Tóka (1999), *Post-Communist Party Systems. Competition, Representation, and Inter-Party Co-operation*, Cambridge, University Press.

—— (2001), 'The Divergent Paths of Post-Communist Democracies', in Larry. J. Diamond and Richard Gunther, eds, *Political Parties and Democracy*, Baltimore, Md., Johns Hopkins University Press.

Knutsen, Oddbjørn and Elinor Scarbrough (1995), 'Cleavage Politics', in Jan van Deth, ed., *The Impact of Values*, Oxford, Oxford University Press.

Krause, Kevin Deegan (2000), 'Public Opinion and Party Choice in Slovakia and the Czech Republic', *Party Politics*, Vol. 6, No. 1, 23–46.

Kriesi, Hanspeter, (2000), 'The Transformation of the National Political Space in a Globalizing World', unpublished manuscript.

Krivý, Vladimír, Viera Feglová and Daniel Balko (1996), *Slovensko a jeho regióny: sociokultúrne súvislosti volebného správania*, Bratislava, Nadácia Médiá.

Lijphart, Arend (1984), *Democracies*, New Haven, Connecticut, Yale University Press.

—— (1999), *Patterns of Democracy: Government Forms and Performance in Thirty-Six Countries*, New Haven, Conn., Yale University Press.

Lipset, Seymour Martin and Stein Rokkan (1967), 'Introduction', in Seymour Martin Lipset and Stein Rokkan, eds, *Party Systems and Voter Alignments*, New York, Free Press.

Madsen, Douglas and Peter G. Snow (1991), *The Charismatic Bond: Political Behaviour in Time of Crisis*, Cambridge, Mass., Harvard University Press.

Mainwaring, Scott (1999), *Rethinking Party Systems in the Third Wave of Democratization: The Case of Brazil*, Stanford, Calif., Stanford University Press.

Mansfeldová, Zdenka (1998), 'The Czech and Slovak Republics', in Sten Berglund, Tomas Hellén and Frank H. Aarebrot, eds, *Handbook of Political Change in Eastern Europe*, Cheltenham, Edward Elgar.

Matějů, Petr (2000), 'Subjektivní mobiliti – rekonstrukce souvislostí mezi objektivním a subjektivním sociálním statusem', in Petr Matějů and Klára Vlachová, eds, *Nerovnost, spravedlnost a politika. Česká republika 1991–1997*, Prague, SLON.

—— and Klára Vlachová (2000), 'Krystalizace politických postojů, politického spektra a role hodnot ve volebním rozhodování', in Petr Matějů and Klára Vlachová, eds, *Nerovnost, spravedlnost, politika: Česká republika 1991–1998*, Prague, Sociologické nakladatelství.

Nedelsky, Nadya (2001), 'The Wartime Slovak State: A Case Study in the Relationship between Ethnic Nationalism and Authoritarian Patterns of Governance', *Nations and Nationalism*, Vol. 7, No. 2, 215–34.

Offe, Claus (1991), 'Capitalism and Democracy by Design? Democratic Theory Facing the Triple Transition in East Central Europe', *Social Research*, Vol. 59, No. 4, 865–92.

Rae, Douglas W. and Michael Taylor (1970), *The Analysis of Political Cleavages*, New Haven, Yale University Press.

Rokkan, Stein, Peter Flora, Stein Kuhnle and Derek W. Urwin (1996), *State Formation, Nation-Building, and Mass Politics in Europe: The Theory of Stein Rokkan – Based on his Collected Works*, Oxford, New York, Oxford University Press.

Šipošová, Elena (1998), 'Z pravidelného mítingu HZDS v Bratislave', http://www.hzds.sk/spravy/Spravy//14_98/MIT1401.htm.

Torcal, Mariano and Scott Mainwaring (2000), 'The Political Recrafting of Social Bases of Party Competition: Chile in the 1990s', Working Paper No. 278, South Bend, Indiana, Kellogg Institute.

Tuček, Milan (1996), 'Srovnání sociální struktury České Republiky s jinými zeměmi', in P. Machonin and Milan Tuček, eds, *Česká společnost v transformaci*, Prague, SLON.

APPENDIX 8.1: ELECTION RESULTS

Results of Elections to the National Council of the Slovak Republic, 1990–2002

Party/Electoral Coalition	Origins in other party	1990		1992		1994		1998		2002	
		Vote %	Seat %	Vote %	Seat %	Vote %	Seat %	Vote %	Seat %	Vote %	Seat %
Public Against Violence	VPN	29.3	32.0								
Civic Democratic Union	ODÚ	Split from VPN		4.0	–						
Movement for a Democratic Slovakia	HZDS	Split from VPN		37.3	49.3	35.0	40.7	27.0	28.7	19.5	24.0
Democratic Union	DU	Split from HZDS				8.6	10.0				
Movement for Democracy	HZD	Split from HZDS								3.3	–
Slovak National Party	SNS		13.9	14.7	7.9	10.0	5.4	6.0	9.1	9.3	3.3	–
Real Slovak National Party	PSNS	Split from SNS								3.7	–
Christian Democratic Movement	KDH		19.2	20.7	8.9	12.0	10.1	11.3			8.3	10.0
Slovak Christian Democratic Movement/Christian Social Union	SKDH /KSÚ	Split from KDH		3.1	–	2.1	–				
Slovak Democratic Coalition	SDK	Coalition of KDH, DU, DS, SDSS and SZS						26.3	28.0	15.1	18.7
Hungarian Coalition/ Hungarian Coalition Party	MK/ MKP	Coalition of ESWS, MKDH, and MPP (after 1992)	8.7	9.3	7.4	9.3	10.2	11.3	9.1	10.0	11.2	13.3
Hungarian Civic Party	MPP				2.3	–						
Communist Party of Slovakia	KSS		13.3	14.7								
Party of the Democratic Left	SDĽ	Renamed from KSS				10.4	12.0	14.7	15.3	1.4	–
Common Choice	SV	Coalition of SDĽ, SDSS, and SZS		14.7	19.3						
Communist Party of Slovakia (reconstituted)	KSS	Split from SDĽ		0.8	–	2.7	–	2.8	–	6.3	7.3
Association of Workers of Slovakia	ZRS	Split from SDĽ				7.3	8.7	1.3	–	0.5	–
Direction	Smer	Split from SDĽ								13.5	16.7

Party												
Social Democratic Alternative	SDA	Split from SDĽ									1.8	–
Party of the Greens	SZ		3.5	4.0	1.1	–						
Party of the Greens in Slovakia	SZS	Split from SZ			2.1	–					1.0	–
Social Democratic Party of Slovakia	SDSS				4.0	–						
Democratic Party	DS		4.4	4.7	3.3	–	3.4	–				
Party of Civic Understanding	SOP								8.0	8.7		
New Citizen's Alliance	ANO										8.0	10.0
All other parties			7.6	–	3.1	–	4.8	–	1.7	–	3.2	–

Results of Slovakia's Presidential Elections, 1999

Candiate	Party	Vote % in First Round	Vote % in Second Round
Rudolf Schuster	SOP	47.4	57.2
Vladimír Mečiar	HZDS	37.2	42.8
Magda Vašaryová	Independent	6.6	
Ivan Majartan	Independent	3.6	
Jan Slota	SNS	2.5	
Other candidates		2.7	

APPENDIX 8.2: GOVERNMENT COMPOSITION

Beg. date	End date	Duration	Prime Minister	Prime Minister's Party	Composition	Share of seats in parliament	Share of seats in gov.ment[*]	Reason for change
27 June 1990	22 April 1991	10 months	Vladimír Mečiar	VPN	VPN	32.0%	52.2%	Dismissal by parliamentary presidium[**]
					KDH	20.7%	34.8%	
					DS	4.7%	13.0%	
					Total	57.3%		
23 Apr 1991[***]	24 Jun 1992	14 months	Jan Čarnogúrsky	KDH	KDH	20.7%	39.1%	Parliamentary election
					VPN/ODÚ	15.3%	52.2%	
					DS	4.7%	8.7%	
					Total	40.7%		
24 June 1992[***]	15 Mar 1994	21 months	Vladimír Mečiar	HZDS	HZDS	49.3% (44.0%)	93.8% (84.2%)	Vote of no confidence
					SNS[****]	10.0% (5.3%)	6.2% (15.8%)	
					Total	59.3% (49.3%)		
15 Mar 1994	12 Dec 1994	9 months	Jozef Moravčík	DU	SDĽ	18.7%	38.9%	Parliamentary election
					DU	15.3%	33.3%	
					KDH	12.0%	27.8%	
					Total	46.0%		
12 Dec 1994	30 Oct 1998	47 months	Vladimír Mečiar	HZDS	HZDS	40.7%	66.7%	Parliamentary election
					ZRS	8.7%	22.2%	
					SNS	6.0%	11.1%	
					Total	55.3%		
30 Oct 1998	15 Oct 2002	48 months	Mikulaš Dzurinda	SDK	SDK	28.0%	45.0%	Parliamentary election
					SDĽ	15.3%	30.0%	
					MK	10.0%	15.0%	
					SOP	8.7%	10.0%	
					Total	62.0%		
16 Oct 2002	–	–	Mikulaš Dzurinda	SDKÚ	SDKÚ	18.7%	38.9%	–
					MK	13.3%	22.2%	
					KDH	10.0%	16.7%	
					ANO	10.0%	22.2%	
					Total	52.0%		

[*] Includes all ministers nominated by a particular party without respect to actual party affiliation (or lack of affiliation).

[**] Procedures from the era of Communist Party rule gave responsibility for appointing ministers to a presidium appointed by parliament.

[***] Because of the rapid shifts in party membership during these periods, distribution of seats by party should be regarded only as an approximation.

[****] Between 24 June 1992 and 10 November 1993, the Mečiar-led government included a representative of SNS without including SNS as a formal partner in government. After 10 November 1993, SNS became a formal coalition member. Numbers in parentheses represent the distribution of seats after the resulting reshuffling of the cabinet.

APPENDIX 8.3: THE ELECTORAL SYSTEM

Since the first post-communist elections of 1990, the citizens of Slovakia have chosen their unicameral parliament – the 150-member National Council of the Slovak Republic – through direct elections on the basis of proportional representation using party lists with a minimum republic-wide threshold that has fluctuated within the range of 3–5, and a maximum term of four years. Slovakia applies a quota system for proportional representation based on the Hagenbach-Bischoff formula, which awards parliamentary mandates on the basis of vote quotas derived from the number of seats (the quota for one seat is approximately equal to the number of votes cast divided by one plus the number of available seats). Unfilled mandates are awarded to parties with the largest numbers of votes remaining after quotas have been filled.

Within these general parameters, there have been several significant changes in Slovakia's electoral framework:

1 *Electoral Threshold*. The electoral law prepared for the 1990 elections introduced a republic-wide threshold of 3 per cent as a condition for obtaining parliamentary mandates. For the 1992 election, parliament raised this threshold to 5 per cent for a single party, to 7 per cent for coalitions of two or three parties and up to 10 per cent for a coalition of four or more parties. Shortly before the 1998 election, parliament raised the threshold for electoral coalitions to an aggregate of 5 per cent for each participating party, such that a three-party coalition would require 15 per cent.

2 *Electoral Districts*. The electoral law prepared for the 1990 elections introduced four electoral districts (Western Slovakia, Central Slovakia, Eastern Slovakia, and Bratislava) based on the country's then-existing administrative regions. These four electoral districts remained in use even after the administrative regions themselves were abolished in administrative reforms. Amendments to the electoral law approved by parliament before the 1998 election abolished these districts and created a single, country-wide electoral district.

3 *List Voting*. The electoral lists prepared for the 1990 election allowed voters to cast preference votes for one candidate from the party list they had chosen. Those candidates receiving the preference votes of more than 25 per cent of a party's voters moved to the top of the list. For the 1992 election, parliament raised the number of preference votes from one to four and lowered the threshold for relevance of preference votes from 25 per cent to 10 per cent.

Slovakia's 1992 constitution established the position of President of the Slovak Republic to be elected by a three-fifths vote of the National Council. A 1999 amendment to the constitution changed the selection procedure to direct election based on a two-round, majoritarian system. Any candidate receiving more than 50 per cent of the vote in the first election round wins the presidency outright. If no candidate receives more than 50 per cent of the vote in the first round, the two candidates receiving the most votes must compete in a second round in which the candidate receiving more than 50 per cent of the votes wins the presidency. Individuals elected to the presidency must suspend party membership for the duration of their stay in office.

All citizens of Slovakia, who have reached the age of 21, possess the right to vote. Permanent residents of Slovakia above the age of 21 are eligible for election to parliament. The office of parliamentary deputy is incompatible with the office of president, judge, prosecutor, or membership in the police corps, prison guard corps or the armed forces. The office of parliamentary deputy is also incompatible with the office of government minister or state secretary; mandates of deputies who are appointed as ministers are suspended during the period in which they serve in government and are restored on resignation from the ministerial positions. Suspended mandates of ministers are filled by substitutes from the ministers' respective party lists.

The details of Slovakia's electoral system are specified by law and not in Slovakia's constitution.

APPENDIX 8.4: THE CONSTITUTIONAL FRAMEWORK

Since its independence at the beginning of 1993, Slovakia has been a unicameral parliamentary system with a relatively weak presidency.

The National Council of the Slovak Republic is the country's highest and only country-wide legislative body. It is elected for four-year terms on the basis of proportional representation. Parliament drafts, debates and approves legislation. Individual members of parliament, parliamentary committees or the Slovak government may introduce parliamentary bills. Parliament approves government ministers and may vote its lack of confidence in the government as a whole or in specific ministers at any time by majority vote. Parliament appoints a variety of executive and oversight boards including the chief prosecutor, the chair of the Slovak National Bank, the ombudsman, and the boards of state television and radio. Parliament also nominates candidates for the Constitutional Court of the Slovak Republic.

The Government of the Slovak Republic is the country's highest executive power. The Prime Minister and other government ministers are appointed by the president and approved by a majority vote of parliament. The government drafts legislation, which it may submit to parliament for approval.

The President of the Slovak Republic is Head of State. Between the establishment of the office in 1992 and 1999, Slovakia's President was chosen on the basis of a three-fifths vote of all parliamentary deputies. In 1999, constitutional changes established a directly elected presidency on the basis of a two-round, majoritarian electoral system. All citizens of Slovakia who have reached the age of 35 and are eligible to be elected to Slovakia's parliament are eligible for the office of President. Slovakia's President represents the Slovak Republic in its international relations, appoints and recalls government ministers with the approval of parliament, acts as supreme commander of the armed forces, declares war and martial law, calls referenda, and grants pardons and amnesty. The President also signs laws or returns them to parliament (with comments), may submit draft legislation, may call meetings of parliament, and may dissolve parliament if the policy statement of the Government of the Slovak Republic is not approved after three attempts totalling more than six months. The President may be recalled by a three-fifths vote of parliament for directly undermining Slovakia's democracy or territorial integrity.

Slovakia's Constitutional Court evaluates the constitutionality of legislation and may strike down laws that do not conform to the constitution. The court consists of ten judges appointed by the President to terms of seven years from a list of nominees submitted by parliament that contains twice as many candidates as there are available vacancies.

9. Hungary

Gábor Tóka*

The institutions squeezed the cleavages: much of the history of Hungarian party competition between 1990 and 2002 could be summed up in this verdict. At the beginning of the period, a relatively fragmented party system articulated a number of crosscutting or just weakly correlated cleavage dimensions. By the end of the period, something very close to a two-party system emerged, and the multiple cleavages were absorbed into the opposition between two poles symbolized by the two major parties, with the more centrist or otherwise idiosyncratic parties apparently approaching extinction.

Yet crisp phrases are rarely accurate: we could equally well argue that it was the weakness of the initial cleavages that allowed their aggregation into a single ideological divide without much apparent anchoring in social identities. Had the vanishing cleavages had a stronger hold over the behaviour of politicians and voters, the codified institutional framework would surely have been adjusted to the reality of a relatively fragmented multi-party system, sustained by a multiplicity of crosscutting divides.

Indeed, even if constitutional law had been hard to change, political practice, if there was a need, could surely have found ways to ameliorate the effect of the institutional arrangements that stole the air from the smaller parties. Their eventual extinction, in this interpretation, found its ultimate cause in a cleavage structure that was only too easy to simplify. Institutional details – most notably the majoritarian component of the electoral system and the overwhelming dominance of the executive by a prime minister whose survival could hardly be called in doubt between two elections – only acted as catalysts for the eventual concentration of the vote on the two parties that became the standard-bearers of the poles on a cleavage that somehow proved more powerful than the others.

Either way, a most striking feature of the Hungarian party system was the spectacular and secular decline in party fragmentation that has taken place since the first free election in 1990, coupled with the strange combination of a stability in the names of the relevant parties with stunning volatility in their relative electoral strength and every election bringing about a wholesale alternation between government and opposition. The two biggest parties' share of the party list votes increased from 46 per cent in 1990 to 53 per cent in 1994, 61 per cent in 1998 and 83 per cent in 2002 (cf. *Appendix 9.1*), and has since settled at around 90 per cent in the polls. The only new party to gain parliamentary representation after 1990 was just a splinter from the party winning the 1990 election – but the two biggest parties in 1998 and 2002 were among the smallest in 1990. Hence, a curious mix of continuity, secular change, and wild fluctuation characterized the party system while the codified institutional framework remained virtually unchanged.

This chapter will not set out to determine to what extent this developmental path was the cause or the result of developments in the cleavage structure. However, while discussing how Hungarian political parties after 1989 mobilized or downplayed potential cleavage lines and how the voters responded, we will make a point of noting wherever possible how the drastic reduction in party system fractionalization may have been related to institutional design and cleavage structure.

Throughout this chapter, the cleavage concept will be used in a colloquial way, so as to avoid the theoretical issue of whether all persistent political divisions can be called cleavages. Thus, cleavage is 'a tendency in rocks or crystals to divide or split in certain directions' and 'the process of division of a fertilized ovum by which the original single cell becomes a mass of smaller cells' (*The New International Webster's Comprehensive Dictionary of the English Language* 1995, 246). In other words, the word cleavage will be used here in a rather broad sense, standing for politically mobilized divisions that in some way pre-exist political mobilization either in the attitudes or other traits of the citizen population. The question whether adopting Knutsen and Scarbrough's (1995) more complex definition of cleavages would be appropriate in the Hungarian – and more generally East Central European – context was explored and answered negatively elsewhere, on the basis of empirical evidence that cleavages defined in their more complex way are not more successful than pure attitudinal divisions in cementing voters' party alignments (Tóka 1998).

The paper first describes the development of the party system over time, then it moves on to analyse electoral alignments with the help of longitudinal and cross-national survey data. The conclusions revisit and summarize the key causal propositions about the causes and effects of the cleavage structure articulated by the parties.

The Origins of the Party System

Once the Iron Curtain came down in 1948, all non-communist parties ceased to exist in Hungary. It was only in the autumn of 1987 that various new civic organizations emerged to support the progress towards more political freedom and various other reforms. After the most stubborn opponents of political liberalization were removed from the Politburo of the ruling Hungarian Socialist Workers' Party (MSZMP) in May 1988, even the key political parties of the short-lived post-war democratic era were formally reorganized in the second half of 1988 and early 1989. Another forty or so non-communist parties emerged in the year after the official recognition of the multi-party system at the MSZP Central Committee meeting in February 1989, but these achieved no lasting significance.

In the course of the democratic transition the key umbrella organization of the democratic opposition was the Opposition Roundtable (EKA), founded in March 1989 by four historical and three newly emerging parties and a trade union federation so as to represent a united voice in the National Roundtable Negotiations. This complex series of negotiations about the terms of the democratic transition took place in June–September 1989 between the MSZP, its satellite organizations and the democratic opposition represented by the EKA. Admission to the EKA in itself signalled a party's potential strength and respectability to the electorate, and the roundtable talks themselves further increased the gap between outsiders and insiders. In the most crucial period of party formation, the talks drew the attention of the media and potential party cadres to EKA-members and accelerated their institutionalization. Not one single one of the opposition parties excluded from the Roundtable was to win more than 2 per cent of the votes in 1990.

On the other side of the Roundtable sat representatives of the Hungarian Socialist Workers' Party (MSZMP), a party soon to disappear. The October 1989 MSZMP congress announced the party's break with Marxism-Leninism and established a new party named the Hungarian Socialist Party (MSZP). The losing Marxist-Leninist faction rejected the new programme and helped organize a relatively orthodox communist party under the old MSZMP label. The reformist wing inherited the government positions and party assets, but not the ideological positions nor the members of the troubled old party – former MSZMP members were not automatically registered as MSZMP members. In the 1990 election campaign, the party emphasized pragmatism, statesmanship, the need for economic reforms, its commitment to democracy, European integration, the party's role in maintaining political stability and the combination of social democratic, patriotic, moderately liberal and technocratic elements in the party's programme and leadership.

The voters presumably had little difficulty guessing what social groups and issue concerns the reorganized historical parties intended to speak for.

From the autumn of 1989, the Independent Smallholders Party (FKGP), a moderately nationalist and religious agrarian centre party before 1948, had come out strongly in favour of the restoration of ex-farmers' pre-1948 property rights, a proposition emphatically rejected by all the other parties. The Social Democratic Party of Hungary (MSZDP) apparently considered the party label self-explanatory and did not bother to tie it to specific issues. Like the fiercely anti-communist FKGP, the MSZDP usually joined the more radical wing of the opposition in the political conflicts of 1989 – the greatest concern, apparently, of the party leaders was to dissociate the MSZDP from the incumbent reform socialists who were also contesting the social democratic field. The Christian Democratic People's Party (KDNP) stressed the traditional religious issues and emphasized its moral commitment to protect the poor. In the 1989 referenda it supported the same option as the Socialist Party, and in other respects as well it usually shared the views of the moderate opposition.

All parties with some historical roots attempted to develop organizations following the traditional mass party model (Enyedi 1996). But the dominant actors in the Opposition Roundtable – the MDF, SZDSZ and FIDESZ – were newly created umbrella organizations of anti-communist mobilization, each representing a fairly broad ideological spectrum. Their future political orientation was also uncertain because their chief issue concern – the transition to democracy – was bound to lose relevance soon. Yet their leading role in the transition process and the relatively great breadth and internal cohesion of the pre-existing social networks of intellectuals upon which these three organizations were based, made them the most successful non-communist actors in mobilizing human and material resources for politics.

The nature of the most important resources was determined by the context. In Hungary's negotiated revolution, the media constituted the main channel of communication from parties to voters. The masters of this technique in Hungarian transition politics – apart from the reform socialists within the MSZP – were the pro-democracy activists in MDF, SZDSZ and FIDESZ. They had the most imagination for creative political initiatives, and were able to react promptly to any event. Unlike the historical parties and the reform socialists, the MDF, SZDSZ and FIDESZ did not have pre-determined fixed positions on any issue: they were free and – due to their doubtless skills and internal cohesion – able to adapt their policies to events and experiences as they saw fit.

The transferability of the initial advantages into electoral superiority over less broadly based parties may seem less mysterious than the mere survival of these umbrella organizations in the ordinary business of party politics. Maybe they were 'organized along tribal lines' (as an insider put it), and – as the late MDF leader József Antall claimed – 'nobody beyond the Grand

Boulevard' (i.e. the dividing line between down-town and mid-town Budapest) was interested in their ideological debates, which reflected only the traditional micro-cleavage dividing the Hungarian intelligentsia (Körösényi 1991). But their founding fathers would never have acquired their undeniable charisma, had they been unable to deduce from their ideological heritage a distinctive position on every single newly arising issue, thus maintaining the ideological cohesion of their emerging parties. The competition among them and between them and the regime provided sufficient incentives to keep each of these three parties united.

Before being formally established in the autumn of 1988, the Hungarian Democratic Forum (MDF) and the Alliance of Free Democrats (SZDSZ) both had at least a decade-long prehistory. The SZDSZ was more or less the direct successor to the informal network of the dissent movement dating back to the late 1970s. For the general public, the only visible difference between them and the MDF until late 1989 was tactical. The founding fathers of the MDF, aiming at a moral reorganization of the nation, advocated *Realpolitik* and tried to cooperate with the reformers in the communist party.

In terms of leadership, the MDF initially relied on a group of intellectuals under the guardianship of the reformist Politburo-member Imre Pozsgay. Many of the most influential founding fathers shared with Pozsgay a left-wing version of the pre-war *népi-nemzeti* (literally populist-national or *völkisch*-national) orientation. The *népi* ideology sought a third way based on participatory democracy between cosmopolitan capitalism and internationalist communism, the building of a new national elite – preferably originating from the countryside – and to some extent collective ownership mixed with small- and medium-size private enterprises. The network of dissenters, reform-economists and sympathizers that rallied around SZDSZ tended to despise the *népi* ideology and missed no opportunity to point out its historical links to anti-Semitic and authoritarian tendencies.

Of all opposition groups, the MDF was the fastest and most efficient in building a nation-wide party organization. By the summer of 1989 it became recognized as the most likely non-communist contender for electoral victory in the next election, which was due no later than June 1990. Its relative moderation may have been a key asset in 1988 and early 1989, but it soon turned into a liability as the breakdown of communist rule speeded up all over the Soviet bloc in late 1989. Through a number of bold political initiatives, the SZDSZ turned from a small party apparently unable to obtain more than 5–8 per cent of votes into a major electoral force matching the MDF both in terms of membership and popularity. The MDF responded to this challenge in two ways. It started presenting itself as a centre-right, strongly patriotic Christian party facing a cosmopolitan, radical and agnostic SZDSZ. On the other hand, the MDF claimed that it was pursuing a more cautious approach to the introduction of market economy than its liberal rival.

Indeed, conventional wisdom has it that the SZDSZ's radical proposals had turned into an electoral liability by the time of the 1990 elections.

The Federation of Young Democrats (FIDESZ) was established by a network of university students and young professionals that crystallized in the second half of the 1980s. Initially, FIDESZ became known mainly for its protest actions. Seeing its electoral niche eroded by its increasingly popular ideological twin, the SZDSZ, the Young Democrats fought for survival during the 1990 election campaign. The campaign strategy was based on maximizing the party's generational appeal so as to differentiate the party from the Free Democrats. In early 1990, the electoral strength of the Young Democrats was fairly limited; after the elections, however, the FIDESZ was the only party able to capitalize on the decreasing popularity of the MDF as well as of the SZDSZ.

Issue dimensions in 1989 and early 1990
Quite apart from the information overflow resulting from the exceptional circumstances of regime change, there was a non-trivial reason why the 1990 distribution of electoral preferences could not have been expected to reflect very closely the distribution of the population along some underlying cleavage dimensions. The point is not, as journalistic accounts often suggested, that the parties had no 'clear programmes' apart from some vague anti-communism. Had the parties not had a considerable ideological cohesion already when they entered the legislature, party discipline within the ranks of the backbenchers would hardly have been as high as it actually was in 1990–91.[1] Rather, while the parties of the transition period clearly and consistently propagated differences in priorities and policies, the many issue conflicts between them were not yet incorporated into one all-embracing ideological super-dimension pitting two comprehensive camps against each other across all controversial issue domains. The future importance of the several partly crosscutting divisions was unclear, since the communism versus Western-style democracy dimension was rightly believed to lose its relevance after the first election. Thus, the post-election period was to determine the dominant divide of the future as well as how the political parties were to unfold on the dominant dimensions.

In 1990, the anti-communism factor, or, in other words, the radicalism versus gradual change divide, pitted the small party of orthodox communists (MSZMP) against the liberals (SZDSZ, FIDESZ), the Smallholders (FKGP), and some smaller right-wing parties. From this perspective, the Socialists (MSZP) were somewhere near the Communists (MSZMP), while the Democratic Forum (MDF) and the Social Democrats (MSZDP) were close to the centre but still on the radical side. The Christian Democrats (KNDP) and the People's Party (MNP), i.e. the two EKA-members that in the November 1989 referendum broke with the SZDSZ-led radical opposition and sided with the socialists to support direct presidential elections, were probably in the centre.

The divide between the pro-market and the social protectionist parties ran mostly, but not entirely, parallel to this first dimension. Here again, the SZDSZ and the FIDESZ were on the one pole and the Communists on the other, but the exact ordering of the Socialist MSZP, the Democratic Forum, the Social Democrats and the Smallholders (all being on the pro-market side) was somewhat uncertain. The Social Democrats and the Smallholders were more in favour of pro-market policies and full-scale privatization than the other two, but the first had an ambiguous attitude towards declining industries, and the second obviously had an affinity for agrarian protectionism. The People's Party and the Christian Democrats unequivocally located themselves on the social protectionist side.

The parties' attitudes towards class interests could not be easily inferred from their respective positions on the pro-market versus social protectionism axis. With recession and an inflation rate in the range of 25 to 30 per cent at the time of the elections, the parties were not inclined to commit themselves to substantial increases in welfare spending, save for education and what was necessitated by the growing rate of unemployment. Under state socialism, the actual flow of cash transfers and benefits in kind favoured middle- and high-status groups (Ferge 1991). Thus, one could easily pledge – as did the pro-market Free Democrats – to divert more public spending to the poor without increasing the overall level of welfare spending.

The Smallholders and the MDF also tended to hold out the prospect of a broad national bourgeoisie as a remedy to social problems, a position that might suggest that they were advocating the interests of would-be proprietors. The Free and Young Democrats, in contrast, saw private property merely as an economic instrument, not as a moral goal in its own right (Körösényi 1991, 10). While it was radically pro-market, the rhetoric of the Free Democrats often rang like that of the Social Democrats and the Socialists, who also called for strong trade unions to protect the interests of wage-earners against what they believed was bound to become a small propertied minority. As if to make things even more obscure, the MDF pledged itself to restrict unemployment and pauperization, and the Socialists, who took pride in speaking for wage-earner interests, were inevitably associated with the former *nomenklatura* and had a tarnished credibility on welfare issues after the austerity measures of the late 1980s. Finally, the Hungarian People's Party and the Christian Democrats loudly committed themselves to protecting the non-propertied poor, but their main issue concerns lay elsewhere.

The situation was much simpler regarding the nationalist–cosmopolitan divide, which was certainly present and fairly important in the 1990 campaign (cf. Glenny 1990). On this dimension, the Hungarian Democratic Forum, the Hungarian People's Party and probably also the Smallholders constituted the 'national' (*nemzeti*) pole, while the pro-Soviet Communists in the MSZMP along with the pro-Western Free and Young Democrats occupied the anti-nationalist end of the spectrum. Although the parties themselves rarely referred to it, commentators took the Christian Democrats' moderately nationalist and the Social Democrats' moderately anti-nationalist stands for granted. The Socialist Party was in a difficult position. As heir to János Kádár's Hungarian Socialist Workers' Party, it was open to the dual charge of having betrayed national sovereignty in and after the 1956 anti-Soviet uprising and for not having made sufficient efforts to protect the Magyar minority in Ceauşescu's Romania. But the presence of Imre Pozsgay in the leadership secured a certain *népi* and 'national' credibility for the Socialists. As a matter of fact, practically no controversial and salient policy issues were associated with the nationalist–cosmopolitan dimension. The 'national' issues of the day – the protection of the Magyar minorities living in neighbouring countries or the political and economic break with the Soviet-bloc – fitted the liberal just as well as the national agenda, and both sides seemed credible and outspoken on these issues.

The alignments on the rural–urban, religious–secular, and moral (as distinguished from narrowly political) libertarianism–authoritarianism dimensions largely coincided with the national–cosmopolitan divide. The Democratic Forum on the one hand and the liberal parties on the other seemed to have opposite, distinct, but moderate positions on these three dimensions. The MDF had its strongholds in provincial cities; it was moderately religious, slightly conservative on moral issues, and demanded a measure of respect for authority. The Free Democrats were a distinctly urban or even metropolitan phenomenon; along with the other liberal party, the FIDESZ, they were plainly secular but outspoken on freedom of religion, mostly libertarian on morality and always suspicious of authorities. In 1990, however, only the urban–rural dimension had salience among these divides. The agrarian–rural parties, particularly the Hungarian People's Party and the Agrarian Alliance (ASZ), were trying to mobilize against the privileges that Budapest and other urban centres were seen to enjoy at the expense of the countryside.

This complexity of ideological divisions would presumably have allowed several different routes of cleavage development in the 1990s. With the socialist government out of power, democratic anti-communism as an ideology was likely to lose its importance for the structuring of the political field, but there were good reasons to believe that the social protectionist versus pro-market divide could replace it as a dominant force in inter-party relations. If so, then the liberal and socialist camps would remain poles apart even after the 1990 elections. Indeed, pre-election commentaries suggested the following coalition formulas to be the most likely: MDF and MSZP with some smaller parties; SZDSZ–FIDESZ–FKGP, probably joined by the MSZDP; and MDF–SZDSZ (probably joined by FIDESZ). This last formula was supposed to have the best odds, and a liberal-socialist alliance to be inconceivable.[2]

However, all these pre-election speculations failed to grasp the full impact of the newly created electoral system. In the elections, the MDF won more than 42 per cent of the mandates with somewhat less than a quarter of the (first round) votes. Altogether, the Hungarian Democratic Forum, the Independent Smallholders and the Christian Democrats had close to 60 per cent of the seats (cf. *Appendix 9.1*), and soon reached an agreement on the composition and programme of the new government.

The coalition that changed the issue agenda

József Antall's coalition formula replaced the previous political divides with a new one between a Christian–National coalition government and its liberal and socialist opposition. Judging from survey data on the sympathy rating of the main parties, the main emotional divide in early 1990 was still between the Socialists and the radical opposition (SZDSZ, FIDESZ, FKGP), with the Democratic Forum close to the centre. By May 1991, however, the main divide became the one pitting the government parties against the liberals and the Socialist Party: by then, the more sympathy a survey respondent had for the Free Democrats, the more likely he or she was to like the Socialists and the Young Democrats, and to dislike the Smallholders and the Democratic Forum (Tóka 1993).

The coalition formula chosen after the 1990 elections strongly affected the future importance and combination of the potential ideological divides too. In a 1990 citizen survey, the conflict over the reforms and the class cleavage were rated the most important among some possible political divides; and analyses of 1990 party manifestos, to some extent corroborated by mass survey data, suggested that these two cleavages pitted the liberal parties against the left (Tóka 1993). However, under the Antall-government liberals and ex-communists found themselves sitting side by side on the opposition benches, and protesting the Christian-national rhetoric of the government as well as its attempts to increase executive influence in public broadcasting and other supposedly non-political spheres of life.

Various shifts in the parties' policy proposals and rhetoric after the 1990 election also contributed to the redefinition of the cleavage structure. Referring to external constraints, until 1992 the MDF leadership opted for monetary and privatization policies along the lines suggested by the liberal parties during the 1990 campaign, and it suspended its erstwhile plans to increase the money supply and investment in education. Some rhetorical and tangible differences certainly remained between the government and the liberal opposition: the latter called for a smaller budget deficit, curtailed spending on bureaucracy, a little spending more on welfare, lower taxes and a quicker pace of privatization. But fiscal policy and privatization became relatively uncontroversial areas in the second half of 1990 and 1991. The constraints on government policy had an impact on the Christian Democrats and the Smallholders too. Quite fittingly, the KDNP's key representative in the government was the Minister of Welfare and the nominal leader of the FKGP became Minister of Agriculture. But as part of a coalition government they could not live up to their party's promises of social protectionism. The opposition parties, including the Socialists, also avoided aligning themselves with any kind of social protectionist rhetoric. Thus, the differences between the parties' attitudes on most socio-economic issues either diminished or lost their relevance altogether.

Some of the major controversial issues in 1990–91 were related to the sectional interests represented by the two smaller coalition partners. In exchange for FKGP support, the Democratic Forum and the Christian Democrats had to give up much of their opposition to the Smallholders' restitution policies. Fearing that the government might score points among former owners of collectivized and nationalized property, the SZDSZ also shifted its position, but the Young Democrats and the Socialists kept rejecting the idea of compensating pre-1949 owners. On the issue of financial compensation to the churches – a pet project of the KDNP – polarization was moderate, but a few details divided the parties into two distinctive and united blocs, with the government parties speaking for a somewhat greater role of organized religion in social life than the opposition parties preferred.

The extent of central government power too was a recurrent issue. The MDF advocated a greater degree of central governmental control over local governments, education, national media, and state-owned companies than the opposition. The liberal and socialist opposition was unified, and the Socialists and the Free Democrats frequently claimed that the MDF wanted to create large clientelistic networks and subject ever more spheres of life to political control.

Finally, a major controversy surrounded issues of retroactive justice, on which the government parties repeatedly showed anti-communist zeal and determination to undo past injustices, while the liberals and the socialists insisted that retroactive justice violated the rule of law.

Overall, the government parties managed to act in concert even on such a matter as restitution, which had caused very pronounced disagreements between them before the 1990 election. The Socialist Party, which sought to affirm its position as a relevant player on the political scene, readily found issues where it could appear as an ally of the liberal parties. The liberal parties, on the other hand, mostly abandoned their anti-communist rhetoric, partly because the content of the practical issues related to it had changed since the Socialists lost power, but possibly also because they found a ready and willing ally in the Socialist Party. The difference between the Socialists and the once united opposition did not disappear entirely: a small number of bills (particularly trade union law) were passed with only the Socialists voting against them. But this divide had no relevance any more to the main controversial issues discussed below. Moreover, the anti-communist pole – previously the domain of the liberal parties and the FKGP – was gradually occupied by the three government parties, and was not associated with the pro-democratic pole on procedural issues any more.

The demise of the traditionalist right

Notwithstanding their unity on most practical matters, the Christian–National bloc started to lose cohesion shortly after the formation of the Antall-government. This was primarily due to disagreements about restitution, foreign policy, and whether Christian-national influence in mass media and social life could be and should be increased by a rapid change of the guards in all spheres of life under government influence. The Antall-government took moderate positions on all these questions but the opposition could still portray it as a captive of the more radical voices in the government benches, while Antall and his party in fact lost the loyalty of the latter.

The internal divisions were only made worse by signs of diminishing support in the electorate. In the September–October 1990 municipal elections, the electoral coalition of FIDESZ and SZDSZ defeated the government parties in virtually every major city. From early 1991 on, Socialist candidates ever more often won parliamentary and local by-elections, but the FIDESZ maintained a huge lead in the opinion polls, with the MDF falling back to 10–15 per cent by late 1991. The heavy losses by the MDF were surely inflicted partly by the economic recession, but the party's newly acquired Christian-radical image must have had something to do with the fact that it lost considerably more support among secular than among anti-market voters (Tóka 1995a).

Premier József Antall's strategy of maintaining the cohesion of the Christian-national bloc by policy compromises and his discrete manipulation of leadership elections in the KDNP and the FKGP worked out with the KDNP, but failed almost completely with the FKGP. József Torgyán, the former FKGP caucus leader, turned out to be an absolutely unacceptable partner for Antall, and the Premier aided those trying to remove Torgyán from all party offices. Torgyán managed to rally most of the FKGP organizations behind him in the conflict with the FKGP MPs who remained loyal to Antall and the government coalition. Once Torgyán had won the battle for party leadership, he expelled his critics (i.e. the majority of the parliamentary club) from the FKGP and took the party into opposition. For most of 1992–94, the parliamentary deputies of Torgyán's FKGP were one or two members short of forming a separate caucus. The 35 expelled MPs remained on the government benches and eventually founded a party of their own, known as the United Smallholders Party (EKGP; see Patáki 1994b). However, the EKGP had very little appeal on the Smallholders rank and file and lost out miserably in the 1994 elections.

A second series of defections from the government benches involved the MDF directly. By mid-1991, some sections of the MDF had lost patience with the failure of the MDF government to purge the economic and cultural elites of what they perceived as a hostile mix of former *nomenklatura* and secular–cosmopolitan liberals. This growing dissatisfaction within the ranks of the MDF found its most radical expression in the newspaper articles of party vice-president István Csurka. The tolerance or even encouragement supposedly shown by the government and the MDF towards various extremists – from Csurka to skinhead gangs masquerading in fascists uniforms – became the most hotly debated issue in Hungarian politics. In a major embarrassment to the government, several MDF deputies questioned the legitimacy and permanence of the current state borders of Hungary, and at least one even called for a peaceful reunification of the entire Carpathian Basin (read: historical, pre-1920 Hungary). In the year following the publication of a notorious Csurka-essay in the semi-official party weekly in August 1992, the Foreign Ministry counted approximately one thousand articles in the mainstream world press (approximately one half of all the entries found on Hungary) discussing Csurka's views, which were labelled fascist even by some fellow party members (Patáki 1992). The MDF was apparently paralyzed: the leadership sensed that Csurka's views faithfully reflected the frustration of many rank-and-file members, yet it could not agree with him either on policy objectives or on pre-election tactics. By way of example, Csurka argued that the 1994 elections were already lost; what remained at stake was the preservation of the ideological integrity of the party and a decisive increase in the social influence of the *népi-nemzeti* forces, requiring radical steps to promote faithful cadres in the media, the privatization agency, the civil service, and in the boards of state-owned companies. At last, even the official silence of the MDF about the widely recognized terminal illness of the Prime Minister was broken when Csurka publicly called upon him to nominate a successor. Coming on top of his public criticism of the beleaguered government, this *faux pas* alienated the bulk of the party from Csurka. Yet the party leadership suspected that a left-liberal alliance aiming at the total delegitimization of the Christian–National bloc was emerging under the guise of the public outrage over Csurka's views. Thus, the MDF leaders were reluctant to turn against him in a concession to 'anti-fascist' voices.

In June 1993, Csurka and his followers were eventually expelled from the MDF; they went on to found the Party of Hungarian Justice and Life (MIÉP) in August 1993. As an illustration of the delicate balance of forces within the MDF, the most vocal critics of Csurka were expelled at the same time (Oltay 1993b; 1993c). Even more important than the public image was the fact that Csurka became a serious threat to the organizational unity of the MDF. First he had developed an organization parallel to the MDF called the Movement of the Hungarian Path; then he organized a strong faction within the MDF caucus that defied the government in the vote on the Basic Treaty signed with Ukraine.[3] Once Csurka had been thrown out, moderate conservatives regained control of the MDF, but the party was unable to change its image accordingly in the run-up to the elections. The period of national mourning following Prime Minister Antall's death induced a surge of support for the MDF in public opinion polls, but this effect proved short-lived and did not translate into increased electoral support, nor into the consolidation of the party's position in the centre-right. The somewhat lax fiscal policies of the last 16 months before the elections, delivering a 7 per cent real wage increase in the last 6 months prior to the elections, were also no avail (see Okolicsányi 1994).

Hence, the last three years of the MDF-dominated government did little to reshape the issue agenda of Hungarian politics compared to where it was after the 1990 election. True, the – more apparent than real – consensus on economic issues was weakened by increasing criticism by the MSZP, KDNP and SZDSZ of the allegedly corrupt and clientelistic practices in the privatization process; by the KDNP and the MSZP calling for greater social justice and a more equal sharing of the burdens of economic transformation by rich and poor; and by the SZDSZ and the FIDESZ talking more and more about cutting corporate taxes. But, if anything, the battles on non-economic issues became ever more bitter as Hungary's media war escalated (Oltay 1993a; Patáki 1994a), and the emergence of the extreme right generated considerable anxiety (Patáki 1992; Oltay 1993b; 1994a) – even making a few pundits publicly panic in late 1993 over the possibility of a right-wing coup.

At the same time, small but steady steps paved the way for a future socialist–liberal coalition through the establishment of the 'Democratic Charter' – a loose framework for protest action, organized by leaders from within the SZDSZ and MSZP along with some public intellectuals who were wary of what they saw as the authoritarian propensity of the MDF government (Bozóki 1996).

Somewhat unexpectedly, the Democratic Charter had its greatest – though first barely visible – impact on those leaders of FIDESZ around charismatic party leader Viktor Orbán, who felt definitely more anti-communist than liberal when it came to a choice between aligning with either the ex-communists or the momentarily unpopular Christian-national right. In late 1992, they engaged in a reorientation of their party. For one thing, they were anxious to prepare voters for the economic policy measures that a liberal government would implement after the 1994 elections. As anybody familiar with the mechanics of the Hungarian electoral system must have realized, the 1992 opinion poll held out the prospect of a two-thirds majority for the SZDSZ–FIDESZ coalition. Hence the FIDESZ could easily afford to lose quite a few pocketbook-oriented and protest voters. Thus, early in 1993, the FIDESZ stopped espousing left-liberal views on religious and 'national' issues, voted against a routine adjustment of state pensions to the increase in nominal wages, and implicitly called for a boycott of the elections of union representatives to the social security council.

Secondly, the strong showing of the Socialists in the 1991–93 by-elections convinced most FIDESZ-strategists that the MSZP was going to be their most serious rival in the electoral arena. Some of them called for cooperation with the socialists in order to replace the Christian-nationalist government with a more agreeable alternative. But the group around Viktor Orbán secured a clear victory over them in the ensuing within-party elections, and the official FIDESZ-line became to stop the SZDSZ from cooperating with the socialists. Hence the party lashed out against the Democratic Charter and the SZDSZ for their supposedly exaggerated anxiety about the nationalist, as opposed to the Red menace.[4]

The 1993–94 period proved electorally disastrous for FIDESZ. First, the rejection of any coalition with the MSZP implied a post-election coalition with the MDF – a prospect unattractive to large sections of the FIDESZ constituency. The image of the party was further tainted by two scandals related to party finances and the party's demonstrative opposition to old-age pension hikes. Within just one year, the FIDESZ dropped from some 40 to less than 10 per cent in the public opinion polls.

Worse yet, the Christian–National constituency was reluctant to switch to the FIDESZ immediately after receiving the news of the party's reconciliation with MDF. The expulsion of Csurka from the MDF put an end to whatever hopes the FIDESZ might have entertained about the more moderate voters of the Christian–National camp switching to FIDESZ. Rather than placing itself into the position of the median party in an MDF-FIDESZ-SZDSZ coalition, Orbán's party was giving way for an overwhelming MSZP victory in the 1994 election.

With the MDF and the SZDSZ, followed by the FIDESZ, falling out of grace with the voters, the MSZP went on to win an overall majority of seats in the 1994 elections without any new items on its electoral platform, save the inclusion of a populist twist to its economic policy rhetoric and a more confident posture on non-economic issues (Oltay 1994b). The MSZP promised much the same as the liberals: competent and pragmatic leadership; economic prosperity; no government-promoted re-socialization of society in the name of systemic change, but a continuation of the economic reforms and privatization; no retroactive revision of past privatization deals but tightened control of privatization by parliament; the implementation of all the restitution laws enacted during MDF rule; and probably some improvements in the relations with Slovakia and Romania.

In pursuing an electorally suicidal course of action, the FIDESZ-leaders were certainly confident that should the 'Warsaw express' – also called 'Lithuanian disease' in reference to the victory of ex-communists in the 1992 Lithuanian and the 1993 Polish elections – arrive in Hungary, they would at least become the major opposition party, most probably doomed to become the leading force on the political right. Compared to these expectations, the most disappointing aspect of the 1994 election outcome was not even the socialist victory, but the Free Democrats' unexpected rise to second place in the polls.

The SZDSZ went through a brief leadership crisis in 1991–92. After the resignation of its founding father, Péter Tölgyessy was elected party leader against strong resistance from veteran dissenters of the 1970s and 1980s. For about a year, the constellation of influential factions and a weak executive paralyzed the party. When Péter Tölgyessy came up for re-election in 1992, the old party establishment had launched a better-known candidate than in the year before, and Tölgyessy suffered a crushing defeat.

In the following years, the SZDSZ tried to adapt to electoral considerations in every respect except on some issues concerning economic policy, civic liberties and the constitutional framework. The nomination of a relatively unknown newcomer instead of the party leader for Prime Minister in the 1994 campaign testified to the new style. By 1994, the SZDSZ was the most united Hungarian party with some lessons learned and moral rising high again among the party faithful. The 1994 campaign of the Free Democrats steered clear of divisive issues and controversial policy pledges, emphasizing the personal qualities and appeal of the parties' leading candidates instead. All this made the Free Democrats an attractive liberal alternative to the triumphant Socialists, who were equally non-nationalist and secular, but somewhat anti-market in the eyes of the voters.[5]

Party positions redefined

Clearly, the issue dimensions that defined the ideological identity of the Hungarian parties changed considerably between 1990 and 1994. The most comprehensive data set available about the issue positions of the Hungarian parties to date serves as the point of departure for an evaluation. These data derive from an international survey conducted by Herbert Kitschelt and his associates in early 1994 (Kitschelt 1995; Kitschelt, Mansfeldová, Markowski and Tóka 1999). In Hungary, 129 mid-level party activists – e.g. heads of regional or municipal party organizations – were interviewed, in nearly equal numbers from each of the six main parties. Among other things, the respondents had to locate seven Hungarian parties on 16 twenty-point balanced issue scales. By way of example, the alternative positions on the first issue were 'social policy cannot protect citizens from all risks, but they also have to rely on themselves. For instance, all costs of medical treatments should be paid either directly by everybody from his or her own pocket, or by joining voluntary health insurance schemes individually'; and 'the social policy of the state must protect citizens from every sort of social risks. For instance, all medical expenses should be financed from the social security fund'.

The original answers were then recoded so that the resulting scores show how much closer to point 1 or point 20 the party in question was placed by the respondents, compared to their average placement of all the seven parties on the given question. Minus scores indicate a placement deviating from the average towards the first of the two response alternatives offered to the respondents, and positive scores the opposite.

Table 9.1: The mean position of seven parties vis-à-vis other parties as perceived by a panel of party activists[6]

Issue scale	Rated party						
	MSZP		KDNP		FIDESZ		MDF
		FKGP		SZDSZ		MIÉP	
Social security	3.2	0.1	1.6	-2.1	-2.8	0.6	-0.7
Market vs. state	4.2	0.4	1.3	-3.3	-3.6	1.8	-0.8
Mode of privatization	-0.3	3.5	2.3	-4.5	-4.4	4.2	-0.9
Inflation-unemployment	3.5	0.9	0.8	-2.3	-2.2	1.7	-2.4
Foreign investment	0.9	-5.2	-1.2	5.4	4.7	-6.0	1.3
Income taxation	0.0	-1.6	-0.9	2.5	2.3	-2.3	0.1
Immigration	2.9	-4.0	-0.9	3.7	3.1	-4.7	-0.1
Women at work	-5.5	4.2	3.1	-3.1	-3.3	3.8	0.8
Abortion	5.9	-5.3	-6.4	6.8	6.6	-6.3	-1.2
Churches and education	7.9	-5.6	-6.7	7.1	6.7	-5.8	-3.6
Urban–rural	0.7	-5.6	-0.6	3.3	2.9	-2.5	1.8
Authority–autonomy	3.6	-5.1	-4.6	7.1	7.1	-5.5	-2.7
Environment	-1.3	-0.1	0.5	0.6	1.8	-0.8	-0.7
Censorship	-3.6	4.1	4.5	-6.3	-6.1	4.9	2.5
Former communists	8.7	-6.2	-2.8	5.1	2.7	-7.0	-0.5
Basic treaties with neighbours	-6.5	6.6	2.0	-5.6	-4.6	7.9	0.2

Table 9.1 shows the mean issue placement of the seven parties by the cross-party jury. With the exception of the question on environmental protection, the respondents apparently saw sizeable differences between the

positions of the different parties on just about every issue. On economic issues, the FIDESZ and the SZDSZ were attributed the most, and the MSZP the least pro-market position. The issues of foreign direct investments and property restitution slightly deviate from this pattern. The socialists and the liberals were seen to be more in favour of foreign direct investment than the average, while the Christian–National parties were believed to favour property restitution and the defence of supposed national interests from the intrusion of foreign capital.

Table 9.2: Principal component analysis of the issue scales in Table 9.1 (N=903). Matrix of factor loadings (after varimax rotation)[7]

	% of variance explained		
	47.6	13.3	7.5
Scale			
Social security	-0.01	0.77	0.09
Market vs. state	-0.12	0.82	-0.20
Mode of privatization	-0.53	0.60	0.01
Inflation-unemployment	-0.02	0.74	0.03
Foreign investments	0.67	-0.25	0.34
Income taxation	0.37	-0.42	-0.13
Immigration	0.77	-0.15	0.03
Women at work	-0.80	0.03	0.18
Abortion	0.88	-0.14	0.13
Churches and education	0.91	-0.06	0.09
Urban–rural	0.55	-0.46	-0.28
Authority–autonomy	0.87	-0.22	0.20
Environment	0.08	0.07	0.92
Censorship	-0.82	0.23	-0.09
Former communists	0.87	-0.02	-0.15
Basic treaties with neighbours	-0.86	0.10	-0.01
Factor scores of rated parties:			
MSZP	1.24	1.21	-0.64
FKGP	-1.04	0.16	0.21
KDNP	-0.63	0.23	0.05
SZDSZ	0.96	-0.69	0.24
FIDESZ	0.81	-0.78	0.55
MIÉP	-1.07	0.31	-0.17
MDF	-0.27	-0.45	-0.24

The next relevant finding emerges in Table 9.2, which derives from a factor analysis of the items in Table 9.1. For every respondent there are seven observations in the analysis on every issue: one for each party. If a small number of factors emerge, and all the original variables have high positive or negative factor loading on at least one of the factors, then party positions on just about any relevant issue can be nicely predicted once we know the position of the party on some other issues. A small number of factors would thus signal a relatively simple party-policy space.

In the given Hungarian data, we encounter essentially two dimensions. Technically speaking, we still see a third dimension with an *Eigenvalue* higher than one, but it merely explains 7.5 per cent of the variance and it is almost exclusively defined by environmental protection, which, as we saw, barely produces any meaningful differences between Hungarian parties. No less than 48 per cent of the variations in party positions across the 16 issues and seven parties can be explained by the first factor, on which all non-economic issues except environmental protection have a very high loading. In other words, inter-party conflict on national, religious and other non-economic issues tends to be structured along a similar pattern; such issue dimensions or cleavages were not crosscutting but overlapping.

Most economic policy items have a high loading on the second, but not on the first factor. This factor only explains a meagre 13.3 per cent of the variance in party positions across issues, and it does not correlate with party positions on non-economic issues. This is clearly an economically defined left–right cleavage, pitting the socialist MSZP against the two liberal parties (SZDSZ and FIDESZ) and the MDF. On the first and primary dimension, the Christian–National, anti-communist and slightly agrarian FKGP, the MIÉP, the KDNP and the MDF are differentiated from the secular, cosmopolitan, and urban MSZP, FIDESZ and SZDSZ.

Thus, the analysis of the elite perceptions of party space lends support to the notion of a fairly simple cleavage structure. It is dominated by a strongly polarizing cultural dimension, which cuts across a much less important and less polarizing economic left–right cleavage. This sets Hungary apart from the Czech Republic and Poland, where economic issues played a much greater role in defining the major lines of conflict in the party system in the mid-1990s and where the number of crosscutting issue dimensions was higher (Markowski 1995).

The Stabilization of the New Cleavage Structure: 1994–98

In the 1994 election the MSZP won 54 per cent of the seats with just one third of the popular vote. On the one hand, they needed no coalition partners – on the other hand, they did not have to be afraid of having one. All factions of the party agreed that some coalition partners would be desirable so as to avoid being locked into an unfavourable position in an ex-communists versus democrats discourse, and in order to broaden the base of support for a new government that had to tackle a mounting budget and trade deficit. The Socialists rejected the FKGP and MDF as potential coalition partners because of their radical nationalist leanings and anti-communism. On the other hand, the FIDESZ and the KDNP refused to cooperate in any way with the MSZP. This left the SZDSZ as the only possible coalition partner. The Free Democrats, with their credentials of anti-communist dissent and monetarist and pro-Western stance, seemed ideally suited to boost the incoming government's legitimacy at home and its credibility among investors, creditors and governments abroad. As coalition partners they might also serve as a handy scapegoat in the event that the Socialist government failed to live up to the expectations of its voters.

When joining the coalition, parts of the SZDSZ entertained high hopes of being able to ally with what they perceived as a like-minded liberal wing of the Socialist Party in overcoming any relics of the communist past as well as the union leaders within the socialist party. Other Free Democrats felt that they might lose too much electoral support if they were to reject an offer of governmental responsibility for reasons that were not readily comprehensible for some of their supporters; in any case, they felt closer affinity with the Socialists than with the Christian–National parties relegated to the opposition benches.[8] Finally, a significant minority of SZDSZ-members left or withdrew from the party in the wake of the coalition with the MSZP.

Conventional wisdom has is that the economic policies of the socialist–liberal coalition were liberal rather than socialist, but in fact the SZDSZ had little visible and direct impact on economic policy making. Like the FKGP before them, the Free Democrats also learnt from bitter experience that even a pivotal coalition partner – not to speak about a numerically dispensable one like the SZDSZ between 1994 and 1998 – has a hard time imposing its will on the prime minister given the constitutional position of the latter. The letters of agreement between the two coalition partners – the MSZP and the SZDSZ – gave extensive veto rights to the junior coalition partner, but in practice they had little choice but to swallow whatever humiliation and embarrassment the socialist prime minister invented for them. Coupled with a financial scandal and the inevitable alienation of some anti-communist supporters from the party, the 1994–98 coalition turned into an electoral disaster for the Free Democrats.

Support for the Socialists also fluctuated, but by the time of the 1998 elections it seemed to be back at the May 1994 level. Although the introduction of the 1995 austerity programme – widely considered 'right-wing' in Hungary in terms of underlying policy preferences – caused serious image problems for the socialists, they eventually persuaded both internal opponents and a significant part of Hungarian society alike that the infamous Bokros-package, named after the most unpopular finance minister in Hungarian history, put the country on the course to sustainable and rapid economic growth.

In stark contrast to the period of MDF rule, economic, social welfare and foreign policy issues dominated the political agenda in 1994–98. Foreign ownership of land, the Basic Treaties with Slovakia and Romania, the sale of electricity and gas companies to foreign investors, and the 1995 austerity programme were among the most divisive issues. All parties of the opposition unequivocally accused the government of betraying strategic national interests, the impoverished middle-class, as well as the Magyar minorities in neighbouring countries. The MSZP and the SZDSZ defined themselves in terms of valence issues, casting themselves as champions of sound macro-economic policy, European integration and foreign direct investment. Thus the issue agenda had changed, but the major divisions remained rooted in conflicting attitudes towards the Christian-national ideology, with the government trying to present an attractive, pragmatic, mainstream contrast to the excesses of the former.

With the government coalition firmly in control of the legislative process, the opposition struggled to form a potentially winning electoral alliance for the upcoming elections. The elections of 1990 and 1994 had taught Hungarian party strategists that the single-member districts were crucial for the success of the political parties. *Ad hoc* alliances formed after the first round, they inferred, were unlikely to influence the voters of the eliminated candidates. This made FIDESZ, MDF and KDNP leaders conclude that they were well advised to form a stable electoral alliance in advance of the 1998 elections. Recognizing its new place in the party system FIDESZ accelerated its own ideological and organizational transformation from a liberal youth organization into a conservative people's party. This prompted the party to change its party label in 1995 – from the Federation of Young Democrats (FIDESZ) to Fidesz-Hungarian Civic Party (Fidesz-MPP).

The parliamentary presence beyond the 1998 elections of the MDF and a number of former KDNP-deputies was made possible thanks to a variety of electoral pacts with the once again popular Fidesz-MPP. MDF was to run joint candidates with Fidesz-MPP in about a third of the single-member districts, so that it would have enough representatives in the next parliament to form its own caucus even if the MDF-lists fail to clear the 5 per cent threshold in the election. The Fidesz-MPP-leaning members of the KDNP, in their turn, simply left their party and scores of them ran as Fidesz-MPP candidates in the 1998 election.

The Move Towards a Two-Party System: 1998–2002

The simple ideological structure notwithstanding, the 1998 election brought the same number of parties into parliament as the elections of 1990 and 1994. But the divisions within the emerging two blocs were becoming much harder to interpret in ideological terms. On the left, the differences between MSZP and SZDSZ were either reduced to matters of style and personality, or seemed largely inconsequential given the limited governmental influence of the junior coalition partner. The right-wing bloc went through a similar process in a climate marked by considerable fractionalization.

Even in 1998, bringing the Fidesz-MPP and the FKGP into a pre-electoral alliance seemed impossible if for no other reason than because of their rivalry for the position as standard-bearer of the right. The MDF and KDNP had also held a grudge against the FKGP leader ever since József Torgyán had led his party out of the embattled Antall-government in 1992. Alas, by 1998 the Fidesz-MPP was not yet an entirely credible partner for many on the right, who saw no genuine commitment to their Christian-conservative, somewhat government interventionist, and at least slightly nationalist policy agendas in a party of young men and women that once joined the Liberal International for other reasons than mere convenience. By 1998, the Fidesz-MPP was in fact advocating much the same policies as the MDF, but words were not always enough to totally eradicate memories of the secular, anti-nationalist and economically liberal stances that the party had once taken.

Hence, electoral coalition building turned out to be an extremely divisive issue within the parties of the right. The Christian Democrats split – essentially into a social-protectionist wing that would have favoured a coalition with the FKGP to any alignment with the MDF and Fidesz-MPP, and into a group supporting the unification of the centre right. The first faction retained control of the party label while the second eventually ran in the 1998 election as Fidesz-MPP candidates. Tellingly, MDF also split for no other visible reason than coalition preferences. In March 1996, a new party – the Hungarian Democratic People's Party (MDNP) – was formed by about half the MDF deputies who defected from their party exclusively because of their opposition to the perceived coalition preferences of the then newly elected party leader. Once again, the winner-take-all logic built into the electoral system and prime ministerial omnipotence within the ruling coalition powerfully focused party political wrestling on questions that could only contribute to conflict and decay in the small parties.

Hence, the 1998 election found the political right bitterly divided, and with the two core components of József Antall's coalition hopelessly below the 5 per cent threshold for parliamentary representation. The MIÉP, the extremist splinter of István Csurka, visibly thrived on the wave of discontent among right-wing voters with the socialist-liberal government and with the seeming inability of the mainstream right to stop the socialists from winning another term in office. But the MIÉP was not likely to gain parliamentary representation and remained unacceptable as coalition partner; so, the swing in its favour only served to erode the prospects of the right even further. With the socialists back in the lead and FIDESZ-MPP constantly denying that they would be ready for a coalition with the FKGP, a change of government seemed unlikely.

It testifies to the remarkably deep divide between the liberals of the SZDSZ and the Fidesz-MPP – by now more of a conservative than a liberal party – that both parties ruled out the possibility of a coalition with one another. In fact, the impossibility of such a coalition had been taken as an absolute certainty ever since the 1994 elections. Not crossing the dividing line between relevant political camps in governmental coalition-making seemed a number one article of faith for nearly all concerned.

The first round of the 1998 election saw the socialists taking a convincing lead in terms of popular vote ahead of Fidesz-MPP, with the FKGP coming in third. However far apart the two latter parties may have been in terms of social background, they shared a commitment to replace the governing socialist-liberal coalition with a right-wing alternative. This paved the way for a last minute electoral alliance prior to the second round of voting, and eventually for a right-wing government coalition based on Fidesz-MPP, FKGP and MDF.

The extent of the voters' willingness to rally under just two flags was neatly demonstrated by the otherwise inexplicable, sudden, but absolutely lasting drop in support for both FKGP and MDF in the polls that they suffered just as they were entering an initially rather popular government as perfectly respected partners. At the same time and equally inexplicably, SZDSZ also lost about 3 per cent in the polls, only to remain at an almost unchanging 4–5 per cent level up until the 2002 election. The MDF, the MIÉP and the SZDSZ experienced a similar loss of support in the wake of the elections of 2002, which confirmed the absolute dominance of Fidesz-MPP and MSZP in the electoral arena. One may be tempted to infer that some citizens only waited to see which party offered the best rate of exchange between their votes and the increased parliamentary presence for one of the two major camps, and they took the answer to this question from the most authentic source: the election results themselves.

Looking at it from a narrowly party political perspective, the 1998–2002 government had numerous major achievements. Firstly, under Orbán's unusually firm leadership the cohesion and internal solidarity of the right-wing bloc increased to a previously unknown level. Unlike previous governments, his parliamentary majority missed no opportunity to stress what divided the government and opposition in policy terms, and to seek partisan advantage everywhere possible within the – arguably rather loosely understood – constraints set by relevant laws. The government and especially Fidesz-MPP delivered on major elements of the Christian-national agenda in both domestic and foreign policy in a way that greatly pleased even the MIÉP, which offered consistent and dependable legislative support for the government from the opposition benches. The government became far more self-assertive *vis-à-vis* foreign investors and Western allies, far more ready to accept political conflicts because of its support for Magyar minorities in neighbouring countries, and a lot more effective than it had been before in promoting a comprehensive change of guards in every sphere of life. The bloc's ideological identity became rooted primarily in anti-communism and a self-assertive foreign policy emphasizing national interest. The friendly ties between the major Christian churches and the right became much firmer than under the Antall-government, but without alienating any one of Fidesz-MPP's secular supporters.

Secondly, Fidesz-MPP added new dimensions to its right-wing identity, linking it to some welfare state and economic issues that proved very popular with large parts of the electorate. The newly introduced subsidies and hefty tax-cuts for middle to high-income families raising children, as well as the reintroduction of tuition-free status for about half the university students did not impose too much of a burden on the budget, but neatly responded to the concerns of the Christian-national right about declining birth rates, especially among the non-Roma, and about limiting the domain of market allocation in society. At the same time, such measures contributed towards the efforts by Fidesz-MPP to create a more caring image for itself. Even more importantly, Orbán's government – undeniably helped by the highly favourable economic trends that prevailed between 1997 and 2002 – eradicated an uncomfortable legacy of the Antall-government – the association of right-wing governments with incompetence and mishaps in the eyes of many voters. Except for some of the smallholder ministers, Orbán's government seemed to function and communicate more smoothly and efficiently than any government before.

Thirdly, the four years in government practically destroyed the FKGP, probably without inflicting too much damage on the electoral prospects of the right-wing bloc as a whole. After passing the budget for the last two years of the Orbán-government in a single stroke in December 2000, the FKGP saw a number of financial scandals emerging around it – partly due to minor wrongdoings of its own ministers, but also because Fidesz-MPP was apparently feeding journalists with damaging information. By the time of the 2002 election, the seemingly untouchable FKGP-leader not only had to concede the state presidency to a Fidesz-MPP nominee, but also had to resign from his cabinet post. His position in the party was undermined, and the party itself fell in the polls from around 7 to 1 per cent one and a half years before the election. Most of these losses apparently benefited Fidesz-MPP, which recaptured its leading position in the polls in September 2001.

Thus, Fidesz-MPP seemed be heading for the 2002 election with good prospects of winning re-election. An electoral pact was signed with the MDF that the two parties would run on a joint list in order to prevent waste of votes on a separate MDF-ticket that would most probably not pass the 5 per cent hurdle.

Meanwhile all the above factors also helped to integrate the socialist and liberal opposition. In 1999, the SZDSZ made a brief attempt to reduce the unbridgeable gap dividing them and Fidesz-MPP but without success. By the time of the 2002 election, there could be no doubt that the MSZP and SZDSZ would join forces for the second round of the election and continue as loyal coalition partners in government, if need be. As it turned out, four years of Orbán's determined leadership, and the opposition's successful allegations about giant proportions of sleaze in government managed to mobilize just enough additional support for the MSZP to topple the government – but only in alliance with SZDSZ, and only because the MIÉP narrowly missed the 5 per cent threshold.

With nearly 90 per cent of the legislative seats in the hands of the two major parties and the future electoral survival of the only smaller parties in the parliament apparently dependent on an alliance with one or another of the big two, the parliament elected in 2002 seems to have confirmed the drastic simplification of the party system since 1990. It is tempting to draw a parallel with Germany and Spain, where the adoption of the constructive vote of no confidence was, despite a proportional electoral system, also followed by a spontaneous move towards something rather close to – though never identical with – a two-party system. To the extent that the constructive vote of no confidence creates a situation where the leader of the biggest parliamentary party is likely to end up as a prime minister who dominates the executive and is next to impossible to remove, this device appears to create a winner-takes-all logic paving the way for something closely resembling a two-party system. It is probably not far-fetched to speculate that under this rule it takes some particularly autonomous cleavages – such as the one dividing the Catalans from the rest of Spain – to sustain a small party in the long run.

Mass Electoral Alignments

Table 9.3 presents data on the determinants of mass electoral behaviour derived from four surveys with national random samples. The surveys were carried out in September 1992, a few weeks before the 1994 elections, and between the two rounds of the 1998 and 2002 elections. The analysis explores the social and attitudinal base of the parliamentary parties over time. For each relevant party, there is a separate dependent variable coded 1, if the respondent preferred that party, and 0 if he or she preferred another party. The MIÉP did not exist in 1992; the KDNP and the MDF did not run as separate parties in 2002; in 1994 the MIÉP received less than 2 per cent of the list votes, a predicament faced by the FKGP in 2002. At these points in time, the parties in question either did not get any votes at all or too few votes to be represented in the samples, and had to be left out of the analyses; thence the empty cells in the matrix.

The predictor variables were identical in all four surveys; they tap socio-demographic traits, religiosity, former communist party membership, and political attitudes. The regression coefficients measure the relative impact of each independent variable at each point in time on the preferences for each of the then relevant parties. Statistically significant coefficients are printed in bold. Since all the independent variables were standardized to have a zero mean and unit standard deviation, the coefficients are comparable across parties, years, and variables. The higher a coefficient in absolute numbers, the more distinctive the composition of the given party's electorate was in the given year, compared to all other voters together.

The first set of regression analyses pertain to the socialist party (dependent variable: MSZP). Throughout the entire period, its most distinctive traits were the overrepresentation among its ranks of secular people and former communist party members, and the underrepresentation of religious and anti-communist voters. Once these factors are controlled for, socialist voters are no different than others in terms of social status and place of living. Most remarkably, left-wing economic policy attitudes only characterize MSZP-supporters in those elections when the party was in opposition, i.e. 1994 and 2002. By contrast, at times when memories of the party's performance in government were still fresh (1992 and 1998), the MSZP-supporters were, albeit insignificantly, more right-wing than all other voters combined. In the same years the socialist voters also seem to have been considerably older than in 1994 and 2002 (see the always positive, but remarkably changing impact of age on MSZP-support). By 2002, finally, the socialist electorate acquired a characteristic that had previously been the hallmark of SZDSZ-supporters only – a significantly less nationalist attitude than the sample average.

The Free Democrats (SZDSZ) are strikingly similar to the socialists. Initially, the party had an anti-communist appeal, but not so any more after having formed a government coalition with the MSZP in 1994. At that point in time there was a large gap between SZDSZ- and MSZP-supporters in terms of age, economic policy attitudes, and religiosity – but by 2002 all these differences had become more or less muted (see the increasing similarity of the respective regression coefficients). By then, there were only a few major differences remaining between the two centre-left parties. SZDSZ-voters stand out as more middle-class and urban as well as far more centrist in terms of religiosity and the pro- versus anti-communist dimension than MSZP-supporters.

The transformation of the Fidesz-MPP electorate over time is even more dramatic. In 1992, at the peak of its popularity, FIDESZ stood out as a party of the young, the cosmopolitan and the secular. By 2002, the very same party had a thoroughly right-wing constituency with all the appropriate attributes of a conservative movement – anti-communism, religiosity, nationalism, and strong pro-market sentiments. It barely differed from other parties in terms of age structure, and it interestingly enough had stronger support among lower- than among middle-class voters. This combination of characteristics was not previously observed amongst right-wing parties in Hungary. The MDF used to have a relatively elderly and middle-class, somewhat pro-nationalist and anti-communist, but overall not very right-wing constituency – see the insignificant impact of religiosity and economic policy attitudes on MDF-support. The only consistent and highly distinctive trait of the Christian Democratic (KDNP) constituency was its religiosity – with predictable consequences for its age composition – without any other trait linking them to the broader right-wing. The smallholders (FKGP), in their turn, appealed to an aging, lower-class, rural, anti-communist and nationalist electorate.

As the MDF, the KDNP and the FKGP disappeared as relevant electoral alternatives, all the distinctive traits they showed separately were merged in the profile of the new Fidesz-MPP electorate. At the same time, anti-communism gained importance as a feature defining the Fidesz-MPP as well as the MIÉP. By the beginning of the 21st century, the small electoral niche that István Csurka's far-right MIÉP managed to carve out for itself was not all that different from the large bloc of voters supporting the Fidesz-MPP: it just displayed even more consistently anti-communist and especially nationalist attitudes than the centre-right electorate, plus a different demography – with men, the young and higher social status predominant on the far right.

Table 9.3: Logistic regression analyses of the determinants of party preferences in four CEU surveys: B-coefficients[9]

	1992 (N=749)	1994 (N=708)	1998 (N=979)	2002 (N=990)
Dependent variable: MSZP				
Gender (High=woman)	-0.16	0.05	**0.16**	**0.18**
Age (High=old)	**0.44**	0.05	**0.22**	0.05
Class (High=high income, high education)	0.07	-0.08	-0.05	-0.01
Rural (High=lives in rural area)	-0.20	0.07	0.03	0.09
Anti-communism (High=anti-communist attitudes; was not a communist party member before 1990)	**-0.64**	**-0.63**	**-0.84**	**-0.93**
Religiosity (High=frequent church-goer)	**-0.27**	**-0.45**	**-0.32**	**-0.35**
Nationalism (High=nationalist attitudes)	0.09	-0.01	-0.08	**-0.29**
Economic policy attitudes (High=left-wing)	-0.09	**0.26**	**-0.16**	**0.26**
Dependent variable: SZDSZ				
Gender (High=woman)	-0.19	-0.02	0.05	-0.08
Age (High=old)	-0.01	**-0.32**	**-0.43**	0.06
Class (High=high income, high education)	-0.16	**0.24**	**0.27**	**0.46**
Rural (High=lives in rural area)	**-0.30**	**-0.29**	**-0.28**	**-0.65**
Anti-communism (High=anti-communist attitudes; was not a communist party member before 1990)	0.14	**0.28**	-0.17	-0.10
Religiosity (High=frequent church-goer)	-0.21	-0.01	-0.03	-0.07
Nationalism (High=nationalist attitudes)	0.09	**-0.36**	**-0.47**	**-0.35**
Economic policy attitudes (High=left-wing)	0.01	**-0.28**	-0.09	0.06

(continued on next page)

Table 9.3 (continued)

	1992 (N=749)	1994 (N=708)	1998 (N=979)	2002 (N=990)
Dependent variable: FIDESZ (from 1995 Fidesz-MPP)				
Gender (High=woman)	0.15	0.18	**0.17**	0.01
Age (High=old)	**-0.88**	**-1.01**	**-0.49**	-0.02
Class (High=high income, high education)	-0.10	-0.05	-0.11	**-0.27**
Rural (High=lives in rural area)	-0.09	-0.05	-0.05	0.00
Anti-communism (High=anti-communist attitudes; was not a communist party member before 1990)	-0.02	0.19	**0.65**	**1.08**
Religiosity (High=frequent church-goer)	-0.16	-0.22	**0.16**	**0.36**
Nationalism (High=nationalist attitudes)	**-0.21**	0.24	0.10	**0.31**
Economic policy attitudes (High=left-wing)	-0.02	-0.16	-0.13	**-0.29**
Dependent variable: MDF				
Gender (High=woman)	0.10	0.02	0.10	
Age (High=old)	**0.52**	**0.39**	**0.73**	
Class (High=high income, high education)	**0.27**	0.04	0.10	
Rural (High=lives in rural area)	0.15	0.18	-0.23	
Anti-communism (High=anti-communist attitudes; was not a communist party member before 1990)	**0.55**	**0.40**	0.36	
Religiosity (High=frequent church-goer)	0.08	0.09	0.36	
Nationalism (High=nationalist attitudes)	0.09	**0.28**	0.29	
Economic policy attitudes (High=left-wing)	-0.03	-0.13	0.30	
Dependent variable: KDNP				
Gender (High=woman)	-0.30	0.04	0.08	
Age (High=old)	**0.37**	0.36	0.43	
Class (High=high income, high education)	-0.09	-0.27	0.54	
Rural (High=lives in rural area)	-0.03	**-0.42**	0.14	
Anti-communism (High=anti-communist attitudes; was not a communist party member before 1990)	0.14	0.12	0.38	
Religiosity (High=frequent church-goer)	**1.17**	**1.15**	**1.12**	
Nationalism (High=nationalist attitudes)	**0.49**	0.12	-0.02	
Economic policy attitudes (High=left-wing)	-0.02	-0.10	-0.03	
Dependent variable: FKGP				
Gender (High=woman)	0.14	-0.24	**-0.33**	
Age (High=old)	**0.42**	**0.49**	**0.41**	
Class (High=high income, high education)	**-0.48**	**-0.53**	**-0.35**	
Rural (High=lives in rural area)	**0.57**	0.21	**0.32**	
Anti-communism (High=anti-communist attitudes; was not a communist party member before 1990)	**0.39**	**0.70**	**0.60**	
Religiosity (High=frequent church-goer)	**0.10**	0.17	0.01	
Nationalism (High=nationalist attitudes)	**0.14**	0.29	**0.22**	
Economic policy attitudes (High=left-wing)	0.13	-0.17	0.14	

(continued on next page)

Table 9.3 (continued)

	1992 (N=749)	1994 (N=708)	1998 (N=979)	2002 (N=990)
Dependent variable: MIÉP				
Gender (High=woman)			-0.28	**-0.62**
Age (High=old)			0.10	**-0.45**
Class (High=high income, high education)			**0.37**	**0.37**
Rural (High=lives in rural area)			0.16	0.23
Anti-communism (High=anti-communist attitudes; was not a communist party member before 1990)			**1.01**	**1.72**
Religiosity (High=frequent church-goer)			0.05	0.10
Nationalism (High=nationalist attitudes)			**1.01**	**1.52**
Economic policy attitudes (High=left-wing)			0.05	-0.23

All in all, the determinants of party preferences varied by party a lot more in the first half of the 1990s than the very nearly one-dimensional structure of party positions that emerged from 1993 would seem to suggest. This is probably why the six-party system was viable for so long. It was possible for the political parties to carve out socio-cultural niches for themselves, more or less independently of the day-to-day political agenda. Until 1998, the FIDESZ, KDNP, and FKGP, with their special appeal among the young, the religious, and the rural population, respectively, were cases in point, as was the large difference between the SZDSZ- and MSZP-supporters in 1994. By 2002, however, most of these differences disappeared – in some cases because the parties themselves disappeared, but also because of increasing attitudinal similarity as evidenced by shrinking distance between the MSZP and the SZDSZ, on the one hand, and between Fidesz-MPP and the MIÉP, on the other. Economic policy issues and social class played just a minor role in party competition whether on the elite or the mass level. Instead, non-economic issues defined party positions, inter-party distances and electoral behaviour. Economic conditions did have an impact on the popularity of government parties, but since performance evaluations remained unrelated to preferences with respect to divisive policy issues and social group identities, they could not translate into a stable socio-economically defined left–right cleavage. As Table 9.3 and previous studies (cf. Markowski and Tóka 1995; Tóka 1995a) suggest, MSZP-support in 1993–94 was to some extent dependent on economic policy attitudes. The more bitter a voter was about market reforms, the more likely he or she was to support the Socialist Party. Yet after winning the 1994 elections, the MSZP decided to form a coalition government with the Free Democrats, the most pro-market formation of all Hungarian parties at the time, since that party was closer to the MSZP than the Christian-national right on non-economic issues. Along with the introduction of a harsh economic austerity programme in 1995, this move served to reinforce the dominance of cultural issues in the determination of partisan attitudes in Hungary. Socio-economic left-right issues either divide Hungarian parties within the two major blocs, or differentiate between supporters of incumbents and opposition – at any rate without having any consistent relationship with the left-right position of the parties.

Table 9.4: Pair-wise correlations between four attitudinal predictors of vote choice: 1992 data above, and 2002 data below the diagonal[10]

	Anti-communism	Religio-sity	Nation-alism	Economic policy
Anti-communism (High=anti-communist attitudes; was not a communist party member before 1990)		0.18	-0.03	0.03
Religiosity (High=frequent church-goer)	0.12		0.01	-0.01
Nationalism (High=nationalist attitudes)	-0.03	0.09		0.21
Economic policy attitudes (High=left-wing)	-0.10	0.03	0.14	

It is very instructive to consider how attitudes regarding economic policy, religion, anti-communism and nationalism were correlated among citizens in the period examined. Three sets of observations are worth making about the data displayed in Table 9.4. Firstly, all the pair-wise correlations between these attitudes were fairly weak throughout the entire period. Some potentially interesting changes over time emerge from the data, but they are statistically insignificant except that by 2002, anti-communism became negatively correlated with economic leftism. Hence, we can hardly argue that the citizen-level links between these issue dimensions determined how they came to be connected to each other by the party system. Rather, it was the parties, and not the structure of these cleavages at the social grassroots, that created strong links between positions on some of the four dimensions, for instance by linking the cause of religion unequivocally to the nationalist and anti-communist causes. In terms of citizens' attitudes, the party space may well have remained multi-dimensional, instead of being reduced to a single axis of ideological differentiation among the parties.

Secondly, the correlations between economic policy attitudes on the one hand, and attitudes on the three non-economic issue dimensions on the other were, on the whole, no weaker than the correlations among positions on the three non-economic issue dimensions. Hence, it was once again the parties, and not some naturally given linkage between these dimensions among citizens that bundled the three non-economic issue dimensions and separated them from the economic left-right dimension. Thirdly, while the most obvious staple of party ideologies became the link between nationalist, pro-church, and anti-communist stances, among citizens anti-communism has not been connected to nationalism at all, and even the weak positive correlation between pro-church and nationalist attitudes may have declined over time. Thus, neither the one-dimensional structure of the party system (coalition alternatives and so forth) at the beginning of the 21st century, nor its disconnection from the socio-economic left-right cleavage can be explained in terms of an underlying cleavage structure.

Rather, it seems that the reduction in the number of parties led to the simplification of the structure of electorally relevant ideological divisions into a single left-right dimension, and that elite consensus – imperfect and qualified, but no less real – excluded economic left-right issues as well as major constitutional and foreign policy issues from becoming consistently and persistently linked to this emerging, non-economic left-right divide. Indeed, all parties kept endorsing and supporting democracy, even though they were not entirely certain that the other parties would comply with the democratic rules of the game.[11] No major political institutional change occurred at the national level after 1990.[12] A broad commitment to market, military and legal reforms, with an eye to integration into the European Union and NATO was also shared by the six main parties and the business, media and academic establishments.[13] This consensus made the major parties extremely wary of political instability and mass mobilization on socio-economic issues in the early years (cf. Greskovits 1998), and allowed for very effective sanctions against any deviants. Several major parties did, at one point or another, violate this gentlemen's agreement, but they backed down very quickly after the invariably unfavourable reception of such moves in the press and among the other parties.

This consensus was not perfect, and major cracks appeared on its surface from the mid-1990s onwards, first regarding the merits of the 1995 economic austerity programme and then increasingly about major foreign policy issues as well. Yet the relatively minor disagreements over the importance of joining the EU and NATO, and the considerably wider, but ideologically not much more articulate inter-party dissent on economic policies, did not serve as major building blocs of party identities. Previous studies of party elites by Kitschelt, Mansfeldová, Markowski and Tóka (1999) showed that party positions on economic issues in Hungary were less polarized, more diffuse, and less crucial for gauging inter-party ideological distances than in the Czech Republic and Poland. However, analyses of mass electoral behaviour repeatedly found that social status and class were less strongly correlated with party preferences in Hungary than in most other East Central European and a number of Western democracies (Evans and Whitefield 1996; Tóka 1996).

As a further confirmation of these observations, Table 9.5 presents bivariate statistics on the impact of various attitudes on party preferences in some East European countries in late 1995. The important finding for the present chapter is that attitudes on foreign and economic policy issues apparently did not become as important correlates of party preferences in Hungary as in most other East European countries.

Because party preference (i.e. which party the respondent would vote for if there were an election) is not a metric scale but a nominal variable, the so-called uncertainty coefficient was used here to measure how well party choice can be predicted on the basis of responses to the three attitude questions. This coefficient tends to have very small numerical values even in the case of relatively strong relationships. For instance, using this measure the impact of a social class variable (coded 1 for blue-collar workers and 0 otherwise) on party preference was just .04 in Great Britain in 1990 (see Tóka 1996, 116).

Table 9.5: The impact of attitudes towards the market, the EU and NATO *on party preferences in November 1995 (uncertainty coefficient)*[14]

	Uncertainty coefficient		
	Market	*EU*	*NATO*
Albania	0.071		
Armenia	0.052		
Belarus	0.044		
Bulgaria	0.081	0.057	0.075
Croatia	0.009		
Czech Republic	0.059	0.053	0.079
Slovakia	0.030	0.019	0.015
Estonia	0.027	0.017	0.019
Hungary	0.017	0.015	0.012
Latvia	0.012	0.011	0.025
Lithuania	0.031	0.017	0.032
Macedonia	0.055		
Poland	0.032	0.013	0.015
Romania	0.025	0.022	0.021
Russia	0.040		
Slovenia	0.015	0.022	0.013
Ukraine	0.053		
Georgia	0.021		
Kazakhstan	0.031		

The data come from the *Central and Eastern Eurobarometer* No. 6, in which the respondents in the Eastern European countries (then) aspiring for EU and NATO membership were asked how they would vote in a referendum on the entry of their country into these organizations. The responses to these two questions were apparently far better predictors of party preference in Bulgaria and the Czech Republic than elsewhere. The explanation seems to be easy: these are the two countries among the nine in the analysis where the (former) communist parties were the least reformed and remained relatively orthodox during and after the transition to democracy. Poland, Estonia, and Hungary, with their thoroughly transformed post-communist parties were the other extreme. There, the issues of NATO and EU membership hardly differentiated between the supporters of the different parties.

A more complicated picture emerges when we move to the approval of a free market economy. This item predicted voting behaviour much better in the unlikely group of Albania, Armenia, Bulgaria, the Czech Republic and Macedonia than elsewhere. The cross-national differences are now less easily explained than those on foreign policy issues. It is true that the attitude in question seems to have had the least to do with voting behaviour in Croatia, Latvia, Slovenia, and Hungary, and none of these countries had significant orthodox communist parties at the time. But the Russian and Ukrainian successor parties of the CPSU were surely ideologically more orthodox formations than the Macedonian, Armenian, and Albanian post-communist parties. Yet, attitudes towards the market did not appear to have had greater impact on party preferences in 1995 in Russia and Ukraine than south of the Balkan and Caucasus mountains.

At first sight, the same comparison seems to defy Peter Katzenstein's ingenious proposal that small countries, because of their greater openness to trade, are more constrained in their economic policy choices than big countries. Thus, adversarial party competition on economic issues is more likely to appear in big countries, and corporatist institutions in small countries (Katzenstein 1985). Obviously, Albania, Macedonia, and Armenia are small even in comparison to Hungary. Note, however, that their openness to trade may well have been lower in critical periods of their recent political development than that of Hungary, Slovenia and the Baltic states – indeed lower than that of Russia and Ukraine. The reasons are Albania's protracted policy of autarchy under Enver Hoxha, and the trade blockade against Macedonia and Armenia by some of their neighbours in the 1990s, coupled with ongoing warfare in neighbouring territories.

Formal testing of the hypothesis is difficult given the difficulties when it comes to evaluating the amount of unregistered foreign trade – i.e. smuggling – across some borders in Eastern Europe. But it seems clear enough that Hungarian party competition in the mid-1990s had little use for some traditional left–right issues related to foreign and economic policy. This, in turn, can probably be explained by two, interrelated factors: the reformist attitude of the former communist party and the high level of trade openness of the country, especially towards Western Europe.

Conclusions

By now it is conventional wisdom that East European cleavage structures are weak by default. Strong cleavage mobilization presumes organizational carriers and collective identities, over and above the political parties themselves. After decades of systematic destruction and officially encouraged erosion of social pluralism, the post-communist countries may have very little in the way of cleavage politics. Ethnicity may at times be an exception, as ethno-linguistic identities were occasionally promoted by the

Soviet-type regimes, but in all other respects East European party politics is likely to be even more fluid than what is usual in new democracies. Established parties will split and decline, and new ones will emerge out of the blue with an astonishing regularity, as politicians will – quite rightly – expect that voters have only the shallowest of loyalties to the parties they supported previously (Mair 1996).

Indeed, aggregate volatility (i.e. the percentage of the vote changing hands between different parties from one election to another) [15] seems to be much higher all over East Central Europe than in Italy and Germany after the Second World War, or in Spain, Portugal and Greece in the 1970s and early 1980s (Tóka 1997).[16] The 28.3 per cent net volatility between the 1990 and 1994 Hungarian elections was three and a half times higher than the West European average between 1885 and 1985, and comparable to the very highest West European figures registered in that period, such as the 32 and 27 per cent figures produced by the first elections in Weimar Germany.[17] Between 1994 and 1998, volatility increased further yet to 33.6 per cent, and remained at 22 per cent even between the third and fourth free elections – despite any major change in the identity or ideological position of the relevant parties since 1993–94.

In 1990 as well as in 1994, the incumbent government suffered a humiliating defeat, with the opposition winning, respectively, over 90 and over 80 per cent of the seats in the incoming parliament (*Appendix 9.1*). Even in 1998 and 2002, when Hungarian economic and income growth nearly topped European league tables, parliamentary elections produced wholesale alternations of government and opposition. And throughout at least the first six to seven years of the 1990s, comparative surveys repeatedly found Hungarians among the economically and politically most dissatisfied nations in Europe – even if not as wary of the transformation process as the peoples of Belarus, Bulgaria, Russia and Ukraine (cf. *Table 8.1* in the first edition of this volume).

Overall political stability in Hungary probably benefited from the fact that the major issues of economic transformation became a matter of partisan controversy only to a limited extent. In this sense, the weakness of this cleavage promoted political stability. However, the dearth of party competition on divisive economic issues probably contributed to the high volatility in the party and electoral arena. Indeed, an analysis of Polish, Czech, Slovak and Hungarian data shows that the less strongly related party preference is to attitudes on persistent and salient issues, the easier it is for voters to move from one party to another (Tóka 1998).

Yet in an East European comparison the Hungarian party system was certainly not among the least stable in terms of electoral volatility[18] – nearly the same six parties won parliamentary representation in each of three elections in the 1990s. Only the smallest of the six was replaced in 1998 by a splinter formation from another parliamentary party. In the 2002 election, two more relatively sectional parties dropped out of parliament, but once again no new formation could pass the threshold of parliamentary representation. The absence of disruption and upheaval in other elements of the political system – the constitution and the electoral system have hardly been altered since the end of the democratic transition – presumably helped stabilize the party system. But this cannot be a sufficient explanation for the steady progress of party system consolidation, as the absence of major changes in the institutional framework was far less unusual in the post-communist world than party-political stability. Rather, the following factors can be emphasized.

Firstly, the Opposition Roundtable (EKA) had dissolved itself by 1990 instead of remaining a heterogeneous and oversized electoral alliance contesting the first elections on its own, doomed to break up like the anti-communist umbrella organizations in all other countries covered in this volume. Hungary was thus 'spared' at least one phase of organizational transformation which nearly all other East European countries went through when their initial pro-democratic popular fronts gradually disintegrated.

Secondly, the parties of the Opposition Roundtable gained early influence through the national roundtable talks with the communist establishment as well as a monopoly of representing the anti-regime opinion in the process of transition. Thus, they attracted the best human, organizational and material resources available for competitive party politics in Hungary in 1989–90. This gave them considerable advantage over other parties founded only after the spring of 1989.

Thirdly, Hungary does have a politically mobilized cleavage line that has some hold over the electorate and the party elites. This cleavage divides society into two camps: a socially conservative, religious, somewhat nationalist, and anti-communist camp, on the one hand, and, on the other, a secular, morally permissive and generally less nationalist camp. The former camp wishes to see undone the historical injustices that occurred under communism. The latter camp – at the core of which are supporters of the former communist regime and those who appreciate what that regime in some ways promoted like modernization and secularization – would prefer to draw a thick line between past and present. This is what left-right came to mean in Hungarian political parlance in the 1990s.

But all this was still not enough to safeguard the electoral viability of all the parties of the EKA,[19] or to prevent the entry of newcomers into the party arena. In the 1994 election campaign, two outsiders – the Agrarian Alliance (ASZ) and the Republic Party (KP) – showed evidence of having electorally attractive leaders, financial resources and grass-root organizations that should have been sufficient for gaining parliamentary representation – provided that their message to the voters was right. Yet they failed, probably because they lacked a truly unique ideological position within the party system. In 2002, the Centre Party (ÖMC) similarly failed to make it to parliament with its middle-of-the road and technocratic appeal. This was probably due to the inability of these parties to step out of the nearly one-dimensional simplicity of the emerging cleavage structure, in which their position was difficult to distinguish from that of the Socialists (MSZP) and Free Democrats (SZDSZ). In other words, given the already high number of parliamentary parties, Hungary's relatively simple cleavage structure acted as a gatekeeper against the entry of new parties.

At the same time, the simplicity of the cleavage structure may have undermined the six-party system as it existed between 1990 and 1997. At the very least, the one-dimensional party system had something to do with the fact that for a long time it seemed very difficult to distinguish between the Young Democrats (FIDESZ) and the Free Democrats (SZDSZ), and between the Christian Democrats (KDNP) and the Hungarian Democratic Forum (MDF) in ideological terms. The ideological reorientation of FIDESZ in 1993–94 and of the KDNP in 1995–96 was directly linked to their failure to carve out unique ideological niches for themselves. This ideological shift contributed – at least indirectly and through its impact on opinion-makers – to the free-fall of these two parties in the public opinion polls of the respective periods. Thus, the tendency for some parties to engage in extremely risky, almost suicidal ideological repositioning seems to have derived from the fact that it was rather hard to define distinctive and electorally viable ideological positions for as many as six parties in the largely one-dimensional ideological space of the post-1993 Hungarian party system. If so, then the dearth of party polarization on economic issues did indeed undermine the relatively fragmented multi-party system that existed between 1990 and 1997.

The logic of the electoral system surely contributed to the simplification of the party scene. Having seen and experienced the electoral system at work in previous elections, more and more party leaders drew the conclusion that in election campaigns the declared coalition preferences were at least as important as policy platforms. In 1994–97, this was to cause dramatic factional fights over the alternative 1998 electoral alliances within the MDF and KDNP. The SZDSZ found itself in a similar dilemma concerning prospective electoral pacts with the MSZP. The incentives stemming from the majoritarian features of the institutional framework – e.g. the electoral system, the strong position of the Prime Minister *vis-à-vis* the cabinet, the constructive vote of no confidence, and the relative absence of checks and balances – made parties strongly dependent on their coalition preferences and forced them to declare them well in advance of an election. The majoritarian features of the electoral system also made it difficult to reconcile six unique ideological niches with the limited variety of conceivable coalition set-ups.

However, it would be wrong to give too much credit to the Hungarian electoral system for the fact that by 2002 the parliament became nearly entirely two-party, with the electoral prospect of the remaining smaller parties being very doubtful. The PR element numerically dominates in this mixed system, and even majoritarian runoff and alternative vote systems – which are the closest parallel to the electoral formula employed in Hungarian single-member districts – tend to produce a more fragmented party system than what emerged in Hungary by the beginning of the 21st century (cf. Lijphart 1994, 104–5). Besides, the comparative evidence from post-communist countries suggests that mixed systems tend to increase the number of parties above the level that we would predict merely by averaging the expected effect of their majoritarian and PR components (Moser 1999). In contrast, by 2002 the number of effective parties in Hungary fell below what we would expect in a pure majoritarian-runoff system.

Looking for other explanations of the very low number of parties – and the consequently very simple cleavage structure – in Hungary around the millennium, we may be struck by the obvious parallel with party system development in Germany and Spain after the adoption of the constructive vote of no confidence. It would seem that this institutional device, which is meant to increase executive stability in parliamentary systems, does indeed have a remarkable historical record of preventing successful (and even unsuccessful) votes of no confidence in the prime minister. Several behavioural consequences follow suit. Likely governmental coalitions become fairly well clarified in advance of elections, and the ticket leader of the biggest party in the winning coalition invariably becomes the chief executive. Enjoying, *de facto*, an almost fixed term of office, the prime minister becomes hugely dominant *vis-à-vis* minor coalition partners unless the latter can credibly threaten to cause an alternation of government and opposition by defecting from the coalition in the next election. As a result, minor parties can easily lose credibility on the issues that distinguish them from their big brother coalition partners, and prospective political entrepreneurs, the media and the voters all obtain strong incentives to focus their attention on the major parties in the feasible governmental coalitions. At the end of the day, the dynamics of *Kanzlerdemokratie* may, after all, be a stronger determinant of party systems and cleavage structures than the often discussed but too often inconsequential features of electoral system design.

It would certainly be wrong to trace the simplicity of the one-dimensional cleavage structure merely to the codified institutional framework. As we saw above, the weak articulation of the socio-economic left-right cleavage in Hungary can plausibly be explained with structural factors and the historical path (i.e. the reformist heritage of the Hungarian ex-communists). Alas, one could speculate that the limited political imagination of Hungarian political entrepreneurs may have been responsible for the nearly perfect overlap between the nationalist, anti-communist and religious issue dimensions at the level of party profiles – despite the absence of such an overlap at the level of citizens' attitudes. Yet the more modest claim that the institutions squeezed the cleavages remains highly plausible.

Acronyms used in the text

ASZ	Agrarian Alliance
EKA	Opposition Roundtable
FIDESZ	Federation of Young Democrats
FIDESZ-MPP	Fidesz-Hungarian Civic Party
FKGP	Independent Smallholders Party
KDNP	Christian Democratic People's Party
KP	Republic Party
MDF	Hungarian Democratic Forum
MDNP	Hungarian Democratic People's Party
MIÉP	Party of Hungarian Justice and Life
MNP	Hungarian People's Party
MSZDP	Social Democratic Party of Hungary
MSZMP	Hungarian Socialist Workers' Party
MSZP	Hungarian Socialist Party
ÖMC	Alliance for Hungary – Centre Party
SZDSZ	Alliance of Free Democrats

NOTES

* Acknowledgement: Research for this chapter and the collection of the data utilized was supported by the Central European University (CEU). The opinions expressed herein are the author's own and do not necessarily express the views of the CEU.

1. For 1990 roll-call data, cf. Hanyecz and Perger (1991).
2. For pre-election analyses of election programmes, cf. Urbán (1990) and Kovács and Tóth (1990).
3. The treaty came under fire from the far right because of a clause confirming that Hungary had no claims on Ukrainian territory. The treaty was nevertheless ratified with unanimous support from the opposition, but in order to avoid further defections the government had to pledge itself not to sign any such treaty with other neighbours for the duration of its term.
4. The dominant faction within the FIDESZ expected the SZDSZ-leaning elements to leave the party as a result of the new strategy. Indeed, former vice-president Fodor ended up as the number two candidate on the SZDSZ national list in 1994 and as one of the three SZDSZ ministers of Gyula Horn's first government. This, however, was a welcome rather than an unwanted by-product of the new strategy: e.g., Fodor was the only potentially serious challenger of party leader Viktor Orbán in leadership races and could well have unseated the latter after the 1994 election fiasco if he had not already left the party.
5. See the Gallup reports in *Magyar Nemzet* (30 May 1994) and *Pesti Hírlap* (1 June 1994); also Tóka (1995a).
6. The responses were recoded as explained in the text. N=129. *Source:* Four-country survey of middle-level party elites by Herbert Kitschelt and associates, Spring 1994, Durham, NC, Duke University.
7. The responses were recoded as explained in the text. N=129. Source: Four-country survey of middle-level party elites by Herbert Kitschelt and associates, Spring 1994, Durham, NC, Duke University.
8. For a different assessment, cf. Körösényi (1995).

9. Parameters significant at the 0.05 level are printed in bold. The regression constants are not reproduced. The table entries are logistic regression coefficients, showing the net impact of each independent variable on party choice when all other variables in the equation are controlled for. Dependent variables are coded one if the respondent named the party in question as his or her preferred choice 'if there were an election next Sunday' in 1992 and 1994, and the party that he or she voted for on the list ballot in 1998 and 2002, and zero if she or he named another party. Respondents without party preference in 1992 and 1994 and non-voters in 1998 and 2002 are excluded from the analysis.

The independent variables in the analysis are:

GENDER: a dichotomous variable, standardized to mean zero and unit standard deviation, with higher values indicating women and lower values men.

AGE: year of birth (last two digits), standardized to mean zero and unit standard deviation.

CLASS: the standardized sum of three standardized variables, two of which measured education (less than primary or more; and completed university or not) and the logarithm of monthly net family income divided by the size of the household.

RURAL: place of residence (1=village; 0=town), standardized.

ECONOMIC POLICY ATTITUDES: the standardized sum of the standardized form of three variables, measuring the importance attached to three political goals on a 9-point scale. The goals were: Increase pensions and social benefits (CEU variable name: Q18L); Help the development of private enterprises and a free market economy in Hungary (Q18B); Speed up privatization of state-owned companies (Q18N). Because of their direction, the last two items entered the index creation with a negative sign, so that high values on the index stand for traditionally understood left-wing economic attitudes.

ANTI-COMMUNISM: the standardized sum of two standardized variables, one recording if the respondent was a member of the former communist party some time before 1990, and the other recording answers to a question (CEU variable name: Q18Q) about how important the respondent thinks it is to 'remove former communist party members from positions of influence', standardized and adjusted to response set effects through subtracting the mean rating of the importance of eight different political goals from the raw score on the original question.

RELIGIOSITY: the standardized sum of two standardized variables measuring frequency of church attendance (weekly church attendance or less; some church attendance or none).

NATIONALISM: answers to a question (CEU variable name: Q18K) about how important the respondent thinks it is to 'strengthen national feelings', standardized and adjusted to response set effects through subtracting the mean rating of the importance of eight different political goals from the raw score on the original question. *Source*: CEU (1992–).

10. The table entries are Pearson-correlations, with parameters significant at the 0.05 level (two-tailed) printed in bold. Respondents without party preference in 1992 and non-voters in 2002 are excluded from the analysis. The sources, the construction of the variables and the number of cases are the same as in Table 9.3.

11. Searching for the roots and motivation of this consensus is well beyond the scope of this paper.

12. Characteristic is the example of election law. Only the legal threshold for party lists winning mandates was raised from 4 to 5 per cent of the list votes. Otherwise, even the constituency boundaries have remained unchanged since 1990.

13. The orthodox communist MSZMP and the radical nationalist MIÉP, which had a small parliamentary representation in 1993–94, were exceptions to this.

14. The wording of the questions and the coding of the responses for this analysis were as follows: *Market*: 'Do you personally feel that the creation of a free market economy, that is one largely free from state control, is right or wrong for [OUR COUNTRY'S] future?' (1=right, 2=wrong, 3=do not know, no answer). *EU*: 'If there were to be a referendum tomorrow on the question of [OUR COUNTRY'S] membership in the European Union, would you personally vote for or against membership?' (1=for, 2=against, 3=do not know, no answer). NATO: 'If there were to be a referendum tomorrow on the question of [OUR COUNTRY'S] membership in NATO, would you personally vote for or against membership?' (1=for, 2=against, 3=do not know, no answer). All coefficients are significant at least at the 0.01 level. Respondents who were not entitled to vote in their country of residence are excluded.

15. More precisely, aggregate level or net volatility means half the sum of the absolute percentage differences between the votes received by each party in two consecutive elections. Suppose that there are three parties contesting the first of two elections, each receiving 33.3 per cent of the vote.

If one of them goes out of business by the time of the next election, and the remaining two receive 60 and 40 per cent of the vote, respectively, then the total volatility between the two elections was $(33.3+|33.3-60|+|33.3-40|)/2=(33.3+26.7+6.7)/2= 33.3$ per cent.

16. Only a few – though certainly not all – elections in Albania, Bulgaria, Croatia, and Romania might have been exceptions.

17. On the West European figures for 1885–1985, cf. Bartolini and Mair (1990).

18. The Baltic states, Poland and Russia, had substantially higher volatility in their legislative elections in the 1990s (cf. Tóka 1997; 1998).

19. The Bajcsy-Zsilinszky Society (BZSBT) did not even contest any election on its own, and two other member organizations, the Hungarian People's Party (MNP) and the Social Democratic Party (MSZDP) dismally failed to win parliamentary representation in 1990.

REFERENCES

Bartolini, Stefano and Peter Mair (1990), *Identity, Competition, and Electoral Availability: The Stabilisation of the European Electorates 1885–1985*, Cambridge, Cambridge University Press.

Benoit, Kenneth (1996), 'Hungary's Two-Ballot Electoral System', *Representation* 33 (4), 162–70.

Bozóki, András (1996), 'Intellectuals in a New Democracy, The Democratic Charter in Hungary', *East European Politics and Societies* 10 (Spring 1996), 173–213.

CEU (Central European University) 1992–, *The Development of Party Systems and Electoral Alignments in East Central Europe,* Machine readable data files, Budapest, Department of Political Science, Central European University.

Commission of the European Communities (1995), *Central and Eastern Eurobarometer No. 6* [Machine readable data file], Cologne, Zentralarchiv.

Enyedi, Zsolt (1996), 'Organizing a Subcultural Party in Eastern Europe', *Party Politics* 2, 377–97.

Evans, Geoffrey and Stephen Whitefield (1996), 'The Social Bases of Electoral Competition in Eastern Europe', paper prepared for presentation at the European Science Foundation conference on *Transition and Political Power Structures* in Cambridge, UK, 19–21 April.

Ferge, Zsuzsa (1991), 'Social Security Systems in the New Democracies of Central and Eastern Europe: Past Legacies and Possible Futures', in Giovanni Andrea Cornia and Sándor Sipos, eds, *Children and the Transition to the Market Economy: Safety Nets and Social Policies in Central and Eastern Europe*, Aldershot, Avebury, 69–90.

Glenny, Misha (1990), *The Rebirth of History: Eastern Europe in the Age of Democracy*, London, Penguin Books, 72–95.

Greskovits, Béla (1998), *The Political Economy of Protest and Patience: East European and Latin American Transformations Compared*, Budapest, Central European University Press.

Hanyecz, Imre and János Perger 1992, 'A Parlament munkája számokban', in Sándor Kurtán, Péter Sándor and László Vass, eds, *Political Yearbook of Hungary 1992*, Budapest, DKMKA – Economix, 92–122.

Katzenstein, Peter (1985), *Small States in World Markets,* Ithaca, NY, Cornell University Press.

Kitschelt, Herbert (1995), 'Patterns of Competition in East Central European Party Systens', Paper prepared for presentation at the 1995 Annual Meeting of the *American Political Science Association*, Chicago, 31 August–3 September.

——, Zdenka Mansfeldová, Radosław Markowski and Gábor Tóka (1999), *Post-Communist Party Systems: Competition, Representation, and Inter-Party Cooperation*, Cambridge, Cambridge University Press.

Knutsen, Oddbjørn and Elinor Scarbrough (1995), 'Cleavage Politics', in Jan W. van Deth and Elinor Scarbrough, eds, *The Impact of Values*, University Press, 492–523.

Kovács, Éva and István J. Tóth (1990), 'Pártok és pártprogrammok 1990', Manuscript, Budapest University of Economics.

Körösényi, András (1991), 'Revival of the Past or a New Beginning? The Nature of Post-Communist Politics', *Political Quarterly,* 62 (1), 1–23.

—— (1995), 'Forced Coalition or Natural Alliance? The Socialist-Liberal Democrat Coalition 1994', in Csaba Gombár, Elemér Hankiss, László Lengyel and Györgyi Várnai, eds, *Question Marks: The Hungarian Government 1994–1995*, Budapest: Korridor, 256–77.

Lijphart, Arend (1994) *Electoral Systems and Party Systems: A Study of Twenty-Seven Democracies 1945–90*, Oxford, Oxford University Press.

Mair, Peter (1996), 'What is Different About Post-Communist Party Systems?', *Studies in Public Policy* 259, Glasgow, University of Strathclyde, Centre for the Study of Public Policy.

Markowski, Radosław (1995), 'Political Competition and Ideological Dimensions in Central Eastern Europe', *Studies in Public Policy* 257, Glasgow, University of Strathclyde, Centre for the Study of Public Policy.

—— and Gábor Tóka (1995), 'Left Turn in Hungary and Poland Five Years After the Collapse of Communism', *Sisyphus: Social Studies* 1 (IX 1993), 75–100.

Moser, Robert G. (1999) 'Electoral Systems and the Number of Parties in Postcommunist States', *World Politics* 51, 359–84.

Okolicsányi, Károly (1994), 'Hungary's Budget Deficit Worsens', *RFE/RL Research Report*, 14 January, 36–8.

Oltay, Edith (1993a), 'Hungarian Radio and Television under Fire', *RFE/RL Research Report*, 24 September, 40–44.

—— (1993b), 'Hungary: Csurka Launches 'National Movement'' *RFE/RL Research Report*, 26 March, 25–31.

—— (1993c), 'Hungarian Democratic Forum Expels Radical Leader', *RFE/RL Research Report*, 30 July, 24–9.

—— (1994a), 'Hungary', *RFE/RL Research Report*, 22 April, 55–61.

—— (1994b), 'Hungarian Socialists Prepare for Comeback', *RFE/RL Research Report*, 4 March, 21–6.

Patáki, Judith (1992), 'István Csurka's Tract: Summary and Reactions', *RFE/RL Research Report*, 9 October, 15–22.

—— (1994a), 'Hungarian Radio Staff Cuts Cause Uproar', *RFE/RL Research Report*, 13 May, 38–40.

—— (1994b), 'Hungary's Smallholders Fail to Unite before National Elections', *RFE/RL Research Report*, 11 March, 15–19.

Tóka, Gábor (1993), 'Changing Dimensions of Party Competition, Hungary 1990–1991', in Gerd Meyer, ed., *The Political Cultures of Eastern Central Europe in Transition*, Tübingen and Basel, Francke Verlag, 165–228.

—— (1995a), 'Parties and Elections in Hungary in 1990 and 1994', in Béla K. Király and András Bozóki, eds, *Lawful Revolution in Hungary, 1989–94*, Highland Lakes, NJ, Atlantic Research and Publications, Inc., 131–58.

—— (1995b), 'The Working and Political Background of the Hungarian Election Law', in Gábor Tóka, ed., *The 1990 Hungarian Elections to the National Assembly*, Berlin, Sigma, 41–66.

—— (1996), 'Parties and Electoral Choices in East Central Europe,' in Paul Lewis and Geoffrey Pridham, eds, *Stabilising Fragile Democracies,* London, Routledge, 100–25.

—— (1997), 'Political Parties in East Central Europe', in Larry Diamond, Marc F. Plattner, Yun-han Chu and Hung-mao Tien, eds, *Consolidating the Third Wave Democracies. Themes and Perspectives*, Baltimore, MD, Johns Hopkins University Press, 93–134.

—— (1998), 'Party Appeals and Voter Loyalty in New Democracies', *Political Studies*, 46, 589–610.

Urbán, László (1990), 'Gazdasági programjavaslatok, koalíciós esélyek,' *Magyar Narancs* 2 (4), 1–5.

APPENDIX 9.1: ELECTION RESULTS

Distribution of list votes in Hungarian parliamentary elections, 1990–2002

	1990, %	1994, %	1998, %	2002, %
Successor parties to MSZMP:				
Hungarian Socialist Party (MSZP)	10.89	32.99	32.89	42.05
Workers' Party (MP; MSZMP in 1990)	3.68	3.19	3.95	2.16
Patriotic Electoral Alliance (HVK)	1.87	–	–	–
Other left-wing parties:				
Social Democratic P. of Hungary (MSZDP)	3.55	0.95	0.12	–
Szociáldemokrata Párt (SZDP)	–	–	–	0.02
Agrarian Alliance (ASZ)	3.13	2.10	–	–
H. Cooperative and Agrarian P. (MSZAP)	0.10	–	–	–
New Left Party (UB)	–	–	–	0.06
Liberal parties:				
Alliance of Free Democrats (SZDSZ)	21.39	19.74	7.57	5.57
Fidesz (FIDESZ, FIDESZ-MPP in 1998)	8.95	7.02	29.45	–
Republic Party (KP)	–	2.55	–	–
P. of Entrepreneurs (VP; LPSZ-VP in 1994)	1.89	0.62	0.09	–
United P. of H. Entrepreneurs (MVEP)	–	–	–	0.01
Christian-conservative parties:				
Joint list of Fidesz-MPP and MDF	–	–	–	41.07
Hungarian Democratic Forum (MDF)	24.73	11.74	2.80	–
Christian Dem. People's P. (KDNP)	6.46	7.03	2.31	–
Christian Coalition of Somogy (SKK)	0.12	–	–	–
Hungarian Dem. People's P. (MDNP)	–	–	1.34	–
Alliance for Hungary – Centre P. (ÖMC)	–	–	–	3.90
Independent Hungarian Dem. P. (FMDP)	0.06	–	–	–
FKGP and its splinter groups				
Independent Smallholders Party (FKGP)	11.73	8.82	13.14	0.75
National Smallholders Party (NKGP)	0.20	–	–	–
United Smallholders Party (EKGP)	–	0.82	–	–
'Reconciliation' Independent Smallholders P. (KFKGP)	–	0.11	–	–
Conservative Party (KP)	–	0.04	–	–
New Alliance (USZ)	–	–	0.49	–
'Reform' Smallholders Party (RKGP)	–	–	–	0.02
Smallholders P. – The Party of the Smallholders Alliance (KGPKGSZP)	–	–	–	0.01

(continued on next page)

Nationalist parties:

Hungarian Independence Party (MFP)	0.04	–	–	–
Hungarian People's Party (MNP)	0.75	–	–	–
Freedom Party (SZP)	0.06	–	–	–
Market Party (PP)	–	0.01	–	–
National Democratic Alliance (NDSZ)	–	0.52	–	–
P. of Hungarian Justice and Life (MIÉP)	–	1.59	5.47	4.37

Miscallenous other parties:

Green Party of Hungary (MZP)	0.36	0.16	0.05	–
Green Alternative (ZA)	–	0.02	–	–
Together for Hungary Union (EMU)	–	–	0.19	–
Forum of Nationalities (NF)	–	–	0.13	–
Roma Party of Hungary (MRP)	–	–	–	0.01

Abbreviations: Dem=Democratic; H=Hungarian; P=Party.

Sources: 'Az Országos Választási Bizottság jelentése (Report of the National Election Committee)', *Magyar Közlöny*, 13 May 1990; 'Az Országos Választási Bizottság jelentése (Report of the National Election Committee)', *Magyar Közlöny*, 24 June 1994; 'Az Országos Választási Bizottság jelentése (Report of the National Election Committee)', *Magyar Közlöny*, 4 June 1998; 'Az Országos Választási Bizottság jelentése (Report of the National Election Committee)', 4 May 2002, posted at http://www.election.hu/ and accessed on 6 May 2002.

Distribution of seats in Hungarian parliamentary elections, 1990–2002

	1990	1994	1998	2002
FIDESZ	22 (5.7%)	20 (5.2%)	**148 (38.3%)**	164 (42.5%)
FKGP	**44 (11.4%)**	26 (6.7%)	**48 (12.4%)**	- (0.0%)
KDNP	**21 (5.4%)**	22 (5.7%)	- (0.0%)	- (0.0%)
MDF	**164 (42.5%)**	38 (9.8%)	**17 (4.4%)**	24 (6.2%)
MIÉP	- (0.0%)	- (0.0%)	14 (3.6%)	- (0.0%)
MSZP	33 (8.5%)	**209 (54.1%)**	134 (34.7%)	**178 (46.1%)**
SZDSZ	94 (24.4%)	**70 (18.1%)**	24 (6.2%)	**20 (5.2%)**
independents	6 (1.6%)	- (0.0%)	1 (0.3%)	- (0.0%)
others	2 (0.5%)	1 (0.3%)	- (0.0%)	- (0.0%)

Note: The majorities of the incoming governments are printed in bold. Deputies elected in single-member districts as joint candidates of more than one party are counted according to the parliamentary party that they joined at the first session of the respective parliament, including two ASZ-candidates (one each in 1990 and 1994, respectively) who joined SZDSZ in exchange for receiving SZDSZ-endorsement in the second round of the election.

Sources: as above plus press reports about the first session of each parliament.

Turnout in Hungarian parliamentary elections (including invalid and blank votes), 1990–2002

Year	1st round, %	2nd round, %
1990	65.1	45.5
1994	68.9	55.1
1998	56.3	57.0
2002	70.5	73.5

Note: In 1990, the turnout in the voting for party lists was 0.1 higher than in the single-member districts, because in that election voters casting their ballot outside of their home constituency were only allowed to vote for regional party lists, but not for the candidates standing in the single-member districts. The table reports the higher of the two figures.

Sources: As above.

APPENDIX 9.2: GOVERNMENT COMPOSITION

Partisan composition of governments and the cause of their termination, 1989–1998

December 1988–23 May 1990
Premier: Miklós Németh
Government parties: MSZMP until October 1989, thereafter MSZP
Overwhelming but not entirely quantifiable and dependable legislative support from virtually all deputies elected in the 1985 non-competitive elections.
Cause of termination: March–April 1990 general elections.

23 May 1990–21 February 1992
Premier: József Antall
Government parties: MDF, KDNP, FKGP
Cause of termination: the FKGP left the coalition, though 35 FKGP deputies (eventually expelled from the party) continued to support the government. Since the Premier did not resign and no non-confidence motion was passed by the Parliament, from the point of view of Hungarian constitutional law no change of government occurred.

21 February 1992–21 December 1993
Premier: József Antall
Government parties: MDF, KDNP, and various splinter groups from FKGP; in June 1993 the Hungarian Justice National Politics Group and from July 1993 the MIÉP also supported the government in the legislature
Cause of termination: József Antall died on 12 December 1993, and a new Prime Minister had to be elected.

21 December 1993–15 July 1994
Premier: Péter Boross
Government parties: MDF, KDNP, FKGP; legislative support from the MIÉP caucus
Cause of termination: May 1994 general elections.

15 July 1994–8 July 1998
Premier: Gyula Horn
Government parties: MSZP, SZDSZ
Cause of termination: May 1998 general elections.

8 July 1998–27 May 2002
Premier: Viktor Orbán
Government parties: Fidesz-MPP, FKGP, MDF
Cause of termination: April 2002 general elections.

27 May 2002–
Premier: Péter Medgyessy
Government parties: MSZP, SZDSZ

APPENDIX 9.3: THE ELECTORAL SYSTEM

The rules of pertaining to parliamentary elections are laid down in Act No. XXXIV of 1989, slightly amended in 1994 and 1997 as indicated below. All Hungarian citizens over 18 years of age are eligible to stand as a candidate and vote in parliamentary elections, with the exception of citizens who have no domicile in Hungary, are abroad on the day of the given election, are under guardianship, have been banned from public affairs, or are serving a sentence of imprisonment or under forced medical treatment ordered in the course of a criminal procedure. Further rules regarding the campaign etc. are formulated by the National Election Committee, which also supervises the elections and announces the election results. The composition of the National Election Committee is based on parity among the parties. The respective municipal council elects the secretary and two members of the local returning boards, and each party and each independent candidate running in the district can delegate one additional member.

Every voter may cast two votes: for a candidate in a single-member district (henceforth SMD) and for a regional party list in a multi-member constituency. If the turnout remains below 50 per cent either in a regional district (henceforth RD) or in an SMD, the result is invalid and the election has to be repeated on the day set by the National Election Committee for the second round of the general elections.

Candidates running in the SMDs are considered elected if they receive an absolute majority of the valid votes in the first round. Barring this, a run-off round takes place between those candidates who received more than 15 per cent of the valid votes or were among the top three vote-winners. If the turnout in the first round is below 50 per cent, all candidates can contest the runoff. In either case, the candidate with the largest number of votes in the run-off round is elected, provided that the turnout was over 25 per cent.

The average RD has 7 seats, which are filled from party lists according to a quota system. The quota equals the number of valid votes divided by one plus the number of seats. If unallocated seats remain after one seat has been awarded to each full quota, the party lists win these remaining seats in the order of their number of remainder votes, provided that their remainder votes are equal to at least two-thirds of the quota. The difference between the full quota and the remainder votes that earned a mandate is subtracted from the party's cumulated remainder votes on the national level. Due to the above mentioned two-thirds rule, about one fifth or more of RD seats remain unallocated on the regional level and are added to the national pool of compensatory mandates. The relatively small multi-member constituencies and the allocation rules significantly favour those parties that obtain at least 10–15 per cent of the vote locally. Apart from this, no party can gain any list mandates if it obtains less than 4 per cent (since January 1994, 5 per cent) of the list votes nationally (henceforth legal threshold). Voters cannot express preferences regarding the ranking of the candidates on the party lists.

Candidates can also win seats on the national lists of the parties. The voters do not vote directly for these lists. Rather, the remainder votes – i.e. votes which, after the completion of the above steps, did not yet go towards obtaining a mandate either in the multi-member or in the single-member constituencies are cumulated on the national level by party. Fifty-eight compensatory mandates plus the unallocated RD seats are distributed according to their cumulated number of remainder votes among the national lists of those parties which surpassed the legal threshold according to the d'Hondt highest average method.

The country is divided into 176 SMDs and 20 RDs. Candidates standing for parliament in a single-member district must collect at least 750 supporting signatures in the district to appear on the ballot. Every party which has nominated candidates in one fourth, but at least in two of all SMDs within an RD have the right to set up a regional list. Parties which have lists in more than six RDs are allowed to have a national list.

Source: Tóka (1995b); Benoit (1996).

APPENDIX 9.4: THE CONSTITUTIONAL FRAMEWORK

The constitutional framework of post-communist Hungary was laid down in the amendments passed in October 1989 and in the summer of 1990, following the political agreements reached in the National Roundtable Talks in 1989, and by the 30 April 1990 MDF–SZDSZ agreement, respectively.

Hungary is a parliamentary republic without any trace of federalism. There are nineteen regional assemblies, which have been directly elected since 1994. Yet their prerogatives and political significance are such that they practically never appear in the news. The parliament is uni-cameral and is elected for four years. The parliament has a specialized committee system and access to generous public funds for party caucuses. Individual members have the right to initiate legislation and propose amendments; they enjoy legal immunity that can only be waived by the assembly; they are entitled to submit interpellations to the Prime Minister and other ministers. The parliament can dissolve itself at any time, but failing that it is likely to serve its full term as the President of the Republic can dissolve it only under highly unlikely circumstances.

The major checks on the power of the parliament are provided by referenda and especially by the Constitutional Court. Members of the Court are elected by a super-majority in parliament from among a relatively broadly defined pool of legal professionals. Anyone can ask the Court to declare a law, decree or rule unconstitutional, even before it comes into effect. The Court has considerable leverage in extending its investigation to related rules not mentioned by the appeal on the table, and routinely interprets the supposed spirit or implications, rather than the letter of the constitution. Referenda can only be called by the legislature, which, however, is obliged to call a referendum if it has been proposed by at least 100,000 (from 1997: 200,000) citizens. However, no referendum may be called on constitutional and budgetary issues and questions that might run counter to an international agreement signed by the government.

The President can single-handedly dissolve parliament if, following an election, the death or resignation of the Prime Minister, no candidate for Prime Minister wins a vote of investiture within 40 days of the first nomination, or, if four different governments are brought down by parliament within a year. The deputies can bring down a Prime Minister either through a constructive vote of no confidence (which can be initiated by one-fifth of the deputies), or by defeating a simple vote of confidence initiated by the Prime Minister. The constructive vote of no confidence, if passed, automatically installs as new Prime Minister the alternative candidate named in the motion. Otherwise, it is the President's exclusive right to nominate a Prime Minister. The PM can be any Hungarian citizen. In practice, presidents always consult the parliamentary parties and the candidate named by the strongest parliamentary caucus is always given the opportunity of the first try to form a government. So far every candidate for premier has succeeded in winning a vote of investiture. A nominee for Prime Minister has to present a programme to the assembly, which then votes on the candidate and the programme. Investiture and constructive no confidence votes need the support of an absolute majority of all members of the Parliament.

Cabinet ministers are nominated by the Prime Minister and appointed by the President. The constitution refers to the responsibility of individual ministers to the assembly, but gives the latter no power to remove the former. Obviously, in actual practice the prospective coalition partners agree on the composition of the cabinet prior to the election of a Prime Minister.

The Head of State is elected by the parliament for a five-year term. One re-election is allowed. If no candidate receives a two-thirds majority in the first two rounds, a candidate can be elected by a simple majority in a third round within three days. The current President, Ferenc Mádl, was elected in 2000 with a simple majority provided by Fidesz-MPP, MDF and FKGP. The previous president, Árpád Göncz, was unanimously elected in May 1990 as part of a comprehensive MDF–SZDSZ deal, and re-elected in June 1995 by a two-thirds majority against the then opposition candidate Ferenc Mádl, when his party of origin (SZDSZ) was a junior coalition partner of the MSZP. Before signing a law, the President can send it back to Parliament once, with comments urging reconsideration, or refer it for judicial review to the Constitutional Court. The President's right to refuse making appointments or dismissals proposed by the Prime Minister is severely limited, but there is no legal remedy against his or her decision. The President has the right to address the Parliament, to initiate legislation and referenda. According to Art. 29 of the constitution the President 'shall express the unity of the nation and safeguard the democratic functioning of the state' and acts as the (nominal) commander-in-chief of the army.

The Prime Minister dominates the executive, as he is the sole focus of parliamentary accountability. The Prime Minister's office has a staff of several hundred. On top of the ten-odd ordinary cabinet ministers, there are – in ever-changing numbers – ministers without portfolios, who are responsible for specific jurisdictions and work out of the Prime Minister's Office.

10. Slovenia

Drago Zajc and Tomaž Boh

The political transformation of Central and Eastern Europe has been a recurrent theme in comparative politics and sociology since the breakdown of the communist regimes in the late 1980s and early 1990s. Some of these studies were inspired by models of democratization developed in other parts of the world, also subject to rapid social and political change such as the third world and Southern Europe. This makes good sense when it comes to the transition from authoritarian to democratic rule, but it does not do justice to the transition from plan to market in Central and Eastern Europe, to say nothing of the changing state boundaries in some parts of the region. Central and Eastern Europe provides the analyst with a much more complex setting than Spain, Portugal and Greece.

The Lipset–Rokkan model of cleavages, deeply rooted value-based (ideological) divisions in modern societies, would seem to have greater explanatory potential within the Central and East European framework, but it is sparingly used for at least two reasons. Critics frequently contest the usefulness of Lipset and Rokkan's cleavage concept in a setting without clearly differentiated social structures and group (class) attitudes. The application of the Lipset–Rokkan concept is moreover a demanding endeavour, particularly considering that the agreement on it is limited (Römmele 1999). In fact, we need several waves of solid demographic and attitudinal data in order to make authoritative statements about the relative importance of the existing cleavages, which may not be adequately translated into the political space because of the insufficiently developed party system or the inadequate performance of some political parties.

Even so, the Lipset–Rokkan model helps us understand the cleavages that are emerging and re-emerging throughout Central and Eastern Europe, some of which are related to the nation- and state-building processes. In many Central and East European countries, the main social cleavages do not fit into the Lipset–Rokkan classification scheme. For that reason it is worthwhile to combine Lipset and Rokkan's approach with that of Herbert Kitschelt (Kitschelt 1992), who sets out to explain the initial configuration of cleavages in the new democracies of Central and East Europe. The multi-dimensional space defined by Kitschelt's main cleavage dimensions – redistribution versus market allocation of resources and libertarian versus authoritarian values and decision-making rules – is most helpful when it comes to classifying and interpreting political controversies over 'matters of principle' as well as practical disagreements and clashes between various political and other actors on specific issues. A number of conflicts could be identified as connected with the authoritarian–libertarian cleavage. Such conflicts typically revolve around the organization of the democratic process, including the separation of powers, the type of electoral system and local self-management. Several conflicts regarding protection of civil rights in general or rights of particular minorities are also related to this dimension, as are occasional conflicts appearing in some countries between the state and the church. These are conflicts particularly related to the religious education of the young as well as to family and gender relationships. On the other side, there are intense allocation conflicts on the 'distributive' dimension. State intervention in the (semi) market economy is a matter of principle for those who favour national solidarity and equality.

The conflicts appearing on these dimensions sometimes interact in such a way that the main protagonists do not always place themselves as might have been expected. The advocates of liberal values in post-communist democracies are favouring an expanded scope of free choice and personal responsibility for the wellbeing of the individuals in the market economy as a motor for quick transformation and modernization. They are also supporting membership in international political, economic and defence organizations. Those defending conservative or nationalist values are likely to reject the notion of the market as the main allocator of resources, though it is conceivable that communist-turned-socialists or new social democrats of various shades may be inclined to support the market economy to demonstrate their commitment to the economic reform process. In a similar vein, it is possible that groups with their roots in the struggle against the communist system may be driven by paternalistic or authoritarian values and be wary of mercerization as well of membership in international organizations.

A number of surveys, research data and practical observations provide sufficient ground for the hypothesis that cleavages have been strongly determining the pace of democratic modernization in all countries of Central and East Europe, regardless of their level of development or the more or less repressive character of the previous communist system. The nature of the cleavages may differ from one country to another. There may be new highly significant cleavages strongly connected with the painful transformation processes as well as cleavages that are simply manifestations of various differentiations of the past (Lawson 1999). Likewise, some cleavages do find an adequate expression and intensity while others may not be clearly manifested, existing only in a latent form.

The social cleavage model applied here offers a wide understanding of the complexity of the political processes and their direction in Central and Eastern Europe. The authors set out to describe the deeply rooted ideological divisions in Slovene society, more or less similar to the divisions in other East-Central European countries, which triggered the process of democratization and were intertwined with the struggle for national independence. The authors will also make an attempt to identify the cleavages that manifested themselves during the processes of democratic consolidation and Europeanization, leading up to EU and NATO accession. Data will also be provided, illustrating how cleavages influenced the emerging party system and determined the main issues of party competition, including the patterns of coalition formation.

As in the other countries of the region, ideological divisions in Slovenia contribute to stable patterns of political polarization – some groups support certain policies or parties, while other groups support opposing policies or parties.

The Major Cleavages of Contemporary Slovenia

Slovene society has been burdened by deep cleavages, characteristic also of the larger states of which its territory was historically part. The dissolution of the Austro–Hungarian, Russian and Ottoman empires less than a hundred years ago solved many tensions in the larger region, but it also led to the creation of a number of new culturally very heterogeneous states greatly different in terms of economic development, such as Yugoslavia, Czechoslovakia and Italy (Lipset and Rokkan 1967). The tensions between the more and the less developed parts or between the new centres and the periphery persisted also after the Second World War when communism was established throughout the region. Certain ethnic groups and nations kept striving for domination over others, using alleged historical or ideological pretexts. In this light, recent developments in South-Eastern Europe are by no means unique.

The sudden conversion of the communist states to liberal democracy and market economy was itself a manifestation of gigantic contradictions and deeply rooted cleavages, which could not be accommodated by the former regimes. This dramatic turning point paved the way for a number of cleavages that are considered normal in democratic societies, some of them 'historical' cleavages or carry-overs from pre-communist and communist times. The abrupt, multi-faceted and sometimes violent transition process was to have a profound impact on the process of cleavage formation in Slovenia, which thus deviates somewhat from the mainstream Central European pattern.

Modern nation-building versus centralizing forces: Until 1991, Slovenia was part of larger nation states. The process of nation-building intensified in 19th century and coincided with similar processes in other European countries. Slovenian culture and national identity were especially important because of the resistance to Germanization (Fink Hafner and Lajh 2003). The Slovenian cultural movement took on distinct political connotations with the 'Programme for United Slovenia' of 1848. Slovenia entered the state of South Slaves (known as the Kingdom of Serbs, Croatians and Slovenians in 1918–29, subsequently as the Kingdom of Yugoslavia) as an ethnically homogenous entity, but with few political experiences.

After the Second World War, Yugoslavia gave the constituent republics some political autonomy in accordance with the federal socialist system (Fink Hafner and Lajh 2003). But by the 1980s, Slovenia's position within the federal state had become increasingly difficult. The centralizing forces, controlled by the Communist Party of Yugoslavia, were resisting demands for democratization, trying to preserve power, which was largely outside of the formal representative institutions (the two-chamber Federal Assembly of Yugoslavia). The attempts to increase the competences of the central institutions to the detriment of the prerogatives of the republics (change of the federal constitution in 1988, etc.) along with the incursions into the Yugoslav financial system by the Republic of Serbia (unauthorized printing of money) were infuriating the Slovenes, who were net contributors to the federal budget. Afraid as they were that the principle of equality of nations was about to be discarded and democratization to be thwarted, Slovenes became more and more convinced that stepping out of the federation was the only rational solution. An overwhelming majority of Slovenes (88.5 per cent) came out in favour of independence in a referendum held on 23 December 1990; only 5 per cent voted against. The outcome testifies to Slovenia's ethnic homogeneity, which goes a long way towards accounting for the relative ease with which Slovenia managed to sever its ties with the former Yugoslav federation. As a result, the nationalist cleavage is virtually absent from Slovenian politics today.

The early steps towards democratization (the passing of the amendments to the constitution of Slovenia on 29 September 1989), the preparations for the plebiscite and the rather elegant separation from the rest of Yugoslavia were to a large extent the result of close cooperation between old communist reformers and the emerging opposition based on the assumption that old resentments must be buried, at least for the time being. The two elite groups formally changed places in April 1990, after the first democratic elections since the Second World War, when the reformed Communist party went into opposition (Zajc 1997). This spelled the demise of the Yugoslav federal state and the beginning of independent political life for Slovenes and other nationalities. It could be argued that the tensions between modern nation-building and the outmoded socialist state had been resolved and become part of history. However, as was soon to be demonstrated, democracy provided new opportunities for old cleavages, which had been repressed but not eliminated by the defunct federal state.

Nation-building versus centralizing forces is a typical historical cleavage, which does not exist in Slovenia any more. Slovenia entered the process of Yugoslav disintegration as a very homogeneous society. There was virtually no resistance to independent statehood because this cleavage was perceived as as a resolved, historical, cleavage. In Slovenia it is impossible to find a political party opposing Slovenian independence.

Cosmopolitan versus national orientation: In Slovenia, political and economic independence was generally perceived as a shift from the Balkans with its ethnic conflicts and Byzantine traditions back to Central Europe with its democratic values and cultural heritage. Independence was also seen as a way of accelerating modernization and integration with international organizations. The country is almost completely devoid of tensions along the cosmopolitan–nationalist continuum. The only 'resistance' is to be found among sympathizers of the small Slovene National Party, representing about 4 per cent of the voters (even among the voters of this party a great many are in favour of the EU). An overwhelming majority of Slovenes came out in favour of joining the European Union and a majority of them also called for NATO membership even at the height of the recent military conflict between the United States and Iraq. The two referenda thus provided solid evidence of Slovenia's commitment to both international organizations.

In December 2002, when Slovenia completed its negotiations with the EU at the Copenhagen Summit Meeting of the European Council and especially on 23 March 2003 when the EU referendum was held, Slovenia finished an important chapter of its independent history (Fink Hafner and Lajh 2003). Slovenia is joining transnational organizations, which are likely to have a profound impact on the social environment of its citizens. With 89.84 per cent of the voters in favour of EU membership in the referendum, European integration is hardly an issue of contention in Slovenia. And with 66.08 per cent of the voters in favour of NATO membership, NATO does not seem to be much of an issue either. Both referenda were held on the same day, and the turnout was quite high (60 per cent) by Central and East European standards.[1]

This commitment to European integration and trans-Atlantic cooperation runs somewhat counter to other attitudes prevalent in Slovenia. Slovenes, proud of their economic achievements even in the period of communism, are only cautiously accepting foreign capital, and oppose the selling out of Slovene banks and companies to foreigners. The approval rating of the EU is therefore likely to drop as the negative consequences become apparent, a pattern familiar from other newcomers to the union. Slovenia is, for example, scheduled to become a net contributor to the EU budget in the near future.[2]

Cosmopolitan versus national orientation is a very weak cleavage in Slovenia. Resistance to Slovenian integration into the EU is almost non-existent. The small Slovenian National Party is the only EU sceptic party in parliament. NATO membership is a somewhat more controversial issue. The Slovenian National Party and the Youth Party of Slovenia are both against NATO membership; other parties are in favour.

The *socio-economic cleavage* is understandably one of the major cleavages in a country still marked by the transition from plan to market. The change was initiated in the early 1990s, and it had the effect of an earthquake in a society where economic life had been governed by the ideological principles of workers' self-government. The transition to market economy was unexpectedly smooth and Slovenia was spared the deep recession that had been anticipated, when it was cut off from the market in other parts of the former Yugoslav federation. But economic performance nevertheless left a great deal to be desired. The transition to market economy was accompanied by a gradual dismantling of the socialist welfare system. The right to work was no longer guaranteed by the state; and on top of this, pensions were cut back. The pensioners responded to this challenge by forming an interest party of their own.

The transition to market economy paved the way for economic polarization. There was a small minority of extremely rich people, who had accumulated great wealth in an extremely short time through dubious privatization schemes by taking advantage of their privileged position within the former political or economic *nomenklatura*. The economic transition of Slovenia did not produce a vast majority of poor people as in some other post-communist countries, but it certainly separated the 'winners' from the 'losers'. Those who somehow could not adapt to the new economic order ended up in the latter category.

The distribution of resources in society and the role of the state as equalizer are typical left-right items. In Slovenia, the liberal part of the spectrum is predominant, as demonstrated by the dominant position of Liberal Democracy of Slovenia in all government coalitions after 1992.

Tensions between the *secular state and the Church* have a long tradition in the lands of the Slovenes, where Catholicism has been the dominant religion since the end of the 16th century when Habsburg rulers suppressed Protestantism. Secularization and separation of state and religion notwithstanding, the Catholic Church kept playing an important role in Slovene political life, not least as a defender of the national interest. The Church also served as an important channel of promotion for young Slovenes who had few career opportunities in other professions or, for that matter, corporations; the nobility was predominantly of foreign extraction. The occupation of all Slovene land by Nazi and Fascist forces at the beginning of the Second World War put an end to the traditional role of the Catholic Church. During the war, it took a most dubious position towards the national liberation movement, led by the national communists, and even helped right-wing conservatives to work out agreements with the occupiers in order to crush the communist guerrilla. After the war severe repressive measures were taken against the Catholic Church. Presenting itself as the stronghold of the anti-communist opposition, the Church remains the only religious organization with substantial political influence. But it has not benefited from the same kind of religious revival that has characterized some of the other Catholic countries in the region. Tensions still run high between the advocates of a strict separation between Church and state and those who argue for the Church to take an active part in policy making. The state-church cleavage is readily apparent in a number of current issues of contention like the reintroduction of religious instruction, abortion, national conciliation and even certain matters of land restitution. A staunch defender of conservative values and the traditional way of life it is frequently meeting fierce opposition from anti-clerical groups within civil society, while the state is trying to play a neutral role.

The attitude towards the Catholic Church and its role in political life is one of the most persistent cleavages in Slovenian society and it is also reflected by the party system. Both conservative parties (SLS and NSI) – and to some extent the SDS – argue for the Church to play an active role in public (and political) life. The SNS, the ZLSD and DESUS adopt the opposing point of view, while the LDS positions itself somewhere in between these two camps.

Ideological cleavage (anti-communism versus smooth adaptation of the former structures and cadres): The roots of anti-communism go back to the period before the First World War. In accordance with conservative encyclicas, the Catholic Church came out against all kinds of reform. Communism of the Soviet type was in the inter-war period rejected by the established political elite and by the vast majority of Slovenes, regardless of political affiliation. In early 1941, a small group of radical communists gained prominence by taking the lead in organizing partisan resistance against the Nazi and Fascist occupiers. The antagonism between leftist adherents of resistance and fervent anti-communists supported by the Church leadership increased to the point that the anti-communists opted for collaboration with the occupiers in an attempt to crush the communist guerrilla (Prunk 1997). The dominant role of the communists within the resistance movement facilitated the communist takeover after the war. A Soviet-style system was introduced along with one innovation – the reorganization of the former unitary Yugoslav state on federative principles.

It was only after the break with Stalin that the communist leaders (Yugoslav and Slovene) eased their grip on society and introduced reforms that brought decentralization and self-management, though under the strict guidance of Communist party.

The collapse of communism in the early 1990s provided the left/right cleavage with additional impetus. There is in fact a deep value-based gap between the two political camps. There are those who emphasize the totalitarian character of the communist system and seek for at least symbolic acknowledgement of its unlawfulness, calling also for the exclusion of former communist cadres from the policy making process. And on the opposite end of the spectrum, there are those who refuse to deal with the past and favour an easy adaptation of the former structures and cadres to the new circumstances and institutions (Fink Hafner 2002). This cleavage is of crucial importance in contemporary Slovenia. Its resilience and intensity make Slovenia unique in the post-communist context, and it provides structure to the Slovene party system.

These different attitudes towards the past have manifested themselves on several occasions – in the mid-1990s in the public and parliamentary debates about the unlawfulness of the communist system and about national conciliation (no agreement was reached) and in the parliamentary discussion in 2002–03 about the arrangement of the graveyards of those people who were killed without due process of law after the Second World War.

This cleavage contributed to the formation of the Christian-Democratic Party, a bearer of Christian values and a representative of the anti-communist heritage, and it has served as an ideological watershed in contemporary Slovene party politics. It is one of the most visible cleavages in Slovenia with a decisive impact on the formation of party clusters. It is a historical cleavage, but it remains unresolved and influences all the other cleavages, most notably the state-Church cleavage.

Urban versus rural: The polycentric structure of Slovenia and the relative small territory serve as obstacles against the emergence of a centre-periphery cleavage. It exists, but in a weak form and particularly after the 1990s (Fink Hafner 2001). It may also be mentioned that the current system of local government goes towards defusing the conflict potential of the centre-periphery cleavage by allowing for the establishment of municipalities according to the desires of citizens in communities of 3000–300,000 inhabitants.

On the other hand, there are pronounced differences between agrarian and urban interests. The government has not quite satisfied the interests of the farming community, even though it got a fair deal within the EU.[3] Rural interests clash with state interests or the interests of some political parties. The countryside is expressing unease about the influence of urban communities on certain policies affecting the countryside. For the time being, there are open conflicts about the middle-level administrative organization (read: the establishment of 'regions') between those who would like to influence decision-making and those who would prefer the state to determine the boundaries without consulting regional interest groups.

The SLS, which developed out of the Slovenian Peasants Alliance (*Slovenska kmečka zveza*), remains the only party representing agrarian interests. It was particularly active during the negotiations on EU accession.

Ecology (environmentalism) versus economy: Protection of the environment is one of the most important issues in modern societies. Ecological issues are modern post-industrial (post-material) issues, which presuppose a high level of economic development. Protection of the environment and economic development are to some extent conflicting goals. Environment protection is always costly. The ecological movement had a particularly high profile as an advocate of social change in the 1980s (Fink Hafner 1992). The greens had objectives that were neutral enough to be tolerated by the socialist regime, but they have lost momentum and been reduced to political insignificance in post-communist Slovenia. The cleavage has basically disappeared from public debate. But environmental protection nevertheless remains a sensitive issue, and the cleavage may very well reappear as a strong cleavage in the future (Boh 2003b). For the time being, though, it exists only in latent form.

The generational cleavage: The impact of political generation is readily apparent in Slovenia. The quick economic transformation of the early 1990s spelled problems for the young as well as the old. But the young were in a much better position to take advantage of the opportunities that opened up with the transition from plan to market. The young have generally accepted the new economic order; they have adapted to individualism and opted for a new life style. The upper age cohorts tend to cling to the values of solidarity and collectivism, which prevailed under communism, and some of the senior citizens are nostalgic about the 'good old days' when all social relations were arranged under the patronage of the state. The generational gap is in fact compounded by an unfavourable demographic structure. A high standard of living and a well-developed health care system have increased life expectancy to the point that there are fewer and fewer in the labour force to provide for a steadily increasing number of old-age pensioners. This process has actually been going on since the 1980s.

As already mentioned, the generation gap carries over into party politics. The Party of Retired People sets out to improve the worsening lot of the old, while the Youth Party of Slovenia tries to mobilize the young, who tend to be politically apathetic.

The Response of the Parties to the Cleavages

Slovene society is divided along several axes. There are historical cleavages, latent cleavages and there are cleavages reflecting the underlying social differentiation. Right now communism–anticommunism, traditionalism–modernism and central ideological orientations (conservative, liberal, neutral) stand out as the most important social cleavages in terms of party system developments (Fink Hafner 2001). But Slovenia is still young as an independent state and the cleavage pattern may change over time.

Cleavages are not necessarily translated into party structures. Some cleavages have an obvious impact on party formation and development; others do not. Parties are not 'prisoners' of cleavages, but play an autonomous role in cleavage mediation and policy-making as well as in the general structuring of the political space (Sartori 1968). New political parties are not only expressions of political cleavages but also agents for them. Whether conflictual or consensual, party strategies, ideologies and orientations may influence the way particular cleavages are transmitted into the party system. When communism collapsed, the political elites in the countries in transition (Hungary, Slovenia, Poland, the Czech Republic, and Slovakia) were divided on the issue of how political conflict was to be structured. Some leaders tried to force visions of past cleavages on a profoundly changed electorate (Márkus 1996), thereby neglecting the actual underlying cleavage structure. These differences are still more articulated in some countries than in others (Zajc 1997).

The transformation of cleavages is determined by a variety of intermediary variables, such as the traditions of political participation, the openness of the political system, and the transparency of political processes and prevalence of democratic, as opposed to autocratic, procedures. A cost-benefit evaluation also comes into play – is it better to attempt to gain individual representation or to join an established political actor? The issue of majority versus proportional representation has strong implications: does electoral victory give a party a disproportionate share of the parliamentary seats, enabling it to bring about major structural changes? The electoral framework also affects the composition of institutions and government formation. Of importance also is the ability of political parties and individual politicians to introduce new alternatives. If they lose the elections, they will set out to formulate or politicize issues likely to attract a majority of voters (Riker 1986).

After the transition from communism, new political parties were formed and shaped within an extremely short period of time, and it was only in parliament that they were tested (Olson 1994). The subsequent fragmentation of many of the pre-transition political organizations, and the emergence of completely new formations, testify to the tentative character of many of these parties. The post-communist leaders and cadres have had limited experience of competitive party politics and have often failed to evaluate correctly the gains and costs of alternative standpoints; at times they even act in contradiction of their declared goals. The post-transition parties and party systems were, in many cases, created 'from above' by political elites. They were weakly defined and often unstable, only imperfectly reflecting the divisions inherited from the socialist regime including the socio-economic and socio-political divisions resulting from the large-scale transformation process.

The latest challenge the political parties have had to face is the process of European integration which has emerged as a major issue for national political parties. The political parties of Central and Eastern Europe will have to blend into a European political framework. They will have to coexist in a multi-level polity in which decisions about further EU integration will affect virtually all of their established (national) economic and political concerns (Marks and Wilson 2000).

The communism versus anti-communism cleavage remains one of the most salient political line of conflict among parties and voters alike. We have seen that this cleavage has deep roots in the history of the Slovene lands, but for the time being it basically revolves around attitudes towards the communist past. Slovenia has a number of political parties with historical and organizational ties to the political institutions of the old regime, pitted against new political parties extolling anti-communist values and calling for the removal of the old *nomenklatura* (Fink Hafner 2002). These two party clusters define the core of Slovenian political space.[4] There are some other parties as well, but as for now they are weak and not likely to gain parliamentary representation. The 'old political parties' favour incremental social change. They stress values of the anti-Nazi and anti-Fascist resistance and call for the political ambitions of the Catholic Church to be curtailed. They see Slovenia's transformation into a democracy mainly as a continuation of the social-political changes of the 1980s. The 'new' political parties' advocate the exclusion of ex-communist cadres from the policy-making process. They are favourably disposed towards the Catholic Church; they condemn the totalitarian communist regime and stress the importance of large-scale privatization.

The strong desire of the 'new' parties to recreate a strong anti-communist bloc suggests that the tensions along the communism versus anti-communism continuum will persist for yet some time. Internal strife has so far thwarted these attempts, but the anti-communists bloc is nevertheless clearly visible as brought out by the presidential elections of 2002. Constitutional provisions prevented the incumbent from running for a third term, and for the first time the 'new' parties had a real chance to win the presidential elections.

It was generally felt that party labels might have a negative impact on the voters; and many candidates therefore refrained from pledging allegiance to either of the two camps and chose to run as independents. This did not prevent the parliamentary parties from having preferred choices in the first round of elections; and by the time of the second round, the two clusters of parties had crystallized very clearly. The 'new' parties of the so-called Coalition Slovenia (*Koalicija Slovenija*) – NSI, SDS and SLS – supported Barabara Brezigar, while the 'old' parties endorsed the candidature of Janez Drnovšek, the leader of the strongest parliamentary party (LDS) and former member and president of the ex-Yugoslav collective leadership. The latter came out on the winning side with a comfortable margin – 56.5 per cent as opposed to 43.5 per cent – but Barbara Brezigar was nevertheless a strong opponent. Together 'old' and 'new' parties account for the lion's share of Slovenia's party space. This is the message conveyed by the recent presidential elections and, for that matter, by time series data on Slovenian voting behaviour (*Figure 10.1*). The graph also provides data on another cluster of parties already mentioned in passing – the residual category 'other parties'.

Figure 10.1: Share of votes for clusters of 'new' and 'old' political parties in Slovenia, 1990–2000 (%)

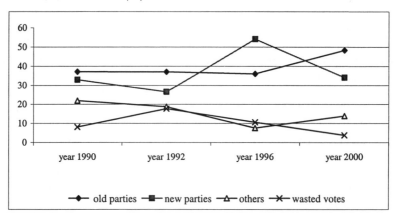

Source: Fink Hafner and Boh (2002).

The residual category, including the SNS, DESUS and the SMS, account for a very limited share of the political space. Representing only fractions of the electorate, these parties are constantly at risk of losing their parliamentary representation; and to the extent that they do lose their seats in parliament, they run the risk of disappearing altogether from the arena of party politics just like the Democrats in 1996. All things considered, a vote for 'other parties' might very well be a wasted vote.

*

The ideological cleavage is not the only cleavage in Slovenia, but it dominates all others cleavages. The attitudes towards the Catholic Church coincide with the ideological cleavage. Anti-communism goes hand in hand with favourable attitudes towards the Catholic Church and the other way around. But with this major exception, the clusters are far from homogeneous. There is a traditional left-right division within each cluster. Similar comments apply to other dimensions of conflict, especially religion-secular, and liberal-social and labour. Theoretically this might open up for coalitions across the ideological divide, but the strength of the ideological divide is such that crosscutting coalitions rarely materialize. The Liberal Party represents the only deviation from this rule. It has managed to attract government coalition partners from both ends of the continuum, pitting communists and anti-communists against each other.

The Slovene party system may thus be seen to fluctuate between extreme simplicity and extreme complexity – simplicity on account of the dominant position of the ideological cleavage and complexity by virtue of the overlapping and crosscutting secondary cleavage. It is therefore not without qualifications that we embark on an attempt at classifying Slovene political parties into the categories familiar from the international literature on party families.

Party families

The Slovene political parties may tentatively be placed according to the traditional left–right typology.

Table 10.1: Share of votes of party families (%)

Year of elections	Left-wing parties, reformed and new ZLSD, SDS	Pro-liberal, centrist parties LS, DS, ZS, LDS	Right-wing parties SKD, SLS, NSi	Other parties
1990	30.5	33.8	25.4	
1992	19.7	32.4	23.1	10.5 (SNS)
1996	25.1	27.1	29.0	7.5 (SNS, DESUS)
2000	27.9	36.2	15.3	14.9 (SNS, DESUS, SMS)

Sources: Fink Hafner and Boh (2002); Zajc (1997).

The left-wing party family

The United List of Social Democrats (ZLSD) and the Social Democrats of Slovenia (SDS) belong squarely on the statist side of the distributive dimension, which in a sense reflects the traditional capital/labour cleavage. An heir to the reformist wing of the Slovene Communist Party, the ZLSD can take credit for contributing towards Slovenia's independence, by defending national sovereignty against the centralist pressure of the Yugoslav communist leadership dominating the institutions of the former federation. Nevertheless, it remains a *nomenklatura* party; it has a heterogeneous core electorate, and it forfeited the chance to take positions on the most urgent transitional problems. Its share of votes declined from 1990 to 2000 from 17.28 per cent to 12.07 per cent (the lowest point was in 1996, when the party got just 9.03 per cent).

The Social Democrats of Slovenia (SDS) was formed as a socialist alternative without ties to the former regime of which it has remained very critical. The SDS has set out to establish close cooperation with the two main right-wing parties (Coalition Slovenia). The SDS has slowly stabilized its electoral base. In 1990, it gained 7.39 per cent of the votes, and in 1992 merely 3.34 per cent; but in 1996 and 2000, it obtained 16.13 per cent and 15.80 per cent, respectively. Though claiming to be ideologically detached, the two social democratic parties are both in favour of increased financial transfers to underprivileged social groups, and of subsidies to financially troubled large enterprises.

Pro-liberal and centrist parties
Liberal Democracy of Slovenia (LDS) is located somewhat towards the market end of the distributive dimension and clearly on the libertarian side of the procedural dimension. The party has its organizational roots in the socialist youth organization of the former Yugoslav federation, and is therefore thought of as part of the 'old' parties. In the first democratic elections in 1990 the party got 14.49 per cent of the votes and remained in opposition. In the 1992 elections, the Liberal Democratic Party won the largest share of votes, and it repeated this feat in 1996, following a merger with two parties of similar orientation, the Democrats (DS), and the Greens (ZS) in 1994. In the last elections in 2000 LDS even improved its result from 1996 (27.1 per cent), getting 36.21 per cent of the votes. The new Democratic Party, established by the group of dissidents who opposed the merger, failed to gain parliamentary representation in 1996.

The LDS promotes individualistic and cosmopolitan values; it has been a promoter of EU integration and NATO membership, and an advocate of sound economic and financial policies. Catering to the secular intelligentsia and young optimistic entrepreneurs and managers, the LDS rules out populism and adopts a pragmatic and unbiased approach towards the communist heritage.

Right-wing parties
There are two parties on the right/traditional side of the Slovenian political spectrum – New Slovenia (NSI) and Slovenian People's Party (SLS). In the 1990s, there were serious attempts to form a united party based on the traditional and Christian values of the pre-war era. Two parties dominated this part of the political space: the Slovene Christian Democrats (SKD) and Slovenian People's Party (SLS). On 15 April 2000 these parties actually merged into the Slovenian People's Party (SLS + SKD). But the new party

disintegrated shortly before the parliamentary elections a few months later on and gave rise to two successor parties: the SLS, a self-proclaimed heir of both founding parties, and New Slovenia (NSI) vying for the slot previously occupied by the former SKD. The NSI strongly supports traditional values and defends the position of Catholic Church in society. Though clearly pro-European, it has brought some of the unresolved issues from the pre-war and post-war eras into the political agenda.

Compared to New Slovenia, the People's Party (SLS) remains a more modern party, accepting practical compromises. It is pro-European like all the major Slovene parties, but sensitive to the problems of Slovene farmers within the European Union. The NSI and the SLS see eye to eye on issues of privatization, and like the SDS they have been known to express unease about the influence of the *nomenklatura* on the transition processes.

Other parties

Conventional wisdom tells us that East European party systems are in the process of consolidating. The number of parties is getting smaller and the cleavage structure is getting more and more simplified (Jackiewicz and Jakiewicz 1996). If so, Slovenia is somewhat of a deviant case. The threshold for parliamentary represention has been increased from 3 to 4 per cent, but that has not prevented new political entrepreneurs, competing on dimensions other than communism versus anti-communism, from making it into parliament. There are in fact three such parties in the parliament elected in 2000.

The Slovene National Party, which was very successful in the 1992 elections, suffered a defeat in 1996 and only just succeeded in making it past the 4 per cent threshold in 2000. It has been promoting strongly nationalist views on citizenship and relations with the neighbouring countries. It has called for rejection of the demands by the Catholic Church for restitution of nationalized Church property, and come out against Slovenia joining the EU and NATO.

The generation cleavage paved the way for parties catering to specific age cohorts. The Party of Retired People (DESUS) reflects the profound division between the oldest generation and the rest of the population. The pension system, introduced more than 30 years ago, was built on the assumption of an unchanging demographic structure and proved untenable in the long run. The reform of the pension system made good sense from a macro-economic point of view, but left many old in a vulnerable social position.

The Youth party of Slovenia (SMS) is also catering for a specific age group. Established prior to the elections in 2000, it advocates the rights and interests of the young, particularly students. It is in favour of EU integration, but against NATO membership.[5]

Figure 10.2: Political cleavages and party competition: party positions on the main axes of party competition

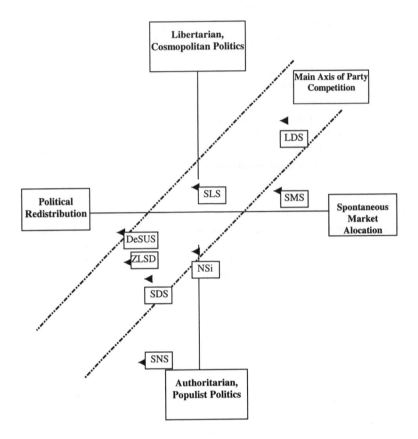

Figure 10.2 represents an attempt to position the Slovene political parties within a space defined by two axes: political redistribution versus spontaneous market allocation and cosmopolitan versus authoritarian. The dominant position of the ideological cleavage in Slovene politics makes this a complicated task. The strong pro-EU sentiments shared by all major parties, regardless of their respective positions on the cosmopolitan-authoritarian scale, complicate things further. The map of Slovenian party space (*Figure 10.2*) should therefore been seen as intuitive and tentative.

Conclusions

Communism versus anti-communism remains the crucial cleavage in Slovene politics after 13 years of transition. Slovene parties will eventually have to relate to the emerging European party system, where the left-right dimension plays an important role. The European party space is also affected by yet another cleavage likely to gain prominence as Europe moves further towards integration: defence of the nation state versus supranational integration (de Haro 2003). It is still too early to say how the Slovene party system will cope with these challenges. All we can say is that old cleavages do not always disappear even when the underlying grievances appear to be resolved.

NOTES

1. Both referenda were held on 23 March 2003. The turnout for the EU referendum was 60.44 per cent and for the NATO referendum 60.43 per cent. The share of 'yes' votes was 89.84 per cent in the EU referendum and 66.08 per cent in the NATO referendum. For more detailed information see www.gov.si/rvk.
2. For more details about the Slovenian position in the EU budgetary system, see also *Slovenija in Evropska unija* ('Slovenia and the European Union'), *Urad vlade za informiranje*, Ljubljana (2003). Available at www2.gov.si.
3. The share of peasants in Slovenia is 6–7 per cent of the population; and the contribution of agriculture, forestry and fishery to the GDP is 3.1 per cent (Statistical Yearbook 2002, Statistical Office of the Republic of Slovenia, Ljubljana; *Analiza gospodarskih gibanj za Slovenijo v letu 2000 in napovedi za obdobje 2001–2003, pomladno poročilo 2001*, UMAR, Ljubljana. Available also at www.sigov.si).
4. The old parties – LDS and ZLSD – developed out of the transformed socio-political organizations of the old regime. The new parties – SDS, SLS, NSi and SKD – were once part of the opposition to the old regime.
5. Declaration of the Youth Party of Slovenia (SMS) on Slovenia joining NATO, 21 January 2003 (www. sms.si, 18.6.2003). Statement of the President of the SMS on the EU accession referendum.

REFERENCES

Analiza gospodarskih gibanj za Slovenijo v letu 2000 in napovedi za obdobje 2001–2003 (2001), UMAR, Ljubljana.
Boh, Tomaž (2003a), 'Varstvo okolja–privilegij bogatih?!', in Martin Klainšek, ed., *Ena znanost– Raziskovalno delo podiplomskih študentov v Sloveniji*, Društvo mladih raziskovalcev Slovenije, Ljubljana.
—— (2003b), 'EU Environmental Policy – Institutional View: The Case of Slovenia', Organising for Enlargement. A Challenge for Member States and Candidate Countries, *II Report on the EU's Fifth Framework Programme*, HPSE-CT-2001-00083.
Fink Hafner, Danica (1992), 'Nova družbena gibanja – subjekti politične inovacije', *Znanstvena knjižnica*, Fakulteta za družbene vede, Ljubljana.
—— (2001), 'Politične stranke', Fakulteta za družbene vede, Ljubljana.
—— (2002), 'Prevzemanje oblasti v kontinuiranem demokratičnem prehodu', in Danica Fink Hafner and Tomaž Boh, eds, *Parlamentarne volitve 2000*, Fakulteta za družbene vede, Ljubljana.
—— and Tomaž Boh, eds (2002), *Parlamentarne volitve 2000*, Fakulteta za družbene vede, Ljubljana.
—— and Tomaž Boh (2003), *Predsedniške volitve 2003*, Fakulteta za družbene vede, Ljubljana.
—— and Damjan Lajh (2003), 'Managing Europe from Home: the Europeanisation of the Slovenian Core Executive', Fakulteta za družbene vede, Ljubljana.

de Haro, Alfonso Egea (2003), 'The European Policy Space: Does Ideology Reduce or Foster Cleavages', Paper proposal prepared for the ECPR Joint Session, Edinburgh, 28 March–2 April 2003.

Jackiewicz, Irena and Zbigniew Jackiewicz (1996), 'The Polish Parliament in Transition: The Search for a Model', in Attila Agh and Gabriella Ilonszki, eds, *Parliaments and Organized Interests: Second Steps*, Budapest, HCDS.

Kitschelt, Herbert (1992), 'The Formation of the Party Systems in East Central Europe', *Politics & Society*, No. 1.

Lawson, Kay (1999), 'Cleavages, Parties and Voters', in Kay Lawson, Andrea Römmele and Georgi Karasimeonov, *Cleavages, Parties and Voters: Studies from Bulgaria, the Czech Republic, Hungary, Poland and Romania*, Westport, Connecticut, Praeger.

Lewis, Paul G. (2003), 'The impact of the Enlargement of the European Union on Central European Party Systems', Paper prepared for the 19th Conference of the International Political Science Association, Durban 29 June–4 July, 2003.

Lipset, Seymour Martin and Stein Rokkan (1967), 'Cleavage Structures, Party Systems and Voter Alignment: An Introduction', in Seymour Martin Lipset and Stein Rokkan, eds, *Party Systems and Voter Alignments: Cross National Perspective*, New York, The Free Press.

Marks, Gary and Carole J. Willson (2000), 'The Past in the Future: A Cleavage Theory of Party Response to European Integration', *British Journal of Political Science*, No. 30, 433–59.

Márkus, György G. (1996), 'Cleavage Dynamics and Party System in Hungary', Paper presented at the Third Regional Conference of the Central European Political Science Association on Conflicts and Consensus, Bled (Slovenia), 22–23 November, 1996.

Olson, David M. (1994), 'The New Parliaments of new Democracies: the Experience of the Federal Assembly of the Czech and Slovak Federal Republic', in Attila Agh, ed., *The Emergence of East Central European Parliaments: The First Steps*, Budapest, HCDS.

Prunk, Janko (1997), 'Kratka zgodovina Slovenije', Založba Grad, Ljubljana.

Riker, William (1986), *The Art of Manipulation*, New Haven, CT, Yale University Press.

Römmele, Andrea (1999), 'Cleavage Structures and Party Systems in East and Central Europe', in Kay Lawson, Andrea Römmele and Georgi Karasimeonov, *Cleavages, Parties and Voters: Studies from Bulgaria, the Czech Republic, Hungary, Poland and Romania*, Westport, Connecticut, Praeger.

Sartori, Giovanni (1968), 'Political Development and Political Engineering', *Public Policy*, No. 17.

Slovenija in Evropska unija ('Slovenia and the European Union') (2003), Urad vlade za informiranje, Ljubljana.

Statistical Yearbook (2002), Statistical Office of Republic of Slovenia, Ljubljana.

Zajc, Drago (1997), 'The Changing Political Systems', in Danica Fink Hafner and J.R. Robbinson, eds, *Making a new Nation: The Formation of Slovenia*, Dartmouth, Aldershot.

—— (2002), 'Četrte demokratične volitve v Sloveniji', in Danica Fink Hafner and Thomaž Boh, eds, *Parlamentarne voilitve 2000*, Fakulteta za družbene vede, Ljubljana.

—— (2003), 'Predsedniške volitve 2002 in pomen volilnih pravil', in Danica Fink Hafner and Thomaž Boh, eds, *Presidential Elections in Slovenia 2002*, Fakulteta za družbene vede, Ljubljana.

APPENDIX 10.1: ELECTION RESULTS

NATIONAL ASSEMBLY ELECTIONS[*]

Party / list[**]	1990		1992		1996		2000	
	%	seats	%	seats	%	seats	%	Seats
LDS (Liberal Democracy of Slovenia)	14.5	39	23.5	22	27.0	25	36.2	34
SDS (Social Democrats of Slovenia)	7.4	17	3.3	4	16.1	16	15.8	14
ZLSD (United List of Social Democrats)	17.3	36	13.6	14	9.0	9	12.0	11
SKD (Slovenian Christian Democrats)	12.9	23	14.5	15	9.6	10		
SLS (Slovene People's Party)	12.6	32	8.7	10	19.4	19		
SLS + SKD (United party)							9.5	9
NSI (New Slovenia)							8.8	8
SNS (Slovene National Party)			10.0	12	3.2	4	4.4	4
ZS (The Greens)	8.8	17	3.7	5	failed	failed	failed	failed
DeSUS (Party of Retired Parsons)					4.3	5	5.2	4
DS (The Democrats)	9.5	30	5.0	6	failed	failed	failed	failed
LS (Liberal Party)	2.5	4	failed	failed	failed	failed		
SMS (Youth party of Slovenia)							4.3	4
SOS (Slovenian Craftsmen Party)	3.5	3						
SSS (Socialist party of Slovenia)	5.4	5						
Nationalities[***]		6		2		2		2
TOTAL		240		90		90		90
DATE	April		10 December		10 November		15 October	
TURNOUT %	83.3		85.8		73.7		70.3	

Source: Fink Hafner and Boh (2002); Zajc (2002).

[*] The 1990 elections were to the three-chamber Assembly of Slovenia (as instituted by the 1974 Constitution of the Socialist Republic of Slovenia) with 80 deputies in each chamber. Only the deputies to the Socio-Political Chamber were elected on the basis of a proportional system. The elections in 1992, 1996 and 2000 were to the one chamber, 90-member National Assembly (Constitution of the RS, adopted in 1991).
[**] Some parties changed their names or merged with other parties. In the table just recent names of the parties or their successors are listed.
[***] Seats reserved for the Magyar and Italian minorities.

Elections 1990 – Chairman of the Presidency of the Republic of Slovenia

Candidate	Share of Votes % 1st round	Share of Votes % 2nd round
Marko Demšar	10.4	
Ivan Kramberger	18.5	
Milan Kučan	44.4	58.6
Jože Pučnik	26.6	41.4
TURNOUT %		

Source: Fink Hafner and Boh (2003).

Elections 1992 – President of the Republic of Slovenia

Candidate	Share of Votes % 1st round	Share of Votes % 2nd round
Ivan Bizjak	21.1	-----
Stanislav Buser	1.9	-----
Jelko Kacin	7.3	-----
Milan Kučan	63.9	-----
Darja LAvtižar-Bebler	1.8	-----
Ljubo Sirc	1.5	-----
France Tomšič	0.6	-----
Alenka Žagar-Slana	1.7	-----
TURNOUT %		

Source: Fink Hafner and Boh (2003).

Elections 1997 – President of the Republic of Slovenia

Candidate	Share of Votes % 1st round	Share of Votes % 2nd round
Jožef Bernik	9.5	-----
Marjan Cerar	7.0	-----
Bogomir Kovač	2.7	-----
Milan Kučan	55.5	-----
Franc Miklavčič	0.5	-----
Anton Peršak	3.1	-----
Janez Podobnik	18.4	-----
Marjan Poljšk	3.2	-----
TURNOUT %		

Source: Fink Hafner and Boh (2003).

Elections 2002 – President of the Republic of Slovenia

Candidate	Share of Votes % 1st round	Share of Votes % 2nd round
France Arhar	7.6	
Anton Bebler	1.8	
Barbara Brezigar	30.8	43.5
France Bučar	3.2	
Jure Jurček Cekuta	0.5	
Gorazd Drevenšek	0.8	
Janez Drnovšek	44.4	56.5
Lev Kreft	2.2	
Zmago Jelinčič pl.	8.5	
TURNOUT %		

Source: Fink Hafner and Boh (2003); Zajc (2003).

Results of EU accession referendums in Slovenia and other ECE countries

	Turnout %	% voting yes
Lithuania	63	91
Slovenia	60	90
Poland	59	77
Czech Republic	55	77
Slovakia	52	92
Hungary	46	84

Source: Lewis (2003).

APPENDIX 10.2: GOVERNMENT COMPOSITION

Period	Prime Minister	Party of Prime Minister	Other parties	Majority status
16. 5. 1990 – 14. 5. 1992	Lojze Peterle	SKD	SKZ, ZS, SDSS, SDZ, LS	Surplus coalition 47 (80)*
14. 5. 1992 – 12. 1. 1993	Janez Drnovšek	LDS	SDSS, ZS, SSS, DS	Minority government 50 (80)*
12. 1. 1993 – 14. 3. 1994	Janez Drnovšek	LDS	SKD, ZLSD, SDSS	Grand coalition 55 (90)
14. 3. 1994 – 6. 4. 1994	Janez Drnovšek	LDS	SKD, ZLSD, SDSS + (Z-ESS, DS, SSS)	Grand coalition 63 (90)
6. 4. 1994 – 31. 1. 1996	Janez Drnovšek	LDS	SKD, ZLSD + (Z-ESS, DS, SSS)	Grand coalition 59 (90)
31. 1. 1996 – 27. 2. 1997	Janez Drnovšek	LDS	SKD + (Z-ESS, DS, SSS)	Minority government 42 (90)
27. 2. 1997 – 7. 6. 2000	Janez Drnovšek	LDS	SLS, DeSUS	Surplus coalition 49 (90)
7. 6. 2000 – 30. 11. 2000	Andrej Bajuk	SLS + SKD	SDS	Minimal winning coalition 45 (90)
30. 11. 2000 – 19. 12. 2002	Janez Drnovšek	LDS	ZLSD, SLS + SKD, DeSUS	Surplus coalition 58 (90)
19. 12. 2002 – present	Anton Rop	LDS	ZLSD, SLS, DeSUS	Surplus coalition 58 (90)

Sources: Zajc (1997); Fink Hafner and Boh (2003); Fink Hafner and Lajh (2003).

* Socio-Political Chamber of Socialist Assembly

APPENDIX 10.3: THE ELECTORAL SYSTEM

The National Assembly (*Državni zbor*), the highest legislative authority endowed with the sole power to enact laws, has 90 deputies. Deputies are elected for a four-year term at equal, direct and secret elections. Every citizen of the Republic of Slovenia who has reached the age of 18 by election day is eligible to vote and stand as a candidate. The Italian and Hungarian ethnic communities in Slovenia are entitled to one deputy each in the National Assembly elected by a preferential voting system. Members of autochthonous Italian and Hungarian national communities have double voting rights. According to the Electoral law of 1992 Slovenia has been divided into 8 constituencies, each of which electing 11 deputies (altogether 88 deputies). Constituencies are defined so as to make sure that deputies are elected by an approximately equal number of inhabitants. Each constituency is divided into 11 geographically divided electoral sub-districts. As a general rule, individual candidates stand in one constituency only, although in exceptional circumstances candidates may be allowed to stand in a maximum of two constituencies. Lists of candidates must contain a minimum of 6 and maximum of 11 candidates for each constituency. A political party nominates candidates in accordance with its own internal rules. Under certain circumstances a party may put up a list in every constituency. The law also permits the formation of pre-election coalitions, so that two or more parties present a joint list of candidates. Such a list, however, must have a single label. Voters may also nominate candidates by collection of signatures. In an individual constituency, a voters' list is accepted if supported by at least one hundred voters with residence in the constituency. Such a list can consist of a number of independent candidates or of one alone, in which case the candidate stands in all 11 sub-districts.

In July 2000, the following amendment to the constitution was adopted: 'Deputies, with the exception of representatives of national minorities, will be elected according to the principle of proportional representation with a 4 per cent electoral threshold for the National Assembly, giving voters a decisive influence on the allocation of mandates.' The Droop quotient has since been used for allocating mandates to constituencies. The new regulation enables each electoral unit to have 11 elected deputies since national lists are not allowed any more. Lists can get one direct mandate in an electoral unit for every 8.33 per cent of the vote. Additional mandates also belong to lists (Fink Hafner and Lajh 2003). For the election of ethnic representatives, special constituencies are formed in regions where the indigenous Italian and Hungarian communities live. These deputies are elected according to the majority principle.

The second chamber, the National Council (*Državni svet*) has 40 members elected for a five-year term. The council is an advisory body with 22 representatives of local interests and a total of 18 representatives of social, economic and professional interests. National Councilors are elected not on the ground of general, but of a special, right to vote, specified in separate law for each interest group. The persons who are entitled to vote and to be elected as members of the National Council are representatives of (a) employers, employees, farmers, small businesses, (b) representatives of professionals, and (c) non-profit activities.

All citizens of the Republic of Slovenia who have reached the age of 18 by election day, and who are not legally barred from voting, have the right to vote and to be elected as a member of the National Council. Foreigners have the right to vote under the same conditions as citizens of Slovenia i.e. if they are engaged in a relevant activity in Slovenia, but cannot themselves be elected members of the National Council.

18 representatives of functional interests are elected by electors who are themselves elected within interest groups and constituted electoral colleges. Four represent the employers and are elected by the chambers of commerce and the employers' associations; four represent the employees and are elected by unions and the associations or confederations of unions; two represent the farmers and are elected by professional farmers' organizations; one representative each for small businesses and independent professionals is elected by their respective representative professional organizations. The six representatives of non-profit organizations are elected as follows: one by the universities and colleges, one for the area of education by the professional teachers' organization; one for the area of sport and culture by the professional organization of cultural and sport workers; one for the field of medicine by the professional organization of medical workers and associations; and one for the area of social care by the

professional social workers' organization. Local communities elect 22 representatives, each in geographically-, historically- and interest-based constituencies.

The President of the Republic of Slovenia is elected in direct, general elections by secret ballot. The candidate who receives a majority of the valid votes cast is elected to office for a term of five years. The President may be elected for a maximum of two consecutive terms.

APPENDIX 10.4: THE CONSTITUTIONAL FRAMEWORK

The 1991 Constitution of Slovenia provides for the separation of church and state and freeing up of political and economic systems. A wide variety of rights and basic liberties are guaranteed with respect to nationality, race, sex, language, religion, political or other convictions, material state, birth, education, social status, or any other personal circumstance, including the right to conscientious objection (Fink Hafner and Lajh 2003).

The Slovene constitution opts for a system of 'incomplete bi-cameralism'. Notwithstanding a certain terminological vagueness in the constitution, the Slovene parliament consists of two chambers. The National Assembly (*Državni zbor*) with 90 deputies is the main chamber. The National Council (*Državni svet*), with 40 seats, is a second chamber with limited legislative competence.

The National Assembly convenes to regular sessions during the last week of each month during the spring and autumn terms, to enact laws and make other decisions. In addition, the National Assembly meets in extraordinary sessions. Bills may be proposed by Government, individual deputies or by a minimum of 5,000 voters signing a petition. The National Council may propose legislation by the National Assembly. The National Assembly debates a bill in three readings. When required due to exceptional circumstances, a bill may be adopted according to a fast-track procedure.

The National Assembly only makes its decisions when a majority of deputies are present, i.e. at least 46. Decisions are taken by a majority of votes of the deputies attending and voting. Individual decisions of exceptional importance (e.g. amendments to the Constitution) require qualified two-thirds majority of all the 90 deputies in the National Assembly. The President of the Republic of Slovenia proclaims laws no later than eight days after their enactment.

The Prime Minister is chosen by a majority of the deputies of the National Assembly in a secret ballot. If a majority of at least 46 deputies is not found even after a few attempts, the president shall dissolve the National Assembly and call new elections. Other Ministers are appointed and dismissed by the National Assembly upon the proposal of the Prime Minister. Ministers are collectively responsible for the work of the government and each Minister is responsible for his or her ministry. The government shall resign when a new National Assembly convenes after an election. The National Assembly may upon the motion of no fewer than 10 deputies and by the vote of a majority of all elected deputies, elect a new Prime Minister. The Prime Minister may himself or herself call for a vote of confidence. If such a vote is not carried by a majority of all elected deputies, the National Assembly must, within 30 days, either elect a new Prime Minister or express its confidence in the incumbent Prime Minister in a fresh vote. If this requirement is not fulfilled, the President of the Republic shall dissolve the National Assembly and call new elections.

According to the Constitution, the National Council may propose enactment of laws by the National Assembly (legislative initiative); communicate to the National Assembly opinions on all matters within its jurisdiction; require that the National Assembly reconsiders laws prior to their proclamation; require that referenda be called on matters regulated by law; call for parliamentary inquiries into matters of public importance; and address requests to the Constitutional Court. In a similar vain, the National Assembly may require the National Council to provide its opinion on a specific matter.

The President of the Republic is empowered to: (1) call elections for the National Assembly; (2) proclaim statutes; (3) appoint State officers in accordance with statute; (4) accredit Slovene ambassadors and consuls and accept the creditials of foreign diplomatic representatives; (5) sign international treaties and agreements; (6) grant pardons; (7) and confer state honours, decorations and honorary titles. In the event of the National Assembly being unable to convene due to a state of war or a state of emergency, the President may, at the request of the Government, issue decrees, which have the binding force and effect of statute.

11. Romania

William Crowther

Nearly all aspects of the post-communist political transition in Central and Eastern Europe have been subjects of contention and alternative explanation. Analysts have raised fundamental questions concerning the applicability of models of political behaviour developed in other political contexts to post-communist conditions. This is notably true of the nature and impact of cleavages in post-communist societies. Lipset and Rokkan's conceptualization of the role of abiding socially based ideological divisions has been a staple of political analysis of the developed democracies (Lipset and Rokkan 1967). Its applicability in the early post-communist context, however, has been sharply contested on a number of grounds, primarily relating either to the presumed lack of a social basis sufficient for ideological structuring, or to a presumed disjunction between elite competition and mass attitudes.[1]

If sceptics are correct, Romania should stand out as a strong case for the inapplicability of social cleavage analysis. Because of the peculiarities of its pre-communist and communist past, Romania is often taken as an arche-typical example of the post-communist countries' dearth of civil society. Given the absence of independent associations; a predominantly Orthodox rather than Protestant or Catholic religious tradition; for the most part Ottoman rather than Habsburg cultural influences; lack of economic development; highly repressive rather than reformist trends during the late communist period; and a near total absence of market forces during communism, Romania would seem to provide the strongest possible case for anyone wishing to argue that the social bases for political cleavages do not pertain in the immediate post-communist context. Conversely, if social cleavages do play a significant role in shaping the first decade of post-communism in Romania, one would be hard pressed to argue that they do not play a role in other post-communist countries.

Cleavages, as the term will be used here, are politically salient ideological divisions that are grounded in the social structure of a particular country. As such, they clearly comprise something more long lasting and deeply rooted than transitory policy disputes. Employing mass public opinion and elite survey data, this chapter argues that Romania has been characterized by a clear cleavage structure from a very early point in the transition.[2] Moreover, it will be shown that cleavages have played a crucial role in determining electoral competition and party political outcomes. First, the social and political background of the Romanian transition will be reviewed in order to better assess the source and nature of post-communist ideological divisions. The character of political cleavages in the society will then be examined, and the impact of cleavages on party competition during the post-communist transition will be assessed.

Precursors to Transition in Romania

Like neighbouring South Eastern European countries, Romania has confronted serious obstacles across the course of the 20th century. A late modernizer, it was marginalized in the international economy, and failed to establish stable democratic politics. In many ways, the already substantial problems of the Romanians were compounded by the incorporation of additional territory after the First World War, and with it a significantly increased minority population. During the inter-war years the country found itself in a state of turmoil, racked by internal divisions and beset by economic problems.[3] Romania's far from perfected democratic institutions were overwhelmed by the associated challenges of the depression and the resurgence of Germany. The dominant democratic parties, the National Peasant Party and the Liberals gave way before the advance of right-wing extremists.[4] Linked with resentment toward the failed democratic regime and its economic policies, xenophobia propelled a powerful indigenous fascist movement in the 1930s. Left-wing forces were, in contrast, notably weak. Identified by many in the largely peasant and Orthodox population as atheist as well as anti-nationalist, the socialist parties failed to attract a strong following.[5]

By the outbreak of the Second World War, the civil consensus had disintegrated almost entirely. In late 1938, members of the fascist Iron Guard movement unleashed a campaign of political terror against the increasingly isolated royalist government. Power passed briefly to the Iron Guard in 1940, after which General Ion Antonescu established a military government and led Romania through the Second World War in military alliance with Germany.

Rather than erasing its national peculiarities, Romania's communist experience acted to reinforce crucial aspects of the country's traditional political culture. While space does not permit a comprehensive exploration of the communist period, it is safe to brand what developed as 'national communism', characterized by a legitimization system and socio-political patterns that differed significantly from those found elsewhere in Central and Eastern Europe (Crowther 1988; Verdery 1991).

Even prior to its public deviation from Soviet orthodoxy, the Romanian communist regime showed signs of singularity. The Communist Party's unresolved internal factionalism retarded efforts to restructure the country's economy and, in contrast to events in most other East European countries, enabled a national communist faction to survive the Stalinist period. Under Gheorghiu Gheorghiu-Dej, the Romanian leadership embarked on an 'independent Stalinist' strategy of industrialization, and took preliminary steps toward a 'national' legitimization strategy. The rise to power of Nicolae Ceauşescu in the second half of the 1960s was accompanied by further turmoil as the new leader purged potential opponents and elevated supporters in order to consolidate his position. Betraying the potential for an independent and more moderate form of communism that many saw in his regime, within five years Ceauşescu was moving Romania in a more intensely nationalist and more authoritarian direction than his predecessor.

The failure by the Ceauşescu regime to reach accommodation with Romanian civil society, from which it was becoming increasingly isolated, strengthened important continuities between the communist period and inter-war political traditions. Sharp divisions between elites and the rest of the population, subject rather than participant attitudes with respect to civil-state relations, an abiding distrust of established authority, and intense nationalism were all conspicuous elements in the pre-communist political culture. These attitudes were reinforced, and in some cases exaggerated to the point of extreme distortion, under Ceauşescu's national communist legitimization formula.

Transition, Proto-Politics and the Founding Elections

With the possible exception of Albania, at the end of the 1980s Romania was arguably less prepared than any other country in Eastern Europe to undertake democratization. Up to the very end of the communist period, the Ceauşescu leadership systematically fostered political alienation and fractured society along class and ethnic lines. The consequences of this strategy for the post-communist body politic were catastrophic. The level of political culture suffered, institutionalized alternatives to the communist party simply did not exist, and reformist tendencies within the Romanian Communist Party (RCP) were limited at best. Immediately after the fall of the RCP dictatorship, elite-level politics resolved into a contest between forces associated with the previous regime and an ineffective liberal opposition. Despite these stark conditions, however, coherent societal level interests rapidly took shape and clearly influenced party competition.

As the edifice of Communist political repression disintegrated, a diverse coalition formed with the intent of guiding the December 1989 popular revolt to a successful conclusion.[6] Its main components were the leaders of the spontaneous uprising, marginalized reform communists, and elements that abandoned the failing Ceauşescu regime. Organized as the National Salvation Front (FSN) and headed by former Politburo member Ion Iliescu, these forces announced their assumption of provisional control over the country on 22 December 1989.

Upon coming to power, the FSN immediately announced a programme of reform, including a call for elections to be held in April 1990.[7] FSN spokesmen asserted that the Front was as a non-political umbrella organization that would act in the interest of all those who fought to bring down the Ceauşescu dictatorship. It pledged to act in a caretaker role until the situation could be regularized and elections could be held to select a freely elected democratic successor regime.

Almost immediately, however, both the character of the FSN and its electoral intentions changed. In essence, the two best positioned elements of the original makeshift coalition (reform communists and representatives of the military) banded together at the expense of the less politically experienced leaders of the mass uprising. A dominant core formed within the ruling council of the FSN around Iliescu. While the RCP itself was abolished in early January 1990, significant elements of the party's administrative network remained intact and passed into the structure of the provisional government. This dynamic strengthened the hand of the former RCP cadre within the FSN Council, and at the same time alienated anti-communists.

Thus transformed, the leadership of the FSN reversed its position on running candidates for office in a successor government. The organization's initial competitive advantage was obvious. Among the general population, the FSN's reputation was on the whole quite positive. FSN leaders were able to successfully associate their organization with the December revolution, and garnered an immediate favourable response by abolishing several hated Ceauşescu policies. Furthermore, unlike other transition regimes, Romania entered the post-communist period with no foreign debt, due to the former dictator's draconian polices directed at repayment in the late 1980s. Hence the FSN was able to take immediate steps to improve public consumption.

Opposition forces were, however, not long in emerging. Already in December the major rivals of the FSN had begun to organize in Bucharest. The first of these were the so-called historic parties FSN, the National Liberal Party (PNL), the National Peasant-Christian Democratic Party (PNT-CD), and the Social Democratic Party of Romania (PSDR). By early January another major force, the Democratic Magyar Union of Romania (UDMR) had begun to function in Transylvania as well.[8] Other less formal organizations, like the student movement, while not explicitly aspiring to power, also brought substantial pressure on the government.

Within weeks – almost days – of Ceauşescu's overthrow this nascent opposition launched public attacks on Iliescu and his colleagues as 'neo-communists'. Faced with growing criticism, the leaders of the FSN decided to take advantage of their immediate broad support to consolidate control over the country through election. Thus on 23 January 1990, the FSN reversed its earlier commitment to neutrality, and announced its intention to participate in the upcoming elections.

The decision to take part in national elections instantly destabilized an already volatile situation, touching off a series of anti-regime demonstrations by the student movement and anti-FSN political parties. Street demonstrations in Bucharest demanding resignation of the FSN were brought to an end only through the use of force. Unable to call on the military to contain the protesters, Iliescu mobilized supportive workers, who responded by rampaging in the capital and attacking presumed opponents of the new regime. Coupled with the extension of compromises to the opposition political parties, the threat of further violence by the workers served to pressure opponents into acceptance of the new political circumstances. After substantial discord and resistance from the opposition parties, an agreement was reached setting 20 May 1990 as the date for elections.

The first round of national elections can only be understood adequately if they are evaluated within this polarized and highly fluid political context, in which the FSN enjoyed nearly unassailable advantages as a quasi-government. This remained the case despite the fact that the Council of the National Salvation Front formally dissolved itself as a government in order to ease opposition from the non-governing parties. In its place, a new body, the Provisional Council of National Unity, was established to govern until elections could be held. The new body retained most of the membership of the old council (fully half of the positions on it were allocated to the FSN) while adding members from the other political parties. But the more experienced and firmly ensconced Front leaders were clearly able to retain control over the state.

As established by law, the legislature (the Assembly of Deputies) was elected with a mechanism combining multi-member districts and proportional representation. The Assembly consisted of 396 seats, of which 387 were determined by election, with the remaining posts reserved for representatives of ethnic minorities. Elections were also held for 119 positions in the Romanian upper house, the Senate. Voters chose among party lists in 41 multi-member districts.

The president was elected simultaneously with the legislature. The presidential elections were direct. If no candidate achieved an absolute majority in a first round, a run-off round was to be held between the two candidates who received the largest numbers of votes in the previous round.

The key contenders in the founding elections were Ion Iliescu's National Salvation Front, the main historical parties; the National Liberals (PNL), the National Peasant Party (PNT), and the Social Democrats; along with the Democratic Magyar Union of Romania (UDMR). In addition, a multitude of smaller parties emerged, representing views across the ideological spectrum; all in all, more than 70 parties participated in the elections. The campaign platform of the National Salvation Front called for the abolition of the most repressive and irrational aspects of the previous dictatorship and for measured reform. At the same time the FSN pledged to protect the population from market forces. In contrast, the traditional parties proposed more rapid economic restructuring, and failed to provide the population with firm assurances that they would be protected during the economic transition. The National Liberal and the National Peasant parties labelled the National Salvation Front 'neo-communist', and charged it with hijacking the revolution.

The results of the elections of 20 May 1990 provide unmistakable evidence of the political dominance of Ion Iliescu and the FSN. In the presidential race, Iliescu won 85.1 per cent of the vote. Radu Campeanu of the National Liberal Party took 10.2 per cent and Ion Rațiu followed with 4.3 per cent. Clearly, no individual political figure could match Iliescu. While not as lopsided, returns for the legislature also testify to the strength of the FSN. The Front captured 68 per cent of the Assembly seats, and 76 per cent of those in the Senate races (*Appendix 11.1*).[9]

Several factors concerning the nature of popular attitudes and party support at the time of the initial transition emerge from examination of the voting returns. Among the most striking results of the initial national vote in Romania was the strength of support for the UDMR. With a population of around two million out of over 24 million in Romania as a whole, the Magyars must have voted almost unanimously in support of the UDMR in order to give it 7.2 per cent of the total vote. Support for the UDMR was intensely concentrated in counties populated by Magyars. In 25 out of 41 counties the UDMR received less than 1 per cent of the vote; in Harghița, with its large Magyar population, it received 85.2 per cent. The historical parties, on the other hand, did worse than expected. The National Liberals (PNL) came in third nationally with 6.4 per cent of the vote, slightly behind the UDMR. The National Peasants (2.56 per cent of the vote) did not take the fourth place, but it was one of the ecological parties, the Romanian Ecological Movement (MER), which attracted 2.62 per cent of the vote.

Nationally, the Front gained 66.3 per cent of the vote. The FSN showed itself strongest in agricultural counties with low levels of industrialization and urbanization. It did least well in the urban setting. In contrast, the PNL did best in urban and industrial counties, and worst in agricultural ones. In regional terms, Ion Iliescu was most successful in Moldavia (94 per cent), Muntenia (93 per cent) and Oltenia (93 per cent), and least successful in Transylvania (72 per cent). Radu Campeanu's strongest showing came in Transylvania, where he won 23 per cent of the vote, presumably due to support from the UDMR. Ion Rațiu, the National Peasant Party candidate, on the other hand, did best in Bucharest, where he achieved 11 per cent of the vote, more than twice the level of the support that he polled nationally.

These election results confirmed the main political tendencies that emerged in the first months after the revolution. The FSN consolidated its early gains, while more militantly anti-communist forces remained fragmented. This outcome was in large part predetermined by the precipitate way in which the elections were held and the Front's near monopolistic access to state resources. The campaign was an unequal contest at best, pitting a cohesive successor communist party with access to state assets against a fragmented opposition. Even so, during the course of the campaign it became clear that the FSN, having successfully co-opted the symbolism of the 1989 revolution, enjoyed a level of popular support that its liberal opponents were unwilling to acknowledge.

The Emergence of Cleavage Politics and Party Formation

Bolstered by electoral success, Iliescu and the FSN government that was formed in the wake of the 1990 elections initiated a programme of limited reform. Their policy initiatives had clear consequences for the population at large as well as at the elite level, and set the stage for the development of more intense party competition in Romania's second electoral cycle.

Within months after the 1990 election, a number of reform laws were passed.[10] Land up to 25 acres held in collective farms was slated for return to former owners. Provision was made for 30 per cent of the value of state enterprises to be distributed to the population through voucher privatization. Private enterprise was legalized. The government called for price controls to be gradually liberalized until market pricing was reached on most goods. But even the cautious reform initiatives by the FSN touched off serious political conflict between pro-reform and anti-reform forces. Social groups affected by the reforms became increasingly active in their opposition. As the year after the elections wore on, strike activity increased and demonstrations by opposition groups became an almost daily routine in the country's capital. At the same time, consensus within the ruling party broke down. As the reform process took hold, improving conditions in some sectors but imposing costs in others, competing factions took shape within the National Salvation Front based on alternative political strategies (Gallagher 1995, 115–17).

Popular reaction against the National Front government and its policies reached a peak in the autumn of 1991, when demonstrations threatened public order in Bucharest for a second time since the revolution. Workers stormed through the streets demanding the resignation of President Iliescu and Prime Minister Petre Roman. Ion Iliescu, however, successfully shifted the burden of responsibility for the consequences of the reforms onto Prime Minister Roman, engineering his resignation in mid-September. Forced to leave the government, Roman became the chief representative of those in the National Salvation Front who argued that reforms should proceed both further and faster. By the spring of the following year, Roman's supporters had become confident enough to force a confrontation at the ruling party's congress. In

March 1992, Petre Roman was re-elected chairman of the party. Ion Iliescu and his supporters responded by breaking off to form their own organization, the Democratic National Salvation Front (FDSN).

Thus some two years after the initial election the relatively heterogeneous communist successor party fragmented into a new reformist FSN, which entered into the spectrum of the non-governing parties, and a relatively more conservative governing party, the FDSN. Iliescu's FDSN then shifted both rhetorically and in terms of policy implementation in the direction of Romania's coterie of 'red-brown' parties: the Socialist Labour Party (PSM), the Party of Romanian National Unity (PUNR), and the Greater Romania Party (RM). Meanwhile, the liberal opposition parties struggled to achieve individual coherence and collective cooperation, but to little avail. Putting aside their rivalries, 14 democratic parties came together to form the Democratic Convention and contest local elections in February 1992.[11] This achievement raised expectations that a new degree of collaboration had been achieved among regime opponents, and that this would allow them to compete successfully in national elections. However, tensions within the opposition coalition were never successfully overcome. As the second post-revolution national election campaign approached, the attention of opposition leaders shifted from efforts to defeat the government to rivalries between the main participants of the Democratic Convention: the National Liberals, the National Peasant Party-Christian Democrat, the UDMR, and the Civic Alliance Party (PAC). Ultimately the National Liberal Party determined that it could more successfully pursue its goals independently, and it withdrew altogether from the Democratic Convention.

With elections coming up, nationalist rhetoric became a progressively more strident element of inter-party debate. The presence of two extremist nationalist opposition parties – the PUNR and the Greater Romanian Party (RM) – insured that the nationalist issue remained part of Romania's political discourse. As the minority question became increasingly salient, a second shift occurred within the Democratic Convention. The UDMR removed itself from the Convention's electoral agreement, apparently in order to avoid hampering the Convention's electoral chances. The UDMR remained a member of the Convention, however, supporting its candidate in the Presidential race and pledging cooperation in the pursuit of common goals in parliament. In the period leading up to the elections, political forces thus consolidated into two broad groupings, which may be characterized as collectivist-nationalist and liberal-universalist. The relevance of this characterization can be validated through an examination of party platforms and leadership behaviour as well as through an inquiry into mass attitudes. For purposes of this study, popular attitudes were analysed through the use of a public opinion survey administered in mid-1992. The key dimensions of differentiation that shaped party-political orientation were associated with attitudes towards economic reform and towards minorities (*Table 11.1*).

Table 11.1: Political attitudes and party confidence

Attitude toward pace of privatization by confidence in party

	R^2	Beta	Significance of F
FDSN	0.051	0.229	0.000
FSN	0.030	0.178	0.000
RM	0.027	0.167	0.000
PSM	0.016	0.133	0.000
PDAR	0.004	0.075	0.012
PNT–CD	0.058	-0.242	0.000
PAC	0.053	-0.233	0.000
UDMR	0.023	-0.155	0.000
PNL–AT	0.029	-0.172	0.000
PNL	0.021	-0.148	0.000

Attitude toward equality scale by confidence in party

	R^2	Beta	Significance of F
FDSN	0.051	0.229	0.000
FSN	0.030	0.178	0.000
RM	0.027	0.167	0.000
PSM	0.016	0.133	0.000
PDAR	0.004	0.075	0.012
PNT–CD	0.058	-0.242	0.000
PAC	0.053	-0.233	0.000
UDMR	0.023	-0.155	0.000
PNL–AT	0.029	-0.172	0.000
PNL	0.021	-0.148	0.000

Minority rights scale by confidence in party

	R^2	Beta	Significance of F
RM	0.018	-0.138	0.000
FDSN	0.015	-0.129	0.000
PUNR	0.014	-0.122	0.000
FSN	0.009	-0.100	0.0005
PDAR	0.009	-0.100	0.0008
PSM	0.005	-0.080	0.0077
UDMR	0.143	0.379	0.000
PAC	0.054	0.234	0.000
PNT–CD	0.036	0.192	0.000
PNL–AT	0.015	0.127	0.000

Note: The R^2 provides a measure of the relationship between an independent variable (for example, the attitude towards the pace of privatization) and a given dependent variable, in this instance attitude toward particular political parties. Beta provides a measure of how much change in the dependent variable is caused by change in the independent variable, and also the direction of change (does an increasing value in one dimension cause an increase value or a decrease in the other dimension). The Significance of F provides a measure of the probability that a given correlation is random. By way of example, a figure of 0.05 would indicate that the correlation in question would have occurred by chance in less than 95 per cent of cases. In essence, this table indicates that the attitudes in question are strongly related to attitudes toward political parties, and that their effect on support for the collectivist–nationalist and liberal–universalist groupings is in opposite directions. For example, the more respondents favour economic equality, the more positively inclined they are towards the collectivist nationalists, and the less positively inclined they are towards liberal universalists.

Source: Random national sample of 1608 respondents taken in late June and early July 1992.

The political significance of these dimensions is immediately clear. On the three measures employed here, the direction of the relationship between attitudes on issues, and attitudes towards the collectivist-nationalist and liberal-universalist parties are consistent, and in opposite directions.

Table 11.2: Political attitudes and social structure

Attitudes towards minorities

	F Ratio	F Prob.
Majority/Minority	405.3656	0.0000
Class	0.8389	0.5221
Respondents' Education Level	0.4292	0.7321
Fathers' Education	5.0728	0.0017
Urban/Rural	7.0701	0.0079
Region	4.3531	0.0002

Attitudes towards private property

	F Ratio	F Prob.
Majority/Minority	12.4200	0.0004
Class	20.5065	0.0000
Respondents' Education Level	55.2005	0.0000
Fathers' Education	33.4482	0.0000
Urban/Rural	87.0958	0.0000
Region	16.3072	0.0000

Note: The F ratio employs the variance of group means as a measure of observed differences among groups. The bigger the F ratio the bigger the variance, and the smaller the F ratio the smaller the variance. The F probability provides a measure of the probability that a given difference in group means is random. For example, a figure of 0.05 would indicate that the correlation in question would have occurred by chance in less than 95 per cent of cases.

Source: Random national sample of 1608 respondents taken in late June and early July 1992.

In addition to being politically relevant, these ideological dimensions are associated with historical divisions located in Romanian social structure, indicating the presence of political cleavages in the society (see *Table 11.2*). Not surprisingly, the strongest indicator of attitudes towards minorities is the divide between Romania's majority and minority communities. But, in addition to this, there are also divisions within the majority group on this dimension. While the direct effect of class and education are not significant, social status does appear to play a role. Examination of the impact of the respondents' fathers' education level produces significant results, indicating that the cultural environment of the family does affect the formation of attitudes toward minorities. Urban/rural differences are also an important determinant of attitudes toward minorities, with urban dwellers being less hostile than their rural counterparts. Attitudes toward minorities differ significantly across Romania's main historic regions as well, with areas of high Magyar population density showing higher levels of ethnic hostility. The effect of region remains strong even if one controls for the effect of urban/rural differences, and for the age and education of the population. Interestingly, attitudes towards minorities are most negative among long-term residents of ethnically mixed regions than among newcomers, indicating a long lasting historical phenomenon rather than a more instrumental effect.

Attitudes towards property are also strongly related to social structural variables. In the case of this dimension, the urban/rural cleavage stands out as the strongest predictor, with the urban population being substantially more favourably inclined towards private property. Class and education play strong roles as well. As one would expect, professionals and those with higher levels of education are more positive with regard to private property, while those with lower levels of education are less so. Finally, as in the case of attitudes toward minorities, regional differences are apparent. Here one finds residents of Transylvania, the Banat, and Bucharest more liberally inclined, while Moldovans and Oltenians appear more collectivist in outlook. This relationship remained valid when controls were introduced for education and urban/rural differences between the regions.

The coherence of the two dominant party groupings in the minds of respondents is further indicated by analysis of the relationship between respondents' attitudes toward individual political parties. This was accomplished by regression analysis examining the relationship between support for each of the major parties and support for each of the other major parties. The results of this process, indicated in Table 11.3, are consistent with the previous analysis: supporters of any of the parties in the collectivist-nationalist grouping of parties are likely to be favourably inclined to other parties in that grouping; those positively inclined to liberal-universalist parties are likely to be positively inclined toward others in the same grouping. The validity of this association was further confirmed by performing a factor analysis on questions reflecting respondents' support for the main political parties.[12]

As Table 11.3 indicates, the FDSN was at the focal point of the collectivist-nationalist cluster of parties, with attitudes towards it and the other parties in the grouping being positively correlated. Following its rupture from the FSN, which under Petre Roman's leadership pursued a more reformist strategy, President Iliescu's FDSN became at least implicitly the party of the status quo, arguing for continuation of reform at a cautious pace, for a strong government sector, and for strong social protection.

The remainder of the collectivist-nationalist grouping consists of four parties that occupy the political space with or to the right of the FDSN on the dimension of nationalism and close to the FDSN or to its left on the reform continuum. These include the Party of Romanian National Unity (PUNR), the Greater Romania Party (RM) and the Socialist Labour Party (PSM), and the Democratic Agrarian Party (PDAR).

Table 11.3: Proximity of party support

		R^2	Beta			R^2	Beta
FSN	FDSN	0.143	0.37	PRM	PUNR	0.297	0.54
					PDAR	0.193	0.44
FDSN	PRM	0.152	0.39		FDSN	0.152	0.39
	PDAR	0.145	0.38		PSM	0.142	0.38
	FSN	0.143	0.37		PR	0.116	0.34
	PUNR	0.142	0.37				
	PSM	0.114	0.34	MER	MR	0.248	0.49
					PNL-AT	0.223	0.47
					PDAR	0.211	0.46
					PNL	0.163	0.40
PNT-CD	PAC	0.427	0.65		PR	0.162	0.40
	UDMR	0.239	0.49		PUNR	0.150	0.38
	PNL-AT	0.161	0.40				
	PNL	0.140	0.34				
	MR	0.137	0.54	PNL	PNL-AT	0.364	0.60
					MER	0.163	0.40
					PR	0.145	0.38
UDMR	PAC	0.289	0.53		MR	0.145	0.38
	PNT-CD	0.239	0.48		PNT-CD	0.139	0.37
					AC	0.106	0.32
PAC	PNT-CD	0.427	0.65				
	UDMR	0.289	0.53	PNL-AT	PNL	0.364	0.60
	PNL-AT	0.178	0.42		MR	0.306	0.48
	MR	0.165	0.40		MER	0.223	0.47
	PNL	0.106	0.32		PR	0.215	0.46
					AC	0.178	0.42
					PNT-CD	0.161	0.40
PDAR	MER	0.211	0.46				
	PRM	0.193	0.44	PR	PUNR	0.220	0.47
	PR	0.193	0.44		PNL-AT	0.215	0.46
	FDSN	0.145	0.38		PDAR	0.193	0.44
					MER	0.162	0.40
					PNL	0.145	0.38
PUNR	PDAR	0.347	0.59		PRM	0.116	0.34
	PRM	0.297	0.54				
	FDSN	0.142	0.37	MR	PNL-AT	0.306	0.55
					MER	0.249	0.49
PSM	PRM	0.145	0.38		PR	0.229	0.47
	FDSN	0.114	0.34		PDAR	0.193	0.44
					AC	0.165	0.40
					FDSN	0.152	0.39
					PNL	0.145	0.38
					PNT-CD	0.137	0.37

Note: The R^2 provides a measure of the association between an independent variable and a given dependent variable, in this instance attitude towards particular political parties. Beta provides a measure of how much change in the dependent variable is caused by change in the independent variable, and also the direction of change. Table 11.3 reports attitudes towards each party and correlates them with attitudes to every other party. Only the positive associations are reproduced. In essence, the analysis indicates that positive attitudes towards any party in the collectivist–nationalist grouping correlate with positive attitudes toward other parties in that grouping, but not with parties outside of the grouping. A similar phenomenon is evident in the case of the liberal–universalist camp.

Source: Random national sample of 1608 respondents, June–July 1992.

While sharing some common characteristics each of these parties has unique attributes that distinguish it from the others and make close cooperation difficult to achieve. PUNR, for example was primarily a regional party of Transylvania. The PSM, led by Ceauşescu lieutenant Ilie Verdeţ, was the most obvious successor to the Romanian Communist Party and is not surprisingly staunchly collectivist. The PDAR, staffed largely by cadre of the former regime's agricultural bureaucracy, closely associated itself with the FDSN.

The second major locus of political power, the liberal–universalist grouping, is located on the opposite extreme of these ideological dimensions. It consists of parties that are often identified as the 'democratic opposition', most of which participate in the Democratic Convention. These include, most prominently, the Civic Alliance Party (PAC), the National Peasant Party-Christian Democrat (PNT-CD), the National Liberal Party (PNL), and the UDMR. These parties were, in general, much more favourably inclined to rapid reform and privatization. They were also much less driven by Romanian nationalism than the former grouping.[13]

The second post-transition national elections were held in September 1992 within this context of shifting party positions. Electoral rules established by the legislature in July of 1992 reduced the number of seats in the lower house from 387 to 328, while the Senate was expanded from 119 to 143 members. A 3 per cent electoral threshold was adopted for participation in the legislature. Coalitions were required to achieve a higher threshold, determined by adding one percentage point for each participating list in the coalition, up to a maximum of 8 per cent. The actual execution of the 1992 campaign was significantly better than in the previous case. While irregularities did occur, as documented by Carry (1995), less violence accompanied the elections, fraud played a smaller role, and access to the media for opposition parties was much improved.

The outcome of voting in September 1992 confirmed that a considerable evolution had occurred in Romanian politics since the 1990 contest. In the presidential race, support for Ion Iliescu was substantiated as a cardinal fact of Romanian political life. With 47.2 per cent of the first round vote and 61.4 per cent in the final contest Iliescu again dominated the field of candidates (*Appendix 11.1*). The Democratic Convention's candidate, Emil Constantinescu, was able to attract 31.2 per cent in the first round, but garnered only an additional 7 per cent in the second round, bringing his total vote to 38.6 per cent. It was a credible showing, but the outcome clearly did not allow the opposition to threaten President Iliescu. On the other hand, the 23.7 percentage point decline in support between 1990 and 1992 could not have been comforting to the President.[14]

Voting in the legislative elections reflected even greater change (*Appendix 11.1*). While still capturing a plurality of the vote in the Chamber of Deputies, FDSN support fell to 27.7 per cent as compared to the 66.3 per cent that the unified FSN won in the previous contest. Petre Roman's rump FSN accounted for only another 10.2 per cent of the vote, leaving a drop of more than 28 percentage points to be accounted for. While no definitive answer as to the destination of these votes can be given, it appears likely that they were distributed across the ideological spectrum. PUNR, for example, won only slightly more than 2 per cent of the 1990 vote, but more than 8 per cent in 1992. Support for the parties that constitute the Democratic Convention also increased dramatically. From a collective vote of less than 5 per cent in 1990 the combined forces captured more than 20 per cent of the legislative vote in 1992; a remarkable feat by any standards. Other parties that enjoyed slight increases include Romania Mare and Verdeț's successor Socialist Labour Party, while support for the Magyar Democratic Union remained approximately constant, as one would expect given the nature of its constituency.

Clearly, the ideological appeal of the FDSN had proved effective in these post-communist second elections. If one considers the differential support for political parties by various social strata, the early strength of the FDSN and the difficulties facing the opposition become even clearer (*Table 11.4*). The 15 per cent of workers expressing 'very much confidence' in the FDSN in late June 1992 was nearly double the figures for any other single party; it was 8.5 per cent for the FSN. Among peasants strong support for the FDSN was even more secure, at 24.6 per cent. Only among professionals with higher education did the FDSN fail to capture the highest level of support, reaching only 11.5 per cent and trailing behind the Civic Alliance Party with 18.5 per cent and the PNT-CD with 16.3 per cent.

Table 11.4: Confidence in political parties by social category

Worker confidence in political parties (%)

	Very much	Much	Moderate	Little
FSN	8.5	22.3	26.7	42.5
FDSN	15.0	21.5	18.1	45.4
PNT-CD	7.1	10.3	21.8	60.9
UDMR	0.1	6.9	15.1	72.8
PAC	6.8	14.5	19.7	59.0
PDAR	4.8	17.1	33.7	44.4
PUNR	7.9	18.9	24.8	48.3
PSM	4.2	9.6	16.7	69.6
RM	6.2	17.8	24.0	52.1
MER	4.3	19.1	29.4	47.2
PNL	6.2	12.6	25.8	55.4
PNL-AT	3.0	17.5	22.8	56.6
RP	3.6	11.5	28.1	56.9
MR	2.1	9.2	17.6	71.1

Peasant confidence in political parties (%)

	Very much	Much	Moderate	Little
FSN	18.1	20.0	25.0	36.9
FDSN	24.6	17.2	13.4	44.8
PNT-CD	2.0	9.9	17.9	72.2
UDMR	4.7	4.8	7.6	85.0
PAC	2.4	5.7	12.2	79.7
PDAR	8.6	25.7	17.1	48.6
PUNR	9.6	13.6	19.2	57.6
PSM	1.7	3.5	8.7	86.1
RM	2.5	10.1	19.3	68.1
MER	6.3	12.5	22.3	61.6
PNL	5.1	5.1	12.4	77.4
PNL-AT	3.1	6.3	14.8	75.8
RP	2.0	9.6	25.5	65.7
MR	2.2	2.2	6.5	89.1

Professionals' confidence in political parties (%)

	Very much	Much	Moderate	Little
FSN	2.5	12.5	27.8	57.0
FDSN	11.5	10.3	15.4	62.8
PNT-CD	16.3	20.0	22.5	41.3
UDMR	7.6	8.9	10.1	73.4
PAC	18.5	19.8	17.3	44.4
PDAR	3.8	13.9	20.3	62.0
PUNR	11.5	12.8	19.2	56.4
PSM	1.3	3.8	12.7	82.3
RM	2.5	11.4	8.9	77.2
MER	5.1	17.9	21.8	55.1
PNL	6.3	17.5	21.3	55.0
PNL-AT	2.5	22.8	30.4	44.3
RP	5.3	20.0	22.7	52.0
MR	9.1	9.1	12.1	69.1

Source: Data taken from a random national poll of 1608 respondents in late June and early July 1992.

Questions concerning support for potential Presidential candidates produced even more disproportionate results (*Table 11.5*), with 46.2 per cent of peasants and 31.9 per cent of workers expressing support for Ion Iliescu. In each of these categories, the only other candidate to attract more than 10 per cent support was then Prime Minister Stolojan. Among professionals, Stolojan gained the highest level of support, 26.2 per cent, followed by Nicolae Manolescu (14.3 per cent) and Iliescu (13.1 per cent). These data confirm strong support for Ion Iliescu and the policies that he represented among a large part of the population, particularly among workers and peasants. The dissatisfaction of the intelligentsia with the government and strong support for the opposition was just as clear. Given the country's demographics, however, intellectual opposition in itself could not lead to a change in regime until the opposition was able to broaden its political base.

Table 11.5: Support for presidential candidates by social category (%)

	Professionals	Workers	Peasants
Raţiu	10.7	9.0	1.7
Druc	2.4	0.3	1.2
Iliescu	13.1	31.9	46.2
Manzatu	0.0	1.9	1.2
Manolescu	14.3	3.1	2.3
Stolojan	26.2	15.8	11.0
Roman	1.2	2.2	4.0
Conescu	1.2	0.6	0.0
Campeanu	1.2	4.6	3.5
Nastase	7.1	5.0	0.6

Source: Data taken from a random national poll of 1608 respondents in late June and early July 1992.

It seems clear in light of the data presented above that policy-relevant cleavages had already appeared within the Romanian electorate early in the post-communist transition. It is further apparent that members of the electorate grouped political parties according to their positions on meaningful ideological dimensions.

A further concern with respect to the role of cleavages in post-communist democracies is the congruity of mass and elite attitudes. Do the positions of constituents systematically correspond with those of the representatives of the parties that they support? If this is the case, then one would be better able to argue both that party formation is proceeding and that party competition and ideological cleavages on the mass level are mutually reinforcing (Kitschelt 1992; 1994).

A comparison of the distribution of attitudes among party legislators and party supporters sheds substantial light on this issue. Despite concern among analysts about the presumably low level of political development and social atomization, a significant differentiation was evident among Romanian political parties on both of the axes described above already by the 1992 elections.

Table 11.6 presents mean scores for legislators elected in 1992 belonging to eight of the country's most significant parties on attitudinal scales measuring views towards property ownership (taken here as an indicator of attitudes toward economic liberalism in general) and attitudes towards ethnic minorities.

Table 11.6: Legislators, party supporters, and non-supporters

Support for private property

		Mean	Std dev	Cases
FDSN	legislator	1.5306	0.2924	119
	supporter	1.8941	0.4346	336
	non-supporter	1.7685	0.5374	967
FSN	legislator	1.2015	0.1380	39
	supporter	1.9374	0.4863	340
	non-supporter	1.7539	0.5183	964
PNT-CD	legislator	1.1673	0.3456	35
	supporter	1.5693	0.4546	266
	non-supporter	1.8603	0.5138	1037
UDMR	legislator	1.1714	0.1472	30
	supporter	1.5694	0.5126	140
	non-supporter	1.8288	0.5092	1163
PAC	legislator	1.1319	0.2764	13
	supporter	0.5850	0.4553	274
	non-supporter	1.8584	0.5157	1029
PUNR	legislator	1.4147	0.2193	31
	supporter	1.7522	0.4419	275
	non-supporter	1.8139	0.5331	1028
PSM	legislator	1.6825	0.2451	9
	supporter	0.0048	0.4402	90
	non-supporter	1.7858	0.5178	1213
PNL	legislator	1.3036	0.1937	8
	supporter	1.6414	0.4714	239
	non-supporter	1.8367	0.5186	1064

Attitude toward minorities

		Mean	Std dev	Cases
FDSN	legislator	1.3150	0.3661	123
	supporter	1.2416	0.3643	329
	non-supporter	1.4694	0.5353	851
FSN	legislator	1.7500	0.6065	36
	supporter	1.3067	0.4035	313
	non-supporter	1.4418	0.5310	868
PNT-CD	legislator	1.7031	0.2940	32
	supporter	0.6084	0.5764	233
	non-supporter	1.3561	0.4717	947
UDMR	legislator	2.8000	0.2013	30
	supporter	2.1022	0.6143	137
	non-supporter	1.3145	0.4074	1043
PAC	legislator	1.7692	0.2385	13
	supporter	1.6820	0.6015	250
	non-supporter	1.3317	0.4464	930
PUNR	legislator	1.0882	0.1834	34
	supporter	1.1742	0.2974	287
	non-supporter	1.4804	0.5334	893
PSM	legislator	1.1818	0.1966	11
	supporter	1.2622	0.3867	82
	non-supporter	1.4167	0.5102	1098
PNL	legislator	1.7143	0.3037	7
	supporter	1.4304	0.4864	212
	non-supporter	1.4006	0.5078	968

The attitudes of the respondents in a 1992 public opinion survey who expressed or did not express support for any of the eight major parties, may be also be gauged from the table above (*Table 11.6*). On both scales, clear differences are evident between legislators associated with the ruling Democratic National Salvation Front (FDSN), its allies (the Socialist Labour Party and the Party of Romanian National Unity), and the democratic opposition parties. The former grouping is less inclined towards private property, and is more hostile to minorities, while the latter group of legislators is more positive towards private property, and less hostile to minorities. On the attitude towards minorities scale, the distinction between the legislative delegation of the Democratic Magyar Union of Romania (UDMR) and the rest of field is obvious. Analysis of variance shows significant differences between parties on both scales.[15]

A comparison of party legislators' positions on the economy with those of their supporters and non-supporters indicates that party supporters in general are less positive towards private property than their respective party legislative groups. The views of the liberal opposition legislative delegations are closer to the views of their supporters than to those of non-supporters, as one would expect if party formation has occurred. This is not the case regarding the Democratic National Salvation Front (FDSN), the Socialist Labour Party (PSM) and the National Salvation Front (FSN), whose supporters are more collectivist than respondents who do not express support for those parties. But there is overwhelming evidence that supporters of these legislative groups are closer to the positions of their legislators than to the opposition party groups.[16]

The data on attitudes towards minorities present a somewhat different picture. Once again the scores of the liberal opposition legislative groups are closer to their supporters than to their non-supporters. This is also the case as regards the PSM and the PUNR, but with the direction of deviation reversed, i.e., legislators are more hostile to minorities than either their supporters or the population at large. FSN legislators here stand out, being substantially more distant from their own supporters than from respondents who do not support their party on this particular issue.[17]

The data indicate that the FDSN–PUNR–PSM grouping is less distant from their supporters than are their liberal opponents, while the FSN suffers from an almost extreme divergence of opinion between legislators and supporters. Differentiation is even more evident in Table 11.6. Clearly, the FDSN and the former communist PSM are substantially closer to the positions of non-supporters than are their opponents. This should potentially provide both parties with competitive advantages. The actual electoral dominance of the FDSN in comparison to the weakness of the PSM may probably be attributed to the weak legitimacy of PSM leaders too closely associated with the Ceauşescu dictatorship, and to the additional advantages accruing to the FDSN as a governing party.

Figure 11.1: Issue positions of Romanian legislators and party supporters

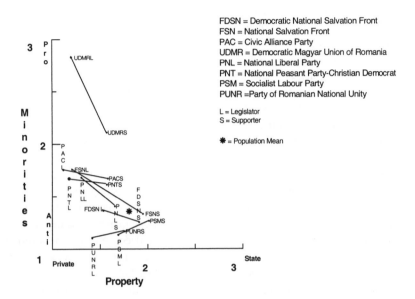

Several of the relationships above are summarized in Figure 11.1, which plots Party–Legislator and Party–Supporter positions spatially on both the property and attitude toward minority dimensions. A number of critical factors can be discerned from the resulting configuration. Clearly, the Democratic Magyar Union of Romania (UDMR) and its supporters stand alone, outside of the general spectrum party competition. The tight grouping of the liberal opposition legislators along with those of the National Salvation Front (FSN), more moderate on minority issues and less collectivist is also clear. Equally striking is the grouping of party supporters who are significantly more collectivist than the legislative groups, while generally more moderate on minority issues than the nationalist party legislators and less moderate than the liberal party legislators.

The advantage of the FDSN within the competitive environment of the early transition is apparent. Ruling party legislators are located between the more extreme nationalist-collectivist parties and the liberal opposition, and quite close to the supporters of both alternative groupings (as well as to the mean position of the entire mass opinion sample). The FDSN strategy following 1990 is clear in light of this configuration. The Iliescu leadership was unlikely to lose votes to the liberal opposition – the supporters of which were actually closer to the ruling party than to their own legislative representatives on property issues – unless the FDSN were to undertake more determined reform measures or become much more moderate on minority issues. It could, however, lose substantial support to the collectivist–nationalist opposition by becoming either more moderate on minority issues or more reformist on property issues, hence it avoided movement in these directions.

While politically expedient in the near term, this political configuration proved unworkable from the point of view of policy formation. The political and economic stagnation that so unfortunately characterized Romania in the years following the 1992 elections can be traced in large part to the nature of the ruling party and its social base. Given the character of its party leadership and its core constituency, the Democratic National Salvation Front, re-labelled the Party of Romanian Social Democracy (PDSR) in July 1993 when it united with three smaller parties, found itself unable to effectively reform, or to competently manage the country's economy.

President Iliescu's post-election strategy relied upon consolidating a base of support among peasants and workers while pursuing limited reform, undertaken at least in part in order to satisfy external constituents. Clearly, given the character of the Iliescu leadership, one can question the depth of the party's commitment to fundamental reform. Indeed, one of the primary considerations that undermined post-election cabinets' ability to govern effectively was the continued influential role that holdover elements of the communist regime continued to play in public life. These included both managers from the state sector enterprises, and the *nomenklatura* class of politically connected individuals who benefited financially from the economy's intermediate stage between market and plan, in essence trading on their access to the state.

Despite these limitations, in the wake of the elections Prime Minister Vacaroiu's government (supported by President Iliescu) did undertake a more serious effort to restructure the Romanian economy than had previously been the case. The government moved to control inflation and initiated a more comprehensive programme of privatization than had previously been in evidence. Romania's tax system was rationalized, and deficit spending was sharply reduced (Roper 2000, 96). These efforts, however, failed to produce any significant increase in growth. As had previously been the case, reform was not allowed to undermine the interests of members of the elite allied with the regime. Inefficient state-owned enterprises were kept afloat through transfers from the state budget and high-level civil servants hostile to market capitalism hindered the activities of businesses in the private sector. Furthermore, even while pursuing limited reform, the FSN fostered popular anxiety concerning rapid social change. It held out the promise of relative stability and continued state protection from the capitalist market. The ruling party also continued to play to nationalist sentiments, and maintained its tacit alliance with the extremist parties.

Under these circumstances, even the limited reforms that were undertaken by Vacaroiu during the 1992–96 period predictably generated high levels of popular opposition, in the face of which they quickly foundered. While centre-right governments or even more autonomous and consolidated centre-left regimes in neighbouring post-communist countries were able to proceed with economic rationalization, the PDSR was not in a situation to marginalize conservative opposition. As a consequence, price reforms were often followed by wage increases, defeating their initial purpose. Similarly, state-controlled financial institutions subsidized non-performing enterprises. Privatization strategies promised decisive action, but implementation was weak, and when serious resistance was encountered, efforts foundered.

A second factor constraining PDSR rule was the party's dependence on its extreme nationalist allies for parliamentary support. The arms-length relationship between the ruling party and these groups in the early 1990s clearly worked to Iliescu's advantage, allowing him to garner electoral support from the nationalist constituency while avoiding direct association with their leaders' most provocative statements. But in 1994 the relationship between PDSR and the extremists was made explicit through the inclusion of two ministers from the PUNR in the Vacaroiu government. This was followed by the conclusion of an open agreement on cooperation with the Greater Romania Party, PUNR, and the Socialist Labour Party in January 1995.

Despite its domestic political benefits, the open alliance between the PDSR and the far right imposed a high external cost on the government, which was increasingly committed to reorient its foreign policy in order to gain acceptance with Western governments and financial institutions. As Romania turned its attention to refurbishing its image with the West, it was clearly recognized by the Iliescu leadership that an improved record regarding minority rights was essential. Therefore, coupled with its European initiative, steps were undertaken to improve relations both with Hungary and with Romania's Hungarian minority community (Phinnemore 2001, 255–6). Among other measures to achieve this end, Bucharest ratified the Charter for the Protection of National Minorities in a highly symbolic move in February 1995. Such moves were far from being appreciated by the nationalists. It became increasingly difficult to manage the alliance with the right-wing parties while acting to accommodate minorities and improve relations with neighbouring states. Conversely Iliescu was limited in his ability to gain international acceptance while he was identified with right-wing extremism. Therefore, even as the 1996 round of elections approached, the PDSR was forced to distance itself from its nationalist allies, aggravating already difficult relations with their volatile leaders, and causing a breakdown in the red-brown coalition that underpinned the regime.

Democratic Consolidation and the 1996 Elections

Romania's third set of elections, held in November 1996, was decisive. It marked the first definitive change in power since the fall of communism. The change in leadership was fundamental, from successors of the communist regime, to proponents of reform who had been excluded from power for the first six years of the transition. The 1996 election results clearly testified to the erosion of support for the PDSR that occurred in 1992–96 as a consequence of its policy failures, and as well as to the increased cooperation among the opposition parties. In the parliamentary elections held on 3 November 1996, the Democratic Convention (CDR) came out a clear winner, with 30.3 per cent of the vote and 122 out of 343 seats in the Chamber of Deputies, and 30.7 per cent of the vote and 51 out of 143 Senate seats (*Appendix 11.1*). The PDSR, in contrast, trailed by nearly 10 percentage points, with 21.5 per cent of the vote and 91 seats in the Chamber of Deputies, and 23.1 per cent and 41 seats in the Senate. The CDR's strong plurality coupled with support from the UDMR, which took approximately 6.5 per cent of the vote, and the Social Democratic Union (USD) with approximately 13 per cent, put the opposition well over the threshold necessary to form a new coalition government under CDR Prime Minister Victor Ciorbea.

In the initial round of the 1996 presidential contest, held simultaneously with the legislative election, Ion Iliescu took the first place with 32.2 per cent of the vote. This represented a significant decline from Iliescu's 1992 performance, when he garnered 47.2 per cent in the first round. The second place position was once again held by CDR candidate Emil Constantinescu, whose vote also decreased slightly between the 1992 and 1996 contests, from 31.2 per cent to 28.2 per cent of the vote. But Constantinescu's decline was clearly accounted for in large part by the fact that the UDMR fielded its own candidate in 1996, and had not done so in 1992. In the earlier contest UDMR supporters can be presumed to have voted overwhelmingly for Constantinescu in the first round. Given this change of conditions, Constantinescu's first-round vote among non-UDMR voters can be assumed to have increased by approximately 3 percentage points.

The results of the second round presidential contest, held on 17 November, represented a decisive success for Emil Constantinescu and the opposition parties. Constantinescu's vote in the run-off increased by 26.2 percentage points to 54.4 per cent of the total vote. Despite President Iliescu's intensified efforts to play on nationalist sentiments and fear of economic change between the first and second rounds, his vote rose by only approximately half as much, 13.4 per cent, to give him a final 45.6 per cent in the final count. As in the previous competition, the role of political cleavages in producing the 1996 electoral outcome was evident. Under the conditions prevailing in 1996 however, cleavage politics did not act in the PDSR's favour. To a certain extent, the basic 1992 pattern was retained, but with a general erosion in support for the PDSR.

Exit polling by the International Foundation for Electoral Support (IFES) and the IRSOP research organization sheds substantial light on the mood of voters. The data indicate that, as in the earlier contest, the rural/urban division was once again significant. Rural voters favoured the PDSR over the CDR by a margin of 8 percentage points (34 per cent against 26 per cent). The peasantry provided the strongest base of support for Iliescu and the PDSR; 53 per cent of peasants voted for the PDSR, 18 per cent for the Democratic Convention. The elderly continued to support the PDSR as well, giving it 42 per cent of their vote, as opposed to 24 per cent for the CDR.

Emil Constantinescu and the Democratic Convention, on the other hand, retained their hold on the upper classes, gaining 65 per cent of the vote from those with higher education. The CDR did very well among young people, who gave it 35 per cent of their vote, as opposed to 17 per cent for the PDSR. The earlier regional pattern of voting was also once again in evidence. Iliescu's vote remained strong in areas that he had dominated in previous campaigns, Oltenia, Muntenia and Moldavia. As one would expect, the Democratic Convention took urban areas, as well as Transylvania and the Banat, but with higher margins than before.

Along with declining margins of support across all categories, the factors that most accounted for the PDSR defeat were its loss of working-class vote, as Michael Shafir (1997) points out, and support of the emerging entrepreneurial class for the opposition parties. The IFES/IRSOP exit polling data show that workers gave the Democratic Convention 32 per cent support, well over the 21 per cent of the worker vote directed to the PDSR. This shift in allegiance was critical in determining the outcome of the election. The 'new middle-class' electorate had an effect as well. While state sector managers no doubt remained a PDSR constituency, six years of post-communism in Romania has produced a more complex economy, and increasing numbers of private owners. This group voted overwhelmingly for the Democratic Convention, giving it 48 per cent of their vote, in comparison to 11 per cent for the PDSR.

In the long term, the failure by President Iliescu and the PDSR government to press through economic reform undercut the Romanian economy's competitive position, engendering hardship for the general population, including workers, and producing the 1996 electoral backlash. This remained the case even though the policy was justified in the name of protecting workers' welfare against the ravages of unconstrained markets. By the time of the elections 60 per cent of voters felt that conditions in Romania had deteriorated, and in every category in which they were questioned, voters felt that the Democratic Convention would be better able to manage the country than the PDSR. The ruling party's abandonment of its coalition with the extreme nationalist parties played a role in its defeat as well. When the seriousness of his situation became apparent and President Iliescu began to more actively pursue an ethnic strategy, his ability to do so was undermined, and support was not forthcoming. In essence the PDSR gave up a more extreme segment of the electorate in the hopes of broadening its appeal, but failed to successfully attract new votes from the centre.

The transformation of Romania's domestic political landscape that followed the 1996 elections cleared the way for a new wave of domestic reform and the further transformation of the country's foreign policy position.[18] Hopes were high among the population that Prime Minister Victor Ciorbea's coalition government, which included the Democratic Convention, Petre Roman's Democratic Party, and the UDMR would serve to open the political process, ending the period of paternalism and insider '*nomenklatura* capitalism' that characterized the previous administration. Extensive changes were introduced in the leadership of both the Ministry of Defence and the Security Services (Deletant 2001; Watts 2002). Encouraged by President Constantinescu, the coalition government formed by Prime Minister Victor Ciorbea committed itself to fulfilling the comprehensive economic reform agenda that, the opposition argued, should have been initiated in the immediate wake of the Ceauşescu regime. In the economic realm, state subsidization of non-profitable firms was curtailed, as was permissive financing by the central bank. Romania's currency was allowed to float, and a more aggressive programme of privatization was initiated (MacFarlan, Martins and Paradis 1998). Constitutional revisions were introduced to address concerns regarding minority rights. Efforts were also undertaken to provide local authorities with increased autonomy in relation to the central authorities (Weber 2001).

The decisive change in Romania's political environment was thus manifest in the post-1996 reform endeavours. With President Constantinescu and the CDR at the helm of government, Bucharest was determined to make up for lost time in pursuing domestic political and economic reform, while at the same time pursuing entry into Western political and economic structures. Unfortunately, despite its advantages, the 'democratic opposition' failed in its efforts to fundamentally redirect Romania's politics. The factors that led to the miscarriage of reforms were manifold. Much of the blame can be attributed to the character of the opposition itself. The government coalition, the Democratic Convention, and the UDMR, and the Democratic Party were themselves politically divided to the extent that Michael Shafir referred to the arrangement as a 'coalition of coalitions' (Shafir 2001, 79–103). Not only did this situation make policy formulation more difficult, it impeded policy implementation as well. As Shafir and others have pointed out, each of the main actors in the coalition supported variants of reform that would have benefited its own supporters, vetoing to the extent possible the initiatives of its partners. Hence the reform process devolved into a chaos of particularism, stalemate, and factional bartering.

Once in power, Constantinescu and the reform coalition were also burdened with the negative consequences of their predecessor's failed policies. The previous government's legacy of international debt, the fiscal imbalance, and the overvalued exchange rate presented a serious obstacle to new reform efforts (Budina and van Wijnbergen 2000). Given the structural imbalances that existed in the Romanian economy, liberalization led to a second round of 'transition shock', not unlike that which occurred at the beginning of the 1990s. In 1997 inflation soared once again to 151 per cent, while real wages declined by one fourth.

Just as serious was the high level of corruption. By the time that President Constantinescu and the liberal coalition assumed power, corruption was already deeply embedded in Romanian public life. Charges were brought against senior officials of the previous administration; it proved difficult to follow through on prosecutions of individuals connected with the political elite (Gallager 2001, 396). Once they assumed power, it very quickly became apparent that the reformers themselves were not free from culpability. Almost immediately after the 1996 elections, charges of insider dealing and influence peddling re-emerged to plague the Ciorbea government and its successors.

Support for the Constantinescu and the centre-right coalition plummeted as the perception grew among Romanians that the government was unable to direct the economy effectively. Prime Minister Ciorbea's replacement by Radu Vasile and the installation of a new government did little to improve the situation. Vasile and his economic team did bring inflation back under control, but fundamental divisions continued to plague the government. While obviously aware of this situation, President Constantinescu was unable to impose order or restore direction to the reforms. In a final effort to salvage the situation, National Bank President Mugur Isarescu was Prime Minister in December 1999. By then, however, new elections were already on the horizon and the government's popular mandate had clearly been lost.

Thus as a new round of elections approached in 2000, Romanians were faced with a failed second chance at reform. Disillusionment with the reformist parties was both deep and widespread. Public opinion surveys entering the elections indicated that while the population generally maintained its commitment to reform, faith in the ability of the liberal parties had been severely eroded by four years of scandal and renewed economic hardship. In polling just before the elections, 75.9 per cent of the population favoured a market economy, with only 9.2 per cent rejecting it. In contrast only 7.6 per cent of the population expressed positive attitudes toward political parties in general, and only one of the governing parties (the PNL with 6.6 per cent) could claim more than 5 per cent popular support. Only 4 per cent of the population expressed any level of positive reaction to the government's efforts to deal with corruption.[19]

The internecine factionalism that plagued reform efforts became even more intense in the run-up to the 2000 elections. Conflict within the coalition that had supported President Constantinescu in 1996 totally undermined the ability of the centre-right to campaign (Pop-Eleches 2001, 156–69). Both the political left and far right were able to exploit these conditions. Former President Iliescu, in contrast to the liberal parties' leaders, had employed the four years intervening since his 1996 defeat to overhaul the PDSR and to restore its internal discipline. The party's electoral message of reform moderated by social protection clearly resonated with the population. Finally, many Romanians were won over by the promise of rule by a single party, which – it was hoped – would be able to restore order in the policy arena.[20]

Under the prevailing conditions of economic hardship and popular disillusionment, the Greater Romania Party (RM) and its leader Corneliu Vadim Tudor emerged as the most significant threat to democratic stability since the disorders of the immediate transition. After poor showing in the 1996 elections (4.5 per cent of the vote and 19 seats in the lower house), most observers felt that the Greater Romania Party would be effectively marginalized by an increasingly stable democratic consensus. Tudor, however, turned out to be both a tenacious politician and a skilled agitator. While maintaining his hold on the ethnic extremist base by playing on anti-Roma and anti-Hungarian sentiments, he became the most prominent critic of Romania's uncontrolled political corruption. Corneliu Vadim Tudor succeeded in establishing himself as the anti-establishment candidate, and his party as the party of the excluded outsiders. Benefiting from both the PDSR's shift away from extreme nationalism and from popular disenchantment with Constantinescu, the Greater Romania Party became a dominant factor in the 2000 elections, reshaping the Romanian political landscape.

The results of the first round in the November 2000 elections devastated the moderate parties, sending shockwaves through Romania. In the presidential elections Ion Iliescu dominated the field, with 36.4 per cent of the vote, followed in second place by Corneliu Vadim Tudor with 28.3 per cent. Liberal democratic candidates Teodor Stolojan and Mugur Isarescu garnered only 11.7 and 9.6 per cent respectively. Returns for Chamber of Deputies results closely mirrored this outcome. The PDSR captured 36.6 per cent of the total followed by Greater Romania, with 19.5 per cent. The Democratic Convention was reduced to 5.3 per cent, the PNL to 7.5 per cent, and the Petre Roman's Democratic Party (PD) to 7.6 per cent. UDMR candidate Gyorgy Frunda won 6.2 per cent of the presidential vote, while the party itself gained slightly more, 6.9 per cent in the Chamber of Deputies. Turnout in 2000 plummeted by more than 20 per cent, and the Democratic Convention failed to maintain its representation in parliament, further indicating the electorate's disenchantment.

Faced with this electoral catastrophe, leaders of the right-wing parties called on their followers to support Iliescu in the second round presidential voting in order to head off a victory by the extreme nationalists. The Media commentators and moderate politicians alike warned that a second round victory by Tudor would lead to the country's complete isolation from Western Europe (Mcaleer and Wagstyl 2000). Taking advantage of the situation, the PDSR moved to position itself as a moderate pro-reform force. Iliescu denounced 'totalitarianism and ethnic extremism', while committing his party to accelerated reform (Iliescu 2000). This strategy clearly succeeded with centrist voters. On 10 December, 2000, Iliescu's share of the second round presidential vote nearly doubled, rising to 66.8 per cent, while Corneliu Vadim Tudor's share increased to 33.2 per cent, only approximately five per cent more than his first round total.

The pattern of party support in the 2000 elections reflects the continued importance of social cleavages that have shaped Romanian electoral competition throughout the transition period. An examination of public opinion surveys carried out in November 2000 shows the influence of class divisions (as reflected in both income and education levels) and urban/rural differences as determinants of party preferences. The two regression analyses of Eurobarometer data reported in full in Appendix 11.5 bear out the significance of each of these factors, while the frequency of selected responses is reported in the three tables that follow. After the widespread popular swing to the liberal opposition parties in 1996, 2000 saw the reassertion of the earlier pattern of strong support by rural voters and less educated voters for Ion Iliescu and the PDSR, while urban and more educated respondents disproportionately favour the liberal parties (see *Table 11.7*). Similarly, the PDSR's advantage among rural voters reasserted itself.

Table 11.7: Party support by residence and education level (%)

	Area of residence		Education level		
	Urban	*Rural*	*Elementary*	*Secondary*	*Higher*
APR	34.5	65.5	63.6	32.7	3.6
CDR	63.3	36.7	45.6	32.9	21.5
PNL	73.5	26.5	42.7	34.2	23.1
PDSR	43.6	56.4	73.0	21.1	6.0
UDMR	63.2	36.8	63.2	28.7	8.0
PD	64.3	35.7	44.6	41.1	14.3
PRM	56.4	43.6	62.6	30.7	6.7

Note: The item reads: 'Which party will you vote for in the November 2000 elections?'

As Table 11.8 indicates, after a decade of transition the 'post-communist' cleavage continued to play a significant role as well. While support for the free market has become increasingly widespread over time, significant differences remain between the supporters of the liberal democratic parties and their opponents. Even more striking is the distribution of support for single party systems. The PDSR and Romania Mare (PRM) voters continue to be approximately evenly divided between those who support and those who oppose the single party option, while supporters of the main liberal parties favour competitive party systems by well over two to one margins.

Table 11.8: Party support by preference for market economy and one-party rule (%)

	Market economy?			Single political party?		
	Yes	*No*	*Don't know/ no response*	*Yes*	*No*	*Don't know/ no response*
APR	78.2	5.5	16.4	36.4	49.1	14.5
CDR	88.6	1.3	10.1	15.2	73.4	11.4
PNL	94.0	1.7	4.3	25.6	68.4	6.0
PDSR	73.6	10.5	15.9	44.5	42.0	13.5
UDMR	69.0	13.8	17.2	28.7	56.3	14.9
PD	82.1	8.9	8.9	25.0	62.5	12.5
PRM	77.9	14.1	8.0	44.8	47.9	7.4

Note: The two items read: 'In your view, is it good to have a market economy?', 'In your view, is it good to have a single political party?'

Finally, the significance of the European integration issue in Romanian politics was also unmistakable. Attitudes toward the EU and other Western institutions have historically been extremely positive in Romania. With regard to integration into economic and security organizations, Romanians have generally been more favourably inclined than any of the other transition countries. Yet even given this general support for integration, clear differences emerge when one examines the distribution of attitudes among party supporters. Once again, the most salient divide is that separating the supporters of the extreme nationalist Romania Mare Party (PRM) and the PDSR. In both of these parties approximately one in five supporters opposed entering NATO. Despite the PDSR leadership's commitment to European integration, the percentage of PDSR proponents (62.4 per cent) favouring entry into the EU is lower than that of any other party (*Table 11.9*).

The results of the 2000 elections gave rise to fundamental questions concerning Romania's democratic transition. The resurgence of political extremism and the return of the post-communist left to power bespeak unequivocal popular discontent with the centre-right reformers' performance in office. The failure of the liberal parties to fulfil the hopes invested in them produced a backlash against the entire political establishment. The return of the PDSR to power, however, also represents a substantial improvement over the initial Iliescu led phase in the transition. Free from its association with the extreme right, the PDSR (merged with the Romanian Social Democratic Party renamed the Social Democratic Party, PSD, in June 2001) is now much less constrained than was the case during the early 1990s. To the extent that its leaders decide to do so, the party is now substantially freer to pursue both ethnic accommodation and international reconciliation without fear of alienating its political base. One clear indication of the extent to which the political landscape had been transformed, was the character of support for the minority government formed following the elections. In order to give it a working majority of votes in the legislature, the PSD was supported by the UDMR, Hungarian party leaders having determined that cooperation with Iliescu was an acceptable price to pay for the exclusion of Greater Romania's influence.

Table 11.9: Party preference by support for NATO and the EU (%)

	NATO?			EU?		
	No	*Yes*	*Don't know/ no response*	*No*	*Yes*	*Don't know/ no response*
APR	20.0	67.3	12.7	9.1	78.2	12.7
CDR	6.3	79.7	13.9	2.5	88.6	8.9
PNL	9.4	80.3	10.3	5.1	88.0	6.8
PDSR	21.1	56.9	22.0	15.4	62.4	22.2
UDMR	4.6	75.9	19.5	2.3	81.6	16.1
PD	16.1	73.2	10.7	8.9	83.9	7.1
PRM	23.3	65.0	11.7	16.6	69.9	13.5

Note: The two items read: 'Do you think that it is useful for our country to enter into NATO?', 'Do you think that it is useful for our country to enter the EU?'

In another positive sign, the selection of Adrian Nastase as Prime Minster signalled the dominance of the more reformist wing of the PSD. During the period leading up to elections, Nastase, the former Foreign Minister, made a series of highly publicized statements in support of European integration and accelerated reform. Prime Minister Nastase's commitment to act on the party's campaign rhetoric became evident in the course of 2001 as his government pressed through a series of reforms that had earlier been stalled. In February 2001, President Iliescu signed a stronger property restitution law. Minority rights issues were also addressed, legislation was introduced that increased access to the communist period security files. The hope that a change in leadership would resolve the country's economic stalemate was also at least in part fulfilled. In 2000, Romanian GDP growth, at 1.6 per cent, was positive for the first time in three years. In 2001 growth reached 5.3 per cent, and inflation declined to 37 per cent.

That the second Iliescu administration has taken a much more affirmative approach to democratization thus appears clear. But serious barriers hinder efforts to further democratize Romania. Primary among the obstacles facing the country are the corruption and lack of transparency that have become embedded elements of the Romanian political system.[21] These issues extend well beyond the status of mere economic problems. As in a number of other post-communist cases, corruption in Romania comprises a system of informal relations and intra-elite bargaining that places a range of activities outside the sector of democratic control. Aurelian Craiuțu has termed the pattern of relations that developed during the first Iliescu administration 'perverse institutionalisation', focusing on the broad and ill-defined powers of the executive, the existence of policy domains exempt from the control of elected officials, and the emergence of widespread clientelism (Craiuțu 2000, 180). These practices clearly survived the Constantinescu interregnum, and currently stand as the primary barrier to further democratic consolidation.

Conclusions

The data presented here suggest a number of conclusions. First, early in the political transition both Romanian mass opinion and that of party elites (legislators) were differentiated along salient and policy relevant ideological dimensions. Second, despite their inexperience with electoral politics, members of the general population assessed particular parties in accordance with their view on salient dimensions, and their attitudes towards a variety of parties is consistent, in accordance with the ideological characteristics of each individual party's ideological characteristics. Furthermore, there was an evident coherence in the position of party legislative groups relative to the positions taken by their supporters along the dimensions examined.

The nature of early party competition is clear, and is explicable in reference to the nature of the cleavage structure that emerged in Romania following the 1989 revolution. The FDSN gained control over the state at the beginning of the transition process as an implicit reform communist party. Its leaders assumed an initially cautious position on economic reform issues, and then backed off from early initiatives as popular resistance to marketization and privatization became apparent. The party took up a relatively nationalist position on minority issues, which played a critical role in its legitimization strategy. The nationalism of the FDSN served to differentiate it further from the liberal parties that were its primary early opponents, while staving off the more extreme collectivist/nationalist parties.

The continual inter-elite attacks and divisions that have plagued the liberal opposition parties and created the impression of personalistic rather than issue-related politics are also partially explained by these data. The liberal opposition legislators (with the exception of the UDMR) were apparently grouped so closely together on both issue dimensions considered here that they felt compelled to resort to non-issue related attacks in efforts to distinguish themselves in their competition for a limited pool of potential supporters. In a similar vein, due to their intra-group competition, none of these parties moved into a less nationalist stance. Any such move risked the loss of support to other parties in the grouping that were equally for privatization of property and might then be closer to potential supporters on minority issues.

The electoral behaviour and to a certain extent the electoral fate of parties in Romania are thus explicable by reference to the parties' proximity to each other and to their potential constituents on crucial cleavages. Say what else one will, the party closest in position to the bulk of the population (the PDSR/FDSN) emerged as electorally dominant in the early phase of the Romanian transition. But both the character of its elite membership and its mass base severely constrained its ability to pursue an effective economic strategy. Thus support for the Romanian former communists declined within the working-class, initially a key element of its electoral base. With its capacity to appeal to nationalists constrained, and unable to attract voters from the emerging post-communist social groups, the leftist government was swept out of office in 1996. It thus seems indisputable that ideological cleavages emerged very early in the Romanian transition, and have played a crucial role in ongoing party competition.

The realignment of political forces that occurred in the context of the 1996 electoral campaign produced a political environment more in line with developments in other Central European countries during the second half of the 1990s. When the fragmented centre-right coalition led by President Constantinescu proved unable to govern effectively, the Romanian electorate predictably and understandably abandoned it. But unlike the first half of the decade, the alternative leadership group that emerged from the 2000 election was a chastened centre-left (if successor Communist in origin) Social Democratic Party. The Greater Romania Party, though it clearly enjoys a limited base of support, found itself without any viable coalition choice in this environment, and was effectively relegated to the margins of the country's political life. While Romania continues to be confronted with daunting challenges, it is now at least free of the coalitional constraints that so disastrously retarded political progress during the early transition.

Acronyms of Parties and Movements

AC	*Alianţa Civică* (Civic Alliance)
ANL	*Alianţa Naţional Liberal* (National Liberal Alliance)
APR	*Alianţa Pentru Romăna* (Alliance for Romania)
AUR	*Alianţa pentry Unitatea Românilor* (Romanian Unity Alliance, electoral wing of *Vatra Romaneasca*)
CDR	*Convenţia Democratică Romăna* (Democratic Convention of Romania)
CIR	*Comunitatea Italiana din România* (Italian Community of Romania)
FDGR	*Forumul Democrat al Germanilor din România* (German Democratic Forum of Romania)
FDSN	*Frontul Democrat al Salvării Naţionale* (Democratic National Salvation Front)
FER	*Federaţia Ecologistă Romăna* (Ecological Federation of Romania)
FSN	*Frontul Salvării Naţionale* (National Salvation Front)
MER	*Mişcarea Ecologistă din România* (Romanian Ecological Movement)
MR	*Mişcarea pentru Romănia* (Movement for Romania)
PAC	*Partidul Alianţă Civică* (Civic Alliance Party)
PAR	*Partidul Alternativă României* (Alternative Party of Romania)
PAN	*Partidul Alianţa Naţional* (National Alliance Party)
PER	*Partidul Ecologist Romăn* (Romanian Ecological Party)
PD	*Partidul Democrat* (Democratic Party)
PDAR	*Partidul Democratic Agrar din România* (Democratic Agrarian Party of Romania)
PDSR	*Partidul Democraţiei Sociale din Romănia* (Party of Romanian Social Democracy)
PNL	*Partidul Naţional Liberal* (National Liberal Party)
PNL-AT	*Partidul Naţional Liberal Aripa Tineretului* (National Liberal Party–Youth Wing)
PNL–C	*Partidul Naţional Liberal–Campeanu* (National Liberal Party–Campeanu)
PNT-CD	*Partidul Naţional Ţăranesc–Creştin Democrat* (National Peasant Party–Christian and Democratic)
PPR	*Partidul Pensionerilor Romăn* (Pensioners' Party of Romania)
PR	*Partidul Republican* (Republican Party)
PRM	*Partidul 'Romănia Mare'* ('Romania Mare' Party)
PS	*Partidul Socialist* (Socialist Party)
PSD	*Particul Social Democrat* (Social Democratic Party)
PSDR	*Partidul Socialist Democrat Romăn* (Social Democratic Party of Romania)
PSM	*Partidul Socialist al Muncii* (Socialist Labour Party)
PSMR	*Partidul Socialist Muncitoresc Romăn* (Party of Socialist Workers of Romania)
PUNR	*Partidul Unităţi Naţionale Romăne* (Party of Romanian National Unity)
PUR	*Partidul Umanist din Romănia* (Humanist Party of Romania)
RCP	*Partidul Comunist Romăn* (Romanian Communist Party)
RM	*Partidul Romănia Mare* (Greater Romania Party)
RP	*Partida Romilor* (Roma Party)
UAR	*Uniunea Armenilor din Romănia* (Armenian Union of Romania)
UBD	*Uniunea Bulgara Banat-Romănia* (Bulgarian Union of the Banate-Romania)
UDMR	*Uniunea Democratică Maghiara din Romănia* (Democratic Magyar Union of Romania)
USD	*Uniunea Social Democrat* (Social Democratic Union)

NOTES

1. For a review of this debate and an extremely useful contribution to it, see Stephen Whitefield and Geoffrey Evens (1997). Whitefield and Evens argue convincingly for the independent role of cleavages in determining political outcomes in post-communist societies (cf. Evens and Whitefield 1993). Ellen Comisso (1997) presents a concise argument to the effect that social cleavages do exist in post-communist Central Europe, but only weakly associated with elite-level politics.

2. The public opinion survey research in Romania cited in this chapter was funded by a grant from the National Council for Soviet and East European Research, contract number 806–20. Fieldwork was carried out by the Center for Rural and Urban Sociology. Approximately 1600 respondents were selected based upon a national probability sample. A stratified sample was drawn based on historical region and type of locality (rural, small towns, and cities). As a sampling frame, voter lists compiled for the 1990 elections were employed. Face to face interviews were used in this project. The questionnaire included 266 questions, and required an average time of approximately one hour to administer. Members of minority communities were recruited to administer the survey in minority districts, and in each case minority language versions of the survey instrument were prepared for the use of members of the larger minority groups. Subjects were provided with an opportunity to choose the language in which they wished to respond. The data on legislators' opinions are based on a 1993 survey of members of the Romanian parliament conducted by William Crowther in collaboration with Gheorgeta Muntean and Informatix, AG in Bucharest. A total of 357 members of both houses responded to the written survey; 102 responses were from the Senate, 255 were from the House. All the parties in parliament were represented in the results.

3. For a thorough treatment of the evolution of Romania's inter-war political economy, see Roberts (1951).

4. On the rise of Romanian fascism, see Weber (1965) or Nagy-Talavera (1967).

5. On the origins and evolution of the Romanian communist movement, see Ionescu (1964).

6. The actual course of events leading to Ceauşescu's overthrow and execution, and the nature of the leadership that emerged from Romania's December revolution immediately became the subjects of intense speculation. Cf. Tismaneanu (1990, 17–21).

7. This decision destabilized an already volatile situation, touching off a series of demonstrations both by the student movement and by anti-Iliescu political parties. In response, the FSN resorted to a combination of force and compromise. In the last week of January 1990, Iliescu mobilized supportive workers who rampaged through the capital attacking supporters of anti-Front political parties. At the same time limited concessions were employed to defuse opposition. The National Salvation Front agreed to dissolve itself as a government and form a new body, the Provisional Council of National Unity, which would rule until elections could be held.

8. For summaries of the programmes of these parties as well as those of the Social Democratic Party and the Ecological Democrats, see Socor (1990, 28–35).

9. Thus, even if all of the opposition groups voted as a bloc, a circumstance that was virtually unimaginable, the Front would still have controlled both new legislative bodies. In fact, on most issues the Romanian Unity Alliance (AUR) – the electoral wing of *Vatra Romaneasca* – and many of the smaller parties could be counted on to in act support of the FSN on most issues, insuring it of control over both executive and legislative branches.

10. For a more detailed discussion of the early post-communist economic reforms in Romania, see Isarescu (1992, 147–65).

11. The Democratic Convention succeeded in gaining 23 per cent of mayoral votes, in comparison with 31 per cent for the still unified National Salvation Front. More significantly, the Convention captured control of seven of the country's largest urban areas, including the capital.

12. The factor analysis was conducted with varimax rotation:

Rotated Factor Matrix

	Factor 1	Factor 2
FSN	0.45624	-0.16666
FDSN	0.69729	-0.17239
PNT-CD	-0.12632	0.81410
UDMR	0.16622	0.67430
PAC	-0.11527	0.82837
PDAR	0.71865	0.24640
PUNR	0.77177	0.14958
PSM	0.58141	0.05967
RM	0.74671	-0.01607
PNL	0.26028	0.62579
PNL-AT	0.31691	0.70326

Factor Transformation Matrix

	Factor 1	*Factor 2*
Factor 1	0.78499	0.61951
Factor 2	-0.61951	0.78499

13. Three other parties that played significant roles in the 1992 elections were not firmly attached to either of these groupings. Led by ex-student activist Marin Munteanu, the Movement for Romania (MR) had ties to the pre-war Legionnaire Movement. It could thus clearly be described as nationalist, but it is also economically liberal, which puts it in an equivocal position between two opposed blocs. Support for the Romanian Ecological Movement (MER) and the Republican Party (PR), on the other hand, did not appear to be determined adequately by the ideological dimensions identified above. Confidence in them does not correlate significantly with attitudes that distinguish supporters of the two main blocs, and their supporters were not consistent in their attitudes toward the parties that participate in the main competing coalitions (*Table 11.4*).

14. This loss, while in part explicable by migration to other parties and their candidates, must also be seen in the context of the artificially inflated support for Iliescu registered in the elections of 1990.

15. Analysis of variance:

Attitude toward minorities by political affiliation

Source	D.F.	Sum of squares	Mean squares	F Ratio	F Prob.
Between groups	7	67.4537	9.6362	72.8793	0.0000
Within groups	288	38.0799	0.1322		
Total	295	105.5336			

Support for private property by political affiliation

Source	D.F.	Sum of squares	Mean squares	F Ratio	F Prob.
Between groups	7	9.2347	1.3192	17.8870	0.0000
Within groups	287	21.1675	0.0738		
Total	294	30.4022			

16. T-tests showed differences between legislators and supporters, and supporters and non-supporters to be significant at the 0.05 level in every case with regard to the property issue.

17. T-tests showed mean score differences on the scale significant at the 0.05 level except in the case of FDSN legislators and their supporters, PSM legislators and their supporters, PAC legislators and their supporters, PNT-CD legislators and their supporters, and PNL supporters and non-supporters.

18. On the significance of the transfer of power to the liberal opposition see Shafir (1997).

19. See the *Open Society Foundation Public Opinion Barometer*. Data available at http://www.sfos.ro/.

20. While support for limited government and democratic norms is apparent in some areas, the same *Open Society* survey cited above indicates that by 2000, 35 per cent of the Romanians preferred a one-party system to multi-party democracy. This clearly reflects a reaction to the disorder associated with multi-party rule.

21. A World Bank study of the problem indicates that two-thirds of the Romanians believe all or most public officials to be corrupt, and highlights the impact of corruption on income inequality, business development, and foreign investment. See *Diagnostic Surveys of Corruption in Romania* (The World Bank 2001).

REFERENCES

Budina, Nina and Swender van Wijnbergen (2000), 'Fiscal Deficits, Monetary Reform and Inflation Stabilization in Romania', The World Bank, *Working Papers Series*, Number 2298, March 2000.

Carry, Henry F. (1995), 'Irregularities or Rigging: The 1992 Romanian Parliamentary Elections', *East European Quarterly*, (Spring) V. 29, No.1.

Comisso, Ellen (1997), 'Is the Glass Half Full or Half Empty?: Reflections of Five Years of Competitive Politics in Eastern Europe', *Communist and Post Communist Studies*, Vol. 30, No. 1, 1–21.

Craiuțu, Aureian, (2000), 'Light at the end of the Tunnel: Romania 1989–1999', in Geoffrey Pridham and Tom Gallagher, eds, *Experimenting with Democracy: Regime Change in the Balkans*, London, Routledge.

Crowther, William (1988), *The Political Economy of Romanian Socialism*, New York, Praeger.

Deletant, Denis (2001), 'Ghosts from the Past: Successors to the Securitate in Post-Communist Romania', in Duncan Light and David Phinnemore, eds, *Post Communist Romania: Coming to Terms with Transition*, New York, Palgrave.

Evens, Geoffry and Stephen Whitefield (1993), 'Identifying the Basis of Party Competition in Eastern Europe', *British Journal of Political Science*, Vol. 23, No. 4, 521–48.

Gallagher, Tom (1995), *Romania After Ceaușescu*, Edinburgh, Edinburgh University Press.

—— (2001), 'Building Democracy in Romania', in Jan Zielonka, ed., *Democratic Consolidation in Eastern Europe, Vol. 2*, New York, Oxford University Press.

Iliescu, Ion (2000), *Rompress News Agency*, 27 November, 2000.

Ionescu, Ghita (1964), *Communism in Romania: 1944–1962,* London, Oxford University Press.

Isarescu, Mugur (1992), 'The Prognosis for Economic Recovery', in Daniel N. Nelson, ed., *Romania After Tyranny*, Boulder, CO., Westview Press.

Kitschelt, Herbert (1992), 'The Formation of Party Systems in East Central Europe', *Politics and Society*, 20 (1), 7–50.

—— (1994), 'Party Systems in East Central Europe: Consolidation or Fluidity', paper prepared for presentation at the 1994 Annual Meeting of the *American Political Science Association*, New York, 4 September.

Lipset, Seymour Martin and Stein Rokkan (1967), 'Cleavage Structures, Party Systems, and Voter Alignments', in Seymour Martin Lipset and Stein Rokkan, eds, *Party Systems and Voter Alignments: Cross-National Perspectives*, New York, The Free Press.

MacFarlan, Maitland, Joaquim O. Martins and Paul Paradis (1998), 'Romana: Macro-Economic Stabilization and Structural Reform', *OECD Observer* (April–May), No. 221, 39–43.

Mcaleer, Phelim and Stefan Wagstyl (2000), 'Rise of Nationalists Throws Romania into Uncertainty, *The Financial Times*, 28 November.

Nagy-Talavera, Nicolas (1967), *The Green Shirts and Others: A History of Fascism in Hungary and Romania*, Berkeley, CA, University of California Press.

Open Society Foundation Public Opinion Barometer. Data available at http://www.sfos.ro/.

Phinnemore, David (2001), 'Romania and Euro-Atlantic Integration since 1989: A Decade of Frustration', in Duncan Light and David Phinnemore, eds, *Post Communist Romania: Coming to Terms with Transition*, New York, Palgrave.

Pop-Eleches, Grigore (2001), 'Romania's Political Dejection', *Journal of Democracy*, Volume 12, Number 3 (July), 156–69.

Roberts, Henry L. (1951), *Rumania: Political Problems of an Agrarian State,* New Haven, Yale University Press.

Roper, Steven D. (2000), *Romania: The Unfinished Revolution,* Amsterdam, Harwood Academic Publishers.

Shafir, Michael (1997), 'Romania's Road to Normalcy', *Journal of Democracy,* Vol. 8 (April), 144–58.

—— (2001), 'The Ciorbea Government and Democratization: A Preliminary Assessment', in Duncan Light and David Phinnemore, eds, *Post Communist Romania: Coming to Terms with Transition*, New York, Palgrave.

Socor, Vladimir (1990), 'Political Parties Emerging', *Radio Free Europe/Radio Liberty Research Reports*, 16 February.

Tismaneanu, Vladimir (1990), 'New Masks, Old Faces', *The New Republic,* 5 February.

Verdery, Katherine (1991), *National Ideology Under Socialism*, Los Angeles, University of California Press.

Watts, Larry L. (2002), 'Reform and Crisis in Romania Civil-Military Relations 1989–1999', *Armed Forces and Society* (Summer), 596–622.

Weber, Eugen (1965), 'Romania', in Hans Rogger and Eugen Weber, eds, *The European Right: A Historical Profile,* Los Angeles, University of California Press.

Weber, Renate (2001), 'Constitutionalism as a Vehicle for Democratic Consolidation in Romania', in Jan Zielonka, ed., *Democratic Consolidation in Eastern Europe, Vol. 1*, New York, Oxford University Press.

Whitefield, Stephen and Geoffrey Evens (1997), 'From the Top Down or the Bottom Up? Explaining the Structure of Ideological Cleavages in Post Communist Societies', mimeo.

The World Bank (2001), *Diagnostic Surveys of Corruption in Romania*, Analysis prepared by the World Bank at the request of the Government of Romania, September 2001.

APPENDIX 11.1: ELECTION RESULTS

PARLIAMENTARY ELECTIONS

1990 Elections
Date: 20 May
Turnout: 86.2%

House of Deputies

Party	%	Seats	Seats, %
National Salvation Front	66.3	263	67.9
Democratic Magyar Union of Romania	7.2	29	7.5
National Liberal Party	6.4	29	7.5
Romanian Ecological Movement	2.6	12	3.1
National Peasant Party	2.6	12	3.1
Alliance for Romania	2.1	9	2.3
Democratic Agrarian Party of Romania	1.8	9	2.3
Romanian Ecological Party	1.7	8	2.1
Socialist Democratic Party of Romania	1.0	5	1.3
Social Democratic Party	0.5	2	0.5
Democratic Group of the Centre	0.5	2	0.5
Democratic Party of Work	0.4	1	0.2
Party of Free Change	0.3	1	0.2
Party of National Reconstruction of Romania	0.3	1	0.2
Party of Young Free Democrats of Romania	0.3	1	0.2
German Democratic Forum of Romania	0.3	1	0.2
Liberal Union 'Bratianu'	0.3	1	0.2
Democratic Union of Romania	0.2	1	0.2
Total	94.9	387	100

Senate

Party	%	Seats	Seats,%
National Salvation Front	67.0	91	76.5
Democratic Magyar Union of Romania	7.2	12	10.1
National Liberal Party	7.1	10	8.4
National Peasant Party	2.5	1	0.8
Romanian Ecological Movement	2.4	1	0.8
Alliance for Romania	2.2	2	1.7
Democratic Agrarian Party of Romania	1.6	–	–
Romanian Ecological Party	1.4	1	–
Social Democratic Party	1.1	–	–
Independent	n/m	1	0.8
Total	n/m	119	100

1992 Elections
Date: 27 September
Turnout: 76.3%

Chamber of Deputies

Party	%	Seats
Democratic National Salvation Front	27.7	117
Democratic Convention of Romania[*]	20.0	82
National Salvation Front	10.2	43
Party of Romanian National Unity	7.9	30
Democratic Magyar Union of Romania	7.4	27
Greater Romania Party	3.8	16
Socialist Labour Party	3.0	13
Democratic Agrarian Party of Romania	2.9	–
National Liberal Party	2.6	–
Romanian Ecological Movement	2.3	–
Republican Party	1.6	–

Senate

Party	%	Seats
Democratic National Salvation Front	28.3	49
Democratic Convention of Romania*	20.2	34
National Salvation Front	10.4	18
Party of Romanian National Unity	8.1	14
Democratic Magyar Union of Romania	7.6	12
Greater Romania Party	3.8	6
Socialist Labour Party	3.2	5
Democratic Agrarian Party of Romania	3.3	3
National Liberal Party	2.1	–
Romanian Ecological Movement	2.1	–
Republican Party	1.9	–

[*] In 1992, the Democratic Convention was an electoral coalition of 12 parties, including the PNT–CD, PAC, PNL, PNL–AT, PDSR, the Romanian Ecological Party, and a number of smaller parties.

1996 Elections
Date: 3 November
Turnout: 76.0%

Chamber of Deputies

Party	%	Seats
Democratic Convention of Romania[*]	30.2	122
Party of Romanian Social Democracy	21.5	91
Social Democratic Union	12.9	53
Democratic Magyar Union of Romania	6.6	25
Greater Romania Party	4.5	19
Party of Romanian National Unity	4.4	18
Socialist Party	2.3	–
Socialist Labour Party	2.2	–
Party of Socialist Workers of Romania	1.7	–
National Liberal Alliance	1.6	–
Pensioners' Party of Romania	1.4	–
Minority Deputies		15
Total	100	343

Senate

Party	%	Seats
Democratic Convention of Romania*	30.7	51
Party of Romanian Social Democracy	23.1	41
Social Democratic Union	13.2	23
Democratic Magyar Union of Romania	6.8	11
Greater Romania Party	4.5	8
Party of Romanian National Unity	4.2	7
Socialist Party	2.3	–
Socialist Labour Party	2.2	–
National Liberal Alliance	1.5	–
Pensioners' Party of Romania	1.5	–
Party of Socialist Workers of Romania	1.3	–
Total	100	143

[*] In 1996, the Democratic Convention was an electoral coalition, including the PNT–CD, PNL, PNL–AT, the Alternative Party of Romania, the Romanian Ecological Party, the Ecological Federation of Romania, the Civic Alliance, the Association of Former Political Prisoners, the University Solidarity, the Movement for Romania's Future, the Association of Revolutionaries '21 December 1989', the World Union of Free Romanians, and the National Union of Unemployed Persons.

2000 Elections
Date: 26 November
Turnout: 65.3% (11,559,458 votes cast)

Chamber of Deputies

Party	%	Seats	
Party of Romanian Social Democracy–			
Social Democratic Party of Romania	36.6	155	(PDSR 142, PSDR 7, PUR 6)
'Romania Mare' Party	19.5	84	
Democratic Party	7.0	31	
National Liberal Party	6.9	30	
Democratic Magyar Union of Romania	6.8	27	
Democratic Convention of Romania 2000	5.0	–	
Alliance for Romania*	4.1	–	
National Liberal Party–Campeanu	1.4	–	
National Alliance Party	1.4	–	
Roma Party	0.7	1	
German Democratic Forum of Romania	0.4	1	
Armenian Union of Romania	0.2	1	
Italian Community of Romania	0.2	1	
Bulgarian Union of the Banate-Romania	0.2	1	
Other parties (minor parties)	10.0	14	
Total	100	346	

Senate

Party	%	Seats	
Party of Romanian Social Democracy–			
Social Democratic Party of Romania	37.1	65	(PDSR 60, PSDR 1, PUR 4)
'Romania Mare' Party	21.0	37	
Democratic Party	7.6	13	
National Liberal Party	7.5	13	
Democratic Magyar Union of Romania	6.9	12	
Democratic Convention of Romania 2000	5.3	–	
Alliance for Romania*	4.3	–	
National Liberal Party–Campeanu	1.4	–	
National Alliance Party	1.2	–	
Romanian Ecological Party	1.0	–	
Other parties (minor parties)	6.7	–	
Total	100	140	

* APR merged into the PNL in 2002.

PRESIDENTIAL ELECTIONS

1990 Elections
Date: 20 May

Candidate	Party	% of vote
Ion Iliescu	FSN	85.1
Radu Campeanu	PNL	10.6
Ion Rațiu	PNT–CD	4.3

1992 Elections
Dates: 27 September (first round) and 12 October (second round)
Turnout: 76.3% (first round), 74.2% (second round)

Candidate	Party	% of vote First round	% of vote Second round
Ion Iliescu	FDSN	47.2	61.4
Emil Constantinescu	CDR	31.2	38.6
Gheorghe Funar	PUNR	11.0	
Caius Dragomir	SN	4.8	
Ion Manzatu	PR	3.1	
Mircea Druc	Independent	2.8	

1996 Elections
Dates: 7 November (first round) and 17 November (second round)
Turnout: 75.9%

Candidate	Party	% of vote First round	% of vote Second round
Emil Constantinescu	CDR	28.2	54.4
Ion Iliescu	PDSR	32.2	45.6
Petre Roman	USD	20.5	
György Frunda	UDMR	6.0	
Corneliu Vadim Tudor	PRM	4.7	
Gheorghe Funar	PUNR	3.2	
Tudor Mohora	PS	1.3	

2000 Elections
Dates: 26 November (first round) and 10 December (second round)
Turnout: 65.3% (11,559,458 votes cast, first round), 57.5% (10,184,715 votes cast, second round)

Candidate	Party	% of vote First round	% of vote Second round
Ion Iliescu	PDSR–PSDR	36.4	66.8
Corneliu Vadim Tudor	PRM	28.3	33.2
Theodor Stolojan	PNL	11.8	
Mugur Isarescu	Independent	9.5	
Gyorgy Frunda	UDMR	6.2	
Petre Roman	PRM	3.0	
Teodor Melescanu	APR	1.9	
Other candidates		2.9	

APPENDIX 11.2: GOVERNMENT COMPOSITION

Time	Prime Minister (Party)	Political orientation	Reason for change of Government
May 1990 – 27 September 1991	Petre Roman (FSN)	Left	Breakdown of initial ruling party (FSN) into factions. President Iliescu became leader of FDSN. Roman stepped down to lead rump FSN.
17 October 1991 – 20 November 1992	Theodor Stolojan (unaffiliated)	Left/technocrat	New elections held. PDSR controlled promulgation of post-communist constitution.
20 November 1992 – 12 December 1996	Nicolae Vacariou (independent, aligned with FDSN/PDSR)	Left/nationalist, PDSR controlled	Change of government following scheduled elections at end of parliamentary term.
12 December 1996 – 16 April 1998	Victor Ciorbea (CDR)	Centre-right	New elections held.
16 April 1998 – 14 December 1999	Radu Vasile (CDR)	Centre-right	Change of Government due to conflict within ruling coalition.
14 December 1999 – 28 December 2000	Mugur Isarescu (CDR)	Centre-right	Change of Government in anticipation of scheduled elections.
28 December 2000 –	Adrean Nastase (PSD)	Left	New elections held. PSD formed minority government.

APPENDIX 11.3: THE ELECTORAL SYSTEM

Law No. 68/1992 for elections to the Chamber of Deputies and the Senate was published on 16 July 1992. It was in force for the 1996 elections. Members of the Senate and the Chamber of Deputies are elected by equal, secret, free, direct vote for a four-year term. Voters have the right to one vote for the Chamber of Deputies and one vote for the Senate. Citizens who have reached the age of 18 on election day have the right to vote. According to Art. 34 of the Constitution, citizens mentally deficient or alienated, laid under interdiction, as well as persons disenfranchised by a final decision of the court cannot vote. Eligibility to run for office is granted to all citizens having the right to vote and who on election day have reached the age of 23 (Chamber of Deputies), or 35 (the Senate and the office of President of Romania).

Deputies and Senators are elected from electoral districts on the basis of proportional representation. The standard for the Chamber of Deputies is one deputy to 70,000 inhabitants. The standard for the Senate is one Senator to 160,000 inhabitants. The number of deputies and senators will be in rapport with the number of inhabitants in each district. One senator or deputy will be added when more than one half of the relevant standard is surpassed. The number of deputies in a district will not be less than four, the number of senators will not be less than two. Recognized national minorities who do not elect a representative have the right to one deputy.

For the 1992 elections, 42 electoral districts were established based on the Romanian administrative districts (*judeţ*). Senators and deputies were assigned to these proportionally, with a total of 328 deputies, and 143 senators. Recognized parties and other political formations propose candidates on separate candidate lists. In each electoral district a party, political formation or coalition of these can propose for each chamber of the parliament only a single list of candidates. A party or formation can participate only in one single coalition. Individuals can participate as independent candidates only if they obtain support from at least 0.5 of the number of permanently registered voters in the district in which they wish to run. Candidates can run for the Senate or the Chamber of Deputies only in one single electoral district.

The government must publicly announce the date of elections at least 60 days in advance of the event. Elections must take place on a single day, and this must be a Sunday. All citizens with the right to vote shall be enrolled on permanent electoral lists in the district of their domicile. Romanian citizens living abroad have the right to be listed in the district where they were born, or where they later moved. Each voter is enrolled on a single electoral list. Voters enrolled on the permanent electoral lists will receive registration cards, which grant them the right to vote. The electoral campaign officially begins on the day that the election is announced, and ends two days before voting takes place.

Only candidates on party lists that receive a minimum of 3 per cent of the national vote may be elected. In the case of electoral coalitions, for 1992 one percentage point is added to the 3 per cent threshold for each party running in the coalition, up to a maximum of 8 per cent.

According to rules established for the 1990 parliamentary elections, 'wasted votes' are aggregated at the national level in order to achieve greater proportionality. In each constituency, an electoral coefficient is calculated by summing the number of valid votes cast for the party lists and independent candidates and dividing this number by the district magnitude. Any 'unused' votes at the district level are transferred to a national level in which a second allocation is made using the d'Hondt method. At the national level, all party votes are combined and divided by the number of mandates not assigned at the district level.

Law No. 69/1992 for election of the President was published on 16 July 1992. It was in force for the 1996 elections. The President is elected by equal, secret, free, direct vote for a four-year term. Citizens over the age of 18 on the day of the election have the right to vote, in accordance with Art. 34 of the Constitution. Voters have the right to one vote in each presidential election in accordance with Art. 81 of the Constitution. Voting for President will take place in the electoral districts established for the Chamber of Deputies and Senate elections. Political parties or other political formations may propose candidates for the presidency, individually or by coalitions. In order to run candidates must be supported by 100,000 voters. Voters may support only a single candidate for election. The date of elections must be publicly announced by the government at least 60 days in advance of the event. Elections must take place on a single day, and this must be a Sunday.

A candidate who receives more than half of the votes cast in the first round is elected. If no single candidate receives a majority of the votes, a second round is held. Second round elections will be held two weeks after the first round, based on the same voting lists as in the first round, and using the same electoral districts. Only the two candidates receiving the highest number of votes in the first round participate in the second round.

APPENDIX 11.4: THE CONSTITUTIONAL FRAMEWORK

The Romanian constitution was adopted on 8 December 1991. The form of the Romanian State is a Republic. Parliament is the supreme representative body of the Romanian people and the sole legislative authority of the country. Parliament consists of the Chamber of Deputies and the Senate. Parliament passes constitutional, organic, and ordinary laws.

The President represents the Romanian State and is the safeguard of the national independence, unity, and territorial integrity of the country. He shall act as mediator between the powers of the State, as well as between the State and society. The President is elected by universal suffrage for a term of four years. The President may preside over meetings of the government debating matters of national interest with regard to foreign policy, defence, and public order, or other matters at the request of the Prime Minister. The President presides over meetings that he attends. The President may dissolve parliament after consultation with the leaders of both chambers if no vote of confidence has been obtained to from a government within 60 days after the first request was made. During the same year, Parliament may be dissolved only once. The President may initiate referenda. The President is Commander-in-Chief of the Armed Forces. He may institute a state of emergency, but must request parliamentary approval within five days. The President may be impeached for grave acts infringing upon the Constitution by a majority vote of the members of the Chamber of Deputies and the Senate, voting in joint session.

The Government shall ensure the implementation of the domestic and foreign policy of the country and exercise the general management of public administration. The Government consists of the Prime Minister, Ministers, and other members as established by an organic law.

The President designates the Prime Minister after consultation with the party that has obtained an absolute majority in Parliament, or if no such party exists, with the parties represented in Parliament. Within ten days the Prime Minister shall present a government list to a joint session of the Chamber of Deputies and Senate and seek a vote of confidence.

The Prime Minister directs the Government and submits to the Parliament reports on its activities. The Government shall adopt Orders and Decisions in order to organize the execution of laws passed by the Parliament. The Government exercises its term in office until validation through general parliamentary elections, or until a withdrawal of parliamentary confidence. The Government must present any information requested by the Chamber of Deputies, Senate or Parliamentary Committees, and members of the Government must attend proceedings of Parliament if requested. The Chamber of Deputies and Senate in joint session may issue a motion of censure, withdrawing confidence from the Government, through a majority of vote. Such motions are initiated by at least one fourth of the Deputies and Senators. The Government may make a programme, policy or bill an issue of confidence before the Chamber of Deputies and the Senate in joint session. If no motion of censure has been passed within three days from such presentation, the bill or programme is considered passed, and becomes binding upon the Government.

APPENDIX 11.5: REGRESSION RESULTS

Nominal Regression: Party Preference by Age, Education, Income, and Residence

Model Fitting Information

Model	-2 Log Likelihood	Chi-Square	Df	Sig.
Intercept Only	1219.980			
Final	1005.464	214.516	54	0.000

Pseudo R-Square

Cox and Snell	0.166
Nagelkerke	0.175
McFadden	0.061

Likelihood Ratio Tests

Effect	-2 Log Likelihood of Reduced Model	Chi-Square	Df	Sig.
Intercept	1005.464 (a)	0.000	0	.
AGE	1051.271	45.807	12	0.000
EDUCATIO	1039.376	33.912	12	0.001
URBRUR	1031.864	26.400	6	0.000
INCOME1	1054.894	49.430	24	0.002

The chi-square statistic is the difference in -2 log-likelihoods between the final model and a reduced model. The reduced model is formed by omitting an effect from the final model. The null hypothesis is that all parameters of that effect are 0.
(a) This reduced model is equivalent to the final model because omitting the effect does not increase the degrees of freedom.

Parameter Estimates

Party Support		B	Std. Error	Wald	df	Sig.	Exp (B)	95% Confidence Interval for Exp (B)	
								Lower Bound	Upper Bound
APR	Intercept	-1.304	0.901	2.091	1	0.148			
	[AGE=1]	0.832	0.494	2.832	1	0.092	2.297	0.872	6.052
	[AGE=2]	0.559	0.422	1.754	1	0.185	1.749	0.765	3.999
	[AGE=3]	0 (b)	.	.	0	.	.	.	.
	[EDUCATIO=1]	0.291	0.831	0.122	1	0.727	1.337	0.262	6.821
	[EDUCATIO=2]	0.459	0.829	0.306	1	0.580	1.582	0.311	8.038
	[EDUCATIO=3]	0 (b)	.	.	0	.	.	.	.
	[URBRUR=1]	-0.918	0.350	6.873	1	0.009	0.399	0.201	0.793
	[URBRUR=2]	0 (b)	.	.	0	.	.	.	.

		B	S.E.	Wald	df	Sig.	Exp(B)		
	[INCOME1=1.00]	0.165	0.593	0.078	1	0.780	1.180	0.369	3.774
	[INCOME1=2.00]	-0.145	0.513	0.079	1	0.778	0.865	0.316	2.367
	[INCOME1=3.00]	-0.772	0.556	1.926	1	0.165	0.462	0.155	1.375
	[INCOME1=4.00]	-0.191	0.440	0.187	1	0.665	0.827	0.349	1.958
	[INCOME1=5.00]	0 (b)	.	.	0	.	.	.	.
CDR	Intercept	0.223	0.572	0.152	1	0.697			
	[AGE=1]	0.319	0.423	0.567	1	0.452	1.375	0.600	3.153
	[AGE=2]	0.100	0.345	0.084	1	0.772	1.105	0.562	2.172
	[AGE=3]	0 (b)	.	.	0	.	.	.	.
	[EDUCATIO=1]	-1.567	0.489	10.293	1	0.001	0.209	0.080	0.543
	[EDUCATIO=2]	-1.052	0.476	4.879	1	0.027	0.349	0.137	0.888
	[EDUCATIO=3]	0 (b)	.	.	0	.	.	.	.
	[URBRUR=1]	0.048	0.316	0.023	1	0.880	1.049	0.564	1.949
	[URBRUR=2]	0 (b)	.	.	0	.	.	.	.
	[INCOME1=1.00]	1.241	0.491	6.372	1	0.012	3.457	1.320	9.059
	[INCOME1=2.00]	0.069	0.492	0.019	1	0.889	1.071	0.409	2.808
	[INCOME1=3.00]	-0.206	0.461	0.199	1	0.656	0.814	0.330	2.010
	[INCOME1=4.00]	-0.373	0.417	0.800	1	0.371	0.689	0.304	1.560
	[INCOME1=5.00]	0 (b)	.	.	0	.	.	.	.
PNL	Intercept	-0.368	0.545	0.457	1	0.499			
	[AGE=1]	1.310	0.399	10.782	1	0.001	3.707	1.696	8.102
	[AGE=2]	0.840	0.344	5.962	1	0.015	2.316	1.180	4.547
	[AGE=3]	0 (b)	.	.	0	.	.	.	.
	[EDUCATIO=1]	-1.434	0.436	10.791	1	0.001	0.238	0.101	0.561
	[EDUCATIO=2]	-1.137	0.429	7.020	1	0.008	0.321	0.138	0.744
	[EDUCATIO=3]	0 (b)	.	.	0	.	.	.	.
	[URBRUR=1]	0.540	0.287	3.540	1	0.060	1.716	0.978	3.012
	[URBRUR=2]	0 (b)	.	.	0	.	.	.	.
	[INCOME1=1.00]	0.716	0.476	2.258	1	0.133	2.046	0.804	5.204
	[INCOME1=2.00]	0.369	0.422	0.764	1	0.382	1.446	0.632	3.309
	[INCOME1=3.00]	-0.395	0.420	0.884	1	0.347	0.674	0.296	1.535
	[INCOME1=4.00]	-0.072	0.341	0.044	1	0.834	0.931	0.477	1.818
	[INCOME1=5.00]	0 (b)	.	.	0	.	.	.	.
PDSR	Intercept	1.463	0.427	11.716	1	0.001			
	[AGE=1]	-0.222	0.282	0.619	1	0.431	0.801	0.460	1.393
	[AGE=2]	-0.023	0.213	0.011	1	0.915	0.978	0.644	1.484
	[AGE=3]	0 (b)	.	.	0	.	.	.	.
	[EDUCATIO=1]	-0.131	0.385	0.115	1	0.735	0.878	0.412	1.868
	[EDUCATIO=2]	-0.337	0.390	0.748	1	0.387	0.714	0.332	1.533
	[EDUCATIO=3]	0 (b)	.	.	0	.	.	.	.
	[URBRUR=1]	-0.305	0.192	2.510	1	0.113	0.737	0.505	1.075
	[URBRUR=2]	0 (b)	.	.	0	.	.	.	.
	[INCOME1=1.00]	1.133	0.360	9.872	1	0.002	3.104	1.531	6.292
	[INCOME1=2.00]	0.433	0.304	2.030	1	0.154	1.543	0.850	2.801
	[INCOME1=3.00]	0.268	0.285	0.883	1	0.348	1.307	0.748	2.286
	[INCOME1=4.00]	-0.260	0.268	0.941	1	0.332	0.771	0.456	1.304
	[INCOME1=5.00]	0 (b)	.	.	0	.	.	.	.
UDMR	Intercept	-0.277	0.609	0.207	1	0.649			
	[AGE=1]	-0.283	0.406	0.486	1	0.486	0.754	0.340	1.669
	[AGE=2]	-0.672	0.322	4.341	1	0.037	0.511	0.271	0.961

		B	Std. Error	Wald	df	Sig.	Exp(B)	Lower	Upper
	[AGE=3]	0 (b)	.	.	0	.	.	.	.
	[EDUCATIO=1]	.110	0.549	0.040	1	0.841	1.116	0.381	3.272
	[EDUCATIO=2]	-0.068	0.554	0.015	1	0.902	0.934	0.315	2.767
	[EDUCATIO=3]	0 (b)	.	.	0	.	.	.	.
	[URBRUR=1]	0.416	0.297	1.964	1	0.161	1.516	0.847	2.711
	[URBRUR=2]	0 (b)	.	.	0	.	.	.	.
	[INCOME1=1.00]	0.042	0.517	0.006	1	0.936	1.042	0.379	2.869
	[INCOME1=2.00]	-0.197	0.439	0.200	1	0.655	0.822	0.347	1.944
	[INCOME1=3.00]	-1.086	0.478	5.160	1	0.023	0.337	0.132	0.862
	[INCOME1=4.00]	-0.405	0.382	1.126	1	0.289	0.667	0.316	1.409
	[INCOME1=5.00]	0 (b)	.	.	0	.	.	.	.
PD	Intercept	-1.246	0.713	3.059	1	0.080			
	[AGE=1]	1.587	0.516	9.443	1	0.002	4.887	1.776	13.442
	[AGE=2]	0.849	0.476	3.178	1	0.075	2.337	0.919	5.941
	[AGE=3]	0 (b)	.	.	0	.	.	.	.
	[EDUCATIO=1]	-0.960	0.562	2.914	1	0.088	0.383	0.127	1.153
	[EDUCATIO=2]	-0.602	0.545	1.222	1	0.269	0.548	0.188	1.593
	[EDUCATIO=3]	0 (b)	.	.	0	.	.	.	.
	[URBRUR=1]	0.077	0.348	0.049	1	0.824	1.080	0.546	2.139
	[URBRUR=2]	0 (b)	.	.	0	.	.	.	.
	[INCOME1=1.00]	0.456	0.603	0.572	1	0.450	1.578	0.484	5.149
	[INCOME1=2.00]	-0.595	0.646	0.846	1	0.358	0.552	0.155	1.958
	[INCOME1=3.00]	0.238	0.460	0.268	1	0.605	1.269	0.515	3.127
	[INCOME1=4.00]	-0.099	0.428	0.054	1	0.816	0.905	0.391	2.095
	[INCOME1=5.00]	0 (b)	.	.	0	.	.	.	.

(a) The reference category is PRM.
(b) This parameter is set to zero because it is redundant.

Nominal Regression: Party Preference by Support for NATO, Support for the EU, Support for Single Party, Support for Free Market, and Evaluation of Standard of Living

Model Fitting Information

Model	-2 Log Likelihood	Chi-Square	df	Sig.
Intercept only	1343.339			
Final	1088.562	254.777	84	0.000

Pseudo R-Square

Cox and Snell	0.205
Nagelkerke	0.216
McFadden	0.076

Likelihood Ratio Tests

Effect	-2 Log Likelihood of Reduced Model	Chi-Square	df	Sig.
Intercept	1088.562 (a)	0.000	0	.
NATO	1110.569	22.007	12	0.037
EU	1114.978	26.416	12	0.009
SPARTY	1123.952	35.390	12	0.000
MARKET	1117.100	28.538	12	0.005
CORRUPT	1109.669	21.107	12	0.049
LIVING	1151.496	62.934	24	0.000

The chi-square statistic is the difference in –2 log-likelihoods between the final model and a reduced model. The reduced model is formed by omitting an effect from the final model. The null hypothesis is that all parameters of that effect are 0.
(a) This reduced model is equivalent to the final model because omitting the effect does not increase the degrees of freedom.

Parameter Estimates

Party Support		B	Std. Error	Wald	df	Sig.	Exp (B)	95% Confidence Interval for Exp (B)	
								Lower Bound	Upper Bound
APR	Intercept	1.720	1.636	1.105	1	0.293			
	[NATO=1]	-.0575	1.284	0.200	1	0.654	0.563	0.045	6.972
	[NATO=2]	-1.209	1.264	0.915	1	0.339	0.299	0.025	3.553
	[NATO=9]	0 (b)	.	.	0	.	.	.	.
	[EU=1]	0.295	1.354	0.047	1	0.828	1.343	0.094	19.078
	[EU=2]	1.393	1.252	1.238	1	0.266	4.029	0.346	46.892
	[EU=9]	0 (b)	.	.	0	.	.	.	.
	[SPARTY=1]	-0.325	0.700	0.215	1	0.643	0.723	0.183	2.851
	[SPARTY=2]	-0.125	0.703	0.031	1	0.859	0.883	0.223	3.499

	[SPARTY=9]	0 (b)	.	.	0	.	.	.	.
	[MARKET=1]	-0.683	0.658	1.079	1	0.299	0.505	0.139	1.833
	[MARKET=2]	-1.393	0.873	2.543	1	0.111	0.248	0.045	1.376
	[MARKET=9]	0 (b)	.	.	0	.	.	.	.
	[CORRUPT=1]	-0.384	0.874	0.193	1	0.660	0.681	0.123	3.778
	[CORRUPT=2]	-0.067	0.897	0.006	1	0.940	0.935	0.161	5.424
	[CORRUPT=3]	0 (b)	.	.	0	.	.	.	.
	[LIVING=1]	-1.706	1.264	1.821	1	0.177	0.182	0.015	2.164
	[LIVING=2]	-2.016	1.265	2.542	1	0.111	0.133	0.011	1.588
	[LIVING=3]	-1.753	1.304	1.808	1	0.179	0.173	0.013	2.230
	[LIVING=4]	-2.689	1.651	2.654	1	0.103	0.068	0.003	1.726
	[LIVING=5]	0 (b)	.	.	0	.	.	.	.
CDR	Intercept	1.763	1.703	1.071	1	0.301			
	[NATO=1]	-3.390	1.050	10.432	1	0.001	0.034	0.004	0.264
	[NATO=2]	-2.906	0.918	10.029	1	0.002	0.055	0.009	0.330
	[NATO=9]	0 (b)	.	.	0	.	.	.	.
	[EU=1]	1.919	1.298	2.186	1	0.139	6.815	0.535	86.751
	[EU=2]	3.130	0.997	9.864	1	0.002	22.872	3.244	161.275
	[EU=9]	0 (b)	.	.	0	.	.	.	.
	[SPARTY=1]	-1.216	0.719	2.860	1	0.091	0.296	0.072	1.213
	[SPARTY=2]	0.298	0.662	0.203	1	0.652	1.348	0.368	4.930
	[SPARTY=9]	0 (b)	.	.	0	.	.	.	.
	[MARKET=1]	-0.415	0.688	0.363	1	0.547	0.660	0.171	2.545
	[MARKET=2]	-2.172	1.226	3.139	1	0.076	0.114	0.010	1.260
	[MARKET=9]	0 (b)	.	.	0	.	.	.	.
	[CORRUPT=1]	-1.201	0.627	3.672	1	0.055	0.301	0.088	1.028
	[CORRUPT=2]	-0.855	0.649	1.737	1	0.188	0.425	0.119	1.517
	[CORRUPT=3]	0 (b)	.	.	0	.	.	.	.
	[LIVING=1]	-1.228	1.479	0.689	1	0.406	0.293	0.016	5.318
	[LIVING=2]	-1.235	1.474	0.702	1	0.402	0.291	0.016	5.228
	[LIVING=3]	-0.437	1.487	0.087	1	0.769	0.646	0.035	11.911
	[LIVING=4]	-0.396	1.562	0.064	1	0.800	0.673	0.031	14.378
	[LIVING=5]	0 (b)	.	.	0	.	.	.	.
PNL	Intercept	-0.129	1.711	0.006	1	0.940			
	[NATO=1]	-2.905	0.982	8.759	1	0.003	0.055	0.008	0.375
	[NATO=2]	-2.423	0.902	7.218	1	0.007	0.089	0.015	0.519
	[NATO=9]	0 (b)	.	.	0	.	.	.	.
	[EU=1]	1.994	1.123	3.155	1	0.076	7.346	0.814	66.312
	[EU=2]	2.783	0.962	8.365	1	0.004	16.174	2.453	106.661
	[EU=9]	0 (b)	.	.	0	.	.	.	.
	[SPARTY=1]	-0.612	0.616	0.987	1	0.320	0.542	0.162	1.814
	[SPARTY=2]	0.026	0.602	0.002	1	0.966	1.026	0.316	3.336
	[SPARTY=9]	0 (b)	.	.	0	.	.	.	.
	[MARKET=1]	0.555	0.706	0.618	1	0.432	1.742	0.436	6.953
	[MARKET=2]	-1.122	1.012	1.231	1	0.267	0.326	0.045	2.364
	[MARKET=9]	0 (b)	.	.	0	.	.	.	.
	[CORRUPT=1]	-0.368	0.643	0.328	1	0.567	0.692	0.196	2.439
	[CORRUPT=2]	-0.128	0.661	0.038	1	0.846	0.880	0.241	3.213
	[CORRUPT=3]	0 (b)	.	.	0	.	.	.	.
	[LIVING=1]	-0.606	1.449	0.175	1	0.676	0.545	0.032	9.329

	[LIVING=2]	-0.495	1.445	0.117	1	0.732	0.610	0.036	10.344
	[LIVING=3]	0.181	1.458	0.015	1	0.901	1.199	0.069	20.880
	[LIVING=4]	0.170	1.529	0.012	1	0.911	1.185	0.059	23.721
	[LIVING=5]	0 (b)	.	.	0	.	.	.	.
PDSR	Intercept	1.850	1.390	1.771	1	0.183			
	[NATO=1]	-1.297	0.701	3.427	1	0.064	0.273	0.069	1.079
	[NATO=2]	-1.350	0.694	3.784	1	0.052	0.259	0.066	1.010
	[NATO=9]	0 (b)	.	.	0	.	.	.	.
	[EU=1]	0.898	0.697	1.659	1	0.198	2.455	0.626	9.629
	[EU=2]	0.907	0.668	1.844	1	0.175	2.476	0.669	9.164
	[EU=9]	0 (b)	.	.	0	.	.	.	.
	[SPARTY=1]	0.035	0.417	0.007	1	0.934	1.035	0.457	2.344
	[SPARTY=2]	-0.082	0.421	0.038	1	0.846	0.922	0.404	2.102
	[SPARTY=9]	0 (b)	.	.	0	.	.	.	.
	[MARKET=1]	-0.473	0.408	1.346	1	0.246	0.623	0.280	1.386
	[MARKET=2]	-0.814	0.461	3.117	1	0.077	0.443	0.179	1.094
	[MARKET=9]	0 (b)	.	.	0	.	.	.	.
	[CORRUPT=1]	-0.253	0.517	0.240	1	0.624	0.776	0.282	2.138
	[CORRUPT=2]	-0.175	0.533	0.108	1	0.743	0.840	0.296	2.385
	[CORRUPT=3]	0 (b)	.	.	0	.	.	.	.
	[LIVING=1]	0.706	1.236	0.326	1	0.568	2.025	0.180	22.819
	[LIVING=2]	0.408	1.235	0.109	1	0.741	1.503	0.134	16.921
	[LIVING=3]	0.549	1.250	0.193	1	0.660	1.732	0.150	20.064
	[LIVING=4]	-0.191	1.334	0.021	1	0.886	0.826	0.060	11.293
	[LIVING=5]	0 (b)	.	.	0	.	.	.	.
UDMR	Intercept	-17.16	1.246	189.75	1	0.000			
	[NATO=1]	-3.505	1.145	9.371	1	0.002	0.030	0.003	0.283
	[NATO=2]	-2.483	0.946	6.886	1	0.009	0.083	0.013	0.533
	[NATO=9]	0 (b)	.	.	0	.	.	.	.
	[EU=1]	1.641	1.369	1.436	1	0.231	5.159	0.352	75.516
	[EU=2]	2.948	0.998	8.724	1	0.003	19.072	2.696	134.904
	[EU=9]	0 (b)	.	.	0	.	.	.	.
	[SPARTY=1]	-0.290	0.639	0.206	1	0.650	0.748	0.214	2.619
	[SPARTY=2]	0.061	0.630	0.009	1	0.923	1.063	0.309	3.653
	[SPARTY=9]	0 (b)	.	.	0	.	.	.	.
	[MARKET=1]	-1.060	0.611	3.011	1	0.083	0.347	0.105	1.147
	[MARKET=2]	-0.041	0.702	0.003	1	0.953	0.959	0.242	3.801
	[MARKET=9]	0 (b)	.	.	0	.	.	.	.
	[CORRUPT=1]	0.054	0.882	0.004	1	0.951	1.055	0.187	5.942
	[CORRUPT=2]	1.041	0.889	1.373	1	0.241	2.832	0.496	16.161
	[CORRUPT=3]	0 (b)	.	.	0	.	.	.	.
	[LIVING=1]	15.874	0.806	388.17	1	0.000	7833302.042	1614866.090	37997343.100
	[LIVING=2]	16.877	0.760	493.30	1	0.000	21351070.91	4815438.328	94668065.152
	[LIVING=3]	17.380	0.793	480.53	1	0.000	35336853.84	7470307.793	167154188.825
	[LIVING=4]	16.636	0.000	.	1	.	16792384.90	16792384.90	16792384.904
	[LIVING=5]	0 (b)	.	.	0	.	.	.	.
PD	Intercept	-16.307	1.125	209.967	1	0.000			

[NATO=1]	-2.512	1.113	5.092	1	0.024	0.081	0.009	0.719
[NATO=2]	-2.565	1.022	6.302	1	0.012	0.077	0.010	0.570
[NATO=9]	0 (b)	.	.	0	.	.	.	.
[EU=1]	2.335	1.295	3.250	1	0.071	10.328	0.816	130.757
[EU=2]	2.949	1.129	6.829	1	0.009	19.090	2.090	174.366
[EU=9]	0 (b)	.	.	0	.	.	.	.
[SPARTY=1]	-1.076	0.698	2.379	1	0.123	0.341	0.087	1.338
[SPARTY=2]	-.0453	0.670	0.456	1	0.499	0.636	0.171	2.365
[SPARTY=9]	0 (b)	.	.	0	.	.	.	.
[MARKET=1]	-.0176	0.762	0.053	1	0.818	0.839	0.188	3.735
[MARKET=2]	-.0173	0.892	0.038	1	0.846	0.841	0.146	4.828
[MARKET=9]	0 (b)	.	.	0	.	.	.	.
[CORRUPT=1]	-.0527	0.721	0.535	1	0.465	0.590	0.144	2.425
[CORRUPT=2]	-.0859	0.768	1.249	1	0.264	0.424	0.094	1.910
[CORRUPT=3]	0 (b)	.	.	0	.	.	.	.
[LIVING=1]	15.781	0.713	489.49	1	0.000	71379 38.824	17637 15.290	2888797 9.217
[LIVING=2]	16.116	0.678	565.65	1	0.000	99827 22.246	26451 40.818	3767464 5.815
[LIVING=3]	17.110	0.697	602.77	1	0.000	26960 232.73	68789 88.361	1056629 42.120
[LIVING=4]	17.022	0.000	.	1	.	24687 925.32	24687 925.32	2468792 5.324
[LIVING=5]	0 (b)	.	.	0	.	.	.	.

(a) The reference category is PRM.
(b) This parameter is set to zero because it is redundant.

12. Bulgaria

Georgi Karasimeonov

Cleavages reflect deep and permanent conflicts and divisions in society. But not all of them become determining factors for party formation and influence electoral behaviour.

The post-communist political system did not inherit a structurally responsive democratic party system. Favourable conditions for the development and the stabilization of a viable party system were absent in most countries in Central and Eastern Europe prior to the communist takeover after the Second World War. In Bulgaria, no conditions for normal party life existed from 1923, when a military *coup d'état* interrupted the democratic process, until 1944. One authoritarian regime followed another. After the 1944–47 period of limited pluralism, the communist power monopoly was established and political pluralism was forcefully eliminated. At the economic level, the market economy and private property were also suppressed and state ownership established.

The communist regime attempted to regulate all societal conflicts in the name of creating a classless society, and in that process tried to 'overcome' or subdue all the cleavages typical for underdeveloped capitalism; Bulgaria was then a predominantly rural country with only a small industrial sector. It expropriated or nationalized existing private companies and politically banned all parties expressing 'bourgeois' interests. The working-class became the leading 'progressive' force and the dictatorship of the proletariat took the place of the capitalist state. The class antagonism between the proletariat and the bourgeoisie was mythologized, with the aim of eliminating all real and potential 'enemies' of socialism. The constitutions of 1948 and 1971 established the leading role of the Communist Party, and – except for the agrarian party, closely linked to the communists – no other parties were allowed to participate in political life.

Although the regime attempted to create an egalitarian society and to subdue or control the expression of conflicts, the communist society was not without cleavages. Various cleavages appeared behind a veil of formal political uniformity and national unity. Periodically, they were reflected in internal party struggles and in attempts at opposition to the regime. They did not have the same scope as in the Central European countries where resistance to the regimes did reach large proportions, but were nonetheless a major factor in the later transition to democracy in Bulgaria. The growth of discontent first showed among intellectuals and among the new generation of technocrats, which did not accept the political and administrative monopoly of the party *nomenklatura*, especially in the late 1970s and 1980s when the communist economic and political system entered a period of deepening crisis.

One line of conflict was provoked by the social structure which replaced the one based on private property. The new class structure was determined by access to power resources at various levels in the party-state system. The so-called 'new class', or *nomenklatura*, emerged as a specific social group, which augmented its privileges to the detriment of other social groups. Retaining political power, it had all but unlimited possibilities to control and distribute economic resources. The power of the *nomenklatura* was challenged by new party *apparachiks* and technocrats who were Western-oriented and recognized the need for major changes in the system – changes which were, in turn, to guarantee their future economic power. They realized the need to transform the power monopoly of the Communist Party into real economic power by changing property relations. Many of them initiated limited reforms towards a market-based economy, which challenged the dogma of state ownership.

Bulgaria experienced a sharpening of ethnic conflict in the 1980s, provoked by the policy of forceful assimilation of the Turkish minority in the Bulgarian nation. This policy further deepened the rift between the nascent opposition and the regime, leading to the growing isolation of the latter.

In the late 1980s, the conflict between modernizers oriented towards the West, and traditionalists tightly linked to the Soviet regime became evident. This cleavage determined the conflict between the reform communists and the hard-liners in the Communist Party as well as the conflict between the nascent opposition and the Communist Party machine.

The 'new working-class' which emerged during the socialist era, never experienced the contradictions inherent in class conflicts that have marked advanced capitalist countries in their historical development. Even though the Communist Party upheld the myth of a 'workers' state', the working-class was marked by lack of 'class consciousness' or solidarity. The development of the rural community showed a similar pattern: in the 1950s the majority of the population lived in rural areas following a rural life-style, but the rural strata 'melted' in the following 45 years as a consequence of rapid urbanization and industrialization processes. Its remnants today are mostly older people who hardly represent a viable social class. Consequently, communist society in Bulgaria was highly atomized;

specific communitarian interests dominated and led to the formation of subgroups of a patrimonial type (family, village), intellectual circles, and so on.

The post-communist changes turned the historical development in the opposite direction – from a centralized state economy and political monopoly to market economy and political democracy. In a relatively short span of time, new cleavages appeared that bear the mark of the radical upturn. The post-communist society in Bulgaria 'inherited' almost none of the 'historical' pre-communist cleavages. This is not the case in the Central European countries.

Some cleavages are still only emerging, some are bound to disappear, and some will appear in the future, determined by the process of transformation of society. Conflicts in non-consolidated post-communist societies differ substantially from the classical four-dimensional cleavage structure analysed by Lipset and Rokkan (1967). Political parties find themselves at the initial mobilization phase and have to establish their identities and links with the electorate. This process is fluid, because parties need time to implement their policies and test them in several rounds of elections until a certain stability of party-voter relationship establishes itself.

Excluding the Communist Party and its ally the Agrarian Party, most of the political parties at the start of the changes were what may be dubbed 'spiritual communities' – circles of friends established more on emotional than rational goals. They also tended to represent clientelist groups for the defence of particular interests. Thus, new issues and conflicts could not be absorbed or transmitted in a rational way onto the political scene, where the antinomy between the privileged and the underdogs of the old system came to the forefront in the bitterest forms. To a large extent, the new conflicts reflected clashes among elites, personal sympathies and animosities. The new political parties were thrust upon society from 'above' with little or no participation of the mass of the population, which mostly accepted the changes without any clear idea of where they would lead. New parties also sprang from the communist parties as kinds of subdivisions.

Bernhard Wessels and Hans-Dieter Klingemann (1994, 12–13) have introduced the concept of 'flattened societies' for the initial phase of post-communism; when citizens were unable to define their political interests as a consequence of the fact that the location of individuals in the societal structure was determined by the state, as the largest and practically only, employer. This may no longer be the case in the Central Europe of 2003, but it remains largely true in South Eastern Europe, including Bulgaria.

Political parties in post-communist societies not only reflect conflicts; they are also agents of conflicts and shape the public agenda. Their policies and ideology, as well as inter-party relations (confrontational or consensus-oriented), are major factors in the transformation of certain conflicts and issues into cleavages. This is a consequence of the domination of 'politics' over the 'economy' at the initial phase of changes.[1]

Lipset's and Rokkan's cleavage theory was formulated on the experiences of a specific group of European countries finding themselves in similar historical conditions. Nonetheless, the methodology can be helpful in the analysis of electoral behaviour and party formation even in transitional societies, like those in South Eastern Europe – with some necessary revisions. I propose a typology of cleavages which reflects the specific historical conditions in which the new democracies have found themselves in recent years. As I see it, post-communist societies reveal at least four types of cleavages: residual (historical), transitional, actual, and potential.

Residual (historical) cleavages are those inherited from the pre-communist society and which, to varying extents, manifest themselves in the post-communist society. In some countries they determine electoral and party preferences. They are particularly evident in the countries of Central Europe, where the communist regimes were less able to eradicate old values and old culture, or where they accepted some elements of market economy and did tolerate forms of private property.

Transitional cleavages are those which determine political divisions and party formation at the initial stage of changes after the fall of the regime, but which later disappear or are 'swallowed' by new cleavages appearing as the post-communist societies are consolidated. They are the products of the initial 'pro-and-contra-communism' axis, which determined many of the party conflicts and divisions immediately after 1989.

Actual cleavages are new cleavages marked by the specific contradictions and conflicts of post-communist societies, resulting from the economic and political reforms. They result from changes in the social structure and property relations. To a great extent, they determine electoral behaviour and party preferences, when the major transitional cleavage based on the communism-anti-communism axis is partially or mostly resolved, and society moves on to resolve new conflicts and issues typical for the consolidation phase.

Potential cleavages represent those major issues and conflicts in post-communist societies which might transform into actual cleavages as a consequence of the evolution of the economic and political system. They are dependent on the nature of the transition and on the effect of the policies of the different political parties in power.

All of these types of cleavages are present in post-communist societies, in different proportions and guises. Their effects on the process of transition and consolidation varies between countries, depending on their development before, during and after communism.

Issues and Divisions at the Initial Stage of Transition

In most post-communist societies, including Bulgaria, the initial stage of transition was dominated by one major division and conflict. Wessels and Klingemann (1994, 12) mention a 'super issue' – reform communism versus liberal democracy – which structured the emerging party systems in the first phase of democratization. The major issue behind that ideological confrontation was the redistribution of power resources between old and new elites, in the process of elimination of the power monopoly of the Communist Party. This transitional cleavage was, in the case of Bulgaria, revealed in the struggle between two main political blocs. On the one side were the supporters and driving political forces of the reform movement, united in the Union of Democratic Forces (UDF); and on the other, the representatives of the old system grouped around the Communist Party. The conflicts and political struggles between them determined initial party formation. Political alignments were mostly psychologically motivated, based on ideological confrontation.

Although both the anti-communists and the reform-communists understood the necessity of change, the struggle for power resources to be redistributed put them into different camps at the round-table talks which paved the way for democracy (Verheijen 1995, 105–16). Both blocs were also socially and ideologically heterogeneous, which caused several waves of differentiation and divisions within them.

The proponents of radical reforms were assembled in the Union of Democratic Forces (UDF), a coalition of new parties that sprang up in the months after the downfall of the old regime. Three major groups could be discerned. One consisted of 'historical parties', such as the Social Democratic, the Bulgarian Agrarian Peoples Party 'Nikola Petkov', the Democratic Party, and the Radical-Democratic Party, to name the most important. They were led by some of the surviving members and leaders of these parties during the pre-communist era. The second group included former dissidents who had taken part in various protest actions preceding the downfall of the communist regime. Most prominent among them were the *Ecoglasnost* movement, the Club for Glasnost and Democracy, and the *Podkrepa* trade union, most of whose leaders and members were former members of the Communist Party. The third group included newly created parties or organizations – such as the Republican Party and the Christian Democratic Party – which joined the newly formed opposition coalition, the UDF (cf. Karasimeonov 1995, 154–79; Karasimeonov 1997).

The supporters of the Union of Democratic Forces could be subdivided into two major groups: the conservatives, i.e. the representatives of the old privileged classes marginalized and suppressed by the communists, who were longing for a 'return to the past'; and the modernists from the newer generation opting for a Westernization of society. Tactically the UDF was also divided between radicals, supporting revolutionary 'de-communization', and moderates who accepted the rules of parliamentary democracy and evolutionary change. At the beginning, the radicals, moderates, conservatives and modernists were united in one camp. Their coalition had to face a most powerful opponent, the ex-communist party, which was renamed the Socialist Party (BSP) a few months after the regime had changed.

The convergence of the groups in the UDF coalition was motivated by a one-dimensional policy and ideology – the removal from power of the former communists. All their internal differences were sublimated in the name of anti-communism and the 'liberty myth'. Most UDF factions were motivated by the perspective of gaining power – a phenomenon typical of 'outsiders' or political 'turncoats'. The parties in the UDF were clientelist circles rather than authentic parties. Their electorates were highly heterogeneous, a fact which prompted internal differentiation and divisions as soon as the major task of eliminating the communists from power had been partly achieved.

The fact that the 'historical' parties very quickly lost their initial advantage and were marginalized, testifies to the irrelevance of the old cleavages. This was particularly true for the Social Democratic Party and the BAPU 'Nikola Petkov' which in the past had reflected, respectively, the labour/capital and the centre/periphery or rural/urban cleavages. By 1989, these 'historical' cleavages had lost their significance as determinants of party formation. When these parties opted for a more moderate policy, defying the radical anti-communists, their influence dwindled dramatically and they were not able to overcome the 4 per cent threshold for parliamentary representation at the 1991 elections.

The communist camp was also divided into two major groups – the supporters of reform and the neo-communists, who in turn were heterogeneous. The bloc of reform supporters was divided into a radical and a moderate wing, of which the first wanted a definite engagement with democratic change and a break with the past, and the latter defended the need to keep the party together, and were keen on preserving as long as possible the party's hold on the power structures. The neo-communist camp included representatives of the 'old guard' fighting to survive and keep their privileges, as well as 'hard-liners' or Marxist ideologues. Yet compared to other ex-communist parties in Central Europe, the Bulgarian party avoided serious rifts between these rival factions and kept its relative strength and cohesion until the founding elections of 1990 and the period thereafter. It did witness an erosion of its membership, but was able to transform gradually into a parliamentary party, preserving the core of its organizational structure, and trying to keep a balance between the various factions from social democratic to neo-communist.

The first period of party formation was characterized by harsh confrontation between the two major political camps. It was engendered by the radicalization of the UDF after the founding elections and its attempts to implement a policy of radical 'de-communization'. This reached its peak after the second round of parliamentary elections in November 1991, when the UDF won a relative majority and formed a government with the support of the ethnic-Turkish Movement for Rights and Freedoms (MRF).

Even so, the BSP remained a powerful opponent. It was able to use the internal divisions in the anti-communist camp and 'allowed' the integration into the political system of moderate representatives of the UDF after the 1990 elections, thus lessening the pressure from the radicals. The policy of 'appeasement' was most clearly demonstrated in the support which the reform communists extended to UDF leader Zhelyu Zhelev, in the elections to the presidency in the summer of 1990. It showed the desire of the communists to compromise in order to avoid a radical 'de-communization' and achieve a consensual relationship with the opposition.

Although the confrontation between the UDF and BSP camps determined the political landscape in the following years, the 'flexibility' of the ex-communists and the internal instability of the UDF kept the political process on a peaceful track. Yet at the same time, the high level of tension between them led to bitter confrontation which blocked the reform process and delayed major changes in the economy.

The integration of the ethnic-Turkish MRF into the political system represents an interesting case of peaceful and constructive resolution of ethnic tensions, which in Bulgaria reached their peak in the late 1980s, as a consequence of the policy of assimilation initiated by the communist regime. Ethnic tensions remained a feature of the post-communist landscape, but they did not escalate into major conflicts endangering the democratic process.

The conflict between the UDF and the BSP was reflected in various political clashes, but the main dividing line between the two concerned who should have the initiative in the reform process, and control the levers of power in a society still dominated by an all-powerful bureaucratic state. The lack of a significant private sector and the weakness of civil society at the outset of the transition process, focused the political struggle on state bureaucracy which controlled the major decision-making resources. For the UDF, de-communization mostly meant the marginalization of the communists in the main state structures. As long as a normal balance between the public and the private spheres remains unestablished and civil service legislation does not create the necessary guarantees against political appointments and reprisals against public officials, state bureaucracy will remain a major area of conflict between the political parties; a fact accentuated by the patronage tradition typical of Southern Europe. Those who retain control of the state bureaucracy command enormous resources and are able to determine who the beneficiaries of the reform process will be. Privatization was, of course, a particular case in point in Bulgaria.

The unresolved struggle for power between the UDF and the BSP – which continued until the parliamentary elections of 1994 – blocked not only the reform process, but kept other issues and conflicts in the shade, preventing them from becoming determining factors for electoral behaviour and party identification. It led to the persistence of a bipolar, confrontational party system and determined government formation, which was marked by instability and the lack of stable parliamentary majorities.

The third post-transition parliamentary elections in December 1994, however, resulted in a resounding victory for the socialists, and a defeat for the radical anti-communists in the UDF and their policy of radical 'de-communization'. The elections also paved the way for the emergence of new political formations in parliament, besides the three previous ones: the Bulgarian Business Bloc (BBB), a nationalist, populist party; and the People's Union, a coalition between BAPU, the main agrarian party, and the Democratic Party, which had left the UDF coalition.

Nevertheless, the socialist government which took office was unable to respond to the expectations of its electorate and began losing popular support about a year after its victory at the polls. Its main deficiencies were an inability to achieve positive results in the economic sphere, and the delay of reforms. This situation led to a deepening financial crisis and a loss of confidence among the population. Early in 1997, after month-long, unprecedented protests by the public against the worsening economic crisis and the drastic fall in living standards, the socialist government was forced to resign and agree to pre-term elections. The April 1997 elections resulted in a radical change in the composition of parliament and in a restructuring of the political arena, with the UDF and its coalition partner, the People's Union, in the United Democratic Forces coalition, winning an absolute majority. The BSP lost a major part of its base support. Moreover, a new coalition known as the BBB – the Union for National Salvation – with the MRF as its main driving force, appeared in parliament. The Euroleft with its distinct social democratic flavour, also entered parliament in 1997.

Voting Behaviour and Citizen Values

The delay of reforms and the lack of progress in the establishment of a market economy, accompanied by a worsening economic crisis, created a situation in Bulgaria which was radically different from post-communist Central Europe, where adaptation to the challenges of capitalism had been much more successful. The fall of the socialist government in Bulgaria in 1997 marked the end of the model of development started in 1989, mostly characterized by the very strong presence of the former communist party.

Another particular Bulgarian phenomenon was the emergence of a post-communist oligarchy, composed of members of the former *nomenklatura* or their stooges, corrupt state officials and politicians, and criminal groups. This new oligarchy was the major stumbling block for reform policy and the beneficiary of the clandestine privatization of state property. It forged a policy of redistribution of national resources through newly created banks, and in bankrupt state companies which amassed bad debts. This uncontrolled absorption of national resources by the post-communist oligarchy left the country with a ruined economy and worsening living conditions.

The inability to engage in serious reforms determined the policy agenda, value orientations, electoral behaviour and party identities in late 1996 and early 1997. Most cleavages were the products of the actual social and economic situation, resulting from the failure of the political class to initiate a successful policy of transformation from plan to market.

By 1997, most of the major issues at the centre of the public agenda were the same as in the period following the change of regime in 1989. There were, however, two major differences: first, a crumbling economy and a drastic fall in living standards; and, second, the failure of the political system to produce effective governments, which brought on growing disappointment with and delegitimization of democracy.

This social and political situation led to a significant change in public attitudes. The majority of the public began to make much more rational assessments of the policy of alternative governments and parties, on the basis of their own experiences. In contrast to the recent past, electoral behaviour and party identification did not depend only, or mostly, on the import of values and evaluations from the parties. Rationalization of public attitudes and voting behaviour meant that cleavages had a stronger determining influence on citizens' political and ideological choices. Voters had a better idea of what they wanted and of how it should be achieved, and accordingly their attitude towards parties and politicians became less ideologically biased and more determined by concrete political results than before. The mood in the country clearly testified to a general antipathy to great designs, promises and electoral programmes, and there was evidence of a more rational and sceptical approach towards the political elite.

The results of the presidential elections in November 1996 were a clear indication of the rationalization of public attitudes and behaviour. They were won by Petar Stoyanov of the United Democratic Forces by an unprecedented margin – the Socialist candidate was defeated by 60 per cent against 40 per cent. These changes were further confirmed in the parliamentary elections in April 1997.

The initial phase of the transition (1989–97) points to a number of major cleavages and issues in post-communist Bulgaria. In different ways, they have been influencing – and are still influencing – electoral behaviour and party support.

The new economic cleavage: One of the major actual and potential cleavages results from the radical changes in the economy and the type of economic policies introduced by the post-communist governments. They are determined by the conversion of state property to private and the contradictions resulting from that process. The transition from plan to market economy leads to fundamental changes in the social structure. Its major trait, in Bulgaria in particular, is the polarization between, on the one hand, a fast-growing class of socially marginalized and poor people and, on the other, a small, oligarchic caste of the very rich. The latter is largely comprised of heirs of the 'red bourgeoisie' who amassed their riches from covert privatization and the redistribution of state property. This process has led to the formation of a 9/10 society, with a great majority of losers and a tiny minority of winners in the transition to market economy. This cleavage has revealed itself in national surveys, where the 77.3 per cent of respondents declare that the conflict between rich and poor is the major contradiction in Bulgarian society (*BBSS Gallup International Yearly Report* 1995, 191; cf. *Figure 12.1*).[2]

Figure 12.1: Attitudes on political confrontation: Do you think there are serious confrontations in your country? (%)

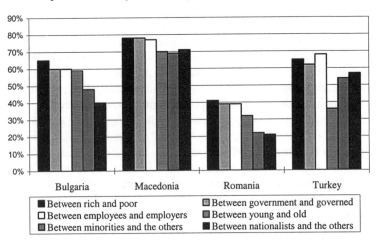

Source: *BBSS Gallup International Yearly Report* (1995, 253).

This economic cleavage is qualitatively different from the class cleavage typical of the early stage of capitalism, as it is not based on a capital/labour conflict. Instead, its roots are in the massive impoverishment of great masses of people in all social, professional and age groups, and in the melting away of the 'levelled' society and the socialist 'middle-class', which enjoyed a certain stability in living conditions and security in the patronage state.

At the same time, society has remained 'flattened': the great majority of the population encounter similar economic conditions. This means that, in the near future, the majority of the electorate will not be influenced by social status and social differences. In the late 1990s, most citizens made the same assessment of the current economic situation and their personal financial standing. Ninety-six per cent of Bulgarians polled thought that the economic situation of the country was bad; 67 per cent said that their personal financial situation was bad or very bad, while only 5.9 per cent declared it to be good or very good (Genov 1997, 48).

It is likely that economically disaffected voters will be greatly influenced by the effect of governmental policies on their immediate financial situation. This will be especially true for that part of the electorate not firmly attached to any of the major parties. The results of the parliamentary elections in 1997 provided ample proof of the massive change of preferences in favour of the UDF after the failure of the socialists. However, with the stabilization of the economic structure following the privatization process and the establishment of a viable market economy based on various forms of property, socio-economic cleavages will probably begin to have a more determining effect on voting behaviour. When social differentiation produces more well-defined economic groups, engaged in various sectors of the economy, a more permanent structure of interests will determine party orientation. This long-term process is only just beginning and will cause a change in the dominant ideological profile of party linkages to the electorate, creating a relationship increasingly based on social and economic interests. The more abstract values associated with left or right will be complemented or replaced by economic and social cleavages and by the parties' concrete policies in response to these cleavages.

Other potential cleavages that will influence electoral behaviour derive from the conflict between the interests of private capital and the interests of the state bureaucracy, which holds in its command great resources in dominant sectors of the economy. The process of privatization undermines the decision-making parameter of the state and its representatives in the various structures. Particularly in the lower echelons of the state machinery, bureaucracy is losing some of its privileges and material benefits (including those obtained through corruption), and this obviously creates resistance.

Another conflict influencing party politics is that between the criminal groups in the 'grey' sector of the economy, prospering in economic anarchy, and economic groups willing to abide by the law. The first group has amassed its fortunes from speculation, tax evasion and various criminal activities (drugs, racketeering) and favours the 'feudalization' of the country, weak democratic institutions, and corruption in politics. The second will opt for the modernization of the country and be ready to cooperate with political groups and parties aiming for similar goals.

Ideological and political cleavages: Ideological cleavages were the major factor determining party allegiances at the start of the political transition. As mentioned earlier, the distribution of the electorate on the *pro et contra* communism axis was typical of nascent post-communist societies. In the late 1990s, a growing differentiation in the ideological preferences of the electorate could be observed. The bipolar cleavage has transformed into a more complex value orientation that corresponds to particular allegiances. These values reflect attitudes towards major conflict areas such as the market economy, state property, privatization, law and order or citizens' rights.

For example, the Bulgarian Presidential elections survey 1996 (part of the Comparative National Elections Project, CNEP) revealed that there were already in 1996 some fundamental differences in value orientation between the electorate and the sympathizers and members of the major parties. UDF sympathizers were more individualistic, pro-market and anti-authoritarian, while BSP sympathizers had a more collectivist, authoritarian and nationalist outlook (*Figures 12.2, 12.3, 12.4*).

Figure 12.2: Attitude to privatization by party affiliation (%)

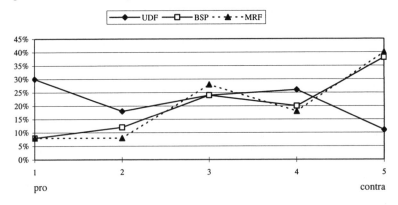

Source: Bulgarian CNEP Survey, Bulgarian Presidential Elections Survey, November 1996.

Ethnic and religious cleavages: Ethnic conflicts in Bulgaria do not have the explosive character typical of other South Eastern European countries. The consequences of the assimilatory policies of the communist regime in the 1980s towards the Turkish minority were rebuffed by all major political parties and the principle of ethnic and religious freedom was established in the post-communist Constitution. Article 11 of the Constitution bans parties based solely on ethnic, racial or religious principles. This article, contested by some constitutional commentators, is a reflection of the specific internal and geopolitical situation of Bulgaria and the fears of most political parties that purely ethnic political parties (particularly parties representing the

Turkish minority, encompassing some 8 per cent of the population) could endanger the sovereignty of the state. This is why the Movement for Rights and Freedoms (MRF), which originally registered itself as a 'political movement' and has its social base mainly among the Turkish population, has declared itself a national party. The subsequent ruling by the Constitutional Court allowing the MRF to participate in political life, the willingness of the MRF to integrate into the political system, and its actual participation in government formation over the past few years, have substantially reduced ethnic and religious tensions.

Figure 12.3: Attitude to private initiative by party affiliation (%)

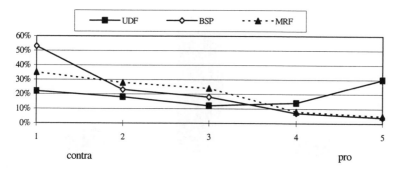

Source: *Bulgarian* CNEP *Survey, Bulgarian Presidential Elections Survey,* November 1996.

Figure 12.4: Nationalist attitudes by party affiliation (%)

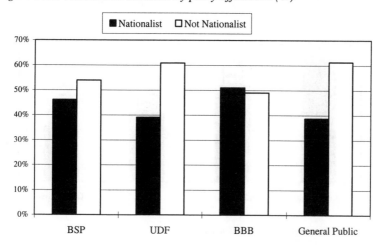

Source: *Bulgarian* CNEP *Survey, Bulgarian Presidential Elections Survey,* November 1996.

The majority of the ethnic Turkish population supports the MRF, and the ethnic cleavage determines electoral attitudes of both major ethnic groups in Bulgaria. However, Bulgarian nationalism as well as religious fundamentalism among the Turkish population are, for the time being, reflected only in the activity of marginal political parties and groups. Nevertheless, a change of orientation of the MRF towards a policy for national autonomy could arguably trigger ethnic conflicts on a larger scale (cf. *Figures 12.5, 12.6*).

Figure 12.5: Attitudes towards MRF: Does the MRF play a positive or a negative role in the country's political life? (%)

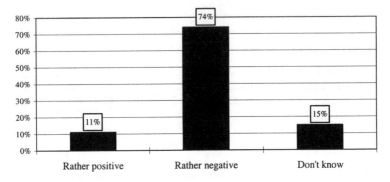

Source: BBSS Gallup International Yearly Report (1995).

Figure 12.6: Views on Islam as a threat to national security (%)

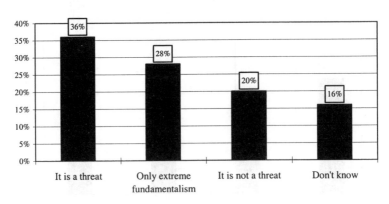

Source: BBSS Gallup International Yearly Report (1995).

There is also potential tension with respect to the so-called Macedonian question. Macedonia has a history and culture intimately linked to that of

Bulgaria. Some groups in Bulgaria, including a small party – the IMRO (Internal Revolutionary Macedonian Organization) – do not accept the existence of a 'Macedonian' nation. The illegal organization 'Ilinden', on the other hand, propagates the idea of 'Greater Macedonia'.

Religion has never played a dominant role in party formation in Bulgaria, but in the aftermath of communist ideological dominance and forced atheism, a spiritual vacuum has appeared, leading to growing disorientation in peoples' minds. As the dominant Greek Orthodox Church has been weakened by internal struggles, a multitude of pseudo-religious groups and sects have been able to 'invade' Bulgaria. This brings to the forefront the issue of safeguarding national identity and culture against groups and values which undermine them.

Cleavages on international policy: Bulgaria's political life has been strongly influenced by its historical development and geopolitical situation. Foreign policy issues and conflicts have often determined political alignments and realignments, and the orientation of political parties.

Post-communist realities reveal similar tendencies. Two major political orientations are influencing party policies: the pro-European, integrationist; and the pan-Slavic, Russia-oriented. In the post-Cold War international setting, the NATO issue best reveals the clash between these two groups. The former orientation has been represented mainly by the UDF; the latter by the BSP which is burdened by its past allegiances to Russia. It is likely that a sharpening of the conflict between Russia and the West will have a great impact on parties' policies and their internal divisions (*Figures 12.7, 12.8*).

Figure 12.7: Attitude towards joining NATO by party affiliation (%)

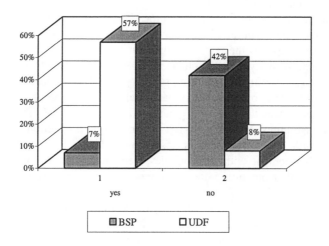

Source: National Centre for the Study of Public Opinion, Sofia, 1996.

Figure 12.8: General public's attitude towards joining NATO (%)

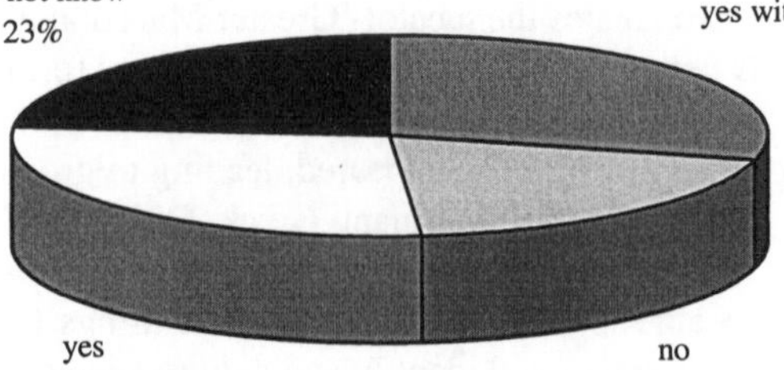

Source: National Centre for the Study of Public Opinion, Sofia, 1996.

The rural/urban cleavage has been of great importance in Bulgaria, determining party affiliation from the 1920s until the 1940s. The agrarian party, the BAPU, was the largest party in the 1920s, won absolute parliamentary majority in 1920 and stayed in power until 1923 when its government was brought down by a right-wing *coup d'état*. In the 1940s, the BAPU was the main opposition party until 1948 when the communists rose to a position of total hegemony.

The policies of the communist regimes brought radical changes to the economic situation of the peasantry, increasingly so in the 1960s and 1970s. The modernization process, focused on industrialization and urbanization, radically transformed Bulgaria's traditional social structure. The peasantry became a minority within the population in the 1970s, and by the 1990s it was mainly composed of old people.

By and large, the rural population profited from the rise in living standards and modernization of the country and overcame the poverty of the past. This fact explains the relatively firm support of this social group for the ex-communist party after the changes in 1989. The attempts of the UDF government (1991–92) to transform property relations radically, with a return to private land ownership – in particular the restitution of land to its former owners – was the source of great conflict in rural areas. This policy generated huge unrest and a drastic fall in agricultural production and rural living standards. The congruence of nostalgia for the old times, patriarchal culture and discontent with UDF policies, generated support for the BSP among the rural population, although some of that support waned in the aftermath of the fall of the socialist government in 1997. The process of restructuring property relations with the conclusion of the programme for restitution of land will have long-lasting consequences for the value orientations and electoral behaviour of the rural population in the coming years. As a result of a worsening demographic situation and increasing unemployment, the rural population will be particularly severely hit by economic reforms.

The generational cleavage: Surveys and electoral results show very clear divisions between age groups in post-communist Bulgaria. They are the products of divergent cultural traditions and value orientations between the older and younger generations. The former carries the values of collectivism and the patronage socialist state, and responds with nostalgia and animosity to the abrupt changes that destroy their professional and personal milieu. The younger generation (the 18–39 year age bracket) accepts the need for radical changes in the economy and supports the values of liberalism and market economy.

Such cultural and ideological divisions lead to opposing, conflicting party allegiances. The younger generation has reacted to the delay of reforms with clearly defined support for the UDF, which it has perceived as an alternative to the socialist state. Consequently, those in the 18–39 age bracket voted massively for the UDF presidential candidate Petar Stoyanov in the November 1996 elections, and for the UDF in the parliamentary elections in April 1997. Conversely, the older generation has overwhelmingly backed the BSP after 1989, and remains the main strongest base of support for that party (*Figures 12.9, 12.10, 12.11*).

Figure 12.9: Main parties' electorate by age (%)

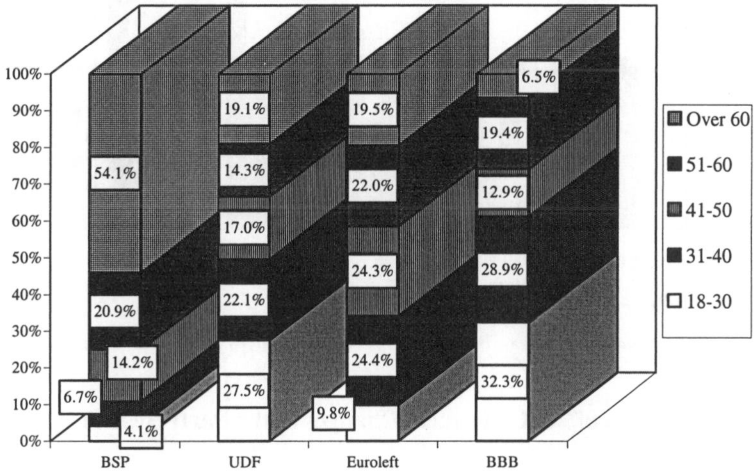

Source: Mediana Agency, March 1997.

Figure 12.10: Affinity with the BSP: How close do you feel to the BSP? (%)

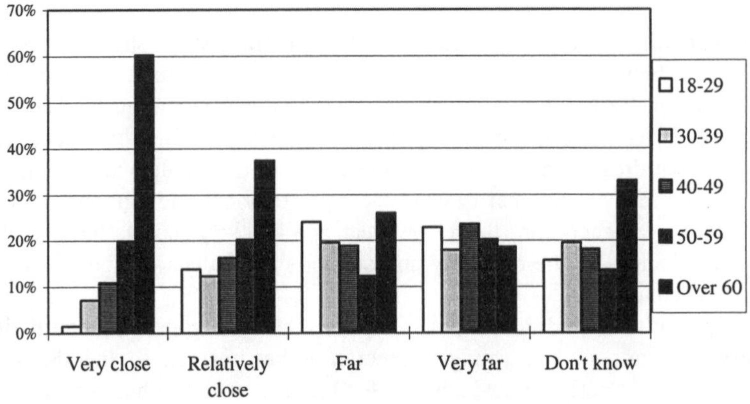

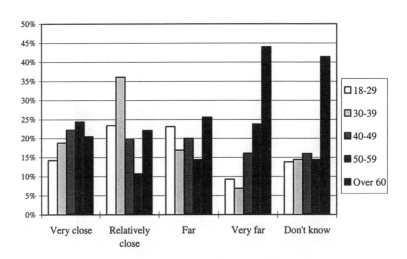

Source: Bulgarian CNEP Survey, Bulgarian Presidential Elections Survey, November 1996.

Figure 12.11: Affinity with UDF: How close do you feel to the UDF? (%)

Source: Bulgarian CNEP Survey, Bulgarian Presidential Elections Survey, November 1996.

The Elections of 2001 – Radical Changes in the Party System

The landslide victory of the UDF at the parliamentary elections of 1997 gave the anti-communist opposition – for the first time since the fall of the communist regime in 1989 – the chance to fulfil its mandate as a party in government. The new government, having a stable majority in the parliament, was able to achieve some major reforms, especially in the fields of social policy and the civil service. It achieved financial stability and in the field of foreign policy it managed to advance the cause of Bulgaria as a future member of NATO and the European Union.

At the same time, the government and the UDF were accused of corruption and of following policies in the interest of its party activists, of creating a new *nomenklatura* and favouring its own economic groupings. Towards the end of its mandate, this led to a substantial loss of public support.

The parliamentary elections of 2001 entailed radical changes in the Bulgarian party system. This was mainly due to the appearance of a new spectacular political formation – the National Movement Simeon II. Virtually out of nowhere came ex-king Simeon II and enjoyed a phenomenal electoral success; his movement received more than 42 per cent of the vote and almost absolute majority in parliament.

What were the causes for this unexpected newcomer and its influence on the political process? Some of the causes are arguably deeply rooted in the character of the transformation itself. Developments in the post-communist countries have shown that the consolidation process does not exclude volatility of the party system. This is a result of the radical transformation of the economic and social structures, which affect interests, values, and lifestyles of millions of people. It will probably take two or more generations to adapt to the market economy and the new principles of redistribution of social goods. The paternalism of the socialist state, which created dependency and civic passivity is being replaced by competitive self-affirmation. Still, many social groups have been unable to adapt to these new realities and have become marginalized. These groups are the 'losers' of the transformation process. Politically they feel disadvantaged; and as outsiders in the system of representation, they are the social basis of new protest movements in the post-communist countries. These groups of 'losers' have been inclined to support protest parties and populist movements, which thrive on nostalgia and anti-system sentiments. Such movements direct their dissatisfaction and anger with present conditions – e.g. political clientelism, corruption and crime – at the 'partitocracia', which in the post-communist countries symbolizes a new privileged class of politicians, party leaders, bureaucrats and the new bourgeoisie.

The emergence, rise and success of such movements and parties – in Romania (Tudor), Slovakia (Mečiar) and lately in Bulgaria (Simeon II) – demonstrate the inability of the regular post-communist parties to respond to the 'losers' and outsiders in their respective societies.

Bulgaria is a particular case in comparison to the other mentioned cases. The political movement founded by the ex-king Simeon II is not a nostalgic, xenophobic, anti-European nationalistic movement, but a modern version of a populist alternative to the post-1989 political parties. The movement is not anti-democratic; it accepts the constitutional framework and does not pose a threat to the political system.

The National Movement Simeon II wants to portray itself as an alternative to the highly confrontational bipolar party system, dominated by the ex-communist BSP and the radical anti-communist UDF. As noted above, this confrontational party system emerged as a consequence of the pro and contra communism ideological cleavage of the early and mid-1990s that constantly divided the country. Furthermore, the National Movement Simeon II has attempted to present itself as a moral challenge to the policies of party clientelism and corruptive practices that have marked Bulgarian politics since 1989. And last but not least, the movement has emphasized the same economic issues that many ordinary Bulgarians care about – the need for economic revival in order to overcome high unemployment, low living standards and stimulate business and entrepreneurship. In its foreign policy, the National Movement Simeon II supported Bulgaria's orientation towards the EU and NATO.

The phenomenal electoral success in the 2001 elections, where the National Movement Simeon II received more than 42 per cent of the vote, should also be ascribed to the charismatic ex-monarch Simeon II himself. He embodied the father figure, the Western educated statesman, the incorruptible politician and the saviour for large groups of the population. At the same time, his movement came across as a spontaneous, heterogeneous and unorganized group of parliamentarians without any political experience, consisting mostly of professionals, young Western educated economists, established lawyers and intellectuals.

Following its coming to power as a governing party, the National Movement Simeon II has faced a number of challenges that will either break the fragile association apart or transform it into a more stable party in the years to come. Some of these challenges are linked to the governing capacities of the new movement and its concrete policies, which at the time of writing are still far away from the promises made at the elections. Other challenges encompass the creation of internal organizational structures, a process that has just started; the establishment of relations to other parties in and outside parliament; and the choice of an ideological identity for the new party.

The disappearance of old and the formation of new cleavages – from transition to consolidation of democracy

In many ways, the 2001 elections marked the end of the initial transition and the 'exhaustion' of the transitional cleavages. After the serious blow inflicted on the UDF at the parliamentary elections, the party entered a period of internal crisis. The ex-prime minister and party leader Ivan Kostov was replaced by Nadeshda Mihailowa, who was faced with the task of renewing the party. The negative aspects of the past had to be overcome, like the aggressive anti-communism associated with the UDF. Also, the old way of monopolizing the 'democratic' alternative was challenged with the emergence of new right-wing and centre-right parties.

The Presidential elections of November 2001 confirmed another important trend in the development of the Bulgarian party system. The ability of the ex-communist Socialist Party to reaffirm its position in the political landscape was reflected in the victory of Georgi Parvanov, the leader of the BSP. With the election of a new party leader – Sergei Stanischev – the BSP took the final steps in the transformation from an ex-communist to a social democratic party. The party is in favour of Bulgaria's membership of NATO, and it has joined the Socialist International as an observer.

In 2001, the ethnic Turkish MRF became a governing party for the first time, thus concluding the cycle of its full integration into the Bulgarian party system. The inclusion of the MRF in a government also indicated a more democratically mature political system.

In the field of foreign policy, a major achievement was the invitation to join NATO in 2004 and the expected membership of the EU in 2007. The inclusion of Bulgaria in both these organizations will dramatically change Bulgaria's geopolitical situation as well as contribute to the consolidation of democracy in the country. In 2002, the EU gave Bulgaria the status of a functioning market economy, which reflected the fact that a major part of the economy nowadays is privately owned and the principles of a market economy are beginning to take hold.

And last, but not least, Bulgarian society is changing from within, as a new, post-communist generation is growing up, bringing with it new values and ideas into society and political life, different from the values and ideas of the socialist and 'transitional' generations.

All of this has had an impact on the cleavage structure of the country. The cleavages that dominated in the early and mid-1990s – the transitional cleavages – are gradually disappearing, giving way to new cleavages. The political-ideological neo-communism/anti-communist cleavage is the most obvious example. This cleavage forged party allegiances to two major political opponents, the UDF and BSP. The changes in the overall political environment in recent years, however, have largely eliminated the basis for such a bipolar, highly polarized party system.

A second indicator of a new cleavage structure is the 'softening' of the ethnic cleavage, indicated by the undisputed acceptance by a majority of Bulgarians of the inclusion of the MRF in the new government formed after the parliamentary elections in 2001.

A third indicator is the loss of significance of conflicts over the geopolitical direction of the country. All major parties – even the BSP – acknowledge the necessity of Bulgaria to join NATO.

Table 12.1: Main problems facing Bulgaria, October 2002 (%)

Unemployment	65
Low income	46
Poverty	41
Corruption	33
Crime	32
Political instability	15
Health care	12
Ecology	2
Ethnic problems	2

Source: *Vitosha Research Agency*, Sofia.

All these 'old' cleavages, typical for the initial transition to democracy, are slowly being replaced by a set of cleavages reflecting the new political, socio-economic and cultural realities. The most significant phenomenon is the growing role of social and economic factors on the formation of a new cleavage structure, and accordingly, of new issues that determine party allegiances. When polled in the fall of 2002, a majority of the Bulgarians emphasized such issues as unemployment, income and poverty as the most salient political problems in contemporary Bulgaria. Political instability or ethnic tensions, in comparison, were not nearly as important in the minds of ordinary people (cf. *Table 12.1*).

Figure 12.12: What separates the people in Bulgaria more – inequality or political beliefs?

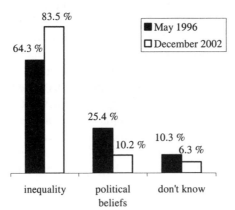

Sources: *National Centre for the Study of Public Opinion*, Sofia, 1996; *Social Democratic Institute and Friedrich Ebert Foundation*, Sofia, December, 2002.

Also, when polled in December 2002, approximately 84 per cent of the respondents stated that inequality was above all what separated people in Bulgaria. Only some 10 per cent felt that political beliefs could be the base for a societal division (*Figure 12.12*). In 1996, the corresponding figures had been 64 per cent (inequality) and 25 per cent (political beliefs).

The radical transformation of the social system has affected the quality of life for almost all citizens. The most enduring effect has been the formation of a new proto-class structure that is quite different from the traditional class structure of developed capitalism. Many analysts define capitalism in post-communist societies as 'wild capitalism', as it in a way reproduces the class structure of early capitalism, where a majority of the population were marginalized and exploited wage labourers. The difference to today's post-communist reality is that a majority of Bulgaria's population has lost its earlier status and has *become* marginalized, as the 'losers' of the transition. According to some surveys, as many as 81 per cent of the population could be categorized as 'losers' (*Alpha Research Agency*, Sofia, August 2002). Other surveys provide a more differentiated picture, categorizing 40 per cent of the population as 'poor', 25 per cent as 'surviving', 25 per cent as 'relatively stable' and 10 per cent as 'upper-class' (*Figure 12.13*).

Figure 12.13: Social stratification 2002 (%)

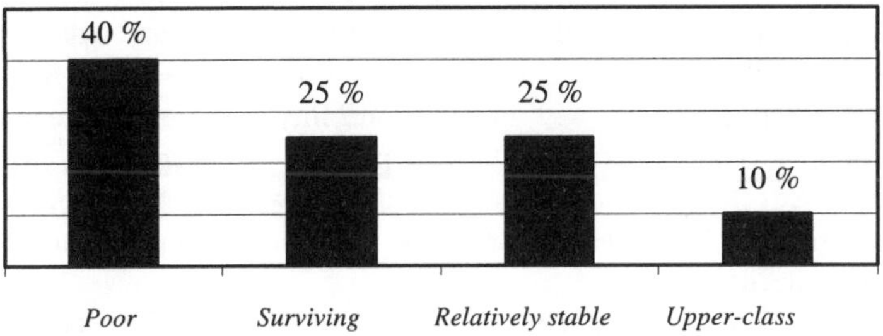

Poor   Surviving   Relatively stable   Upper-class

Source: *Social Democratic Institute and Friedrich Ebert Foundation*, Sofia, December 2002.

The enduring process of marginalization has thus created a proto-class, composed of various social groups and individuals with different professional background and social status, who have in common rather negative attitudes to the post-communist transformation. These 'losers' have become a relative stable 'class' as their situation has worsened or has not changed for the better in recent years. This in turn has made this 'class' an increasingly more important political actor, with unpredictable political behaviour. The political values found among large shares of the 'losers' are based on a combination of nostalgic, authoritarian, anti-European, nationalistic orientations and ideals. Its is precisely these volatile voters that have shaped the outcome in the Bulgarian elections, characterized by drastic changes of allegiances from one election to another and, most recently, the victory of a king's party which was expected to do 'wonders'. At the same time, it could be noted that the 'losers' have not remained loyal to the National Movement. In coming elections, they are just as likely to vote for any other populist alternative.

The 'losers' are countered by a new proto-class of 'winners' (approximately 20–35 per cent of the population) which is also made up of various groups – 'new rich' who amassed fortunes from the initial disintegration of state ownership, crime and corruption, the upper layer of the 'new middle-class', and professionals and entrepreneurs who have profited from the establishment of a market economy and the closer ties to the European Union. This 'class' of 'winners' supports the modernization of Bulgaria, are pro-western orientated, and are to a much lesser extent influenced by the conflicts of the distant and recent past (*Alpha Research Agency* 2002; *Figure 12.13*).

What about the future development, then? As the post-communist societies will develop and become more like the established democracies of Western Europe, the group of 'winners' will grow. In the meantime, however, we should expect the loser/winner cleavage to determine for a relatively long time party politics and policies. It will influence the volatility of the party system and internal party conflicts in the years to come.

Furthermore, it is likely that the centre/periphery cleavage will reappear as a result of the economic transformation in Bulgaria. The capital Sofia and several other big cities will in all probability become the centres of economic revival, where the largest part of the population will be concentrated. The smaller cities and villages will be marginalized and characterized by high rates of unemployment, impoverishment and general economic decline.

Another new cleavage that is emerging, and that will probably have significant implications for the party system in the years to come, has to do with the globalization process, e.g. the increased impact of the global economy and the integration of Bulgaria into the EU. The kind of cleavage that could emerge here has to do with economically motivated nationalism, anti-European sentiments and anti-globalization. An indication of this potential cleavage is the fact that the initial unconditional support for the integration of the country into the EU has been replaced by more sceptical and even inimical attitudes, as the debate on the closure of four reactors of the nuclear plant in Kosludui has revealed. The BSP has in fact turned the Kosludui debate into a major issue, and the party has even demanded a referendum to be held. As other of the (perceived) negative effects of the integration process will appear in the coming years, this cleavage has the potential of determining party politics and even of leading to the formation of new, nationalistic oriented parties.

Concluding Remarks

The changing political landscape and the recent transformation of the Bulgarian party system indicate the validity of the typology of post-communist cleavages used in this chapter – residual, transitional, actual and potential cleavages. The downfall of the communist system and the transition to democracy and market economy gave birth to a cleavage structure that reflected the initial phase of the transition. This was a critical juncture in the development of the country that fundamentally changed the conditions for the political process, as it replaced the political monopoly of the communist party with party pluralism. A multitude of new parties quickly emerged. Their different policies and relations reflected specific cleavages that proved to be of a transitional nature. These cleavages determined 'the first' party system, which evolved around the fundamental divides and issues concerning the nature of the transformation to democracy, like the question of which political actors should engage in and lead this process, as well as questions about the redistribution of economic and political resources and the privatization of former state property. In practise, all of this entailed the formation of a highly polarized party system, up until the elections of 2001 dominated by the ex-communist BSP and the anti-communist UDF.

The only other significant cleavage in the 1990s, the ethnic one, ensured a place in the party system of a small, but relatively stable ethnic party, with its base in the Turkish population, the Movement for Rights and Freedom (MRF).

At the beginning of a new century, these transitional cleavages have lost their formative effect on the party system. As shown in this chapter, these changes in the cleavage structure have led to the emergence of 'a second' party system. New major divides and issues have appeared on the political agenda. Most of these cut across the major parties, like the issues of living standards, law and order, and ethics in politics. Such divides reflect a great disenchantment and disappointment of a majority of the population (the 'losers' of the transformation) in the policies of the two major parties – the BSP and the UDF.

The stunning success of the populist National Movement Simeon II in the 2001 elections was an expression of such widespread feelings of disappointment and a longing for a new kind of politics, as well as an indicator of the failure of the 'old parties' to respond to such sentiments. At the same time, the failure of the National Movement Simeon II to respond adequately to the very same popular attitudes since the election has created something of a power vacuum. The unsatisfied voters have not remained loyal to the National Movement, and virtually anything can happen in the future (cf. *Table 12.2*).

Table 12.2: Party preferences by social groups, December 2002 (%)

	Poor	Surviving	Relative stable	Uppe- class
NMSII	11	12	14	19
UDF	5	7	16	18
BSP	22	13	10	8
Other parties	8	11	11	10
Will not vote	54	56	50	46

Source: *Social Democratic Institute and Fridriech Ebert Foundation*, Sofia, December 2002.

What is most striking is perhaps the tendencies of a crisis of legitimacy in the party system. According to sociological surveys, almost 50 per cent of the population – in all social categories – has declared that they will not vote in the coming elections (*Table 12.2*). Furthermore, other surveys indicate that 85 per cent of the respondents do not trust political parties (*Trud Daily*, 3 March 2003).

The development of the 'second party system' will depend on two major factors. Firstly, the future development will depend upon the governing capacities of the political parties and their ability to respond with concrete policies to people's needs and aspirations. Secondly, the establishment of stable party identities and the mobilizing capacities of the political parties vis-à-vis civil society will shape the future development of the Bulgarian party system. This means that the party system will be influenced to a major extent by the way political parties respond to new political issues and electoral preferences. In comparison to the 'first' party system, it is highly probable that the second one will be more pluralized, less polarized, and more coalition oriented. It is also likely that we will see the emergence of a number of new parties in the years to come. This pluralization of the Bulgarian party system will reflect the difficult process of consolidation of democracy.

NOTES

1. For example, laws pertaining to restitution of property, privatization laws, or legislation concerning ethnic questions, and so on, are most likely to provoke, sharpen or calm certain conflicts and issues that could evolve into cleavages. In Bulgaria, the restitution of land did become a major issue and one of the major permanent dividing lines between political parties.
2. Data show that GNP fell about 50 per cent between 1990 and 1996.

REFERENCES

Alpha Research Agency, Sofia, August, 2002.

BBSS Gallup International Yearly Report 1995, UNDP, Sofia.

Bulgarian CNEP Survey, Bulgarian Presidential Elections Survey, November 1996.

Genov, G. (1997), *Bulgaria Today and Tomorrow*, Sofia.

Karasimeonov, Georgi (1995), 'Differentiation Postponed: Party Pluralism in Bulgaria', in Gordon Whightman, ed., *Party Formation in East-Central Europe*, Frank Cass.

—— (1997), *The 1990 Elections to the Bulgarian Grand National Assembly and the 1991 Election to the Bulgarian National Assembly*, Berlin, Edition Sigma.

Lipset, Seymour Martin and Stein Rokkan (1967), 'Cleavage Structures, Party Systems and Voters Alignments: An Introduction', in Seymour Martin Lipset and Stein Rokkan, eds, *Party Systems and Voter Alignments: Cross-National Perspectives*, New York, The Free Press.

Mediana Agency, Sofia, March 1997.

National Centre for the Study of Public Opinion, Sofia, 1996.

Social Democratic Institute and Friedrich Ebert Foundation, Sofia, December, 2002.

Trud Daily, 3 March 2003.

Verheijen, Tony (1995), *Constitutional Pillars for New Democracies: The Cases of Bulgaria and Romania*, Leiden, DSWO Press.

Wessels, Bernhard and Hans-Dieter Klingemann (1994), 'Democratic transformation and the prerequisites of democratic opposition in East and Central Europe', Wissenschaftszentrum Berlin für Sozialforschung, FS III, 94–201.

APPENDIX 12.1: ELECTION RESULTS

PARLIAMENTARY ELECTIONS

	1990	*1991*	*1994*	*1997*	*2001*
Turnout	89.0	83.9	75.2	62.4	67.0
Party/coalition					
Bulgarian Socialist Party[*]	47.2	33.1	43.5	22.1	17.2
Union of Democratic Forces[**]	36.2	34.3	24.2	52.3	18.2
Movement for Rights and Freedom[***]	6.0	7.6	5.4		7.5
Bulgarian Agrarian People's Union	8.0	3.9			
BAPU–'Nikola Petkov'[***]		3.4			
Union of Democratic Forces–Centre		3.2			
Union of Democratic Forces–Liberals		2.8			
Bulgarian Business Bloc		1.3	4.7	4.9	
Confederation 'Kingdom Bulgaria'[***]		1.8	1.4		
People's Union[**]			6.5		
Democratic Alternative for the Republic			3.8		
Euroleft				5.5	0.9
Union for National Salvation[***]				7.6	
National Movement Simeon II					42.7
Gjorgjovden–IMRO					6.6

[*] In the 1997 Elections, the BSP formed the coalition 'Democratic Left' together with Ecoglasnost. In the 2001 Elections, the BSP was a part of the 'Coalition for Bulgaria', together with 14 other left parties.
[**] 1997 and 2001 Elections: Coalition 'United Democratic Forces' (UDF and the People's Union).
[***] 1997 Elections: Coalition 'Union for National Salvation' (MRF, BAPU–'Nikola Petkov', the Confederation 'Kingdom Bulgaria', the Green Party, and New Choice).

PRESIDENTIAL ELECTIONS

	1992		*1996*		*2001*	
	First Round	*Second Round*	*First Round*	*Second Round*	*First Round*	*Second Round*
Turnout	75.4	75.9	62.7	69.8	41.6	54.9
Candidate (Party)						
Zhelyu Zhelev (UDF)	44.6	52.8				
Vulko Vulkanov (BSP)	30.5	47.2				
George Ganchev (BBB)	16.8		21.9			
Petar Stoyanov (UDF)			44.0	59.7	34.9	45.9
Ivan Marasov (BSP)			27.0	40.3		
Alexander Tomov (ind.)			3.2			
Hristo Boychev (ind.)			1.3			
Georgi Parvanov (BSP)					36.4	54.1
Bogomil Bonev (Civic Party)					19.4	

APPENDIX 12.2: GOVERNMENT COMPOSITION

Bulgarian Prime Ministers since 1989

Name	Affiliation	In office	Out of office
Georgi Atanasov	Bulgarian Communist Party	November 1989	January 1990
Andrei Lukanov	BCP (later renamed BSP)	January 1990	November 1990
Dimitar Popov	Non-party	December 1990	October 1991
Filip Dimitrov	UDF	November 1991	December 1992
Luben Berov	Non-party	December 1992	October 1994
Reneta Injova	Non-party	October 1994	January 1995
Zhan Videnov	BSP	January 1995	January 1997
Stefan Sofianski	UDF	February 1997	May 1997
Ivan Kostov	UDF	May 1997	May 2001
Simeon Sakskoburgotski	NMSII/MRF	July 2001	

The 'palace coup' against Todor Zhivkov, staged on 10 November 1989, initiated rapid changes towards democracy and market economy in Bulgaria. During the course of the Roundtable talks, which started at the beginning of 1990, the cabinet of Georgi Atanasov, who had been one of the main executors of the dethronement of Zhivkov, had to resign on 1 February 1990 in order to pave the way for the formation of a new government.

The national Roundtable, initiated by the representatives of the ruling party and the opposition, lasted from January until May 1990. The agreements signed by the participants in the talks were attributed legislative status. The acting National Assembly was supposed to carry out the legislative initiatives by the Roundtable without any corrections or amendments whatsoever. The main participants in the talks were the BCP (since April 1990 known as the Bulgarian Socialist Party, BSP) and the Union of Democratic Forces (UDF), an anti-communist coalition founded on 8 December 1989. The talks were held in contact groups and plenary sessions in three rounds: 22 January–12 February 1990; 12 February–30 March 1990; and 14–15 May 1990.

Meanwhile, a congress of the Communist Party was held in January 1990. Immediately after the congress a new government was formed, headed by Andrey Lukanov. It took office on 8 February 1990. Lukanov, at the time a symbol of the reformist trend within the BCP, faced potential coalition partners reluctant to join the BCP in a government of national salvation, and Lukanov had little choice but to form a one-party cabinet. By the time he handed in its resignation – on 7 August 1990 – only six months had passed, and the election campaign had been in full swing since early May.

The first free, 'founding' elections were won by the Socialist Party. It obtained 211 seats out of a total 400 in the new parliament, known as the Greater National Assembly, while its main rival, the Union of Democratic Forces, gained 144 seats. Andrei Lukanov kept trying to form a coalition government relying on a 'gentleman's agreement' with the opposition, whose leaders had promised to support a coalition government provided that one of the opposition representatives was elected President of the Republic. In September 1990, however, the BSP formed yet another one-party government, again with Lukanov as Prime Minister. In the vote of confidence, the government was supported by 234 deputies and rejected by 104.

The problematic economic and social situation, including severe deficiencies in food supply, brought down the second Lukanov government on 29 November 1990. The ensuing parliamentary crisis forced a political agreement between all political forces represented in Parliament, the main point of which was the formation of a national government for the peaceful transition to democracy, headed by the independent premier, Dimitar Popov, and backed explicitly by all political forces. The main ministries were distributed on an equal basis between the BSP and the UDF, while the sensitive Ministry of the Interior was assigned to a politically neutral cabinet member. On 20 December 1990, an 18-member cabinet was formed, consisting of eight socialists, three members of the UDF, two Agrarians, and five independents. The government included representatives of all parliamentary forces with the exception of the Movement for Rights and Freedoms. Though the term 'coalition' was strictly avoided, the government was generally supported in accordance with the political agreement of January 1991. It was actually a cabinet dominated by the UDF, as the key economic posts were held by its representatives.

The cabinet of Dimitar Popov enjoyed broad parliamentary and public support and was relatively independent. It was able to embark on a programme of economic reform inspired by the then recent Polish experiences. The reforms set in motion in February 1991 were perhaps the most daring in the whole of Eastern Europe. They included an almost total liberalization of prices, a high degree of liberalization of the trading and currency regime, sharp interest rate increases, and the introduction of a floating exchange rate. However, in the summer of 1991 the reform process lost momentum as structural reform did not take off. This was due to increased confrontation in the parliament and to the process of fragmentation within the UDF.

Parliament was nevertheless able to adopt a new constitution; it was enacted on 12 July 1991. Before the Grand National Assembly adjourned, it also adopted legislation providing for the restoration of agricultural land to its former owners and promoting economic reform in general, but the new laws were hardly implemented. The elections were held on 10 October 1991, and the cabinet of Dimitar Popov resigned on 5 November 1991. The elections were won by the anti-communist coalition of the UDF, but by a small margin. The UDF coalition did not have a majority in its own right and had to look for support in the only other parliamentary group with an openly anti-communist outlook, the ethnic-Turkish MRF. The MRF had no particular desire to assume ministerial responsibility, since the party was well aware that such an unprecedented position of political prominence for the ethnic-Turkish minority might arouse nationalist feelings, kindled by the main opposition party, the ex-communist BSP.

Filip Dimitrov, the leader of the UDF coalition, became Prime Minister, and he immediately initiated legislation on restitution of nationalized property and agricultural land. The programme set in motion by the UDF did lead to a resurgence of private business, but even so, privatization remained a distant goal. Powerful interests and bureaucratic snags halted privatization of state enterprises, which accounted for 95 per cent of national property, one of the highest ratios in Eastern Europe. In the area of foreign policy, the government made a *rapprochement* with the United States and Western Europe, much to the chagrin of the socialist opposition which accused the government of giving up the friendly relations with Russia.

The UDF coalition was heterogeneous, and prone to internal discord. The government faced its first open crisis in April 1992, when Dimitrov sacked the Minister of Defence, Dimitar Ludzhev, a politician with close ties to President Zhelev. In addition to this, the UDF's parliamentary coalition partner, the MRF, was becoming increasingly dissatisfied with the failure by the Dimitrov government to improve the conditions of the impoverished Turkish population and by the attempts to isolate the MRF. By September 1992, the Dimitrov government found itself in a state of siege without an absolute majority in parliament. Dimitrov decided to risk a vote of confidence in October 1992, and when the government lost the vote, it was forced to resign.

The second-largest non-socialist parliamentary formation, the MRF, was offered an opportunity to form a new government, and it nominated presidential advisor Luben Berov as Prime Minister. He was to form an expert non-party government with the aim of implementing pressing economic reforms. The government of Luben Berov received the support of a so-called 'dynamic majority' formed by the socialists, the MRF and 19 defectors from the UDF parliamentary group. Luben Berov's government was not predicted to stay in power for long; pre-term parliamentary elections were widely expected, as the government was dependent on parliamentary support from political groups which had until recently been hostile to one another. Nevertheless, the cabinet of Luben Berov was surprisingly long-lived and remained in power until September 1994, by which time even the President had withdrawn his support.

Dimitar Ludzhev, a former UDF activist, and his parliamentary group *'Nov Izbor'* (New Choice) then made an unsuccessful bid to form a government. When he did not receive the support of the two main parliamentary groups, the UDF and the BSP, the President dissolved the National Assembly and called new elections for 18 December 1994. Up to that date, Bulgaria was governed by a caretaker government of non-party officials, appointed by the President in accordance with the Constitution. The new Prime Minister was Reneta Injova, who until then had chaired the Agency for Privatization.

The elections resulted in a landslide victory for the Socialist Party, which received a parliamentary majority in its own right. Socialist leader Zhan Videnov formed a new government in January 1995. Within a few months, the new government felt the negative effects of the delayed reform and privatization processes. Under increasing pressure from the population at large as well as from the rank and file within his own party, Videnov's government was unable to pursue a coherent and consistent policy. By mid-1996, Videnov had encountered growing economic instability and popular discontent; at the end of the year he had to resign as party chairman, and in January 1997, as Prime Minister. The Socialists presented a new candidate for the premiership, but mass rallies and the opposition boycott of parliament forced them to agree to pre-term elections in April 1997. In the meantime, a caretaker government led by Sofia's popular Mayor Stefan Sofianski was appointed by the President. With the support of the International Monetary Fund, it was able to halt the downward spiral in the economy.

The elections of 1997 were won decisively by the UDF and its ally, the People's Union. A new government, led by UDF chairman Ivan Kostov, was appointed in May. It continued the stabilization programme begun by its predecessor and by the end of 1997 it could boast that it had kept the country on a course of stabilization and reforms; among various measures, it introduced a currency board which kept inflation under control.

The elections of 2001, won by the newly formed National Movement Simeon II, led to a new government, headed by exiled king Simeon Sakskoburgotsky. For the first after its formation, the ethnic Turkish party, MRF was included as junior partner in the government. The policies of the new government followed the general line of the previous one.

APPENDIX 12.3: THE ELECTORAL SYSTEM

The first free multi-party elections for the Grand National Assembly were held in June 1990. The main task of the Assembly was to adopt a new Constitution and a new electoral law. The Assembly was elected through a combination of simple majority and proportional representation; the electoral system was a compromise between the political groups which had taken part in the national Roundtable talks. Fifty per cent of the MPs were to be elected on the basis of simple majorities in single-member constituencies, and the remaining 50 per cent by proportional representation. Bulgaria was divided into 200 single-member and 28 multi-member districts.

During its short existence, the Grand National Assembly fulfilled its main task: the drafting and ratification of the new democratic Constitution of the Republic of Bulgaria; a new electoral law (the Law on the Election of National Representatives, Local Councillors and Mayors); and certain other basic laws. The political parties and coalitions represented in the founding parliament approved a system of proportional representation but with a 4 per cent electoral threshold. As a result of this restriction, the smaller political parties (43 parties were registered for the 1991 elections to the National Assembly) were well advised to enter coalitions. The electoral law was drafted under considerable time pressure, and the law contains significant gaps, disparities and contradictory regulations which have caused uncertainty pertaining to the electoral procedure, requiring the Central Election Commission to redouble its efforts to interpret the legislation.

The new electoral law divided Bulgaria into 31 electoral constituencies, the size and borders of which were to be determined by presidential decree. The number of mandates for each electoral region depended upon the size of the population. The 31 districts were predominantly medium-sized with 6–10 mandates each; a few were larger. The Constitution envisages a single-chamber Parliament, comprised of 240 MPs elected for a period of four years.

Any eligible individual who can collect 2,000 signatures, may run as an independent candidate in one of the 31 constituencies (the required age for candidates is 21; for voting it is 18). An independent candidate is elected if he or she obtains more votes than the regional quota (the total number of ballots cast in the constituency divided by the number of seats allotted to this constituency). This is the first step in the calculation of the outcome, and the only one that may allocate seats at the constituency level. All remaining seats are allocated on the basis of list votes aggregated to the national level. The formula used is the d'Hondt system.

Parties, independent candidates, coalitions of political parties and coalitions of parties are obliged to run on non-amendable elections lists. The voters must vote *en bloc* for a particular electoral list, i.e. vote without expressing preferences for the selection of candidates and/or the rank order of the listed candidates. The major political parties prefer non-amendable lists, since they promote discipline within the parliamentary caucuses.

The electoral legislation itself did little to ensure real or adequate proportional representation of diverse social interests in the legislative body. The 4 per cent electoral barrier proved too high for post-totalitarian Bulgaria. It favoured the two main political formations, the UDF and the BSP, which had little political tolerance for each other. A less cumbersome electoral threshold would have provided representation for political parties and social formations now largely excluded. Some analysts argue that such an amendment would have opened up the Assembly for liberal, environmental, social democratic and agrarian groups, which together enjoy the support of some 25 per cent of the electorate. Given the strength of party competition, social polarization and the complicated nomination and registration procedures, independent candidates had little chance of being elected; in fact, not a single candidate running independently was elected in 1991.

The President of the Republic of Bulgaria is elected directly by the people, and may serve a maximum of two five-year terms in office. Candidates for President and Vice President may be nominated by political parties or party coalitions, or by 5,000 voters signing a petition. The elections are carried out in two rounds, on the basis of the simple majority system. A Bulgarian-born citizen, who is at least 40 years of age, has lived in Bulgaria for the previous five years and satisfies the conditions required of prospective MPs, can be elected President.

The first local elections in democratic conditions were held in November 1991, on the basis of the law adopted by the Grand National Assembly. In 1995, a special law on local elections was adopted, introducing the proportional system for candidates to local councils. Mayors, however, are elected according to the majority principle. If no candidate in a mayoral race wins an outright majority in the first round, a run-off round is held between the three candidates with the largest vote in the first round.

APPENDIX 12.4: THE CONSTITUTIONAL FRAMEWORK

The Constitution approved on 12 July 1991 played a major role in the transformation of Bulgaria. The founding constitutional principles are republican parliamentary rule, the sovereignty of the people, the rule of law, political pluralism and the separation of powers. The principle of separation of powers is established in Article 8 of the Constitution: 'The power of the state shall be divided between a legislative, an executive and a judicial branch'. The Constitution proclaims the supremacy of the Parliament (the People's Assembly) as a permanent, representative institution embodying legislative power. The strict application of the principle of separation of powers finds its expression in the incompatibility of the mandate of a deputy with any other state office, including a ministerial post: 'A Member of Parliament elected as a Minister shall cease to serve as a member during his term of office as Minister ' (Article 68 [2]).

In accordance with its constitutional status, the Parliament enjoys a wide range of prerogatives. The main functions of Parliament are three: legislative; creative (relating to the formation of Cabinets); and control (relating to the exercise of parliamentary control over the Government). Legislation rests with the People's Assembly, but not with the People's Assembly alone. The President of the Republic has the right to promulgate the laws passed by Parliament and to return them for a second review, and the Council of Ministers has the right of legislative initiative.

The People's Assembly elects the Government and exercises control over its activities. The permanent committees exercise parliamentary control over the government on behalf of Parliament. Parliamentary control can be preliminary (preventive), current and subsequent. The means for parliamentary control are established by the Constitution, and in greater detail, by the internal rules of the Assembly: the use of questions and interpellations by MPs addressed to the Council of Ministers or to the various Ministers; votes of no confidence, or of confidence, in the Government or its individual members; the right of inquiries and investigations on issues which concern state or social interests.

In accordance with its constitutional status the Council of Ministers (CM) 'heads the implementation of the domestic and foreign policy of the state in observance of the Constitution and the laws' and 'ensures general management of the state bureaucracy and of the Armed Forces'. The CM manages the implementation of the state budget; organizes the management of state assets; concludes, confirms and rejects international treaties in certain cases specified by law; and rescinds any illegal and improper acts by the Ministers.

The Council of Ministers consists of a Prime Minister, Deputy Prime Ministers and Ministers. The Prime Minister heads and coordinates the overall policy of the Government and bears responsibility for it. He or she appoints and dismisses the deputy Prime Ministers. The Ministers head the various ministries, unless Parliament decides otherwise. They are responsible to Parliament for their acts. Only Bulgarian citizens qualified to be elected to Parliament are eligible for membership in the Council of Ministers.

The Constitution itself creates the premises for the strength of power of the Council of Ministers and of the Prime Minister, who is authorized to lead and coordinate the overall policy of the Government. An example of the wide prerogatives enjoyed by the Cabinet is the number of legal acts which may be issued by the Government and by the various Ministries: the Government issues decrees, ordinances, resolutions, rules of administration and regulations; the Ministers issue rules of administration, regulations, instructions and orders.

Parliament is to control the Government by means of questions and interpellations, and through the Cabinet's dependence on Parliament for approval. The two-way relationship is strengthened by the opportunity given to members of the Government to take part in parliamentary proceedings and in the work of the permanent committees, where they can take the floor upon request. The procedure for the termination of the prerogatives of the Government is spelled out in the Constitution. The Government must submit its resignation in the following cases: a vote of no confidence in the Government or in the Prime Minister; the resignation of the Government or the Prime Minister; the death of the Prime Minister; and when a newly elected National Assembly convenes.

The Constitution envisages limited prerogatives and mainly representative functions for the President of the Republic. By way of example, the President has the right to propose to Parliament a candidate for the post of the Prime Minister, but only a candidate endorsed by the largest parliamentary group and after consultations with the other parliamentary groups. The prerogatives of the President in the legislative process are limited. The President does not have the right to propose legislation and has only a suspensive veto. The application of the presidential veto is not unlimited: it is applicable only in instances of obvious violations of the Constitution and the procedures of the legislative process. A presidential veto can be overturned by a repeated majority vote in the Assembly. The Constitutional Court has the right to scrutinize the President for the legality of his actions, and may initiate proceedings against the President in cases of High Treason or violation of the Constitution.

According to Article 98 of the Constitution, the President: (1) calls elections for the National Assembly and for the bodies of local self-government; (2) has the right to address the nation and the National Assembly; (3) signs international treaties in the cases established by law; (4) promulgates laws; (5) appoints and dismisses the heads of Bulgaria's diplomatic and permanent missions at international organizations upon a motion by the Council of Ministers, and receives the credentials and letters of recall of the foreign diplomatic representatives to Bulgaria; (6) grants asylum. The President appoints four of the 12 members of the Constitutional Court. The President is the Supreme Commander-in-Chief of the Armed Forces, appoints and dismisses the High Command and presides over the Consultative National Security Council.

Within the prerogatives vested in him, the President can issue decrees, addresses and messages. Presidential decrees must be signed by the Prime Minister or by the respective Minister, excepting decrees with which the President: (1) appoints a caretaker government; (2) assigns a mandate for the formation of government; (3) dissolves the National Assembly; (4) returns a law passed by Parliament for further debate; (5) organizes the work of the offices of the Presidency and appoints presidential staff; and (6) schedules elections and referendums and promulgates the laws.

The Bulgarian constitution states that the President bears the duty to contribute to the preservation of the unity of the nation. A number of constitutional guarantees exist to that effect: the incompatibility of the presidential post with a mandate as a member of parliament, as well as with participation in the leadership of political parties.

In recent years, however, a number of factors have contributed to the opposite effect, like the dependence of the President on political parties, the election legislation concerning the President, and various conflicts which arose between former president Zhelev and the government leading to what some experts defined as an 'institutional war'.

Although the current Constitution does not contain legal provisions which allow the dominance of the President in the overall government system, the demands for a stronger presidency are becoming more actual. A constitutional change strengthening presidential powers has been on the agenda of some political parties, including the UDF, which came to power in 1997. But fear among a significant part of the political elite that this could lead to an authoritarian regime is still strong enough to restrict any serious attempts for a regime change. If the transitional process is accompanied by instability and weakness of the parliamentary institution, attempts at a regime change are not be excluded (as was the case with the 4th French republic).

13. Croatia

Nenad Zakošek and Goran Čular

As Eastern Europe was gradually integrated into comparative and sociological research, the former Yugoslavia remained somewhat of a white spot: the states which emerged out of the collapsed Yugoslav federation were usually left out from comparative studies due to war, nationalist conflicts, deficient democratization and incomplete and/or contested state-building.[1] This experience was particularly painful for those social scientists who had had excellent relations with the West long before other East European researchers and who were abruptly cut off from these ties. Scientific work did go on despite the relative isolation; and as a result, there is a solid foundation of empirical data that may be used for the purpose of comparative research.[2]

However, if we leave aside objective obstacles to international cooperation (war and nationalist conflicts), it must be said that the research subject itself, namely the post-socialist transition and the emerging political systems in the post-Yugoslav societies, were difficult to grasp from a comparative perspective since they were clearly different from other East European cases. This is indeed also true for Croatia: there are some specific features of the Croatian transition from the socialist system, which heavily influenced the character of the new regime and made a comparative evaluation rather difficult. While the first stage of transition displays some similarities with other Central and East European countries (e.g. the electoral victory of the anti-communist opposition in the founding elections, and the peaceful acceptance of the election results by the communists), there is one characteristic of the Croatian transition that is unique: the simultaneity of democratic transition, state-building and war, which significantly influenced later political developments.

Other post-socialist systems emerging out of collapsed communist federations (Czechoslovakia, Soviet Union) experienced the combination of the first two processes without war. Though similar to Croatia, Bosnia-Herzegovina and the Federal Republic of Yugoslavia (Serbia and

Montenegro) have a different background. In Bosnia-Herzegovina the war impeded state-building in an early phase and the common state framework was finally secured through intervention by international forces, which *de facto* made Bosnia-Herzegovina into an international protectorate. Also, these conditions resulted in an incomplete democratic transition. In the Federal Republic of Yugoslavia, on the other hand, there was a different combination of processes: due to an early and effective mobilization of nationalism the socialist regime secured its legitimacy and was able to postpone effective regime change until October 2000. State-building was contradictory, since both regime and opposition pursued a variety of options, so that borders and population of the state remained unclear. The issue of war was also unclear, since Serbia and Montenegro never officially admitted to be at war, although they sent their troops to Croatia and Bosnia-Herzegovina. The territory of the Federal Republic was not directly affected by war until the escalation of violence in Kosovo in 1998 and the NATO intervention in 1999.

The specific dynamics of conflict and change in Croatia also testify to the great impact of some long-term historical developments and political legacies. Thus, in explaining the historical setting – in which the Croatian political drama unfolded – we very early discovered the usefulness of the Lipset/Rokkan's cleavage paradigm, also for the Croatian case.[3] The methodological and substantive questions pertaining to the application of this paradigm on Croatia are discussed at some length below.

Croatian Political Dynamics in the First Decade of Post-Socialist Transformation

Before turning to a detailed discussion of the nature of cleavage politics in Croatia and its impact on voters' behaviour and party development, we will give a brief overview of the entire transformation period from the late 1980s until today.[4]

Democratization in Croatia was initially triggered by an external threat and not by internal development: this threat came in the form of Serbian nationalism and the regime of Slobodan Milošević, whose aggressive politics destabilized the entire region from the late 1980s and onwards. Due to the weakness of the reformist forces in the society, the old communist elite controlled the initial stage of transition until the founding elections of April/May 1990. In 1988–89, the attempts by Belgrade to topple communist leaders hostile to the Milošević regime constituted the major challenge to the communist regime in Zagreb. The Croatian leaders were initially defending the status quo, which also explains why reformists were blocked by a strong hard-line wing of the Communist Party (SKH). It was only after this strategy proved unsuccessful that democratization became possible: at the SKH Congress in December 1989 the reformist wing took power and proclaimed its acceptance of political pluralism and free elections.

Despite the very brief period between the legalization of pluralism (end of 1989) and the elections in April 1990 (1st round of elections), the anti-communist opposition was able to organize effectively. Two main Croatian opposition blocs were formed: a broad right-wing nationalist party-movement HDZ, led by charismatic Franjo Tuđman (former Second World War partisan army general and nationalist historian) and a four-party coalition KNS, representing a 'liberal nationalist' option, including the nationalist-populist Democratic Party (HDS), Christian Democrats (HKDS), Social Liberals (HSLS) and Social Democrats (SDH). The Serbian nationalist movement in Croatia was rather unprepared for the rapid change, but was able to organize its own party (SDS).

The nature of political conflict in the first free elections was clearly dichotomous: it was a vote for or against the regime, which was mainly interpreted by the political elites and voters as a quasi-referendum on the future status of Croatia. HDZ, the strongest and most convincing Croatian nationalist party, won a clear electoral victory: it received 42 per cent of the votes and about 60 per cent of the seats in the three-chamber parliament (*Sabor*), while the left bloc received 35 per cent of the votes and 29 per cent of the seats. Since all other political forces were only marginally present in the parliament, it can be said that the founding elections produced a two-party system, in which the major parties, HDZ and the reformed communists, represented the two opposing state-building options: formation of an independent Croatian state (though initially portrayed as a part of a Yugoslav confederation) or continuation of the Croatian status as a constitutive republic of the Yugoslav federation.

The first stage of regime change was smooth, but the conflict with Belgrade was far from resolved. Quite on the contrary, the rift was rapidly deepening. Milošević was not prepared to accept the transformation of Yugoslavia into a loose federation, as proposed by Slovenia and Croatia, and the breakdown of the federal state became more and more probable. Croatian preparations for a unilateral declaration of independence were met by a violent rebellion of Serb nationalists in Croatia, who were supported by the federal army. As the Serb-Croat conflict intensified, the political opposition between the ruling HDZ and the strongest left party, the reformed communists (renamed into Social Democrats, SDP) decreased. The growing inner-Croatian political consensus on the crucial question of state-building made it possible to adopt the new Constitution in December 1990 and prepare a referendum on Croatian independence, which took place in May 1991. After the declaration of independence on 25 June 1991, the Serbian insurgence and the sneaking intervention by the federal army escalated into open aggression and war.

The consequences of war were very serious and cannot be accounted for here in detail. Between the summer of 1991 and August 1995, Serbian rebels occupied about one third of Croatia's territory; more than 300,000 persons were temporarily displaced, serious human losses and material damage were suffered. Croatia eventually liberated the bulk of the occupied territories, which prompted 200,000 Serbian refugees to leave the country; the remaining occupied part in Eastern Slavonia was reintegrated with Croatia under UN-control in January 1998. The direct political consequences of the war were also very significant: mass mobilization for defence narrowed the space for political competition, and during the most serious period of war (August 1991 to August 1992) an all-party government was formed. Also, a certain level of nationalist ideological mobilization shaped Croatian public opinion and left lasting imprints, which may still be felt today, especially in debates about cooperation with the Hague tribunal and the question of how to cope with atrocities and human rights violations committed by the Croatian side.

The Croatian party system was transformed in the subsequent elections to the House of Representatives (August 1992, October 1995), the elections to the second chamber, the House of Counties, which was conceived as vehicle of a regional representation (February 1993, April 1997), and the elections for the presidential office (August 1992, June 1997). In all these elections, the ruling HDZ was able to confirm its position as a dominant party: due to the disproportional effects of the electoral system 43–45 per cent of the votes were transformed into a safe parliamentary majority of about 60 per cent of seats in both chambers. Franjo Tuđman won both presidential elections by a high margin (56.7 and 60.3 per cent respectively). A number of other parties also managed to carve out electoral niches for themselves during the 1990s: the reformed communists of the SDP, the 'nationalist liberals' of the HSLS and (initially) the HNS, regionalist IDS, agrarian-conservative HSS, and right-wing nationalist HSP and HKDU, both of which were politically close to HDZ. The dominant party system of the 1990s, in which the HDZ rule could not seriously be challenged by the weak opposition, was characterized by several features: HDZ used its hegemonic position to control crucial economic and social resources (public companies, public electronic media) and, at the same time, to destabilize its main opposition competitors (by manipulating individual opposition leaders and by promoting internal splits in the opposition parties). However, HDZ itself was not immune to factional conflicts and a major split occurred in February 1994 on the issue of Croatian policy towards Bosnia-Herzegovina. The party that emerged out of this conflict, HND, did not prove successful. The semi-presidential system, combined with the authoritarian political style of Tuđman and his uncontested authority in the HDZ, resulted in a high degree of personalization and concentration of political power. Finally, the

HDZ regime developed a complex network of clientelistic organizations, which were directly dependant on state funds and other resources administered by HDZ officials.

The monopolization of power by Tuđman and his party made the Croatian regime semi-authoritarian (or semi-democratic). Its legitimacy was not undermined until the late 1990s, and then only as the result of different converging factors: the failure of economic and social policies, widespread dissatisfaction with the unjust consequences of privatization, and the international isolation of the regime. The death of Franjo Tuđman in December 1999 added the final blow to the legitimacy of the HDZ regime. In the system of personalized power his death left a leadership vacuum that could not be filled. Also, in the late 1990s a specific regime political divide emerged among the opposition parties, which criticized democratic deficits and united against HDZ. In the elections of January 2000 a broad coalition of six opposition parties (SDP, HSLS, HSS, IDS, HNS and LS) made a firm agreement to cooperate before and after the elections. As a result of these developments HDZ experienced a serious electoral defeat (winning only 24.4 per cent of the votes and 30.5 per cent of the seats), while the six opposition parties (including two minor regionalist parties, PGS and SBHS) could win a safe majority of the votes (56.4 per cent) and the seats (63.5 per cent).

The political development after the January 2000 elections and the change of government made democratic reforms possible. The semi-presidential system was abandoned through constitutional amendments and a parliamentary system with a strong government was introduced. However, the broad six-party ruling coalition proved very unstable and not sufficiently efficient. In July 2002 the coalition fell apart and the second strongest party, HSLS, left the government. The Social Democratic Prime Minister Račan formed a minority cabinet, which is expected to continue the reforms until the elections in late 2003. The party system experienced further transformation. Though afflicted by internal tensions, which gave rise to splinter movements (DC, HB), the HDZ was able to preserve its electoral support on the same level as in the 2000 elections and thus remains the strongest right-wing party. The SDP stands out as its main opponent at the other end of the left-right continuum, and between the poles defined by these two parties there is a variety of parties competing for the favours of the voters. The Croatian party system is apparently developing towards moderate pluralism.

Historical, Ideological and Socio-Structural Roots of Party Politics

We have initially stated that certain historical continuities in Croatian politics indicate that cleavages exist and form the basis of political bloc formation. In this section we would like to explain in what way we intend to use the concept of cleavages. The starting point of our analysis is the classic account of cleavages given by Seymour M. Lipset and Stein Rokkan (1967).

When using the Lipset and Rokkan's paradigm, we cannot just take the results they report and expect them to be valid in Eastern Europe. The paradigm was developed on the basis of a limited set of West European cases over time, but we can use it as a source of inspiration in analyses of the social and political transformation of contemporary Eastern Europe. If we investigate the existence of cleavages as structures determining political behaviour, we ask about the historically grown 'identity patterns', which reflect membership in social groups combined with a certain 'world view' and political orientation. Thus, on a very abstract level, it can be said that cleavages describe a certain coincidence of structural and action elements. The level and intensity of stabilization of structural factors (i.e. cleavages) may be conceived of as the result of the interrelation of action and structure: action produces outcomes, outcomes add up to structures, and structures determine or limit action. Human action produces different types of outcomes: economic structures, social strata, cultural products, which serve as the basis of group formation (class, ethnic, religious groups).[5] Therefore, the answer to the question whether cleavages do exist and determine politics in Eastern Europe depends on the conceptual framework that describes the mutual relationship between structure and action and makes it operational for historical or sociological research. In the Lipset/Rokkan paradigm this is precisely the purpose of introducing an abstract scheme based on Parsons' theory of social action (the so called 'AGIL-scheme' – a scheme depicting four functional aspects of social action which correspond to four dimensions of cleavage formation: political, economic, cultural and social). Similarly, the cleavage model of Herbert Kitschelt (1992; 1995) uses an equally abstract argument of the rational choice theory: it presupposes a hierarchy of political conflicts, ranging from identity conflicts over the definition of boundaries of the polity to value conflicts and socio-economic interest conflicts.

For the purpose of our empirical analysis we think that the theoretical assumptions and historical accounts, made by Lipset and Rokkan as well as Kitschelt, may be combined with the operationalization of the cleavage concept launched by Oddbjørn Knutsen and Elinor Scarbrough (1995). For the two latter, cleavages include structural, value and political dimensions. The cleavages are 'rooted in a relatively persistent social division', that is groups 'according to class, religion, economic, or cultural interests'. Furthermore, cleavages 'engage(s) some set of values common to members of the group', who share the same value orientation: of which Knutsen and Scarbrough distinguish three basic types in West European societies: religious-secular, left-right materialism and materialism versus post-materialism. Finally, the cleavages are 'institutionalized in some form of organization – most commonly a political party, but also in churches, unions, and other associational groups' (Knutsen and Scarbrough 1995, 494).

Conceptually grounded also in Bartolini and Mair (1990), the theoretical framework has been somewhat refined at the operational level (Tóka 1998). Along the way the theory has lost part of its historical dimension and has been almost completely turned into a statistical model for assessment of the impact of each and every dimension on the stability of party preferences. In this way, a crucial element of the cleavage theory – its potential for accounting for long-lasting effects of the social and political development on party system stability – has been lost. When presenting the cleavage politics of post-socialist Poland, Markowski (2002) therefore makes a point of highlighting the theoretical and methodological aspects all at once. Conceptually still following Bartolini and Mair (1990), Knutsen and Scarbrough (1995) and Tóka (1998), he introduces a research design without models that ascribe motives to and assign probabilities at the individual level. As Markowski sees it, statistical analyses of cleavage politics should be carried out on the aggregate level for different kinds or groups of voters. We are inclined to agree with him and propose that a definition of cleavages should include the following elements:

- cleavages are based on long-term oppositions or conflicts, which involve distinct social groups with particular 'world views', value orientations and certain patterns of political behaviour;
- cleavages describe a bipolar or dichotomous interest constellation of groups;
- cleavages include both elite and mass beliefs and actions;
- cleavages are historically created by political mobilization of group values or interests;
- cleavages presuppose coincidence between social group identity and political/party blocs, although there may be groups without adequate political expression (which might be referred to as 'latent cleavages') and party politics without socio-cultural basis (issue or candidate voting, party identification);
- cleavages explain the long-term stability of party systems and long-term voting behaviour; they cannot account for short-term volatility.

Formation of the Historical Cleavages in Croatia and Their Mobilization in the 1990 Founding Elections

As indicated above, already in the phase of transition and in the founding elections the evident impact of historical conflict lines suggested the existence and great impact of long-term polarizing structures, i.e. of cleavages. In our earlier studies we have developed a model, which depicts the main features of cleavages in Croatia (Zakošek 1991; 1998). We think that the historical account of the cleavage development in Eastern Europe by Tomas Hellén, Sten Berglund and Frank Aarebrot in the 1998 version of *The Handbook of Political Change in Eastern Europe* corresponds with our description of the development in Croatia.

Based on these previous findings we would like to suggest that Croatian politics is determined basically by three types of cleavages. In Croatia, the traditional conflict between the centre and periphery, evolving around opposing concepts of the status and the level of autonomy of Croatia, could be labelled the territorial-cultural cleavage. It can be traced back to the 19th century and to the very beginning of modern politics in Croatia. The beginning of party politics in the then part of the Austrian-Hungarian Monarchy was clearly structured according to that cleavage. Later on, in the Kingdom of Yugoslavia the same conflict dominated Croatian politics completely and had a major impact on Yugoslav politics. In Croatia, which was part of larger states until 1991, this cleavage long had a dual character. It implied opposition against the state centres to which Croatia was subjected and against which it advocated the interests of the periphery, but it also implied the presence of an internal opposition against the centre of Croatian state-building efforts by minority and/or regional collective actors who constituted the periphery. In the founding elections, the relationship between Belgrade and Zagreb represented the former, while the relationship between Zagreb and the Serb-dominated regions in Croatia was expressed by the latter. During the democratic transition, the cleavage emerged in the form of opposing national identities: Croats versus Serbs or Yugoslavs (Zakošek 1998, 47). The centre-periphery cleavage has also a cultural component fuelled by opposing ideological concepts of Croatian national and state integration: 'centre' symbolizes an exclusive concept of the Croatian nation, hostile to minority cultures and external cultural influences, while 'periphery' is compatible not only with minority cultures but also with various concepts of a non-exclusive national identity (historically mainly variations of a Yugoslav national ideology). The latter concept also includes ideas of an open national culture.

The ideological-cultural cleavage in Croatia is primarily based on strong religious and secular identities. It is a product of cultural modernization and the emergence of a secular culture, and an expression of the historical conflict over the role and status of the Catholic Church, especially in the field of education and moral instruction. This cleavage deepened during the socialist regime due to its explicit anti-Catholic politics and its radical secularization of all cultural segments. The ideological-cultural cleavage progressively became more and more intertwined with the centre-periphery cleavage, when the Catholic Church came out as one of the major proponents of Croatian national autonomy, strongly connecting Catholic religious identity[6] with anti-communism and Croatian nationalism. After the demise of the socialist system the cleavage expresses the divide between religious-traditionalist and secular-modernist concepts of culture, both of which are very prominent in Croatian society. This dimension showed the strongest correlation with the 'left-right' spectrum, which goes to prove that Croatian voters did not connect the terms left and right with the socio-economic dimension of the political conflict in a meaningful way (left-right in the classical sense), but with the ideological-cultural dimension, i.e. modern/liberal versus traditional/conservative (Šiber 1991, 116–28; Šiber 2001, 85–8).

Functional or socio-economic cleavages consist of several structural cleavages (urban–rural, working-class–middle-class) and are after the collapse of socialism based on the opposition of different socio-economic interests and concepts of economic distribution of resources. These cleavages existed also before the socialist regime, but were radically altered by it. The contemporary interest constellation is therefore based on the consequences of the economic transformation after 1990, although some of its structures emerged already during socialist market reforms in the 1960s.

Figure 13.1: Ethnic and religious determinants of mass attitudes on the Yugoslav federation, multiparty system, and self-management in 1990

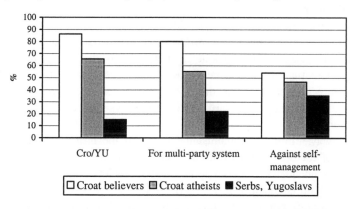

Note: Percentages of respondents grouped as Croat devout Catholics, Croat atheists, and Serbs or Yugoslavs. 'CRO/YU': support for Yugoslavia as a confederation or for Croatian independence; 'For multi-party system': unconditional support for a multi-party system; 'Against self-management': support for the abolishment of the system of self-management in the economy. Croat traditional Catholics not shown.

Source: FPS (1990).

The historical cleavage structure was mobilized openly for the first time during the founding democratic elections in 1990. This also marked the emergence of political parties (1989–90) and the formation of a party system. Though the emphasis was on national independence and system change, the emerging party system was defined by existing cleavage lines from the very beginning. The parties to which the voters rallied in 1989–90 virtually conquered the political space and survived over the next twelve years as the only relevant actors. The role the parties played in the founding elections goes a long way towards accounting for this achievement. It has in any event left a more lasting impression on the voters than subsequent ideological manoeuvres and leadership changes.

The territorial-cultural and ideological-cultural cleavage significantly determined the pattern of political competition in the 1990 elections, not only because the relationship between Croatia and Yugoslavia was the mobilizing issue but also because the cleavage affected public attitudes on the communist regime, democracy and market institutions (Zakošek 1991, 182–4). Figure 13.1 clearly shows to what extent Serbs/Yugoslavs in Croatia were ideologically connected not only with the Yugoslav federation but with the socialist institutions as well. These figures can be explained by the fact that Serb nationalism in the late 1980s strongly mobilized fears based on the genocide Croatian Serbs suffered in the fascist Independent State of Croatia from 1941–44 and by the fact that this group enjoyed the most favoured position in socialist Yugoslavia. The Croatian Serbs were in fact one of the ethnic groups most loyal to the communist regime in the entire federation.

As we have seen, there is a large difference between the most and the least religious ethnic Croats. The difference is particularly pronounced on the issue of independence. About 27 per cent of the strong believers supported Croatian independence (which was more than half of all the independence advocates at that time), but only 5 per cent of the Croatian atheists and virtually none of Serbs/Yugoslavs opted for Croatian independence.[7]

In this way, through communist mediation of the historical cleavages, two types of socio-cultural identity lines crosscut at the structural level and created four unequal segments within Croatian society. However, when a value dimension is added, it becomes obvious that belonging to the ethnic majority religious segment reinforces pro-independence and anti-socialist attitudes to a large extent. In 1990 the HDZ mobilized the bulk of its voters from this segment. Thus, around 70 per cent of all devoutly Catholic Croats voted HDZ; nine out of ten HDZ voters were in fact either devout Catholics or traditional Catholic believers. The SKH-SDP, on the other hand, relied on secular Croats along with Serbs and Yugoslavs (also largely secular) for the bulk of its popular support.

While the overall cleavage structure clearly distinguished the SKH-SDP from the HDZ and the KNS (see *Figure 13.2*), it was primarily the structural component of the ideological-cultural cleavage that distinguished the HDZ from the centre-oriented KNS (Zakošek 1991, 185). Unlike the HDZ and the SKH-SDP, whose supporters belonged to the structurally opposed electoral segments, the KNS had a mix of devout Catholics, traditional Catholics and 'non-believers' that comes quite close to the national average. In this way, the KNS represented a rather small segment of 'national liberals' (the actual electoral support of the KNS was 15 per cent), for whom value and issue voting was much more important than their structural position.

Figure 13.2: Party preferences and attitudes on the Yugoslav federation, multiparty system, and self-management in 1990

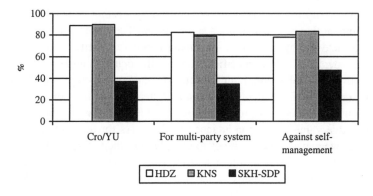

Note: Percentages of respondents grouped as HDZ, KNS and SKH-SDP voters expressing the following attitudes: 'CRO/YU': support for Yugoslavia as a confederation or for Croatian independence; 'For multi-party system': unconditional support for a multi-party system; 'Against self-management': support for the abolishment of the system of self-management in the economy.

Source: FPS (1990).

A peculiarity of the development of the Croatian party system was the fact that the communist–anti-communist divide from the very beginning was absorbed by the issue of Croatian independence, which made the Croatian case much different from e.g. the Czechoslovakian case, but also from other post-communist cases in which the founding elections were dominated solely by the regime divide. However, in this context, the institutionalization of the semi-authoritarian movement produced a new regime divide. This combination of cleavages was imposed as a fundamental constraint on the voters' party preferences throughout the 1990s and including the last parliamentary elections in 2000. Reinforced by the regime divide, the overlapping territorial-cultural and ideological-cultural cleavages eventually reduced the space for the national liberal segment, almost like a pair of scissors. The functional or socio-economic cleavages were never mobilized sufficiently to make an impact on party competition in any of the democratic elections held so far.

Cleavages as Constraints on Party Competition: 1992–99

In this part of the chapter we set out to assess the degree to which party competition and voting behaviour have been constrained and determined by the cleavage structure as it emerged in the 1990 founding elections. To this end, we have to measure the strength of particular cleavages over time and describe the overall trend, including the relative strength of cleavages over time. The analysis draws on partly longitudinal surveys conducted in 1992, 1995 and 1999.[8]

In this analysis, we have to go beyond the rather general level of measurement that has been applied so far. We will search for the *territorial-cultural* cleavage by looking at the linkages between parties and ethnic or regional identities. More specifically, we will focus on attitudes towards nationalism, federalization, multi-culturalism and cosmopolitanism. We will tap the presence of the *ideological-cultural* cleavage by analysing electoral behaviour in terms of religious-secular identities with the liberal-conservative value dimension attached to them. As for the *socio-economic* cleavage, we expect political blocs to comply with the urban-rural and class divides with significant attitudinal differences between them on the left-right scale.[9] For further details on the operationalization of the variables see Appendix 13.5.

Croatia has two peculiarities worth noting in this structural context. Religious denomination loses its significance in the Croatian case, as it overlaps almost completely with ethnicity. Thus, the distinction between Catholic and Orthodox Christians is mainly covered by the distinction between Croats and Serbs.

Another point refers to the ethnic structure. The size of the Croatian core population increased from 78 per cent before the war (1991) to 90 per cent after war (2001). This is primarily a consequence of drastic demographic changes caused by extensive war actions and the ethnic cleansing in Croatia and its neighboring country Bosnia-Herzegovina, which created more ethnically homogeneous territories on both sides of the border. In this process, the size of the Serbian population decreased from almost 12 per cent in 1991 to a meagre 4 per cent in 2001. The exodus of Serbs started with the outbreak of hostilities between Belgrade and Zagreb in 1991 and culminated with military defeat of the Serbian insurgents in 1995. In this way, the demographic base of the most important political cleavage at the founding elections shrank so much that the Serbian segment of the population lost its political relevance. In our analysis, we do not treat Serbs separately from other non-Croat ethnic groups, but take all minorities as one entity.

With regard to other traits visible already at the socio-structural level of analysis, it is important to point to a certain, though not strong, association between urban-rural and class criteria on the one hand and religious identity on the other. The probability of finding devoutly religious people in rural areas and in working-class neighbourhoods is somewhat higher than in the population as a whole. This feature of the cleavage structure in Croatia remains stable throughout the period under investigation.

Table 13.1: Strength of socio-structural and political aspects of cleavages 1992–1999

Value dimensions	Centre /periphery			Liberal /conservative			Socio-economic left		
Socio-structural divisions	1992	1995	1999	1992	1995	1999	1992	1995	1999
Territorial -Cultural									
Regional	–	0.27	0.53	–	0.39	0.42	–	–	n.s.
Ethnic	0.48	0.63	0.53	0.62	0.50	0.38	n.s.	–	n.s.
Ideological -Cultural									
Religious-Secular	0.41	0.26	0.70	0.88	0.80	0.92	0.12	–	0.26
Socio-economic									
Rural/urban	0.16	n.s.	0.28	0.23	0.24	0.41	0.09		0.30
Class	0.29	0.27	0.34	0.42	0.48	0.55	n.s.	–	0.46

Note: Entries are differences in arithmetic means of two sub-samples. The sub-samples are: regional (Istra and Rijeka versus all others), ethnic (Croats versus all others), religious beliefs (convinced believers versus all others), rural/urban (dwellers in villages and suburban areas versus urban dwellers), class (workers, peasants, housewives, retired, unemployed versus administration, entrepreneurs, professionals, students). All differences are significant at the 0.01 level, unless otherwise indicated (n.s.). For some socio-structural and value dimensions in some years data is missing (–). The construction of the value scales are explained in Appendix 13.5.

Source: FPS (1992, 1995, 1999).

The initial question is whether voters belonging to different socio-structural segments also have different attitudes on the value dimensions that correspond to their social position? Explanations of party system stability in terms of cleavage theory presuppose that the social groups cultivate value orientations predicted by the theory.[10] As may be gauged from Table 13.1, all the socio-structural segments display differences on the value dimensions except regional and ethnic identities that do not differ on the left-right value dimension. However, the ideological-cultural cleavage and eventually also the territorial-cultural cleavage tend to be most pronounced where they connect with dimensions with which they are theoretically linked. The situation is somewhat unclear in the case of the functional cleavage, which consistently correlates with all the three value dimensions, albeit less strongly with the left/right dimension. If we control for party bloc vote intention (not shown in *Table 13.1*), some of the 'unexpected' correlations lose their significance. But the religious segment does remain different from the secular when it comes to attitudes pertaining to the centre-periphery dimension, while the class and urban-rural divisions perform somewhat erratically on the liberal-conservative value dimension. The former may be attributed to the close connection between the centre-periphery and liberal-conservative value dimensions that might be collapsed into one single dimension (Kitschelt 1992, 14–15); the latter may be seen as a by-product of the partial overlapping of class and urban-rural with the religious-secular socio-structural divisions. It may also be attributed to a tendency towards conservatism in working-class and rural settlements, regardless of religious identity. The implication is that we should treat the urban-rural divide as the socio-structural base of the ideological cultural cleavage.

The ideological-cultural cleavage is clearly the most pronounced cleavage, though less so in 1999 than in 1992. Its socio-structural strength coincides with the impact of political parties on value preferences and it seems that these two aspects reinforce the ideological-cultural value cleavage. This cleavage is clearly at the very centre of the cleavage structure in Croatia. It was a force to be reckoned with already during the formative years in the early 1990s and it has since reduced other cleavages to a secondary position.

The territorial-cultural cleavage, on the other hand, lost most its significance after 1990 for reasons already mentioned. The Serbs were reduced to an almost insignificant minority position as a result of the war; national independence ceased to be a real and major political issue, and its symbolic impact on later ideological and political debates got a somewhat more complex expression. Of relevance in this context is also the process of political mobilization of the early 1990s, which brought the centre-periphery value dimension so close to the liberal-conservative value scale that the two dimensions eventually became indistinguishable from one another. The HDZ still attracted some liberal voters back in 1990, but soon turned into an authoritarian and conservative party. At the same time, the SDP gradually, though in a rather traumatic way, got rid of the Yugoslav conservative part of its electorate inherited from the socialist past and opened up to younger and more liberal voters who accepted national independence as a matter of fact. The new regime divide – about the nature of the HDZ regime (Čular 2000, 2001) – that developed after the war against Serbia contributed towards the gradual withering away of the ideological space originally occupied by the KNS, namely pro-independence liberals. As a result the centre-periphery dimension was gradually integrated into the ideological-cultural cleavage (*Table 13.1*). This process coincided with the gradual transformation of centre-periphery from a predominantly ethnic into a predominantly regional dimension, as evidenced by the appearance of a strong regional party, the IDS, in Istria, a region in Western Croatia.

The functional cleavages have been much less pronounced. It may also be noted that class and urban-rural distinctions originally had a greater impact on centre-periphery and liberal conservative value orientations than on the economic left-right dimension. The salience of the functional cleavages increased somewhat in 1999; but they seem to matter more on the socio-structural level than on the level of political preferences. The implications are twofold. The functional cleavages are obviously neutralized – rather than mobilized – by the existing political divide, but they clearly have potential as a platform for political parties.

Table 13.2: Independent (controlled) effects of structural and value dimensions on cleavages in Croatia 1992–1999

Socio-structural divisions	1992 left–right	1992 within left	1992 within right	1995 left–right	1995 within left	1995 within right	1999 left–right	1999 within left	1999 within right
Territorial -Cultural									
Regional	–	–	–	**0.09**	**0.16**	n.s.	n.s.	**0.09**	n.s.
Ethnic	**0.07**	**0.20**	n.s.	0.05	n.s.	n.s.	0.05	n.s.	n.s.
Ideological -Cultural									
Religious -Secular	**0.11**	n.s.	n.s.	**0.12**	n.s.	n.s.	**0.07**	n.s.	n.s.
Socio- economic	**0.07**	n.s.	n.s.	n.s.	n.s.	n.s.	n.s.	n.s.	n.s.
Rural-urban	0.03	n.s.	**0.08**	0.04	n.s.	n.s.	n.s.	n.s.	**0.16**
Class									
Value dimensions									
Liberal -Conservative	**-0.21**	**-0.13**	n.s.	**-0.22**	n.s.	**-0.11**	**-0.22**	**-0.12**	n.s.
Centre -Periphery	**0.18**	**0.10**	n.s.	**0.08**	n.s.	n.s.	**0.18**	n.s.	**-0.18**
Socio-economic left	n.s.	n.s.	**0.10**	–	–	–	n.s.	0.07	n.s
Correctly predicted (%)	74.45	76.83	63.47	71.33	63.80	83.06	77.00	65.87	79.39
Odds ratio	8.45	5.47	2.78	5.71	4.90	1.78	11.09	2.63	4.14
N	2012	958	1054	830	395	425	739	463	276

Note: Entries are logistic regression coefficients from logistic regression analyses of the three 'party bloc' variables on socio-structural and value variables for each year. For the way in which the variables are constructed, see Apendix 13.5. Values printed **bold** are significant at 0.01, other values at the 0.05 level; 'n.s.' indicates not significant at 0.05. Undecided respondents are excluded from the analysis. Odds ratios are generated from two by two contingency tables of statistically predicted party bloc preference (predicted group membership from logistic regressions) and the dependent variables.

Source: FPS (1992, 1995, 1999).

In order to get a clearer and more precise picture of cleavage voting during the observed period, we look at the independent impact of socio-structural and value variables on party bloc voting. In this way it is possible to see how much each variable contributes to vote preferences grouped into party blocs. We have already seen that some parties of the left as well as of the right are consistently over-represented in certain segments of the population, and we therefore made a point of testing two additional cleavage lines on the political level (*Table 13.2*).

The overall picture ties in nicely with our previous findings. The value dimensions such as liberal-conservative and centre-periphery are more crucial for left-right bloc voting than the socio-structural variables. In this respect, Croatia stands in line with other Central European countries, which display similar characteristics (Tóka 1998). It may also be noted that the impact of the socio-structural divisions has weakened over time. As opposed to 1992, religious-secular identities no longer serve as strong predictors of party bloc vote, and urban-rural and class no longer have an independent impact on voting behaviour. Though somewhat weaker in 1999 than in 1992, the two value dimensions have become the primary determinants of left-right bloc voting.

The suspicion that the parties respond in different ways to the existing cleavage lines has also been confirmed. While a special form of the territorial-cultural cleavage seems to be at work within the left-wing bloc, the right-wing bloc is divided on the class cleavage. Although somewhat blurred at times, these two additional cleavage lines help us identify consistent patterns of competition within each bloc. Unlike patterns dividing the two main political blocs, the patterns within blocs are much more based on socio-structural segments than on the corresponding value dimensions. On the whole, though, these two divisions are of secondary importance in determining the limits of party competition and future party system changes. This is why references to the crosscutting nature of the cleavage structure in Croatia are only partly true. With all due respect for the IDS, the dominant party in Istria in the 1990s and the only proper organizational representative of a regional segment, Croatian politics has been dominated by the religious-secular divide, which after independence absorbed the historical centre-periphery cleavage. Figure 13.3 provides a visual summary of the Croatian cleavage structure in the 1990s.

Finally, as may be gauged from the last three rows in Table 13.2, it is relatively easy to predict party bloc vote on the basis of information on the social and value position of the respondents; the percentage of correct predictions falls within the range of 63–83 per cent. A longitudinal analysis reveals that the dominant left-right cleavage has been increasing its predictive power along with the class determinants within the right-wing bloc. On the other hand, the centre-periphery cleavage line has been loosing its predictive power among the left-wing parties.[11]

Figure 13.3: Spatial positions of the Croatian parties according to cleavage lines, 1992–1999

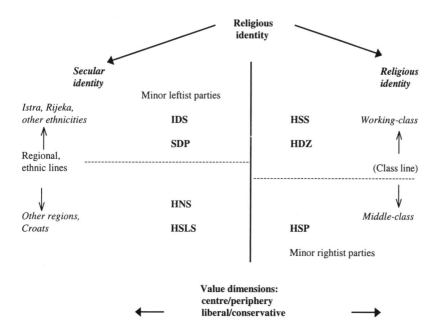

On the whole, the cleavages produce the bloc choices that we would expect. But class voting is an exception from this rule. In Croatia, 'working-class' is linked with the right rather than with the left.[12] There are two explanations for this 'anomaly' and they both include certain assumptions about the nature of party competition and the structure of the main issues. We have already suggested that the relationship might be spurious; in other words, class is just a proxy for a number of other variables, primarily related to the salient religious-secular divide. Recent political developments in Central and Eastern Europe have paved the way for a more elaborate hypothesis. Transitional politics revolves not only around classical issues of redistribution and welfare, but also around problems of privatization and monetary stability. This cluster of issues has a bias towards a quite different value domain – the relationship between national interests and international requirements – whether for free trade and foreign investments or for restrictive IMF policies. In this way, advocating national interests and sovereignty coincides with the opposition against free market allocation and neo-liberal economic policies, thereby providing a 'natural' linkage between the two value dimensions. The forces of party competition can cement this link in the economically least advantageous and most nationalistic and authoritarian part of the population creating a 'counter-intuitive' bloc of working-class socialists voting for parties of the right.[13]

In the end, we should bear in mind that cleavage theory is useful for describing the logic of party systems and patterns of political competition only if empirically tested. If cleavages really serve as constraints on the voters, the existing pattern of voting behaviour should contribute towards party system stability. We are therefore well advised to change our focus from single elections to stable voting patterns over time. Although operationalized and measured differently, the very conceptualization of cleavage voting follows in principle the reasoning elaborated by Knutsen and Scarbrough (1995), Tóka (1998), and Markowski (2002). In a nutshell, the idea rests on the assumption that the correspondence between social status or identity of the individual citizen, on the one hand, and his/her value judgments, on the other hand, should yield more solid ties to a certain party bloc than would be the case if the two aspects do not coincide.[14]

Table 13.3: Size and stability of the cleavage voting pattern (C) 1992–1999

Type of cleavage	1992				1995				1999			
	Size (%)	Stability			Size (%)	Stability			Size (%)	Stability		
		left b.	right b.	mean		left b.	right b.	mean		left b.	right b.	mean
Territorial -Cultural												
Ethnic	51	2.26	1.50	1.88	31	1.67	1.41	1.54	48	1.99	1.58	1.79
Regional	–	–	–	–	34	2.04	1.46	1.75	50	1.73	1.61	1.67
Ideological -Cultural												
Religious -Secular	65	1.72	1.79	1.76	63	1.84	1.71	1.77	68	1.56	2.23	1.90
Socio- economic												
Class	51	1.06	1.20	1.13	–	–	–	–	62	1.20	1.33	1.27
Rural -Urban	50	1.16	1.21	1.19	–	–	–	–	57	1.35	1.28	1.32

Note: Samples have been split into two sub-samples: cleavage voters (*C*) and other, non-cleavage voters (*NC*). *C* contains all the respondents whose value position on the assumed dimension fits with their socio-structural position, and *NC* contains all other respondents. For instance, working-class socialists and middle-class neo-liberals both belong to *C*, while working-class neo-liberals and middle-class socialists belong to *NC*. For the purpose of the analysis, ordinal value scales are dichotomized with their mean values as cut-points. On the other side, from respondents' actual and recalled party choice in earlier elections, we constructed a new variable on which there emerged three groups of respondents: consistent right voters, consistent left voters and voters with discontinuity in voting behaviour. Stability in voting behaviour of *C* is then compared to the stability in the whole sample. However, voting stability is recognized only if it emerged in the corresponding segment. In this way, for instance, stable voting for the right bloc of a not religious liberal is not considered as evidence of stability determined by cleavage voting, but rather as the opposite. 'Size' is the percentage of the *C* pattern in the sample. 'Stability' is the ratio of the percentage stable voters in the corresponding *C* and all stable voters.

Source: FPS (1992, 1995, 1999).

The results are summed up in Table 13.3. First, the table contains information on the size of the sub-sample of cleavage voters (*C*) within the entire sample in 1992, 1995 and 1999 respectively. The match between religious-secular identity and liberal-conservative values creates the biggest and the most stable *C*-group, ranging from 63 to 68 per cent of all voters. The territorial-cultural cleavage displays variations over time that are not easy to explain.[15] As for the class cleavage, there is an enlargement of the segment occurring between 1992 and 1999.

On the whole, the analysis of the effects of cleavages on the stability of voting behaviour corroborates previous findings about the strength of particular cleavages. Thus, by 1995 the ideological-cultural cleavage had emerged as the most effective constraint on political preferences, and it subsequently kept proving its ability to cultivate stable voters. The strongly disproportional stability of the right-wing bloc in 1999 goes a long way towards accounting for the relative success of the HDZ and the entire right-wing bloc in the face of the extremely unfavourable electoral swing at the beginning of 2000. Inter-bloc volatility went up, but most of the changes that occurred must be attributed to a flow out of the main segment. The ideological-cultural cleavage thus proved to be the most pronounced constraint on party competition. It has been the strongest cleavage line on all relevant counts – strength, size of segments and stability potential.

The territorial-cultural cleavage has also displayed a rather high level of stability at times. Its periphery and minority segments have served the interests of the left by coming out in favour of decentralization, minority rights and openness *vis-à-vis* the European Union rather than by adopting the opposing points of view. The small size of the segment may have something to do with this, but it probably has much more to do with what is at stake. Minority rights and regional autonomy are at the very core of the interests of regional and ethnic minorities, and of limited importance to the centre-majority segments. Last but not least, the class cleavage gained a bit in size and became a somewhat better predictor of voting stability as time went by, but it still remains of marginal importance.

The Role of Political Parties in Maintaining the Cleavage Structure

Two interconnected questions arise from this analysis. The first question pertains to the role of political parties themselves. To what extent – if at all – did the type of organizational development of the parties and the electoral strategies of the party leaders affect the changing structure of cleavages? The importance of these factors certainly should not be exaggerated. The demographic changes and the fact that the project of national independence – initially an issue of partisan contention that eventually gained the overwhelming support of the political community – played the crucial role.

However, there is room for an institutional explanation on at least two other counts: the role of the regime divide at the level of political elites and the role of individual parties, their strategies and organizations. In 1995–2000, a strong manifest divide between the HDZ regime and the opposition against the democratic deficits marked Croatian politics; it had several consequences for party institutionalization (Kasapović 1996; Čular 2001). The divide greatly overlapped with the existing territorial-cultural and ideological-cultural cleavage lines; it blurred the differences between the cleavages and reinforced their effects. The divide was more distinct on the elite level than on the mass level, and it helps account for the seemingly counter-intuitive party strategies between 1995 and 2000. The regime divide can also partly explain the drastic political changes that took place in the 2000 elections, in spite of a rather closed cleavage structure.[16]

Other parties also contributed to the mobilization of certain cleavage lines, including the HDZ and the SDP both of which modified their ideological profiles in the early 1990s. The emergence of a small but strong regional party in Istria (IDS) and the failure of similar attempts in other parts of Croatia may be attributed to favourable socio-cultural conditions in Istria, but the organizational profile of the IDS may also have something to do with it.[17] The HSS has also played an interesting role, well worth highlighting. It is a traditional party with a broad organizational base and several rural strongholds. It has operated within the exiting cleavage structure, but on a deliberately diffuse ideological platform that has made it possible for the party to change coalition partners with impunity. The HSLS is another case in point. It is ideologically close to the liberal nationalists of 1990; it has suffered several setbacks, including a party split in 1997, but it has nevertheless survived and may possibly be listed as a case of institutional resistance and organizational encapsulation of segments under pressure.

This leads us to the second question, the question of future party strategies and their effects on the cleavage structure. It seems reasonable to expect the class cleavage to gain impetus. In the short run, we would expect it to overlap with the existing cleavage lines rather than crosscut them. It is hard to see how a political party could mobilize voters by calling for state interventionism, a slow-down of the process of privatization and resistance against IMF recommendation, while promoting liberal and cosmopolitan values. Such an economic platform is in fact more likely in the authoritarian and conservative part of the political space in Croatia than in the opposite corner, leaving possibly the representation of empty political segments to non-political actors like social movements, NGOs, interest groups and trade unions.

Conclusions

The concept of cleavages as it is defined and used in this analysis appeared to be a rather suitable theoretical tool in accounting for the main features of the political development of Croatia from 1990 and onwards. We have primarily focused on the development of the party system and the patterns of party competition, and in the process we have seen how Croatian politics has been shaped by the political and social dynamics of the underlying cleavage structure. We have also accounted for the emergence of the authoritarian HDZ regime with all its democratic deficits in terms of the historical cleavage structure in Croatia.

We are by no means saying that the historical cleavage structure automatically determines the dynamics and institutional landscape of the party system, independently of the political actors. On the contrary, we have demonstrated the importance of political elite action for cleavage mobilization, particularly in times of political and social change. The historical cleavages were there from the very beginning, but it was up to the political elites to determine which of them to mobilize and how to mobilize them. Once mobilized by ideological and political strategies of the political elites, the cleavages were incorporated into the very identity of main political parties and the party system.

Nor do we suggest that the current patterns of political competition will prevail forever. The political institutionalization of cleavages formed a lasting pattern of political competition in Croatia; it is not always productive and favourable for democratic consolidation, but we have also seen that it does not exclude fundamental political change. The Croatian cleavage structure is also subject to the same gradual changes as cleavage structures everywhere. Our hypothesis is that changes in the future will be strongly contingent upon the existing cleavage structure, which does not mean that they will be gradual or insignificant. Any future changes of the Croatian party system, be it in number of parties, new issue dimensions or patterns of coalition-building, will not be comprehensible without linking them to the existing cleavages as structural components of the party system.

List of Party Acronyms with a Brief Description

ASH (*Akcija socijaldemokrata Hrvatske*) Social Democratic Action of Croatia. Small left socialist party.

DA (*Dalmatinska akcija*) Dalmatian Action. Regional party of Dalmatia. Not active at the national level anymore.

DC (*Demokratski centar*) Democratic Centre. Moderate conservative party. Founded after the presidential elections in 2000 by the defeated HDZ candidate Mate Granić. See under HDZ.

HB (*Hrvatski blok*) Croatian Bloc. A right-wing nationalist party. Founded in 2002 after the defeat of the right-wing faction of HDZ at the party congress. See under HDZ.

HDS (*Hrvatska demokratska stranka*) Croatian Democratic Party. See under HKDU and KNS.

HDZ (*Hrvatska demokratska zajednica*) Croatian Democratic Union. Founded in June 1989. The leading party of the right, with nationalist and conservative appeal. The ruling party in Croatia from 1990 to 2000. As of 2003, still the strongest Croatian party. Founded in June 1989. Until his death (in 1999), the leader of the party was Franjo Tuđman, the President of Croatia. Splinter parties: HND (1994), DC (2000) and HB (2002).

HKDS (*Hrvatska kršćanska demokratska stranka*) Croatian Christian Democratic Party. See under HKDU and KNS.

HKDU (*Hrvatska kršćanska demokratska unija*) Croatian Christian Democratic Union. Small rightist conservative and nationalistic party. Founded in December 1992 as the result of the merger of HDS and HKDS.

HND (*Hrvatski nezavisni demokrati*) Croatian Independent Democrats. Founded in 1994 by HDZ moderates (including current President of Croatia Stipe Mesić) who opposed the Croation policy towards Bosnia and Herzegovina. Today of marginal importance. See under HDZ.

HNS (*Hrvatska narodna stranka*) Croatian People's Party. Liberal party, recently more to the left. Founded in October 1990 under the leadership of several prominent political leaders of the 1971 national movement in Croatia, who were non-partisan leaders of the KNS in the 1990 elections. The party follows the political ideas of the KNS. Party of the President of Croatia Stipe Mesić. Member of the governing coalition since 2000.

HSLS (*Hrvatska socijalno-liberalna stranka*) Croatian Social Liberal Party. A national liberal party of right-centre flavour, but recently moving further to the right. Founded in May 1989 as the first established party within the so-called 'democratic alternative'. In 1990, it was the leading force of the KNS. After the breakdown of the coalition it remained the most successful party of the KNS. The party split in 1997. A faction formed LS in 1998, later member of the governing coalition in 2000. HSLS was a member of the winning coalition HSLS-SDP in 2000 and also a member of the governing coalition from 2000 to 2002, when the party split again and left the government. The rest formed a new party – *Libra* – which stayed in the coalition government.

HSP (*Hrvatska stranka prava*) Croatian Party of Rights. Radical nationalist party, recently getting rid of radicalism and neo-fascism. Founded in 1990 as a political follower of the party from 1861. The party entered Parliament in 1992, but split in 1993. A faction established HSP-1861 in 1995, but with no success at the national level.

HSS (*Hrvatska seljačka stranka*) Croatian Peasant Party. Centrist traditional party catering to agricultural and handicrafts interests. The only traditional Croatian party with organizational continuity since 1904, when the party was established under a slightly different name. After 1945, the party existed in exile. In December 1989, it was legally re-established in Croatia, and, after factional disputes, consolidated in 1991. It is part of the governing coalition since 2000. It will in all likelihood be a rather important potential coalition partner for both sides of the political spectrum in the future.

IDS (*Istarski demokratski sabor*) Istrian Democratic Assembly. Founded in February 1990. Regional party acting on the territory of the region of Istria, where it controls all local governments. Member of the governing coalition from 2000 to 2001.

KNS (*Koalicija narodnog sporazuma*) Coalition of People's Agreement. Coalition of HDS, HKDS, HSLS and SDH at the 1990 elections. Ideologically mixed centrist coalition. The coalition broke down between the first and the second round of the 1990 elections when HDS left the Coalition. At the 1992 elections the parties competed individually. SDH collectively joined the SDP in April 1993.

Libra A new liberal party founded in 2002 by a part of the parliamentary fraction of HSLS. See under HSLS.

LS (*Liberalna stranka*) Left-liberal party founded in 1998 by the deafeted faction of HSLS. See under HSLS.

PGS (*Primorsko-goranska stranka*) Party of Primorsko-Goranska Region. Formerly RIDS. In 1992 coalition partner of other regional parties. In the 2000 elections minor partner in the HSLS-SDP coalition.

RIDS (*Riječki demokratski savez*) Democratic Alliance of Rijeka. See under PGS.

SBHS (*Slavonsko-baranjska hrvatska stranka*) Croatian Party of Slavonia and Baranja. In the 1995 elections minor coalition partner of HSS, HNS, IDS and HKDU. In the 2000 elections minor partner of the coalition HSLS-SDP.

SDH (*Socijaldemokratska stranka Hrvatske*) Social Democratic Party of Croatia. See under KNS.

SDP (*Socijaldemokratska partija Hrvatske*) Social Democratic Party of Croatia. The leading force of the centre-left, with moderate social democratic policies. The party is the legal successor of the SKH (*Savez komunista Hrvatske*), League of Communists of Croatia, reformed and formally founded in November 1990 by the reformist wing of the SKH. Initially the party was called SKH-SDP, and since 1992, SDP. In 1994, it merged with a small social democratic party (SDH), which was founded in 1989. A member of the winning HSLS-SDP coalition in 2000 and the main pillar of the governing coalition since 2000.

SDS (*Srpska demokratska stranka*) Serbian Democratic Party. Party of the Serbian ethnic minority in Croatia and Bosnia and Herzegovina. Participated in the first elections 1990, later engaged as the leading force of the armed rebellion of parts of the Serbian minority. Legally banned by decision of the Constitutional Court in 1992.

SKH-SDP (*Savez komunista Hrvatske-Stranka demokratskih promjena*) Communist League of Croatia-Party of Democratic Changes. See under SDP.

SNS (*Srpska narodna stranka*) Serbian People's Party. A small party of the Serbian ethnic minority, active since 1992.

NOTES

1. Slovenia was an exception. After an initial reluctance, during the first years after the collapse of Yugoslavia, it was integrated into the network of international cooperation in comparative political science and sociology. Croatia and FR Yugoslavia were included in a limited number of important comparative research projects such as *Founding Elections in Eastern Europe*, led by Hans-Dieter Klingemann of the Science Center (*Wissenschaftszentrum*) in Berlin, which resulted in the publication of a series of country specific studies. For the Croatian contribution, see Šiber (1997).

2. A group of scholars at the Faculty of Political Science (FPS) of the University of Zagreb has monitored voting behaviour and party system development in Croatia from 1990 and onwards. Included in this group are Ivan Šiber, Mirjana Kasapović, Ivan Grdešić and the two authors of this chapter.

3. The results of the first electoral survey conducted by the FPS research team were interpreted on the basis of this cleavage model. See Zakošek (1991).

4. For the detailed accounts of the transition in Croatia, see Kasapović (1996), Kasapović and Zakošek (1997). The development of the Croatian political system during the 1990s is described in Kasapović (2000), Čular (2000; 2001), and Zakošek (1994; 1997; 2001; 2002a; 2002b).

5. For an interesting account of these processes in the East European transformation processes, see Offe (1998).

6. Emphasizing only the importance of a Catholic religious identity and Croatian nationalism, and not the Orthodox Church, is justified by empirical results, which show an exceptionally low level of religious identity among Croatian Serbs and Yugoslavs. While in 1990, only about 34 per cent of Croats were considered to be neither committed nor traditional believers, 80 per cent of Serbs and 90 per cent of Yugoslavs were not in those categories. Although the intensity of religious identity among the Serbian population in Croatia partly explains their choice to vote for the SKH-SDP or the SDS (a Serbian ethnic party), it is still a marginal phenomenon, considering the competition from mainstream parties in the 1990 elections.

7. This is not shown, because in Figure 13.1, supporters of the Croatian independence were aggregated together with the respondents advocating Croatian sovereignty within confederative Yugoslavia. In that period, namely, only around 10 per cent of the Croatian citizens openly opted for Croatian independence due to the fact that complete independence did not seem feasible. After the military actions of the Serb rebels and the Yugoslav Army, support for Croatian independence rapidly increased within only a year, and eventually led to the overwhelming support for Croatian sovereignty in the referendum held in the spring of 1991.

8. Structured face-to-face interviews were conducted around ten days prior to each parliamentary election. Respondents were selected among citizens of Croatia using a two-step selection procedure: stratification in the first step and systematic random procedure in the selection of respondents in each locality. Sample sizes were 2608 in 1992, 1144 in 1995, and 1126 in 1999. We refer to the surveys in the text as to FPS 1992, 1995 and 1999.

9. The classification of the rural-urban divide as functional cleavage is problematic. Though grounded in the original Lipset–Rokkan theory, the historical development of Croatian society

suggests that the rural-urban divide should be treated as a base of ideological-cultural cleavage. As shown later, this is confirmed also by the contemporary voting patterns in Croatia.

10. We would thus expect devout believer to express more conservative views than others. In a similar vein, we would expect the majority core population to adopt a more nationalistic and centralistic position than those who belong to an ethnic minority and/or live in the periphery, who should be more likely to express multi-cultural and federalist views. We would finally expect working-class voters to advocate socialist (left) values on socio-economic questions and middle-class voters neo-liberal or conservative attitudes. If our expectations are not borne out by the data, we are well advised to investigate to what extent these deviations may be accounted for in terms of historical peculiarities.

11. Here we rely on *odds ratios* as a measure of association, not dependent on differences (or changes over time) in the size of the party bloc sub-samples.

12. According to data on class-voting, this is not the case in most other democracies (Evans 1999).

13. Kitschelt initially published this thesis in 1992 (Kitschelt 1992, 16–19). Kitschelt et al. put the theory to an empirical test in 1999.

14. For the exact construction of the cleavage pattern of voting (*C*-voters) see note in Table 13.3.

15. The rather low percentage in 1995 is a result of an entirely different distribution of answers on the same questions as in 1992 and 1999.

16. There are two reasons why we do not consider the regime cleavage as a proper cleavage in this paper, although the cleavage is conceptualized (Sartori 1976, 336; Lijphart 1990, 254) and used in the analysis of the democratic changes in Central and Eastern Europe (Merkl 1997; Kitschelt et al. 1999). Firstly, we are not yet sure that the cleavage has had long-lasting effects on party competition and voting behaviour, which we consider one of the decisive criteria for cleavages. Secondly, the cleavage lacks clear socio-demographic identities and party organizations (since the HDZ has lost this role) as bearers and future transmission belts of the cleavage.

17. The two Croatian regions of Dalmacija and Slavonia differ significantly from Zagreb and inner Croatia with respect to the issue of decentralization. These two regions have a strong historical record of separate regional identities, but they do not seem strong enough to produce new party formations.

REFERENCES

Bartolini, Stefano and Peter Mair (1990), *Identity, Competition, and Electoral Availability: The Stabilisation of European Electorates 1885–1985*, Cambridge University Press, Cambridge.

Čular, Goran (2000), 'Political Development in Croatia 1990–2000: Fast Transition – Postponed Consolidation', *Politička misao*, Vol. 37, No. 5, 30–46.

—— (2001), 'Vrste stranačke kompeticije i razvoj stranačkog sustava', in Mirjana Kasapović, ed., *Hrvatska politika 1990–2000. Izbori, stranke i parlament u Hrvatskoj*, Zagreb, Fakultet političkih znanosti, 123–46.

Evans, Geoffrey, ed. (1999), *The End of Class Politics?: Class Voting in Comparative Context*, Oxford, Oxford University Press.

Faculty of Political Science (FPS), University of Zagreb, surveys conducted by Ivan Šiber, Mirjana Kasapović, Ivan Grdešić, Nenad Zakošek, and Goran Čular, 1990 and onwards.

Hellén, Tomas, Sten Berglund and Frank Aarebrot (1998), 'The Challenge of History in Eastern Europe', in Sten Berglund, Tomas Hellén and Frank Aarebrot, eds, *The Handbook of Political Change in Eastern Europe*, Cheltenham, Edward Elgar, 13–54.

Kasapović, Mirjana (1996), *Demokratska tranzicija i političke stranke*, Zagreb, Fakultet političkih znanosti.

—— and Nenad Zakošek (1997), 'Democratic Transition in Croatia: Between Democracy, Sovereignty and War', in Ivan Šiber, ed., *The 1990 and 1992/93 Sabor Elections in Croatia. Analyses, Documents and Data*, Berlin, Sigma, 11–33.

—— (2000), 'Ten Years of Democratic Transition in Croatia 1989–1999', in Henriette Riegler, ed., *Transformation Processes in the Yugoslav Successor States between Marginalization and European Integration*, Baden-Baden, Nomos, 45–63.

Kitschelt, Herbert (1992), 'The Formation of Party Systems in East Central Europe', *Politics and*

Society, Vol. 20, No. 1, 7–50.

—— (1995), 'Formation of Party Cleavages in Post-Communist Democracies. Theoretical Propositions', *Party Politics*, Vol. 1, No. 4, 447–72.

——, Zdenka Mansfeldová, Radosław Markowski and Gábor Tóka (1999), *Post-Communist Party Systems: Competition, Representation, and Inter-Party Cooperation*, Cambridge, Cambridge University Press.

Knutsen, Oddbjørn and Elinor Scarbrough (1995), 'Cleavage Politics', in Jan W. van Deth and Elinor Scarbrough, eds, *The Impact of Values*, Oxford, Oxford University Press, 492–523.

Lijphart, Arend (1990), 'Dimensions of Ideology in European Party Systems', in Peter Mair, ed., *The West European Party System*, Oxford, Oxford University Press, 253–65.

Lipset, Seymour M. and Stein Rokkan (1967), 'Cleavage Structures, Party Systems, and Voter Alignments: An Introduction', in Seymour M. Lipset and Stein Rokkan, eds, *Party Systems and Voter Alignments: Cross-National Perspectives*, New York, Free Press, 1–64.

Markowski, Radosław (2002), '*Polski system partyjny po wyborach 2001 roku*', in *Przyszłość polskiej sceny politycznej po wyborach 2001*, Warsaw, Instytut Spraw Publicznych.

Merkel, Wolfgang (1997), 'Die Bedeutung von Parteien und Parteiensystemen für die Konsolidierung der Demokratie: ein interregionaler Vergleich', in Wolfgang Merkel and Eberhard Sandschneider, eds, *Systemwechsel 3. Parteien im Transformationsprozess*, Opladen, Leske + Budrich, 337–371.

Offe, Claus, (1998), 'Introduction: Agenda, Agency, and the Aims of Central East European Transitions', in Jon Elster, Claus Offe and Ulrich K. Preuss, eds, *Institutional Design in Post-communist Societies*, Cambridge, Cambridge University Press.

Sartori, Giovanni (1976), *Parties and Party Systems: A Framework for Analysis*, Cambridge, Cambridge University Press.

Šiber, Ivan (1991), 'Nacionalna, vrijednosna i ideologijska uvjetovanost stranačkog izbora', in Ivan Grdešić et al., *Hrvatska u izborima '90*, Zagreb, Naprijed, 98–130.

——, ed. (1997), *The 1990 and 1992/93 Sabor Elections in Croatia: Analyses, Documents and Data*, Berlin, Edition Sigma.

—— (2001), 'Političko ponašanje birača u izborima 1990–2000' in Mirjana Kasapović, ed., *Hrvatska politika 1990–2000: Izbori, stranke i parlament u Hrvatskoj*, Zagreb, Fakultet političkih znanosti, 65–98.

Tóka, Gábor (1998), 'Party Appeals and Voter Loyalty in New Democracies', *Political Studies*, Vol. 46, No. 3, 589–610.

Vjesnik, 31 July 2002.

Zakošek, Nenad (1991), 'Polarizacijske strukture, obrasci političkih uvjerenja i hrvatski izbori 1990', in Ivan Grdešić et al., *Hrvatska u izborima '90*, Zagreb, Naprijed, 131–87.

—— (1994), 'Struktura i dinamika hrvatskoga stranačkog sustava', *Revija za sociologiju*, Vol. 25, No. 1–2, 23–39.

—— (1997), 'Political Parties and the Party System in Croatia', in Ivan Šiber, ed., *The 1990 and 1992/93 Sabor Elections in Croatia. Analyses, Documents and Data*, Berlin, Sigma, 34–49.

—— (1998), 'Ideološki rascjepi i stranačke preferencije hrvatskih birača', in Mirjana Kasapović, Ivan Šiber and Nenad Zakošek, *Birači i demokracija. Utjecaj ideoloških rascjepa na politički život*, Zagreb, Alinea, 11–50.

—— (2001), 'Struktura biračkog tijela i političke promjene u siječanjskim izborima 2000', in Mirjana Kasapović, ed., *Hrvatska politika 1990–2000. Izbori, stranke i parlament u Hrvatskoj*, Zagreb, Fakultet političkih znanosti, 99–122.

—— (2002a), 'Das politische System Kroatiens', in Wolfgang Ismayr, ed., *Die politischen Systeme Osteuropas*, Opladen, Leske + Budrich, 639–79.

—— (2002b), *Politički sustav Hrvatske*, Zagreb, Fakultet političkih znanosti.

APPENDIX 13.1: ELECTION RESULTS

1990 *Sabor* elections

Registered voters[1]	3,528,579
Votes cast	2,980,663
Turnout	84.5%
Non-valid votes	115,852 (3.89%)
Valid votes	2,864,811

Party or coalition	Votes in %[2]	Distribution of seats in the Socio-political Council (DPV)		Distribution of seats in all three Chambers	
		No.	%	No.	%
HDZ	41.9	55	68.8	209	59.5
SKH-SDP, SSH	35.0	20	25.0	101	28.8
KNS	15.3	3	3.8	21	6.0
SDS	1.6	1	1.3	5	1.4
Other parties	2.0	–	–	2	0.6
Independent	4.1	1	1.3	13	3.7
Total	99.9	80	100.2	351	100.0

Notes: (1) The number indicates voters registered for the election of the first parliamentary chamber (DPV), which was the only chamber elected on the basis of general and equal suffrage. The electorate for the other two chambers (Council of Municipalities and Council of Associated Labour) differed significantly. The turnout figure indicates first round of elections. (2) Calculated as the sum of votes for the party candidates in the first round of elections.

1992 elections for the House of Representatives (*Zastupnički dom*) of the *Sabor*

Registered voters	3,558,913					
Votes cast	2,690,873					
Turnout	75.6%					
Non-valid votes	59,338					
	(2.21%)					
Valid votes	2,631,535					
Party or coalition	Votes in %[3]	Distribution of 120 seats		Distribution of seats for ethnic minorities representatives	Distribution of all 138 seats	
		No.	%		No.	%
HDZ	44.7	85	70.8	–	85	61.6
HSLS	17.7	13	10.8	1[4]	14	10.1
HSP	7.1	5	4.2	–	5	3.6
HNS	6.7	4	3.3	2	6	4.4
SDP	5.5	3	2.5	3	6	4.4
HSS	4.3	3	2.5	–	3	2.2
IDS[1]	3.2	6	5.0	–	6	4.4
SNS[2]	1.1	–		3	3	2.2
Independent representatives of Serbian minority	–	–	–	5[5]	5	3.6
Representatives of other ethnic minorities	–	–	–	4	4	2.9
Independent	–	1	0.8	–	1	0.7
Other parties	9.8	–	–	–	–	–
Total	100.1	120	99.9	18	138	100.1

Notes: (1) In coalition with regionalist parties RIDS and DA. (2) The Constitutional Court decided that the 3 per cent electoral threshold does not apply to SNS as a Serbian ethnic minority party and that it may participate in the distribution of additional seats necessary for proportional representation of Serbs. (3) The number indicates percentage of votes in the proportional segment of elections. (4) Representative of the Jewish minority was appointed by the decision of the Constitutional court from the HSLS list. (5) Appointed from the SDP list, but left the party before they started their mandate.

1995 elections for the House of Representatives (*Zastupnički dom*) of the *Sabor*

Registered voters	3,634,233				
Votes cast	2,500,040				
Turnout	68.8%				
Non-valid votes	82,666				
	(3.31%)				
Valid votes	2,417,374				

Party or coalition	Votes in %[1]	Distribution of 108 seats		Distribution of seats for Diaspora representatives[3]	Distribution of seats for ethnic minorities representatives	Distribution of all 127 seats	
		No.	%			No.	%
HDZ	45.2	63	58.3	12	–	75	59.1
United list incl.:	18.3			–	–		
HSS	–	10	9.3	–	–	10	7.9
IDS	–	4	3.7	–	–	4	3.1
HNS	–	2	1.9	–	–	2	1.6
HKDU	–	1	0.9	–	–	1	0.8
SBHS	–	1	0.9	–	–	1	0.8
HSLS	11.6	12	11.1	–	–	12	9.4
SDP[2]	8.9	10	9.3	–	–	10	7.9
HSP	5.0	4	3.7	–	–	4	3.1
Representatives of Serbian minority:							
SNS	–	–		–	2	2	1.6
ASH	–	–		–	1	1	0.8
Independent representatives of other ethnic minorities	–	–		–	4	4	3.1
Other parties	11.0	1	0.9	–	–	1	0.8
Total	100.0	108	100.0	12	7	127	100.0

Notes: (1) The number indicates the percentage of votes in the proportional segment of elections. (2) On the SDP electoral list, one candidate of the regionalist PGS was elected. (3) Out of 398,841 registered Diaspora voters, 109,389 (27.4 per cent) participated in the elections; 1,617 (1.5 per cent) votes were non-valid, while 107,772 votes were valid.

2000 elections for the House of Representatives (*Zastupnički dom*) of the *Sabor*

Registered voters	3,686,378
Votes cast	2,821,020
Turnout	76.5%
Non-valid votes	46,740 (1.66%)
Valid votes	2,774,280

Party or coalition	Votes[1] in %	Distribution of 140 seats		Distributions of seats for Diaspora representatives[4]	Distribution of seats for ethnic minorities representatives	Distribution of all 151 seats	
		No.	%			No.	%
HDZ	24.4	40	28.6	6	–	46	30.5
SDP/HSLS[2] incl.:	40.8	71	50.7	–	–	–	–
SDP	–	44	31.4	–	–	44	29.1
HSLS	–	24	17.1	–	–	24	15.9
PGS	–	2	1.4	–	–	2	1.3
SBHS	–	1	0.7	–	–	1	0.7
HSS/LS/HNS/IDS[3] incl.:	15.6	24	17.1	–	–	–	–
HSS	–	15	10.7	–	1	16	10.6
IDS	–	4	2.9	–	–	4	2.6
LS	–	2	1.4	–	–	2	1.3
HNS	–	2	1.4	–	–	2	1.3
Independent[3]	–	1	0.7	–	–	1	0.7
HSP/HKDU incl.:	5.3	5	3.6	–	–	–	–
HSP		4	2.9	–	–	4	2.6
HKDU		1	0.7		–	1	0.7
Representatives of ethnic minorities:							
SNS	–	–	–	–	1	1	0.7
Independent	–	–	–	–	3	3	2.0
Other parties	14.0	–	–	–	–	–	–
Total	100.1	140	100.0	6	5	151	100.0

Notes: (1) The number indicates the percentage of valid votes in all 10 electoral districts. (2) In two districts, candidates of two regionalist parties were elected (PGS and SBHS) on the SDP-HSLS-list. (3) An independent candidate was nominated by HSS and elected on the coalition list. (4) Out of 360,110 registered Diaspora voters, 126,841 (35.2 per cent) participated in the elections; 1,186 (0.9 per cent) votes were non-valid, while 125,655 were valid.

1993 elections for the House of Counties (*Županijski dom*) of the *Sabor*

Registered voters	3,580,396				
Votes cast	2,303,782				
Turnout	64.3%				
Non-valid votes	76,019				
	(3.30%)				
Valid votes	2,227,763				
Party or coalition	Votes	Distribution of 63		Distribution of all 68 seats	
	in %[5]	No.	%	No.	%
HDZ	45.5	37	58.7	39	57.4
HSLS[1]	27.9	16	25.4	16	23.5
HSS	11.6	5	7.9	5	7.4
IDS[2]	4.5	3	4.8	3	4.4
SDP[3]	2.8	1	1.6	1	1.5
HNS[4]	1.0	1	1.6	1	1.5
Other parties or independent candidates	6.7	–	–	–	–
Appointed by the President:	–	–	–	5	7.4
HDZ	–	–	–	2	2.9
others	–	–	–	3	4.4
Total	100.0	63	100.0	68	100.1

Notes: (1) Including joint lists with SDP, HNS and HKDU. (2) Including joint lists with RIDS. (3) Without joint lists with HSLS and HNS, but including joint lists with smaller parties. (4) Including joint lists with smaller parties. (5) The number indicates percentage of valid votes in all 21 electoral districts.

1997 elections for the House of Counties (*Županijski dom*) of the *Sabor*

Registered voters	3,664,693				
Votes cast	2,615,474				
Turnout	71.4%				
Non-valid votes	86,062				
	3.29%				
Valid votes	2,529,412				
Party or coalition	Votes	Distribution of 63		Distribution of all 68 seats	
	in %[5]	No.	%	No.	%
HDZ[1]	42.7	39	61.9	42	61.8
HSLS/HSS[2] incl.:	23.0	–	–	–	–
HSLS		7	11.1	7	10.3
HSS		9	14.3	9	13.2
SDP/HNS[3] incl.:	16.0	–	–	–	–
SDP		4	6.3	4	5.9
HNS		–	–	–	–
IDS	2.6	2	3.2	2	2.9
HSP[4]	0.5	2	3.2	2	2.9
Other parties	15.2	–	–	–	–
Appointed by the President:	–	–	–	5	7.4
HDZ	–	–	–	3	4.4
others	–	–	–	2	2.9
Total	100.0	63	100.0	68	99.9

Notes: (1) Including joint lists with HSP, HKDU and a minor regionalist party. (2) Results of separate lists by these two parties were added together. (3) Including joint list with PGS; results of separate lists by these two parties were added together. (4) HSP participated in the elections in only one County, independently and without success. However, two HSP candidates were elected on HDZ lists. (5) The number indicates percentage of valid votes in all 21 electoral districts.

PRESIDENTIAL ELECTIONS (1992 AND 1997)

	1992	1997	
		Only voters in Croatia	All voters, incl. Diaspora
Registered voters	3,575,032	3,683,774	4,061,479
Votes cast	2,677,764	2,129,720	2,218,448
Turnout	74.9%	57.8%	54.6%
Non-valid votes	50,703	39,174	39,656
	(1.9%)	(1.8%)	(1.8%)
Valid votes	2,627,061	2,090,546	2,178,792

	Votes in %[*]	Votes in %[*]	
Candidates		Only voters in Croatia	All voters, incl. Diaspora
Franjo Tuđman (HDZ)	56.7	59.0	60.3
Dražen Budiša (HSLS)	21.9	–	–
Savka Dapčević-Kučar (HNS)	6.0	–	–
Dobroslav Paraga (HSP)	5.4	–	–
Silvije Degen (SSH)	4.1	–	–
Marko Veselica (HDS)	1.7	–	–
Ivan Cesar (HKDS)	1.6	–	–
Antun Vujić (SDH)	0.7	–	–
Zdravko Tomac (SDP)	–	21.4	20.7
Vlado Gotovac (HSLS)	–	17.8	17.3
Total	98.1	98.2	98.3

[*] The percentage indicates the candidate's share of all votes cast, following the requirements of the Croatian Constitution (Art. 94), i.e. an absolute majority of votes cast in order to win in the first election round.

PRESIDENTIAL ELECTIONS (2000)

	2000, 1st round		2000, 2nd round	
	Only voters in Croatia	All voters, incl. Diaspora	Only voters in Croatia	All voters, incl. Diaspora
Registered voters	3,856,418	4,252,743	3,858,893	4,252,921
Votes cast	2,602,684	2,677,845	2,519,010	2,589,120
Turnout	67.5%	63.0%	65.3%	60.9%
Non-valid votes	12,895	13,217	29,361	29,779
	(0.4%)	(0.5%)	(1.2%)	(1.2%)
Valid votes	2,589,789	2,664,628	2,489,649	2,559,341
	Votes in %[1]		Votes in %[2]	

Candidates	Only voters in Croatia	All voters, incl. Diaspora	Only voters in Croatia	All voters, incl. Diaspora
Dražen Budiša (HSLS)	28.2	27.7	43.1	44.0
Stjepan Mesić (HNS)	42.0	41.1	56.9	56.0
Mate Granić (HDZ)	21.2	22.5	–	–
Slaven Letica (independent)	4.2	4.1	–	–
Anto Đapić (HSP)	1.8	1.8	–	–
Ante Ledić (independent)	0.9	0.9	–	–
Tomislav Merčep (HPS)	0.9	0.9	–	–
Ante Prkačin (NH)	0.3	0.3	–	–
Zvonimir Šeparović (independent)	0.2	0.3	–	–
Total	99.7	99.6	100.0	100.0

Notes: (1) The percentage indicates the candidate's share of all votes cast, following the proposition of the Croatian Constitution (Art. 94), which requires an absolute majority of votes cast in order to win in the first election round. (2) Percentage in the second round indicates candidate's share of valid votes.

APPENDIX 13.2: GOVERNMENT COMPOSITION

Prime Minister	Mandate period	Reasons for government dissolution	Type of government (parties participating in the government)	Government composition			Parliamentary basis of the government	
				Vice-presidents of government	No. of ministries	Ministers	No. of seats	%
Stjepan Mesić	30.5.1990– 24.8.1990	Presidential decision	One party government (HDZ), including independent, HDS and KNS ministers	3	19	24[1]	209[2]	59.5
Josip Manolić	24.8.1990– 17.7.1991	Presidential decision	One party government (HDZ), including independent, HDS and KNS ministers	4	18	31	209[2]	59.5
Franjo Gregurić	17.7.1991– 12.8.1992	Elections	Coalition of all parliamentary parties[3] (HDZ, SDP, HSLS, HNS, HDS, SDH, SSH, independent)	4	21	41	All parliamentary parties	
Hrvoje Šarinić	12.8.1992– 3.4.1993	Presidential decision	One party government (HDZ), including independent ministers	5	14	18	85	61.6
Nikica Valentić	3.4.1993– 7.11.1995	Elections	One party government (HDZ), including HSS and independent ministers	6	15–18[4]	36	85[5]	61.6
Zlatko Mateša	7.11.1995– 27.1.2000	Elections	One party government (HDZ), including independent ministers	6	22	44[6]	75	59.1
Ivica Račan I	27.1.2000– 30.7.2002	Resignation	Coalition government (SDP, HSLS, HSS, HNS, LS, IDS), including independent ministers	3	19	19	95	62.9
Ivica Račan II	30.7.2002–		Coalition government (SDP, HSS, HNS, LS, *Libra*), including independent ministers	4	19	21[7]	78/83[8]	51.7/ 55.0

Notes: (1) The difference between the number of ministries and the number of ministers results from the fact that several ministers were exchanged during the government's term in office, while some ministers were without portfolio. (2) The number indicates HDZ seats in all three Chambers of the parliament. Initially, all Chambers equally participated in the decision on confidence in the government. (3) The escalation of war and the rebellion of Serbian extremists prompted all parliamentary parties to form the 'Government of democratic unity'. (4) The number of ministries varied during the government mandate. (5) After May 1994, the parliamentary majority of HDZ was reduced to 75 seats (54.3 per cent), after a group of representatives left the party and formed a new one, HND. (6) The number includes 6 vice-presidents of the government. Some of them also performed ministerial duties. (7) The number includes vice-president of the government Željka Antunović, who also acts as defence minister. (8) The first number indicates the parliamentary seats of the parties represented in the government coalition; the second number indicates the seats of the parliamentary majority of the government, including those of three regionalist parties (IDS, PGS, SBHS) not represented in the government.

Source: http://www.hidra.hr/rh/, February 2002; *Vjesnik*, 31 July 2002.

APPENDIX 13.3: THE ELECTORAL SYSTEM

From a comparative perspective, the Croatian electoral legislation during the first decade after the fall of communism has some unique features: in this short period, each election for the first parliamentary chamber has been organized on the basis of a different electoral system (majority, segmented and proportional). These frequent changes have been enforced by the ruling party, due to its safe parliamentary majority and the fact that amendments to the electoral law have not required a qualified majority (since it was not part of the Constitution). The main purpose of these changes was to increase the electoral chances of the ruling party and to maximize its number of mandates.

The first parliamentary elections were held in April and May 1990. The Croatian parliament, the *Sabor*, was composed of three chambers, which were originally established within the framework of the communist political system, based on different principles of representation. The Socio-Political Council was the only truly representative body, based on general and equal suffrage; its members were elected in 80 electoral districts. The Council of Municipalities was a representative body of 115 territorial units (municipalities). It was based on general but disproportionate suffrage, since there were huge differences between the electoral units in terms of size (the ratio between the biggest and the smallest electoral unit in terms of number of voters was more than 200:1). The Council of Associated Labour was set up in order to represent functional interests, based on restricted and unequal suffrage, since only employed persons (including self-employed and students) were entitled to vote. The size of the 160 special single-member districts (and thus the weight of individual votes) varied greatly also in this case.

The absolute majority system was chosen to meet the requirements of the three forms of representation. The main elements of the electoral system included single-member districts, run-off elections, winning either by an absolut majority (and a minimum of one-third of all registered voters) in the first round, or by a relative majority (plurality) in the second round, whereby only candidates winning more than 7 per cent of the votes could participate.

The new constitution, adopted in December 1990, established new parliamentary structures: the House of Representatives – the first chamber – was the main legislative chamber, based on general and equal suffrage, while the House of Counties – the second chamber – was created to represent the 21 Croatian regional units (counties). The Constitution also determined that the regular term of both parliamentary chambers is four years, and that elections must be held within 60 days after the expiry of the term. Elections to the first chamber were held in 1992, 1995 and 2000, and for the second chamber in 1993 and 1997. The second chamber was abandoned by amendments to the Constitution in March 2001.

The 1992 elections to the House of Representatives were organized on the basis of a segmented electoral system, combining plurality and proportional elections. Half of the 120 parliamentary seats were to be elected by proportional vote in a single, countrywide electoral district, with a 3 per cent threshold for representation and the d'Hondt method of transforming votes into seats. The other 50 per cent of seats were to be elected by plurality vote in 60 single member districts.

Additional propositions defined rules of electing parliamentary representatives of ethnic minorities. The Serb minority was entitled to a proportional number of seats relative to the share of Serbs in the population of Croatia (12.2 per cent according to the 1991 census). Other, smaller ethnic minorities were entitled to five seats, of which Italian, Hungarian, Czech/Slovak and Ruthenian/Ukrainian/Austrian/German minorities each elected one representative in special electoral districts, while the fifth one, representing the Jewish minority, was appointed after the elections by the Constitutional Court from the HSLS party list. The principle of ethnic minority representation was widely debated, contested and eventually changed. In 1995, the provision about proportional representation of the Serb minority was abandoned and the number of Serb representatives elected in special districts reduced to three, while the number of representatives of other ethnic minorities was reduced from five to four. In 1999, the number of Serb minority representation was reduced even further – to just one, and thus made equal in relation to the status of other ethnic minorities. The total number of ethnic minority seats was reduced to five. The latest amendments to the Electoral Law (April 2003) again saw an increase in the number of reserved minority seats elected through special electoral districts to eight, whereby three seats were to be reserved for the Serb minority and five seats for the other, less numerous minorities (Italian, Hungarian and 19 other ethnic groups which are explicitly mentioned in the Law).

The 1995 elections to the House of Representatives brought about changes in the ratio of seats elected by proportional and plurality system, introducing a new system that involved the Croatian diaspora. The number of seats distributed through proportional elections in the countrywide electoral district was increased to 80, and a higher threshold for representation was introduced: 5 per cent for single parties; 8 per cent for coalitions of two parties; and 11 per cent for coalitions of three or more parties. The plurality segment of the electoral system was reduced to 28 seats, elected in single-member districts. However, the most important innovation was the introduction of a special electoral district for Croatian citizens living abroad – often having dual citizenship but without permanent residence in Croatia – in which 12 seats were to be elected through proportional elections, with a 5 per cent legal threshold, and distributed according to the d'Hondt method. An electorate that effectively did not participate in the political life and legal order of Croatia thus elected nearly 10 per cent of parliamentary seats. Although the ruling party claimed that the institutionalization of the diaspora vote was a necessary consequence of the constitutional stipulation that ensures the voting rights to all Croatian citizens, several aspects of this solution were highly questionable (and indeed criticized by the opposition parties). Most of the diaspora voters lived in Bosnia-Herzegovina, where they formed a constitutive part of that state, while at the same time they were mainly loyal supporters of the Croatian ruling party, HDZ, which harboured irredentist goals towards Bosnia-Herzegovina. Last but not least, the entire electoral process involving the diaspora voters was procedurally incorrect and heavily biased in favour of the HDZ. It is thus hardly surprising that the HDZ won all diaspora seats in the 1995 and 2000 elections. Despite fierce criticism, the inclusion of a separate diaspora quota has not been entirely scrapped: the electoral reform in 1999 merely reduced the share of parliamentary seats for Croats abroad. Moreover, the elections in January 2000 were held on the basis of a completely new electoral law, adopted in November 1999. The segmented electoral system was abandoned and a proportional system introduced. Important features of the new system include proportional voting for closed party lists in ten multi-member electoral districts (each with 14 seats), a 5 per cent electoral threshold on the district level, and the d'Hondt method of transforming votes into seats. As for the Croatian diaspora, a so-called non-fixed quota was introduced, in which the number of diaspora seats was made dependent on the level of participation both abroad and in Croatia. In effect, this amendment reduced the share of diaspora seats in the 2000 elections from approximately 10 to 4 per cent.

Elections to the now defunct House of Counties were organized on the basis of a proportional system: 21 counties were defined as three-member electoral districts, in which seats were distributed according to the d'Hondt method. However, proportional representation in small districts produces highly disproportional results, similar to those produced by plurality elections, heavily favouring the strongest party – the ruling HDZ. In addition to the 63 elected representatives, the President was entitled to appoint five representatives according to choice.

The President of the Republic is elected in direct elections. In order to obtain a straight win in the first round, a candidate must receive more than 50 per cent of the votes cast, without further requirements for minimum electoral turnout. If no candidate wins straight away, a run-off between the two frontrunners is to be held after 14 days. The term of the Presidential office is five years and limited to two terms.

APPENDIX 13.4: THE CONSTITUTIONAL FRAMEWORK

The current Constitution of Croatia was adopted on 22 December 1990, only some eight months after the first free elections. Since then, the Constitution has been amended three times: in December 1997, November 2000 and March 2001. While the first amendments included only minor changes, the second saw the end of the semi-presidential system, and the third transformed the *Sabor* into a single-chamber assembly.

One of the most visible features of the constitutional system, which emerged in the early 1990s, was the semi-presidential system of government, which gave significant powers to the President of the Republic. The core of the semi-presidential system was defined by the following presidential powers: to appoint and relieve of duty the Prime Minister and other members of the Government; to convene sessions of the Government and preside over them; and to issue decrees in case of emergency or state of war. However, the highly concentrated and centralized power structure that emerged during the 1990s, accumulating vast powers in the hands of the President, was not simply a consequence of constitutional provisions, but also of several additional political factors: first, the fact that the President at the same time acted as the leader of the ruling party, HDZ, which during the time of his rule enjoyed a safe parliamentary majority and followed his directives in a disciplined manner; second, extensions of the presidential powers through statutes and other legal regulations; and, finally, the creation of an influential presidential apparatus in the form of the Office of the President, as well as the establishment of a network of advisory bodies, which gave the President the power not only to concentrate all decision-making in the executive branch of government, but also to influence the working of the legislature and judiciary. The death of the first Croatian President, Franjo Tuđman, in December 1999, and the subsequent electoral defeat of his party – HDZ – opened up for the abolishment of semi-presidentialism and a de-concentration of power.

The new constitutional system, adopted in November 2000, introduced a parliamentary system of government and abandoned the chief constitutional pillars of the presidential power. Furthermore, the President is not any longer entitled to act as party leader: after being elected as President he or she must disband party membership. However, the new system did not see the abolishment of a directly elected president. Moreover, the President still enjoys important constitutional prerogatives, including (1) to call elections to the *Sabor* and referenda (upon Government proposal), (2) to nominate a Prime Minister (on the basis of consultations and respect for the parliamentary majority), (3) to dissolve the *Sabor* upon Government proposal, (4) to nominate the President of the Supreme Court (elected by the parliament), (5) to promulgate laws (without a suspensive veto, but with the right to call upon the Constitutional Court to rule on their conformity with the Constitution), (6) to pass decrees with the force of law during state of emergency or state of war, (7) to cooperate with the Government in coordinating the work of intelligence services and in shaping foreign policy (including the right to establish diplomatic missions and appoint ambassadors), (8) to act as the Commander-in-Chief of the Army, and (9) to appoint and relieve of duty military commanders.

The main Government prerogatives include implementation of laws and other parliamentary decisions, proposing laws and national budgets, issuing decrees that are deemed necessary for the implementation of laws, guidance and control of public administration. The constitutional amendments in November 2000 significantly strengthened the Government, which during the 1990s had to exercise its powers in the shadow of a constitutionally and politically dominant President. The Government is now able to determine its policies and seek parliamentary approval autonomously, although it has to cooperate with the President in the fields of foreign, defence and security policies. The Government consists of the Prime Minister, Vice-Premier and Ministers. Being a member of the Government is incompatible with a parliamentary mandate: a member of the *Sabor* who enters the Government has the possibility to 'freeze' his or her parliamentary mandate, which he or she may reclaim after leaving the Government (this possibility is often applied in practice). Previously, ministers, including the Premier, were appointed by the President, and only afterwards (within 15 days) had to be approved by the Parliament. After the amendments of 2000, government formation is a lengthy process, involving presidential nomination of a prospective Prime Minister with mandate to form a Government (after formal consultations), negotiations over Government formation and a parliamentary vote of confidence. During the regular four-year parliamentary term, the Government may lose a vote of confidence, which does not directly lead to the dissolution of parliament and early elections. After consultations with party leaders, the President may give the outgoing Prime Minister or a prospective candidate the mandate to seek a new parliamentary majority to form a new government.

Since 1990, the Croatian parliament – the *Sabor* – has undergone significant changes. Croatia inherited a complex and inefficient tri-cameral structure from the old communist system. The only reason why the system actually worked at all was due to the fact that the new ruling party, HDZ, possessed a safe majority in all three chambers. The new constitution from December 1990 introduced a bi-cameral parliamentary structure: the *Sabor* was composed of the House of Representatives (*Zastupnički dom*) as the main legislative and decision-making body, and the House of Counties (*Županijski dom*), conceived as the chief representation of the 21 regional entities and endowed with advisory, deliberative and suspensive functions. In practice, the House of Counties had only marginal influence on the working of the House of Representatives and was unable to establish itself as the parliamentary voice for the regions, mainly due to the fact that the ruling party continued to dominate it. It was thus almost inevitable that the second chamber was scrapped under the constitutional amendments of March 2001.

The Constitution stipulates that the *Sabor* has between 100 and 160 members. Since 1992 it has had 138 (1992), 127 (1995) and 151 (2000) members. The regular term of the Parliament is four years, although it may be dissolved at any time by a majority decision passed by the *Sabor*. Members of the *Sabor* enjoy immunity. The main prerogatives of the *Sabor* include decisions on enactments and amendments of the Constitution, passing of laws and state budgets, proclaiming war and peace, controlling the work of the Government, and to call national referenda. The *Sabor* also elects members of the Constitutional Court, members of the State Judicial Council (see below), the President of the Supreme Court, the Chief Public Prosecutor and the Ombudsman, who acts as the commissioner of the parliament in protecting constitutional and legal rights of the citizens in proceedings before public administration. A two-thirds majority is required for the enactment and amendments of the Constitution and the laws that regulate the rights of national minorities. The so-called organic laws, including those which concern the protection of constitutional rights, elections, the structure and operation of the government bodies and public administration, regional and local self-government, have to be passed by a majority of all representatives (absolute majority). All other laws are passed by a simple majority, provided that more than half of the representatives take part in the vote.

A national referendum may also be initiated by 10 per cent of all registered voters. A referendum is valid if more than 50 per cent of registered voters take part in it, and if it is decided by a majority of the votes cast. The outcome is binding.

Under constitutional provisions, judicial power is exercised by an independent judiciary that is bound only by the Constitution and additional laws. The Constitution also provides that the Judicial Office is permanent, which in practice means that judges, after being appointed, enjoy life-long tenure until reaching the mandatory retirement age of 70. The appointment of judges is performed by a specialized body, the State Judicial Council, which consists of 11 members (15 until 2000): seven judges, two lawyers, and two law professors. The members of the State Judicial Council are elected by the *Sabor* for a term of four years (eight years until 2000), with the possibility to be re-elected for one additional term, in a procedure which involves the Supreme Court, the Croatian Bar Association, deans of the Croatian faculties of law, and the Minister of Justice, coordinated by the parliamentary Judicial Committee. The Croatian courts are organized in a three-tiered structure. Lower courts of general jurisdiction are organized into 102 municipal courts and 19 county courts. Petty offences are dealt with by 109 petty offence tribunals and one high petty offence tribunal. In addition, there are eight specialized commercial courts, with a high commercial court as an appellate body, and the Administrative Court, which acts as a reviewing body for administrative proceedings. At the top of the judicial hierarchy is the Supreme Court, which among other things serves as a court of instance for special legal remedies in civil actions and as an appellate court in criminal cases decided in first instance by the county courts. It also has the task of ensuring the uniform application of law in Croatia.

As a specialized judicial body outside the court system, Croatia has a separate Constitutional Court, whose task is the protection of constitutional order. The Croatian parliament elects 13 judges of the Constitutional Court (11 until 2000) for a term of eight years. The Court is entrusted with ruling on abstract conformity of laws and regulations with the Constitution and with protection of constitutional rights in concrete cases in which their violation is pleaded. In addition, the Court supervises national elections, decides jurisdictional disputes between different branches of government, and controls the constitutionality of political parties and rules on the impeachability of the President of the Republic.

The Constitution guarantees the right to local self-government, which is practiced through 122 cities and 424 municipalities. The constitutional amendments in March 2001 introduced a right to regional self-government, which was the basis for the transformation of the existing 20 counties into entirely self-governed entities (earlier they were conceived of as both administrative entities of the state and self-government bodies). The capital city, Zagreb, which is at the same time a self-governed city and an independent regional entity, enjoys special constitutional status.

APPENDIX 13.5: SPECIFICATIONS

A note on the use of the concept of 'cleavages'

Following the conceptualization of cleavages in the first part of the chapter, we add here some brief remarks on operationalization and measurement issues. Firstly, cleavages are operationalized through three levels. The socio-structural level is represented by variables capturing respondents' place of living (region, rural/urban), ethnicity, religious identity, and class status (viewed as a mixture of occupation, education and degree of dependence on the welfare state). It is important to notice that while region, urban-rural and class status are pure objective variables which entail a certain degree of organizational closure, the 'consciousness of belonging' and the life-style and identity of respondents, ethnic group and religious beliefs are subjective measures of respondents' identity. These variables are dichotomized. The value aspect of cleavages is represented through three dimensions: attitudes of respondents on the dimension centre-periphery, where centre overlaps with nationalism and periphery with decentralization, multiculturalism and cosmopolitanism; attitudes on the liberal-conservative dimension; and attitudes on the economic or materialist left-right dimension. Each dimension is represented by a single index variable or in some cases by a single variable. These are continuous variables which are in some cases for purpose of the analysis dichotomized around mean value. Finally, the political aspect of cleavages is operationalized through respondents' vote intentions, dichotomized and grouped in party blocs. The reason why party blocs rather than parties themselves serve as political variables follows from two assumptions. First, cleavage lines divide society and political space in two parts; more parts (segments) can be only consequence of two or more crosscutting cleavage lines. When trying to capture the crosscutting nature of cleavages, we divided each political bloc in two, 'within left' and 'within right' blocs. Second, as convincingly argued earlier (Bartolini and Mair 1990, 63–5), the notion of cleavages derived from Lipset and Rokkan's work does not count with individual parties but party blocs representing a social segment. Therefore, cleavage theory can not and should not be expected to account for inter-party competition and changes in the strength of individual parties, but rather for constraints and limits of the party competition over cleavage lines. For these reasons, it is clear why cleavage theory, in principle, aims at explanation of the static nature and not the dynamics of a party system.

But, when dealing with dichotomized variables (such as socio-structural variables and party choice) we have to make decisions on the cut-points, since all these variables initially contained several categories. Sometimes, as in the case of ethnic origins, the decision was rather simple – majority ethnic group (Croats) versus minority groups was a theoretically straightforward expression of the centre-periphery divide. In other cases (e.g. region of living, the strength of religious identity) we tried to get the best possible fit between the socio-structural divide and the corresponding value dimension, even if it did not follow from the theoretical assumption. For instance, since there was no significant difference between the Zagreb region (inner Croatia) and the other, periphery regions in the country with regard to the centre-periphery value dimension (as assumed by theory), we have decided to employ the empirically existing social divide, the one between the Istra and Rijeka regions on the one hand and other Croatian regions on the other hand. Only this division yields statistically significant differences in the centre-periphery value orientations of the two groups of respondents. Again, in some other cases (class cleavage line) a theoretically based mix of criteria also found empirical confirmation in different vote intentions. With regard to the party bloc variable, the party grouping in the left and right bloc is founded in the very manner vote intentions have split political space over longer periods rather than in the programmatic stances derived from party platforms or expert judgements of ideological positions of parties. In this way, we accept the existing political divide in the electorate, regardless of whether such a division is 'logically' and consistently reflected in the programmatic positions of party elites.

Construction of the variables used in the analysis

Socio-structural segments (identities)

1. Ethnic: Croats versus others (Serbs, Italians, etc.)
    Regional: Istra, Rijeka versus other regions (Zagreb, Slavonia, Dalmacija)
2. Religion: devout believer versus others (traditional believer, atheist)
3. Class: workers, peasants, housewives, retired, unemployed (working-class) versus
    administration, professionals, entrepreneurs, students (middle-class)
    Urban/rural: villages and suburban settlements versus towns

Value dimensions

1. Centre/periphery:

q69 (1992), q56 (1995), q27 (1999)
Attitudes on the relationship between centre and regions in Croatia

q70 (1992), q58 (1995), q28 (1999)
Attitudes towards position of Serbian minority in Croatia

q72 (1992), q61 (1995), q30 (1999)
Attitudes on Croatian priorities in cooperation with other states in the region (including EU integration)

Standardized values (range 0–1) on each variable are summed up
A new index variable was transformed into z-scores with positive values indicating periphery

2. Liberalism/conservatism:

q91–q101	(1992)	Items tapping this dimension:
q83–q92	(1995)	attitudes on church, nation, freedom,
q24	(1999)	tradition, women and critical worldview

Values (range -1– (+)1, in 1999: 1–5) are summed up
A new index variable was transformed into z-scores with positive values indicating conservatism

3. Economic left/right:

q73	(1992)	Attitudes on the role of the state in the economy
	(1995)	No items tapping this dimension
q29	(1999)	Attitudes on the role of the state in the economy

A new variable was transformed into z-scores with positive values indicating economic left

Political blocs

Right block   HDZ, HSP, HSS, HKDU (1999) and minor right parties
Left block   SDP, HNS, HSLS, IDS (regional parties 1992) and minor left parties
              (An exception in 1995, when HSS is grouped within the left block)
'Within left'   SDP, IDS (regional parties 1992), LS (1999), minor left parties versus HSLS, HNS
'Within right' HDZ, HSS versus HSP, HKDU (1999), minor right parties

Party positions on the main dimensions, as determined by voters' attitudes

Party positions on three value dimensions (1992)

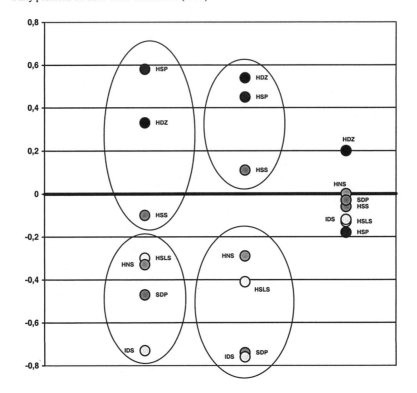

Centre (+) /periphery (−)   Liberal (−) /conservative (+)   Economic left (+)

Note: Circles indicate party blocs as defined in the chapter.

Party positions on two value dimensions (1995)

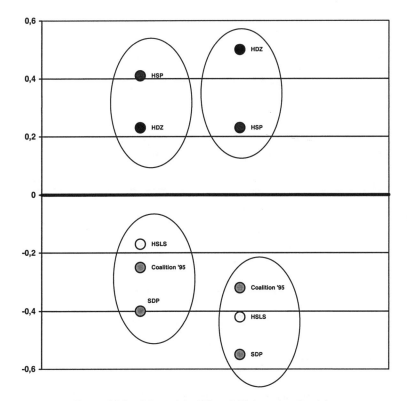

Centre (+) /periphery (–)   Liberal (–) /conservative (+)

Note: Circles indicate party blocs as defined in the chapter.

Party positions on three value dimensions (1999)

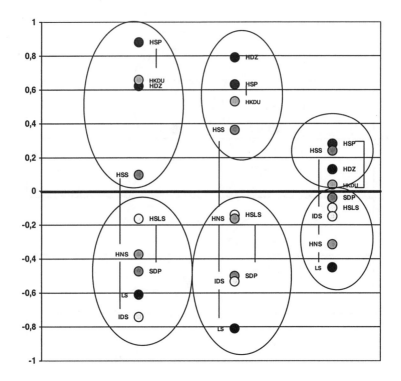

Centre (+) /periphery (−)   Liberal (−) /conservative (+)   Economic left (+)

Note: Circles indicate party blocs as defined in the chapter. Lines indicate actual electoral coalitions.

14. Serbia

Bojan Todosijević*

Politics in Serbia has often been described as an epic struggle between the good and the evil, or the evil and the somewhat lesser evil. This simplistic image has its roots, among other factors, in the conspicuous absence of serious academic investigation into the political processes in this country. Tucker's (2002) review, for example, shows that Yugoslavia/Serbia is among the least studied post-communist countries in terms of voting and elections.[1]

The particularly painful transition makes Serbia unique, but the integration of this case into the general scholarship on post-communist politics is nevertheless both necessary and feasible. The country experienced a number of competitive elections which, though neither fair nor completely free, reflected the political preferences of the citizens. Academic studies and public opinion surveys have been carried out regularly, generally at an appropriate professional level. These two kinds of sources of information provide the researchers with sufficient data for assessing the profile of the main political blocs. The present chapter intends in part to fill this gap of knowledge about Serbia, relying on the aforementioned databases. The focus is on the existence, character and role of socio-political cleavages.

Cleavage politics is often associated with political stability (Whitefield 2002). The presumed intricate link between the two phenomena suggests that in a country that experienced such a degree of instability as Serbia, cleavage politics can play only a marginal role. One rather expects a scene where charismatic and populist leaders are the dominant actors. And indeed, most parties in Serbia are better recognized for their leaders than for their political programmes. Among literally hundreds of parties which tested their luck over the last dozen years, responsible programmatic parties have certainly been a rarity. This chapter, however, argues that there is a system in this apparent political chaos.

The *political system* – but not *society* at large – did display some features of stability. The fact that it took ten years for the first crucial political change to materialize testifies to the underlying political stability, which kept producing a party system with few electorally relevant actors. The chapter sets out to demonstrate that the ensuing political immobilism was an expression of a particularly deep political divide based on different socio-structural categories, and different values and world-views.

The chapter is divided into three major parts. The first one is a review of political developments in Serbia since the introduction of the multi-party system. Here, the focus is put on the evolution of the party system, and on the issues over which the parties conflicted. This largely qualitative approach will primarily consider elite politics. Although the paper deals with Serbia, equal attention is paid to Yugoslav (i.e. Serbia and Montenegro) federal (parliamentary and presidential in 2000) elections, since first, they are equally valid tests of popular political preferences, and second, their consequences were relevant for Serbia.[2] The second part of the chapter contains empirical analysis of socio-structural bases of party preferences. The analysis of the influence of sociological variables such as age, ethnicity, and rural-urban residence will take place in conjunction with the examination of specific ideological orientations, and general value orientations or world-views, such as authoritarianism. The final section integrates the findings from the first two sections, and discusses the character and the role of socio-political cleavages in Serbian politics.

Elections, Parties, and Issues: Development of the Party System

Political pluralism was introduced in Serbia more as a reaction to external processes and events than as a result of the internal pressure coming from popular democratizing forces (Vukomanović 1998, 35). There was certainly no such strong popular anti-communist opposition as in Hungary, Poland, or the Czech Republic; nor was there a strong nationalist opposition of the kind found in Croatia and Slovenia. On 15 December 1989, the ruling communist party has simply declared the introduction of political pluralism.

Two factors are crucial for the understanding of the initial transition to pluralist politics in Serbia: the destruction of Yugoslavia and the Kosovo problem. Studies from the communist period show strong support for the system of self-management, and widespread identification of democracy with socialism (e.g. Rot and Havelka 1973; cf. Goati 1998, 16). Part of the explanation can be found in the fact that the Yugoslav version of socialism was rather liberal and comfortable for the masses compared to the countries from the Warsaw Pact. In addition, Serbs have identified with the Yugoslav state because they saw it as the only possible solution to the 'national question', i.e. the inclusion of all Serbs into one state. Thus, the dissolution of Yugoslavia and the secession of the other republics reopened the Serbian national question, at a time when marketization threatened the widely accepted social and economic order.

Even before the collapse of the Yugoslav state, the ethnic conflicts in Kosovo had already prepared the public for a nationalist course. In fact, Milošević came to power in the late 1980s with the programme to reverse the alleged injustices by previous non-national communists who had 'betrayed' Serbian national interests. Since both Kosovo and the break-up of Yugoslavia are linked to the Serbian national question, it is not surprising that the national question dominated the first elections, or that it remained a dominant issue throughout the 1990s (Sekelj 2000). These two factors, thus, can go far in explaining the initial appeal of the ideological blend of nationalism and redistributive economy provided by the quasi-reformed communists.

The first pluralist elections for the Serbian Parliament, December 1990
Since the Serbian communists were neither overthrown nor seriously threatened by a popular anti-communist movement, they were able to adapt to political pluralism with relatively mild reforms, and to inherit the assets of the dissolved League of Communists of Serbia (SKS) and some other related organizations (Vukomanović 1998). In July 1990, SKS merged with other related communist organizations and formed the Socialist Party of Serbia (SPS) under the firm leadership of Slobodan Milošević. Being in control of the inherited infrastructure, electronic media, and the state, it was easy for the party to refuse round-table talks, which might have secured more equal status for all competitors.

Thus, when the first multi-party elections came the Socialist party had huge infrastructural advantages, and felt no need for major ideological changes. The Socialists promised a large degree of continuity with socialist Yugoslavia, a solution to the Kosovo problem, and moderate reforms in economy. They faced a highly fragmented opposition – and won easily, obtaining 194 (77.6 per cent) out of 250 seats with just 46.1 per cent of the votes cast (thanks to the majoritarian two-round electoral system). The rest of the 56 seats were divided among 13 parties and coalitions and eight independent candidates. Among these, only some proved viable and deserve to be mentioned here.

The strongest opposition party was the Serbian Renewal Movement (*Srpski pokret obnove*, SPO), headed by a well-known writer Vuk Drašković, winning 15.8 per cent of the ballots cast (19 seats). This party, and some subsequent party formations within the nationalist bloc, has its roots in various non-political nationalist organizations, which had been engaged in revising the history of the Second World War, particularly the role of the Chetniks (troops loyal to the exiled King Peter), and their leader, Draža Mihailović.

The Democratic Party (DS), at the time headed by Dragoljub Mićunović, offered a liberal-democratic perspective and adopted a moderate position on the national issue. DS won seven seats in the Parliament, with about 7 per cent of the votes. Another important bloc consisted of parties representing national minorities. The party of ethnic Hungarians (DZVM) entered the first Serbian pluralist parliament as the third strongest party with eight elected representatives. The Party of Democratic Action (SDA), representing the Muslim minority from Sandžak, also participated and won three seats.

The Serbian Presidential elections, held at the same time, clearly show the balance of power between the Socialists and the opposition: Milošević won approximately four times more votes than the main challenger, Vuk Drašković. However, the socialists' hold on power was not absolute. In local elections, the opposition parties took power in localities where national minorities were in absolute or relative numerical majority, often in coalition with the parties of the democratic opposition.

These initial pluralist elections were not simply about communists and anti-communists. The central theme of the elections was the national issue, but more as a valence issue, since all parties but those of national minorities claimed to be fighting for supposedly threatened national interests. In 1990, the opposition, especially the SPO, was more nationalist than the socialists (Slavujević 1998, 89; cf. *Table 14.1*). However, it was difficult to beat Milošević on the nationalist ground, since he was already perceived as a statesman (i.e. not only a 'politician') defending the Serbian state and the national interest (Goati 1998).

The central role of the national issue is not surprising. The ongoing secession of Croatia and Bosnia and Herzegovina meant that some 25 per cent of Serbs would remain outside of Serbia, while Kosovo – a hot problem since the early 1980s – galvanized the Serbian public with almost daily reports about the exodus of Serbs from that 'heartland' of medieval Serbia and the place of the most important religious sites of the Serbian Orthodox Church. Albanians, for their part, firmly pursued the secessionist strategy from the very beginning, and never showed any interest in participating in the Serbian political system (Goati 1998).[3]

SPO, the main opposition party, pursued a strongly nationalist and anti-communist rhetoric, largely neglecting the issues of economy and democratization. However, frequent references to the potential restoration of monarchy, and occasional clericalism were not appealing to the highly secularized masses attached more to socialism than to the former Karađorđević dynasty.

The strength of the SPS was in its ability to appeal to voters in several different ways – by promising a degree of continuity with the former socialist regime while at the same time distancing itself from the 'anti-Serb' rhetoric of non-national communists, by presenting itself as a true defender of Serbian national interests especially concerning the Kosovo problem, and by promising moderate economic reforms which were supposed to increase living standards without the risks associated with quick marketization.

The formation of the authoritarian–democratic division

After the first pluralist elections, SPS and Milošević continued to ignore all demands for substantive democratization. This resulted in massive demonstrations in Belgrade on 9 March 1991, lead by Vuk Drašković and SPS. The opposition demanded – with rather limited success – a new, democratic constitution, a new election law, and the liberation of mass media from partisan control.

The new constitution of April 1992, though not of Serbia but of Yugoslavia, was written without consultations with the opposition parties. Yugoslavia was defined as a federal republic consisting of Serbia and Montenegro. Simultaneously, a new electoral law was announced, which replaced the majoritarian system with a proportional one.

On the party scene, this was a year of further diversification of the opposition bloc. Two new important actors appeared there: the Citizens' Alliance of Serbia (*Građanski Savez Srbije*, GSS) representing the most pro-western, anti-nationalist, liberal and libertarian orientation, and the Democratic Party of Serbia (*Demokratska stranka Srbije*, DSS) combining a commitment to democracy with a concern for national interests and tradition. The leader of the DSS, Vojislav Koštunica, left the DS in 1991 after disagreements concerning the cooperation of DS with the regime (Vukomanović 1998).

This was also a year of elections in Serbia: federal parliamentary elections were held in May and again in December, now together with the Serbian presidential and parliamentary elections. The federal parliamentary elections of 31 May 1992 were boycotted by the democratic opposition[4] as a sign of protest for not being consulted in creating the electoral law, and generally against the unfair media coverage. However, this boycott was ineffective since the party of the Hungarian minority (DZVM) and the extreme nationalist Serbian Radical Party (SRS) took part in the elections. Milan Panić, a Serbian-born US businessman, was appointed Federal Prime Minister by the Socialists soon to become their main opponent in the issues of cooperation with the international community and the liberalization of the economy. He scheduled extraordinary Federal Parliamentary elections for December 1992, and was soon dismissed.[5]

Meanwhile, the democratic opposition managed to form a loose coalition named DEPOS, within the framework of which some smaller parties joined the SPO. Altogether 14 parties participated in this new formation. The results of the extraordinary elections for the Federal parliament in December 1992 revealed that the communist heirs in Serbia and

Montenegro could not win an absolute majority against the relatively united opposition. In Serbia, SPS won 44 per cent of the seats, SRS won 28 per cent, DEPOS managed to win 20 per cent of the seats, the DS participated on its own and won five seats, while the Magyar party (DZVM) took three seats. These results made the Radicals a necessary partner for securing a comfortable majority, thus marking the beginning of the so-called 'red-brown coalition', though based on varying agreements between the coalition partners over the next ten years. The other side of the barricade was occupied by the democratic opposition, still headed by the SPO and joined by parties of the national minorities. This conflict between parties of authoritarian and democratic orientations was to be the central divide in Serbia for the rest of the 1990s.

In the elections to the Serbian parliament DEPOS did not participate as an integral coalition. Instead, SPO and DSS formed a mini-coalition, and won 50 seats (20 per cent). SPS remained the strongest single party with 40 per cent of the seats (101), while the Radicals came in second with 73 seats (nearly 30 per cent). The Hungarian minority defended its position and obtained nine representatives.[6] The Democratic Party was reduced to six MPs.

Although SPS remained the strongest single party, it obtained about one million votes less than in the 1990 elections (now they won 1.3 million of votes, which was about 29 per cent of the votes cast). Obviously, an increasing number of voters felt that the country was heading in the wrong direction. Yet, many of them opted for the Radicals and the effective nationalist-populist rhetoric of their charismatic leader, Vojislav Šešelj. Nevertheless, the support for the opposition was still too weak to seriously challenge the Socialists' rule. In the direct electoral clash between Milošević and Panić, the opposition's candidate for the Serbian presidency, Milošević obtained approximately one million votes more than his opponent.

War and peace

While the tone for the 1990 elections was set by the secession of the former Yugoslav republics and the gradual escalation of the Kosovo problem, the elections of 1992 were framed by the war in Croatia, and by the sanctions imposed by the UN Security Council in 1992. The national and state issue was still on the top of the agenda, but now it was filtered through the attitude towards the wars in Croatia and Bosnia and consequently the attitude towards the sanctions and the 'international community'.

The Socialists appealed to the voters by presenting themselves as fighting for the 'salvation' of Yugoslavia. In cooperation with SRS, they pursued an aggressive campaign that pictured the entire opposition as 'traitors' of the national interests. The SPS-controlled media propagated the idea of a worldwide conspiracy against the Serbs, not that difficult a task given the objective situation. The attitude towards the international community became one of the central political issues, dividing those who preferred isolationism and/or friendship with Russia from those who were in favour of cooperation with the 'West'. This division largely coincided with the authoritarian-democratic divide.

On the opposition side, there were important ideological changes. The SPO abandoned its romantic-nationalist rhetoric, and started campaigning against the on-going wars. At the time, most of the opposition still believed that Serbs should be given the right to stay in one state (Slavujević 1998, 94). Yet generally, the opposition remained fragmented and deeply divided ideologically, as clashes between republicans and royalists, and nationalists and cosmopolitans exemplified.

During the campaign for the December elections, SPS and SRS intensified their nationalistic rhetoric, while DEPOS started insisting on democratization and reduced its earlier heavy nationalist tone (Slavujević 1998). The main issue dimension was defined on the one side by hyper-patriotism and full support for the Serbs abroad, while the other side argued for yielding to the pressure of the international community for democratization and economic reforms.

Although the DS tried to emphasize economic issues in its campaign, this was a topic rarely addressed by the two camps, despite the sharply deteriorating economy (Slavujević 1998, 97). In practice, by the introduction of the new privatization law the Socialists actually slowed down the process of privatization, while the state assumed a strong redistributive role. Various policies were introduced designed to retain the control of the economy in the hands of the ruling party, and on to secure the basic survival of the population under the conditions of the UN sanctions. Printing money mostly financed the new welfare programmes and the support for the Bosnian and Croat Serbs. The result was hyperinflation, especially in 1993.

On 20 October 1993, President Milošević dissolved the Serbian parliament, since the SPS lost the parliamentary majority due to conflicts with SRS over policy towards Bosnian Serbs (SPS decided to accept the Vance-Owen Plan). In the third Serbian parliamentary elections, held on 23 December 1993 and 5 January 1994, the SPS won 123 seats (49 per cent) with a somewhat larger share of the votes than in 1992. But without the support of the SRS, they were three seats short of an absolute majority. DEPOS, again headed by Vuk Drašković, obtained 45 seats (18 per cent), Šešelj's radicals won 39 seats, DS had 29 MPs, and DSS seven; the Magyar party won five seats, and the Muslims of Sandžak had two representatives. After the elections, in a surprise move, New Democracy (ND) left the DEPOS coalition and its six MPs joined the SPS to form the government.[7]

The SPS 'repositioned itself as a party advocating peace' (Slavujević

1998, 101). Since Milošević accepted the Vance-Owen Plan for Bosnia, the socialists attempted to present it as a success for the Serbian side. The nationalist rhetoric was calmed down, while topics such as peace, social and economic recovery, and fight against crime were emphasized (Slavujević 1998, 101). The changes advocated were moderate and slow, particularly within the sphere of economics.

The opposition bloc now consisted of radical nationalists (SRS), the more democratically oriented DEPOS, DS and DSS, and ethnic minority parties. Under the influence of the SPO, DEPOS kept insisting on anti-communism. The Radicals continued their aggressive nationalist-populist rhetoric, but now also directed their attacks against the SPS and Milošević, blaming them for corruption and links with organized crime. The democratic opposition again had problems with building a coalition: two important parties, DS and DSS, remained outside of DEPOS. They expected to benefit from public discontent, and therefore emphasized the scale of the problems and their own ability to solve them (e.g. lifting of the sanctions).

The fight between the opposition and the regime party was bitter, but conflicts among the opposition parties and leaders were not much friendlier. This is one of the reasons that accounts for the continued weak electoral support for the opposition, despite the country's deteriorating conditions. Further splits in the opposition parties were inevitable. The most important event was Đinđić's 'ex-communication' of Mićunović from the DS in 1994, apparently because of personal conflicts (Vukomanović 1998, 38). Mićunović had been one of the main figures within the democratic opposition since 1990. He soon formed his own party, the Democratic Centre (DC).

Nationalism is out of fashion: Elections from 1995 to 1997
The events of 1995 had a particularly strong impact on Serbian politics. The wars in Bosnia and Croatia ended as a result of direct and indirect military intervention by NATO. The Dayton and Erdut agreements were signed, but some half a million Serbs fled from Croatia to Serbia. The dream of all Serbs in one state seemed increasingly hopeless. Milošević's position on the national issue weakened, and now not only nationalists blamed him for abandoning and betraying the Krajina Serbs.

In order to contest the third Federal parliamentary elections on 3 November 1996, the opposition formed a coalition, known as *Zajedno* ('Together'). At the same time, SPS formed a coalition with JUL (Yugoslav United Left, Milošević's wife's party), and ND. The Radicals, the party of the Magyar minority (SVM), and a coalition of regionalist parties from Vojvodina ran in their own right.

The regime parties again won, with about 43 per cent of the votes (64 seats), while the *Zajedno* coalition polled some 22 per cent of the votes (22 seats). Šešelj's radicals won about 18 per cent of the vote, or 16 seats, somewhat less than previously. The party of the Magyar minority (DZVM had been replaced by the Alliance of Vojvodina Hungarians, SVM) obtained three representatives, Coalition Vojvodina two, and Coalition Sandžak (Muslim minority) ended up with a single representative.

Throughout 1996, and especially during the electoral campaign, the SPS presented the events of 1995 as a triumph for their 'peace-making politics', arguing that the interests of Bosnian Serbs had been well preserved and protected by the signed agreements. The emphasis switched from the national issue to the issue of economic recovery (as a result of the Dayton accord, the sanctions had been partially lifted). With the notable exception of the SRS, the opposition parties followed suit and reduced the nationalist rhetoric despite the massive exodus of the Krajina Serbs. The opposing blocs again competed on the valence issue of economic recovery and reintegration into international institutions.

Politically, the local elections held simultaneously with the elections for the federal parliament were the most consequential event in 1996. The *Zajedno* coalition was victorious in most of the major cities including Belgrade. The government attempted to annul the results of these elections, but under the pressure of massive public demonstrations and the OSCE, the initial results were finally acknowledged. With this victory, the democratic opposition gained control over some local media and access to additional financial resources. These results also demonstrate the importance of the urban-rural cleavage.

Milošević's monopoly on political power suffered several additional blows in 1997. In this year, the communist heirs in Montenegro (DPS) split into two wings. The stronger one, led by Đukanović, switched from collaboration towards increasingly open confrontation with the SPS and Milošević. In addition, the socialists suffered a defeat in presidential elections for the first time. In the second round of elections for the Serbian presidency in September 1997, Šešelj won against the socialist candidate Zoran Lilić. However, since the turnout was below the required 50 per cent, the elections were not valid. Repeated elections were held in December, but this time the socialist candidate, Milan Milutinović, was victorious (Milutinović 59.23 per cent, Šešelj 37.57 per cent).

On 15 July 1997, Milošević switched from being Serbian President to becoming President of the FRY, since his second term in the previous post was expiring.[8] The new position was largely symbolic, but he was able to control the political system through informal channels.

The fourth Serbian parliamentary elections were held in the same year, together with the presidential elections. Once again, the opposition parties had serious problems in forming a coalition. Despite the existing agreement within the democratic opposition to support Drašković for the Serbian presidency, the rest of the opposition decided to boycott the elections. Although some 12 parties participated in the boycott, the turnout was hardly affected. The so-called 'left coalition', consisting of SPS, JUL and ND, won the relative majority (some 34 per cent of the votes cast). The Radicals came in second with nearly 30 per cent, and the SPO third with about 20 per cent of the votes. The relatively clear trend of decreasing support for the SPS thus continued.

These elections were a triumph for Šešelj, since the number of votes for the Radicals increased by about 400,000. The democratic opposition was the main loser. The boycott clearly failed, and Drašković did not even get into the second round of the presidential elections. Only the SPO was in the parliament, yet too weak to exhibit any influence and open for charges of collaboration with Milošević. The main issue dimensions had remained largely unchanged since the 1996 elections: the national issue, economic recovery, and the demands for democratization (Sekelj 2000). Only the emphasis changed somewhat: the wars were lost, and only the Radicals heavily exploited the national issue.

Kosovo and NATO

1998 marks the transformation of the Serbian political system from a semi-democratic into an increasingly authoritarian system. Goati (2001a) divides the rule of the socialists into two periods: the period of 'pseudodemocracy' between 1990 and 1998, when certain minimal rules of democracy were observed, and the period between 1998 and 2000 when the regime became increasingly authoritarian. The coalition government – formed on 24 March 1998 by the right-wing parties (SPS, JUL and SRS) – passed a number of openly undemocratic laws, such as the Law on Public Information, the Law on Universities, and the law regulating local self-government. Instances of open repression of the opposition had become increasingly frequent. And on 31 May 1998, the relationship between Serbian and Montenegrin institutions were almost entirely broken.

These events took place against the background of increasingly violent conflicts in Kosovo. Between 1991 and 1998, Albanian rebels in Kosovo killed 128 policemen and 199 civilians in 2,018 incidents.[9] In the beginning of 1998, Kosovo Albanians started an open armed rebellion under the leadership of the Kosovo Liberation Army (*Ushtria Çlirimtare e Kosovës*), and soon Serbia lost control over more than a third of the province's territory (Antonić 1999). The increasingly repressive measures – to which Serbia resorted in its attempts to regain control – finally provoked a military intervention by NATO. After 78 days of NATO bombing, which started on 24 March 1999, and in which all neighbouring countries more or less actively participated, Kosovo was placed under the protection of the UN (UN Resolution 1244, of June 10, 1999).

Internal politics in Serbia started taking on an increasingly bizarre shape. The ruling SPS claimed victory in this war,[10] and promised extremely fast reconstruction of the devastated country without external assistance.[11] The reconstruction work actually went on at a rather fast pace, further exhausting already weak resources.

The first regime change

Milošević's claim that Serbia had won the war, despite the loss of Kosovo and vast human and material losses, was perhaps too much even for his most faithful supporters. His popularity and that of his party and its coalition partners dropped sharply in the opinion polls, to the advantage of the opposition. The SPS-JUL leadership was not yet ready to recognize that *their* war was lost. Political repression marked the following period, featuring two aborted assassination attempts on Vuk Drašković (in October and June 2000 respectively). The efforts of the opposition were coordinated by a loose coalition known as the Alliance for Changes (*Savez za promene*), which was later transformed into the Democratic Opposition of Serbia (DOS). In the autumn 1999, the coalition organized mass demonstrations against the regime.

On 6 July 2000, the federal government loyal to Milošević introduced two constitutional amendments, which instituted popular election of the federal president and of the second chamber of the federal parliament. The rationale was to give Milošević additional terms in power.[12]

The elections were held in September 2000. The opposition formed a broad coalition, the DOS, consisting of 18 parties (including ethnic minority parties and a syndicate). The joint list was headed by Vojislav Koštunica, the leader of the DSS and the opposition politician with the highest rating in the opinion polls. However, the SPO could not reach agreement with the rest of the opposition and remained outside of the coalition. In addition, strong explicit support came from non-political organizations, such as the Serbian Orthodox Church, and the Serbian Academy of Arts and Sciences. An exceptionally important role was played by various NGOs, such as *Otpor* ('Resistance'), which organized a number of creative and provocative actions.[13] There was a general feeling that broad social consensus had been reached on regime change. And that was essentially the 'programme' of the DOS, as brought out by popular slogans like 'He is finished'. The governing parties, on the other hand, presented an extremely anti-West campaign, branding all opposition parties and leaders as 'servants of the West and NATO' (Matić 2002).

The federal presidential elections took the shape of a referendum for or against Milošević. As the results were counted, it became obvious not only that Milošević obtained considerably less votes than his challenger, but also that Koštunica was about to win the first round. The Federal Election

Commission decided that a second round must be organized, while the Federal Constitutional Court ruled that the election was invalid. Koštunica, however, relying on independent counting, proclaimed victory in the first round and decided not to participate in the second round, nor, for that matter, in new elections. A series of demonstrations ensued throughout the country, which culminated in the storming of the Federal Parliament and the building of the national TV, on 5 October 2000 (the so called 'bulldozer revolution'). Milošević finally stepped down and congratulated Koštunica on his victory.

The elections to the federal parliament provided the opposition with a convincing victory, particularly considering the high voter turnout (74 per cent). The DOS coalition won 53 per cent of the seats. SPS and JUL ended up with about 41 per cent of the seats, while the election spelled defeat for the Radicals (five representatives).

After the inauguration, President Koštunica signed the so-called 'Political Agreement' with the socialists, which included extraordinary elections for the Serbian parliament. These elections were held on 23 December 2000. DOS won an even larger majority (70.4 per cent of the seats), the Socialists and the Radicals together won only 24 per cent of the mandates (14.8 and 9.2 respectively) while the JUL and SPO remained without a single MP. A new party, known as the Party of Serbian Unity (SSJ), programmatically close to the Radicals, won 14 seats (5.6 per cent).

National and state issues dominated the elections of 2000 as well, though the main themes had to be different after the disastrous events of 1999. The incumbents emphasized the importance of economic reconstruction and of not giving in to international pressure. The opposition claimed that it was in Serbia's best interest to get rid of a regime that had brought disaster and isolation upon the country. Thus, after the war against NATO and the loss of Kosovo, the opposition now took the opportunity to market itself as a reliable defender of Serbian national interests. Nationalists were angered by the loss of Kosovo, while the need for cooperation with the international community was appealing to those in the liberal segment of the political spectrum. The supply offered by the opposition elites was well matched by the demand of the population. By the end of 1999 and beginning of 2000, public opinions surveys were showing a marked decrease in nationalist attitudes and an increasing concern for the declining standard of living (Mihailović 2001, 67).

Two years in democracy: Split within the democratic bloc

The elections of 2000 spelled the transition to more genuinely democratic politics in Serbia, the gradual removal of UN sanctions, and the reintegration of the country into international institutions. The division of power agreed upon among the DOS members stated that since Koštunica was supported in the presidential campaign, the position of the Serbian prime minister was reserved for the leader of the second largest opposition party – DS and Zoran Đinđić. Soon after the two occupied their places, a series of clashes within DOS started. On the level of rhetoric, the division revolved around the relative priority of economic reform and cooperation with international organizations, such as ICTY, and IMF versus building of democratic institutions. The government, headed by Đinđić, emphasized the former, while the DSS emphasized the need for constitutional reform, and for establishing other institutional prerequisites of democratic consolidation. In addition, DS had been promoting a self-image as a strongly pro-European and liberal party, while DSS was perceived as more nationalist and traditionalist.

The increasing polarization between the DS and the DSS is evident if we compare correlation coefficients between respondents' perceived distance to these parties. In 1996, the correlation coefficient was $r=0.78$ ($p<0.001$); in 2002 the correlation disappeared ($r=-0.05$, $p>0.05$). Likewise, the loss of power brought voters of the SPS and SRS closer to each other. In 1996, this correlation was negative $r=-0.15$ ($p<0.01$), while in 2002 it increased to $r=0.64$ ($p<0.01$).[14]

The division between these two key players in the post-Milošević period dominated the political agenda throughout 2001 and 2002. The test of their public support came in September–October 2002, when Serbian presidential elections were held. The three main candidates were Koštunica, representing DSS, Šešelj as the candidate of the Radicals, and Miroljub Labus, a member of DS, supported by the government parties. The socialists could not agree on a candidate, although Milošević advised them from the Hague prison to support Šešelj. Koštunica won approximately twice as many votes as Labus in the second round, but the turnout was below 50 per cent, and new elections had to be organized. DOS-without-DSS decided not to have a candidate for the new elections, since public opinion surveys and the just failed elections showed that their candidate was determined to lose against Koštunica (e.g. Goati 2001b). Before the new elections some of the DOS member-parties openly called for boycott.

An amendment to the electoral law removed the 50 per cent turnout requirement for the second round, but preserved it for the first round of elections. With a turnout of some 45 per cent, the new elections clearly did not live up to this requirement. Koštunica was not elected President of Serbia in spite of his convincing performamce at the polls (58 per cent of the votes cast). The Chairman of the Parliament, Nataša Mićić (DS), was appointed caretaker president, and new elections were postponed pending the adoption of a new constitution. Serbia will thus have to do without an elected president for quite some time yet.

On 12 March 2003, Serbia suffered another shock when a criminal clan assassinated Prime Minister Zoran Đinđić in collusion with members of certain special security forces. The assassins were apparently motivated by the desire to obstruct democratic reforms, and to stop further extraditions to the Hague tribunal. Vice president of the DS, Zoran Živković, who was appointed new Prime Minister, pledged to continue the policies of his predecessor. The tragic death of Zoran Đinđić and the following clampdown on organized crime, when hundreds of members of various criminal gangs were arrested, contributed to the upsurge in sympathy for the assassinated Prime Minister and his party. Public opinion polls from April 2003 list the DS as the most popular party in the country, with the DSS, the newly formed G17,[15] and SRS as its major rivals.

It remains to be seen how the latest developments will reflect on the party scene in Serbia, particularly considering that the ruling coalition has not always managed to resist the temptation to use the situation offered by the extraordinary measures to discredit its competitors. The DSS remain without any institutional levers of power, while the Radicals are considerably weakened since their charismatic leader Vojislav Šešelj joined Slobodan Milošević in the Hague. We should thus expect the Serbian political landscape to be dominated by the two opposing blocs – on the one hand, economically neo-liberal, and culturally relatively libertarian and elitist DS and affiliated smaller parties, and, on the other hand, the DSS and other parties tending to embrace a more conservative, traditionalist, or even populist worldview.

Résumé: political transformations on the level of elite politics

The purpose of this qualitative review of the development of the party system in Serbia is to provide a basis for understanding political conflicts primarily on the level of political elites. We can identify three stages in the development of the Serbian party system. Political pluralism started with the opposition between the former communists and anti-communist nationalists, just as in other countries in the region. The Serbian peculiarity was that the anti-communist side was far too weak and fragmented to seriously challenge the semi-reformed communists, partly because the communists had earned a strong nationalist reputation.

Since this unequal balance meant bleak prospects in the long term, the opposition reframed the divide as the conflict between authoritarianism and democracy. This marks the second phase, which lasted throughout most of the 1990s. Socialists and radical nationalists laid claim to the authoritarian part of the spectrum; the democratic opposition was ideologically rather heterogeneous, united by the desire to remove Slobodan Milošević from power.

In the third phase, after the 'bulldozer revolution', it seems that two central divisions are consolidating. One is the emerging opposition within the democratic camp between the nationalist and conservative perspective represented by the DSS, and the economically liberal and culturally libertarian option promoted by the DS and some smaller affiliated parties from the DOS coalition. The second division is continuing the divide between authoritarianism and extreme nationalism (represented by the Radicals and the remains of the SPS), and liberal democracy.

The regime change in 2000 represents the main change on the political scene since political pluralism was introduced. It produced several major consequences for the party system. The Socialists lost a huge number of voters. For example, their candidate in the first round of the 2002 presidential elections won only slightly more than 100,000 votes. Moreover, they seem to be in a prolonged crisis, and have already suffered several splits. SRS initially seemed weakened too, but their recovery was fast: Šešelj was able to win about one million votes in the unsuccessful December 2002 presidential elections. However, he will have difficulties in leading the party from the Hague. Although the extreme nationalist bloc got another party in the parliament, namely the SSJ, this orientation, at least temporarily, lost popularity after the Đinđić assassination. The SPO and Vuk Drašković are also on the losing side. Drašković fared rather poorly as a presidential candidate in October 2002, and the SPO remained without a single representative in the Serbian parliament. Thus, once the main leader of the democratic opposition, he seems to be on the way out of the political stage in Serbia. Perhaps, there remained little room for this 'romantic' brand of nationalism between the discredited extremists associated with the Radicals, and the conservative traditionalists who are now closer to Koštunica.

The former democratic opposition remains divided into two main blocs. The DSS has cultivated an image of a party firmly committed to democracy and the rule of law, and committed to pursuing vital national interests. Culturally, they are more traditionalist and conservative. The DS, with particularly firm roots in the elite circles of the capital, is ideologically liberal, oriented towards market reforms and European integration.[16] Among the other parties from the DOS coalition, there is an ongoing differentiation according to their proximity to DSS or DS, since most of them are too small for independent electoral competition.

Determinants of mass level political preferences

This section presents empirical analyses of the connection between social structure, ideology and party preferences. Most of the data presented come from Serbian and Yugoslav election studies, provided by the Central Archive in Cologne (*Zentralarchiv für Empirische Sozialforschung*), hereafter referred to as ZA Studies.[17] The second main source of data is the present author's survey of a random sample of Belgrade residents (*N*=502), conducted in the spring of 2002.

First the role of the basic socio-demographic characteristics, such as age, residence, occupation and education will be analysed. These are not necessarily 'cleavage variables' in the traditional sense, but they reveal social groups that differ politically. The next section presents a multivariate analysis of party preferences, including socio-structural and ideological variables. The analysis focuses on the five most influential parties, with the strongest electoral base and continuity over time: SPS, SRS, DS, DSS and SPO.

Figure 14.1: Relationship between age and party preferences over time[18]

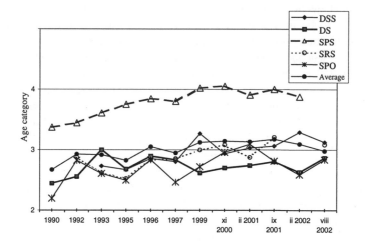

Note: Age categories: 2 (30–39 years); 3 (40–49 years); 4 (50–59 years).

Source: Recalculated on the basis of Slavujević (2002).

Social structure: Bi-variate relationships

Age: In the post-communist countries older generations are more likely to support parties of the former communists, and Serbia is no exception to this. As Figure 14.1 clearly shows, SPS supporters are considerably older than the voters of other parties. This trend spans the whole decade, and if anything, it has become more pronounced over time. As the SPS was loosing its support, mostly the older generations remained faithful. Thus, in the late 1990s, the average SPS voter was approximately in his/her fifties. Age differences among supporters of other parties do not show a clear pattern. SPO had occasionally particularly young supporters, but it seems that DS recruits voters consistently from the youngest cohorts. DSS displays a pattern similar to the DS, but with the increasing popularity of the party DSS supporters are now approaching the average age. It is clear that this 'generation gap' does not coincide with the authoritarianism-democracy dimension, since supporters of the Radicals do not differ from the more liberal and democratic parties. Age differentiates primarily communists from anti-communists.

Urban-rural residence: Urban versus rural residence has important consequences for voting patterns, as shown by Figure 14.2. Socialist and Radical parties attracted a disproportionate share of voters from rural environments, while DS and DSS were clearly more urban parties, at least until 1996. The SPO and the DEPOS coalition it headed were also disproportionately urban parties in the early 1990s, but in the mid-1990s SPO occupied an intermediate positions. The differences, though significant as the presented contingency coefficients show, are not large enough to allow us to talk about 'two Serbias' – one rural and authoritarian and the other one urban and democratic (e.g. Goati 1998, 29).

Figure 14.2: Party preferences and urban/rural divide (%)

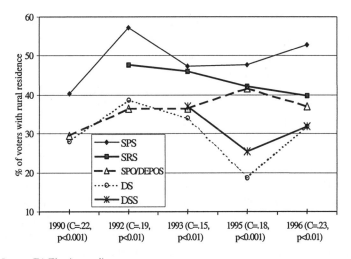

Source: ZA Election studies.

Predictably, the profile of the DSS changed somewhat after the 2000 elections, when its support became evenly distributed (*Figure 14.3*). In 2002, the urban/rural cleavage was relevant for the SPS and DS. The former remained predominantly popular in rural, and the latter in urban settings.

Figure 14.3: Urban-rural divide and party support, August 2002 (%)

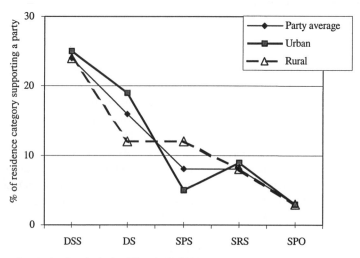

Source: Recalculated on the basis of Slavujević (2002).

Occupation: Occupation also exhibits significant bi-variate relationships with party preferences. Peasants and, somewhat less consistently, blue-collar workers disproportionately supported the SPS (Antonić 1998; Mihailović 2000). Throughout the last decade the parties of the democratic bloc have attracted disproportionately many white-collar workers. In 1990 the Socialists and the SPO had relatively more white-collar workers than the DS, but since then the DS is continuously the most white-collar party in Serbia (Slavujević 2002). Blue-collar workers tend to be relatively more attracted to nationalist parties (SRS, SPO, and recently DSS). Socialists were popular in this occupational category in the early 1990s, but especially since the regime change, the proportion of SPS voters who are blue-collar workers is as low as for the DS (Slavujević 2002; Mihailović 2000). There are, however, occupational categories that exhibit clearer voting patterns, but they tend to coincide with some other social categories. For example, the category of peasants/farmers largely coincides with the urban/rural division. Although pensioners are perhaps the most uniform category in terms of voting, this category strongly coincides with age.

Education: Education is doubtlessly one of the major factors influencing party choice. As Figure 14.4 shows, the authoritarian-democratic division correlates with the education of voters. Parties of the authoritarian orientation, i.e. SPS and SRS, attract less educated voters, while parties more committed to liberal-democratic values are hardly popular among citizens with elementary education. SPO is somewhere between the SPS and DS. The increasing proportion of less educated among the DSS voters of 2000 is a logical consequence of the party's rise to electoral prominence.

Figure 14.4: Education and party preferences (%)

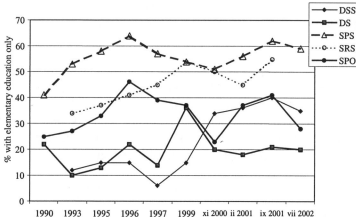

Source: Recalculated on the basis of Slavujević (2002).

Religion: One of the two main cleavages emanating from the process of nation-building in the West, according to Lipset and Rokkan (1967), is the state versus church cleavage. In Serbia, however, differences in the degree of religiosity are not associated with relevant political divisions. In 1992, for example, religiosity did not correlate with preferences for any of the most important political leaders of the time. The correlation between religiosity and opinion about leaders including Milošević, Drašković, Panić, and Ćosić (four-point positive-negative scale), was not different from zero.[19] One year later, the religious were more sympathetic towards Šešelj (r=0.17, p<0.01).[20] In 1995, the only significant correlation of religiosity was with *sympathy* for a socialist candidate Zoran Lilić (r=0.10, p<0.01).[21] In 2002 church attendance and religiosity correlated only with preference for SPO and SRS, and even with these parties rather weakly (coefficients were about 0.10).[22] National state formation may very well be an unfinished project in Serbia, but the heavily secularized context seems to deprive the religious factor of its political power.

The presented bi-variate analyses show that age and residence primarily differentiate voters of the SPS who tend to be older and rural. These variables do not coincide with authoritarian-democratic dimension since in this respect the Radical voters appear closer to the parties of democratic orientation. Voters of the SPS and SRS are, however, close to each other when occupational categories, and especially education, are examined.

In general, the underprivileged strata, with poorer chances in a competitive economy, have been less attracted to the parties of the democratic opposition. This tendency is also revealed by economic attitudes. For example, support for privatization correlates negatively with preference for the Socialist party and its candidates. In 1995, support for privatization correlated negatively with sympathy towards Milošević ($r=-0.32$, $p<0.01$), while the coefficient was positive, though lower, for Đinđić ($r=0.20$, $p<0.01$).[23] Contrary to their 'objective' economic situation, however, supporters of Milošević tended to express satisfaction with the state of the economy. Satisfaction with 'economic situation in FRY' ($r=0.56$, $p<0.01$) correlated positively with preference for Milošević and negatively but weakly with preference for Đinđić, Šešelj, and Koštunica. The popularity of the then most important opposition leader Vuk Drašković was entirely unrelated to these variables. Thus, the opposition leaders did not manage to extract stronger support from the dissatisfied.

Figure 14.5: Opinion about socialism and vote preferences in 1995 (%)

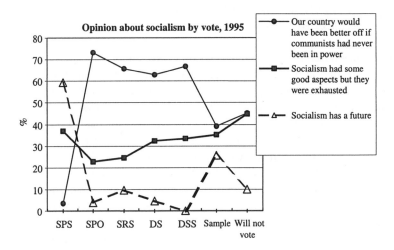

Source: ZA Study 2910, 1995.

Although the public has regarded the issue of economy as the most pressing one,[24] it is clear that some other forces are behind the underprivileged SPS voters' satisfaction with economy. The explanation lies perhaps in their ideological commitments. Figure 14.5 clearly shows that SPS is the only party with voters who strongly disagree that 'the country would have been better if communists had never been in power'. At the same time, they are the only voters who believe that 'socialism has future prospects'. Likewise, in 1990, 47.7 per cent of the SPS voters said that they had never been members of the SKJ, while approximately three quarters of all SPO voters said the same. Supporters of the DS were close to the SPO.[25] Hence, the communist/anti-communist divide separated the SPS voters from all other relevant parties. The Radicals were closer to the rest of the opposition than to their occasional coalition partners.

During the 1990s, the lower strata supported the socialists and radicals, depending on their attitude towards communism. After the decline of the SPS, the DSS seems to be taking over the representation of part of these strata. It seems that the regime change in 2000 was possible only when the underprivileged realized that there was a party acceptable to them also within the democratic bloc.

Multivariate models, 1996 and 2002

The established bi-variate connections do not necessarily imply that each relationship represents a separate cleavage. Age, residence, education, and related variables may exhibit both direct and indirect effects. Therefore, we now present an attempt to construct a causal model of party support that does include socio-structural variables, ideological dimensions, and intermediary variables.

Instead of analysing single items, we now set out to construct relatively reliable multi-item measures of some of the key ideological dimensions relevant for political behaviour. The data sets from 1996 and 2002 contain a sufficient number of items for this objective. In both sets, items were first grouped according to their ideological content, and then re-scaled according to their first principal component. Items composing these ideological scales, and corresponding Alpha reliability coefficients, are given in Appendix 14.5.

Causal modeling of party preferences

In order to examine how socio-structural characteristics are integrated with ideological orientations and party support a series of regression analyses is performed. Support for political parties (now operationalized not as a vote choice, but as proximity towards each political party) [26] is regressed on the scales of ideological orientation, and on basic socio-demographic indicators. The complete model is constructed in the following way: first, the principal dependent variable is regressed on all independent variables, then, relevant ideological variables are regressed on so-called mediating variables, which in the present case are authoritarianism and left-right ideological orientation, and the background variables. Authoritarianism and left-right identification are conceived as explanatory variables to the ideological orientations, since they represent more general orientations, or world-views, rather than concrete political attitudes.[27] Finally, authoritarianism and left-right self-identification are regressed on socio-demographic indicators. In this way, it should be possible to establish the main paths of influence, starting from the social structure, via more general world-views to concrete ideological dimensions, and party preferences.

Causal model, 1996

Multivariate models of party support explanation are presented in Table 14.1. Although each equation is statistically significant, the amount of explained variance varies greatly, from the relatively modest $R^2=0.19$ in the case of the DS, to a respectable 52 per cent of variance in the case of the socialists. There are several features common for all examined parties. Socio-demographic variables display very weak direct influence. Basically only age matters – it increases sympathies for the SPS and decreases for the Radicals and SPO. Mediating variables, i.e. authoritarianism and left-right ideology, are much more influential. Authoritarianism increases support for the SPS and decreases for parties of the democratic opposition. Preference for the SPS is related with left-wing identification, while the relationship is reversed for all other parties.

Table 14.1: Multivariate model of party preferences, 1996. Table entries: statistically significant (p<0.05) standardized regression coefficients (beta)

	SPS	DS	DSS	SRS	SPO
Age	0.09			-0.16	-0.18
Education					
Self-assessment of class					
Religiosity					
Authoritarianism	0.23	-0.16	-0.18		-.023
Left-right self-placement	-0.39	0.21	0.28	0.30	0.19
Liberalism	-0.07				
Democratic orientation		0.10	0.10		
Nationalism				0.29	
International integration				-0.12	0.10
Media censorship	0.20			-0.10	-0.09
R^2	0.52	0.19	0.25	0.32	0.27

Source: ZA Study 2911, 1996.

Different ideological dimensions matter for different particular parties. The Socialist sympathizers are distinguished by a lower degree of liberalism (this factor includes elements of economic liberalism too) and support for media control. Support for the DS and for the DSS is related to endorsement of democratic orientation, though the coefficients are modest. The radicals appear to have clearer ideological roots than the other parties: support for the SRS is explained by strong nationalism, rejection of international integration, and support for media freedom. Support for the SPO, still the main opposition party at the time, is marked by support for international integration and rejection of media censorship. The socialist party supporters were not in the isolationist bloc, probably because after the Dayton accord Socialists were emphasizing the need for international reintegration.

The findings are generally in line with the image of the parties, but it is somewhat surprising that SPO support was not related to nationalism in 1996, although nationalism was the principal ideology of this party some years earlier. The general impression is that specific ideological dimensions matter less than one would expect, while more general orientations, represented by the left-right dimension and by authoritarianism, exhibit surprisingly broad and strong effects.

When the second and third steps in the modeling analysis are examined, we can observe that some of the specific ideological dimensions can be fairly well explained by the model (*Table 14.2*). This applies primarily to the attitude towards media censorship (33 per cent of variance explained) and liberalism (23 per cent of variance), that is, for dimensions closely related to the more general conflict between authoritarianism and democracy. The other three specific ideological dimensions are somewhat less successfully explained but the relationships are statistically significant.

Table 14.2: Multivariate model of ideological and mediating variables, 1996. Table entries: standardized regression coefficients (significant coefficients shown)

	Autho-ritarianism	Left–right	Media censor-ship	Natio-nalism	Libera-lism	Intern-ational integr-ation	Demo-cratic orient-ation
Age	0.18	-0.14	0.11	-0.10			
Education	-0.24	-0.13		-0.17			0.21
Self-assessment of class				-0.10	0.08		-0.09
Religiosity							
Autho-ritarianism	–	-0.31	0.43	0.29	-0.40	-0.11	-0.22
Left–right self-placement	–	–	-0.18	0.27	0.17	-0.12	
R^2	0.13	0.13	0.33	0.15	0.23	0.03	0.08

Source: ZA Study 2911, 1996.

Concerning the explanatory variables at this stage, it is clear that authoritarianism and left-right ideology are both strong determinants, but this is especially true for the former. The effect of authoritarianism is strong for each of the concrete ideological dimensions, and even for the left-right identification.[28] Authoritarianism shows especially strong effects on pro-censorship attitudes, nationalism (positive effect), and liberalism (negative effect).

The demographic variables have varying effects on the different ideological dimensions, but the coefficients are rarely high. Education has a relatively broad effect, influencing nationalism (negatively) and democratic orientation (positively); it also reduces authoritarianism and right-wing identification.[29] Age increases authoritarianism, left-wing identification, and preference for media control, but older respondents, other things being equal, tend to be less nationalistic. Self-ascribed class position has a small and somewhat inconsistent negative influence on nationalism and democratic orientation, and a positive impact on liberalism (higher class – more liberal orientation). Mediating variables are both related to age and education, the effect of education on authoritarianism being the largest one among any of the demographic variables shown.

Certain conclusions seem to be clear. According to the 1996 data, party preferences are determined by specific ideological orientations and general world-views more than directly by socio-demographic variables. Concrete ideological dimensions are in turn influenced by more general world-views, i.e. authoritarianism and left-right ideology, but also to a certain extent by socio-demographic variables. I would like to emphasize the particular role of authoritarianism and left-right identification (but especially the former): these variables exhibit direct and (via concrete ideological dimensions) indirect effects on party support, and they transfer the influence of the background variables. Thus, taking into account both the role of specific ideological dimensions and the role of authoritarianism, the most general finding is that in 1996 those variables were the most relevant for mass party preferences in Serbia which were – in one way or another – indicative of the authoritarianism-democracy opposition. It appears that the fight was much more about general principles than about concrete policies.

Causal model, 2002

The model for 2002 includes a somewhat broader set of variables, but this fact did not help much in increasing the explained variance. The model explains about one third of the variance in the preferences for the included parties, apart of the DSS where the explained variance is approximately half of that (*Table 14.3*).

However, the findings seem to be simpler to interpret. Basically two ideological dimensions are worth discussing in 2002: the attitude towards international integration and nationalism. The former correlates positively with the preference for the DOS, DS and DSS, and negatively with the preference for the SPS and SRS. The division reflects the positions of the conflicting political elites perfectly.

Table 14.3: Multivariate model of party preferences, 2002. Table entries: statistically significant (p<0.05) standardized regression coefficients (beta)

	SPS	SRS	DOS	DS	DSS
Age	0.09				
Education		-0.08			
Church attendance					
Religiosity					
Subjective economic wellbeing					
Family income					
Authoritarianism	0.12				
Left-right self-placement	-0.21	-0.09	0.16	0.13	0.15
International integration	-.020	-0.32	0.35	0.38	0.17
Punitiveness					
Traditionalism		-0.16			
Feminism					
Militarism					
Clericalism					
Elitism					
Nationalism	0.30	0.30	-0.35	-0.29	0.20
Socialism				-0.10	
Environmentalism					-0.15
Economic liberalism					
R^2	0.37	0.32	0.30	0.34	0.17

Source: Author's survey, Spring 2002.

Nationalism shows a more interesting pattern. It correlates positively with the preference for the Socialist and Radical parties, but also for Koštunica's DSS. These three parties currently constitute the nationalist bloc, as the SPO is not on the stage for the time being.

There are only few additional significant effects of the ideological variables. Radical supporters tend to have fewer traditionalists than the average. Supporters of the DS are negatively disposed towards socialist ideology, while DSS supporters tend to reject environmentalism.[30]

This time, authoritarianism does not have a direct impact on party preferences, except in the case of the socialists.[31]The left-right ideology, on the other hand, is still directly influential. An interesting difference is that the preference for the Radical party was related to right-wing identification in 1996, while in 2002 the coefficients suggest relatively leftist identification. Socio-demographic variables remain poor direct predictors of party preferences.

Table 14.4: Multivariate model of ideological and mediating variables, 2002. Significant coefficients shown (p<0.05)

	Authoritarianism	Left-right identification	International integration	Nationalism
Age	0.26	-0.13		
Education	-0.29		0.10	-0.12
Subjective economic well-being				-0.08
Family income	-0.16			
Church attendance				
Religiosity		0.11		
Authoritarianism	–		-0.20	0.56
Left-right self-placement	–	–		
R^2	0.21	0.03	0.09	0.41

Source: Author's survey, spring 2002.

The explanation of the ideological orientations repeats the general findings from 1996 (*Table 14.4*). The model accounts for no more than 9 per cent of the variance in the support for international integration, the most relevant predictors being authoritarianism and education. Thus, although this factor is a stronger predictor of political preferences than in 1996, the background model can explain only a small portion of the individual differences along this variable, just as in 1996.

Nationalism can be explained better (41 per cent of the variance), again by the strong influence of authoritarianism, and by education and subjective economic wellbeing. Authoritarianism itself can be relatively well explained by the background variables, especially when the effects of age and education are strong, but low income is also influential. Only a rather small percentage of the variance in left-right ideology may be attributed to age and religiosity (the older are more left-wing, while the religious are more right-wing, as expected).

Thus, in 2002, the voters' party preferences are determined directly by the attitude towards the international community, by nationalism, and by left-right orientation. Authoritarianism strongly influences the two specific ideological orientations, especially nationalism. It also largely mediates the influence of background variables, especially age and education. The main cleavage does not seem to run between the general principles of authoritarian or democratic rule. The basic ideological markers of the opposing political camps are now two closely related issues – nationalism and international integration. But, the parties are not simply divided in the same two blocs on both issues. The issue of international integration divides parties into an authoritarian and a democratic bloc, but nationalists are divided into supporters of the Radicals and Socialists, and democratically oriented supporters of the DSS. This may be a positive sign that nationalism in Serbia does not necessarily have to be undemocratically oriented.

From the theoretical point of view, the most interesting result is that social-structure does not directly transfer into party preferences. Its influence, according to the Serbian evidence, works via more general world-views. As Gabennesch (1972) argued, authoritarianism is a psychological reflection of particular social conditions marked by material and – especially – educational deprivation. The role of what here is termed 'mediating variables' is perhaps particularly strong in contexts where social structure is still not crystallized, and where it is not easy to establish clear connections between particular economic interests, political actors, and policies.

Discussion
At the initial stage of political pluralism in Serbia, communist heirs faced anti-communist nationalists. The situation was therefore similar to most of the other countries in the region. Social-structural roots were not exceptional: former *nomenklatura*, i.e. elites whose privileges were in various way tied with the communist rule, and older, less educated, and rural segments were pitted against younger, better educated, urban and pro-West oriented segments of the population. These tendencies were still quite modest in 1990. The anti-communist side was too weak and disunited in Serbia.

The early conflict between SPS and SPO testifies to the presence of this cleavage. In subsequent elections, the SPO continued insisting on the anti-communist rhetoric, but with evidently limited public response. After all, most of the anti-communist politicians and MPs were members of the Communist Party, and many of them held important offices. Thus, despite its relative depth, this cleavage did not prove strong enough to mobilize voters for the initial regime change. In Kitschelt's early model (1992), the strength of the libertarian-pro-market camp is dependent on economic development, but Serbia's relative economic backwardness is only part of the story. Another part lies in the popular attachment to self-management socialism. Finally, it is difficult to overemphasize the importance of the then contemporary political processes. The dissolution of socialist Yugoslavia and the secession of the other Yugoslav republics forced the national and state issue to the foreground, and decreased the salience of the communist–anti-communist cleavage. This proved to be, then, a short-term transitional cleavage. Unlike the other countries of the region, this cleavage faded away without provoking regime change.

The dual issue of state and nation has been on the surface of virtually all political controversies in Serbia during the 1990s. It is perhaps the most important *theme* or style of framing concrete issues, rather than a cleavage that strongly divides parties and reflects distinct social categories. However, the parties are distinguishable according to the *kind* of nationalism they represent. Radicals and Socialists represent a more extreme, expansionist and populist nationalism, although it is difficult to exactly interpret the nationalism of the socialists and to determine to what extent their particular policies were motivated by sincere nationalism or by simple desire to retain power. Drašković's nationalism could be termed romantic and anti-communist. Koštunica has integrated a kind of traditionalist nationalism with commitment to the rules of democracy, and the DS has recently distanced itself from its more nationalist past. Thus, we can refer to indications of the nationalism-cosmopolitanism conflict.

The attitude towards the international community, which has played an extraordinarily important role in Serbia for obvious reasons, is very close to, though not identical with, the nationalism-cosmopolitanism dimension. The parties within the authoritarian bloc have been particularly negatively oriented towards cooperation with the international community (except with countries perceived as 'friends', such as Russia or Greece), while liberal parties within the democratic opposition have been outspokenly pro-Western. The empirical analyses we have carried out clearly show the relevance of this issue for party preferences.

The exceptional salience of these two issues, nationalism and attitude towards the international community, is probably a transitional phenomenon, too, related to a decade of border disputes and conflictual relations with the outside world. These issues could perhaps be interpreted as value cleavages, rather than social cleavages in the classical sense, regardless of their correlation with certain socio-economic indicators.

Throughout the 1990s, the deepest division on the party scene in Serbia has been that between authoritarianism and democracy, often represented by the parties involved as the struggle between good and evil. The authoritarian parties were part of the 'red-brown' coalition of the socialists, radicals and the JUL, while SSJ joined the camp more recently. The main players in the democratically oriented bloc have been SPO, DS, DSS, and their numerous coalitions and coalition partners. Despite the party leadership, the radical supporters were often closer ideologically to the other opposition parties. The controversy essentially revolved around the respect for the rules of the democratic game, as manifested by the reactions to the attempts by the SPS to control the mass media and the economy, and especially the police and the army. In many respects, this ties in well with Kitschelt's early model of cleavages in post-communist Eastern Europe (1992, 1995), where pro-market libertarians are opposed to anti-market authoritarians, though with less emphasis on market attitudes. This cleavage has a long history in Serbian politics, but its contemporary manifestation could also be interpreted as a prolonged transitional cleavage (Karasimeonov 1998), which replaced the original pro- and anti-communist division. On the one side of this divide we find communist heirs, and on the other a heterogeneous set of parties and organizations united by the desire to remove the former from power.

Multivariate analyses of party preferences in 1996 and 2002 showed that preference for authoritarian *political* options was tied to authoritarianism as an individual difference variable. Authoritarianism conceived as a personality or attitudinal dimension has frequently been used for explaining anti-democratic political preferences (e.g. Adorno et al. 1950; Altemeyer 1988). Already the first studies of multipartism in Serbia showed significant differences in the degree of authoritarianism between supporters of different parties (e.g. Mihailović 1991). Authoritarianism, presently conceived as a general worldview in line with Gabennesch (1972), proved a very influential variable, both directly on political preferences, and indirectly via specific ideological orientations. Authoritarianism was a key determinant of the two most relevant ideological orientations – nationalism and international integration, especially in 2002. Although the socio-economic indicators exhibited their influence largely through authoritarianism, it seems that the authoritarianism-democracy cleavage is still based more on values and worldviews than on conflicting interests of different social categories. Thus, in the context of 'flattened societies' (Wessels and Klinge-mann, 1994), the formation of politically relevant groups may be based more on values and worldviews than on social categories, even though there is a strong connection between them. It seems that social structure exhibits its influence more implicitly, through particular worldviews, rather than explicitly through ideologies expressing group interests.

The divide between the authoritarian and democratic blocs was thus not only political and ideological, but also psychological and cultural. Political immobilism in Serbia during the 1990s can at least partly be explained by the depth of this division and by the impossibility – both for voters and politicians – to cross the border between the two positions.

The strength of the division, or the extreme political polarization, was reinforced by the fact that it mostly coincided with a number of basic socio-structural categories such as age and education, and with most of the important specific ideological dimensions, such as nationalism or the attitude towards the international actors. Especially in 2002, the model explaining party support was very simple: the same predictors were valid for authoritarian and liberal-democratic parties; only the signs of the coefficients were different.

The ethnic cleavage is perhaps the cleavage that comes closest to Rokkan's cleavage concept, including clear group borders, institutional encapsulation, and distinct group identity. Its importance in Serbia has been clear from the beginning. Even if we disregard Kosovo, which is a case of secession, ethnic divisions still play a significant role in Serbian politics. Parties of national minorities do exist in Serbia; they have representatives in the parliament, and control virtually all votes in their subgroups (cf. Todosijević 2002). On the local level, the minority parties are typically in control of self-governments in regions where they are concentrated. In Serbian and Federal parliaments they have typically been in coalition with parties of the democratic bloc. Beyond that, their role in structuring the national party system is modest, since the two most relevant minorities, i.e. Magyars and Muslims of Sandžak, are numerically relatively small, and none of the major Serbian parties obtains any significant proportion of votes from the minorities (Goati 1996, 131).

This issue, however, extends into several other manifestations of the centre-periphery cleavage. One concerns the issue of state centralization. The Socialists and the Radicals are on the one side of this issue, favouring state centralization, while minority parties and regionalist parties, especially from Vojvodina, have been strongly in favour of decentralization, and more extensive territorial autonomies. The other major parties are in-between these extremes. SPO and perhaps DSS are for more centralization, while DS is for less. Regionalist parties have managed to receive some electoral support in their own right, not only through broader opposition coalitions.[32] Regional differences are observable in general patterns of voting as well. Throughout the 1990s, the socialists were more popular in central and southern Serbia than in Vojvodina. This line of division coincides to a certain extent with the rural-urban division, and with the ethnic composition of the population. In regions, where national minorities are concentrated, the DS candidate Miroljub Labus won a majority of the votes in the first round of the presidential elections on 29 September 2002. For example, in Kanjiža where Magyars have an absolute majority, Labus won more than 80 per cent of the votes, while his national result was about 27 per cent.[33] In regions populated by Serbs who experienced more open ethnic conflicts, such as regions bordering on Kosovo, or Srem in Vojvodina, the extreme nationalist candidate Šešelj received the strongest support.

The definition and measurement of the socio-economic cleavage is always a complex task in the post-communist context. In Serbia this divide is not manifested in the classical shape as a conflict between capital and labour.[34] It is more manifest on the ideological level, in the shape of different economic philosophies, such as attitudes towards privatization or protectionism.[35] It is clear that the Socialists and the Radicals favour protectionist policies, while the democratic opposition has been for economic reform and privatization. Under the Socialist government, the state played a very extensive redistributive role, as most of the large firms were under direct state control. The economy was probably more centralized than during the times of socialist self-management.[36] In this way, the controlled economy served as an efficient clientilistic network (Antonić 2000, 609). If the Radicals disagreed, it was because they demanded more egalitarian and less corrupt redistribution.

Concerning the other parties, nationalists of various shades seem to be closer to the protectionist economic philosophy. Recently it has become clear that economic neo-liberalism can be associated with the Democratic Party, and to some degree with some other liberal-democratic parties as well (e.g. GSS). DSS is nominally in favour of privatization and marketization too, but advocates a slower pace. On the level of rhetoric, however, the economic issue has been mainly framed as a valence issue – who is better able to provide the expected economic benefits for society. The near future will probably clarify the economic interests of the different strata and then transfer them into the realm of politics.

The socio-economic cleavage is also manifested in recurrent patterns of voting preferences in different socio-economic categories. As demonstrated by the empirical analyses, variables such as age, education, rural residence, occupation, or income, clearly matter when it comes to voting. It is clear that potential 'losers of transition' have been more ready to vote for the Radicals and the Socialists. On the other hand, those with greater social and cultural capital seem to be more open towards economic reform, and support parties such as DS and GSS. In this sense, the socio-economic cleavage is certainly relevant in Serbia (cf. Kitschelt et al. 1995).

Finally, it is worth mentioning the cleavages that appear *not* to be relevant in Serbia. This applies to the rural-urban aspect of the economic cleavage, for example. Although several parties have tried to appeal to the agrarian interests, they have remained basically irrelevant as political actors in their own right. This does not mean that there are no clear urban-rural differences in voting patterns – it was found in a number of studies that peasants/farmers disproportionately supported the SPS (Antonić 1998; Mihailović 2000). After all, the democratic opposition was for the first time victorious in the largest urban centres in the local elections of 1996. This only means that no influential party builds its support on a successful appeal to agrarian interests. Similarly, the state-church, or religious-secular cleavage has not played any significant role in party politics in Serbia.

Parties and cleavages in historical perspective

An important question is to what extent there is historical continuity of cleavages in Serbia, either in terms of the connection between contemporary and historical political parties, or in terms of relevant issue dimensions.

There is of course continuity between the communists prior to the Second World War and contemporary SPS, but the difference between the small, often illegal revolutionary party and its distant offspring in the 1990s is huge. Perhaps the connection historical and symbolic rather than institutional or even ideological.

The Democratic and Radical parties also have predecessors in earlier periods of pluralist politics in Serbia. However, none of them have exploited the connection much, although the Radicals occasionally stressed their ideological affinity with the Radical Party of Nikola Pašić.[37] Despite the lack of the institutional continuity, the DS and the SRS are both surprisingly close to their historical namesakes. The old Radical Party – while playing an important democratizing role in Serbia – was nationalist and populist, just as its modern successor (cf. Stokes 1990). The Democratic Party was liberal, elitist and urban also before the Second World War.

Continuity of cleavages is perhaps more interesting than institutional continuity. First of all, state and nation have been on the agenda in Serbia for nearly two centuries. In brief periods of democratic rule, the issue has been politicized in a way reminiscent of the 1990s. The conflict between the authoritarian and democratic blocs is by no means new to the 1990s; it was equally dominant and salient in the 1920s (Antonić 1998). The social forces mobilized by the opposing camps also testify to a high degree of continuity. The authoritarian parties of the inter-war era could thus rely on support from the ruling political elite, the capitalist elite connected with the state through concessions and other privileges, the military elite, parts of the administrative and academic elites, and lower social strata with negative attitudes towards marketization such as smallholders, unqualified workers and the upper-age brackets (Antonić 1998).

Ethnic cleavages have characterized Serbia since it became a multinational state, i.e. after the Balkan Wars, and even more since the First World War.[38] National minorities gained parliamentary representation in the 1920s just as in the 1990s.

But there are also some structural differences between the two time periods well worth highlighting. Most notably, in the 1920s all major parties had to rely on peasant votes, since peasants constituted a vast majority (around 90 per cent) of the population. There were very few large landowners, only some 4 per cent of land was in estates of 100 hectares or more.[39] The situation was thus more favourable for populist politics than for the development of a strong agrarian cleavage.

In the 1990s, the social structure is more differentiated, and in a way favourable to the liberal-democratic bloc (a high level of education, a large service sector, and a relatively small agricultural sector).[40] On the other hand, the time is not yet ripe for the emergence of the classical capital/labour, left-right cleavage, in spite of the growing number of industrial workers. In the 1920s, the working-class was a rather insignificant social force; and in the 1990s workers were employed by the state more often than by private owners.

Conclusion

The utility of the narrowly defined concept of cleavage may be legitimately questioned. In the last decades, cleavage-politics has been declared irrelevant for Western Europe on numerous occasions. In other parts of the world, like in Northern America, models other than Lipset and Rokkan's have been called upon to describe mass political behaviour. Finally, post-Communist Europe is characterized by contradictory tendencies such as the re-emergence of community-based conflicts, on the one hand, and high-scale electoral volatility driven by the influence of mass media and by the fragility of party organizations, on the other.

The evidence presented here shows that a certain part of the variance in voting behaviour may be explained with reference to basic socio-economic categories. Supporters of different parties tend to come from somewhat different socio-economic and socio-cultural groups, and to hold different political attitudes. The central political divide throughout the 1990s – that between authoritarianism and democracy – is well reflected on the level of party and voter characteristics. The less educated, older, and rural population proved to be more authoritarian, nationalist, negatively oriented towards the international community, and tended to support the SPS and SRS. The opposing camp included those with greater social and cultural capital, and those with better prospects in liberalized conditions in a market economy. After the regime change in October 2000, many of the dissatisfied voters who abandoned the SPS opted for the DSS, thus opening an increasingly important divide within the democratic bloc. The division between the two new key players on the political scene in Serbia, that is DS and DSS, is not only ideological, but also social. Ideologically, DSS is more traditionalist, conservative and nationalist. Socially, DS is more urban and elitist. The Radical Party remains consistently associated with relatively young, urban and working-class members of the lower social strata. Finally, in accordance with the cleavage model, the most important issues and divisions have a clear historical background. The central political divide, authoritarianism versus democracy, with its associate oppositions (rural versus urban, nationalism versus cosmopolitanism, market versus plan), has always been part of Serbian history.

The question is: to what extent can the cleavage model capture the political divisions described in this chapter? The cleavage concept can definitely be applied to ethnic oppositions. Borders between voters of different ethnic origin have proved remarkably impermeable. National minorities posses distinct identities; they are institutionally encapsulated, and overwhelmingly support 'their own' single party. Identity politics clearly matters (cf. Whitefield 2002). But the overall picture suggests that party politics basically is not determined by conflicts between organized groups having distinct socio-structural profiles and elaborate identities. The major structural variables such as the rural-urban division, ethnicity or region, and social stratification, are clearly relevant, but their influence is relatively small, and tends to disappear in multivariate models. However, even to the degree that these variables work, they do not work because of organizational encapsulation or closure of relevant social groups (again ethnic minorities are an exception). Age and education are particularly strongly related to party preferences, but these groups are not 'groups for themselves', and in general they 'lack that kind of social closure and/or temporal stability which are necessary preconditions for the functioning of the freezing effect' (Tóka 1998). Moreover, the parties are rarely explicit in their appeal to specific social categories. The SPS and the SRS have perhaps had the most specific appeal to 'ordinary people', while the elitism of the DS and the GSS, and more recently of the DSS, has been more implicit than open and direct.

The relatively weak socio-structural roots of the Serbian parties are explainable from the point of view of all the three key factors that matter in cleavage theory: parties, society, and voters. Serbian political parties are often described as clientilistic networks led by charismatic or would-be charismatic leaders (e.g. Sekelj 2000, 69; Antonić 2002), rather than mass parties with extensive membership and developed infrastructure through which they can establish the connection with targeted social groups. The objective social situation has its role too. Weak social differentiation is often quoted as an important factor in hindering cleavage politics across the region (Wessels and Klingemann 1994). Serbia is an exception only in the sense that it was not flattened by the communist regime: it was a rather flat, or egalitarian society, consisting basically of small peasants when it gained independence in the 19th century. In a society, which is still in flux and turmoil, we see that characteristics related to *potential* success in the transitional struggle predict libertarian-democratic attitudes rather well (cf. Kitschelt 1992). More than anything else, Serbian society had experiences that forced the social cleavages into the background: the dissolution of the former state, conflicts with secessionist republics and provinces (Kosovo), and conflicts with the international community (UN sanctions, NATO attack). In our causal models, attitudes, or ideological orientations proved important as a proximal causal factor determining political preferences. The two most influential orientations are clearly reflections of the most traumatic contemporaneous processes. When borders of the national community are disputed, it is not surprising that nationalism-related attitudes play a major role in dividing the respective camps. The conflict with the international community lies behind the salience of the attitude towards international integration.

Political actualization of potential social cleavages, especially the development of active group-solidarity, presupposes organizational work by political entrepreneurs. That is a lengthy process with uncertain outcomes. Distinct attitudinal characteristics or negative stereotypes about political enemies can be represented and moulded via mass media as well. When these attitudinal features divide the national political field into specific camps across which there is little trust, let alone cooperation, and the range of coalitional alternatives is determined by camp-borders, then national politics resembles the politics of those countries where socio-economic groups are pitted against each other. Stable political orientations, thus, can be rooted in political attitudes, values, or ideologies. This is not a particularly novel argument. Tóka, for example, concluded that 'pure structural voting, on the basis of social class, religion, or place of residence, seldom makes a contribution to the stabilization of critical alignments [...] Value preferences seem to provide for the relatively more solid, stable basis for enduring partisan attachments' (Tóka 1998).

This brings us to the role of individual-dispositional variables. Authoritarianism and left-right ideological self-identification exhibited strong direct and indirect (via ideological orientations) effects on political preferences, but they also mediated the influence of the background variables. Authoritarianism as an individual disposition correlated strongly with the authoritarian-democratic political divide, and with the most influential proximal ideological dimensions (especially nationalism and national integration factors in the 2002 data).

This emphasis on attitudinal and psychological elements in the reconstruction of group-formation does not eliminate socio-demographic background characteristics. Psychological dispositions are formed in interaction with an individual's social position, and therefore the connection between the social structure and political behaviour should be conceived as mediated by attitudinal orientations such as authoritarianism.

Since dispositional variables have a broader influence, they could be helpful in predicting orientations of particular segments of the population in case particular issues become politicized, or predicting reorientations in case of major changes in the party system. During the 1990s all social strata suffered, yet the popularity of the SPS remained high. The voters started to desert the SPS only when military defeat and the zigzags of the party elite undermined the image of the party. Thus, it could have been predicted that in case of the decline of SPS, these voters would be attracted to conservative-traditionalist parties. More to the point, the question is about the consequences of the fact that the DSS attracted most of the former SPS and SRS voters. Perhaps, the nationalist and traditionalist reputation of the DSS might satisfy them, while the firm democratic orientation of the party might help navigate Serbia into safer, more stable and democratic waters.

Acronyms of Parties and Coalitions

DC	Democratic Centre (*Demokratski centar*)
DEPOS	Democratic Movement of Serbia (*Demokratski pokret Srbije*); 1992–93 electoral coalition; principal members SPO, ND, GSS.
DOS	Democratic Opposition of Serbia (*Demokratska opozicija Srbije*); 2000 electoral coalition, principal members DSS, DS, GSS, ND, SVM, LSV, DC.
DRSM	Democratic Reform Party of Muslims (*Demokratsko reformska stranka Muslimana*)
DS	Democratic Party (*Demokratska Stranka*)
DSHV	Democratic Alliance of Croats in Vojvodina (*Demokratski zavez Hrvata u Vojvodini*)
DSS	Democratic Party of Serbia (*Demokratska stranka Srbije*)
DZVM	Democratic Community of Vojvodina Hungarians (*Demokratska zajednica vojvođanskih Mađara*)
GSS	Citizens' Alliance of Serbia (*Građanski savez Srbije*)
JUL	Yugoslav United Left (*Jugoslovenska ujedinjena levica*)
LSV	League of Vojvodina Social Democrats (*Liga socijaldemokrata Vojvodine*)
ND	New Democracy (*Nova Demokratija*)
RDSV	Reform Democratic Party of Vojvodina (*Reformsko-demokratska stranka Vojvodine*)
Savez za promene	Alliance for changes; coalition of DS, GSS, DHSS, and New Serbia (*Nova Srbija*)
SDA	Party of Democratic Action (*Stranka demokratske akcije*)
SKS	Communists League of Serbia (*Savez komunista Srbije*)
SNP CG	Socialist People's Party of Montenegro (*Socijalistička narodna partija Crne Gore*)
SPO	Serbian Renewal Movement (*Srpski pokret obnove*)
SPS	Socialist Party of Serbia (*Socijalistička partija Srbije*)
SRS	Radical Party of Serbia (*Srpska Radikalna stranka*)
SSJ	Party of Serbian Unity (*Stranka srpskog jedinstva*)
SSS	Peasants' Party of Serbia (*Srpska Seljačka Stranka*)
SVM	Alliance of Hungarians of Vojvodina (*Vajdasági Magyar Szövetsége/Savez Vojvođanskih Mađara*)
Zajedno	Coalition 'Together'; 1996 electoral coalition; principal members SPO, DS, GSS, DSS.

NOTES

* Acknowledgements: Zsolt Enyedi and Markian Prokopovych provided useful comments on a draft version of this chapter.

1. In Tucker's database of articles on voting and election studies in all post-communist countries published in 16 leading journals, there was only one article that included Serbia/Yugoslavia. Only the former Soviet republics in the Caucasus and Central Asia are less studied.
2. Kosovo is excluded from the analysis since throughout 1990s it was outside the sphere of Serbian politics.
3. On 7 September 1990, in Kačanik, Kosovo, a secret meeting of 111 representatives of the dissolved Kosovo Assembly, all of Albanian nationality, announced the 'Constitution' of what was termed the 'Kosovo Republic' – defined as an independent state (Vukomanović 1999).
4. The term 'democratic opposition' refers to the Serbian parties who opposed Milošević, with the exception of SRS.
5. Dobrica Ćosić, another famous writer with a political background, was appointed Federal President. He also came into conflict with Milošević, and was consequently dismissed in June 1993.
6. SDA boycotted the 1992 elections.
7. New Democracy (ND) has had a political influence highly disproportional to its electoral base. The only time this party participated in an election on its own was in 1990, and it won only 1.3 per cent of the vote and no representatives. Interestingly, ND was a member of the DOS coalition when Milošević was removed after the elections of 2000. Its leader Dušan Mihajlović became Minister of the Interior in the Đinđić government.
8. At the time, the Federal President was elected by the federal parliament, i.e. not directly. Montenegrin representatives, under Đukanović's control, fully supported Milošević's appointment.
9. Federal Government Report of 14 January 1999 (quoted in Antonić 1999).
10. Milošević distributed some 4,200 decorations after the 'victory' against NATO (Antonić 2000, 595).
11. It was estimated that the immediate war damage was above 4 billions of dollars. The indirect costs exceeded 100 billion dollars (Antonić 2001, 37).
12. The ruling coalition in Montenegro immediately declared that they did not recognize these constitutional changes, and refused to participate in the scheduled elections.
13. Foreign financial intervention was decisive in this respect. According to Antonić (2001), more than 40 million dollars were 'invested' from abroad in the campaign for removing Milošević from power.
14. Data sources: 1996 data: ZA Study 2911; 2002 data: author's survey. In 1996, support for SRS was positively associated with sympathy towards the opposition parties (e.g., with DS r=0.32, p<0.01).
15. G17 transformed from an expert group closely affiliated with DOS (provided several ministers in the contemporary government), into a political party under the leadership of former presidential candidate Miroljub Labus. It is programmatically close to DS.
16. However, party programmes and ideological commitments are not always reliable predictors of promoted policies once a party comes to power. For example, a minister from the GSS – one of the most liberal and libertarian parties within the DOS – introduced religious classes into Serbian schools.
17. Neither the original collectors nor the Central Archive in Cologne (ZA) bear any responsibility for the analysis or the interpretation presented here.
18. Data from Slavujević (2002) are generally based on surveys and election studies with national random samples.
19. Data source: ZA Study 2904, 1992. In the same study, for the sake of comparison, age was correlated with preference for each one of the included leaders, with Milošević coming out on top (r=-0.29, p<0.001).
20. Data source: ZA Study 2907, 1993.
21. Data source: ZA Study 2910, 1995.
22. Author's data, 2002.
23. Data source: ZA Study 2910, 1995.

24. In 1990, 36.7 per cent of the respondents (the highest percentage) believed that the most pressing issue of the day was 'living standard and economic development'. Five years later 'economic problems' were once again selected as the most pressing issue (chosen by more than 38 per cent of the respondents). Data source: ZA Study 2901, 1990, and ZA Study 2910, 1995. In both surveys, the second most often chosen issue trailed some 20 percentage points behind.

25. Data source: ZA Study 2901, 1990.

26. This strategy is chosen because this variable strongly co-varies with the expressed vote preference; it increases the number of available observations, and enables more powerful and elegant statistical methods.

27. Authoritarianism is interpreted here more in the sense of a worldview rooted in social conditions (Gabennesch 1972), than as a personality disposition (Adorno et al. 1950).

28. More detailed analysis of the relationship between authoritarianism and the left-right scale shows a U-shaped curve, indicating higher authoritarianism on the extremes, but the increase is stronger on the left side of the spectrum.

29. When the bi-variate relationship between education and left-right ideology is examined, a reverse U-shaped curve appears: those on the ideological extremes are less educated, but left-wing extremists are still better educated than those on the right-wing.

30. The negative relationship between DSS support and environmentalism suggests that this party attracts voters with materialist value orientation in Inglehart's sense of that term. Some of the smaller parties from the DOS coalition, such as regionalist and libertarian LSV, tend to be more post-materialist.

31. The reason for the lack of a direct effect of authoritarianism might partly be in the content of the authoritarianism scale in 2002. Namely, in 1996 the scale was more ideological, while in 2002 it was somewhat more psychological.

32. For example, coalition Vojvodina had two representatives in the Federal parliament after the 1996 elections, and four representatives after the Serbian parliamentary elections in 1997.

33. *Subotičke Novine*, No. 40, 4 October 2002.

34. Antonić (1998) calculated the so-called Alford index of class voting in Serbia for data from 1996, and found that it was extremely low (approximately 1), suggesting that workers did not give disproportional support to parties of the 'Left Coalition'.

35. On the mass level, as shown in the multivariate models, economic liberalism was basically not related to party preferences.

36. SPS stopped privatization by law in 1996 (Antonić 2000, 608–9). It was estimated that approximately 85 per cent of basic capital remained under state ownership (Goati 1996, 19). The present DOS government, on the other hand, started privatization at a very fast pace.

37. Šešelj's Radicals are only one of many parties with 'Radical' in their name to claim ties with Pašić's Radical Party, but the other parties are generally very small.

38. The destiny of Serbs in Kosovo was an important symbolic issue even before the territory was incorporated into modern Serbia. Radoje Domanović, a well-known Serbian writer, in one of his famous political satires written in 1903 ridiculed a political meeting where one of the speakers laments the fate of Serbs being harassed by Albanians and calls for revenge.

39. Quoted in Antonić (1998); 71.9 per cent of the land was in possessions smaller than 5 hectares (Grbić 1991).

40. However, FR Yugoslavia still has a large proportion of rural population (48 per cent of the population in 2000), larger than the 'Visegrad Four', or even larger than in the 'Balkan six' countries, i.e. the average for Albania, Bosnia and Herzegovina, Bulgaria, Croatia, Macedonia, and Romania (IMF Country Report No. 02/103, May 2002).

REFERENCES

Adorno, Theodor W., Else Frenkel-Brunswik, Daniel J. Levinson and Nevitt R. Sanford (1950), *The Authoritarian Personality*, New York, Harper and Row.

Altemeyer, Bob (1988), *Enemies of Freedom: Understanding Right-Wing Authoritarianism*, San Francisco, CA, Jossey-Bass Publishers.

Antonić, Slobodan (1998), 'Stranački i društveni rascepi u Srbiji', *Sociologija*, Vol. 40, No. 3, 323–56.

—— (1999), 'Kosovo i demokratska Srbija', *Nova srpska politička misao*, Vol. VI, No. 3–4, 131– 69.

—— (2000), 'Priroda poretka u Srbiji u poslednjim godinama Miloševićeve vlasti', *Sociologija*, Vol. 42, No. 4, 585–616.

—— (2001), 'Priroda petooktobarskog prevrata, "Miloševićevo zaveštanje" i demokratska Srbija', in I. Spasić and M. Subotić, *R/Evolucija i poredak: O dinamici promena u Srbiji*, 33–40, Belgrade, Institut za filozofiju i društvenu teoriju.

—— (2002), 'Politički sistem i elite u Srbiji pre i posle 5 oktobra', *Nova srpska politička misao*, available on: http://www.nspm.org.yu.

Gabennesch, Howard (1972), 'Authoritarianism as World View', *American Journal of Sociology*, 77, 857–75.

Glas javnosti, 18 February 2003.

Goati, Vladimir (1996), *Stabilizacija demokratije ili povratak monizmu: 'Treća Jugoslavija' sredinom devedesetih*, Podgorica, Unireks.

—— (1998), 'Introduction: Political Developments in the Federal Republic of Yugoslavia (1990– 1996)', in Vladimir Goati, ed., *Elections to the Federal and Republican Parliaments of Yugoslavia (Serbia and Montenegro) 1990–1996: Analyses, Documents and Data*, 12–34 Berlin, Edition Sigma.

—— (2001a), 'Priroda poretka i oktobartski prevrat u Srbiji', in I. Spasić and M. Subotić, *R/Evolucija i poredak: O dinamici promena u srbiji*, 43–55, Belgrade, Institut za filozofiju i društvenu teoriju.

—— (2001b), *Izbori u SRJ od 1990 do 1998: volja građana ili izborna manipulacija: Drugo izdanje sa Dodatkom: Izbori 2001*, Beograd, CeSID.

—— et al. (2002), *Partijska scena Srbije posle 5 oktobra 2000*, Belgrade, Friedrich Ebert Stiftung and Institut društvenih nauka.

Grbić, Vladimir (1991), 'Agrarne neusklađenosti u Srbiji', in M. V. Popović, ed., *Srbija krajem osamdesetih: sociološko istraživanje društvenih nejednakosti i neusklađenosti*, 157–92, Belgrade, Institut za sociološka istraživanja Filozofskog fakuleta u Beogradu.

Karasimeonov, Georgi (1998), 'Bulgaria', in Sten Berglund, Tomas Hellén and Frank H. Aarebrot, eds, *The Handbook of Political Change in Eastern Europe*, Cheltenham, Edward Elgar.

Kitschelt, Herbert (1992), 'The Formation of Party Systems in East Central Europe', *Politics and Society*, Vol. 20, No. 1, 7–50.

—— (1995), 'The Formation of Party Cleavages in Post-Communist Democracies', *Party Politics*, Vol. 1, No. 4, 447–72.

——, Dimitar Dimitrov and Assen Kanev (1995), 'The Structuring of the Vote in Post-Communist Party Systems: The Bulgarian Example', *European Journal of Political Research*, 27, 143–60.

Lipset, Seymour Martin and Stein Rokkan (1967), 'Introduction', in Seymour Martin Lipset and Stein Rokkan, eds, *Party Systems and Voter Alignments: Cross-National Perspectives*, 1–64, New York, The Free Press.

Matić, Jovanka (2002), *Mediji i izbori*, Beograd, CeSID.

Mihailović, Srećko (1991), 'Izbori '90: mnenje građana Srbije', in Srećko Mihailović and Vladimir Goati, eds, *Od izbornih rituala do slobodnih izbora: sondaža javnog mnenja uoči prvih višestranačkih izbora u Srbiji*, 27–126, Belgrade, Institut društvenih nauka.

—— (2000), 'Politička i stranačka identifikacija', in Srećko Mihailović, ed., *Javno mnenje Srbije: Između razočaranja i nade (septembar 1999)*, Belgrade, CPA/CPS, UGS Nezavisnost i UUEI.

—— (2001), 'Političke formule održanja i promene režima u Srbiji', in I. Spasić and M. Subotić, *R/Evolucija i poredak: O dinamici promena u srbiji*, 57–69, Belgrade, Institut za filozofiju i društvenu teoriju.

Official Gazette of the FR Yugoslavia, Vol. 9, No. 55, October 2000

Rot, Nikola and Nenad Havelka (1973), *Nacionalna vezanost i vrednosti kod srednjoškolske omladine*, Belgrade, Institut za psihologiju.

Sekelj, Laslo (2000), 'Parties and Elections: The Federal Republic of Yugoslavia – Change without Transformation', *Europe-Asia Studies*, Vol. 52, No. 1, 57–75.

Slavujević, Zoran Đ. (1998), 'The Issues: Dimensions of Electoral Confrontations', in Vladimir Goati, ed., *Elections to the Federal and Republican Parliaments of Yugoslavia (Serbia and Montenegro) 1990–1996: Analyses, Documents and Data*, 86–108, Berlin, Edition Sigma.

—— (2002), 'Socijalna utemeljenost političkih stranaka pre i posle izbora 2002', in Vladimir Goati et al., eds, *Partijska scena Srbije posle 5 oktobra 2000*, 159–94, Belgrade, Friedrich Ebert Stiftung and IDN.

Stokes, Gale (1990), *Politics as Development: The Emergence of Political Parties in Nineteenth-Century Serbia*, Durham, Duke University Press.

Todosijević, Bojan (2002), 'Minority Political Parties and Ethnic Voting in Subotica', *Nationalism and Ethnic Politics*, Vol. 8, No. 3, 95–109.

Tóka, Gábor (1998), 'Party Appeals and Voter Loyalty in New Democracies', *Political Studies 46*, 589–610.

Tucker, Joshua A. (2002), 'The first decade of post-communist elections and voting: What have we studied and how have we studied it?', *Annual Review of Political Science*, Vol. 5, 271–304.

Vukomanović, Dijana (1998), 'A short history of political parties', in Vladimir Goati, ed., *Elections to the Federal and Republican Parliaments of Yugoslavia (Serbia and Montenegro) 1990–1996: Analyses, Documents and Data*, 35–51, Berlin, Edition Sigma.

—— (1999), 'Kosovska kriza: Upravljanje etničkim sukobom (1981–1999)', *Nova srpska politička misao*, Vol. VI, No. 3–4, 35–59.

Wessels, Bernhard and Hans-Dieter Klingemann (1994), *Democratic Transformation and the Prerequisites of Democratic Opposition in East and Central Europe*, Wissenschaftszentrum Berlin für Sozialforschung, FS III, 94–201.

Whitefield, Stephen (2002), 'Political Cleavages and Post-Communist Politics', *Annual Review of Political Science,* Vol. 5, 181–200.

APPENDIX 14.1: ELECTION RESULTS

Parliamentary elections (250 members, four-year term)

Party	December 1990		December 1992		December 1993		September 1997		December 2000	
	Seats	%	Seats	%	Seats	%	Seats	%	Seats	%
SPS (coalition with JUL and ND in 1997)	194	77.6	101	40.4	123	49.2	110	44.0	37	14.8
SPO (DEPOS in 1992 and 1993)	19	7.6	50	20.0	45	18.0	45	18.0		
SRS			73	29.2	39	15.6	82	32.8	23	9.2
DS	7	2.8	6	2.4	29	11.6				
DSS					7	2.8				
DOS									176	70.4
DZVM (SVM from 1997)	8	3.2	9	3.6	5	2.0	4	1.6		
SDA[a,b]	3	1.2			2	0.8	3	1.2		
SRSJ (Vojvodine)	2	0.8								
NSS	1	0.4								
SSS	2	0.8	3	1.2						
SDS	1	0.4								
UJDI	1	0.4								
DSHV	1	0.4								
PDD	1	0.4								
SJ	1	0.4								
DRSM	1	0.4								
Independent candidates	8	3.2								
Vojvodina coalition							4	1.6		
DA							1	0.4		
SSJ									14	5.6
DS-RDSV coalition			2	0.8						
Arkan[c]			5	2.0						
DRSM			1	0.4						
Preševo-Bujanovac coalition							1	0.4		
Total	250	100.0	250	100.0	250	100.0	250	100.0	250	100.0
Turnout %	71.5		69.7		61.3		57.4		57.7	

[a] Coalition of the Party for Democratic Action and Democratic Party of Albanians in 1993.

[b] *Sandžak* coalition in 1997.

[c] Citizen's group 'Ž.R. Arkan'.

Sources: Republican Election Commission 1990, 1992, 1993, 1997, 2000; Goati 2001b; Goati et al. 2002.

Elections to the Chamber of Citizens of the Federal Assembly of the FR Yugoslavia (Veće Građana Saveznog Parlamenta)

138 members, four-year term; results for Serbia (108 representatives)

	May 1992[a]		December 1992		November 1996		September 2000	
	Seats	%	Seats	%	Seats	%	Seats	%
SPS (with JUL and ND in 1996; with JUL in 2000)	73	68.9	47	43.5	64	59.3	44	40.7
SRS	30	28.3	30	27.8	16	14.8	5	4.6
DEPOS in December 1992; *Zajedno* in 1996			20	18.5	22	20.4		
DS			5	4.6				
DOS							58	53.7
DZVM; SVM from 1996	2	1.9	3	2.8	3	2.8	1	0.9
DS/RDSV			2	1.9				
DS/RDSV/GSS			1	0.9				
Vojvodina coalition					2	1.9		
Sandžak coalition					1	0.9		
Independent	1	0.9						
Total	106	100.0	108	100.0	108	100.0	108	100.0
Turnout %	56.0		67.4		60.3		74.4	

[a] Boycotted by some opposition parties.

Source: Federal Election Commission reports; Goati (2001b).

Chamber of Republics of the Federal Assembly

September 2000

Serbia	Votes	%	Seats	%
DOS	2,092,799	44.0	10	50
SPS–JUL	1,479,583	31.1	7	35
SRS	472,820	9.9	2	10
SPO	281,153	5.9	1	5
Total for Serbia		90.9	20	100

Note: Representatives for the Chamber of Republics of the FRY were elected directly for the first time in September 2000. The Chamber of Republics has 40 members, 20 from each republic.

Source: Federal Election Commission (2000); Goati (2001b).

Elections to the Parliament of Serbia and Montenegro

Date: 25 February 2003

Parliamentary caucus	Mandates in the SMN Assembly
DSS	17
DOS	37
SPS	12
SRS	8
SSJ	5
SDP (Social Democratic Party)	5
DA	2
DHSS	2
New Serbia	1
Srbija	1
SNS	1
Total	91

Note: Indirect elections based on Serbian parliamentary caucuses. Unicameral federal parliament, total 126 seats, 91 representatives from Serbia.

Source: *Glas javnosti*, 18 February 2003.

SERBIAN PRESIDENTIAL ELECTIONS

1990 elections

Date: 9 December

Turnout: 71.50%

Candidate (Party)	Votes	%
Slobodan Milošević (SPS)	3,285,799	65.34
Vuk Drašković (SPO)	824,674	16.40
Ivan Đurić (UJDI)	277,398	5.52
Sulejman Ugljanin (SDA)	109,456	2.18
Vojislav Šešelj (citizens' group)	96,277	1.91
Blažo Petrović (YU blok)	57,420	1.14
Slobodan Matić (*Savez svih Srba u svetu*)	28,978	0.58
Dragan Jovanović (*Zelena partija*)	22,458	0.45
Ljuben Aleksov (citizens' group)	19,123	0.38
Ljubomir Grujić (citizens' group)	17,675	0.35
Total	4,739,258	94.24

Source: Republican Election Commission (1990); Goati (2001b).

1992 elections

Date: 20 December

Turnout: 69.7%

Candidate (Party)	Votes	%
Slobodan Milošević (SPS)	2,515,047	53.24
Milan Panić (citizens' group)	1,516,693	32.11
Milan Paroški (People's Party and Serbian Opposition)	147,693	3.13
Dragan Vasiljković (citizens' group)	87,847	1.86
Jezdimir Vasiljević (citizens' group)	61,729	1.31
Miroslav Milanović (citizens' group)	28,010	0.59
Blažo Petrović (Democratic-Patriotic Coalition)	20,326	0.43
Total	4,377,345	92.66

Source: Goati (2001b).

1997 elections (failed)

Date: 21 September (first round) and 5 October (second round)

Turnout: 57.47% (first round), 48.97% (second round)

First round			Second round		
Candidate (Party)	Votes	%	Candidate (Party)	Votes	%
Zoran Lilić (SPS)	1,474,924	35.70	Zoran Lilić (SPS)	1,691,354	47.90
Vojislav Šešelj (SRS)	1,126,940	27.28	Vojislav Šešelj (SRS)	1,733,859	49.10
Vuk Drašković (SPO)	852,800	20.64			
Mile Isakov	111,156	2.69			
Vuk Obradović	100,523	2.43			
Nebojša Čović	93,133	2.25			
Sulejman Ugljanin	68,446	1.66			
Milan Paroški	27,100	0.66			
Milorad Vidojković	14,105	0.34			
Predrag Vuletić	11,463	0.28			
Dragan Đorđević	10,864	0.26			
Milan Mladenović	10,112	0.24			
Đorđe Drljača	9,430	0.23			
Branko Čičić	7,097	0.17			
Gvozden Sakić	3,293	0.08			
Radomir Tukmanović	2,647	0.06			

Source: Republican Election Commission (1997); Goati (2001b).

1997 elections, Second attempt

Date: 7 December (first round) and 21 December (second round)

Turnout: 52.75 % (first round), 53.47 (second round)

First round			Second round		
Candidate (Party)	Votes	%	Candidate (Party)	Votes	%
Milan Milutinović (SPS, JUL, ND)	1,655,822	43.44	Milan Milutinović (SPS, JUL, ND)	2,181,808	56.47
Vojislav Šešelj (SRS)	1,227,076	32.19	Vojislav Šešelj (SRS)	1,383,868	35.82
Vuk Drašković (SPO)	587,776	15.42			
Vuk Obradović (SDP)	115,850	3.04			
Dragoljub Mićunović (DC)	86,583	2.27			
Miodrag Vidojković (citizens' group)	29,180	0.77			
Miodrag Vuletić (LDS)	21,353	0.56			

Source: Republican Election Commission (1997); Goati (2002).

2002 elections (failed)

Date: 29 September (first round) and 13 October (second round)

Turnout: 55.50 % (first round), 45.31% (second round)

First round			Second round		
Candidate (Party)	Votes	%	Candidate (Party)	Votes	%
Vojislav Koštunica (DSS)	1,123,420	30.89	Vojislav Koštunica (DSS)	1,991,947	66.86
Miroljub Labus (citizens' group)	995,200	27.36	Miroljub Labus (citizens' group)	921,024	30.91
Vojislav Šešelj (SRS)	845,308	23.24			
Vuk Drašković (SPO)	159,959	4.40			
Borislav Pelević (SSJ)	139,047	3.82			
Velimir Živojinović (SPS)	119,052	3.27			

Source: http://www.cesid.org.

2002 II elections, second attempt (failed)

Date: 8 December

Turnout: 45.17%

Candidate (Party)	Votes	%
Vojislav Koštunica (DSS)	1,699,098	57.66
Vojislav Šešelj (SRS)	1,063,296	36.08
Borislav Pelević (SSJ)	103,926	3.53

Source: Republican Election Commission (via http://www.statserb.sr.gov.yu).

Elections for the President of FR Yugoslavia

2000 elections

Date: 24 September

Turnout: 71.55%

Candidate (Party)	Votes	%
Vojislav Koštunica (DOS)	2,470,304	50.24
Slobodan Milošević (SPS, JUL, SNP CG)	1,826,799	37.15
Vojislav Mihailović (SPO)	145,019	2.95
Tomislav Nikolić (SRS)	289,013	5.88
Miodrag Vidojković	45,964	0.93

Note: Boycotted by the ruling coalition in Montenegro.

Source: *Official Gazette of the FR Yugoslavia*, Vol. 9, No. 55, October 2000.

APPENDIX 14.2: GOVERNMENT COMPOSITION

Date	Prime minister	Government parties	Political orientation	Reason of termination
February, 1991	Dragutin Zelenović (SPS)	SPS (majority)	Communist	Premier resigned on 11 December 1991
December, 1991	Radoman Božović (SPS)	SPS (majority)	Communist	Elections of 1992
February, 1993	Nikola Šainović (SPS)	SPS (minority, with informal support from SRS)	Reformed communist	President of the Republic dissolved the parliament (20 October1993); new elections December 1993
March, 1994	Mirko Marjanović (SPS)	SPS, ND, DS	'Government of national unity'	Elections of 1997
March, 1998	Mirko Marjanović (SPS)	SPS, JUL, SRS (majority)	Authoritarian	Government resignation, 21 October 2000 (in fact regime change of 5 October: The 'political agreement' included the formation of a transitional government)
October, 2000	Milomir Minić (SPS) and Nebojša Čović (DOS)	SPS-DOS	Transitional government	Extraordinary elections, 23 December 2000
December, 2000	Zoran Đinđić (DS)	DOS (majority)	Reformist	Assassination of the Prime Minister, 12 March 2003
March, 2002	Zoran Živković (DS)	DOS without DSS (majority)	Reformist	

APPENDIX 14.3: THE ELECTORAL SYSTEM

Serbia

Parliament

The first pluralist election law was passed by the one party Assembly of the Socialist Republic of Serbia 1990, and was based on the two-round majoritarian principle. The system was changed in 1992 into a proportional system with nine electoral districts (increased to 29 in 1997) and a 5 per cent elimination quota on the constituency level.

The current system is based on the Law on the Elections of Representatives (*Official Gazette of the Republic of Serbia*, No. 35/2000) from October 2000. The National Assembly of the Republic of Serbia (*Narodna Skupština*) consists of 250 representatives, elected for a period of four years.

Elections for representatives are called by the President of the *Narodna Skupština*. Not less than 45 days, and no more than 90 days may pass between the day of calling for elections and the day of holding of elections.

The right to elect a representative, as well as to be elected as a representative, is given to legally competent citizens over the age of 18 residing on the territory of the Republic of Serbia. The Republic of Serbia forms a single electoral district, and representatives are elected on the basis of lists submitted by political parties, coalitions of parties, other political organizations or groups of citizens. An electoral list is confirmed when accompanied by the signatures of not less then 10,000 voters. Each electoral list is apportioned a number of mandates proportional to the number of votes it has gathered, provided that it meets the 5 per cent clause.

The mandates are apportioned according to the system of the largest quotient. The total number of votes received by each separate electoral list is divided by numbers from one to 250. The quotients thus arrived at are sorted by size, and the 250 largest quotients are taken into account. Each electoral list is apportioned a number of mandates corresponding to the number of quotients. If two or more electoral lists get the same quotient on the basis of which a mandate is to be apportioned, and there are no more mandates to be apportioned, the mandate is apportioned to the list which has received the overall largest number of votes.

The electoral law stipulates that the mandates belong to the parties or organizations that submitt the electoral lists. However, on May 28, 2003, the Constitutional Court found this provision unconstitutional and decided that the mandates belong to the electoral representatives.

Authorities responsible for conducting the elections are the Republican Electoral Commission and polling boards. The *Narodna Skupština* appoints a President and 16 permanent members of the Republican Electoral Commission; the organizations behind the various electoral lists are entitled to appoint on representative each for the sessions of the enlarged electoral commission. .

The municipalities keep the records of eligible voters. There have been serious controversies about their accuracy, especially in connection with the 2002 presidential elections.

President

According to the Law on Election of the President of the Republic of Serbia (passed in 1990, amended in 1992 and 2002) the President is directly elected, by secret voting, for a mandate of five years. The same person can be elected only twice.

The President of the *Narodna skupština* announces elections for the President of the Republic of Serbia. Any legally competent citizen of Serbia, above the age of 18, who has resided in Serbia for at least one year, may be nominated for President. Political parties and groups of citizens, may submit candidacies, provided that they collect at least 10,000 signatures for their respective candidates.

A candidate, polling an absolute majority, is considered elected if at least 50 per cent of the eligible voters have taken part in the election. If none of the candidates obtains an absolute majority, voting is repeated in a second round of elections within the next 15 days. The two candidates with the largest number of votes participate in the second round. If less than 50 per cent of the eligible voters cast their vote, the election is considered invalid, and repeated. The President of the *Narodna Skupština* has to announce repeated elections within 60 days, and the elections must be held no later than 90 days after the announcement. The President of the *Narodna*

Skupština performs the function of the president until a new president is elected (Article 87). The law was amended in the autumn 2002 when the 50 per cent turnout requirement was removed for the second round of elections (but retained for the first round).

Sources:
The Law on the Elections of Representatives, *Službeni glasnik Republike Srbije*, No. 35/2000.
The Law on Electing the President of the Republic, *Službeni glasnik RS*, No. 1/90, 79/92.
The Constitution of the Republic of Serbia, *Službeni glasnik RS*, No. 1/1990).
Politika, June 14, 2002, No. 31826.

The State Union of Serbia and Montenegro

The Parliament of the State Union of Serbia and Montenegro (SMN) is unicameral, consisting of 126 members, 91 coming from Serbia. For the first term of two years, the representatives were elected indirectly and proportionally (d'Hondt system) to the parliamentary caucuses in the republican parliaments. In the future, the representatives are to be elected directly for a term of four years. The President of the SMN is elected indirectly by the parliament, for a two-year term (four years subsequently) by majority vote, upon a proposal submitted by the Speaker and Deputy Speaker of the Parliament. If the Parliament fails to elect a President twice, the Parliament is dissolved and elections are called.

FR Yugoslavia (1992–2003)

Federal Parliament

The *Savezna Skupština* (Federal Assembly) consisted of two chambers: the *Veće Građana* (Council of Citizens; 138 members, 108 members elected in Serbia), and the *Veće Republika* (Council of the Republics; 40 members, 20 from each of the Republics).

Initially, elections for the *Veće Građana* were based on a mixed system (valid in May 1992; 60 members were elected in single-seat constituencies and 78 members by proportional representation). A proportional system has been in use since December 1992. The republican assemblies originally appointed the representatives of the *Veće Republika*, but direct elections were introduced in 2000 (Amendment 3). Until 2003, both chambers of the federal parliament were elected through proportional representation with a 5 per cent threshold at the constituency level in 27 constituencies. Serbia was divided into 26 constituencies, while Montenegro constituted a single constituency. In Serbia, typically 3 to 5 representatives were elected in a single constituency. The President of the FRY called elections for the federal parliament, both houses of which were elected for four-year terms.

In order to be considered valid, electoral lists had to be signed by a minimum of 1,000 voters in constituencies of up to one million voters, and by 2,500 voters in constituencies larger than one million of voters. The seats were apportioned according to the principle of the largest quotient. One third of the seats were assigned according to candidates' place on the electoral list, while two thirds were distributed according to preferences of the list submitter. Mandates could be assigned only to candidates on the list.

Federal President

Direct and secret elections for the Federal President were introduced by constitutional amendments in 2000. The term was four years, with the possibility of re-election (Amendment 5 of 2000 introduced the possibility of re-election).

Presidential candidates had to be above the age of 18, residents of Yugoslavia and holders of Yugoslavian citizenship for at least 10 years before the day of submitting the candidacy. Elections for the federal presidency were called by the *Veće građana* of the *Savezna skupština*. Political parties, other political organizations, or groups of citizens may nominate a candidate provided that the candidate enjoy the support of at least 25,000 voter signatures.

A candidate winning a majority of votes cast was considered elected. If none of the candidates obtained a majority, voting had to be repeated in a second round. The two candidates with the largest number of votes (or more candidates in the unlikely event of vote parity) could participate in the second round. No minimum turnout was required.

Sources:
Amandmani na Ustav Savezne republike Jugoslavije, *Službeni list SRJ*, No. 29, July 6, 2000.
Zakon o izboru i prestanku mandata Predsednika republike, *Službeni list SRJ*, No. 32, July 24, 2000.
Zakon o izboru saveznih poslanika u Veće građana Savezne skupštine, *Službeni list SRJ*, No. 57/93 and 32/2000.
Zakon o izboru saveznih poslanika u Veće republika Savezne skupštine, *Službeni list SRJ*, No. 32, July 24, 2000.
Zakon o izboru poslanika Skupštine Srbije i Crne Gore, *Službeni glasnik,* 10/03.

APPENDIX 14.4: THE CONSTITUTIONAL FRAMEWORK

Serbia

The contemporary constitution dates back to 28 September 1990. It was passed by the one-party Assembly of the Socialist Republic of Serbia, elected in 1989. Constitutional and legislative power belongs to the *Narodna Skupština* (National Assembly). The President represents the Republic and symbolizes state unity. Executive power belongs to the Government, while judicial power belongs to the courts. The Constitutional Court assesses the constitutionality of laws and the constitutionality and legality of regulations and other general enactments.

The *Narodna Skupština* is entitled to schedule referenda; to elect the President and the Vice-President of the *Narodna Skupština*; to elect the President, Vice-Presidents and Ministers of the Government; to elect the President and Justices of the Constitutional Court, Supreme Court and other courts; and to elect the Republican Public Prosecutor and Public Prosecutors; to appoint the Governor of the National Bank. The President of the *Narodna Skupština* represents it in the country and abroad, and calls parliamentary and presidential elections. Citizens are also entitled to propose laws, if they have the backing of 15,000 citizens. Constitutional changes require a two-thirds majority in parliament, and subsequent confirmation in a referendum. Referenda may also be initiated by the public, if the request is supported by 100,000 voters.

The President of the Republic of Serbia (Article 83) nominates a candidate for the position as Prime Minister and candidates for the positions as President and Justices of the Constitutional Court; proclaims laws by decree, and handles the foreign relations of the Republic of Serbia. The President is Head of the Armed Forces in war and peace, and orders general and partial mobilization. The Presidents of the Republics and the President of the FRY are automatically members of the Defence Council. The President can return a law to parliament for reconsideration, but if the law is passed for the second time, it must be promulgated. A two-thirds majority can overrule a presidential veto.

The *Narodna Skupština* can initiate recall proceedings in the event that the President is in violation of the constitution, but only if recall enjoys the support of two thirds of the elected representatives. The President may also be recalled, if more than 50 per cent of the voters vote for recall. If initiated recall proceedings fail, the *Narodna Skupština* is dissolved.

Upon the proposal of the Government, the President of the Republic may dissolve the *Narodna Skupština*. With the dissolution of the *Narodna Skupština*, the Government's mandate is also terminated. In the event of the dissolution of the *Narodna Skupština*, the election for a new *Narodna Skupština* must be held within 60 days of its dissolution. The *Narodna Skupština* may not be dissolved during a state of war, an immediate threat of war or a state of emergency. The *Narodna Skupština* may express no confidence in the Government or in any of its members. A proposal for a no confidence vote must be submitted by at least 20 representatives.

The Republic of Serbia includes two Autonomous Provinces – Kosovo and Vojvodina.

The State Union of Serbia and Montenegro

The State Union of Serbia and Montenegro (SMN) was established on 4 February 2003, by adoption of the Constitutional Charter of the SMN. The SMN is defined as a federal state consisting of two states, Serbia and Montenegro. The unicameral Parliament of the SMN consists of 126 members, of whom 91 come from Serbia and 35 from Montenegro. For the first term of two years, the representatives were elected indirectly and proportionally to the parliamentary caucuses in the republican parliaments. The Charter stipulates that member states have the right to initiate proceedings for terminating the state union after the expiry of a three-year period. If the union continues to exist, the representatives will be elected directly for a term of four years. Parliament makes decision by majority vote, provided that the decision gains the approval of parliamentary majorities in the two member states.

The President of the SMN represents the SMN at home and abroad, chairs the Council of Ministers and runs its activities, nominates candidates for the Council of Ministers, sits on the Supreme Defence Council, proclaims laws passed by the Parliament of the SMN and decrees, adopted by the Council of Ministers, and calls elections for the Parliament of the SMN.

The President is elected for a four-year term, upon proposal submitted by the Speaker and Deputy Speaker of the Parliament. If the Parliament fails to elect a President twice, the Parliament is dissolved and new elections are called. The President of the SMN cannot come from the same member state twice in succession, and is accountable to the Parliament. The Parliament may remove the President if he/she has been found to be in breach of the Constitutional Charter.

The Supreme Defence Council acts as Commander-in-Chief of the Armed Forces of the SMN; it includes the President of the SMN and the presidents of the member states. The Supreme Defence Council takes decisions by consensus.

Executive power is in the hands of the Council of Ministers, headed by the President of the SMN. The Council of Ministers takes decisions by majority vote. In the event of an equal number of votes, the casting vote belongs to the President, provided that at least one minister from the other member state votes in favour of the decision. Ministers are elected for a four-year term, on a list, i.e., not individually. The Council includes the following ministers: the Minister of Foreign Affairs, the Minister of Defence (after a period of two years, these ministers have to switch posts with their respective deputies, each coming from another member state than the minister), the Minister for International Economic Cooperation, the Minister for Internal Economic Cooperation, and the Minister for Human and Minority Rights.

Judiciary power is administered through the Court of Serbia and Montenegro, which has an equal number of judges from both member states. The justices are elected for a six-year period by the Parliament of Serbia and Montenegro upon the proposal of the Council of Ministers.

FR Yugoslavia (1992–2003)

The Federal Republic of Yugoslavia (FRY) was established on 27 April 1992. The FRY Constitution was promulgated by the former federal parliament that consisted of representatives of the two republics, Serbia and Montenegro. FRY was defined as a federal state, composed of two federal units, Serbia and Montenegro.

The Federal Assembly was the highest representative and legislative body of the federation. The bicameral assembly comprised the Chamber of Citizens and the Chamber of Republics. The 138-member Chamber of Citizens represented the citizens of Yugoslavia. There were 65,000 voters to every deputy, but each republic was entitled to a minimum of 30 deputies (Article 80). The latter proviso was basically designed for the benefit of Montenegro, the smaller of the two republics. It ensured that the Chamber of Citizens always included 108 deputies from Serbia and 30 Montenegrin deputies.

The Chamber of Republics consisted of 20 representatives from each republic, representing the interests of the federal units within the federation. The Federal Assembly made decisions in a bicameral procedure, which meant that all decisions had to be harmonized between the two chambers.

Executive power was in the hands of the President of the Republic and the Federal Government. Until 2000, the Federal Government elected the President of the Republic, but the constitutional amendments paved the way for direct elections. The President could be recalled by a two-thirds majority vote in the Federal Assembly, if the Federal Constitutional Court found that he/she violated the Constitution.

The Federal Government was elected by the Federal Assembly, and formed by a candidate nominated by the President of the Republic. The President of the Republic and the Prime Minister had to be from different republics. Furthermore, the number of ministers from the two republics had to be strictly proportionate. The Federal Government performed the executive power falling in the domain of federal competence, and was responsible to the Federal Assembly. A vote of no confidence in the Federal Government required a majority in both chambers, and the initiative by no fewer than 20 federal deputies of one chamber of the Federal Assembly. The Federal Assembly could be dissolved at the request of the federal government.

The Federation administered judiciary powers through the Federal Court, the Federal Attorney General and the Federal Constitutional Court. The Justices of the Federal Court were appointed (for nine-year terms) and dismissed by the Federal Assembly.

Sources:
The Constitution of the Republic of Serbia, *Službeni glasnik Republike Srbije*, No. 1/1990. (English language version available on: http://www.parlament.sr.gov.yu/english/Acts.htm)
The Constitution of the Federal Republic of Yugoslavia.
Amandmani na ustav Savezne republike Jugoslavije, *Službeni list SRJ*, No. 29, 6 July, 2000.

The Constitutional Charter of the State Union of Serbia and Montenegro; The Law on the Implementation of the Constitutional Charter of the State Union of Serbia and Montenegro (accessible via http://www.mfa.gov.yu/).

APPENDIX 14.5: SPECIFICATIONS

Variables used in 1996 and 2002 multivariate models

Ideological dimensions, 1996 survey

Ideological dimension	Number of items	Alpha	Items
Liberalism	5	0.81	Private ownership and free enterprise necessary for economy.
			Freedom of individual expression necessary for political life.
			Freedom more important than equality.
			Private ownership is guarantee of freedom.
			Private interests more important than group interests...
Authoritarianism	8	0.90	The purpose of the police is to control opponents...
			Government should control universities.
			Citizens who misbehaved abroad should be deprived of a passport.
			Children and youth should not be allowed to express disobedience.
			Without a leader every nation is like a man without a head.
			Young people need strict discipline.
			Citizens should behave according to instructions from above...
			We should follow our leaders.
Workers' participation	4	0.70	Participation in management would stimulate employees to work better.
			If everyone were allowed to participate in management ... this would cause more harm than good.
			Workers not capable of management.
			Participation in management would stimulate faithfulness...
Democratic orientation	3		Democracy is dangerous.
			Majorities are entitled sometimes to deny some right to minorities.
			Democracy may have weaknesses, but is still better than other forms of government.
Nationalism	8	0.85	Different nationalities can live together in one state.
			National minorities should be given all the rights...
			Serbs should have priority in getting a job.
			Every nationality should preserve its ethnic purity...
			Openness toward the world brings harm.
			We should be careful in dealing with other nationalities...
			Mixed marriages are doomed to failure.
			It is essential for every nation to be open.

International integration	3		In favour of joining the EU.
			Attitude towards EU.
			In favour of joining the 'Partnership for Peace'.
Media censorship	4	0.36	Published material should never be banned for political reasons.
			Media should have more consideration for those who do not want to hear bad news.
			Censorship of films and magazines...
			Private media are more objective.

Note: Reliability not calculated for scales with less than four items.

Representative items included in the ideological dimensions, 2002 survey

Ideological dimension	Number of items	Alpha	Sample items
International integration	4	0.73	We should welcome openings of international companies, banks and other firms in Yugoslavia.
			Yugoslavia's future is joining the EU.
			The Western world is ready to accept and help democratic Serbia and Yugoslavia.
Nationalism	11	0.85	Serbs should be proud of their people.
			There are few nations that contributed to the world's culture and science as ours.
			No nation has such a glorious and at the same time tragic history as the Serbs.
Militarism	4	0.82	More money from the budget should be devoted to modernizing our army.
			It is a great honour to serve in our army.
			Strong army is the only guarantee of our security.
Socialism	6	0.60	For workers it is better to be employed in state-owned firms, than in private or privatized companies.
			The state should provide jobs to everybody who wants to work.
Authoritarianism	10	0.84	The most important virtues a child has to learn are obedience and respect for authority.
			All true patriots are obliged to take measures against those condemned by the leaders of the country.
			Young people need strict regulations and determination to fight for their families and their country.
Economic liberalism	8	0.52	Every individual has to take care of him/herself and it is no state business to worry about individual welfare.
			The state ought to be involved in economy as little as possible.
Clericalism	3	0.76	The role of the Serbian Orthodox Church should be increased in managing the country's matters.
			Religious teaching should be compulsory, not only an optional course in all elementary and secondary schools.

Tradition-alism	4	0.69	Sexual relationships between people of the same sex are always wrong.
			There are certain life-styles the state (law) should not allow, such as for example, smoking of marijuana, religious sects, and homosexual relations.
			Television should support more the nation's traditions.
Punitiveness	4	0.50	The problem of crime cannot be solved without harsher punishments for criminals.
			The death penalty is the best punishment for the worst criminals.
Environmen-talism	4	0.53	There are more important problems the state should care about than environmental pollution.
			It is more important to preserve and improve nature than to achieve economic development.
Feminism	2		Sexual discrimination is not a serious problem in contemporary Yugoslavia.
			Women should organize politically in order to fight against sexual discrimination.
Elitism	3		In this life, it is important to rise above other, ordinary people.
			No amount of education can make up for the wrong breeding.
			Great art is not meant for common folks.

Note: Reliability not calculated for scales with less than four items.

15. Moldova

William Crowther and Yuri Josanu

This chapter sets out to analyse the first decade of Moldova's post-communist transition, exploring the role that social cleavages have played in shaping the course of events. The argument will be advanced that the Moldovan transition, particularly in the immediate post-Soviet years, was crucially influenced by deep seated social divisions deriving from the ethno-linguistic structure of the republic, national identity issues, and by sharp political divisions centring on the pace and direction of reform. The Moldovan transition was also increasingly influenced as the transition progressed by the character of elite politics, and by institutional factors.

The chapter begins by examining the historical context of the Moldovan transition, assessing the impact of both the pre-communist and communist periods. This examination focuses on the ethnic composition of the region, and on the role of ethnic mobilization in the movement for independence. While relations between the diverse populations that inhabit Moldova have on the whole been positive, substantial strains developed in the course of the Soviet period, and these played a defining role in the transition. A second legacy of the past that clearly affected the course of the transition was a deep division within the Romanian-speaking population of the republic regarding national identity. While a committed minority among this population identified as 'Romanian' and worked for unification with the Romanian state, the majority gravitated toward Moldovan identification and political independence. The conflict between these divergent cultural strains was crucial to the course of the transition.

Pre-Soviet and Soviet Moldova

The history of the Moldova is inextricably intertwined with that of Romania. Like the Romanians, the Moldovans trace their own origin to the period from approximately 105–207 AD, when Roman colonists settled the region. A short-lived independent principality including the territory of the present

Republic of Moldova was established in the mid-14th century. Moldova re-emerged as an independent political actor only in the 20th century. In the intervening years Moldova's identity was closely tied to that of the Romanian-speakers to its west. Over the years, however, differences did emerge between eastern and western Romanian-speaking populations, in part as a consequence of externally determined political divisions. The bulk of current Moldova, Bessarabia, was annexed by Russia following the Russo–Turkish war of 1806–1812.[1] During the period of Imperial Russian control, Tsarist authorities encouraged immigration. The colonists included Russians, Ukrainians, Bulgarians, and Gagauz from the Balkan Peninsula. Moldovan cities became very diverse ethnically, as did some rural zones. The most concentrated ethnic Romanian population was found in the central region, while large numbers of Ukrainian and Russian villages were established in the north and east, and Gagauz and Bulgarian in the south.

Bessarabia was reunited with Romania as a consequence of the Russian revolution, but, despite the high hopes of nationalists, the inclusion in 'Greater Romania' did not result in substantial progress for Moldova. Administrators from Bucharest did little to improve economic conditions, and generated substantial local hostility. Assimilationist policies on the part of the majority created a legacy of antipathy toward Romania that continues to play a role in Moldovan politics today.

Rather than simply accepting the loss of Bessarabia as a *fait accompli*, the new Soviet government established an alternative Moldovan administrative entity, in October 1924, which could serve as a basis for forwarding claims to the entire territory. This Moldovan Autonomous Soviet Socialist Republic (MASSR), whose capital was Tiraspol, encompassed 14 districts (*raions*) on the east bank of the Dniestr river and was administered as part of Ukraine.

Along with the Baltic republics, Bessarabia was among those territories annexed by the USSR as a consequence of the Ribbentrop–Molotov pact. Its forced re-incorporation into the USSR was traumatic. Agriculture was collectivized, and large numbers of 'kulaks' were deported.[2] Many educated ethnic-Romanians migrated to Romania proper. This, along with a population influx from other parts of the USSR, substantially altered the character of the republic's population. Non-Moldovans' presence in the urban economy was reinforced, leaving Moldovans in less skilled and less highly paid urban occupations and in the agricultural sector. As of 1970 Moldovans made up only 35 per cent of the republic's urban population, while 28.8 per cent was comprised of Russians, and another 19.6 per cent was Ukrainian.[3] Towards the end of the Soviet period, the trend toward 'Russification' of the urban population reversed itself. The last Soviet census (1989) indicated that the Romanian-speaking proportion of the urban population had increased to 46 per cent, while Russians declined to 23.4 per cent (Nedelciuc 1992, 16). The perception of inequality, however, remained strong among Moldovans.

Soviet culture policy was also a source of hostility in Moldova, which presented a particular problem because of its separation from Romania. Responding to this issue, Soviet authorities put forward the argument that the Romanians and Moldovans were two separate and distinct nations. While some historical basis exists to support the view that 'Moldovan' identity is distinct from that of Romania, the artificiality of Soviet efforts to differentiate the two populations became the basis of substantial popular resentment.[4]

Moldovan economic development did not fare well under Soviet administration. Even relative to the rest of the former USSR, the republic remained a 'backward' region. In the early 1980s Moldova produced lower income per capita than any other non-central Asian republic. Not entirely surprising given the political culture of the Balkan region, Moldova also suffered from extreme corruption. During the Brezhnev period, Moldovan Communist Party First Secretary (and Brezhnev crony) Ivan Ivanovich Bodyul presided over an administration that is said to have siphoned off millions of roubles. Bodyul's successor as leader of the Communist Party of Moldova, Simion K. Grossu (the last of the pre-Gorbachev republican First Secretaries to be removed), assumed the rhetoric of *perestroika* and *glasnost* when pressured to do so by the Gorbachev leadership, but acted purposefully to resist restructuring and to marginalize reform proponents in the republic.

Thus on the eve of the transition from communism, Moldova suffered poor economic development, serious ethnic divisions within the population, and a very wide gap separating the population as a whole and the entrenched Soviet era political elite. Further, Moldova had no history of pre-Soviet national level democratic institutions to fall back upon. Its inter-war political life was focused on Bucharest, and provided little useful guidance in developing sovereign institutions.

As in a number of other former republics of the USSR, serious opposition to the Soviet regime began to crystallize in the context of elections to the All Union Congress of Peoples Deputies in the spring of 1989. Despite the formally democratic nature of the rules imposed by Moscow, the Moldovan Party establishment was easily able to manipulate the campaign process and win a large majority of seats. However, the electoral process itself was extremely useful to members of the nascent opposition, who employed the relative security conferred by the status of official candidate to publicize their reform message. Furthermore, the electoral victory of a handful of highly visible opposition leaders proved critical in succeeding months by providing a channel of communication to moderates within the Communist Party.[5] Attesting to the changes in political environment, in early June 1989 official recognition was extended to the Popular Front of Moldova, which held its first public meeting (attended by wavering Party and state representatives) on 11 June 1989 (*Moldova Socialistă*, 13 June 1989, 4).

In their efforts to attract mass support, opposition leaders focused on the highly charged language issue. The republic's language laws mandated that Russian serve as the language of public communication and that Moldovan be written in Cyrillic script. On 27 August 1989 activists organized a mass demonstration in order to bring pressure on the government to undertake reform. In a concession that marked the beginning of the end of Communist power, on 31 August 1989, the republic's Supreme Soviet revised the state language law. Having achieved this concession the Moldovan Popular Front became increasingly assertive.[6]

While expedient in the short run, playing the language issue had a price tag attached to it in terms of undermining popular unity. The heavily nationalist appeal of the anti-Soviet opposition almost instantaneously generated a sharp increase in inter-ethnic conflict.[7] Faced with the prospect of dominance by the Romanian-speaking majority, many Russian-speaking inhabitants of the republic gravitated toward *Edinstvo*. This pro-Soviet mass movement, with its strongest base of support in the industrial cities on the east bank of the Dniestr river, became the main political vehicle of the russophone population. A second anti-Romanian movement, *Gagauz-Halki*, representing Moldova's Gagauz minority in the south, aligned itself with the Russian minority, and demanded that the districts where the Gagauz population is concentrated should be granted autonomy.

The 1990 campaign for the republican legislature was opened within this context of heightened political mobilization. This election, like similar contests in other former Soviet republics, is better understood as a bridge to the post-Communist era rather than as a founding democratic election. The law governing the election provided for quite substantial competition. Opposition candidates were able to campaign actively, and were provided with space in official newspapers. Moldova's most prestigious cultural journal, *Literatura și Artă*, published the Popular Front's electoral platform, which called for full sovereignty, demilitarization, private property, a free market, and political pluralism.[8] In the context of the campaign an alliance began to take shape between Communist Party moderates and the Popular Front. The candidacies of many Communist Party moderates seeking an alternative to communist party affiliation were officially endorsed by the Popular Front. Among these was Mircea Snegur, a Central Committee Secretary since 1985, who was appointed President of the Moldovan Supreme Soviet in July 1989. By early 1990, he had clearly associated himself with the Popular Front and its political programme.

While the 1990 campaign focused in part on issues of political and economic reform, given the divisions existing in the republic it very quickly took on a strongly ethnic character. The Popular Front emerged as the political vehicle of the Romanian-speaking majority, and benefited from heightened ethnic mobilization. Approximately one third of deputies elected to the republican Supreme Soviet were Popular Front members.[9] With the support of allies among the deputies of the Communist Party, the Popular Front was able to command a majority of the votes in the new legislature. The 1990 election thus fundamentally altered the political landscape of the republic. Mircea Snegur, still a Communist, was named President of the Supreme Soviet. Critically, the avowedly Pro-Romanian Popular Front leader Mircea Druc was appointed Prime Minister. Under the influence of Druc and other nationalists among the Popular Front leaders, the legislature introduced a series of extremely divisive measures, which heightened the growing anxiety of the Russian-speaking minorities.[10]

The process of anti-Soviet mobilization that preceded the dissolution of the USSR thus reinforced the ethnic cleavage that was already extant in the Republic. Once initiated, inter-ethnic hostility quickly took on a life of its own. The more extremist faction of the Popular Front became increasingly open and aggressive in its pursuit of power, hastening the descent into violence. Radical Front leaders orchestrated a succession of street demonstrations in central Chişinău designed to intimidate their opponents. In protest, 100 opposition deputies withdrew from the Supreme Soviet citing fears about their personal safety. In localities where Russian-speakers comprised a majority, city and district authorities began to set up independent political instiutions. Local governments in the cities of Tiraspol, Bender (*Tighina*), and *Ribniţa* all passed laws suspending application of central government edicts within their administrative limits.[11] The Gagauz minority went even further, announcing the formation of their own republic in the southern region on 21 August 1990. Local Communist leaders in the region on the eastern bank of the Dniestr river (Transdniestria) followed suit, declaring the formation of the Transdniestrian Moldovan Soviet Socialist Republic.

The divisions generated by the early transition were solidified by the August coup in Moscow. President Snegur and the Chişinău government denounced the coup and declared independence on 27 August 1991. Separatist leaders followed the opposite course with equal vigour, first declaring for the coup plotters, then reasserting their independence from the new Republic of Moldova.

Post-Soviet Moldova

The transition from Soviet rule in Moldova produced a complex network of competing interests and no clear victor. On the popular level, ethnic divisions were evident, but so were strains of conflict between those favouring political and economic reform on the one hand, and those committed to resisting it on the other.[12]

The ethnic communities of the republic were deeply divided on a wide range of minority issues. Three times more Russians and Ukrainians than Moldovans believed that minority rights were not being protected. Other issues related to minority/majority relations bear out this picture of sharp differentiation.[13] The Romanian- and Russian-speaking communities were equally divided on fundamental questions of sovereignty and statehood. While nearly 70 per cent of Romanian speakers wanted complete national independence in 1992, only 31 per cent of Ukrainians and 51 per cent of Russians agreed. 56 per cent of Ukrainians and 40 per cent of Russians wanted to participate in the Commonwealth of Independent States (CIS); only 12 per cent of Romanian speakers supported this outcome (*Figure 15.1*).[14]

Figure 15.1: Preferred international orientation by ethnicity (major groups)

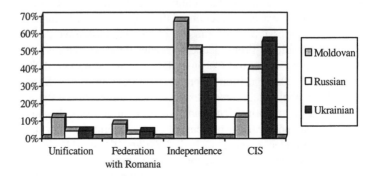

A very different picture appears when attention is shifted to reform issues. Social divisions on reform were substantially less overall, and coincide much less with ethnic divisions. In general, the Moldovan population was highly cautious with regard to change in the early 1990s. While a majority of the population favoured reform in principle, in 1992, less than 10 per cent of the population favoured complete privatization of industrial property, and approximately half favoured retaining state ownership intact.[15] Despite their characterization as supporters of the successor communists, in fact ethnic Russians expressed a slightly more reformist disposition than Moldovans (see *Figure 15.2*). Analysis bears out the fact that, unlike other social cleavages (urban/rural residence and social status), ethnicity did not have a strong impact on attitudes towards reform policy. In other domains, however, ethnicity was clearly a crucial determinant of attitudes.[16]

Questions regarding national identity did not just separate ethnic groups; they also divided the Romanian-speaking majority. Despite the pan-Romanian convictions of many Popular Front leaders, the self-identification of Romanian-speakers in Moldova was overwhelmingly 'Moldovan' (87.5 per cent) as opposed to Romanian (12.5 per cent).[17] Romanian-speakers thus in a sense felt 'Moldovan' rather than 'Romanian', even at the outset of the new state's independence. The strongly pro-Romanian Popular Front therefore failed to inspire broad popular support even at a time when inter-ethnic conflict was relatively intense. Only approximately 15 per cent of Moldovans would express 'much confidence' or 'very much confidence' in the Popular Front, and only 12.2 per cent supported unification with Romania.

Figure 15.2: Necessity of reform by ethnicity (main groups) 1992

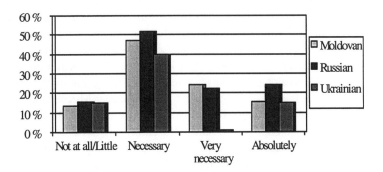

These data testify to the extent of the differences separating Moldova's ethnic communities, and to the tactical difficulties confronting moderate leaders as long as political discourse focused on inter-ethnic issues. But the data also provided some basis for optimism, in that public opinion on reform crosscut rather than reinforced ethnic lines and clearly provided the basis for a non-ethnic appeal, if the salience of the ethnic cleavage could be reduced. This distribution of popular attitudes was crucial in establishing the parameters within which elite factions competed for political power.

The newly emerging political elite was similarly fragmented. Moldova suffered from the absence of any coherent opposition. Nothing of the sort of cohesive alternative political structure produced by the decade-long Solidarity movement in Poland was in evidence, and with the effectiveness of Soviet era institutions eroding, Moldovan politics became increasingly disordered. Competition for power was carried out in an environment of escalating social crisis. As elsewhere in the former Soviet Union, during the first phase of the transition the economy experienced a massive decline. In part this was an inevitable result of the generalized failure of the Soviet economy. The decline of Moldova's traditional agricultural export market into Russia badly hurt the rural sector. Simultaneously, the secession of the territory on the left bank of the Dneistr, the Transdniestrian dispute, dislocated industrial production throughout the entire republic. But Moldova's economic decline was also a consequence of the new leaders' failure to provide any clear policy direction, and the new government's general administrative disorganization. As the economic crisis deepened (GDP declined by approximately 14 per cent in

1991), the government vacillated, unable to produce a comprehensive reform policy. Further complicating the situation, Prime Minister Druc himself came under intense scrutiny for questionable financial dealings. In this context, pro-reform and anti-reform factions proposed radically different policy directions.

The role of ethnic conflict in the competition for leadership control was also evident. Clearly, escalation benefited radicals within the Popular Front, many of whom favoured reunification with Romania and the construction of a single 'Greater Romanian' state. The greater the level of conflict, the greater was their influence within the Romanian-speaking majority. Just as clearly, moderates (mostly drawn from among the former Communists) recognized their vulnerability, and acted to achieve consensus between the majority and minority communities. Mircea Snegur, a key figure in the reformist camp achieved a first step along the course of reorienting the government in May 1991 by replacing the intensely nationalist Prime Minister Mircea Druc with the more moderate Valeriu Muravschi. Druc's dismissal was followed by a number of confidence-building measures. The citizenship law of 5 June 1991, for example, gave citizenship rights to everyone who lived in Moldova before Soviet occupation in 1940, all those who resided in the territory at independence, or who had at least one parent who was born there. In an effort to establish a power base independent of the Popular Front legislators, Snegur cast himself in the role of a moderate advocate of efficient reform. He successfully argued for direct presidential elections in order to clarify the leadership situation, and was confirmed in the office of President through a December 1991 election, in which he ran unopposed.[18] The nationalist faction thus lost the ability to dominate policy unilaterally, but the Popular Front remained a powerful force within the legislature.

In Tiraspol few signs of such moderating tendencies were evident. On the contrary, under the leadership of Transdniestrian President Igor Smirnov, the separatist regime moved in an increasingly aggressive direction. The Transdniestrians were quick to build bridges to nationalists in Moscow, through which they recruited volunteers, and sought to influence Russian political and military leaders.[19] Moscow provided access to an alternative financial infrastructure that minimized the impact of the secession. Links between Russian industry and Transdniestria assured enterprises in the breakaway region of markets and access to raw materials.[20] The Smirnov leadership's increasing intransigence, and conflict between the two sides over control of the city of Bender, led to a major escalation of the conflict in 1992. When Moldovan forces threatened to gain the upper hand, Russia's 14th Army forces intervened decisively on the side of the separatists.

Moldovans' discontent with the war and the stalemate that ensued provided a crucial opening for ethnic moderates within the Romanian-speaking elite. Rallying support from among the ranks of former communists, Moldova's penultimate Communist Party leader, Petru Lucinschi, began to make his way back into power, assuming the post of Ambassador to Russia. A second prominent former communist, Andrei Sangheli, assumed the Prime Ministership in June 1992.[21] Sangheli's government immediately distanced itself from the policies of the Popular Front. Sangheli increased russophone representation in the government and pursued a strategy based on reducing inter-ethnic tensions. He and his colleagues also promised (but notably did not deliver) a more efficient economic reform programme.

Sangheli's government, working with the equally accommodating President Snegur, was in fact able to reduce significantly the level of ethnic hostility in the area under its control. Seeing their support wane and their policies reversed, the remaining Popular Front MPs pursued a course of obstructionism in parliament. Rather than serving their cause, these parliamentarians merely provided their enemies with the opportunity to accuse them of responsibility for the country's deepening economic plight. Adding to the general misery, severe droughts occurred in both 1992 and 1994. Agricultural output is estimated to have declined 33 per cent between 1989 and 1993, and World Bank estimates put Gross Domestic Product loss at 21 per cent in 1992 (*The World Bank* 1994, 5). When Alexandru Moşanu, the pro-Popular Front President of the Parliament, offered his resignation in protest against the changing direction of politics, former First Secretary Petru Lucinschi immediately took advantage of the opening provided, returning from Moscow to assume leadership of the parliament (*Moldova Suverana*, 6 February 1993, 1).

President Snegur, Prime Minister Sangheli, and Lucinschi (former colleagues on the CPM Politburo) took little time in reaching the conclusion that the sitting legislature was no longer viable. The Agrarian Democratic parliamentary faction, formed in great part from among Romanian-speaking members of the former Communist Party's rural apparatus, orchestrated a parliamentary vote calling for the dissolution of the legislature. New elections were called for 27 February 1994. The restructuring of the republican leadership and the decision to call new elections reflected a critical realignment. The moderates' success in regaining control of the state resulted in part from their greater experience and ability to turn political opinion to their own advantage. Their decision to risk elections was necessitated in part by the relatively strong institutional role played by the Moldovan legislature, and in part by the logic of intra-elite competition. In contrast to the experience of many former Soviet republics, Moldova's executive assumed a relatively weak stance in comparison to an active legislature. This outcome was in large part determined by President Snegur's early political isolation. His break with the Popular Front left Snegur without a secure base of parliamentary support. Nor could he count upon unchallenged control over his own executive branch, many of whose members were under the influence of their former leaders in the Agrarian and Socialist parties. As the transition progressed, divisions among Romanian-speakers over the identity issue led to fragmentation of the majority in the parliament, leaving in its wake a legislative vacuum. President Snegur threw his weight behind the ethnically moderate, though reform averse, Agrarians as they sought to develop a new and more effective legislative coalition.

Entering the campaign, the Agrarians enjoyed substantial advantages over their competitors. As in most other post-communist countries, party structures were generally weak in Moldova. Little organization existed outside of the legislature and a limited popular base in the capital. As elsewhere, deputies did little to maintain contact with constituents. Parties in parliament lacked discipline and were subject to continuous fragmentation. The Agrarians, however, were initially able to maintain a remarkable degree of cohesion. Their success is attributable to a variety of factors: the Agrarian deputies were, for the most part, associated with the agricultural sector, having served either as village mayors or collective farm managers. In addition to a common ideological perspective, they shared mutual interests with respect to questions of reform and resource allocation. They enjoyed a powerful base in the Ministry of Agriculture, which served to coordinate their activities, and provided a sizeable reserve of resources that could be used to sway supporters in rural constituencies.

In contrast to Agrarian consolidation, the Popular Front forces progressively broke apart. Moderate supporters of the cause, distressed with the increasingly provocative agenda of the militant leadership, defected to form an alternative electoral vehicle, the 'Congress of Intellectuals'. Similarly, those concerned primarily with reform were discouraged by the Popular Front's failure to pursue an effective economic policy, and established independent centre-right parties promoting their agendas. Thus entering the campaign for the second legislative elections, the Popular Front's parliamentary representation was reduced to only 25 deputies.

The rules governing the 1994 legislative elections called for a dramatically smaller legislature (104 as opposed to 380 deputies). A closed list proportional representation system was employed in the election. In order to avoid any impasse concerning representation from Transdniestria and the Gagauz region, the legislature established a single national electoral district.[22] The campaign focused on alterative approaches to the separatist crisis, and on economic reform. On the left, the Socialist Party and the Agrarian Democrats called for cautious reform, social protection, and a slow transition to market capitalism. These parties also favoured close relations with the Russian Republic, full participation in the Confederation of Independent States, and a conciliatory approach to both majority/minority relations and the separatist crisis. At the opposite ideological extreme, the Popular Front and the National Christian Party argued for unification with Romania. Moderates within the Romanian-speaking community, most of whom rallied to the Congress of

Intellectuals, campaigned for Moldovan independence in the near term but held to the long-range goal of unification. In addition to this primary competition, several small liberal parties, mostly supported by urban professionals, campaigned for rapid marketization and privatization.

The 1994 campaign appears to have been fairly contested for the most part. Some complaints were lodged, primarily by members of the pan-Romanian parties, who protested that they were subjected to harassment. Complaints focused in particular on the rural constituencies where Agrarian support was strongest. While some irregularities undoubtedly did occur, the weak showing of the Romanian nationalist parties outside of urban areas was largely a consequence of poor organization outside of the cities and the limited appeal of pan-Romanianism to rural voters. In the breakaway Gagauz region voting took place without disruption. Transdniestrian leaders, on the other hand, refused to allow any polling places to be set up in their territory, but did permit those who wished to cross into Bessarabia to participate. International observers concluded that the elections were 'open and fair', and there appears to be no reason to conclude that fraud or coercion played a decisive role in the result.

Moldova's first truly democratic legislative election reflected the sharp reversal that had occurred since independence (see *Appendix 15.1*). Turnout was heavy, with 79.31 per cent of registered voters participating (International Foundation for Electoral Systems 1994, 3–5). The most significant outcome was rejection of the parties identified with 'pan-Romanianism' in favour of those supporting Moldovan identity and ethnic accommodation. The Agrarian Democrats won 43.2 per cent of the vote and were awarded 56 of the 104 seats in the new parliament. The Socialist Bloc (the Socialist Party and *Edinstvo*) captured 22 per cent of the vote and 28 seats. The geographic pattern of the vote indicates a great deal about the character of Moldovan politics in the mid-1990s. The Socialist Bloc dominated the urban vote, taking first place in five out of Moldova's seven cities. In essence, these parties did well where industrial workers and Russian-speakers were concentrated. The Agrarian Democrats, on the other hand, won in all of the rural districts and in the two cities not won by the Socialists.[23] The pan-Romanian nationalists suffered massive reversal. The Bloc of Peasants and Intellectuals (the electoral vehicle of the Congress of Intellectuals) did best, winning 9.2 per cent of the vote and 11 seats. The Popular Front took only 7.5 per cent of the vote and was reduced to nine seats in parliament. Neither the strongly pro-reform Social Democratic Party nor the main parties of the emerging managerial interests, the Democratic Labour Party and the Party of Reform, gained sufficient votes to enter parliament.

The 1994 parliamentary election reinforced the preceding elite realignment. It is fair to conclude that a considerable part of the explanation for both resulted from the positioning of competing elite factions in relation to potential constituents on salient issue cleavages in the society. This conclusion is sustained by analysis of the issue positions taken by members of parliament in relation to the distribution of attitudes within the general population (Crowther 1997a). Examination of the attitudes of MPs and the general population indicates both the existence of clear divergence of opinion among political elites and a systematic relationship between public opinion and party support. With respect to economic reform, differences separate the more collectivist Agrarian and the Socialist Parties from Popular Front legislators. On attitudes toward minorities, differences separate all three parties, with the Popular Front occupying the most extreme nationalist position, the Socialists holding views supportive of non-Romanian-speaking minorities, and the Agrarians falling approximately between the extremes. Mass attitudes on these issues were critical in determining the outcome of elite level political competition. While committed activists supported the more extreme positions of the Socialist Party and the Popular Front, the predominance of moderate opinion worked substantially to the advantage of the Agrarian Democratic Party. The Agrarians were able to turn this advantage into a massive electoral success in 1994. Unlike many other cases, in Moldova party competition at this point in the transition therefore favoured a strategy of ethnic inclusion.

Institutional Deadlock, Elite Competition and the Failure of Politics

The 1994 legislative election brought to a close the turbulent initial phase of the Moldovan democratization process. Top leadership positions changed little, but the election consolidated moderates' hold on the political system and provided a working majority in the parliament. Previously deadlocked legislative items were placed on the agenda and enacted. Agreement was reached on extending local autonomy to the Gagauz region. This resolved one of the republic's separatist crises, and was intended to serve as a model for the resolution of the other.[24] A new constitution was ratified by the parliament on 29 July 1994. This established Moldova as a democratic republic with a semi-presidential system, separation of powers, judicial review, and guarantees for basic human rights.[25] The President is conferred with the right to submit issues to the people through referendum, and to suspend acts of government, which he feels contravene the law, until the Constitutional Court settles the matter. He is also empowered to dissolve Parliament after 45 days if it is unable to form a government, or if passage of a law is blocked for three months. The 'Moldovan' national orientation of the new legislative majority was incorporated into the document by removing references to Romanian language that had appeared prominently in earlier drafts. References to a 'national' state were similarly eliminated. As a further indication of the new leadership's policy of accommodation with the minorities, Article 13 committed the state to 'recognize and promote' the development and functioning of Russian and other languages spoken in the territory of the country.

Upon coming to power the Agrarian government also appeared willing at least initially to fulfil the party's commitment to economic reform. Despite some questions concerning the sincerity of their efforts, the new leadership moved to reorganize and invigorate Moldova's privatization programme. A new Ministry of Privatization was established in April 1994. In June, a pilot auction of medium-sized enterprises was held, after which an ongoing privatization programme was initiated. According to World Bank reports, more than 800 enterprises were privatized in 1994, and a new privatization programme approved in March 1995 called for a further 1,450 firms to be privatized by the end of 1996. In the rural sector substantial progress was made through the conversion of state enterprises into joint stock companies. By the close of 1995 reform progress was evident, and Moldova was widely considered by Western governments and international agencies to be among the more progressive of the post-Soviet states.

While Moldova appeared to be on a positive trajectory of economic reform and stabilization, a number of factors came together in the wake of the 1994 elections to undermine further progress. Primary among these was the unremitting struggle for political dominance among the highest-ranking members of the leadership. Discord at the pinnacle of power was exacerbated by the country's semi-presidential system, which left lines of authority between the President and the legislature unclear. This, in combination with Moldova's lack of a constitutional tradition, created a situation in which no actor was able to impose definitive decisions. Lines of authority blurred, and policy stalemate rapidly ensued.

Furthermore, the festering Transdniestrian issue added to the perception of government deadlock. Resolving the separatist crisis was profoundly complicated by the involvement of the Russian Republic. Despite official support for conciliation, Moscow's record of involvement in Transdniestria was ambiguous at best. The July 1992 cease-fire agreement, which brought an end to the worst of the fighting in Moldova, was reached with the support of President Yeltsin, but no final resolution of the conflict was achieved. Russian negotiators publicly supported a political settlement of the crisis based on substantial Transdniestrian autonomy within Moldova, but were not willing to impose this outcome on Transdniestria. Meanwhile the continued presence of Russia's 14th army made the military suppression of the Tiraspol government impossible, and encouraged the Transdniestrians not to compromise.[26] On 10 August 1994, Russia and Moldova initialled an agreement, over the objections of Tiraspol, calling for the withdrawal of the 14th Army within three years. In a major concession, Moldova accepted that the troop withdrawal should be synchronized with a political solution to the separatist conflict. But this agreement, which was immediately denounced by leaders in Tiraspol, was followed by more months of controversy, and little or no actual progress.

In this context of unresolved sovereignty, an open struggle for leadership broke out during the run-up to the 1996 presidential election. President Snegur initiated his fight for a new term early in the year by seeking to assume the political 'niche' formerly occupied by the now marginalized Popular Front. Taking nearly all political observers by surprise, early in the year Snegur began to insert increasingly nationalist rhetoric into his addresses. Reversing his previously held position, he introduced legislation declaring Romanian the official language of the republic. This act, intended to attract the support the ethnic Moldovan voters, was rebuffed by the parliament in early February. Discord deepened in March, when Snegur attempted to dismiss Defence Minister Pavel Creanga over the objection of Prime Minister Andre Sangheli. Snegur's decision was appealed successfully to the Constitutional Court, which found on 4 April that ministers could only be removed by the Prime Minister or through a parliamentary vote.

Far from being disheartened by these highly publicized setbacks, Snegur made the confrontation with the parliament the centrepiece of his campaign, arguing that his primary opponents, Prime Minister Sangheli and President of the Parliament Petru Lucinschi, were using their control over the legislature to block reform. He proposed that Moldova be transformed into a 'Presidential Republic'. In addition to emerging as the most vocal proponent of reform, he argued that Moldova should quickly be integrated more fully into West European political and economic structures.

The outcome of the 1996 Presidential elections indicated popular hesitation concerning this course. President Snegur came in first out of nine candidates in the first round on 16 November, with 38.8 per cent of the vote in comparison to 27.7 per cent for runner-up Petru Lucinschi. Vladimir Voronin, leader of the Communist Party (which had returned to activity in April 1994 after having been banned from political activity in 1991) took 10.2 per cent. The relegation of the Agrarian candidate Andre Sangheli to a fourth place, with 9.5 per cent of the vote, strikingly exemplified the extent of that party's decline since the 1994 legislative election. Second round polling revealed both the very near parity of opinion in Moldovan society and the balance of political forces. President Snegur's strongest support was among pro-reform voters, and within the Romanian-speaking community. Limited to this base, he was able to garner only approximately an additional 6 per cent in the second round vote, bringing his total to 46 per cent. In contrast, a much broader grouping united behind Petru Lucinschi. This faction included ethnic moderates within the Russian-speaking population, as well as those Moldovans who were less supportive of rapid reform. Lucinschi also benefited from a general perception that because of his strong links to

Moscow he would be more able than other leaders to resolve the Transdniestrian standoff. With support in both Romanian-speaking and minority communities, Lucinschi captured 54 per cent of the second round vote, and returned to the peak of political power.

The 1996 presidential elections highlighted the continued influence of conservatism in the political culture of the electorate, much of which remained both attached to socialist-egalitarian values and concerned by the inevitable difficulties that would accompany more thoroughgoing economic reforms. Despite hopes to the contrary, Petru Lucinschi's experience as President of the Parliament and former Communist Party leader did not bring to an end the infighting and institutional deadlock that had plagued Moldova for the previous four years. The new government established under Prime Minister Ion Ciubuc (independent) and backed by President Lucinschi was composed in majority by holdovers from the previous administration, but now including two ministers from the Party of Communists of the Republic of Moldova (PCRM). While officially pro-reform, Ciubuc's government proved largely indecisive, especially with regard to privatization of industrial enterprises. Reform progress also continued to be hindered by the Parliament, due both to the continued presence of many anti-reform MPs and the growing political fragmentation of the membership.

Promises of improvement notwithstanding, following the elections the economy continued to falter. The specifics of Moldova's circumstances made the republic even more vulnerable than a number of other transitional countries. First, Moldova is virtually entirely energy dependent, having no hydrocarbons and almost no other sources of power. Second, within the context of the former Soviet Union, Moldova was a large-scale producer of agricultural commodities. With the break-up of the USSR and the decline of Russia's economy, Moldova's agricultural exports were devastated. Its balance of trade became negative almost immediately, and it began to accrue enormous debts, particularly in the energy sector. Finally, as in both neighbouring Romania and Ukraine, official corruption quickly grew to epidemic proportions. Members of the former *nomenklatura* took advantage of their positions to sell access to the state, and to engage in arbitrage between plan and market.

According to World Bank figures, Moldovan real GDP declined at an average of 10 per cent per year through the 1990s (more than 30 per cent in 1994 alone). By 1997, Moldova was poorer than any country in Central Europe, and poorer than any former Soviet republic except Tajikistan and Uzbekistan with a per capita GDP of $527 in 1997 (*The World Bank* 2002, 4). Compounding the situation, the Russian economic crisis of 1998 delivered a further blow to the Moldovan economy. While unemployment levels were kept relatively under control, the impact of the continuous decline on the standard of living was disastrous.

Under these conditions, the growth of incertitude regarding the future was evident, as was an increasing perception of social crisis on the part of the population. The impact of popular discontent was unmistakable in the 1998 parliamentary contest. Of the 15 parties and electoral blocs that campaigned, only one had as much as 15 per cent of popular support in the months leading up to the election, and this was Voronin's Communist Party, which became the primary outlet for those opposed to reform. As in other post-Soviet states, the Communists' core constituency included pensioners, who were both dependent on the state, and older people in general, who were nostalgic for the previous regime. The PCRM also enjoyed disproportionate support from the Russian-speaking population in general, and in particular Russian-speaking industrial workers. In the months leading up to the elections the Communists campaigned for better social protection, closer future integration into the CIS, and for joining to the Russian-Belarus Union.

The recovery of the PCRM under Vladimir Voronin clearly presented a significant challenge to President Lucinschi. While the party was banned, Lucinschi benefited from the support of its otherwise disenfranchised supporters. Now forced to compete openly for their backing, he established the Movement for a Democratic and Prosperous Moldova (MDPM). The MDPM described itself as a social democratic party, and campaigned for social justice, and retaining a strong system of social protection. In comparison to the Communists, Lucinschi's MDPM was more neutral with respect to foreign policy alignment. Tactically, taking a middle of the road position in international affairs increased Lucinschi's appeal to left-oriented elements of the Romanian-speaking majority. The MDPM made the strengthening of president's role a central tenant of its electoral campaign, arguing that establishing a stronger executive would resolve the republic's policy deadlock and allow reform to go forward.

Right-wing forces also remained deeply divided when entering the 1998 elections. Following his break with the Agrarian Democrats in August 1995, former President Snegur also established a political party, the Party for Revival and Conciliation in Moldova (PRCM) in order to advance his political agenda. In addition to its personalistic appeal, the PRCM espoused a pro-reform and pro-Romanian platform. The PRCM entered the 1998 campaign in an electoral alliance, known as the Democratic Convention of Moldova (CDM). This reunited Snegur in an uneasy partnership with former Popular Front allies now organized as the Christian Democratic Peoples Party (PPCD). A third right-wing party, Party of Democratic Forces (PFD), headed by Valeriu Matai, decided to contest the elections separately. Matei took an extremely critical stance on the political establishment, and argued for eventual (but not immediate) reunification with Romania. By doing so, he hoped to become the choice of the disaffected Romanian-speaking majority.

The outcome of the 1998 election, like the preceding presidential contest, reflected the abiding divisions in the society. Four parties surpassed the 4 per cent threshold: the Communists with 30 per cent (40 seats), the Democratic Convention with 19.4 per cent (20 seats), Lucinschi's Bloc for a Democratic and Prosperous Moldova with 18.2 per cent (24 seats), and finally the Party of Democratic Forces with 8.8 per cent (11 seats). This outcome in essence gave the main left-wing parties 48.9 per cent of the vote and a potential 64 seats, and the main right-wing parties 28.3 per cent and a potential 37 seats. Intra-elite politics, however, dictated otherwise. Despite their substantial differences, the leaders of all of the non-Communist parties were united in opposition to the PCRM. A period of intense post-election negotiation led to the formation of a new organizational vehicle, the Alliance for Democracy and Reform (ADR), through which Voronin and the Communists could be blocked from government. The ADR counted 61 MP's representing the CDM, the PDF and MDPM. A coalition agreement between the parties was signed on the day of the new Parliament's inaugural sitting, 21 April 1998. It called for development of a joint programme and the allocation of offices proportionally to all three factions. The legislative leader of the MDPM (and Lucinschi lieutenant) Dumitru Diacov was voted in as Parliamentary Chairman, with Valeriu Matai and Iurie Rosca as his deputies. While not in the parliamentary leadership the Democratic Convention's second leader, Mircea Snegur, was named president of the Alliance for Democracy and Reform.

Bringing together as it did reform and anti-reform, and nationalist and anti-nationalist factions, this 'alliance' proved to be anything but functional. Diacov and the MDPM were (at least initially) a pro-presidential party. From the outset the leaders of each of the other coalition parties were long-standing opponents of Lucinschi with aspirations for capturing control over the executive branch themselves. They thus had no interest in promoting the President's agenda or in seeing his governmental proposals succeed. Further complicating the situation, Dumitru Diacov very quickly came to see his position as Parliamentary Chairman as an institutional base from which he too might be able to pursue power independently of President Lucinschi. Following months of wrangling, Diacov broke with Lucinschi and formed his own party, the Democratic Party of Moldova (PDM), further aggravating the factional dispute within the legislature. Therefore, rather than clarifying lines of authority and providing a stable base for governance, the 1998 legislative outcome condemned Moldova to a further round of infighting and institutional deadlock.

The course of legislative politics following 1998 is a testament to the disfunctionality of the anti-Communist coalition. Blocking an effort by Mircea Snegur's supporters to name one of their own as prime minister, President Lucinschi engineered the retention of Ion Ciubuc. The new government, including ministers from the three coalition parties, faced a daunting task. While the Ciubuc cabinet struggled to meet the minimum requirements of international lenders regarding privatization and fiscal discipline, the country's economy continued to decline. The government's ability to either cut services or reduce subsidies to failing enterprises was limited by its reliance on left-wing MPs who would, if pushed too far, abandon the coalition. Furthermore, no formula was found to deal with the country's ever-mounting debt to Russian energy providers. As Moldovan payment errors reached 590 million dollars, Gazprom threatened to cut off Moldova's energy supplies. Finally, the public politicization of corruption bitterly divided the elite. Charges concerning high-level involvement in financial fraud were met with counter-charges against their initiators. New rounds of attacks followed, centring on favouritism in prosecution, selective leaking of information by the authorities, and a massive cover-up by President Lucinschi and his supporters.[27] Under these conditions the ability of the ADR to govern was limited at best. Under constant attack from both right and left, Prime Minister Ciubuc found his position untenable, and resigned in November 1998.

Prospects for a successor government formed under Ion Sturza were hardly any better. Considered a moderate reformer, Sturza served as Deputy Prime Minister under Ciubuc, and retained all but four members of the Ciubuc cabinet. His government was voted into office only after two failed attempts, and with great difficulty.[28] Communist MPs voted against it on the first two ballots. The PPCD opposed Sturza as well, on the grounds that the proposed government included corrupt elements from the preceding cabinets. While his pro-reform stance gained the support of Western governments and multi-lateral lenders, his appointment ultimately did little to break the deadlock that had plagued his predecessor. Indeed, as Prime Minister Sturza struggled to govern the country; President Lucinschi ever more openly questioned the functionality of the existing constitutional order. Arguing that it was no longer possible to effectively govern the country because of the institutional power struggle, Lucinschi called for a referendum asking whether the population supported a Presidential form of government.

While the results of the referendum indicated that a majority of the population did in fact support the transition to a 'Presidential Republic', the verdict was not considered valid because the constitution requires three fifths of the population to participate; and in this case only 58 per cent did so. President Lucinschi, however, was not dissuaded in his purpose. On 1 July, he pressed forward, establishing a special commission to draft a law altering the form of government in order to strengthen the role of the president.[29] Far from resolving the situation, Lucinschi's initiative predictably further polarized the elite, undermining the President's already extremely limited support from the centre-right parties. A large majority of Moldovan politicians were vehemently against increased presidential powers. The PCRM contended that Lucinschi's initiative was contrary to democratic principles and warned that it could lead to a totalitarian regime. Similarly, the Democratic Convention and the Party of Democratic Forces both argued that Lucinschi's proposal was an effort to introduce in Moldova the type of authoritarian 'super-presidency' that had emerged in many other former Soviet republics. Even the normally compliant MDPM deputies questioned the necessity of the initiative, causing a schism within that organization. Eleven Deputies (supporters of Lucinschi) withdrew from the MDPM, forming a faction of independents.[30]

In the midst of this controversy, the Sturza government struggled to stabilize the economy and to revive the stalled privatization effort. Reform opponents in parliament worked to undermine what little headway the government did make. When parliament failed to pass privatization legislation affecting major tobacco and wine holdings the international financial institutions reacted sharply. In early November the World Bank postponed structural-adjustment credit, and the IMF suspended its Moldovan operations. Under criticism from all sides, Sturza's cabinet was brought down on 9 November 2000, through a vote of no confidence jointly engineered by the Communists and the Christian-Democratic People's Party.[31] Supporters of the ADR vilified the PPCD and its leader Iurie Roşca for cooperation with the Communists, arguing that the far left and far right were working together to produce political chaos. For its part the PPCD leadership contended that the primary problem facing the country was the imbedded system of political corruption, and that it was unwilling to support the continuation in government of persons, who were known to be engaged in graft. The failure of Sturza's government led President Lucinschi into an effort to govern from the left. Initially he proposed Vladimir Voronin as Prime Minister, hoping that the 40-member Communist legislative faction would at least provide the basis for a stable parliamentary majority. But Voronin's candidacy was predictably blocked by the centre-right. A second candidate, Valeriu Bobutac, also fell short of the necessary number of votes. Lucinschi, increasingly public in his frustration with conditions, threatened to dissolve parliament and call early elections, which would in all probability have resulted in large electoral gains for the PCRM. In order to avoid this outcome, on 22 December, legislators accepted the President's nomination of Dumitru Braghis as Prime Minister.[32]

The Braghis cabinet included a number of technocrats, and committed itself to a programme of more efficient reform and anti-corruption efforts. It was supported in parliament by a politically awkward and ultimately unworkable alliance between the Communists and the PPCD. Like his predecessor in office, Braghis was faced with nearly insurmountable difficulties. The country's economy was in a state of near collapse, the government had accumulated massive arrears in pension and wage payments, and international lenders were increasingly sceptical regarding

Moldova's creditworthiness. Furthermore, while the Braghis government committed itself publicly to reform, its dependence on the support of PCRM MPs for its survival severely circumscribed its ability to act. Given these conditions, and the ongoing power struggle between President Lucinschi and his parliamentary rivals, it is hardly surprising that the Braghis government failed to revive the failing economy and to resolve the political stalemate. Throughout his term in office Prime Minister Braghis was plagued by the country's seemingly interminable infighting, which led to government reshuffles, hindered his ability to develop a coherent programme, and undermined implementation once a policy was (in theory) agreed upon. Ultimately, however, it was the ongoing elite conflict rather than any intrinsic failure of the Braghis Cabinet that led to dissolution of parliament.

Under what they considered to be a considerable threat from Petru Lucinschi's constitutional reform initiative, legislators struck back with an alternative of their own. The PPCD put forward the idea of a 'parliamentary republic', which was quickly taken up by the Communist delegates and gained the support of a large parliamentary majority. The basic premise of this proposal was simple: reduce the role of the chief of state in domestic affairs and have the President indirectly elected by the Parliament with the goal of reigning in the power of Petru Lucinschi. Consequently, on 22 September 2000, legislation was passed according to which parliament elects the Moldovan president. The candidate is elected by the vote of three fifths of the deputies. If none of the candidates receives the required number of votes, then a second-round election must be organized within three days between the two candidates with the highest number of votes in the first round. If no candidate obtains the required majority, repeat elections must be conducted within 15 days. If the repeat balloting fails to elect the President of the Republic, then the incumbent President must dissolve the Parliament and set the date for parliamentary elections (see *Appendix 15.3 and 15.4*).

By enacting this change legislators sought to block Lucinschi from winning a second term through direct national elections, and to place his successor more firmly under parliamentary control. Instead, the new electoral procedure precipitated the dissolution of the parliament. In preparation for the December 2000 presidential elections, the PCRM deputies nominated their leader, Vladimir Voronin, while the Democratic Convention and the Party of Democratic Forces jointly put forward Pavel Barbalat. Neither candidate gained the necessary three-fifths majority in the first round of balloting. The same result was repeated in the mandated second round. On 21 December, the day designated for the third ballot, the centre-right factions boycotted the session in an attempt to avoid the election of a Communist. Only the forty PCRM MPs and eight independents appeared in parliament. After obtaining a ruling from the Constitutional Court on 26 December that under these circumstances the third ballot could be considered to have failed, Lucinschi announced the dissolution of the parliament in mid-January, and set early elections for 25 February 2001 (*East European Constitutional Review* 2001).

The 2001 legislative electoral campaign unfolded much as the previous contest, with the exception of the addition of the newly formed Braghis Alliance, which had the support of President Lucinschi.[33] With 50.7 per cent of the vote 71 parliamentary seats out of 101, the PCRM was the overwhelming victor. The Braghis Alliance came in a distant second, with 13.4 per cent of votes and 19 parliamentary seats. Only one other party, the CDPP, surpassed the 6 per cent threshold, gaining 8.2 per cent of the vote and 11 seats. Two parties, the Party of Rebirth and Reconciliation with 5.8 per cent, and the Democratic Party of Moldova with 5 per cent would have been included in the legislature under the threshold rule that governed previous legislative elections, but were now excluded.

Figure 15.3: Party support in Moldova (January 2001)

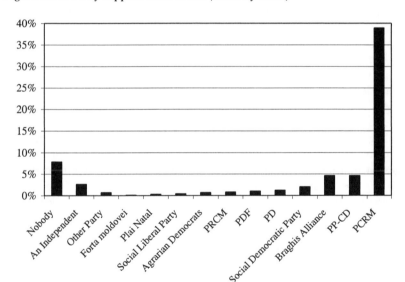

The determinants of this electoral outcome were quite clear. As a consequence of the collapse of the Moldovan economy and continual infighting among the parties and political leaders associated with the government, support for alternatives to the Communists plummeted in the months leading up to the election (see *Figure 15.3*). While the PCRM enjoyed more support than any other single party in virtually every social category, the social cleavages that were evident in the early transition did continue to express themselves. Analysis of January 2001 *Eurobarometer* data indicates that the Communists enjoyed disproportionate support among the less educated, the older population, and among non-Moldovans (see

Appendix 15.5). The PCRM benefited strongly from a growing perception within the population that the country was headed in the wrong direction. Those dissatisfied with the performance of political parties in general, and those who felt they were most at risk economically, were also significantly more likely to support the Communists, as did proponents of a pro-Russian international orientation (see *Appendix 15.5*).

The 2001 electoral outcome completely redefined Moldova's political landscape. After being first banned and then held in check for most of the preceding decade, the PCRM was now transformed into an utterly dominant political force. Its 71 seats not only gave it the numbers required to choose the country's next President, but also provided more than the two thirds majority required to amend the country's constitution. The new parliament set 4 April as the date for the presidential election. Communist parliamentarians put forward two candidates, Vladimir Voronin and Valeriu Cristea, while the Braghis Alliance nominated Dumitru Braghis. Voronin was elected President of Moldova with the support of all 71 Communist deputies. Cristea received 3 votes, and Braghis, 15. CDPP deputies, not wanting to add legitimacy to the election of a Communist President by their participation, boycotted the proceedings.

On 20 April, a new government was formed under Prime Minister Vasile Tarlev. The appointment of Tarlev, a successful business manager, and the retention of 11 members of the previous technocratic Braghis cabinet were seen as concessions to the Western diplomatic community, and as an indication of the Communists' willingness to take a flexible approach to ruling the country. But at the same time, having gained a level of political control in Moldova that was unprecedented since the beginning of the post-Soviet transition, the Communists laid out an agenda designed to reverse those of their predecessors' initiatives, which they found most objectionable. With respect to the economy, the country's new leadership expressed the intention of halting decollectivization, re-establishing the state's taxing authority, re-nationalizing those privatized enterprises that went into default, and strengthening Moldova's economic relationship with the Russian Federation. The Communist Party also committed itself to attacking the problem of corruption, and to paying the arrears in state employee wages and pensions.

Many elements of the PCRM programme clearly enjoyed widespread popular support, as evidenced by the party's domination of the 2001 elections. Other Communist proposals, such as the revision of the language laws and the intention to join the Russia-Belarus Union, while highly popular with the more militant PCRM members, proved more controversial. In early June a plan was announced calling for the reversion of local administration to the Soviet pattern of *raions*. This move would reverse a major administrative reform carried out under Lucinschi with the support of the European Union and World Bank that had reduced the number of local administrative units from 40 *raions* to 12 larger *judets*. The Communists objected to the earlier reform not only on substantive grounds, but also on account of its symbolic character (*judeţ* being the traditional Romanian unit of sub-national administration). Further raising concerns of Russification among nationalist elements of the Romanian-speaking population, President Voronin concluded and Moldova's Parliament ratified a bilateral treaty with the Russian Federation. This agreement named Russia as the guarantor of the Transdniestrian peace settlement and recognized the special status of the Russian language (Tomiuc 2001). Equally controversial, the PCRM initiated actions to make Russian language instruction mandatory in early grades and introduced a new history text into the national curriculum written by scholars widely associated with the Soviet regime.

Even moderates in the non-Russophone population took these initiatives as a direct assault on reforms that were seen as central to the national independence movement. In late 2001, the Christian Democratic People's Party, which had been vainly opposing President Voronin for months, became the focal point of a growing popular protest movement. Unable to make any headway in parliament against the Communist legislative majority, Iurie Roşca and other PPCD leaders organized a series of demonstrations in Chişinău's National Assembly Square. Led by the PPCD Deputies, demonstrators denounced the return to Soviet Communism and called for mass action to save democracy. As the protests escalated through February and March, isolated incidents of violence occurred and rumours circulated that the regime was preparing to declare a state of emergency and deploy its armed forces against the protestors.

Faced with opposition to its programme, the ruling party employed increasingly heavy-handed tactics in an effort to marginalize critics. The state controlled media was subjected to heightened levels of political direction; judicial pressure was brought to bear on the regime's more outspoken critics. On 22 January, Justice Minister Ion Morei banned the PPCD for a period of 30 days while threatening yet harsher sanctions against the party's leaders, should they continue their protest activities (*Financial Times Information*, 22 January 2002). Similarly, teachers and administrators from educational institutions whose students participated in the demonstrations were threatened with dismissal. Moldovan politics thus polarized between supporters of President Voronin and the CPRM and an increasingly militant and growing minority that gravitated toward the Christian-Democratic People's Party. While the Communists' backing remained strong and the party was easily able to contain its opponents, the political cost of its confrontational approach to governance rose dramatically over time.

The tensions, produced by the early programme of the PCRM, generated equally negative fall-out in the international arena. Even prior to the beginning of the protest movement plans to reverse the territorial-administrative reform roused a universally negative response from Western entities, including the European Union. Moldova's relationship with multilateral financial institutions deteriorated sharply in response to the government's retreat from economic reform. Finally, perception that the protests threatened to spiral out of control, as well as concern regarding the regime's heavy-handed tactics in dealing with its opponents, generated a high level of concern within the diplomatic community. Representatives of the Council of Europe lodged a series of protests against the regime's actions.[34] Equally disconcerted with the rise of ethnic tension (and accusations that Bucharest was encouraging extremists inside Moldova), the Romanian government issued a communiqué accusing Chişinău of anti-Romanian rhetoric. Collectively, these reactions raised the very real possibility of diplomatic isolation; an extremely unpalatable prospect given Moldova's debt and economic dependence.

In the face of growing opposition, and in all probability on the advice of Russian political leaders with whom President Voronin consulted frequently, the PCRM sharply altered its position in the course of early 2002. Plans to make the study of the Russian language mandatory were dropped, as was the intention to introduce a new history text. Even more striking, Minister of Education Ilie Vancea, the official most directly connected with the language and history curriculum issues, publicly apologized to protestors for his mistakes, and was then dismissed by President Voronin (*Associated Press*, 26 February 2002). These moves very rapidly defused support for anti-Communist demonstrations by removing the most incendiary issues from public discourse. Relations with the international community were similarly smoothed over. While not dropped all together, the plan for territorial-administrative reform was placed on hold. In order to regain access to international credits the Tarlev government agreed to maintain its budget within limits established by the IMF and to conform to IMF recommendations regarding exports (*Basa Press-Economic*, 30 November 2002). Finally, President Voronin and the Communist leadership agreed to participate in an effort by the Council of Europe to mediate in the confrontation with the PPCD led opposition. This initiative, which brought the competing parties together in Strasbourg in mid-April marked the end of the mass demonstrations in Chişinău and a clear turning-point in the re-engagement between the Moldovan government and the Western diplomatic community (*The James Town Institute Monitor*, April 2002).

Thus, while by no means abandoning their ideological foundations, the Moldovan Communists appear to have recognized the constraints imposed by the international environment and their own vulnerable economic conditions. At least for the time, party leaders pulled back from the most provocative of their early initiatives, and have made an effort to respond to requirements put to them by the international financial community. After months of difficult negotiations, the World Bank approved resumption of SAC-III funding to Moldova (*Basa Press*, 27 June 2002). This decision was absolutely critical to the Tarlev government, which was by that point facing default on 75 million dollars of Eurobond debt. With the conditional support of the World Bank and the International Monetary Fund, Moldova was able to negotiate debt restructuring with its main Western creditors in early August 2002. The country was thus able to stave off the financial disaster that would have followed default and to shore up its foreign exchange position. In the longer term, however it continues to face daunting difficulties.[35]

Further brightening the general outlook, even while the country's political environment was markedly fractious in the months following the 2001 legislative elections, Moldova's economy showed steady improvement, growing by 6.2 per cent in 2001 and approximately 7 per cent in 2002. In part this dramatic recovery was attributable to the turn-around in the Russian economy following the economic collapse of 1998. Moldova's economic growth also resulted from the positive effects of reforms that were undertaken during the late 1990s, and improvement of fiscal policy following 1998 (*The World Bank* 2003, 5). Whatever the source of the recovery, the standing of the PCRM with the public benefited both from the economic upturn, and from the improvement in governance that resulted from its control over both parliament and the presidency. As public perception of conditions improved following the legislative and presidential elections, support for the Communist Party and its leader increased as well (see *Figure 15.4*).

Figure 15.4: Evaluation of conditions and political support 1998–2002

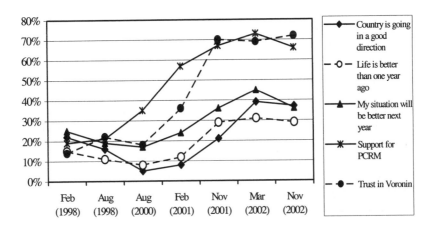

In the period following the elections support for the Communists increased among nearly all demographic categories. Most striking was the inroad that the CPRM made among ethnic Moldovans. Asked if they would vote for the Communists in early 2001, 23.5 per cent of Moldovans answered in the affirmative, as compared to 44.4 per cent of Russians. By April of the following year 47.7 per cent of Moldovan respondents expressed support for the CPRM, while support from the Russian minority had risen to 59.1 per cent (*Moldovan Eurobarometers*, January/February 2001, April 2002). As born out by analysis of public opinion data from these two periods, at least with respect to the willingness to support the Communist Party, the impact of ethnicity was significantly reduced. Urban/rural differences, on the contrary, have become increasingly salient following the elections.[36] As the government moved to repay pension arrears and reverse the decline in living standards in Moldovan villages, support of the rural population shifted sharply in the direction of the PCRM.

Conclusions

Moldova's post-Communist transition began under markedly negative circumstances. As central authority eroded during the late Soviet period, social cleavages played a dominant role in shaping the initial phase of the transition. While the democratic opposition pressed for the end of Soviet rule, conservatives within the Communist Party worked to retain what was possible of the status quo. Simultaneously, nationalists in the majority community pursued an increasingly open agenda of reunification with Romania. In reaction, minority activists gravitated toward the former communists, and in two instances resorted to separatism, seeking to establish independent political entities in order to defend their interests. The very rapid mobilization of these competing forces drove the republic into civil conflict even as it struggled to establish its independence.

In sharp contrast to a number of similar cases, however, in Moldova the cycle of ethnic mobilization was broken, and the country succeeded in stepping back from civil war. The complex issue structure that characterized the republic was crucial in determining this outcome. Entering the post-communist transition, popular opinion was split on attitudes toward inter-ethnic relations. While ethnic extremists were present in both the majority and minority communities, moderate opinions predominated. Furthermore, in addition to the inter-ethnic divide, a second dimension emerged, based on reform issues that cut across communal lines. Finally, a serious dispute over national identity (Romanian versus Moldovan) separated Romanian-speakers.

The interplay of these factors was critical in shaping the initial phase of the post-communist transition. Initially, majority/minority differences caused a collapse in the attempts to establish an ethnically inclusive regime. As efforts at cooperation failed, the extremist leadership of the Popular Front gained control over the national government, precipitating an open conflict with russophone separatists. But divisions within the majority community undermined the nationalists' endeavour to consolidate their hold on power. This division, pitting those identifying as 'Romanian' nationalists against those identifying as 'Moldovan', provided an opening for an alternative (Agrarian Democrat) leadership group which expressly rejected pan-Romanian identification and appealed across ethnic lines, basing its platform on reform rather than national identity.

While playing a positive role in the moderation of ethnic conflict during the initial phase of the post-Soviet transition, intra-elite infighting was prominent among the factors that led to political bankruptcy in the second half of the 1990s. Key members of the elite vied for control over the republic, each employing their various public positions as bases of support, and seeking to form personal parliamentary factions. Elite conflict was exacerbated by Moldova's institutional structure, and weakly established constitutionalism, which left lines of authority between the president, parliament and government unclear. Nearly continuous infighting among political leaders both impeded the development of a coherent reform strategy and frustrated efforts to establish stable patterns of administration. In conjunction with admittedly difficult external economic circumstances, poor governance utterly devastated the Moldovan economy, casting a large proportion of the population into poverty, and discrediting the reform enterprise.

It is within this context of failed democratization that one must view the resurgence of the Moldovan Communists. With virtually no other popularly acceptable alternative on the horizon, the PCRM became the inheritor of the political system, largely because it could claim to have had no role in the failures of the preceding decade. Whether the resurgence of the Communist Party represents a decisive break with the preceding political pattern remains an open question, the conclusion to which will depend largely on whether the Voronin leadership succeeds in reasserting coherent governance, and whether the centre-right is able to consolidate while in opposition.

Acronyms of Parties and Movements

ACF	Electoral Bloc of the *Furnica* (The Ant) Civic Alliance (*Blocul Electoral Alianţa Civică Furnică*)
AFD	Alliance of Democratic Forces Electoral Bloc (*Blocul Electoral Alianţa Forţelor Democratice*)
AFPCD	Alliance of the Popular Christian Democratic Front (*Blocul Electoral Alianţa Frontului Popular Creştin Democrat*)
BEAB	Electoral Bloc 'Braghis Alliance' (*Blocul Electoral 'Alianţa Braghis'*)
BSDS	Social Democratic Electoral Bloc 'Hope' (*Blocul Electoral Social-Democratic 'Speranţa'*)
CDM	Electoral Bloc Democratic Convention of Moldova (*Blocul Electoral Convenţia Democrată din Moldova*)
PCRM	Party of Communists of the Republic of Moldova (*Partidul Comuniştilor din Moldova*)
PD	Democratic Party of Moldova (*Partidul Democrat din Moldova*)
PDAM	Democratic Agrarian Party of Moldova (*Partidul Democrat Agrar din Moldova*)
PDSM	Moldovans' Party of Economic and Social Justice (*Partidul Dreptăţii Social-Economice din Moldova*)
PFD	Party of Democratic Forces (*Partidul Forţelor Democratice*)
PMDP	Electoral Bloc For a Democratic and Prosperous Moldova (*Blocul Electoral Pentru o Moldova Democratică şi Prosperă*)
PPCD	Christian Democratic Peoples Party (*Partidul Popular Creştin Democrat*)
PR	Party of Reform (*Partidul Reformei*)
PRCM	Party of Rebirth and Conciliation of Moldova (*Partidul Renasterii şi Concilierii din Moldova*)
PS	Party of Socialists (*Partidul Socialiştilor*)
PSDM	Social Democratic Party of Moldova (*Partidul Social Democrat din Moldova*)
PUMM	United Party of Labour of Moldova (*Partidul Unit al Muncii din Moldova*)
UCDM	Christian Democratic Union (*Uniunea Crşstin-Democrată din Moldova*)
US	Electoral Bloc Socialist Unity (*Blocul Electoral Unitatea Socialistă*)

NOTES

1. Western Moldova was united with Walachia in 1859, through the joint election of Alexandru Ion Cuza as Prince of both principalities in January 1859, forming the basis of modern Romania (Vlad Gheorghescu 1991, 146–8). For a more complete treatment of the history of the entire region, including the history of the entities that have become both Romania and Moldova, see Barbara Jelavich (1983).

2. Post-Soviet accounts of this event suggest that many of those subjected to it were in no way better off economically than their neighbours. Hence very often the reason for their exile appears to have been more closely related to their attitudes toward the new regime than to actual class status (Tikhorov 1989, 3).

3. See Kozlov (1988, 64). On the other side of the coin, in 1970 Moldovans made up 78.2 per cent of the rural population (Arutyunyan 1980, 36).

4. On the complexities of culture policy during the Soviet period, see King (2000).

5. Among those reformers who became Peoples Deputies were I. Cabana, M. Camp, N. Dabija and I. Hadarca.

6. The Moldovan Popular Front was formed out of a popular movement initially set in motion by the Democratic Movement in Support of Restructuring and the Mateevich Circle. It included in its ranks many of the leaders of these two crucial early reform organizations.

7. On the political dynamics of this period see Crowther (1991).

8. For the full text of the Popular Front's platform see *Literatura si Artă* (8 February 1990, 2).

9. Eighty-one per cent of deputies were members of the Communist Party. Confusing matters

somewhat, some of these, like President Mircea Snegur, were both Communist Party members and supported by the Popular Front. Due to the growing friction between the reform and conservative branches of the Communist Party and the breakdown of the Party's central authority, it is difficult to ascertain in some cases what the affiliation of particular individuals was.

10. These included changes such as reinstating the pre-revolutionary flag as the emblem of the republic, and an effort (narrowly defeated) that would have changed the name of the legislature from Supreme Soviet to the National Council (*Svatul Țurii*). While of little practical consequence, such issues were of great symbolic significance to both the majority and minority communities. For a discussion of the confrontation of the issue of renaming the republican parliament see 'Strain Without Precedent', *Moldova Socialistă* (28 April 1990, 1), or 'Agenda of the Day', *Sovietskaya Moldavia* (28 April 1990, 1).

11. For the central government's response to these actions, see *Moldova Socialistă* (13 May 1990, 1). On conditions in Bender, see S. Ionel, 'Meetings during Work Time', *Moldova Socialistă* (4 May 1990, 3).

12. The public opinion data for this analysis and the following discussion of social cleavages during the early 1990s were drawn from a survey administered by personnel of the ethnography and sociology institutes of the Moldovan Academy of Sciences and the National Institute of Sociology of Moldova, in June and July of 1992. Approximately 1,600 respondents were selected based upon national probability samples. A stratified sample was drawn based on historical region and type of locality (rural, small towns, and cities). Face-to-face interviews were employed in this project. Members of minority communities were recruited to administer the survey in minority districts, and minority language versions of the survey instrument were prepared for the use of members of the larger minority groups. Subjects were provided with an opportunity to choose the language in which they wished to respond.

13. While half of Moldovans considered the situation of minorities to be 'good', only approximately 17 per cent of Russians and Ukrainians agreed. In the crucial area of language policy differences were equally striking. Attitudes concerning language use have been very highly charged since independence. In this crucial area more than 78 per cent of Moldovans felt that Romanian language education should be required for the minority populations, while less that half of Russians and Ukrainians agreed. Conversely, more than one third of Russians and Ukrainians felt that each nationality should learn only its own language, while less than 15 per cent of Moldovans agreed. For a more complete examination of these divisions, see Crowther (1997b).

14. On the Transdniestrian question approximately 80 per cent of Moldovans favoured the continuation of a unitary state with Moldova, while considerably less than half of Russians and Ukrainians did so. Conversely, approximately 29 and 38 per cent of Russians and Ukrainians respectively favoured a solution that would create a federation between Moldova and Transdniestria. Only about 7 per cent of Moldovans were willing to accept this solution to the separatist crisis (Crowther 1997b).

15. Support for private ownership in other sectors of the economy was greater, but the sharp division concerning property ownership remained obvious. When one considers attitudes concerning other policy issues related to reform a similar image emerges. For a more detailed discussion of majority and minority attitudes on reform and inter-ethnic relations, see Crowther (1996).

16. The two following regressions indicate the significance of ethnicity in determining attitudes regarding international orientation, and its lack of relevance in shaping reform opinion. The results reported here are consistent with regression results examining similar dependent variables: privatization, pace of reform, language policy, Transdniestria policy, etc. Parameter estimates are not reported.

Nominal Regression: Necessity of Reform by Urban/Rural, Education, and Ethnicity

Model Fitting Information

Model	-2 Log Likelihood	Chi-Square	df	Sig.
Intercept Only	398.736			
Final	330.430	68.306	24	0.000

Likelihood Ratio Tests

Effect	-2 Log Likelihood of Reduced Model	Chi-Square	df	Sig.
Intercept	330.430 (a)	0.000	0	–
URBAN	331.969	1.539	4	0.820
Education	383.447	53.017	12	0.000
Ethnicity	342.492	12.061	8	0.0148

Pseudo R-Square

Cox and Snell	0.054
Nagelkerke	0.058
McFadden	0.021

The chi-square statistic is the difference in -2 log-likelihoods between the final model and a reduced model. The reduced model is formed by omitting an effect from the final model. The null hypothesis is that all parameters of that effect are 0.

(a) This reduced model is equivalent to the final model because omitting the effect does not increase the degrees of freedom.

Nominal Regression: International Orientation by Urban/Rural, Education, and Ethnicity

Model Fitting Information

Model	-2 Log Likelihood	Chi-Square	df	Sig.
Intercept Only	588.915			
Final	301.261	287.654	30	0.000

Pseudo R-Square

Cox and Snell	0.188
Nagelkerke	0.209
McFadden	0.091

Likelihood Ratio Tests

Effect	-2 Log Likelihood of Reduced Model	Chi-Square	df	Sig.
Intercept	301.261 (a)	0.000	0	–
Urban/Rural	335.218	33.957	5	0.000
Education	340.123	38.862	15	0.001
Ethnicity	522.867	221.606	10	0.000

The chi-square statistic is the difference in -2 log-likelihoods between the final model and a reduced model. The reduced model is formed by omitting an effect from the final model. The null hypothesis is that all parameters of that effect are 0.

(a) This reduced model is equivalent to the final model because omitting the effect does not increase the degrees of freedom.

17. Making this orientation even more clear, 83 per cent of those identifying as Moldovan, given the opportunity to describe themselves as exclusively Moldovan, or primarily Moldovan and secondarily of some other nationality, including Romanian, identified as *exclusively* Moldovan.

18. The results of the election, held on 8 December 1991, were overwhelming. Snegur, who ran unopposed, received 98.2 per cent of the votes cast.

19. Appointment of General Aleksandr Lebed to command of the 14th army in mid-1992 further complicated the situation. Lebed, an outspoken nationalist, immediately became politically engaged. Once in Transdniestria he promptly indicated his strong support for the Russian minority, if not for the Tiraspol government, with which he often found himself at odds. Despite repeated warnings from his superiors to restrain himself, Lebed became a constant presence in both the local and Russian mass media. He stated flatly that he would not 'abandon' Transdniestria's Russians.

20. For a more detailed discussion of the political situation in the Transdniestrian region during this period, see Vladimir Socor (1993).

21. Sangheli was a long term member of the CPM apparatus, serving first as Party *Raion* Committee First Secretary and later as member of the republican Council of Ministers. He played a prominent role in the removal of the extremely reactionary Simion Grossu from the position of Party First Secretary at the end of the Soviet period.

22. While not ensuring participation in the separatist region this mechanism allowed elections to go forward, selecting a body of delegates whose constituency was the entire republic, regardless of their individual places of residence (Resolution on the Procedure for Enacting the Law on Elections to Parliament, 19 October 1993).

23. One of the two cities where the Agrarians took a plurality of the vote was clearly a special case. This was Bender, which was the site of substantial conflict and population movement.

24. For a complete account of the Gagauz agreement, see Vladimir Socor (1994).

25. *Constituţia Republicii Moldova* (Chişinău, Direcţia de Stat pentru Asigurarea Informaţională, MOLDPRES, 1994).

26. The force, which was estimated at several thousand in 1995, is deeply imbedded in the local population. Many of its officers settled their families in the region. Enlisted personnel have been locally conscripted. Hence 'withdrawing' the force in large part amounted to an agreement to dismantle the command structure, demobilize forces, and withdraw weapons stockpiles rather than to physically withdraw troops. A key issue for Moldovan leaders faced with this situation has thus been the fate of these soldiers (they should not be transferred to the authority of the Tiraspol government), and the final disposition of their weaponry. On Moscow's role in supporting the Transdniestrian separatists, see Kaufman (1996).

27. The highest profile of these charges related to the sale to the United States of 21 Moldovan MIG fighters. Critics claimed that the sale, carried out in secret, resulted in a massive misappropriation of state funds. The report of a special commission, which investigated the affair named President Lucinschi, Prime Minister Ion Ciubuc, Minister of Defence Valeriu Pasat, Deputy Prime Minister Ion Sturza, and Minister of Foreign Affairs Nicolae Tabacaru as officials involved in the sale.

28. Sturza was finally successful by inclusion in the vote count of a letter of support from Ilie Ilascu, a parliamentary deputy who was imprisoned in Transdniestria. This proxy, with the support of the Snegur, Diacov and Matei factions provided the 52 votes necessary to empower the government. In reaction, the PPCD withdrew from the centre-right coalition. It was at this juncture that the far left PCRM and far right PPCD found common interest and entered into a *de facto* political alliance.

29. According to the commission's proposal, the government would be selected by the president and subsequently would be accountable to him alone. The president would have the right to name and dismiss the prime minister, and cabinet. The presidential term was extended from four to five years. The number of deputies in parliament was to be reduced from 101 to 70, and a single member district plurality electoral system would be introduced for legislative elections.

30. President Lucinschi certainly recognized that his proposal for a change in the form of government would not be supported by the parliament. Rather, it appears that he was positioning himself for presidential elections in the autumn of 2000, intending to campaign on the platform that the deterioration of conditions was the result of Parliament's obstructionism. Once having gained a second term, he could then force the parliament's dissolution, work with supportive elements to achieve a manageable majority in the legislative contest, and revise the government as he desired.

31. While the crisis was precipitated by the privatization vote, Prime Minister Sturza was already under attack. In addition to the Communists and PPCD deputies in parliament, President Lucinschi had also withdrawn his support, leaving little hope that Sturza could survive politically.

32. The 43-year old Dumitru Braghis was a moderate former communist. Braghis was the last First Secretary of the Moldovan Komsomol, a position that he held from 1988 to 1991.

33. The Braghis Alliance was composed of members of the Braghis government and 11 formerly independent Members of Parliament who supported Lucinschi.

34. Invoking Article 52 of the European Convention, the Council of Europe Secretary General requested an explanation from Moldovan officials as to how their domestic laws ensured effective implementation of the European Convention. The fact that this procedure had only been employed once previously (in the case of Russia's activities in Chechnya) was a clear indication of the seriousness with which European diplomats viewed the situation (Council of Europe Press Division, 4 February 2002).

35. Relations between the PCRM-controlled government and the International Financial community remain difficult at best, and while economic conditions overall have improved, the country's balance of trade remains seriously negative. Furthermore, Moldova is unable to pay the enormous debts that it has accumulated with Gazprom, which, in the beginning of 2003 were in the order of $119 million for consumed gas, $270 million in interest and penalties, and $400 million in gas debts accumulated by Transdniestria.

36. Logistic Regression, of *Eurobarometer* data, January/February 2001, and April 2002. Intention to vote for the PCRM by residence and ethnicity. Changes in the influence of these factors was evident. Residency (urban/rural) did not play a significant role in the 2001 model (Sig. = 0.132) but was highly influential (Sig. = 0.000) by 2002. While the overall influence of ethnicity was substantial in both models, the predictive value of being a Romanian speaker dropped dramatically, from (Sig. = 0.000) in 2001 to (Sig. = 0.425) in the 2002 model.

REFERENCES

Arutyunyan, Yu. V. (1980), *Oput. Etnosotsiologicheskovo Issledovaniya Obraza Zhizni: Po Materialam Moldavskoy SSR*, Moscow, Nauka.

Associated Press, 26 February 2002.

Basa Press, Chişinău, 27 June 2002.

Basa Press-Economic, Chişinău, 30 November 2002.

Crowther, William (1991), 'The Politics of Ethno-National Mobilization: Nationalism and Reform in Soviet Moldavia', *The Russian Review*, Volume 50, Number 2 (April), 183–203.

—— (1996), 'Nationalism and Political Transformation in Moldova' in Donald Dryer, ed., *Studies in Moldavian: The History, Culture, Language and Contemporary Politics of the People of Moldova*, Boulder, East European Monographs.

—— (1997a), 'The Politics of Democratization in Post-communist Moldova', in Karen Dawisha and Bruce Parrott, eds, *Democratic Changes and Authoritarian Reactions in Russia, Ukraine, Belarus, and Moldova*, London, Cambridge University Press, 282–329.

—— (1997b), 'The Construction of Moldovans National Consciousness', in Laszlo Kurti and Juliet Langman, eds, *Beyond Borders: Remaking Cultural Identities in the New Eastern and Central Europe*, Boulder, Westview Press, 39–62.

East European Constitutional Review (2001), Volume 10, No. 1 (Winter).

Eurobarometers: Moldova, (various years), Results and data available through the Public Policy Institute, Chişinău, Moldova, http://www.ipp.md/publications/en.html.

Financial Times Information, 22 January 2002.

Gheorghescu, Vlad (1991), *The Romanians*, Columbus, Ohio, The Ohio State University Press.

International Foundation for Electoral Systems (1994), *Republic of Moldova: Parliamentary Elections, February 1994, Chişinău*, TISH, Ltd., 3–5.

The James Town Institute Monitor, Volume 8, Issue 77, 19 April 2002.

Jelavich, Barbara (1983), *History of the Balkans: Eighteenth and Nineteenth Centuries*, New York, Cambridge University Press.

Kaufman, Stuart J. (1996), 'Spiraling to Ethnic War: Elites, Masses, and Moscow in Moldova's Civil War', *International Security*, Vol. 21, Nr. 2 (Autumn), 108–38.

King, Charles (2002), *The Moldovans: Romania, Russia and the Politics of Culture*, Stanford, California, Hoover Institution Press.

Kozlov, Viktor (1988), *The Peoples of the Soviet Union*, Bloomington, Indiana, Indiana University Press.

Literatura si Artă, 8 February 1990, 2.

Nedelciuc, Vasile (1992), *Republica Moldova, Chişinău*, Universitas.

Socor, Vladimir (1993), 'Moldova's "Dniester" Ulcer', *RFE/RL Research Report*, Vol. 2, No. 1 (1 January), 12–16.

—— (1994), 'Gagauz Autonomy in Moldova: A Precedent for Eastern Europe?', *RFE/RL Research Report*, Vol. 3, No. 33 (26 August), 20–28.

Tikhorov, A. (1989), 'Collectivization: Against White Spaces', *Moldova Socialistă*, 3 February.

Tomiuc, Eugen, (2001), 'Moldova: Moscow and Chişinău Initial Bilateral Agreement', *Radio Free Europe/Radio Liberty Weekly Magazine* (6 November).

World Bank (1994), *Moldova: Moving to a Market Economy*, Washington, DC, The World Bank.

—— (2002), *Interim Poverty Reduction Strategy Paper* (Prepared by the Moldovans authorities) (21 April) Washington, DC, The World Bank.

—— (2003), 'Moldova: Public Economic Management Review', Report No 25423-MD, 20 February.

APPENDIX 15.1: ELECTION RESULTS

PARLIAMENTARY ELECTIONS

1994 Elections
Date: 27 February 1994
Number of registered voters: 2,356,614
Turnout: 79.31%
Total votes cast: 1,869,090
Valid: 1,775,377

Party/grouping	Votes	% Votes	Seats	% Seats
PDAM Democratic Agrarian Party of Moldova (*Partidul Democrat Agrar din Moldova*)	766,589	43.18	56	53.85
PSMUE Socialist Party and 'Unitate-Edinstvo' Movement Bloc (*Blocul electoral Partidul Socialist şi Miscarea 'Unitate-Edinstvo'*)	390,584	22	28	26.92
BTI Peasants' and Intellectuals' Bloc (*Blocul Ţaranilor şi Intelectualilor*)	163,513	9.21	11	10.58
AFPCD Alliance of the Popular Christian Democratic Front (*Blocul electoral Alianţa Frontului Popular Creştin Democrat*)	133,606	7.53	9	8.65
BSD Social Democratic Bloc (*Blocul electoral social democrat*)	65,028	3.66	0	0
AFM Association of Women of Moldova (*Asociaţia femeilor din Moldova*)	50,243	2.83	0	0
PDMM Democratic Party of Labour (*Partidul Democrat al Muncii din Moldova*)	49,210	2.77	0	0
PR Party of Reform (*Partidul Reformei*)	41,980	2.36	0	0
PD Democratic Party of Moldova (*Partidul Democrat din Moldova*)	23,368	1.32	0	0
AVRTM Association of Victims of the Communist Totalitarian Regime (*Asociaţia Victimelor Regimului Totalitar Comunist din Moldova*)	16,672	0.94	0	0
PRM Republican Party of Moldova (*Partidul Republican din Moldova*)	16,529	0.93	0	0
PEM Ecological Party 'Alianţa Verde' – Green Alliance (*Partidul Ecologist 'Alianţa Verde'*)	7,025	0.4	0	0
PNC National Christian Party (*Partidul Naţional Creştin*)	5,878	0.33	0	0
Independent Candidates (20)	45,152	2.54	0	0
Total	1,775,377	100	104	100

1998 Elections
Date: 22 March
Number of registered voters: 2,431,218
Turnout: 69.12%
Total votes cast: 1,680,470
Valid: 1,622,987

Party/grouping	Votes	% Votes	Seats	% Seats
PCRM Party of Communists (*Partidul Comuniştilor din Moldova*)	487,002	30.01	40	39.6
CDM Electoral Bloc Democratic Convention of Moldova (*Blocul Electoral Conventia Democrată din Moldova*)	315,206	19.42	26	25.74
PMDP Electoral Bloc For a Democratic and Prosperous Moldova (*Blocul Electoral Pentru o Moldova Democratică şi Prosperă*)	294,691	18.16	24	23.76
PFD Party of Democratic Forces (Partidul Forţelor Democratice)	143,428	8.84	11	10.89
PDAM Democratic Agrarian Party (*Partidul Democrat Agrar din Moldova*)	58,874	3.63	0	0
ACF Electoral Bloc of the Civic Alliance *Furnica* (The Ant) (*Blocul Electoral Alianţa Civică Furnica*)	53,338	3.29	0	0
AFD Alliance of Democratic Forces Electoral Bloc (*Blocul Electoral Alianţa Forţelor Democratice*)	36,344	2.24	0	0
PDSEM Moldovan Party of Economic and Social Justice (*Partidul Dreptătii Social-Economice din Moldova*)	31,663	1.95	0	0
PSDM Social Democratic Party of Moldova (*Partidul Social Democrat din Moldova*)	30,169	1.86	0	0
US Electoral Bloc Socialist Unity (*Blocul Electoral Unitatea Socialista*)	29,647	1.83	0	0
BSDS Social Democratic Electoral Bloc 'Hope' (*Blocul Electoral* 'Speranta')	21,282	1.31	0	0
PS Party of Socialists (*Partidul Socialiştilor*)	9,514	0.59	0	0
PR Party of Reform (*Partidul Reformei*)	8,844	0.54	0	0
UCDM Christian Democratic Union (*Uniunea Creţtin-Democrată din Moldova*)	8,342	0.51	0	0
PUMM United Party of Labour of Moldova (*Partidul Unit al Muncii din Moldova*)	3,124	0.19	0	0
Plugaru Anatol	17,736	1.09	0	0
Renita Valeriu	2,983	0.18	0	0
Gheorghe Porcescu	2,892	0.18	0	0

Pavel Creanga	2,573	0.16	0	0
Other independent candidates (55)	64,813	3.99	0	0
Total	1,622,987	100	101	100

2001 elections (pre-term)
Date: 25 February
Number of registered voters: 2,379,491
Turnout: 67.52%
Total votes cast: 1,606,703
Valid: 1,587,257

Party/grouping	*Votes*	*% Votes*	*Seats*	*% Seats*
PCRM Communist Party (*Partidul Comuniştilor din Republica Moldova*)	794,808	50.07	71	70.3
BEAB Electoral Bloc 'Braghis Allianc' (*Blocul Electoral 'Alianţa Braghis'*)	212,071	13.36	19	18.81
PPCD Christian Democratic Popular Party (*Partidul Popular Creştin Democrat*)	130,810	8.24	11	10.89
PRCM Party of Rebirth and Conciliation (*Partidul Renaşterii şi Concilierii*)	91,894	5.79	0	0
PDM Democratic Party of Moldova (*Partidul Democrat din Moldova*)	79,757	5.02	0	0
PNL National Liberal Party (*Partidul Naţional Liberal*)	44,548	2.81	0	0
PSDM Social Democratic Party of Moldova (*Partidul Social Democrat din Moldova*)	39,247	2.47	0	0
PNTCD National Peasant Party Christian Democratic (*Partidul Naţional Ţaranesc Creştin Democrat*)	27,575	1.74	0	0
Valeriu Ghiletchi (independent candidate)	27,511	1.73	0	0
BEPN Electoral Bloc 'Plai Natal' [Native Land] (*Blocul Electoral 'Plai Natal'*)	25,009	1.58	0	0
MSPOD Socio-political Movement 'For Order and Justice' (*Mişcare Social-Politică 'Pentru Ordine şi Dreptate'*)	23,099	1.46	0	0
PFD Party of the Democratic Forces (*Partidul Forţelor Democratice*)	19,405	1.22	0	0
PDAM Democratic Agrarian Party of Moldova (*Partidul Democrat Agrar din Moldova*)	18,473	1.16	0	0
AJE Electoral Bloc 'Alliance of Lawyers and Economists' (*Blocul Electoral 'Alianţa Juriştilor ţi Economiştilor'*)	14,810	0.93	0	0
BECD Electoral Bloc 'Fait and Justice' (*Blocul Electoral 'Credinţa şi Dreptate'*)	10,686	0.67	0	0

BEE Electoral Bloc 'Edinstvo' (*Blocul Electoral 'Edinstvo'*)	7,277	0.46	0	0
MSPRR Republican Socio-Political Movement 'Ravnopravie' (*Miscarea Social-Politică Republicană 'Ravnopravie'*)	7,023	0.44	0	0
PȚCD Peasant Party Christian Democratic (*Partidul Țaranesc Creștin Democrat*)	4,288	0.27	0	0
Ilie Donica (independent candidate)	1,475	0.09	0	0
Valeriu Lapinschi (independent candidate)	1,332	0.08	0	0
Mihail Kulev (independent candidate)	1,075	0.07	0	0
Ana Golubenco (independent candidate)	1,053	0.07	0	0
Vasile Severin (independent candidate)	1,025	0.06	0	0
Vasile Trofim (independent candidate)	975	0.06	0	0
Iacob Mogoreanu (independent candidate)	971	0.06	0	0
Ion Pomana (independent candidate)	582	0.04	0	0
Dumitru Solomon (independent candidate)	478	0.03	0	0
Total	1,587,257	100	101	10

PRESIDENTIAL ELECTIONS

1991 Elections
Date of first round: 8 December 1991
Turnout: (first round) 82.9%

Candidate	% Voters
Mircea Snegur	98.17

1996 Elections
Date of first round: 17 November; second round: 1 December 1996
Number of registered voters: (first round) 2,399,156; (second round) 2,441,074
Turnout: (first round) 68.13%; (second round) 71.61%
Total votes cast: 1,634,661 (first round); 1,748,139 (second round)
Valid: 1,557,860 (first round); 1,702,764 (second round)

Candidates	Nominated by	Votes	% Voters	Votes Second Round	% Votes Second Round
Mircea Snegur	PRCN	603,652	38.75	782,933	45.98
Petru Lucinschi	Independent	430,836	27.66	919,831	54.02
Vladimir Voronin	PCRM	159,393	10.23	–	–
Andrei Sangheli	PDAM	147,555	9.47	–	–
Valeriu Matei	PFD	138,605	8.9	–	–
Marina Livitchi	Independent	33,115	2.13	–	–
Anatol Plugaru	Independent	28,159	1.8	–	–
Lulia Gorea-Costin	Independent	9,926	0.64	–	–
Veronica Abramciuc	Independent	6,619	0.42	–	–
Total		1,557,860	100	1,702,764	100

2000 Elections
Date of first round: 1 December 2000
Voters: Indirect Elections by 101 Members of Parliament
Valid: 85% (first round)

Candidates	Nominated by	Votes	% Voters
Vladimiar Voronin	PCRM	48	47.5
Pavel Barbalat	ADR	37	36.6
Invalid Ballots		15	14.8
Total		100	99

Note: After only 48 deputies appeared at the special parliamentary secession called for second round elections (61 being required to elect a president), the Constitutional Court found that the sitting President was enjoined under the election law to dissolve parliament and hold new legislative elections. A new attempt to elect the president was called for following legislative elections.

2001 Elections
Date of first round: 4 April 2001
Voters: Indirect Elections by 101 Members of Parliament
Valid: 89% (first round)

Candidates	Party nominated by	Votes	% Voters
Vladimiar Voronin	PCRM	71	70.0
Dumitru Braghis	Braghis Alliance	15	14.86
Valerian Cristea	PCRM	3	3.0
Total		89	88.1

Note: 11 deputies from the PPCD boycotted the special secession of Parliament called to hold presidential elections. Vladimir Voronin was elected after receiving more than the necessary 60 votes in the first round.

APPENDIX 15.2: GOVERNMENT COMPOSITION

Time	Prime Minister (Party)	Political orientation	Reason for change of government
26.05.90–28.05.91	Mircea Druc (Popular Front)	Right/nationalist	Dismissed, disagreement with President and Parliament, widespread popular dissatisfaction
28.05.91–01.07.92	Valeriu Muravschi (unaffiliated)	Centre	
01.07.92–24.01.97	Andrei Sangheli (Democratic Agrarian Party of Moldova)	DAPM controlled	President Lucinschi proposed new candidate
24.01.97–01.02.99	Ion Ciubuc (unaffiliated)	Centre	Dismissed, disagreement with parliament about reform
19.02.99–09.11.99	Ion Sturza (Electoral Block for a Democratic and Prosperous Moldova)	Centre/technocrat	Disagreement with President and Parliament
21.12.99–19.04.01	Dumitru Braghis (unaffiliated)	Centre/left	Communists proposed a new candidate after parliamentary elections
19.04.01–	Vasile Tarlev (unaffiliated)	Communist-Party controlled	

APPENDIX 15.3: THE ELECTORAL SYSTEM

The first semi-democratic legislative elections in Moldova were organized in spring 1990, in accordance with a single member district majority system. Labour collectives and public organizations had the right to nominate candidates in 380 circumscriptions for the Republican Supreme Soviet. On 23 June 1990, the Parliament adopted the Declaration of sovereignty and, one year later, on 27 August 1991 – the Declaration of Independence of the Republic of Moldova. In 1993 a new Law on Parliamentary Elections was adopted. The law on Moldovan legislative elections was passed on 19 October 1993. It called for the formation of a new national parliament that differed significantly from its initial legislature. In a key shift, it was decided that Moldova's first entirely post-communist legislature would be comprised of 104 delegates. After years of deadlock, it was hoped by republican leaders that this smaller body would be more manageable than the 380-member Soviet institution, in which it was often difficult even to achieve a quorum. Rules governing the electoral mechanism were also fundamentally altered. Under the new system delegates were elected on the basis of proportional representation from closed party lists. A 4 per cent threshold was established in order to avoid excessive fragmentation. In a move that distinguished it from the vast majority of proportional representation systems, the Moldovans adopted a single national electoral district for the 1994 elections. While not ensuring participation in the separatist region, this mechanism allowed elections to go forward, selecting a body of delegates whose constituency was the entire republic, regardless of their individual places of residence. Transdniestrian leaders refused to allow voting in their region, but did agree to permit those who wished to cross over into Moldovan territory in order to participate in the elections. Some six thousand people took advantage of this opportunity to cross the Dniestr and vote in specially established west bank polling places.

As established in the 1994 constitution, the President is chosen through a two-round popular election, with a requirement that more than 50 per cent of the vote must be gained for victory in the first round. If no candidate achieves such a majority, a run-off between the top two candidates determines the outcome in the second round. Until March 2000, independent candidates had to pass the 4 per cent electoral threshold, the same threshold as for political parties and electoral blocs. At that time this threshold was decreased for independent candidates to 3 per cent. In March 2000, Parliament increased the threshold to 6 per cent.

On 22 September 2000, new legislation was enacted according to which the Moldovan President is elected by the members of the Parliament. The winner has to get the backing of two thirds of the deputies. If none of the candidates obtains the required number of votes, then a second-round election shall be organized within three days between the two candidates who received the highest number of votes in the first round. If no candidate is elected the first repeat elections shall be conducted within 15 days. If the repeat elections fail to elect the President of the republic, then the incumbent President shall dissolve the Parliament and establish the date of parliamentary elections.

APPENDIX 15.4: THE CONSTITUTIONAL FRAMEWORK

The Constitution of the Republic of Moldova, adopted on 29 July 1994, calls for the formation of a democratic republic, guaranteeing human rights and representative political pluralism. Citizens are protected against retroactive application of laws, and have the right to be informed about their rights and legal obligations (Articles 22 and 23). Like many of the post-Soviet Constitutions, Moldova's basic law established strong 'labour rights'. Article 42 guaranteed the right of workers to form or join unions. Article 43 establishes the right to work and the protection of work. It establishes a right to a healthy work place, establishes a forty-hour-work week, and provides for protection against unemployment. Article 13 established Moldovan as the language of state. Article 13, clause (2) 'recognizes and promotes the development and functioning of Russian and other languages spoken on the territory of the country'.

Institutionally, power at the national level is divided between the President of the Republic, a unicameral legislature, and a Constitutional Court. The Parliament, described as the supreme representative body of the republic, is made up of deputies elected to four-year terms by means of direct universal vote. It elects a President of the Parliament by secret majority-vote of the deputies, and may remove him by a two-thirds vote. Parliament meets in four-month sessions, twice per year, and may be called into extraordinary session by the President of the Republic, the President of the Parliament, or a two-thirds vote of the deputies. The Parliament passes laws, may call for a referendum, and exercises control over the executive as called for in the constitution.

On 22 September 2000, legislation was passed according to which the members of the Parliament elects the Moldovan President (see *Appendix 15.3*). The candidate is elected by the vote of three fifths of the deputies, for a term of four years. Holding office for more than two consecutive terms is prohibited. The election is validated by the Constitutional Court. The President is charged with guaranteeing the independence and unity of the republic, and overseeing the efficient functioning of public authorities. The President has the right to submit issues to the people through referendum, and to suspend Acts of Government, which he feels contravene the law until they are decided upon by the Constitutional Court (Article 88). The President may be impeached by vote of two-thirds of the total number of deputies elected to Parliament. The President's case is then heard by the Supreme Court of Justice. The President can take part in meetings of the Government, and presides when he does so. The President can take part in the work of the Parliament, and is called upon to deliver to the Parliament messages concerning issues of national concern. The President names the Prime Minister following consultation with the parliamentary majority and names the Government on the basis of a vote of confidence by the Parliament. The President can dissolve parliament if it was unable to form a Government for a period of 45 days. This could be done only once in one year, not during the last six months of the life of a Parliament, and not during a state of emergency or war.

The Government is comprised of the Prime Minister, and other ministers as determined by law. Once selected by the President, the Prime Minister selects a Government and establishes a programme, which is then submitted to Parliament for a vote of confidence. The Government and its members are responsible to Parliament. They must submit to parliamentary questioning, and if requested, members of the Government must participate in the work of Parliament. Parliament is given the power to dismiss the Government through a vote of no confidence by a majority vote of the members (Article 101).

The judicial system consists of a Supreme Court of Justice, a Court of Appeals, subordinate tribunals, the Superior Council of the Magistracy, the Procuracy, and a Constitutional Court. The Superior Council of the Magistracy is responsible for discipline in the judicial system. It is made up of judges. Under Article 122, its eleven judges include the Presidents of the Supreme, Appeals, and Economic Courts, the Minister of Justice, the Procurator General; and six elected members, (three by the Parliament, and three by judges of the superior courts). The Procuracy, itself overseen by a Procurator General named by the Parliament, oversees the execution of law by public institutions, protects public order, and protects the rights of citizens. The Constitutional Court is comprised of six judges, two selected by the President, two by the Parliament, and two by the Superior Council of the Magistracy. It is named as the sole authority with constitutional jurisdiction in the republic, and described as entirely independent, subordinated only to the constitution itself.

APPENDIX 15.5: REGRESSION RESULTS

Multi-Nominal Logistic Regression 1: Support for the PCRM by Education, Age, Residence, and Nationality

Model Fitting Information

Model	-2 Log Likelihood	Chi-Square	Df	Sig.
Intercept Only	695.222			
Final	556.940	138.282	16	0.000

Pseudo R-Square

Cox and Snell	0.102
Nagelkerke	0.143
McFadden	0.086

Likelihood Ratio Tests

Effect	-2 Log Likelihood of Reduced Model	Chi-Square	df	Sig.
Intercept	556.940 (a)	0.000	0	–
Age	586.051	29.110	4	0.000
Residence	557.522	0.582	1	0.446
Nationality	616.295	59.355	5	0.000
Education	582.210	25.270	6	0.000

The chi-square statistic is the difference in -2 log-likelihoods between the final model and a reduced model. The reduced model is formed by omitting an effect from the final model. The null hypothesis is that all parameters of that effect are 0.
(a) This reduced model is equivalent to the final model because omitting the effect does not increase the degrees of freedom.

Parameter Estimates

Vote for PCRM	B	Std. Error	Wald	df	Sig.	Exp (B)	95% Confidence Interval for Exp(B)	
							Lower Bound	Upper Bound
Intercept	-0.281	0.393	0.510	1	0.475			
[AGE=1.00]	-0.933	0.218	18.259	1	0.000	0.393	0.256	0.603
[AGE=2.00]	-0.358	0.211	2.879	1	0.090	0.699	0.462	1.057
[AGE=3.00]	-0.517	0.217	5.688	1	0.017	0.596	0.390	0.912
[AGE=4.00]	0.141	0.217	0.417	1	0.518	1.151	0.751	1.763
[AGE=5.00]	0 (a)	–	–	0	–	–	–	–
[RESIDENC=1.00]	-0.107	0.140	0.580	1	0.446	0.899	0.683	1.183
[RESIDENC=2.00]	0 (a)	–	–	0	–	–	–	–
[NATION=1.00]	-0.934	0.353	7.007	1	0.008	0.393	0.197	0.785
[NATION=2.00]	-0.001	0.379	0.000	1	0.998	0.999	0.475	2.101
[NATION=3.00]	0.229	0.370	0.384	1	0.536	1.258	0.609	2.599
[NATION=4.00]	-0.344	0.468	0.541	1	0.462	0.709	0.284	1.773
[NATION=5.00]	0.469	0.538	0.761	1	0.383	1.599	0.557	4.591
[NATION=6.00]	0 (a)	–	–	0	–	–	–	–
[EDUCAT=1.00]	0.073	0.345	0.045	1	0.833	1.076	0.547	2.117
[EDUCAT=2.00]	0.525	0.234	5.026	1	0.025	1.691	1.068	2.676
[EDUCAT=3.00]	0.856	0.196	19.116	1	0.000	2.354	1.604	3.456
[EDUCAT=4.00]	0.596	0.197	9.120	1	0.003	1.816	1.233	2.674
[EDUCAT=5.00]	-0.166	0.802	0.043	1	0.836	0.847	0.176	4.084
[EDUCAT=6.00]	0.136	0.296	0.211	1	0.646	1.146	0.641	2.047
[EDUCAT=7.00]	0 (a)	–	–	0	–	–	–	–

(a) This parameter is set to zero because it is redundant.

Multi-Nominal Logistic Regression 2: Support for the PCRM by Estimation of Income Sufficiency, Assessment of Country's Direction, International Orientation and Confidence in Political Parties' Performance

Model Fitting Information

Model	-2 Log Likelihood	Chi-Square	Df	Sig.
Intercept Only	458.766			
Final	248.401	210.365	15	0.000

Pseudo R-Square

Cox and Snell	0.151
Nagelkerke	0.212
McFadden	0.131

Likelihood Ratio Tests

Effect	-2 Log Likelihood of Reduced Model	Chi-Square	df	Sig.
Intercept	248.401 (a)	0.000	0	–
Income Sufficiency	293.187	44.786	5	0.000
International Orientation	362.194	113.793	3	0.000
Country's Direction	259.485	11.084	3	0.011
Confidence in Political Parties	279.743 (b)	31.342	4	0.000

The chi-square statistic is the difference in -2 log-likelihoods between the final model and a reduced model. The reduced model is formed by omitting an effect from the final model. The null hypothesis is that all parameters of that effect are 0.
(a) This reduced model is equivalent to the final model because omitting the effect does not increase the degrees of freedom.
(b) There is possibly a quasi-complete separation in the data. Either the maximum likelihood estimates do not exist or some parameter estimates are infinite.

Parameter Estimates

Vote for PCRM	B	Std. Error	Wald	Df	Sig.	Exp(B)	95% Confidence Interval for Exp(B) Lower Bound	Upper Bound
Intercept	-2.450	1.094	5.012	1	0.025			
[SELFINC=1.00]	0.143	0.896	0.026	1	0.873	1.154	0.199	6.686
[SELFINC=2.00]	-0.565	0.899	0.395	1	0.530	0.568	9.753E-02	3.311
[SELFINC=3.00]	-1.072	0.934	1.317	1	0.251	0.342	5.483E-02	2.137
[SELFINC=4.00]	-1.093	0.993	1.211	1	0.271	0.335	4.789E-02	2.348
[SELFINC=5.00]	-19.64	0.000	–	1	–	2.956E-09	2.956E-09	2.956E-09
[SELFINC=9.00]	0 (a)	–	–	0	–	–	–	–
[A64=1.00]	0.811	0.477	2.897	1	0.089	2.251	0.884	5.729
[A64=2.00]	2.127	0.474	20.163	1	0.000	8.388	3.315	21.224
[A64=5.00]	1.256	0.649	3.742	1	0.053	3.510	0.984	12.528
[A64=99.00]	0 (a)	–	.	0	–	–	–	–
[DIRECT=1.00]	-0.075	0.448	0.028	1	0.867	0.928	0.385	2.234
[DIRECT=2.00]	0.025	0.381	0.004	1	0.948	1.025	0.486	2.165
[DIRECT=3.00]	-0.815	0.455	3.216	1	0.073	0.443	0.182	1.079
[DIRECT=9.00]	0 (a)	–	–	0	–	–	–	–
[A42=1.00]	0.283	0.305	0.859	1	0.354	1.327	0.730	2.413
[A42=2.00]	0.649	0.315	4.242	1	0.039	1.914	1.032	3.550
[A42=3.00]	1.352	0.348	15.101	1	0.000	3.866	1.955	7.645
[A42=4.00]	1.272	0.836	2.316	1	0.128	3.568	0.693	18.357
[A42=9.00]	0 (a)	–	–	0	–	–	–	–

(a) This parameter is set to zero because it is redundant.

16. Concluding Remarks

Joakim Ekman, Sten Berglund and
Frank Aarebrot*

The study of political cleavage formation in post-communist Central and Eastern Europe offers a rare opportunity to investigate the dynamics of how support for political parties is shaped by varying circumstances. In a global perspective these states are all complex, modern societies. Moreover, most of the countries emerged as independent states with relatively democratic constitutions at the time when mass politics was consolidated throughout the industrialized world in the wake of the First World War. Finally, all the states experienced profound regime changes prior to, and in the immediate aftermath of, the Second World War, as well as in the early 1990s. Central and Eastern Europe does provide students of political conflict with a fascinating laboratory for comparing the impact of very different historical and structural contexts on the patterns of political cleavages.

The current volume does not pretend to offer a final account of the conditions conducive to linking support for current political parties to societal conflicts, past and present. We would nevertheless argue that the analytic contributions provided by the authors of the country-specific chapters may serve as a good starting point for future systematic, comparative investigation.

In his contribution to the first edition of the *Handbook of Political Change in Eastern Europe* (1998), Georgi Karasimeonov presented a classification of regimes based on their degree of democratic consolidation (cf. Linz and Stepan 1996). His typology testifies to the relatively high degree of variation among the ten nations covered by the handbook at that point in time. None of them could be classified as consolidated democracies, but most of them were seen as being on the road towards democratic consolidation. Only Romania and Bulgaria were unequivocally what Karasimeonov would define as transitional democracies; Slovakia stood out as something of a borderline case, at best a transitional democracy, but perhaps an authoritarian democracy like Serbia (Karasimeonov 1998). There were thus intimations of a North/South divide with South Eastern Europe lagging behind the Northern Tier in terms of democratic consolidation. Five years later, the ten countries covered by the first edition of the handbook had all been invited to join the European Union in two waves of accession – the three Baltic countries, Poland, Hungary, the Czech Republic, Slovakia and Slovenia in May 2004, followed by Bulgaria and Romania in 2007. The historical decision by the EU summit in Copenhagen in December 2002 testifies not only to the successful consolidation of democracy in Central and Eastern Europe, but also to the resilience of the North/South divide astutely identified by Georgi Karasimeonov in 1998. The present volume, which includes chapters not only on Bulgaria and Romania but also on Serbia and Croatia, only goes towards highlighting the importance of the North/South divide. There is, in fact, a good case to be made for the notion that the resilience of authoritarian features in the Balkans has much to do with the clientelistic heritage in that particular region.

The country-specific chapters make it abundantly clear that democratic consolidation has been possible without cleavage crystallization and a freezing of the party systems. The East European party systems remain weakly anchored in the fluid and poorly differentiated post-communist social structure. The fact that democratic consolidation may occur in a setting of weak cleavage crystallization goes against the grain of established theory. How can this paradoxical fact be accounted for?

Chapter 2 lists several factors which go a long way towards explaining why the current, post-communist try at democracy has better prospects than the inter-war and immediate post-war experiments in democratic rule; and the importance of these factors has indeed been brought out by all the country-specific chapters.

East European political leaders and voters alike have vigorously pursued integration into Western political, economic and military structures. This has given Western governments and institutions strong leverage to enforce adherence to the principles of participatory democracy, the rule of law, the free market and minority protection. In short, democratic consolidation is a prerequisite for, as well as a by-product of, integration with the West. The swift and relatively smooth integration of ex-communists into the democratic framework is but one aspect of the broad commitment to democratic principles. There is a climate favouring co-optation of the organizations and individuals tainted by communism, who for their part, have all but given up their hegemonic ambitions. Moreover, the countries of Eastern Europe have successfully applied creative electoral engineering in order to avoid political fragmentation. By now, all the countries in the region have introduced electoral thresholds and several of them have electoral systems combining majority and proportional representation; designs set to produce strong and stable government and to counter immobilism.

The impact of more than 40 years of communism has also, somewhat counter-intuitively, improved the prospects for democracy. The comprehensive modernization of Eastern Europe during communism has provided a social setting more conducive to democracy than ever before. By way of example, the high level of education (Berglund and Aarebrot 1997, 93; Lewis 1994, 132) makes it inconceivable for the countries of contemporary Eastern Europe to restrict balloting in a way similar to Hungary in the inter-war era, when rural voters had to state their voting preferences openly or were not allowed to vote at all (Rothschild 1974, 160). Another aspect of communist modernization conducive to democracy was the emergence of social groups with interests – at least potential – that political parties could set out to represent. The post-communist societies have sometimes been referred to as 'flattened societies' (Wessels and Klingemann 1994); they were certainly marked by class differences, but did not have an independent middle-class in the Western sense. Nevertheless, these flattened societies contained embryos of a modern class structure. Of particular importance are the well-educated middle strata, which have the potential of developing into a Western-style propertied middle-class.

Civil society alone did not bring down Soviet-style communism, but the increasing strength of autonomous organizations in Eastern Europe throughout the 1980s and the early 1990s is easy to document and was certainly an unintended by-product of communist-initiated modernization. It is no coincidence that the transition was violent and/or an elite-level affair in the least modern societies, where civil society was not developed enough to challenge the clientelistic structures. While the peoples of the Baltic republics organized a 'singing revolution', and the Czechs and Slovaks embarked on their Velvet Revolution, the transfer of power was a backroom affair in Bulgaria and Romania; in Romania, eventually spilling over into a regular shoot-out between competing factions of the beleaguered regime. In Croatia, Moldova and Serbia the transition from communism was elite-driven and accompanied by the revival of deeply seated ethnic and religious tensions.

Cleavage Typologies: Three Different Approaches

The seminal Lipset–Rokkan classification scheme (Lipset and Rokkan 1967; Rokkan 1970; 1975) draws on a wide range of historical data mainly from Western Europe; it identifies manifest cleavages rooted in the long-running processes of national and industrial revolution, such as urban/rural, centre/periphery, church/state, labour/capital and social democracy versus communism (*Figure 16.1*).

Cleavages are operative on three levels of analysis – the demographic level, the attitudinal level and the behavioural level. Some of the contributing authors, most notably Kevin Deegan-Krause (Chapter 8) and

Zakošek and Čular (Chapter 13), make a strong case for reserving the term 'cleavage' for cases where all three levels overlap. Though operating within a framework inspired by Lipset and Rokkan, the editors are inclined to be somewhat less demanding and extend the term 'cleavage' also to what Deegan-Krause would refer to as 'divides'. This is also in line with the terminology applied by Tóka (Chapter 9) and Karasimeonov (Chapter 12).

In Chapter 2, the editors take an intermediate position on the relevance of historical cleavages in contemporary Central and Eastern Europe. They were repressed during several decades of dictatorship before, as well as after, the Second World War; they may re-emerge, but not necessarily in the same form. By way of example, the rural/urban dimension has been thoroughly transformed by communist-style modernization. Collectivization of agriculture reduced the farmers to workers, and to all intents and purposes wiped out the constituencies of the inter-war agrarian parties, with the exception of the peasant parties of Poland and Slovenia. Advocating privatization of agricultural land was not a successful strategy for the reborn agrarian parties of the early 1990s; agricultural workers adjusted well to being workers rather than farmers, and they are now rallying to parties associated with the defunct communist regimes, which serve as parties of rural defence.

Figure 16.1 provides an overview of the scope of conceptual variations in the usage of terms related to the cleavage concept throughout this volume. First, Lipset and Rokkan's distinction between manifest and latent cleavages is taken as a point of departure. We would argue that this book deals primarily with cleavages manifested through the representation of and the electoral support for political parties. Thus, Figure 16.1 indicates that latent cleavages – or, in Karasimeonov's typology: 'potential cleavages' – are not subject to investigation by the authors. Second, we have classified the categories proposed by Karasimeonov and ourselves in terms of their respective origins. We would argue that some of the manifestations of political parties in contemporary Eastern Europe originate from social conflicts present already in the inter-war period. As mentioned above, these 'historical' or 'residual' cleavages are not necessarily represented by the same parties or even by the same ideologies today as after the First World War. In fact, in most cases it is new parties, which today capitalize on old societal cleavages.

Another set of manifest cleavages is derived from contemporary social conflicts. Such cleavages are referred to by the editors as 'contemporary' cleavages; by Karasimeonov as 'actual' cleavages. Lack of precedence from the inter-war period is the common denominator behind this class of conflicts. Finally, both the editors and Karasimeonov have defined a class of manifest 'transitional' cleavages. These are conflicts related to the dramatic days and months following the fall of the Iron Curtain and the collapse of the Soviet Union. In order for a cleavage to be classified as transitional, parties which still identify themselves with the early popular fronts or, conversely, with the besieged pro-Soviet communists, must be present on the parliamentary level throughout the 1990s.

Figure 16.1: Cleavage typologies and their origins

Origins	*Lipset and Rokkan*	*Karasimeonov*	*Editors*	*Cleavages discussed in the country-specific chapters*
Pre-war social structure	MANIFEST • urban–rural • centre–periphery • Church–State • labour–capital • social democracy–communism	Residual (historical) cleavages	*Historical* • core populations versus minorities • religious–secular • urban–rural • workers–owners • social democracy–communism	• ethnic–linguistic • religious • urban–rural • regional • left–right
Contemporary social structures		Actual cleavages	*Contemporary* • national versus cosmopolitan • protectionist versus free-market • generational	• mode of distribution • rent-seekers versus wage-earners • education • generation
Regime transition from authoritarian to democratic		Transitional cleavages	*Transitional* • apparatus versus forums/fronts	• communist regime versus civic forums/fronts • apparatus versus civil society • professionals (competence) versus dissidents ('amateurs')
Long-term developmental trends	LATENT	Potential cleavages		

In the right-hand column of Figure 16.1, we have listed terms for classification of cleavages employed in the various country-specific chapters. Thus, we will argue that, despite some terminological ambiguities, a conceptual consistency exists throughout the volume.

The relevance of the left-right dimension is an important finding in the country-specific chapters. The party systems in all countries, with the exception of Estonia, Moldova, Serbia and, possibly, Latvia and Croatia (cf. *Table 16.1*) are structured along a left-right dimension, either explicitly or implicitly. As convincingly demonstrated by Zdenka Mansfeldová (Chapter 7), Czech voters place the parties and the parties place themselves explicitly along a left-right continuum defined in socio-economic terms. In the remaining countries, the political parties somehow end up on a left-right scale anyway. Lithuania and Hungary are cases in point, but they also serve as a reminder that the East European party systems have not frozen yet. The legacy of communism has added one important component to the left-right cleavage: the conflict of interest between winners and losers in the transition process, between what may be classified as wage earners and rent-seekers. This component has some features in common with the Lipset–Rokkan labour/capital cleavage, which also revolves around questions of distribution and redistribution. Yet it is important not to overstate the particularity of the East European case. The left/right or labour/capital cleavage in Western Europe has undergone a profound change since Lipset and Rokkan developed their classification scheme in the 1960s. The welfare state has contributed to a weakening of class linkages, and created a growing constituency of subsidy-seekers who use political parties to extract resources from the state. With the public sector accounting for more than half of GDP in many West European countries, the state has seen fit to take over many of the distributive functions formerly attributed to private capital.

Several parties compete for the different segments of the rent-seeking electorate in Eastern Europe. The rent-seeking electorate has occasionally found representation through the ex-communist parties, but some of the former ruling parties have developed into paragons of pro-market virtue – the Lithuanian Democratic Labour Party (LDDP) is a case in point; as evidenced by William Crowther's chapter on Romania, legislators affiliated with the three main communist party-derived formations (FDSN, FSN, PSM) are more pro-market than the population average. All East European parties, including the ex-communists, are constrained by voters conditioned to seeing the state as a source of subsidies, and by external economic factors, as well as by the need to make a clean break with communism and the planned economy.

The 1998 version of the handbook made the editors conclude that many of the countries had gone through a metamorphosis and acquired genuine democratic credentials. This tendency was particularly strong in Poland, Hungary, Slovenia and Lithuania and particularly weak in Slovakia, Bulgaria and Romania. In the five years that have passed since then, the three latter have edged much closer to the Central and East European mainstream. Slovakia is no longer a deviant case in the Central European context; and though marked by clientelism as well as occasional political turmoil, Bulgaria and Romania are now well beyond the transitional stage.

Moldova and Serbia clearly are not. William Crowther and Yuri Josanu bluntly refer to Moldova as a case of 'failed democratization'; and in a similar vein, Bojan Todosijević refers to the level of violence in contemporary Serbian politics. Croatia is obviously in a more favourable position, but it is nevertheless grappling with the recent transition from authoritarianism under Franjo Tuđman.

With the exception of the Balkans, the issues of nationalism and ethnicity have been of less importance than might be expected, given Eastern Europe's legacy of ethnic politics. Even so, it is legitimate to ask whether this will be a permanent state of affairs. The countries in South Eastern Europe remain ethnically heterogeneous in spite of the 'population transfers' of the early 1990s within the former Yugoslav federation; the Baltic states are more ethnically heterogeneous than they were before they were annexed by the Soviet Union in 1940; and Polish 'anti-Semitism without Jews' (Lendvai 1971) and anti-German resentments without Germans in the Czech polity testify to the potential explosiveness of ethnic tensions, even long after they have lost their underlying substance. External constraints, operative on the elite level, may go a long way towards accounting for the limited degree of exploitation of ethno-linguistic cleavages. EU and NATO intervention has certainly played a major role in defusing, or at least suspending, the Trianon issue between Hungary and her neighbours.

Identity politics is an important feature of state- and nation-building, and it still plays a role in Central and Eastern Europe. State- and nation-building was not completed by the end of the inter-war era, and in many cases, communism slowed down the process. In this respect, the Baltic states and Moldova had the dual disadvantage of being not only communist but also under direct Soviet rule and subject to intense attempts at Russification. It should therefore come as no surprise that identity politics plays such a prominent role in these four countries, in Moldova to the extent of overshadowing all other cleavages.

Contemporary Cleavage Structures in Central and Eastern Europe

Capitalizing on the conceptually consistent pattern defined in Figure 16.1, we will seek to define and compare the cleavage patterns for all the thirteen countries analysed in the previous chapters of this volume. In order to do so, it is necessary to define a set of historical, contemporary and transitional cleavages at a rather high level of abstraction. We do this in order to be able to compare variations in cleavage patterns across the countries of Central and Eastern Europe. The results are reported in Table 16.1 below.

The first five cleavages are historical, closely related to Lipset and Rokkan's classification of 1967:

- *Core populations versus ethno-linguistic minorities*: Here we refer to political parties which are clear-cut representatives of a linguistic or ethnic minority, or to any party appealing to the core population by negative references to national minorities;

• *Religious versus secular*: This dimension is captured by parties seeking to gain votes by defending religious values or by parties attacking religious values and arguing for a secular society;

• *Urban versus rural*: This cleavage is manifested by parties that represent cities or rural areas and have some roots in the politics of the inter-war era;

• *Workers versus owners*: This cleavage, also known as labour/capital or left/right, manifests itself through parties which derive their support primarily from within organized labour, or from within employers' organizations such as federations of industry. Traditional social democratic parties would be typical examples;

• *Social democrats versus communists*: This cleavage is tapped by parties derived from the traditional conflict between internationalist and nationally-oriented socialism.

The next four cleavages are contemporary:

• *National versus cosmopolitan*: At the poles of this cleavage we find parties with the nation-state as the focal point, and parties strongly oriented towards international cooperation as a way of solving political problems. To be listed as an exponent of this cleavage, nationalist or cosmopolitan rhetoric must be a dominant feature of the party's appeal;

• *Protective versus free market*: At one end of this spectrum are parties which try to preserve subsidies for unprofitable industries; at the other are parties which launch themselves by arguing that the free market will benefit the country, irrespective of negative short-term consequences such as unemployment and social tension;

• *Generational*: This cleavage is manifested by parties, which derive their support from people with a common generational experience, such as pensioners and youth;

• *Socio-economically disadvantaged versus occupational and managing elites*: This cleavage is manifested by parties drawing support from, on the one side of the spectrum, 'ordinary people' who feel that they have become 'losers' in contemporary Central and Eastern Europe, and on the other end of the spectrum, the 'winners' of the transformation, the emerging middle- and upper-middle classes. This cleavage may cut across traditional cleavages based on issues such as left/right, urban/rural, generation and ethnicity.

Finally, we have listed one transitional cleavage:

• *Apparatus versus popular forums/fronts*: In order for this cleavage to be manifest, the party system must include parties which are derived from the old communist ruling apparatus, or parties which represent a direct continuation of the early anti-communist popular forums and fronts.

For a cleavage to be listed as relevant in Table 16.1, a party representing it must have returned at least 5 per cent of the vote in recent general elections (see the appendices to the country-specific chapters). The same party may be salient as a mobilizing agent on more than one cleavage. For a party to be considered 'mobilizing' on the basis of a historical cleavage, it is not necessary for it to have had organizational continuity since the inter-war and immediate post-war eras. Cleavages do not have to be bipolar in order to be registered as salient for any specific country: it is sufficient for the party system to include a party, or a group of parties, seeking to capitalize on one end of a given dimension. For example, a country is considered to have a religious/secular cleavage if it has a religious party polling more than 5 per cent of the vote; a secular counterpart is not necessary.

If each significant party in a country attempts to mobilize voters on the basis of the same position on a given cleavage, we do not classify that cleavage as salient. For example, in countries where all relevant parties are in favour of NATO and EU membership, the national versus cosmopolitan cleavage is not considered salient.

Following these rules of classification we arrive at the pattern of salient cleavages presented in Table 16.1. A '+' marks a salient cleavage, whereas a '+' within brackets indicates marginal salience relevant to one of our criteria. But the patterns emerging in the table should nevertheless only be seen as indicative of the underlying cleavage structures.

Table 16.1 makes it possible to make a rough distinction between countries with simple versus complex cleavage structures. Countries like Estonia, Lithuania, Poland and Croatia with only one salient contemporary cleavage clearly qualify for the first category. And with three salient contemporary cleavages, Latvia, Hungary and Slovenia obviously qualify for the latter category. With two salient contemporary cleavages, the Czech Republic, Slovakia, Romania, Bulgaria and Serbia land in-between these two groups. Moldova finally ends up all by itself with no salient contemporary cleavages at all. Moldova is grappling with historical cleavages that revolve around ethnicity, state- and nation-building, to the extent that the contours of the contemporary cleavages are barely visible.

The summary table (*Table 12.1*) in the 1998 version of the handbook made the editors conclude that there was ample evidence of a North-South divide, with the Northern Tier – encompassing Estonia, Latvia, Lithuania and Poland – having the most simple cleavage structure. The updated summary table (*Table 16.1*) does not lend itself to such straightforward conclusions; and the outcome clearly is not just a simple function of the inclusion of three additional countries in this volume. The three new countries – Croatia, Serbia and Moldova – are all located in South Eastern Europe, and they all seem to have rather simple cleavage structures. This is not what we would have hypothesized given the pattern in the 1998 version of the handbook. The same data set (*Table 12.1*) would also have led us to expect Latvia to stay put among the Northern Tier countries with a simple contemporary cleavage structure. But Latvia has obviously moved towards greater complexity (*Table 16.1*).

Table 16.1: Patterns of cleavage types in Central and Eastern Europe

	Est	Lat	Lith	Pol	Cze	Slvk	Hun	Slvn	Rom	Bul	Cro	Ser	Mol
Historical													
Core population versus ethno-linguistic minorities	+	+				+			+	+	+	+	+
Religious versus secular	+		+	+	(+)	+	+	+			+		
Urban versus rural	+	+		+			+	+	+	(+)	+	(+)	
Workers versus owners	(+)	+	+	+	+	+	+	+	(+)	(+)			
Social democrats versus communists		+	+	(+)	+	+	+	+	+	+			
Contemporary													
National versus cosmopolitan		+		+	+	+	+	+	+	+	+	+	(+)
Protectionist versus free-market		+	+	+	+	+	+	+	+	+		+	(+)
Generational							+	+					
Socio-economically disadvantaged versus occupational and managing elites	+	+											
Transitional													
Apparatus versus forums/fronts	+		+	+	+				+	+	+		(+)

Est: Estonia; Lat: Latvia; Lith: Lithuania; Pol: Poland; Cze: Czech Republic; Slvk: Slovakia; Hun: Hungary; Slvn: Slovenia; Rom: Romania; Bul: Bulgaria; Cro: Croatia; Ser: Serbia; Mol: Moldova

A word of caution might be appropriate at this stage. Table 16.1 tells us which cleavages are represented by the relevant parties in each of the 13 East European countries; it does not convey any information about cleavages represented by non-relevant parties, i.e. parties polling less than 5 per cent of the valid votes cast. More important still, the table does not say anything about the relative importance of the various cleavages that we have identified. And not all cleavages are of equal importance.

We know from Mikko Lagerspetz and Henri Vogt's analysis that contemporary Estonia is uni-dimensional to all intents and purposes. Identity politics is pervasive to the extent that Estonia might even be classified as a case of non-party politics, though with left-right lurking in the background. This of course does not preclude the existence of enough actors in the market to fill a few more cells in the matrix than just one. Similarly, Hermann Smith-Sivertsen convincingly demonstrates the increasing salience of the left-right cleavage in contemporary Latvian politics. Kjetil Duvold and Mindaugas Jurkynas document the resilience of the left-right cleavage in Lithuania also in times of political turmoil. There is in fact an almost overwhelming agreement among the contributing authors that East European parties may be classified in terms of left, right or centre. These terms often carry other than socio-economic connotations, however. Right-wing parties may, for instance, be seen to campaign on a platform of traditional conservative and religious values, while left-wing parties adopt a secular and cosmopolitan platform. This is the case in Hungary, the Czech Republic, Poland and Slovenia, to some extent even in Slovakia, Bulgaria and Romania.

We are basically saying that a complex cleavage structure may turn into something rather simple and straightforward, if the cleavages are correlated as tends to be the case in Central and Eastern Europe. In the extreme scenario, the cleavages are literally superimposed on one another. This would seem to be at least part of the secret behind the relative simple cleavage structure in Croatia, Moldova and Serbia. The transition to pluralism and democracy in these countries has been dominated by historical cleavages to the extent that other cleavages or divides have been subordinated to the dominant cleavage. This is most strongly pronounced in Serbia, where all latent cleavages were subsumed by the historical national cleavage. But Croatia and Moldova have also had more than their fair share of polarization and are not that far removed from the Serbian model.

*

Whether broadly or narrowly defined, the cleavage concept remains an analytical concept. Voters do not necessarily relate to political parties in terms of cleavages, even though they might seem to do so when we analyse their attitudes and political behaviour. This does not mean that politics does not make sense to the voters. On the contrary, voters are also capable of identifying stable patterns and underlying structures as brought out by numerous election studies.

In the *New Europe Barometer* (2001), respondents were explicitly asked about their understanding of existing cleavages in society that parties can draw on. The item reads: Here are some reasons that people give about the differences between political parties in this country. Which of the following best explains these differences:

1. Some parties believe the Communist regime did much more harm than good, while others want to preserve many of its achievements.

2. Some parties represent big cities, while others defend rural and peripheral regions.

3. Some parties want the government to manage the economy, while others prefer the market.

4. Some parties represent ethnic minorities, while others oppose special policies for minorities.

5. Big personalities are the chief appeal of some parties, while others ask voters to support their political ideas.

6. Some parties promote national traditions, while others emphasize integration in Europe.

The respondents were explicitly instructed to select the two alternatives that explain the most. Table 16.2 provides information on both, on the first and second most important cleavages as perceived by the respondents.

Table 16.2: Perception of cleavages (%)

Country	Communist past	Market vs. state	Urban vs. rural	Ethnic minority rights	Nation vs. Europe	Ideas vs. persons	No opinion
Bulgaria	45	29	17	16	24	23	21
Czech Republic	45	44	14	6	32	41	3
Estonia	24	29	35	17	35	33	12
Hungary	29	24	20	9	31	24	28
Latvia	13	27	12	12	31	33	31
Lithuania	29	50	24	10	33	40	6
Poland	42	20	18	5	31	39	18
Romania	30	26	16	17	34	33	19
Slovakia	22	30	14	25	31	36	16
Slovenia	25	25	19	6	40	25	24
Average	30	30	19	12	32	33	18

Source: New Europe Barometer (2001).

Unfortunately, the *New Europe Barometer* does not cover all the countries in Central and Eastern Europe that are included in this volume. Serbia, Croatia and Moldova are excluded, and we are thus left with a sample of 10 countries instead of 13. Nevertheless, Table 16.2 provides us with some insights into the way ordinary citizens perceive the relevant cleavages in post-communist Europe.

Looking at the average scores, we find that four types of cleavages stand out as particularly important: *ideas versus persons* (or populism versus ideology); *nation versus Europe*; *market versus state*; and *communism versus anti-communism*.

We have encountered the populism/ideology cleavage in Karasimeonov's chapter on the vicissitudes of Bulgarian politics, and most chapters do contain some references to charismatic personalities. Its salience in the minds of East European voters is hardly surprising. The importance attributed to nation versus Europe and market versus state also goes towards confirming previous expectations. In fact, the history of Central and Eastern Europe from 1989–90 and onwards might very well be summarized in terms of these very cleavages. Communism versus anti-communism is a prominent topic in all country-specific chapters, but the importance of this cleavage in the minds of the voters nevertheless comes as somewhat of a surprise, particularly in consolidated democracies like Poland and the Czech Republic. The editors would be inclined to see this a lingering impact of what was a salient transitional cleavage in the early part of the 1990s rather than an indication that the cleavage is about to become a permanent fixture. The communist past remains relevant, but it is by no means decisive any more.

The Normalization of Eastern Europe

It is standard operating procedure to conclude a volume like ours with an evaluation of the prospects for democracy in Central and Eastern Europe. This is easily done. The reader will undoubtedly have noticed that the vast majority of our indicators pull in favour of democracy. Nine out of the 13 countries in our sample qualify as being well on the road towards democratic consolidation, if not already consolidated democracies. Only Croatia, Romania, and particularly Serbia, lag behind. Yet even the laggards in our sample have made considerably more progress on the bumpy road towards democracy than other post-communist states, such as Russia, Ukraine and Georgia (cf. *Table 1.1*). It would nevertheless be foolhardy to exclude the possibility of setbacks. Democracy is not a one-way street, as illustrated by the failed democratization in Moldova.

In the 1998 edition of *The Handbook of Political Change in Eastern Europe*, we felt obliged to include a word of caution. We feel that such caution is called for today as well. The countries of Central and Eastern Europe do still have features which may turn out to be problematic for democratic consolidation in the long run. As evidenced by the country-specific analyses in this volume, cleavage crystallization remains far from complete and the linkages between parties and voters are weak. The net result is party system fluidity and a high degree of electoral volatility. These are weaknesses which can be offset by what we have referred to as 'creative electoral engineering' – but only to a degree, as shown throughout the 1990s as well as in recent years by the surprising success of outsiders like presidential contenders Stanisław Tymiński in Poland, Valdas Adamkus in Lithuania, or the ex-king Simeon II in Bulgaria; or, for that matter, of parties such as the Czech Republican Party, the People's Movement for Latvia (Siegerist Party), and Estonia's Res Publica. As if this were not enough, there is still the potential explosiveness of ethnic and national grievances, currently checked by pressure from the international community, and by a strong wish on the part of East European leaders to bring their countries into the European Union and NATO.

The problems of the new democracies in Central and Eastern Europe are closely monitored by Western political science, and frequently discussed on the implicit assumption that West European democracy may be taken for granted and serve as a model. This attitude may be captured by substituting 'the West' for 'the Soviet Union' in an East German communist party slogan of the 1950s (Leonhard 1994): 'Who learns from the West learns how to triumph'. We believe things are slightly more complicated than that.

Contemporary Western Europe is in fact beset by many of the problems encountered in the East European context, albeit in different forms and to a different order of magnitude. Most of Western Europe is in the middle of a transition process of sorts. Harsh economic realities undermine the welfare states which were built from the 1950s and onwards, on the dual assumptions of continuous growth and the primacy of politics. The increasing inability of the welfare state to deliver on its outstanding promises erodes the legitimacy of the political system as well as attachments to political parties. There is in fact ample evidence of decreasing levels of party attachment in Western Europe (cf. Schmitt and Holmberg 1995; Biorcio and Mannheimer 1995). There is even a case to be made for the notion that Western Europe is currently undergoing a process of party system 'unfreezing'. As a rule, established parties all over Europe have found it increasingly difficult to defend their position against new political entrepreneurs such as the Greens in Finland, Sweden and Germany, or against various kinds of populist movements such as the Progress parties of Denmark and Norway, the Austrian Freedom Party (FPÖ) and the National Front of France.

Last but not least, the breakdown of Soviet-style communism has had an impact on Western Europe well beyond the obvious economic and strategic implications. With the spectre of communism removed from the political agenda, the conceptual and ideological space in Western Europe was substantially reduced. It is probably premature to proclaim the demise of ideology in Western Europe, but like their East European counterparts, West European parties face the necessity of reformulating and rethinking their ideological positions. There is, thus, a very strong case to be made for broad all-European comparative research, as opposed to more narrow East–East and West–West comparative research designs.

* This chapter is partly based on Chapter 12 in the 1998 version of *The Handbook of Political Change in Eastern Europe*, written by Tomas Hellén, Sten Berglund, and Frank Aarebrot.

REFERENCES

Berglund, Sten and Frank H. Aarebrot (1997), *The Political History of Eastern Europe in the 20th Century: The Struggle Between Democracy and Dictatorship*, Aldershot, Edward Elgar.

Biorcio, Roberto and Renato Mannheimer (1995), 'Relationships Between Citizens and Political Parties', in Hans-Dieter Klingemann and Dieter Fuchs, eds, *Citizens and the State*, Beliefs in Government Volume 1, Oxford, Oxford University Press.

Karasimeoniv, Georgi (1998), 'Bulgaria', in Sten Berglund, Tomas Hellén and Frank H. Aarebrot, eds, *The Handbook of Political Change in Eastern Europe*, Cheltenham, Edward Elgar.

Lendvai, Paul (1971), *Anti-Semitism without Jews: Communist Eastern Europe,* Garden City, Doubleday.

Leonhard, Wolfgang (1994), *Spurensuche: 40 Jahre nach Die Revolution Entläßt Ihre Kinder*, Cologne, Kiepenheuer & Witsch.

Lewis, Paul G. (1994), *Central Europe since 1945,* Singapore, Longman.

Linz, Juan and Alfred Stepan (1996), *Problems of Democratic Transition and Consolidation: Southern Europe, South America and Post-Communist Europe*, Baltimore and London, Johns Hopkins University Press.

Lipset, Seymour Martin and Stein Rokkan (1967), 'Introduction', in Seymour Martin Lipset and Stein Rokkan, eds, *Party Systems and Voter Alignments*, New York, Free Press.

New Europe Barometer (2001), Centre for the Study of Public Policy (CSPP), Glasgow, University of Strathclyde/Conditions of European Democracy, Örebro University.

Rokkan, Stein (1970), *Citizens, Elections, Parties: Approaches to the Comparative Study of the Process of Development*, Oslo, Universitetsforlaget.

—— (1975), 'Dimensions of State Formation and Nation-Building: A Possible Paradigm for Research on Variations within Europe', in Charles Tilly, ed., *The Formation of National States in Europe*, Princeton, Princeton University Press, 562–600.

Rothschild, Joseph (1974), *East Central Europe Between the Two World Wars,* Seattle and London, University of Washington Press.

Schmitt, Hermann and Sören Holmberg (1995), 'Political Parties in Decline?', in Hans-Dieter Klingemann and Dieter Fuchs, eds, *Citizens and the State*, Beliefs in Government Vol. 1, Oxford, Oxford University Press.

Wessels, Bernhard and Hans-Dieter Klingemann (1994), 'Democratic Transformation and the Prerequisites of Democratic Opposition in East and Central Europe', Wissenschaftszentrum Berlin für Sozialforschung, FS III, 94–201.

Name Index

609

Subject Index